Srimad Bhagavad Gita

Srimad Bhagavad Gita

A User's Manual for Every Day Living

Transliterated Sanskrit Text
Free Translation & Brief Explanation for
The Modern Generation

T.N. SETHUMADHAVAN

PARTRIDGE
A Penguin Random House Company

ISBN:	Hardcover	978-1-4828-4611-9
	Softcover	978-1-4828-4610-2
	eBook	978-1-4828-4609-6

Print information available on the last page.

To order additional copies of this book, contact
Partridge India
000 800 10062 62
orders.india@partridgepublishing.com

www.partridgepublishing.com/india

DEDICATED
TO
JAGADGURU ADI SANKARACHARYA
(788 – 820 CE)

*Who retrieved it from the mighty tomes of the epic,
the Mahabharata, and presented it to the
world through his brilliant commentary*

"When I read the Bhagavad Gita and reflect about how God created this universe everything else seems so superfluous."
– Albert Einstein

Contents

About the Book

Srimad Bhagavad Gita has been a source of inspiration and enlightenment for generations. The message of the Gita is not merely a general spiritual philosophy or ethical doctrine but it has a bearing upon the practical aspects in the application of such principles in our day-to-day lives. It is indeed "A Users' Manual for the Practice of the Art of Right Living".

The Bhagavad Gita was first translated into English by Charles Wilkins in 1785 and published by the British East India Company with an introduction by Lord Warren Hastings, the first British Governor-General of India, in which he prophetically wrote: "The writers of the Indian philosophies will survive when the British Dominion in India shall long have ceased to exist, and when the sources which it yielded of wealth and power are lost to remembrance". He further wrote "I hesitate not to pronounce the Gita's performance of great originality, of sublimity of conception, reasoning and diction almost unequalled and a single exception amongst all the known religions of mankind".

The radiance of such Bhagavad Gita is being presented by the author to the readers of the modern generation covering the subject in an informal style with transliterated Sanskrit Verses, their lucid translation and explanatory notes. At the end of each chapter its Outline View has also been provided for a quick recapitulation. The author has steered clear off all the scholastic debates and intellectual controversies with a view to reach out to the average modern educated young people who require the strength of the Gita to wade through the current day troubled waters.

The language employed is very plain and down to earth with no frills attached with a view to help the readers at the early stages of their life to understand the essential message of the Gita so that they will blossom into integrated grown-ups full of equanimity of mind, speech and action. Their needs in the context of the present day living styles and habits of study have been kept in view in this process.

If this effort ignites the minds of the readers and prepares them to take a dip into the *Gita Ganga* on their own, the efforts of the author would be amply rewarded.

Introducing Srimad Bhagavad Gita
A User's Manual for Every Day Living

"Live in the world but don't be of the world. Live in the world but don't let the world live within you. Remember it is all a beautiful dream, because everything is changing and disappearing. If you become detached you will be able to see how people are attached to trivia and how much they are suffering. And you will laugh at yourself because you were also in the same boat before". - Osho

THE GITA'S WIDE APPEAL

The Bhagavad Gita was first translated into English by Charles Wilkins in 1785 and published by the British East India

Company with an introduction by Lord Warren Hastings, the first British Governor-General of India, in which he prophetically wrote: "The writers of the Indian philosophies will survive when the British Dominion in India shall long have ceased to exist, and when the sources which it yielded of wealth and power are lost to remembrance". He further wrote "I hesitate not to pronounce the Gita's performance of great originality, of sublimity of conception, reasoning and diction almost unequalled and a single exception amongst all the known religions of mankind".

The Gita deals with human problems in a human way. That is why it has a tremendous appeal. It has inspired the human mind in India for centuries and today it casts its spell on millions of people across the world. It remains the most translated work in the Globe. The modern technology like the Internet has further increased its reputation by carrying its message to every nook and corner of the world. An incredible reach for any scripture!

Among the great and extraordinary people who were inspired and found their outlook changed by the timeless wisdom of the Gita are thinkers, writers, scientists and philosophers like Mahatma Gandhi, B.G.Tilak, Sri Aurobindo, Albert Einstein, Dr. Albert Schweitzer, Herman Hesse, Ralph Waldo Emerson, Aldous Huxley, Walt Whitman, Henry David Thoreau, Annie Besant, Robert Oppenheimer Sir Edwin Arnold and Carlyle to name but a few.

In India it was left to Adi Sankara who lived in the 8th century A.D. to reveal the greatness of the Gita to the world. He retrieved it from the mighty tomes of the epic, the Mahabharata, and wrote a brilliant commentary on it.

It is this commentary which prevails as a classic text even today. Later great *acharyas* like Ramanuja, Madhva, Vallabha and others came out with their own commentaries which are popular among their followers. In modern times Sant Jnanesvar, B.G.Tilak, Aurobindo contributed their original thinking on the text.

Despite this enormous popularity, the Bhagavad Gita remains a less understood but a better known text; people know more about it than what it is about. On the analogy of what the Bhagavad Gita says in Chapter 2, Verse 29 some look upon the book as marvelous, a scripture of extraordinary or mysterious value, some others speak of the book as wonderful. And still others though hearing its teachings do not comprehend its wonderful significance!

Bhagavan Sri Krishna also says in the Gita (7.3) "Among thousands of men, one by chance aspires for perfection; even among those successful aspirants only one by chance knows Me in essence."

A question arises why such enlightened persons are so rare in our midst and why such an achievement is not within the reach of everyone.

Vedanta being a subjective science, rarely one tries to know how to remove one's weaknesses and develop inner strength much less one tries to live up to the ideals propounded by it and bring about consequent re-adjustments in one's life. Very few feel this urge to evolve themselves and most of us do not even find the need for self improvement. We grope along by the voice of tradition, authority, herd-instinct and group-mentality. Of those who strive to see the truth and reach the goal, only a few succeed. Of those who gain the sight, not even one learns to live by the sight.

No wonder once a teacher wanting to educate a child about the Gita asked him "Do you know Gita"? The child replied "Yes, I know, that is the name of my next door aunty". The child obviously heard of Gita and had his own meaning of it in his mind and remained happy about it. That is the case with most of us today including the large mass of modern educated sections. Then where do we go from here? There is no other way than a constant study of the Gita and practicing its teachings.

WHAT IS THE GITA?

The dictionary meaning of the word 'Gita' is a song or poem containing an inspired doctrine and the word 'Bhagavat' means a blessed or adorable or venerable or divine One. Hence Srimad Bhagavad Gita is variously called as 'The Song of God', 'The Divine Song', 'A Song of Fortune', 'The Lord's Song', 'The Holy Song of God', 'The Song of the Lord', *Gudartha Deepika, Gita Rahasya, Jnaneshwari, Bhavaarthadipika, Sadhaka Sanjeevani* and so on. The noted English poet, journalist and a Principal of the Government Sanskrit College at Pune, Sir Edwin Arnold (1832-1904) called his famous poetic version of the Bhagavad Gita as 'The Song Celestial'. The Bhagavad Gita's another title is *'moksha sastra'* or 'Scripture of Liberation'. However, it is more popularly known as "The Gita".

The Bhagavad Gita is a sacred Hindu scripture, considered among the most important texts in the history of literature and philosophy. It finds a place in the Bhishma Parva of the Mahabharata. It comprises of 18 chapters spread out in 700 verses. Its author is Veda Vyasa, the compiler of the Mahabharata who wrote this epic through the hands of the Lord of Wisdom, Sri Ganesha. Its teachings are considered timeless and the exact time of revelation of the scripture is considered of little spiritual significance. The teacher of the Bhagavad Gita is Lord Krishna, who is revered as a manifestation of God, The Bhagvan, Parabrahman.

The content of the Gita is the conversation between Lord Krishna and Arjuna taking place on the battlefield of Kurukshetra before the start of the war between the two clans of brothers - the Kauravas and the Pandavas.

Responding to Arjuna's confusion and moral dilemma about fighting his own cousins, Bhagavan Krishna explains to Arjuna his duties as a warrior and prince and elaborates on different Vedantic concepts. This has led to the Gita being described as one of the *prasthana traya*, the triumvirate of the canons of Hindu Philosophy, the other two being the Upanishads and the Brahma Sutras.

It is considered as a concise, practical, self-contained guide to play the game of life. The subject of the Bhagavad Gita is the crisis of the active human in the midst of worldly obligations. The analysis and insight it provides are true for all times to come because the character of human mind and its interactions with the world are changeless.

During the discourse, Krishna reveals His identity as the Supreme Being *(Svayam Bhagavan)*, blessing Arjuna with an awe-inspiring vision of His divine universal form.

The Gita itself tells us about what it is. At the end of the first chapter we find a narration reading as under:

om tat sat iti srimad bhagavadgeetaasu upanishatsu brahma vidyaayaam yogashaastre sri krishnaarjuna samvaade arjuna vishaada yogo naama prathamo'dyaayah ||

"THUS IN THE UPANISHADS OF THE GLORIOUS BHAGAVAD GITA, THE SCIENCE OF THE ETERNAL, THE SCRIPTURE OF YOGA, THE DIALOGUE BETWEEN SRI KRISHNA AND ARJUNA, ENDS THE FIRST DISCOURSE ENTITLED: THE YOGA OF THE DESPONDENCY OF ARJUNA"

The narration as given above at the end of the first chapter occurs at the end of all the other subsequent chapters, the only difference being the respective title of the chapters. This narration is called '*sankalpa vakya*' meaning an epilogue for the chapter. It reveals in a very concise form the glory and greatness of the Gita and states the theme of the concerned chapter.

The meaning of this recital is as under:

- Om Tat Sat: A designation for the Absolute enabling everybody to turn towards Godhead.
- Gita is called: Upanishad because it contains the essence of all the Upanishads which are the revelations of the ancient sages.
- Brahma Vidya or the science of the Eternal because it teaches about the changeless Reality behind the ever-changing phenomenal world of perceptions, emotions and thoughts.
- Yoga Shastra because it is a scripture that explains the technique of right living and provides a practical guide to work it out in the form of Jnana Yoga, Karma Yoga, Bhakti Yoga and Raja Yoga.

- Samvad because it is in the form of a dialogue between Krishna and Arjuna, the Divine and the human, the former teaching the latter how to function successfully and efficiently in a community.
- This chapter is entitled 'Arjuna Vishaada Yogah' or the Yoga of despondency of Arjuna.

STORY OF THE MAHABHARATA

In the north of India, there flourished a kingdom with its headquarters at Hastinapur. King Pandu was ruling the kingdom after his father's death, as his elder brother, Dhritarashtra, was born blind and therefore not qualified for the rulership according to the tenets of that age. King Pandu had five sons who were known as Pandavas. Dhritarashtra had one hundred sons who were called as Kauravas, the eldest of whom was Duryodhana. Bhishma was the uncle of Pandu and Dhritarashtra.

After Pandu's death his children, Pandavas, were brought up and educated along with Kauravas under the supervision of Bhishma and patronage of Dhritarashtra. Drona was a skillful teacher who taught them all the techniques of warfare. Pandavas were intelligent and brave. Within a short time they could master the art of warfare. Yudhishtira, the eldest of the Pandavas, succeeded his father as the king.

Duryodhana was jealous of the Pandavas. When Yudhishtira was proclaimed a king Duryodhana could not keep quiet and watch. He was not only burning with envy over what the Pandavas had but also by the covetous thoughts of denying them what he himself possessed. He employed all foul means to destroy Pandavas and every time he tried to kill them he met with failure. On Bhishma's advice the kingdom was divided into two parts - the better one with Hastinapur as capital was taken by the Kauravas while the Pandavas took the other half and built a new beautiful capital called Indraprastha for themselves.

Dhritarashtra was equally affectionate towards his sons and Pandavas but had the weakness to be sympathetic towards his eldest son's sorrows and disappointments.

Once Duryodhana invited Yudhishtira for a game of dice wherein the former with the help of his cunning and deceitful uncle, Sakuni, defeated Yudhishtira by using all fraudulent means. As a result, Yudhishtira lost not only all his kingdom and possessions but also Draupadi, the wife of all the Pandava brothers. Draupadi was humiliated by the Kaurava brothers to such an extent that an attempt was made to disrobe her in public. Her honor was saved by Bhagavan Sri Krishna, a great family friend of the Pandavas.

Finally it was settled that Pandavas should live in the forest for twelve years in exile and further one year incognito untraced by any one. After successfully completing these thirteen years of ordeal when the Pandavas claimed their kingdom Duryodhana refused to part with even that much little land as could be covered by the point of a needle.

The good offices of Sri Krishna to bring sanity to Duryodhana who was intoxicated with power and greed proved futile. The Pandavas were left with no alternative but to take up arms against Kauravas to regain their kingdom lost through tricks, treachery and chicanery.

A war between Pandavas and Kauravas became inevitable and the preparations for the epic battle started. Both the sides mobilized their troops and took their respective positions in the battlefield at Kurukshetra, near modern Delhi.

Bhagavan Sri Krishna was the charioteer of Arjuna, the mightiest of the Pandava brothers. Arjuna asked Sri Krishna to place their chariot between the two armies to enable him to have a look at all those with whom he had to fight. Although till that time he was in full fighting spirit, when he saw his teachers, elders, brothers, relatives and friends standing before him ready for the fight, his determination gave way to weakness of head and heart. He lost his enthusiasm to fight and told Sri Krishna that he did not want to wage the battle against his seniors, relations and friends for the sake of a paltry kingdom.

When Arjuna refused to fight, Sri Krishna gave him a good peace of advice enlightening him upon where his duty lay. This marvelous advice delivered by The Bhagavan in the battlefield at Kurukshetra is the immortal poem, the song divine, the glorious SRIMAD BHAGAVAD GITA which epitomizes the whole gamut of knowledge contained in all the Scriptures.

Sage Vyasa offered Dhritarashtra the power of sight which would enable him to see the events of war. Unwilling to see the inevitable massacre of his sons, the blind king desired to know the full details of the war. To fulfill Dhritarashtra's request Vyasa bestowed Sanjaya, the trusted minister of Dhritarashtra, with the divine intuitive vision by which he could know not only the incidents of the battlefield but also the ideas in the minds of the warriors.

After ten days of war, Bhishma, the commander of the Kaurava army was severely wounded and thrown off his chariot. When Sanjaya informed Dhritarashtra about this incident the blind king became very sad and asked him to tell him all the details of the war. The reporting of Sanjaya about the events of war including the dialogue between Sri Krishna and Arjuna at the battlefield is contained in the Bhishma Parva of Mahabharata wherein The Gita text finds place. The Gita opens with the question of the blind king to Sanjaya asking him what happened on the battlefield when the two armies faced each other in the battle formation.

CENTRAL THEME OF THE GITA

The Bhagvad Gita can be studied from different angles such as a historical document, a spiritual treatise, a scriptural text for daily chanting and prayer, a sublime poetry, an exposition of Grammar and meter, or a management manual, depending on one's own outlook and purpose.

The objective here is to study it as a spiritual text and try to find out its main theme. Our ancient Rishis have given us a six-point test to determine the main theme of a text. This is called *'sadvidvidha tatparya nirnaya linga'*. In the light of this six-factor test let us look at the Gita to discover its central theme.

The 1st point is called *upakrama* and *upasamhara* - the beginning and conclusion of a text. The crux of the subject in the text starts with Arjuna's confusion, his acceptance of the delusion and surrender to the Lord as a *sishya* with a request to teach him what is the best for him. The text ends with his statement that all his doubts were cleared, his delusion is gone and he regained his memory of the Self. This kind of beginning and end of the text shows that the Bhagavad Gita contains the Knowledge that removes the delusion and bestows the Supreme Good.

Even from the teacher's view point, the text starts from Sri Krishna telling Arjuna that he is grieving for that which should not be grieved for thereby explaining how sorrow is borne of delusion. It ends by asking Arjuna whether the delusion had gone. This makes it clear that the entire purpose of the dialogue between Krishna and Arjuna was aimed at removing spiritual ignorance which is the cause of delusion. Thus the removal of sorrow and delusion *(soka moha nivritti)* is the main theme of the Gita.

The 2nd point is called *abhayasa* - repetition and emphasis in the text. The 2nd chapter gives ample evidence to this aspect. Krishna frequently tells Arjuna not to grieve and puts forward the reasons for that view from several angles like the true knowledge, duty, ignominy etc. Similarly, the concept of *sthitaprajna* has been highlighted in several ways at various places. This shows imparting Self-Knowledge is the key note in the text.

The 3rd point is called *apurvata* - the novelty or uniqueness of the theme. Sri Krishna calls this Self-Knowledge as a secret, *guhyam* because normal extroverted minds cannot grasp it and hence very few succeed in knowing it. Similarly, moderation in all walks of our lives has been stressed at many places. The teachings of the Gita are thus unique.

The 4th point is *phalam* or the fruit or the end result of the study of the text. Removal of sorrow and confusion and attainment of clear thinking and supreme knowledge - enlightenment - are the end result of the study of the text.

The 5th point is *arthavada* - positive praise of the subject and negative condemnation of the opposite. We find many slokas in the text extolling the supreme Self-Knowledge and condemning spiritual ignorance. Thus attaining the Supreme Knowledge is the goal of the Gita.

The 6th and the last point is *upapatti* - illustration and reasoning. We find in the text that Krishna has been giving a number of logical explanations and reasoning to convince Arjuna about his teachings. He uses profusely the word *'tasmat'* meaning 'therefore'. His arguments are given from many angles, the main goal of all His efforts being elimination of sorrow and delusion through Self-Knowledge. The nature of Self is also revealed through examples and reasoning. These indicate the Supreme knowledge *(tattva jnanam)* as the main subject matter of the Gita.

Therefore Self-Knowledge *(atma jnana)* which eliminates ignorance and its problems and which bestows the ultimate good for all *(shreyas)* is the core theme of the Gita.

OVER-VIEW OF THE GITA

The entire Bhagavad Gita can be divided into five topics viz.

1. Identifying the problem (covered in the 1st and the starting portions of the 2nd chapters of the Gita).
2. Finding a solution (covered in the major portion of the 2nd chapter and reiterated in the 7th, 9th and 13th chapters.
3. Implementing the solution (This theme is dealt with in the 3rd, 5th, 12th and 18th chapters).

4. Understanding the values of life (stated in many places in the Gita and particularly in the 16th chapter) and
5. Achieving perfection (elaborated in the 2nd, 5th, and 14th chapters).

Arjuna's misunderstanding, his inability to see things as they are and consequent grief and self-pity just at the crucial moment of war are the problems. The solution to them can be short term which will only be of temporary nature or long term which will be of permanent nature. The Gita offers a long term solution with which anybody can face any situation in life at any time anywhere. This spiritual solution teaches us to look at life as a whole and live a whole life. Finding a solution is just not enough. We must know how to implement it. The Gita provides us with a practical guidance that helps us to understand how to live according to the guidelines offered.

But living a life according to the guidelines offered is also not adequate unless it is spiced with certain basic vision and values. If a person's vision of life is limited to mundane happiness derived from the senses, he will merely spend his life time in eating, drinking and making merry. His value system will revolve round making money by any means to satisfy his never ending needs. But the value system of a person with a philanthropic bent or an animal lover or an environmentalist or spiritually oriented will be entirely different. The Gita provides us with such an enlarged vision of life laying the foundation for a sense of fulfillment.

Finally, the Gita gives us the vision of a person who has gained the supreme Knowledge and lives anchored in it. One who faces problems and crisis in life gains the vision of Truth, puts it into practice, and lives according to that value system. He becomes a *jivan mukta*, liberated in this very life. He is called a *sthita prajna* and the Gita gives us a vivid description of his nature.

MAIN CONCEPTS OF THE GITA

The main philosophical subject matter of the Bhagavad Gita is the explanation of five basic concepts.

- Jiva, the individual soul or the living being
- Jagat, the universe he lives in or nature or matter
- Jagadishvara, the creator of the universe or the Supreme Controller and the relationship between Jiva, Jagat and Jagadishvara.
- Dharma (Duty in accordance with Divine law)
- Kaala (Time)

Krishna counsels Arjuna on the greater idea of dharma, or universal harmony and duty. He begins with the tenet that the soul (Atman) is eternal and immortal. Any 'death' on the battlefield would involve only the shedding of the body, whereas the soul is permanent.

In order to clarify his point, Krishna expounds the various Yoga processes and understanding of the true nature of the universe. He describes the yogic paths of devotional service -Bhakti Yoga, action - Karma Yoga, meditation - Dhyana Yoga or Raja Yoga and knowledge - Jnana Yoga.

Fundamentally, the Bhagavad Gita proposes that true enlightenment comes from going beyond identification with the temporal ego, the 'False Self', the ephemeral world, so that one identifies with the truth of the immortal self, the absolute soul or Atman.

Through detachment from the material sense of ego, the Yogi, or follower of a particular path of Yoga, is able to transcend his/her illusory mortality and attachment to the material world and enters the realm of the Supreme.

Krishna does not propose that the physical world must be abandoned or neglected. Rather, one's life on Earth must be lived in accordance with greater laws and truths; one must embrace one's temporal duties whilst remaining mindful of timeless reality, acting for the sake of service without consideration for the results thereof. Such a life would naturally lead towards stability, happiness and, ultimately, enlightenment.

In the Bhagavad Gita Krishna refers to the war about to take place as 'Dharma Yuddha', meaning a righteous war for the purpose of justice. He also states that he incarnates in each age (*yuga*) to establish righteousness in the world.

WHY STUDY THE GITA?

Srimad Bhagavad Gita has been a source of inspiration and enlightenment for generations. The message of the Gita is not merely a general spiritual philosophy or ethical doctrine but it has a bearing upon the practical aspects in the application of such principles in our day-to-day lives. It is indeed "An Users' Manual for the Practice of the Art of Right Living".

The centuries old Bhagavad Gita continues to be the most relevant beacon light for all of us today. The modern man, like Arjuna, is at the crossroads where the focus is more on improving the Standard of Living rather than the Quality of Life, more on the Stock Exchange or Cost of Living Index than on the Human Development Quotient. This has resulted in his disorientation and imbalance in an environment of shifting values. While science aims to enhance the comfort of human life, spirituality teaches us how to be comfortable with what we have. That is the difference. In this scenario, the Gita is the only source of strength for the development of an integrated personality, a complete man, within us.

The Gita teaches how to achieve harmony with divinity in the midst of disharmony by subduing all outward energies and remaining in equanimity with pairs of opposites like pain and pleasure, aversion and attraction, success and failure etc. The focus of the Gita is moderation and its aim is the total surrender of man before the Supreme while continuing to perform his duties in the spirit of Yoga.

The problem that is facing us today is that while the world is coming closer physically it is drifting apart mentally and emotionally. Hence all the conflicts and violence, destruction and damage across the globe. The urgent need, therefore, is the reconciliation and reconditioning of the human mindset, to inculcate a global vision and bring about the universal brotherhood. The Gita is specially suited for the purpose, as it attempts to bring together varied and apparently antithetical forms of the consciousness and emphasizes the root conceptions of humanity which are neither ancient nor modern, belonging neither to the east nor the west, but eternal and universal. Its beauty and sublimity lie in its everlasting relevance to the daily problems of human life, either occidental or oriental. It prescribes the methods which are within the reach of all. It has a message of solace, freedom, salvation, perfection and peace for all human beings. It is indeed a recipe for sane living for every man and woman.

<<<000>>>

Chapter 1

Arjuna Vishaada Yogah:

Yoga of the Despondency of Arjuna

INVOCATION

It is customary to study the meditation verses on the Gita called *Gita Dhyanam* before commencing the study of the Bhagavad Gita text. It is not known who composed them. It is a set of 9 verses recited as invocation, dedication and prayer to the Gita Knowledge and its glory. Let us take up one of the verses and understand its meaning.

Prapanna paarijaataaya totra vetraika paanaye |
Jnaanamudraaya krishnaaya geetaamrita duhe namah ||

SALUTATIONS TO BHAGVAN KRISHNA, WITH HIS RIGHT HAND IN JNANA MUDRA, THE BESTOWER OF ALL NEEDS TO THOSE WHO SURRENDER TO HIM COMPLETELY, THE MILKER OF THE DIVINE NECTAR OF THE BHAGAVAD GITA, THE HOLDER OF THE WHIP IN ONE HAND FOR DRIVING THE COWS.

This verse describes Sri Krishna with His right hand held in *Jnana Mudra* - in knowledge posture - wherein the thumb is joined to the forefinger and all the other three fingers are stretched out, the gesture symbolizing knowledge. This is a remarkable concept in Indian Vedantic philosophy and spirituality which indicates that our body postures have psychological counter parts. As the mind is, so is the body; bodily expressions being the manifestation of the working of the mind or the effect of psyche. This is what we call 'body language' in the modern business school terminology. It means that there is nothing in this world so purifying as Knowledge.

We offer our obeisance to Sri Krishna who is the embodiment of Knowledge and who imparts such knowledge to all those who seek it from Him. This is what Arjuna does in the Gita. That knowledge is the Supreme Knowledge - the knowledge of the Absolute Reality, the knowledge of Dharma, the knowledge of righteousness, the knowledge about the right way of living.

With this prayer let us start our journey in the Gita Ganga and crave for enlightenment.

PREAMBLE

The 1st Chapter in the Bhagavad Gita introduces the scene, the setting, the circumstances and the characters involved determining the reasons for its espousal. The scene is the sacred plain of Kurukshetra. The setting is the battlefield. The situation is that the war between the two clans of brothers, the Kauravas and the Pandavas is about to begin.

The main characters are Bhagavan Sri Krishna and the valiant Arjuna from the side of Pandavas and Duryodhana from the side of Kauravas in the midst of large armies on both the sides led by their respective commanders.

After noticing the principal warriors on both the sides, Arjuna falls into the mood of deep dejection and melancholy due to the fear of destruction of friends and relatives in the course of the impending war leading to his resolve not to take up arms against his kith and kin. This subject of *vishaada* or grief is the major content and message of this Chapter and hence it is called "Arjuna Vishaada Yogah: The Yoga of the Despondency of Arjuna". Sorrow is the setting and compulsion which made Arjuna search for the truth. The answer to this search shows that the Gita is not a spiritual gospel meant for ascetics to have a better life hereafter but a helpful tool in the hands of those who want to practice right living here and now.

THE TEXT

THE QUESTION

dhritaraashtra uvaacha
dharmakshetre kurukshetre samavetaa yuyutsavah
maamakaah paandavaashchaiva kimakurvata sanjaya // 1.1 //

DHRITARASHTRA SAID
WHAT DID THE SONS OF PANDU AND ALSO MY PEOPLE DO WHEN THEY ASSEMBLED TOGETHER ON THE HOLY FIELD OF KURUKSHETRA, EAGER TO FIGHT, O SANJAYA?

In the entire Gita this is the only uttering of the blind king, Dhritarashtra. All the remaining verses are Sanjaya's report to him about the happenings at the battlefield of Kurukshetra just before the war.

The battlefield is called *dharmakshetra* or the sacred field because The Lord who is the protector and embodiment of

Dharma was actively present in it. Kurukshetra means the field of the Kurus, a leading clan of that era. This question of Dhritarashtra exhibits a sense of anxiety in him on two counts. If Pandavas decide not to undertake the war, his sons will automatically get the kingdom and in such an event, the stigma of waging the unrighteous war might not stick to his covetous and deceitful sons. If his sons decide not to wage the war they will lose the kingdom that was earlier acquired by them through deceit, because of which they will be as good as dead. Such was the anxiety in the king's mind due to the prominence and spiritual atmosphere of the field of battle.

Mamakaah: My people. And 'Pandu's sons'. - This sort of divisive reference to one and the same family members indicates the absence of the sense of belonging, inclusiveness and closeness with regard to the Pandavas and thereby betrays the King's hostility towards them.

This sense of a pair of opposites 'mine-ness' and 'not-mine-ness' is the result of *ahamkara* or 'I - ness' which is the source of all evil. The conflict between the two cousin groups represents the clash between two sets of values of life - one standing for virtue, justice and righteousness staking a legitimate claim for the kingdom lost through deceit and treachery and the other for vice, jealousy, injustice, hatred, greed, hunger for power and the foul means employed to justify the ends. It indirectly indicates that life itself is a battle between good and evil.

TWO ARMIES

sanjaya uvaacha
drishtwaa tu paandavaaneekam vyoodham duryodhanastadaa
aachaaryam upasamgamya raajaa vachanam abraveet // 1.2 //

SANJAYA SAID
HAVING SEEN THE ARMY OF PANDAVAS DRAWN UP IN BATTLE ARRAY, KING DURYODHANA THEN APPROACHED HIS TEACHER, DRONA, AND SPOKE THESE WORDS.

Duryodhana was thinking all along that it might not be possible for the Pandavas to mobilize forces strong enough to face his own huge army. But what he saw on the battlefield unnerved his position and hence he rushed to his teacher, Drona and exclaimed:

pashyaitaam paanduputraanaam aacharya mahateem chamoom
vyoodhaam drupadaputrena tava shishyena dheemataa // 1.3 //

BEHOLD, O TEACHER, THIS MIGHTY ARMY OF THE SONS OF PANDU, ARRAYED BY THE SON OF DRUPADA, YOUR WISE DISCIPLE.

atra shooraa maheshwaasaa bheemaarjunasamaa yudhi
yuyudhaano viraatashcha drupadashcha mahaarathah // 1.4 //

HERE ARE HEROES, MIGHTY ARCHERS, EQUAL IN BATTLE TO BHIMA AND ARJUNA, YUYUDHANA, VIRATA AND DRUPADA, THE GREAT CHARIOT WARRIOR.

dhrishtaketush chekitaanah kaashiraajascha veeryavan
purujit kuntibhojashcha shaibhyashcha narapungavah // 1.5 //

DHRISHTAKETU, CHEKITANA AND THE VALIANT KING OF KASI, PURUJIT, KUNTIBHOJA AND SAIBYA, THE BEST AMONG MEN.

yudhaamanyushcha vikraanta uttamaujaashcha veeryavan
saubhadro draupadeyaashcha sarva eva mahaarathaah // 1.6 //

THE COURAGEOUS YUDHAMANYU, THE BRAVE UTTAMAUJA, SAUBHADRA AND THE SONS OF DRAUPADI - ALL GREAT CHARIOT-WARRIORS.

asmaakam tu vishishtaa ye taan nibodha dwijottama
naayakaa mama sainyasya samjnaartham taan braveemi te // 1.7 //

KNOW ALSO, O THE BEST AMONG THE TWICE BORN, THE NAMES OF THOSE WHO ARE MOST DISTINGUISHED AMONGST US, THE LEADERS OF MY ARMY. THESE I RELATE TO YOU FOR YOUR INFORMATION.

bhavaan bheeshmashcha karnashcha kripashcha samitinjayah
ashwatthaamaa vikarnashcha saumadattis tathaiva cha // 1.8 //

YOURSELF AND BHISHMA AND KARNA AND KRIPA, THE VICTORIOUS IN WAR, ASWATTHAMA AND VIKARNA AND JAYADRATHA, THE SON OF SOMADATTA.

anye cha bahavah shooraa madarthe tyaktajeevitaah
naanaashastrapraharanaah sarve yuddhavishaaradaah // 1.9 //

AND MANY OTHER HEROES ALSO, WELL-SKILLED IN WARFARE AND ARMED WITH MANY KINDS OF WEAPONS ARE HERE; READY TO LAY DOWN THEIR LIVES FOR MY SAKE.

aparyaaptam tad asmaakam balam bheeshmaabhirakshitam
paryaaptam twidam eteshaam balam bheemaabhirakshitam // 1.10 //

OUR ARMY DEFENDED BY BHISHMA IS INSUFFICIENT BUT THE ARMY OF THEIRS DEFENDED BY BHIMA IS SUFFICIENT.

ayaneshu cha sarveshu yathaabhaagam avasthitaah
bheeshmam evaabhirakshantu bhavantah sarva eva hi // 1.11 //

NOW ALL OF YOU BEING STATIONED IN YOUR RESPECTIVE POSITIONS IN THE DIVISIONS OF THE ARMY GUARD BHISHMA ALONE BY ALL MEANS.

By using the words 'your talented pupil' Duryodhana sarcastically told Drona that he was a mere simpleton to teach the art of warfare to the son of Drupada [Drstadyumna] who was standing before him to kill no other person than his teacher himself.

Duryodhana perceived the army of Pandavas as formidable because of his own guilty consciousness and doubts about the loyalty of his chief warriors. A list of all the names of the mighty warriors in the Pandava army was given.

Dwijottama means 'twice born' which refers to the Brahminical background of Drona. Duryodhana implied that Drona, a Brahmin and therefore being timid by nature and given to peaceful life, might be soft towards his students no matter to whichever side they may belong to.

Receiving no response from Drona despite his long speech and to make amends for his censuring him, Duryodhana enumerated the names of the warriors of his side also exaggerating their qualities in order to look self-confident and hide his nervousness. Duryodhana felt that his army led by Bhishma was insufficient because of the latter's softness towards Pandavas and the other led by Bhima as sufficient because of its high morale and efficiency. He ordered full protection to Bhishma from all sides and by all means not only to please him but to emphasize his important place in the entire Kaurava army. He was fully aware that once Bhishma were to be eliminated his whole edifice would collapse.

SOUNDING OF THE CONCH SHELLS

tasya sanjanayan harsham kuruvriddhah pitaamahah
simhanaadam vinadyocchaih shankham dadhmau prataapavaan
// 1.12 //

THEN THE POWERFUL BHISHMA, GRANDSIRE AND OLDEST OF THE KAURAVAS, ROARED LIKE A LION AND BLEW HIS CONCH IN ORDER TO CHEER UP DURYODHANA.

tatah shankaashcha bheryashcha panavaanakagomukhaah
sahasaivaabhyahanyanta sa shabdastumulo bhavat // 1.13 //

THEN (FOLLOWING BHISHMA) CONCHES, KETTLE DRUMS, TABORS, TRUMPETS AND COW-HORNS SUDDENLY BLARED FORTH FROM THE KAURAVA SIDE CREATING A TUMULTUOUS NOISE.

tatah shvetair hayair yukte mahati syandane sthitau
maadhavah paandavashchaiva divyau shankhau pradadhmatuh
// 1.14 //

THEN STATIONED IN THEIR MAGNIFICENT CHARIOT, YOKED WITH WHITE HORSES, MADHAVA (KRISHNA) AND THE SON OF PANDU (ARJUNA) ALSO BLEW THEIR DIVINE CONCHES WITH A FURIOUS NOISE.

paanchajanyam hrisheekesho devadattam dhananjayah
paundram dadhmau mahaashankham bheemakarmaa vrikodarah
// 1.15 //

HRISHIKESHA (KRISHNA) BLEW THE CONCH, PANCHAJANYA, DHANANJAYA (ARJUNA) BLEW THE DEVADATTA AND BHIMA, THE DOER OF TERRIBLE DEEDS, BLEW THE GREAT CONCH, PAUNDRA.

anantavijayam raajaa kunteeputro yudhishthirah
nakulah sahadevashcha sughoshamanipushpakau // 1.16 //

KING YUDHISHTIRA, THE SON OF KUNTI, BLEW THE ANANTAVIJAYA, NAKULA AND SAHADEVA BLEW THE SUGHOSHA AND MANIPUSHPAKA CONCHES RESPECTIVELY.

kaashyashcha parameshwaasah shikhandee cha mahaarathah
dhrishtadyumno viraatashcha saatyakishchaaparaajitah // 1.17 //

THE KING OF KASI, AN EXCELLENT ARCHER, SIKHANDI, THE MIGHTY CHARIOT-WARRIOR, DHRSHTADYUMNA, VIRATA AND SATYAKI, THE UNCONQUERED.

drupado draupadeyaashcha sarvashah prithiveepate
saubhadrashcha mahaabaahuh shankhaan dadhmuh prithak prithak // 1.18 //

DRUPADA AND THE SONS OF DRAUPADI, O LORD OF THE EARTH, AND THE SON OF SUBHADRA, THE MIGHTY ARMED, BLEW THEIR RESPECTIVE CONCHES.

sa ghosho dhaartaraashtraanaam hridayaani vyadaarayat
nabhashcha prithiveem chaiva tumulo vyanunaadayan // 1.19 //

THE TUMULTUOUS SOUND OF THE CONCHES PIERCED THE HEARTS OF THE MEMBERS OF THE DHRITARASHTRA'S SIDE, MAKING BOTH THE SKY AND EARTH RESOUND.

Bhishma understood the mental agony of Duryodhana. In order to cheer him up he roared like a lion and blew his conch which was misunderstood as a signal for commencement of war. The Kaurava army blared forth its various conches and martial musical instruments signifying the declaration of war from its side.

In these verses Sanjaya had given the reaction of Pandavas to the war-cry raised from the opposite side and the names of various conches blown by the respective heroes. The most famous among them is the conch 'Panchajanya' blown by Krishna. The uproar seemed to penetrate the hearts of Kauravas deeply and abnormally because of their guilty conscience.

Metaphorically, the chariot represents the human gross body, the horses are the senses and their reins are the mind that controls the senses. The charioteer is the guiding spirit or the Self or Atman in the human beings. Bhagavan Sri Krishna, the divine charioteer, is the Self in all of us.

By addressing Dhritarashtra as the lord of the earth (Verse 18) and hinting about the superiority of the Pandava side Sanjaya implied that as the ruling monarch he would take a decision even at that catastrophic moment to preserve the integrity of the country from the impending ruinous warfare. But that was not to be.

ARJUNA'S DESIRE TO SURVEY THE TWO ARMIES

atha vyavasthitaan drishtwaa dhaartaraashtraan kapidhwajah
pravritte shastrasampaate dhanurudyamya paandavah // 1.20 //
hrisheekesham tadaa vaakyamidamaaha maheepate -1.21

THEN, O LORD OF THE EARTH, SEEING DHRITARASHTRA'S MEN BEING POSITIONED AND THE DISCHARGE OF WEAPONS ABOUT TO BEGIN, PANDAVA (ARJUNA), WHOSE ENSIGN WAS HANUMAN, RAISING HIS BOW, SPOKE THE FOLLOWING WORDS TO KRISHNA.

The critical situation prevailing just at that moment when the war was about to begin was described. The hero of the Mahabharata war, Arjuna, arrived at the battlefield. Tension prevailed everywhere. Crisis was at its zenith.

Arjuna appeared impatient to fire the first shot. He raised his bow to position it and at that crucial juncture he spoke to Krishna the following words which turned out to be historic as the starting point for the dialogue between them in the form of the great Srimad Bhagavad Gita.

arjuna uvaacha
senayor ubhayormadhye ratham sthaapaya me'chyuta // 1.21 //
yaavad etaan nireekshe'ham yoddhukaamaan avasthitaan
kair mayaa saha yoddhavyam asmin ranasamudyame // 1.22 //

ARJUNA SAID
O ACHYUTA (KRISHNA) PLACE MY CHARIOT IN BETWEEN BOTH THE ARMIES SO THAT I MAY SURVEY THOSE WHO STAND HERE EAGER TO FIGHT. LET ME KNOW ON THE EVE OF THIS BATTLE WITH WHOM I HAVE TO FIGHT.

yotsyamaanaan avekshe'ham ya ete'tra samaagataah
dhaartaraashtrasya durbuddher yuddhe priyachikeershavah // 1.23 //

FOR, I DESIRE TO HAVE A LOOK AT THOSE WHO ARE ASSEMBLED HERE TO FIGHT, WISHING TO PLEASE THE PERVERTED SON OF DHRITARASHTRA.

Arjuna thus expressed his bravery, readiness, impatience, gallantry and determination to face the battle. This is an important stage in the story because up to this time Arjuna was an invincible hero full of self-confidence and enthusiasm with no signs of mental aberrations. However, a little later he became a completely changed personality.

SRI KRISHNA ENTERS THE SCENE

sanjaya uvaacha
evamukto hrisheekesho gudaakeshena bhaarata
senayor ubhayormadhye sthaapayitwaa rathottamam // 1.24 //
bheeshma drona pramukhatah sarveshaam cha maheekshitam
uvaacha paartha pashyaitaan samavetaan kuroon iti // 1.25 //

SANJAYA SAID
O BHARATA (DHRITARASHTRA), THUS REQUESTED BY GUDAKESHA (ARJUNA), HRISHIKESHA PLACED THE MAGNIFICENT CHARIOT BETWEEN THE TWO ARMIES IN FRONT OF BHISHMA AND DRONA AND THE OTHER RULERS OF THE EARTH AND SAID 'O PARTHA (ARJUNA), BEHOLD ALL THESE KURUS ASSEMBLED HERE'.

Gudakesha, one who has controlled sleep i.e. Arjuna. It implies that once a goal is set by him he will not rest contended till it is achieved. Partha means the son of Prtha (Kunti) i.e.

Arjuna. Krishna placed his chariot with sagacity at such a point wherefrom Arjuna could see clearly his kinsman, Bhishma and preceptor, Drona and other kings and warriors of Kaurava side.

As a dutiful driver Krishna told Arjuna 'Behold, O Arjuna, all the Kauravas gathered here'. These are the only words spoken by Krishna in the first chapter of the Gita which proved to be a spark to ignite the process of burning down the false perceptions of the mighty Arjuna.

WHAT DID ARJUNA SEE?

tatraa pashyat sthitaan paarthah pitrin atha pitaamahaan
aacharyaan maatulaan bhraatrun putraan pautraan sakheemstathaa
// 1.26 //

THEN ARJUNA SAW STATIONED THERE IN THE ARMIES, UNCLES, GRANDFATHERS, TEACHERS, MATERNAL UNCLES, BROTHERS, SONS, GRANDSONS AND FRIENDS TOO.

shvashuraan suhridashchaiva senayorubhayorapi
taan sameekshya sa kaunteyah sarvaan bandhoon avasthitaan
// 1.27 //
kripayaa parayaa'vishto visheedannidam abraveet - 1.28

HE SAW FATHERS-IN-LAW AND FRIENDS ALSO IN BOTH ARMIES. KAUNTEYA (SON OF KUNTI) ARJUNA SEEING ALL THESE RELATIVES ARRAYED THERE, BECAME OVERWHELMED BY SUPREME COMPASSION AND SAID THIS SORROWFULLY.

Arjuna seeing his elders and other relations, teachers, friends and well wishers arrayed in the battle ready to fight suddenly developed extreme self-pity and compassion. His manliness gave way to faint-heartedness thinking about consequences that will follow in waging the war with his kinsmen which will result in destroying his own race.

The valiant hero, Arjuna, transformed himself into a kinsman of the opposite side i.e. as a son, a brother, a student etc. This change of disposition was verily spontaneous. It was not due to any discrimination, but on account of the very absence of it and because of an erroneous understanding called delusion and mental confusion called grief which prevented right perception of the situation.

ARJUNA'S REACTION

arjuna uvaacha
drishtwe mam swajanam krishna yuyutsum samupasthitam // 1.28 //

ARJUNA SAID
O KRISHNA, SEEING THESE RELATIVES AND FRIENDS GATHERED HERE EAGER TO FIGHT,

seedanti mama gaatraani mukham cha parishushyati
vepathushcha shareere me romaharshashcha jaayate // 1.29//

MY LIMBS FAIL ME AND MY MOUTH GETS PARCHED UP, MY BODY TREMBLES AND MY HAIRS STAND ON END.

gaandeevam sramsate hastaat twak chaiva paridahyate
na cha shaknomyavasthaatum bhramateeva cha me manah // 1.30 //

THE GANDIVA (BOW) SLIPS FROM MY HAND AND MY SKIN BURNS ALL OVER; I AM UNABLE EVEN TO STAND STEADY AND MY MIND IS REELING.

nimittaani cha pashyaami vipareetaani keshava
na cha shreyo'nupashyaami hatwaa swajanam aahave // 1.31 //

AND I SEE EVIL OMENS, O KESAVA (KRISHNA), I DO NOT SEE ANY GOOD IN KILLING MY OWN PEOPLE IN THIS BATTLE.

Arjuna's attention to omens indicates that his mental tenacity had gone down. It started showing its weak spot and volatility. The image of the world he was seeing till a short while ago, now presented him with a different picture on account of his change of perception. Subjectivity replaced objectivity on account of his mental bewilderment. Losing self-control, he landed in the abyss of ignorance. His words make us think of the loneliness of man oppressed by doubts and emptiness from whom the comforts of human life are slipping away. This sadness is the first experience of those who aspire for the vision of the Reality.

ARJUNA'S ANGUISH

na kaangkshe vijayam krishna na cha raajyam sukhaani cha
kim no raajyena govinda kim bhogair jeevitena vaa // 1.32 //

FOR, I DO NOT DESIRE VICTORY, O, KRISHNA, OR PLEASURES OR KINGDOMS. OF WHAT AVAIL IS KINGDOM TO US O, GOVINDA (KRISHNA), OR PLEASURES OR EVEN LIFE?

Indifference to acquisition of worldly pleasures is a sign of ethical and spiritual progress. However, Arjuna was far from it. It is only his delusion which is masquerading as mental achievement. It is nothing but a momentary temptation to adopt the method of renunciation in times of great sorrow and crisis bordering on escapism from the reality.

yeshaam arthe kaangkshitam no raajyam bhogaah sukhaani cha
ta ime'vasthitaa yuddhe praanaams tyaktwaa dhanaani cha // 1.33 //

THOSE FOR WHOSE SAKE WE DESIRE KINGDOMS, ENJOYMENTS AND PLEASURES, STAND HERE IN BATTLE STAKING THEIR LIFE AND WEALTH.

aachaaryah pitarah putraastathaiva cha pitaamahaah
maatulaah shwashuraah pautraah shyaalaah sambandhinas tathaa // 1.34 //

TEACHERS, FATHERS, SONS AND ALSO GRANDFATHERS, UNCLES AND FATHERS-IN-LAW, GRANDSONS AND BROTHERS-IN-LAW AND OTHER RELATIVES

etaan na hantum icchaami ghnato'pi madhusoodana
api trailokya raajyasya hetoh kim nu maheekrite // 1.35 //

O, MADHUSUDANA (KRISHNA), THOUGH THESE WERE TO KILL ME, I DO NOT WISH TO KILL THEM EVEN FOR THE SAKE OF DOMINION OVER THE THREE WORLDS, LEAVE ALONE KILLING THEM FOR THE SAKE OF THE EARTH.

nihatya dhaartaraashtraan nah kaa preetih syaaj janaardana
paapam evaashrayed asmaan hatwaitaan aatataayinah // 1.36 //

BY KILLING THESE SONS OF DHRITARASHTRA, WHAT PLEASURES CAN BE OURS O, JANARDANA (KRISHNA)? ONLY SIN WILL ACCRUE BY KILLING THESE FELONS.

The term 'felon' refers to the one who sets fire to the house of another, runs with a sword to kill, poisons others, plunders the wealth and land of others or usurps the wife of somebody else. Duryodhana committed all these crimes against the Pandavas. According to Artha Sastra no sin is committed if such felons are killed. But Arjuna overwhelmed with a sense of sentimental sympathy for his near and dear ones takes the help of the general principle of Dharma Sastra which forbids the sin of killing one another. He is talking in terms of misdirected wisdom.

tasmaan naarhaa vayam hantum dhaartaraashtraan swabaandhavaan
swajanam hi katham hatwaa sukhinah syaama maadhava // 1.37 //

THEREFORE, WE SHOULD NOT KILL THE SONS OF DHRITARASHTRA, OUR RELATIVES; FOR, HOW CAN WE BE HAPPY BY KILLING OUR OWN PEOPLE, O, MADHAVA (KRISHNA)?

yadyapyete na pashyanti lobhopahatachetasah
kulakshayakritam dosham mitradrohe cha paatakam // 1.38 //
katham na jneyam asmaabhih paapaad asmaan nivartitum
kulakshayakritam dosham prapashyadbhir janaardana // 1.39 //

O JANARDANA, THOUGH WITH THEIR INTELLIGENCE OVERPOWERED BY GREED THEY DO NOT SEE ANY EVIL OR SIN IN THE DESTRUCTION OF FAMILIES OR HOSTILITY

TOWARDS FRIENDS, WHY SHOULD NOT WE WHO CLEARLY SEE EVIL IN THE DESTRUCTION OF A FAMILY, LEARN TO TURN AWAY FROM THIS SIN.

Arjuna was reinforcing his arguments for saving the Kaurava desperadoes due to his attachment for his relatives and friends by putting forward a philosophy of non-resistance to evil. Krishna in his discourses that will follow proved the hollowness of these arguments and their dangerous implications.

kulakshaye pranashyanti kuladharmaah sanaatanaah
dharme nashte kulam kritsnam adharmo'bhibhavatyuta // 1.40 //

IN THE DESTRUCTION OF A FAMILY, ITS ANCIENT RELIGIOUS TRADITIONS PERISH; ON THE DESTRUCTION OF SPIRITUALITY, LAWLESSNESS OVERTAKES THE WHOLE FAMILY.

Dharma or spirituality means the duties, rites and ceremonies practiced by the family in accordance with the injunctions of the scriptures. War tends to tear us away from our natural home surroundings and uproot us from social traditions which are the essence of the mature will and experience of the people.

adharmaabhibhavaat krishna pradushyanti kulastriyah
streeshu dushtaasu vaarshneya jaayate varnasankarah // 1.41 //

AND WHEN LAWLESSNESS PREVAILS, O KRISHNA, THE WOMEN OF THE FAMILY BECOME CORRUPT AND WHEN WOMEN BECOME CORRUPTED IT RESULTS IN INTERMINGLING OF CASTES O, VARSHNEYA (KRISHNA-THE DESCENDENT OF VRSHNI CLAN).

The idea is that when women are associated with their husbands who flouted their family traditions of righteousness, they may also feel emboldened to commit transgressions.

sankaro narakaayaiva kulaghnaanaam kulasya cha
patanti pitaro hyeshaam luptapindodaka kriyaah // 1.42 //

ADMIXTURE OF CASTES LEADS THE FAMILY AND THE SLAYERS OF THE FAMILY TO HELL BECAUSE THE SPIRITS OF THEIR ANCESTORS FALL DEPRIVED OF THE OFFERINGS OF RICE AND WATER.

doshair etaih kulaghnaanaam varnasankarakaarakaih
utsaadyante jaatidharmaah kuladharmaashcha shaashwataah // 1.43 //

BY THESE EVIL DEEDS OF THE DESTROYERS OF THE FAMILY, WHICH CAUSE CONFUSION OF CASTES, THE TRADITIONAL DUTIES OF THE CASTE AND THE FAMILY ARE DESTROYED.

utsannakuladharmaanaam manushyaanaam janaardana
narake niyatam vaaso bhavateetyanushushruma // 1.44 //

O, JANARDANA, WE HAVE HEARD THAT DWELLING IN HELL FOR AN INFINITE PERIOD IS INEVITABLE FOR THOSE PEOPLE WHOSE FAMILY DUTIES HAVE BEEN DESTROYED.

Arjuna argued that impiety will predominate in the families because the death of the experienced persons in the battle field will leave none to control and guide them in good conduct and right behavior. This would lead to the womenfolk of these families going astray causing intermingling of castes.

The word 'caste' meant a division of society based on one's mental tendencies and qualifications for taking up a particular type of work or avocation in the community. The division of society was never intended to be based on mere accident of birth. Therefore admixture of castes implies people choosing their avocations not suitable to their own inherent aptitude and tendencies resulting in the loss of professional ethics and excellence.

With the intermingling of castes, progeny would not perform 'Sraaddha' ceremonies to their deceased ancestors which would cause them a downfall in the other world. It was feared that the traditions of the individual families called *Kula Dharma* and those of a social group called *Jati Dharma or Varna Dharma* might get disturbed due to social upheaval as a consequence of war.

The import of Arjuna's arguments was that when the fundamental harmony of the domestic life gets broken, when purity of living and sanctity of thought were destroyed, when the ideals enshrined in immemorial traditions were shattered, when the social equilibrium is disturbed, chaos alone will reign supreme in the world.

aho bata mahat paapam kartum vyavasitaa vayam
yadraajya sukhalobhena hantum swajanam udyataah // 1.45 //
yadi maam aprateekaaram ashastram shastrapaanayah
dhaartaraashtraa rane hanyus tanme kshemataram bhavet // 1.46 //

ALAS, WHAT A PITY THAT WE HAVE RESOLVED TO COMMIT A GREAT SIN BY BEING EAGER TO KILL OUR OWN KITH AND KIN OUT OF GREED FOR THE PLEASURES OF

A KINGDOM! IT WOULD, INDEED BE BETTER FOR ME IF THE SONS OF DHRITARASHTRA, ARMED WITH WEAPONS, WERE TO KILL ME IN THE BATTLE WHILE I REMAIN UNARMED AND UNRESISTING.

The idea is that instead of committing the heinous sin of killing his own relatives and friends, Arjuna feels that purification from even such a thought itself will come from the amends in the form of an end to his own life itself.

Arjuna, exhibiting lack of self- confidence, became a victim of emotions instead of a master of the situation. In his weak state of mind he was imputing ulterior motives to a righteous war which he himself was stoutly defending up to the very day it was to start. He went to the extent of telling Krishna that non-injury was a virtue preferable to defending oneself against other's attacks. He was not aware that his attachment, selfishness and delusions were responsible for his faint-heartedness and cold-feet in the face of a crisis. His despondency ultimately culminated in his meek pulling out from the situation in which he finds himself.

CONFOUNDED AND DISTRESSED, ARJUNA COLLAPSES

sanjaya uvaacha
evamuktwaa'rjunah sankhye rathopastha upaavishat
visrijya sasharam chaapam shokasamvignamaanasah // 1.47 //

SANJAYA SAID
HAVING SPOKEN THUS IN THE MIDST OF THE BATTLEFIELD, ARJUNA, THROWING AWAY HIS BOW AND ARROWS, SANK INTO THE SEAT OF THE CHARIOT, WITH HIS MIND AFFLICTED BY SORROW.

Arjuna finally decided not to fight. He threw away his arms and sank into his seat. This is really strange for a warrior of Arjuna's caliber. For all these outpourings, Krishna did not respond. The Lord allowed him to exhaust himself so that the message He was going to deliver shortly to Arjuna and through him to the entire humanity would be fully effective.

om tat sat iti srimad bhagavadgeetaasu upanishatsu brahma vidyaayaam yogashaastre sri krishnaarjuna samvaade arjuna vishaada yogo naama prathamo'dyaayah ||

THUS IN THE UPANISHADS OF THE GLORIOUS BHAGAVAD GITA, THE SCIENCE OF THE ETERNAL, THE SCRIPTURE OF YOGA, THE DIALOGUE BETWEEN SRI KRISHNA AND ARJUNA, ENDS THE FIRST DISCOURSE ENTITLED: THE YOGA OF THE DESPONDENCY OF ARJUNA

AN OUTLINE VIEW OF THIS CHAPTER

The opening chapter of the Bhagavad Gita prepares the scene at the battlefront where Krishna will unveil the philosophy of Vedanta to Arjuna. Poised for battle, outstanding warriors in both the Kaurava and Pandava armies assemble at the battlefield. Arjuna looks at his respected elders, teachers, friends and relatives in both armies, all prepared to die. This sight overwhelms him with emotion. He falls into a state of utter despondency. Hence this chapter is entitled the 'Yoga of Arjuna's despondency.'

I - DHRTARASHTRA'S QUESTION TO SANJAYA - VERSE 1

In the opening verse Dhrtarashtra asks Sanjaya to report the proceedings on the battle fought between his sons and the Pandavas.

II - DURYODHANA BETRAYS HIS VANITY AND FEAR - VERSES 2 -11

Betraying his mixed feelings, Duryodhana boasts that his army is superior to the Pandava's while really fearing their strength and valour.

III - SOUND OF CONCHES TERRIFIES KAURAVAS - VERSES 12 – 19

This topic describes the outstanding warriors on both sides blowing their conches, drums, tabors and trumpets to mark the beginning of battle. Heaven and earth reverberate with that tumultous sound which rents the hearts of the Kauravas.

IV - EMOTIONS OVERPOWER ARJUNA - VERSES 20 – 30

Arjuna bids Krishna to drive his chariot between the two armies to behold the Kurus assembled in the opposing forces. There he sees his own Guru Drona, his grandsire Bhishma and a host of his relatives and friends. This sight drives him into an emotional stuper in which he loses his control of his body. Overwhelmed with despondency, Arjuna lets his great bow Gandiva fall from his hands.

V - ARJUNA TRIES TO JUSTIFY HIS FALSE RENUNCIATION -VERSES 31- 39

Arjuna displays a false sense of vairagya. He tries to justify his indifference by telling Krishna that he has no desire for victory, kingdom or the pleasures therefrom. He claims he will not destroy his own kinsmen, not even for all that the world can offer.

VI - CONFOUNDED & DISTRESSED, ARJUNA COLLAPSES ON THE BATLEFIELD - VERSES 40 - 47

Arjuna condemns the Kauravas as greedy, evil-minded and sinful. He raises a series of one-sided arguments in favour of withdrawing from the battle while Krishna remains silent. He asserts that the involvement in the battle will lead to the atrocious sin of destroying families, religious rites and piety. He would rather let himself be killed unarmed than commit such a heinous crime. So saying, Arjuna sinks to the ground with a distressed mind and lays down his bow and arrows.

<<<000>>>

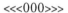

A Critical Look at Chapter One

When the Gods deal defeat to a person, they first take his mind away, so that he sees things wrongly. Time does not raise a stick and hit a man's head; the power of Time is just to project this topsy-turvy view of things. -- Dhritarashtra (Mahabharata - The Book of the Assembly Hall)

As we take up our seats in the comfortable opera house at Kurukshetra, the panorama unfolding before us on the stage is the gigantic field of the battle between the Kauravas and the Pandavas. While the text mentions the names of a number of characters about to play their roles on both the sides, we are concerned with only three of them for our critical evaluation. They are 1. King Dhritarashtra 2. The valiant Arjuna and 3. Bhagavan Sri Krishna, who assumed the role of a charioteer to Arjuna.

If we analyze their mindsets we automatically understand the concepts and issues involved and their complexity. The immortal appeal of the Gita lies in the guided tour the JagadGuru, Sri Krishna, takes us through the annoying wide-spread pot-holes of ignorance (lack of right knowledge, *avidya* in Sanskrit) on the road and who ultimately makes it possible for us to reach the destination of enlightenment, free from the shackles of bondage. This journey from darkness to light is definitely exasperating at times but yet manageable.

DHRITARASHTRA

Dhritarashtra already heard several reasons for the likely victory of the Pandavas. He was afraid of the possibility of loss of kingdom for his own sons, the Kauravas. He therefore asks Sanjaya "what did my sons, Duryodhana and others, as well as Pandu's sons, Yudhishthira and others, actually do on the battlefield at Kurukshetra? Did they undertake the war according to their earlier plan for fighting or did they act otherwise or do something else as a result of sagging of the will to fight due to some reason?

Apart from the inbuilt fear complex in the mind of Dhritarashtra, a significant aspect of his question is his making a distinction between his own sons and the sons of Pandu. Although the question in the form 'What did my sons do?' would have been sufficient, he, by separately mentioning his sons and Pandu's sons exhibits an absence of family homogeneity and harmony in his mind.

The image of the King here is that he is not only physically blind but also is deprived of the vision of personal kindness and a human touch and inclusiveness. He is engrossed totally in his affection exclusively towards his sons.

In the entire Gita this is the only verse which the old king Dhritarashtra gives out. All the rest of the seven hundred stanzas are Sanjaya's report on what happened on the Kurukshetra battlefield, just before the war.

The old king is certainly conscious of the palpable injustices that he had done to his nephews, the Pandavas. Dhritarashtra knew the relative strength of the two armies, and therefore, was fully confident of the larger strength of his son's army. And yet, the viciousness of his past and the consciousness of the crimes perpetrated seem to be weighing heavily upon his heart, and so he has his own misgivings on the final outcome.

Dhritarashtra is physically blind. But passion and desire do not disappear with the absence of physical sight. Even if all the sense organs were lost, the desires hidden within the mind would not vanish and so his mind is curious, eager and troubled to know what is happening on the battlefield.

ARJUNA

Arjuna is intelligent and where there is intelligence there is doubt and where there is doubt there is dilemma. Arjuna is rational and where there is rationality, there lies the capacity to think from a totally different perspective. Where one has these qualities, it is difficult to enter into a dangerous situation like war with closed eyes.

Remember that life does not end the same way as it begins; the end is always unknown and invisible. In this war Duryodhana's focus was entirely on Bheema. He overlooked the fact that Krishna was on the side of Pandavas and particularly as the charioteer of Arjuna. He could not visualize that Krishna would retrieve Arjuna from his shortcomings and consequently the whole story took a different turn and Duryodhana lost.

Arjuna requested Krishna to place his chariot between the two armies so that he can observe with whom he has to fight. The points to be noted here are:

Once observation starts, analysis is not far too behind and analysis always leads to wavering of mind. So Arjuna analyses the question to fight or not to fight and comes to the conclusion that he should not fight. In all his arguments in support of that conclusion he puts forward several pleadings which apparently look valid and very wise but in fact are very hollow as Krishna proves them to be subsequently.

At this stage although it looks that Arjuna is not obsessed with war, he is not against war either and has no aversion to violence. All his life he fought many wars and his whole life's education and training and his lifelong conditioning is all violence and war. Then why he turns his face against war? *We have to understand this paradoxical situation very clearly because this is the very seed for all the teachings contained in the Bhagavad Gita. Had there not been this ironical situation, the Bhagavad Gita would not have come into existence.*

ARJUNA SYNDROME - ORIGIN AND CURE

Arjuna was overpowered by an emotional upheaval. He suddenly started exhibiting several symptoms of weakness both physically and psychologically. He was afflicted with great depression of mind masquerading as compassion. Arjuna himself described his physical symptoms in graphic terms. It was of the nature of a Fever of Unknown Origin (F.U.O.) or a *Bhava-roga* in Sanskrit. This disease is the oldest known to human kind. Its origin is traced to *ajnana* or *avidya* or ignorance in Vedantaic terms. The divine potion or elixir *(amrita)* that cures this disease is *Jnana* or Knowledge, grace of God, issuing from self-surrender, prayer and freedom from desire *(bhakti, sharnagati, prapatti, nirvasana)* and so on.

What makes the Gita, a unique medicine for *bhava-roga* is that it contains all the ingredients stated above, fit to be consumed by peoples of all ages, climes, genders - monastic or lay. The Arjuna syndrome, analyzed and diagnosed by the master physician Sri Krishna is the starting point of the preparation of this unique brew.

Adi Shankaracharya's description of the Arjuna syndrome is simple and remarkable. It is not that Arjuna was unwilling to do his duty as the Army General when he came for war. Arjuna is a picture of courage and self-confidence before the war. In the verses 21 and 22 of the 1st chapter he roars like an impatient lion waiting to pounce on its prey.

Afterwards, Arjuna's mood suddenly changes. At what point of time and for what reasons did he become a victim of the Arjuna syndrome?

Verses 28-46 of the 1st Chapter, if properly analyzed word for word, give us the clue. Arjuna saw in the huge armies his own people, *(svajana)*-fathers, grandfathers, brothers, teachers, friends etc., and was overcome with pity. The key word here is *svajana*, people who are one's very own. It may be noted that Arjuna uses the word 'svajana' four times in these verses. Arjuna's lament and depression are rooted in this feeling of *svajanatva* - one's own-ness. Arjuna's ego that strongly felt this attachment engendered by possessiveness - own ness or svajanatva- plunged him into the abyss of sorrow and delusion *(shoka* and *moha)*

This pathological aberration of Arjuna can be traced to psychological roots that define the Arjuna syndrome. Arjuna displayed feelings of grief and delusion caused by ignorance and confused understanding and his attachment for and the sense of separation from dominion, the elders, sons, friends, kinsmen, relatives - all these arising from the notion that '*I* am theirs and they are *mine*'. It was when discriminative faculty (knowledge) was thus over powered by grief and delusion that Arjuna, who had of himself naturally and spontaneously been engaged in battle as warrior's duty, abstained from fighting and prepared to lead a mendicant's life which was a duty alien to him.

It is thus that in the case of all creatures whose minds come under the sway of the defects of sorrow, delusion, etc. there verily follows, as a matter of course, abandoning their own duties and resorting to prohibited ones.

Even when they engage in their own duties their conduct in speech, thought and deed is certainly motivated by hankering for rewards, and is accompanied by egoism. Egoism consists in thinking that one is the agent of some work and therefore the enjoyer of its reward.

Such being the case, the cycle of births and deaths, characterized by passing through desirable and undesirable births, and meeting with happiness, sorrow, etc. from the accumulation of virtue and vice, continues without any end. Thus, sorrow and delusion are the sources of the cycles of births and deaths. Their cessation comes from nothing other than the knowledge of the Self which is preceded by the renunciation of all attachment to duties. Hence, wishing to impart that (knowledge of the Self) for the welfare of the whole world, Lord Krishna, making

Arjuna the medium, said, 'You grieve for those who are not to be grieved for,' etc. (Chapter 2)

Thus the Arjuna syndrome analyzed could be reduced to the following flow-chart. Ignorance®confused understanding®feeling of I and Mine (*ahamkara* and *mamakara*) ®sorrow and delusion (*shoka* and *moha*)®overpowering of discriminative faculty® abandoning one's own duty *(svadharma)* and adopting alien duty *(para dharma)*, even in own duty craving for reward and egoism®accumulation of merit and demerit (*dharma* and *adharma)*®endless cycle of birth and death, *samsara,* consisting of getting the experiences of the desirable and the undesirable, pleasure and pain.

The remedy prescribed by Krishna is Self-Knowledge *(atma jnana)* which He starts unfolding from the verse 11 of the 2nd chapter. This is the greatest relevance of the Bhagavad Gita for the modern world particularly to the youth - stress filled, strife torn, panic stricken, and conflict ridden, modern world. *Atma jnana* is the source of strength, infinite power, eternal knowledge and wisdom.

Like Arjuna we too are weak, we too have wavering minds. The will power has been lost in our never-ending debate 'What to do and what not to do? What is proper and what is not proper?' The ground beneath our feet is slipping like quick-sand. The Arjuna in us is in suspended animation, is in limbo. We too require a shock treatment.

Krishna is holding Arjuna's hands and starting to resolve his problems from the very place where Arjuna is. That is why the Gita is very dynamic psychological address. As Arjuna evolves step by step the Gita also rises and unfolds gradually. Krishna reforms Arjuna at Arjuna's level. Arjuna is the focus all the time in the Gita and not Krishna.

KRISHNA, THE MASTER STRATEGIST

It is better to quote Swami Vivekananda here. He says: "I have heard about Krishna's life. I take it for granted there must have been a man called Krishna, and his Gita shows he has left a wonderful book. He is the most rounded man I know of, wonderfully developed, equally in brain, heart and hand. Every movement of his is alive with activity, either as a gentleman, warrior, minister or something else. Great as a gentleman, as a scholar, as a poet. This all-rounded and wonderful activity and combination of brain and heart you see in the Gita and other books. Most wonderful heart, exquisite language and nothing can approach it anywhere.

In Krishna we find two ideas stand supreme in his message. The first is the harmony of different ideas and the second is non-attachment. A man can attain to perfection, the highest goal, sitting on a throne, commanding armies, working out big plans for nations. In fact, Krishna's great sermon was preached on the battlefield!

How hard it is to arrive at this sort of non-attachment? Therefore Krishna shows us the lower ways and methods. The easiest way for every one is to do his or her work and not take the results. It is our desire that binds us. If we take the results of actions, whether good or evil, we will have to bear them. But if we work not for ourselves, but all for the glory of the Lord, the results will take care of themselves. To work you have the right, but not to the fruits thereof. The soldier works for no results. He does his duty. If defeat comes, it belongs to the General and not to the soldier. We do our duty for love's sake-love for the General, love for the Lord".

With such a kind of the Charioteer guiding the eminent soldier Arjuna, let us see what strategy Krishna adopted in the very first scene of the Gita to achieve the purpose of his *avatar*, his descent from the *Vaikuntha.*

When Arjuna asked Krishna to place his chariot between the two armies, Krishna placed it with his sagacity, at such a point from where his kinsmen such as Bhishma, teachers like Drona and other chief kings and warriors of the Kaurava army, could be clearly seen. After keeping the chariot at a crucial spot he told Arjuna, "O Partha (the son of Prtha, Kunti, and Krishna's aunt) behold all these Kurus, assembled here". This statement has got a deep significance.

In the word 'Kuru', the sons of both Dhritarashtra and Pandu are included because of both of them belong to the Kuru lineage. Krishna by saying 'behold all these Kurus assembled here' means that they are all one, whether they are on his side or opposite side and whether they are good or bad and thus a feeling of kinship may develop in Arjuna. This feeling of kinship may lead to attachment and make him inquisitive. Thus, by making Arjuna an instrument, Krishna wants to preach the gospel of the Gita for the humanity as a whole. Therefore, Krishna instead of using the word *'Dhartarashtran'* used the word *'Kurun'*. Had he used the former word, Arjuna would have become enthusiastic (as could be observed from Arjuna's dialogues using this word) and there would not have been any occasion to expound the Gita.

Krishna considered his duty to destroy Arjuna's delusion by first arousing it and then destroying it as in the case of certain medical procedures for achieving his avowed purpose of establishing and protecting Dharma in the world through his several incarnations.

The relationship between Arjuna and Krishna in this scene is that of a car owner and his driver. The driver just drives the car to the place where its owner wants him to go. The driver does not question the owner or pass any comments on the owner's instructions or wish. But here Krishna tells or directs Arjuna "Behold these Kurus". There is no need for these remarks as Arjuna will see the assembled warriors anyway and Krishna could have placed the chariot without uttering any words. But he intentionally used the words *'Kurun Pasya'* to arouse attachment in Arjuna.

The main reason of Arjuna's grief is that when Krishna placed the chariot between the two armies and asked Arjuna to behold the Kauravas, he saw his relatives, teachers and friends etc. and thus his sense of attachment was aroused. He perceives good in turning away from war and overwhelmed with grief he sinks into the chariot laying down his arms. Thus we see that it is delusion which changes a hero's great courage into anxiety and worry state neurosis.

Dr.S.Radhakrishnan says that Arjuna's cry or demand was simple yet tremendous and damaging one, "significant of the tragedy of man, which all, who can see beyond the actual drama of the hour, can recognize. The mood of despair in which Arjuna is found in the 1st Chapter of the Gita is what the mystics call the dark night of the soul, an essential step in the upward path. Krishna stands for the voice of God, delivering the message in the thrilling notes, warning Arjuna against dejection of spirit. As the dialogue proceeds, the dramatic element disappears. The echoes of the battlefield die away and we have only an interview between God and man".

LIVE AS THE GITA TEACHES YOU TO LIVE

The core teaching of Krishna in the Gita is that where there is virtue there is the prospect of victory and glorious life, both in this world and hereafter and wherever there are vice, unrighteousness, injustice and immorality, there is destruction, physical, moral and spiritual.

The senses of 'I', 'Me', and 'Mine' are the root of all evils and bondages in the world and the senses of 'you' and 'your' bring freedom to the soul. A wise man is the one who goes beyond the sense of 'I', and knows the secret of 'you' by which he gets rid of the senses of 'I' and 'Mine'. As long as we remain selfish we are caught in the net of desires and the world, so long we shall not be able to realize the real essence of the Gita. So Krishna says detachment is freedom and attachment is bondage. Therefore he instructs everybody to perform work disinterestedly without asking for results thereof because desire for the result of works is the chain that binds men and drags them into the den of delusion or *maya*.

Krishna represents the realized soul free of all conditioning, capable of seeing the truth as it is. He is the Self in a state of *sat-chit-ananda*. Arjuna is consciousness crumpled by conditioning. The chariot he rides is the body. The horses are the senses. The two wheels are the desire and destiny. As a charioteer, Krishna does two things - 1. He helps Arjuna to realize the true nature of life and 2. He overpowers the forces that threaten social order.

He classifies all actions into reaction and response; the former is guided by one's ego, motivated by one's desires and the latter is guided by one's intellect motivated by one's duty. The former focuses on result while the latter focuses on action. Krishna proves that by responding rather than by reacting, by maintaining equanimity and not getting provoked by worldly stimuli, it is possible to satisfy the demands of worldliness, fulfill one's obligation to the society, repay one's debts to ancestors and still attain *moksha*, liberation.

The *varnashrama dharma* categorizes life into four stages to be lived sequentially viz., *brahmacharya, grihasta, vanaparstha and sanyasa.* Krishna's message is that simultaneous rather than sequential achievement of material joy and spiritual bliss is possible.

FREQUENTLY ASKED QUESTIONS

1. Is the Gita a scripture that propagates war?

The answer is that it is concerned neither with violence nor with non-violence. It neither condones nor condemns war. The point it makes is to look at the root of any action. What is the yardstick that makes one war noble and the other ignoble? It is the motivation behind it - is it the ego or the common welfare based on justice that distinguishes the two.

Before the battle of Kurukshetra begins, Arjuna asks Krishna to drive their chariot into the open space between the two armies, so that he may see the men he must fight with. When Krishna does this, Arjuna recognizes many of his kinsmen and old friends among the ranks of the enemy. He is appalled by the realization that he is about to kill those whom he loves better than life itself. In his despair, he exclaims: 'I will not fight!'

Krishna's reply to Arjuna occupies the rest of the book. It deals not only with Arjuna's immediate personal problem, but with the whole nature of action, the meaning of life, and the aims for which man must struggle here on earth. At the end of their conversation, Arjuna has changed his mind. He is ready to fight. And the battle begins to fight the evil on the clear understanding that non-resistance to evil is as good as committing evil.

To understand the Gita, we must first consider what it is and what it is not. We must consider its setting. Krishna and Arjuna are on a battlefield. Arjuna is not a dedicated monk but a householder and a warrior by birth and profession. His problem is considered in relation to the circumstances of the moment.

In the background of Gita is a war, between two families, ready to start. Arjuna the main hero on one side looks at the family members, elders and friends on the other side and experiences a strong sense of frustration for infighting in the family. Although he was a great warrior, he merely broke-down by thinking on the utter futility of this war and in that moment of depression he asks his mentor about what he should do.

The answer given by Shri Krishna is equally unexpected. He says "your present reluctance to fight is illusion. Your problem is not regarding the fight as such but the fight against what you call my relatives, my brothers, my friends". Krishna says that "your real fight has to be against 'I' and 'My' rather than the fight outside". It is in this context of how to come out of our ego i.e. 'I' and the result of the ego 'My' that all the other seventeen chapters have been strung into one garland.

In teaching Arjuna, Krishna employs two sets of values, the relative and the absolute. He begins by dealing with Arjuna's feelings of revulsion, on general grounds. Arjuna shrinks from the act of killing. Krishna reminds him that, in the absolute sense, there is no such act called killing. The Atman, the indwelling Godhead (soul) is the only reality. This body is simply an appearance; its existence, its destruction, is likewise, illusory.

Having said this, Krishna goes on to discuss Arjuna's individual problem. For Arjuna, a member of the warrior caste, the fighting of this battle is undoubtedly 'righteous'. His cause is just. To defend it is his duty. Running away from the battle is avoiding duty and escapism.

Socially the caste system is graded, but spiritually, there are no such distinctions. Everyone, says Krishna, can attain the highest sainthood by following the prescribed path of his own caste duty. There have been instances of men everywhere who grew into spiritual giants while carrying out their duties as merchants, peasants, doctors, priests, or kings.

In the purely physical sphere of action, Arjuna is, indeed, no longer a free agent. The act of war is upon him; it has evolved out of his previous actions. It is his *svadharma*. At any given moment in time, we are what we are; and we have to accept the consequences of being ourselves. Only through this acceptance can we begin to evolve further. We may select the battleground. We cannot avoid the battle.

Arjuna is bound to act, but he is still free to make his choice between two different ways of performing that action. In general, mankind almost always acts with attachment; that is to say, with desire and fear. Desire for a certain result and fear that this result will not be obtained. Actions with attachments bind us to the world of appearances; to the continual doing of more actions.

But there is another way of performing action, and this is without desire and without fear. The doer of the non-attached actions is the most conscientious of men. Freed from desire and fear, he offers everything he does as a sacrament of devotion to his duty (surrenders all his actions to the Lord). All work becomes equally and vitally important. It is only toward the results of work- success or failure, praise or blame- that he remains indifferent. When action is done in this spirit, Krishna teaches, it will lead to the knowledge of what is behind action, behind all life; the ultimate Reality. And, with the growth of this knowledge, the need for further action will gradually fall away from us. We shall realize our true nature, which is God, *sat-chit-ananda*.

It follows, therefore, that every action, under certain circumstances and for certain people, may be a stepping-stone to spiritual growth – if it is done in the spirit of non-attachment. All good and all evil is relative to the individual point of growth. For each individual, certain acts are absolutely wrong. Indeed, there may well be acts that are absolutely wrong for every individual alive on earth today. But, in the highest sense, there can be neither good nor evil. Krishna, therefore speaking as God Himself, advises Arjuna to fight. The Gita thus neither sanctions war nor condemns it. Regarding no action as of absolute value, either for good or for evil, it cannot possibly do either. (Swami Prabhavananda).

Dharma and *satya* were at stake in Kurukshetra. So, preventing *adharma* from gaining victory over *dharma* was the purpose of Mahabharata war and fighting for *dharma* against *adharma* is the message of Gita.

However, we have forgotten this message of Gita and have distorted it in the name of *ahimsa* as our *dharma* unconditionally. Our dharma was satya (truth), and our duty was to fight and protect dharma and satya from every enemy. *Dharmao rakshati rakshitah* - dharma protects those who protect it - is our creed. And violence was not prohibited in this fight for satya and dharma. Otherwise Rama would not have killed Vali or Ravana. Actually, violence committed for ensuring dharma by a Kshatriya is no violence. That is why Krishna asks Arjuna in each and every chapter of the Gita "Arise Arjuna, pick up your weapon and fight to defeat adharma".

To sum up, war is justified only when it is meant to fight evil and injustice and not for the purpose of self aggrandizement.

2. How such a long discourse like the Gita took place in the midst of two impatient armies ready to fight it out?

The rules of time and space as we understand them today were not applicable to the age when the Mahabharata war took place during which the discourse was delivered by God. What seems to us a long dialogue must have taken place in the blink of an eye on the battlefield! We come across many stories indicating that silence is more powerful and penetrating than speech and a teacher taught his students by maintaining silence - thought transference or telepathy. These instances, probably, were like a pre-cursor to the modern developments in the field of information technology.

3. This chapter is entitled "Arjuna Vishaada Yogah: The Yoga of Arjuna's despondency". How despondency or grief can be yoga?

The word *Yoga* means to join. Any conscious attempt on the part of an individual to lift his present personality and adjust it to a higher, perfect ideal is called *Yoga*. The title of this chapter is self-contradictory. It is named as the *Vishaada Yoga* or Yoga of Arjuna's grief, depression. If 'grief' could be *Yoga*, everybody on the earth would be Yogins. It is not so for obvious reasons.

Arjuna's condition of utter despair is the most appropriate mental attitude wherein the seeds of the Gita can be ideally sown for their glorious flowering. The scriptural texts by themselves cannot help any one unless the seeker's mental condition is prepared to absorb their teachings. Therefore, even the initial mental condition of Arjuna is called as *Yoga* as this darkness of the soul is an essential step in the progress to spiritual life.

"Most of us go through life without facing the ultimate questions. It is in rare crises, when our ambitions lie in ruins at our feet, when we realize in remorse and agony the sad mess we have made of our lives, we cry out "Why we are here? What does all this mean? Where do we go from here? My God, why have you forsaken me?" Draupadi cries "I have no husbands, no sons, no kinsmen, no brothers, and no father, not even You, O Krishna". Arjuna passes through great spiritual tension. When he detaches from his social obligations and asks why he should carry out the duty expected of him by society, he gets behind his socialized self and has full awareness of himself as an individual alone and isolated. He faces the world as a stranger thrown into a threatening chaos. The new freedom creates a deep feeling of anxiety, aloneness, doubt and insecurity. If he is to function successfully, these feelings must be overcome". - Dr. S. Radhakrishnan

Thus for learning and living the Gita, the Arjuna-Syndrome is the initial *Sadhana*, a pre-requisite and hence his grief is considered as Yoga.

4. Why in the courts of law in India does one take the oath by putting one's hand on the Gita and not on the other scriptures like the Ramayana?

The main reason for this practice is that the *avatar* of Krishna is considered as *Purnavatar* i.e. a complete and perfect incarnation. Krishna is multi-dimensional, touching all aspects of human personality while Rama is a *maryada purushottam*. The dictionary meanings of the word *maryada* are mark, landmark, boundary, limit, end, goal, strictly defined relation, bounds of morality, moral law. Thus *maryada purushottam* implies a uni-dimensional nature possessing one note and hence its appeal is bound by the limits of such nature while Krishna's appeal is universal. A thief, a dancer, a Gopika, a cow-herd, a warrior, an enemy, a *rakshasa* and of course a *jnani*, a saint uniformly are crazy about him from their own points of view.

Krishna is like an orchestra where many instruments are simultaneously played and each one is bound to fall in love with the note emanating from the instrument he likes. That is the reason why all people like some part of Krishna and nobody knows the whole of Him as the Gita itself says. To put it in terms of music performances, *Rama tattva* is like a solo performance while *Krishna tattva* is like a *jugalbandi* with a bout of *sawal-jawab.*

Generally only disputants go to the courts of Law. If anybody really swears by or believes in Rama he would never go there. For him courts are redundant. But a person coming before a court can love Krishna because Krishna is accessible even to the sinners and He opens the doors for criminals also as He says in the Gita. Therefore it is the practice to use the Gita text for the purpose of taking oath.

<<<000>>>

Chapter 2

Saankhya Yogah:

Yoga of Knowledge

PREAMBLE

In the 1st Chapter we have seen that Arjuna asked Krishna to place the chariot in the midst of the two armies. Krishna placed the chariot between the two armies particularly in front of Bhishma and Drona and asked Arjuna to behold the Kurus. Having seen the kinsmen, Arjuna was filled with compassion and sadness and threw away his arms and sank into the seat of the chariot. His personality was destroyed by his overwhelming emotions erupting at the sight of his near and dear ones on the battlefront.

The 2nd Chapter begins with Sanjaya telling Dhritarashtra about the dialogue between Krishna and Arjuna when the latter continues to remain under the spell of melancholy and dejection. Arjuna, with a phony sense of renunciation, argues that he would rather live on alms than slay the noble elders like Bhishma and Drona and that even an undisputed sovereignty over all the worlds would not drive away his grief. Arguing thus, he expressed his unwillingness to fight and became silent completely burnt out.

This is one of the longest Chapters in the Gita.

THE TEXT

KRISHNA REBUKES ARJUNA

sanjaya uvaacha
tam tathaa kripayaavishtam ashrupoornaakulekshanam
visheedantam idam vaakyam uvaacha madhusoodanah // 2.1 //

SANJAYA SAID
TO HIM WHO WAS THUS OVERWHELMED WITH PITY AND SORROW AND WHOSE EYES WERE DIMMED WITH TEARS, MADHUSUDANA (KRISHNA) SPOKE THESE WORDS.

The second chapter starts with a brief reference to the miserable mental condition of Arjuna. His pity was not compassion but a form of self-indulgence. It is the shrinking of the nerves from an act which compels him to hurt his own people. Arjuna recoils from this task in a mood of self-pity. His teacher, Sri Krishna, therefore rebukes him particularly because Arjuna was knowing all along that he had to fight against his own people.

sri bhagavaan uvaacha
kutastwaa kashmalam idam vishame samupasthitam
anaaryajushtam aswargyam akeertikaram arjuna // 2.2 //

SRI BHAGAVAN SAID
O ARJUNA, AT THIS MOMENT OF CRISIS, WHEREFROM HAVE YOU GOT THIS WEAKNESS, UN-ARYAN LIKE, DISGRACEFUL AND WHICH IS NOT CONDUCIVE TO THE ATTAINMENT OF HEAVEN?

The Lord is called Bhagavan because He possesses six *'bhagas'* or divine traits viz. wealth, virtue, glory, greatness, knowledge and dispassion. Krishna, who was silent all along, started speaking.

During His very first utterance in these verses the core of the message of Gita was delivered with a tremendous force. Sri Krishna addresses him as Arjuna which means pure in heart, implying that despite this quality he became faint-hearted instead of showing valor and zeal. It is quite unbecoming of him. Krishna was surprised about this change in Arjuna.

The term 'Arya' refers to a highly evolved and cultured man who scrupulously adheres to Dharma. Arjuna, in whom manliness was in full all along, suddenly sunk into un-manliness at the moment of a crisis. The Lord rouses him from this set-back. Sri Krishna classified Arjuna's mind as confused. Consequently all the utterances of such confused Arjuna would be meaningless and devoid of discrimination. Hence he is termed un-Aryan.

Kirti or fame attends on the one given to laudable life on earth. But Arjuna's way was entirely to the contrary. For him who was wavering in facing a decisive moment there would be nothing but disgrace, neither this world nor the next for such confused and dejected minds.

The message of Krishna is that the goal of life or success cannot be attained by the weak. To be firm in body, mind and character is born of strength. This world and the next are for the strong. Strength brings forth right conduct and straightforwardness leading to enjoyment of this world and reaching Godhood. All divine traits have their source in strength. Strength is life; weakness is death.

The three words used by the Lord are *'anaryajushtam'*, *'asvargyam'* and *'akirtikaram'*. They mean respectively three types of persons. 1. Thoughtful whose aim is to Bliss. 2. Virtuous whose aim is to achieve heaven by performing honest actions and 3. Ordinary who want name and fame in this world. Arjuna is indicted that he belongs to none of these because of his affliction.

klaibyam maa sma gamah paartha naitattwayyupapadyate
kshudram hridaya daurbalyam tyaktwottishtha parantapa //2.3//

O PARTHA (SON OF PRITHA, KUNTI), YIELD NOT TO UNMANLINESS. IT DOES NOT BEFIT YOU. CAST OFF THIS PETTY FAINT-HEARTEDNESS AND ARISE, O PARANTHAPA (SCORCHERER OF FOES - ARJUNA).

The man, who fails to face a critical situation, speaking and acting irrelevantly, is denounced as unmanly. But Arjuna was not really made of that stuff. He was a vanquisher of his foes. The Lord seems to have deliberately used the strongest language to make him get out of his stupor and to goad him to perform his primary duty to wage war for which he came fully prepared.

The use of the words 'Partha' and 'Kaunteya' with reference to Arjuna is with a purpose. These words mean the son of Pritha, Kunti who is Krishna's father's sister. Krishna thus attempts to show his nearness to him and thereby convey something special to him for his welfare.

ARJUNA'S DOUBTS ARE UNRESOLVED

arjuna uvaacha
katham bheeshmamaham sankhye dronam cha madhusoodana
ishubhih pratiyotsyaami poojaarhaav arisoodana //2.4 //

ARJUNA SAID
BUT O MADHUSUDANA, HOW CAN I STRIKE BHISHMA AND DRONA WITH ARROWS IN THIS BATTLE, FOR THEY ARE WORTHY OF WORSHIP, O ARISUDANA (DESTROYER OF ENEMIES - KRISHNA)?

guroon ahatwaa hi mahaanubhaavaan
shreyo bhoktum bhaikshyam apeeha loke
hatwaarthakaamaamstu guroon ihaiva
bhunjeeya bhogaan rudhirapradigdhaan // 2.5 //

IT IS BETTER TO LIVE IN THIS WORLD BY BEGGING THAN TO SLAY THESE HONORED TEACHERS. BY SLAYING THEM I WOULD ENJOY IN THIS WORLD PLEASURES WHICH ARE STAINED WITH BLOOD.

na chaitad vidmah kataran no gareeyo
yad waa jayema yadi vaa no jayeyuh
yaan eva hatwaa na jijeevishaamas
te'vasthitaah pramukhe dhaartaraashtraah // 2.6 //

I CAN HARDLY TELL WHICH WILL BE BETTER - TO FIGHT OR NOT TO FIGHT, THAT WE SHOULD CONQUER THEM OR THEY SHOULD CONQUER US. THE VERY SONS OF DHRITARASHTRA AFTER SLAYING WHOM WE DO NOT EVEN WISH TO LIVE STAND FACING US.

kaarpanya dosho pahata swabhaavah
pricchaami twaam dharma sammoodha chetaah

yacchreyah syaan nischitam broohi tanme
shishyaste'ham shaadhi maam twaam prapannam // 2.7 //

WITH MY NATURE STRICKEN WITH WEAKNESS OF SENTIMENTAL PITY AND MY MIND BEWILDERED ABOUT MY DUTY, I REQUEST YOU TO TELL ME FOR CERTAIN WHAT IS GOOD FOR ME. I AM YOUR DISCIPLE. PLEASE TEACH ME. I AM SEEKING REFUGE IN YOU

na hi prapashyaami mamaapanudyaad
yacchokam ucchoshanam indriyaanaam
avaapya bhoomaav asapatnam riddham
raajyam suraanaam api chaadhipatyam // 2.8 //

FOR, EVEN AFTER OBTAINING AN UNDISPUTED SOVEREIGNTY AND AN AFFLUENT KINGDOM ON THIS EARTH AND LORDSHIP OVER THE GODS, I DO NOT SEE ANY MEANS OF DRIVING AWAY THIS GRIEF WHICH IS DRYING UP MY SENSES.

Arjuna wondered as to how he was being asked to fight Bhishma and Drona, who were not his enemies but respected elders and teachers worthy of reverence. When even using soft words against them was considered sin, Arjuna was surprised about his being exhorted to wage war against them with arrows.

Arjuna continued that it would be better for him to eat food by begging, which was most unbecoming for a man of warrior class, than to slay his noble elders on the Kaurava side. He felt that even if they were killed, his subsequent enjoyment would be stained with their blood and therefore not worth anything and the life in this world would be nothing but hell.

A question arises, why is it that Bhishma and Drona, who are not his enemies, are on the side of Duryodhana? They are there because as Arjuna says Bhishma and Drona are *'arthakaman'*, which means even though they never approved the criminal ways of Duryodhana, they still sought, accepted and enjoyed the royal hospitality of Duryodhana for so long that they now feel obligated to him so much that they simply cannot abandon Duryodhana in his time of need. That is how Bhishma and Drona are now caught on the side of Duryodhana. Arjuna feels that it is their problem and he has nothing to do with it and so he sticks to his point of view that they are worthy of his worship.

He had also said that Duryodhana and his companions being goaded by greed were prepared to wage war; but for him if he wages war, he will enjoy only blood-stained pleasure in the form of wealth and sensual enjoyment. Thus he perceives nothing but evil in waging war.

When an evil comes to us in the form of an evil, it is easier to do away with it, than when it comes in the garb of something good. Ravana could not be recognized by Sita because he disguised himself as a sage while Krishna killed Kamsa and others recognizing them as evil forces. Similarly Arjuna perceives that it is virtuous not to wage war and it is an evil to wage war. Hence Krishna had to give an elaborate explanation to convince Arjuna about the real wisdom and his erroneous interpretation of it.

When sentiment overtook and clouded his understanding Arjuna lost the faculty of judgment and started doubting as to who should conquer whom?

Realizing his complete helplessness in knowing the nature of his duty and admitting his incapacity to face the crisis and the challenges presented before him, he surrendered himself to Sri Krishna. He confessed before The Lord that he was his disciple and requested Him to tell him for certain what was good for him.

Arjuna does not ask for a philosophical solution as he is not a seeker of knowledge; as a man of action he asks for the law of action, for his dharma, for what he has to do in this difficulty. "Master, what would you have me to do?" that was his question.

Arjuna made it clear that in spite of the victory in the war which will in any case bring him an affluent kingdom on this earth and lordship over the Gods, he could not see any way to drive away his grief which was eating away his vitals. He appealed to The Lord to show him a definite way which would remove his grief and guide him in his Dharma.

sanjaya uvaacha
evam uktwaa hrishikesham gudakeshah parantapah
na yotsya iti govindam uktwaa tooshneem babhoova ha // 2.9 //

SANJAYA SAID
HAVING THUS SPOKEN TO HRISHIKESA (KRISHNA), ARJUNA THE DESTROYER OF FOES (PARANTAPA), SAID TO GOVINDA (KRISHNA) I WILL NOT FIGHT AND BECAME SILENT.

tam uvaacha hrisheekeshah prahasanniva bhaarata
senayor ubhayor madhye visheedantam idam vachah // 2.10 //

O DESCENDENT OF BHARATA (DHRITARASHTRA), THEN KRISHNA, AS IF SMILING, SPOKE THESE WORDS TO HIM (ARJUNA) THUS DEPRESSED IN THE MIDST OF THE TWO ARMIES.

Even after taking refuge in The Lord and seeking His grace, the great warrior Arjuna decidedly told Sri Bhagavan that he would not fight and became silent and quiet. Becoming silent and quiet in the face of a crisis was an expression of bewilderment and helplessness. We may notice that despite asking his teacher to advise him, Arjuna already made up his mind not to fight without even waiting for the advice sought. This signifies the confused state of his mind. In this situation the teacher's task becomes all the more difficult to convince the student.

The depiction of Arjuna as a person sorrowing in the midst of the two armies was in contrast with his description as an enthusiastic warrior ready to fight when he requested Krishna to place their chariot in between the two armies.

Sri Krishna's virtual smile indicates that He saw through Arjuna's attempt at rationalization of his wishful thinking. The attitude of the savior Lord who knows all the sins and sorrows of the suffering humanity is one of the tender pity and thoughtful understanding and not of reproach or censure.

We have seen the dejection of Arjuna and his determination not to wage the war. Since Bhagavan Krishna has discovered that the deep-rooted delusion and grief of Arjuna cannot be removed without the knowledge of reality, He immediately starts His discourse on the immortality of the Soul with a virtual smile on His face,

In that moment of depression, the sinking heart of Arjuna heard the Divine voice of Krishna. Krishna's virtual smile indicates that he saw through Arjuna's attempt at rationalization of what is now known as wishful thinking.

Krishna starts the sermon of the Gita by stating that

- The wise grieve neither for the living nor for the dead.
- The Self within is eternal, indestructible.
- The bodies enveloping the Self are ephemeral. They have a beginning and an end.
- Death is certain for the born and birth for the dead.
- Beings constantly pass through the repeated stages of unmanifest, manifest and again unmanifest. So why grieve over the inevitable?
- The indwelling Self remains eternally the same.

The 2nd Chapter is considered as the epitome of all that stands for in the Gita.

THE DISTINCTION BETWEEN THE SELF AND THE BODY: WE SHOULD NOT GRIEVE FOR WHAT IS IMPERISHABLE.

sri bhagavaan uvaacha
ashochyaan anvashochastwam prajnaavaadaamshcha bhaashase
gataasoon agataasoomshcha naanushochanti panditaah // 2.11 //

SRI BHAGAVAN SAID
YOU GRIEVE FOR THOSE WHO ARE NOT TO BE GRIEVED FOR; AND YET YOU SPEAK WORDS OF WISDOM! THE LEARNED DO NOT GRIEVE FOR THE DEPARTED AND THOSE WHO HAVE NOT DEPARTED.

There are four propositions in this verse. 1. Arjuna is grieving 2. He is grieving for those not to be grieved for. 3. He speaks the words of the wise though he is not so, and 4. The wise do not grieve for the living or for the dead.

Let us have a closer look at these statements.

1. The cause for Arjuna's suffering and distress is because when he looked at his relatives, friends and teachers lined up on the opposite side, the feeling of 'me' and 'mine' became very strong in him, the central point being the sense of 'I.' A man is grieved when he categorizes some objects or persons as his own and some others as not his own. This sense of mine and not-mine - attachment for things considered as one's own and indifference for things considered as not one's own - is called ego which is the source of all grief, worry, fear and confusion. Rediscovering one to be really higher than one's ego is the end of all sorrows arising out of false identification or relationship.

So Krishna went to the bottom of this grief, sorrow, misery and suffering and explained that a wise man does not have the sense of 'I', 'me' and 'mine'. Such a man is not bound by any tie or attachment of any kind.

2. Here the phrase 'those not to be grieved for' refers to Bhishma and Drona. Why they are not to be grieved for? It is because they are beyond the sense of attachment and the feeling of "I' 'my' and 'mine'. That is the reason why they are on the side of the Kaurava army despite the Pandavas being equally dear to them. They are aware of the difference between the real and the unreal, the soul and the body respectively. They are wise because they have realized the eternal reality behind the phenomenal changes and therefore do not grieve at the decay and death of the finite and the mortal in the form of the physical bodies.

When we go to the sea shore we do not grieve over each wave that rises and dissolves for we know that they are unreal and the real thing is the water in the waves. Waves are like the physical bodies which appear and disappear while the indweller of the body, the self or soul is like the water. Those who have realized this eternal truth have no sorrow for the change they perceive in the world of happenings.

Thus both real and unreal are not to be grieved at as the real is imperishable and therefore should not be grieved for. The unreal is bound to perish, as it is perishing at every moment, so it should not also be grieved at. It follows that Arjuna's grief over the bodies of his relatives getting perished is misplaced and is the consequence of his ignorance, lack of right knowledge, *avidya* although his words apparently look wise which in fact they are not. Hence Krishna says that he is grieving for those who should not be grieved for.

What Krishna means is "Arjuna, Look at those standing before you not as human beings; look at them as the souls *(atman)* and the soul is immortal; you cannot kill the soul if you have the real knowledge". The idea is, "You are sorrowing for those who are eternal in the real sense, and therefore who are not to be grieved for. Hence you are a fool".

"The wise do not mourn for the dead or for the living," says Krishna to Arjuna. Why? Because there are no "living" or "dead" in the sense that those with bodies are alive and those divested of a body are dead. Nor is there such a duality called life and death. These are only the illusions produced by the distorting veils of ignorance. "Lead me from death to immortality" is not a petition to gain a state where we will nevermore experience bodily death, but a plea to be led from the outward-turned consciousness that produces death to the inward-turned consciousness that produces life. It is spirit itself that is immortality–nothing else.

In order to remedy this myopic view of Arjuna, Krishna administered the strongest medicine of the Knowledge of the Self to him at the very first stroke from the 11th verse of this chapter which is considered as the key verse of the Gita. All the subsequent teachings are an elaboration of the principle laid down in this verse.

He advised Arjuna to renounce his physical, emotional and intellectual estimate of his grand-sire and teacher and to re-evaluate the situation from his spiritual understanding whereby his problem at the battlefield would vanish.

na twevaaham jaatu naasam na twam neme janaadhipaah
na chaiva na bhavishyaamah sarve vayam atah param // 2.12 //

IT IS NOT THAT I DID NOT EXIST BEFORE, NOR YOU NOR THESE KINGS. NOR IS IT THAT WE SHALL CEASE TO EXIST IN FUTURE.

There are two things in the world, the soul which is real and the body which is unreal. Both of these are not to be grieved for because the soul never ceases to be and the body is ever perishable. Thus Sri Krishna speaks here of the immortality of the Self or the soul. The Self exists in the three periods of time - past, present and future.

He declares that the embodied soul in every one identifies itself with varied forms temporarily to gain preordained experiences. Neither Krishna himself nor Arjuna nor the other kings who have assembled in the battlefield is mere accidental happening nor shall it cease to exist in future. It is not that they came from nowhere nor at their death they become nothing or non-existent. The soul remaining the same, it gets apparently conditioned by different body equipments and comes to live through its self-ordained environments.

All the living creatures existed before their birth; they exist now and would exist even after the disappearance of their present bodies. A man experiences his existence before sleep, after sleep and during sleep. While his existence is continuous, his body is changing every moment and ultimately perishes one day. Thus existence is beyond time while biological body is bound by time and space. Waves arise, they play and die away. But the ocean ever remains the same.

Prior to the pot, in the pot and after the pot it was only the mud or clay which has continuous existence. Just as the destruction of a pot does not lead to the destruction of clay, so also destruction of the physical body does not lead to destruction of the Soul. Therefore, Arjuna should not grieve for his relatives out of fear of their destruction.

IMMUTABLE CHARACTER OF THE SOUL

dehino'smin yathaa dehe kaumaaram yauvanam jaraa
tathaa dehaantara praaptir dheeras tatra na mhuhyati // 2.13 //

JUST AS IN THIS BODY THE EMBODIED SELF PASSES INTO CHILDHOOD, YOUTH AND OLD AGE, SO ALSO DOES HE PASS INTO ANOTHER BODY; CALM MAN DOES NOT GRIEVE AT IT.

Embodied self means the soul assuming a physical body. Calm man means he who has Self-Knowledge and does not grieve at it means that he does not grieve at death.

In the progress of growth of the body, childhood dies when youth is born and youthhood dies when the old age sets in. Even when childhood or youthhood no longer remains at the old age, man remembers his early days fairly well. Thus 'something' is common throughout the various stages of growth which could remember the past experiences and none feels unhappy about these changes.

For the SELF in this body, the change in the experiences of childhood, youth and old age and the change in the experiences on obtaining another body are one and the same. A wise person is not confused or overpowered by such modifications in experiences.

Let us elaborate this statement. The Indweller - The self in one's body is the same in one's childhood, youth and old age; similarly, on obtaining another body, the Indweller in that new body also is the same self or *atman.*

Childhood, youth and old age are only with respect to one's physical body. The SELF, without undergoing any change, remains the same in all the three stages of bodily experiences. It is the same *atman* which is the Indweller in any new body one may assume later, after the present body falls. There can never be a time when *atman* is not there. Thus at all times, "I am" does not change, but "what I am" may change. A wise person is not confused or overpowered by such changes. If one thinks that "I" changes from "childhood I" to "youth I" to "old-age I" and to another "I" in another body, one must simply ask oneself the question who is "That I" who recognizes all these changes in "I"s. That "I" - That Recognizer I - That Seer I - "That Knower - I" is indeed *atman*, The SELF which is Eternal - All-pervading, and is never subject to change.

The Self does not die at the cessation of the childhood stage nor is it born again at the commencement of the youth stage and so also with the next stage of the old age. As the Self passes unchanged from one stage of the physical body into another stage so it passes unchanged from one body into another. As one does not grieve for the body when it passes through childhood, youth and old age, similarly one should not worry or get himself deluded over when the soul passes over to another body at physical death. Thus birth and death are spoken of with regard to the physical body and not the soul.

At the moment of death, there is no extinction of the individual. The embodied ego of the dead body (the subtle and causal bodies) leaves its previous structure and according to vasanas or mental impressions gained during its embodiment it gets itself identified with another physical body where it can express itself completely and seek its perfect fulfillment.

The entire existence with respect to an individual is divided into two categories: 1. 'I' or *aham* and 2. 'This' or *idam*. Atman is 'I' and the rest is 'This' *idam*. But due to the ignorance of my real nature, I am always identified with my body, mind and intellect and thus developed a false notion about myself. This false notion is ego.

If I can differentiate what is different from me, I can apprehend my own nature. Thus the enquiry is to know first what is not I and then to assert what is I. In other words it is about knowing what is not I (the body, mind and intellect) and knowing my real nature i.e. Atman (I). This is the study of the nature of the atman and the body which is called *Sarira Traya Prakriya.*

The personality of an individual is considered to consist of three bodies or *'sarira'* viz. gross body *(sthula sarira),* subtle body *(sukshma sarira)* and causal body *(karana sarira).*

Gross body *(Sthula Sarira):* It is that which is composed of the five great elements viz. space, air, fire, water and earth. The volume of the body occupies 'space', the breathing and respiratory system is due to 'air', the warmth in the body is due to 'fire' and the body is made up of 'water' and the 'minerals'(earth). This physical body is considered to have been acquired as a result of past good deeds. This body is the locus or the hutment or the counter for experiencing pain and pleasure and such other pairs of opposites. It is subject to six modifications *(shad vikaras)* viz. existence, birth, growth, change, decay and death.

Subtle body *(Sukshma Sarira or Linga Sarira):* It is the counterpart of the gross body that keeps the latter alive, performs all the physiological functions and operates the organs of action and perception. The physical body dies when the subtle body departs. The subtle body consists of seventeen components. They are the five organs of perception, the five organs of action, the five vital airs *(Pancha Pranas),* the mind and the intellect.

The five organs of perception are 1. Ear (sense of hearing), 2. Skin (sense of touch), 3. Eyes (sense of vision), 4. Tongue (sense of taste) and 5. Nose (sense of smell). The five organs of action are 6. Mouth, 7. Hands, 8. Legs, 9. Anus and 10. Genitals. The five vital airs are: 11. Prana - its function being respiration - located in Nose 12. Apana - Evacation or Excretion - Anus & Genitals 13. Vyana - Circulation - Entire Body 14. Udana - Reaction or Throwing out upwards - Throat 15. Samana-Assimilation or Digestion - Central Region of the Body. 16. The Mind - Receives Stimuli through organs of perception from external sources and 17. The Intellect - Analyses situations or stimuli received and determines - Cognition faculty.

According to some the mind and intellect only are treated as the causal body and the other fifteen components mentioned above form part of the gross body. The subtle body is the instrument of experience while the gross body is the hutment or the place of the experience.

Causal body *(Karana Sarira):* It is inexplicable, beginingless and in the form of ignorance of the Reality and the cause for the other two bodies, ignorant of one's own real nature, free from duality or division. According to some our inborn tendencies or *vasanas* are treated as causal body.

Atman (Self, Soul): It is not any of the three bodies mentioned above. It is the "awareness" or "consciousness" by which we are aware of the three bodies. It is called *'chit'*. The Atman does not undergo any change during the three states of consciousness viz. waking, dream and deep sleep *(avastha traya)* or during the passage of time because it is beyond time. It is therefore called *Sat* or ever-existent. The atman is also beyond the limitations of body, mind and intellect. It is also beyond space and time because space and time also are creations of the mind.

It is in a constant state of bliss or *ananda*. Atman is therefore *sat-chit-ananda* or Existence-Knowledge-Bliss. It is the principle that is self-effulgent, that pervades everything including space and which is complete *(Purna)*. The *Sat-Chit-Ananda Svaurpa* is the natural state of every living being but it is not experienced because we are struggling in a wrong direction and squandering our energies on inconsequential matters. Thus the purport of Krishna's advice to Arjuna is that the latter should change the direction of his mindset from the unreal to the real.

Now Arjuna may say: Well Krishna, all this talk about atman is interesting. It is nice to know that all of us are in fact eternal, and atman is *ananda svarupa*, Atma is All-Happiness. I have not experienced That Atma yet. Our scriptures say so; you say so; I accept all that to be true. But that does not help me much just now. The ups and downs of daily life do create pain and sorrow. This is common experience. Whether it is justified or not, it is still a fact that I am suffering from sorrow and distress at this time. Please tell me how I must handle this situation. Anticipating such a request from Arjuna, Bhagavan says:

maatraa sparshaastu kaunteya sheetoshna sukha dukhadaah
agamaapaayinonityaas taamstitikshaswa bhaarata //2.14 //

THE CONTACTS OF THE SENSES WITH OBJECTS, O SON OF KUNTI, WHICH CAUSE HEAT AND COLD, PLEASURE AND PAIN HAVE A BEGINNING AND AN END; THEY ARE IMPERMANENT; ENDURE THEM BRAVELY, O DESCENDENT OF BHARATA (ARJUNA).

Objects are perceived not by the sense organs viz. skin, ear, eye, nose and tongue but through them. The sense organs are the channels through which the perceiving-ego gathers the knowledge of the objects such as touch, sound, form, smell and taste. If this process of perceiver contacting the objects through sense organs does not take place the objects as such can not bring any response or reaction in any individual.

The object remaining the same it can give different experiences to the same individual at different times or at the same time to different individuals. Cold is pleasant at one time and unpleasant at another. Heat is pleasant in winter and not in summer. Food is welcome to a hungry person but not to the one who just finished his lunch. So the sense contacts that give rise to feelings of heat and cold, pleasure and pain, favorable and unfavorable experiences come and go. They are therefore impermanent in nature, giving pleasure at one moment and pain at another. One should bear all the pairs of opposites patiently and thus develop a balanced state of mind. Do not give yourself to joy or grief on their account.

Joys and sorrows are all responses of the mind to the conducive and non-conducive world around us. They are but mental reactions - thoughts. Learn to be observer of these emotions rather than get identified with them. Do not react but reflect. Stand apart - be aloof in yourself - be just an uninterested witness to the tumults of the mind. This attitude gives poise and balance.

The pairs of opposites like heat and cold are impermanent as distinguished from the Permanent Self, the Indweller. Actually there is no affinity between the Self and the unreal pairs of opposites. But it assumed this affinity which can be rooted out only when we cease to accept it. If anyone called a woman bereaved of her husband say fifty years ago as the wife of Mr. so and so (her late husband) she becomes alert and feels sad even today. It shows that the assumed affinity has not yet broken off which means that though the objects are lost, yet the assumed affinity persists which continues to cause anguish. The more one is able to distance oneself with this assumed affinity and identifies himself with the permanent Self, the less one is affected by the agreeable and disagreeable conditions of life.

Mere knowledge of agreeable and disagreeable senses is not bad. But attachment with and aversion to them is a fault. Not to be affected by such an evil is expressed by the term 'endure them'. Moreover, body, the sense organs and their actions have a beginning and an end. But the perceiver, the 'I" never changes and therefore one should remain unaffected by such transitory and fleeting experiences which is called 'endurance'.

WHAT GOOD COMES TO HIM WHO ENDURES THESE DESIRABLE AND UNDESIRABLE SITUATIONS?

yam hi na vyathayantyete purusham purusharshabha
samaduhkha sukham dheeram so'mritatwaaya kalpate // 2.15 //

THAT CALM MAN WHO REMAINS UNCHANGED IN PAIN AND PLEASURE, WHOM THESE CANNOT DISTURB, ALONE IS ABLE, O GREATEST AMONGST MEN, TO ATTAIN IMMORTALITY.

Titiksha or the power of endurance of the pairs of opposites advocated here does not mean a meek submission to sorrows in life (Stoic philosophy) but signifies the equipoise of mind in both pleasure and pain entertained by a wise man based on the knowledge of the Soul's immortality.

Endurance, coupled with the discrimination between the real and the unreal and detachment from the worldly objects and pleasures, prepares the aspirant for right knowledge, which alone leads to liberation.

Vedanta defines endurance as the bearing of all afflictions without wishing to redress them, while being free from all anxiety or regret on their account.

This perfect sameness or equanimity amidst the ills of life means full and unbroken consciousness of our oneness with the immortal Self. At that stage a person becomes fit for attaining immortality or knowledge of Self - the ultimate goal of life. Immortality means the infinite experience of the Eternal and the Permanent. Eternal life does not mean survival of physical death, but it is the transcendence of life and death.

HOW THE SOUL IS ETERNAL AND HOW THE CONTACTS WITH SENSORY OBJECTS ARE TRANSITORY? THE DISTINCTION BETWEEN THE REAL AND THE UNREAL: ADDITIONAL EXPLANATIONS.

naasato vidyate bhaavo naabhaavo vidyate satah
ubhayorapi drishto'ntastwanayos tattwadarshibhih // 2.16 //

THE UNREAL HAS NO EXISTENCE. THE REAL NEVER CEASES TO BE (NEVER CEASES TO EXIST). MEN POSSESSED OF THE KNOWLEDGE OF THE TRUTH FULLY KNOW BOTH THESE.

This verse indicates that the mental tranquility can accrue only through right interpretation of life. Right interpretation of life involves knowing what is Real and what is un-Real. The distinction between these two is dealt with here.

The Real is that which has no change and remains the same in all periods of time - past, present and future. It always is. The unreal is that which does not remain the same for two successive moments. Whatever did not exist in the past or will not exist in the future cannot really exist in the present. That which is not in the beginning and which will not be in the end, but which seemingly exists in the present is called un-Real. Any object conditioned by the law of cause and effect is not absolutely real because every effect is a change brought about in a cause and every cause is temporary till it becomes an effect.

The life is finite. The body changes every moment, mind evolves and intellect grows with the passage of time. Each change in the body for example from childhood to youth and from youth to old age results in the constant death to its previous state. Body, mind and intellect constitute the continuous succession of the changes and all of them cannot be real. A thing which never remains the same for any given period is un-Real. The whole of the phenomenal world must be unreal because no one state in it endures even for a fraction of the time.

But there must be some real entity behind these changes. For the changes to take place there must be some changeless substratum just as a river bed is necessary for the rivers to flow. In order to hold together innumerable experiences at the levels of body, mind and intellect and to give them a cohesive whole which is called life, a changeless substratum is required for all.

That something which remains unchanged all through the changes is The Real and it is nothing other than the Self in all, the Pure Awareness, and Consciousness. What is changing must be unreal and what is constant must be real. When the soul is overpowered by ignorance, the un-Real which is the names and forms of the phenomenal world, veil the unchanging reality - the Atman, Consciousness - which is for ever manifest and which is not conditioned by causality. This Self is the unchanging Witness of the changes in the relative world as in the case of the river bed and a flowing river.

This Awareness by which one becomes conscious of things in one's life - because of which one is considered alive, but for which one will have no existence in the given embodiment - That Spiritual Entity, Eternal, All Pervading, Unborn and Undying, the One Changeless factor is the Infinite in him. And this is the Atman, Consciousness which is the Real.

Therefore the men of knowledge and wisdom have known the implications of these - the Real and the Un-Real, the Self and the Non-Self, which in combination is called the world.

Embedding this exposition into the practical world, we notice that Arjuna is grieved by thinking that the warriors will die. So, the Lord explains that the real never dies and the unreal never exists as it is continuously dying (changing). Therefore it is not wise to grieve.

WHAT THEN IS THAT WHICH IS ALWAYS REAL ?

avinaashi tu tad viddhi yena sarvam idam tatam
vinaasham avyayasyaasya na kaschit kartum arhati // 2.17 //

KNOW 'THAT' TO BE INDESTRUCTIBLE, BY WHOM ALL THIS IS PERVADED. NONE CAN CAUSE THE DESTRUCTION OF THAT, THE IMPERISHABLE.

'That' is Brahman or the unchangeable Consciousness. It is the self of all. It is The Real that envelops everything that exists. It is the very substance of all the world of perceptions, the world of names and forms, which we experience. Brahman is the Witness and the innermost essence of the changeable world.

Different mud pots have different names and shapes depending upon the things they contain or the purposes for which they are made use of. Yet all of them are permeated with the same stuff i.e. mud without which no pot can exist. All the pots come from mud exist in mud and when they are destroyed all their forms and names merge back in mud. So the mud is The Reality holding all the pots together.

So too, the world of finite objects and changes is enveloped by The Real, the Changeless Brahman. Sri Krishna says that there is no possibility of this Real ever getting destroyed at all. Destruction of an object is caused by the loss of its parts as in the case of the body or by the loss of something belonging to it. As Brahman is without parts and is One without a second, there cannot be any question of its destruction.

The immutable Consciousness or Atman in the individual is the same as the all pervading Consciousness or Brahman in the universe.

The idea here is that while the soul is imperishable, the body is perishable and is perishing every day. Nobody can check the process of such destruction. Whether Arjuna wages the war or withdraws from it, the imperishable cannot be destroyed and the perishable cannot be saved from destruction.

WHAT IS THE UNREAL WHOSE NATURE IS SUBJECT TO CHANGE?

antavanta ime dehaa nityasyoktaah shareerinah
anaashino'prameyasya tasmaad yudhyaswa bhaarata // 2.18 //

ONLY THE BODIES, OF WHICH THIS ETERNAL, IMPERISHABLE, AND INCOMPREHENSIBLE SELF IS THE INDWELLER, ARE SAID TO HAVE AN END. THEREFORE, O DESCENDENT OF BHARATA (ARJUNA) FIGHT.

Arjuna's grief which deters him from his duty is born of ignorance as to the true nature of the soul. Hence Sri Bhagavan's continuous attempts to illumine him on the subject.

The physical body may be injured or destroyed by illness or death. The Self is subject to neither of these. The Self is said to be incomprehensible because it is not comprehended by the senses, by the mind, or by any other instrument of knowledge. The self is *svatah-siddha,* determined by Itself. Being the knowing Consciousness, It cannot be known by any other instrument. Everything is known by the Self just as no other light is required to see the light of the Sun which is self-effulgent.

Here the earlier advice about the Permanent and Non-Permanent is repeated with an added call to Arjuna to fight. Krishna is not really commanding Arjuna to fight as it is commonly understood. Arjuna, following his Dharma, had come to the battlefield to fight. He refused to fight on account of his erroneous perception of the true nature of the soul and the body. The efforts of the Lord are towards removing this erroneous awareness and leave him to do what he (Arjuna) considers to be right.

This is really not a command in war mongering but a call to Arjuna and through him to all of us to discard the defeatist mentality and face whole heartedly and sincerely all the situations in every field of activity at any given moment of existence in life.

IT IS IGNORANCE TO THINK THAT THE SOUL IS CAPABLE OF KILLING OR CAN BE KILLED.

ya enam vetti hantaaram yashchainam manyate hatam
ubhau tau na vijaaneeto naayam hanti na hanyate // 2.19 //

HE WHO LOOKS ON THE SELF TO BE THE SLAYER AND HE WHO LOOKS ON THE SELF AS THE SLAIN - NEITHER OF THEM APPREHENDS CORRECTLY. THE SELF NEITHER SLAYS NOR IS SLAIN.

The Self is a non-doer and as it is immutable; it is neither the agent nor the object of the act of slaying. He who thinks 'I slay' or 'I am slain' really does not comprehend the true nature of the Self. The Self is indestructible. It exists in all periods of time - past, present and future. It is The Existence itself i.e.*'Sat'*. The physical body undergoes inevitable changes every moment but the Self is not affected in the least by such changes. When the body is destroyed, the Self is not. Both of them who think that they have been slain when their bodies have been slain and those who feel that they are the slayers of the bodies of others do not understand the real nature of the Self.

The agent of slaying is the ego *(aham)* and the object of slaying is the body. Therefore the Self which is different both from the ego and the body is neither the slayer nor the slain. But by identifying with the body It assumes itself as the doer of actions performed by the body. If the man does not identify himself with the body he is not at all doer of any activity. One who holds the soul as slain is also ignorant because the soul remains unaffected and unchanged. Only that which is perishable and changeable can be slain. How could the imperishable and unchangeable be slain?

HOW IS THE SELF IMMUTABLE AND IMMORTAL?

na jaayate mriyate vaa kadaachin
naayam bhootwaa bhavitaa vaa na bhooyah
ajo nityah shaashwato'yam puraano
na hanyate hanyamaane shareere // 2.20 //

HE IS NEVER BORN NOR DOES HE EVER DIE; AFTER HAVING BEEN, HE AGAIN DOES NOT CEASE TO BE. UNBORN, ETERNAL, CHANGELESS AND ANCIENT. HE IS NOT KILLED WHEN THE BODY IS KILLED.

This verse describes the absence of the six kinds of modification inherent in every living being viz., birth, subsistence, growth, transformation, decay and death. The Self is altogether changeless. These changes are the source of all sorrows and miseries in every mortal's life. All these are denied to the Self to prove Its changelessness. Birth and death are for the physical bodies only and they cannot touch the immortal Self just as the waves are born and die in the ocean but the ocean itself is not born with the waves nor does it die when the waves disappear.

Arjuna was grieved about the death of his kinsmen in the war. So the Lord explains that the soul is not killed when the body is slain and hence he should not grieve.

WHY THE SOUL DOES NOT KILL ANYBODY?

vedaavinaashinam nityam ya enam ajam avyayam
katham sa purushah paartha kam ghaatayati hanti kam // 2.21 //

WHOSOEVER KNOWS HIM TO BE INDESTRUCTIBLE, ETERNAL, UNBORN AND IMMUTABLE, HOW CAN THAT MAN SLAY O ARJUNA, OR CAUSE ANOTHER TO SLAY?

An enlightened person who knows the changelessness and the indestructibility of the Self cannot perform the function of slaying or cause another to slay. When we know the Self to be invulnerable, how can anyone slay it? The words 'how can he slay' refer to Arjuna and 'cause another to slay' refer to Krishna's own role.

Summarizing what has been said so far Krishna emphasizes that those who know the nature of the Self shall have no dejection or sorrow in the face of the realities of life. Therefore, while slaying anyone or causing anyone to be slain when discharging his duty, one should not grieve, but perform that act in accordance with the ordinance of scriptures.

ILLUSTRATION REGARDING INDESTRUCTIBILITY OF THE SOUL.

vaasaamsi jeernaani yathaa vihaaya
navaani grihnaati naro'paraani

tathaa shareeraani vihaaya jeernaa
nyanyaani samyaati navaani dehee // 2.22 //

JUST AS A MAN CASTS OFF HIS WORN-OUT CLOTHES AND PUTS ON NEW ONES, SO ALSO THE EMBODIED SELF CASTS OFF ITS WORN OUT BODIES AND ENTERS THAT ARE NEW.

Here *'dehi'* means the *jiva* - the individual person, who is made up of the perceptible gross physical body, the imperceptible subtle and causal bodies, together with the *atman*.

The verse says: Just as an individual person gives up worn out or old clothing and takes up new ones, similarly, the same jiva, on giving up the worn out or old gross physical body, naturally takes up an appropriate new gross physical body. By giving up the old clothes and putting on new ones, the person does not change. Similarly, by giving up the old body and assuming a new one, the atman in the jiva - the individual person - does not change. The 'worn out condition of the body' does not refer to its biological condition but to the capacity of the body, mind and intellect equipments to earn the required experiences from the available environment for facilitating their evolutionary journey. This evolution and change is for the physical bodies and not for the Self.

The verse also tells something more about every individual person. By virtue of one's own 'karma' the jiva already becomes ready to assume a new body, prior to casting out the old worn-out body which has served its purpose. In other words, the mental make-up of a person does not die along with the death of the gross body. The mental make-up of the person, along with its karma-born tendencies and dispositions is called the subtle-body which is the core of every jiva and it survives the death of the physical frame. In its next step of evolution, the jiva assumes a new physical frame more suited to the fulfillment of its natural tendencies and dispositions. In all these changes, the self or soul or the Atman remains unchanged. In reality, the soul being immobile and non-active does not migrate from one body to another; it is ever fixed and steady and does not undergo any change whatsoever.

But just as when a pot is carried from one place to another, the space within the pot also appears be carried, even so when the subtle body leaves a gross body and enters another, it appears that the soul also has moved from one body to another. Therefore, the acts of leaving one body and entering into another are attributed to the soul in order to explain the phenomenon of death to the lay people. The word *'dehi'* is indicative of the soul identifying itself with gross body when it appears to be leaving and entering into another. In this sense it is said that the soul leaves a worn-out body and enters into a new one.

Now a question arises why this cycle of birth and death has been going on from times immemorial. While this question can be answered from the Jnana, Bhakti and Karma points of view, the basic factor behind this never-ending cycle is that God has granted the choice to the living beings to make proper use of their lives and to rediscover ultimately their own transcendental nature. Through innumerable births in the relative world they gain experience, through experience, knowledge and through knowledge, attain freedom or liberation or *moksha* from this cycle.

So far Krishna explained the permanent nature of the Soul and the impermanent nature of the physical body wherein the Lord proved it unreasonable to grieve over the process of a living being exiting one physical frame and entering another.

Continuing the discussion from another angle the Lord in the next three verses reiterates the eternal and changeless character of the soul and proves that grieving for fear of its destruction is unbecoming and improper on the part of Arjuna.

nainam chhindanti shastraani nainam dahati paavakah
na chainam kledayantyaapo na shoshayati maarutah // 2.23 //

WEAPONS CANNOT CUT IT, NOR CAN FIRE BURN IT; WATER CANNOT WET IT, NOR CAN WIND DRY IT.

Here the unseen has been explained by means of the seen to indicate its nature. The changeless Self is explained with the aid of ever changing world which is familiar to Arjuna and others. In the world of change, objects meet their end by means of instruments of destruction like weapons, fire, water and wind.

Arjuna's grief was based on the assumption that he would be killing the elders and other realtives by striking them with lethal weapons. Hence in order to remove his grief the Lord demonstrates the immortality and formlessness of the soul by pointing out the inability of all the four elements of earth, water, fire and air to destroy it. The body is perishable and possessed of a form; the soul is everlasting and formless. Therefore, the soul can never be destroyed by the elements of earth in the form of weapons or by the elements of water, fire and air and so it is sheer ignorance to lament for it.

acchedyo'yam adaahyo'yam akledyo'shoshya eva cha
nityah sarvagatah sthaanur achalo'yam sanaatanah // 2.24 //

THIS SELF CANNOT BE CUT, BURNT, WETTED OR DRIED UP. IT IS ETERNAL, ALL-PERVADING, STABLE, ANCIENT AND IMMOVABLE.

Continuing the import of the previous verse, The Lord says that if a thing cannot be annihilated by any means of destruction discovered by man such an object must be everlasting. Since the Self is indestructible, It is necessarily everlasting. That which is everlasting or eternal will pervade everywhere. All-pervading indicates that It has only itself all around It and it is unconditioned by anything other than Itself.

That which is eternal and all-pervading must be stable meaning no change can ever happen to It. That which is stable is immovable. Mobility or moving implies the transfer of an object or person from one set of time and place to another set of time and place where they were not there already. Since Self is all-pervading there cannot be any place or period of time where It was not there before. As the Self is unconditioned by the concept of time It is said to be ancient.

Sri Bhagavan explains nature of immortal Self in a variety of ways giving several illustrations in order that the underlying idea can be easily grasped.

avyakto'yam achintyo'yam avikaaryo'yam uchyate
tasmaad evam viditwainam naanushochitum arhasi // 2.25 //

THE SELF IS UNMANIFEST, UNTHINKABLE AND UNCHANGEABLE. THEREFORE, KNOWING IT TO BE AS SUCH, YOU SHOULD NOT GRIEVE.

The Self is not an object of perception. It cannot be perceived by any one of the senses. Therefore, it is unmanifest. The mind can think only about an object perceived by the senses. As the Self cannot be perceived by the senses, It is unthinkable and beyond comprehension.. As the Self is infinite and without any form it cannot undergo any change. Hence It is changeless or immutable.

Arjuna's grief is misplaced as the Self cannot be hurt or slain. Forms may change; things may come and go but that which remains behind them all is for ever. The Lord, therefore, advises Arjuna not to grieve on that account and he should not think that he is the slayer and that the others are slain by him.

In the next two verses the lord shows that it is improper to grieve for the soul even if it is assumed to be subject to birth and death.

atha chainam nityajaatam nityam vaa manyase mritam
tathaapi twam mahaabaaho nainam shochitum arhasi // 2.26 //

BUT EVEN IF YOU THINK OF IT AS BEING PERPETUALLY BORN AND PERPETUALLY DYING, EVEN THEN, O MIGHTY ARMED (ARJUNA), YOU SHOULD NOT GRIEVE.

Sri Krishna, for the sake of argument, takes up the popular assumption here. Granting that the Self is repeatedly born whenever a body comes into being and dies whenever the body dies, even then one should not grieve, because birth is inevitable to that which dies and death is inevitable to that which is born. This is the inexorable law of the nature. As such, the occasion that Arjuna faces is not the one for lament.

jaatasya hi dhruvo mrityur dhruvam janma mritasya cha
tasmaad aparihaarye'rthe natwam shochitum arhasi // 2.27 //

DEATH IS SURE TO HAPPEN TO THAT WHICH IS BORN. BIRTH IS SURE TO HAPPEN TO THAT WHICH DIES. BIRTH AND DEATH ARE CERTAINLY UNAVOIDABLE. THEREFORE YOU SHOULD NOT GRIEVE OVER AN INEVITABLE OCCURRENCE.

Here Krishna continues to view the whole situation from the materialistic angle. Even from this stand point, if life is a constant flow of appearances and disappearances one should not shed tears over the unavoidable and inevitable.

It is not proper to grieve for beings which are mere combination of cause and effect.

avyaktaadeeni bhootani vyaktamadhyaani bhaarata
avyakta nidhanaanyeva tatra kaa paridevanaa // 2.28 //

BEINGS ARE UNMANIFEST IN THEIR BEGINNING, MANIFEST IN THEIR MIDDLE STATE AND UNMANIFEST AGAIN IN THEIR END O, ARJUNA. WHAT IS THERE TO GRIEVE ABOUT?

The world of beings which we see and experience i.e. the world which is manifest follows the law of causation. Effects rise from the causes. The effects are manifest i.e. visible while the causes are unmanifest. Projection from the unmanifest to the manifest is called the creation of a thing.

The manifest world of today was in a condition of unmanifest before its creation. Now temporarily it is manifest or available for cognition. It shall fade away one day again into unmanifest. The present came from the unknown past and will return to the unknown future. The physical body is a combination of the five elements. It is perceived by the physical eye only after the five elements have entered into such combination. After death the body disintegrates and the five elements return to their source. The body cannot be perceived then. Therefore the body can be perceived only in the middle state.

Thus before birth, beings had no connection with the bodies; after death too they would maintain no connection with these gross bodies. During the intermediate period alone viz. from birth to death, they are manifest and maintain relationship with their bodies.

The relationships such as son, wife, father, mother, brother, sister and teacher etc., are formed through the body because of delusion and attachment. Such relationships are only temporary as long as the bodies can perceive and are mere correlations as causes and effects just as we perceive the dream world only as long as the dream lasts and which was not existent before or after the dream.

It is just like a pot which was not there before it was made nor would it be there when it is destroyed. The only constant factor was the mud out of which the pot was made. The existence of the pot is visible only in the middle state and hence its existence is illusory. So also there is no body in the beginning or in the end. That which does not exist in the beginning or in the end must be having no real existence in the middle state as well; it can only be an illusory perception. He who thus understands the nature of the body and all human relationships based upon it will not allow them to have any influence upon his mind and therefore there would be no point in lamenting over the situation.

MARVELOUS NATURE OF THE SOUL

aashcharyavat pashyati kashchid enam
aashcharyavad vadati tathaiva chaanyah
aashcharyavacchainam anyah shrinoti
shrutwaapyenam veda na chaiva kaschit // 2.29 //

SOME LOOK ON THE SELF AS A WONDER; SOME SPEAK OF IT AS A WONDER; SOME HEAR OF IT AS A WONDER; STILL OTHERS, THOUGH HEARING, DO NOT UNDERSTAND IT AT ALL.

The Self is incomprehensible because it is not known by the ordinary means of knowledge. Though the knowledge of the Self is freely accessible to all mankind, it is attained only by a very few who are willing to pay the price in the form of self-discipline, steadfastness and non-attachment. Though the truth is open to all, many do not feel any urge to seek. Of those who have the urge, many suffer from doubt and vacillation. Even if they do not have doubts, many are scared away by difficulties. Only a few rare souls succeed in braving the perils and reaching the goal.

Although it is difficult to comprehend the idea of the Self, if one starts the practice of listening *(sravanam),* continuous reflection *(mananam)* and long contemplation *(nidhidhyasan)* it is possible to realize the Self in him.

END OF DISCUSSION ABOUT THE SOUL AND THE BODY

dehee nityam avadhyo'yam dehe sarvasya bhaarata
tasmaat sarvaani bhootani na twam shochitum arhasi // 2.30 //

THIS SELF, THE INDWELLER IN THE BODY OF EVERYONE, IS ALWAYS INDESTRUCTIBLE. O, ARJUNA, THEREFORE YOU SHOULD NOT GRIEVE FOR ANY CREATURE.

The body of any creature may be destroyed but the Self dwelling within it cannot be killed. Therefore, grief on account of death is improper, be it Bhishma or anyone else.

So far Krishna argued establishing the infinite nature of the soul and finite nature of the bodies. This verse concludes the idea opened in verse 11.

GRIEVING IS NOT PROPER TO ARJUNA AS A KSHATRIYA

swadharmam api chaavekshya na vikampitum arhasi
dharmyaaddhi yuddhaachhreyo'nyat Kshatriyasya na vidyate // 2.31 //

FURTHER HAVING REGARD TO YOUR DUTY (YOUR OWN DHARMA) YOU SHOULD NOT WAVER, FOR THERE IS NOTHING HIGHER FOR A KSHATRIYA THAN A RIGHTEOUS WAR.

Sri Krishna, so far talked to Arjuna on the immortality of the Self and the perishable nature of the body to justify why he should fight. He now gives him worldly reasons for fighting. He tells Arjuna that fighting is the ntural duty of a Kshatriya or the one born in the ruling class. His *svadharma* or law of action requires him to engage in battle for upholding law, justice and righteousness. To him nothing is more ennobling than a fair fight. Arjuna should therefore wage the war and ought not to waver from his duty.

yadricchayaa chopapannam swargadwaaram apaavritam
sukhinah Kshatriyaah paartha labhante yuddham eedrisham // 2.32 //

HAPPY ARE THE KSHATRIYAS WHO ARE CALLED UPON TO FIGHT IN SUCH A BATTLE THAT COMES OF ITSELF UNSOUGHT AS AN OPEN DOOR TO HEAVEN, O ARJUNA.

Arjuna's opponents had precipitated the war by their own indiscretion and hence this war has been called to come of itself unsought. A Kshatriya who gives up his life in a righteous war is said to go to heaven.

atha chettwam imam dharmyam samgraamam na karishyasi
tatah swadharmam keertim cha hitwaa paapam avaapsyasi // 2.33 //

BUT IF YOU WILL NOT FIGHT IN THIS LAWFUL BATTLE, THEN, HAVING ABANDONED YOUR OWN DHARMA AND HONOR, YOU SHALL INCUR SIN.

akeertim chaapi bhootaani kathayishyanti te'vyayaam
sambhaavitasya chaakeertir maranaad atirichyate // 2.34 //

PEOPLE TOO WILL RECOUNT FOR EVER YOUR INFAMY; TO A MAN WHO HAS BEEN HONORED, DISHONOR IS WORSE THAN DEATH.

With these stinging words Krishna seeks to stiffen Arjuna's spirit.

bhayaad ranaad uparatam mamsyante twaam mahaarathaah yesham cha twam bahumato bhootwaa yaasyasi laaghavam // 2.35 //

THE GREAT CHARIOT-WARRIORS (SUCH AS BHISHMA, DRONA, KRIPA ETC.) WILL THINK THAT YOU HAVE WITHDRAWN FROM THE BATTLE THROUGH FEAR AND YOU WILL BE RIDICULED BY THEM WHO HELD YOU IN MUCH ESTEEM.

avaachyavaadaamshcha bahoon vadishyanti tavaahitaah
nindantastava saamarthyam tato duhkhataram nu kim // 2.36 //

YOUR ENEMIES ALSO, FINDING FAULT WITH YOUR ABILITIES, WILL SPEAK MANY A WORD THAT SHOULD NOT BE UTTERED. WHAT COULD BE MORE PAINFUL THAN THIS?

hato vaa praapsyasi swargam jitwaa vaa bhokshyase maheem
tasmaad uttishtha kaunteya yuddhaaya kritanishchayah // 2.37 //

IF YOU ARE KILLED IN THE BATTLE, YOU WILL GO TO HEAVEN; IF YOU WIN, YOU WILL ENJOY THE EARTH. THEREFORE ARISE, O SON OF KUNTI, RESOLVED TO FIGHT.

The idea is that whatever may be the outcome of the war, Arjuna will be the gainer. Krishna implies that everyone should discharge his duty very sincerely and enthusiastically, to the best of his power and ability, in whatever circumstances, he is placed. Humanity demands it.

sukhaduhkhe same kritwaa laabhaalaabhau jayaajayau
tato yuddhaaya yujyaswa naivam paapamavaapsyasi // 2.38 //

TREATING ALIKE PLEASURE AND PAIN, GAIN AND LOSS, VICTORY AND DEFEAT, ENGAGE IN BATTLE FOR THE SAKE OF THE BATTLE, THUS YOU SHALL NOT INCUR SIN.

Arjuna was thinking that by killing his kinsmen he would incur sin. So Krishna clarifies that it is the desire for and attachment to the result of an action that create bondage; but when an action is performed without any such desire, it leads to freedom of the soul. The injunction to fight is only incidental.

Pain and pleasure are the intellectual awareness of the unfavorable or favorable experiences. Gain and loss are such awareness at the mental level. Victory and defeat are the experiences felt at bodily level or physical fields. Arjuna's goal is not to think of victory and defeat etc. but to discharge his duty by treating the agreeable and disagreeable alike. By doing so he would not commit any sin. i.e. he would be free from bondage.

Up to the verse 2.38 we have seen the Lord establishing the propriety of Arjuna engaging in the war from the point of view of Sankhya Yoga or the Yoga of Knowledge about the soul and the body as also from the angle of duty of a Kshatriya. In conclusion He advised Arjuna to fight in a spirit of equanimity. Now Bhagavan Krishna advocates the same theme from the point of view of Karma Yoga

THE INSIGHT OF YOGA

eshaa te'bhihitaa saankhye buddhir yoge twimaam shrinu
buddhyaa yukto yayaa paartha karma bandham prahaasyasi
// 2.39 //

WHAT HAS BEEN DECLARED TO YOU SO FAR IS THE WISDOM OF SANKHYA. NOW LISTEN TO THE WISDOM OF YOGA, ARMED WITH WHICH, O SON OF PRITHA, YOU WILL BREAK THROUGH THE BONDS OF KARMA.

Sri Krishna taught knowledge or Jnana to Arjuna till now. This is called Sankhya Yoga which is the path of Vedantic philosophy by which the true nature of the Self and the methods of attaining Self-Realisation can be comprehended through logic of reasoning.

From this verse onwards the focus of the Gita in this chapter is to explain the technique of Karma Yoga having known which one can break through the bonds of Karma or vasanas.

Let us see what these two yogas mean in the Bhagavad Gita and what is meant by the bondage of karma. Yoga means the technique of attaining knowledge or wisdom.

Sankhya or Jnana Yoga is the path of knowledge about the Absolute reality. It teaches discrimination between the Real and the Unreal and urges the renunciation of the unreal. The knowledge of Reality directly destroys ignorance, which is the cause of birth and death in the relative world and of grief and delusion inevitably associated with it.

Yoga or Karma Yoga is the path of action. The follower of this path engages in action without any desire for or attachment to the result of such action. He regards himself as an instrument of God. It is desire and attachment that create the subtle impressions in the mind *(vasanas)* which are the seeds of future action. Action performed without attachment and care for the result does not create new karma, but leaves the will free to devote itself to the achievement of Self-realization. This is the secret of Karma Yoga. What are the bonds of karma? Merit and demerit, virtue and sin, pain and pleasure, likes and dislikes, love and hatred and other such pairs of opposites constitute the bondage of all actions performed with a motive. These are the shackles that overpower and enslave those who undertake desire-oriented actions which make them happy or miserable because the results may or may not be of their expectations..

Sankhyayoga or the path of knowledge, which directly reveals the true nature of the self, is meant for very rare seekers, endowed with keen intellect for discrimination and undaunted will-power for renunciation. But the large majority does not belong to this category. Hence they should first of all purify their minds, through the discipline of Karma Yoga. They will then become fit to follow the path of knowledge. The pure in heart attain Self-knowledge through the grace of God.

Arjuna can qualify for the highest knowledge only through performance of his duty. Krishna all along adduced various arguments from the Upanishadic, materialistic, mundane standpoints to persuade him to perform his duty. Now Krishna describes Karma Yoga which is the special contribution of the Gita to the philosophy of life, ***a user's manual for every day living.***

THE SPECIAL MERIT OF KARMA YOGA

nehaabhikramanaasho'sti pratyavaayo na vidyate
swalpamapyasya dharmasya traayate mahato bhayaat // 2.40 //

IN THIS NO EFFORT IS EVER LOST AND NO HARM IS EVER DONE. EVEN VERY LITTLE OF THIS DISCIPLINE (DHARMA) SAVES A MAN FROM THE GREAT FEAR.

If a religious ceremony is left incomplete it is a wasted attempt as the performer will not derive any benefit like a house left unroofed. Again in the worship for an object, any imperfection in the process produces positive harm or loss instead of gain as in the case of sickness non-use of right medicines brings about adverse results. But it is not so in the case of Karma Yoga where every action and worship performed without desire brings about immediate purification of heart and protects one from the cycle of birth and death which is termed here as the great fear.

KARMA YOGA LEADS TO THE HIGHEST GOOD

vyavasaayaatmikaa buddhir ekeha kurunandana
bahushaakhaa hyanantaashcha buddhayo'vyavasaayinaam
// 2.41 //

O JOY OF THE KURUS (ARJUNA), IN THIS BLESSED PATH, THERE IS A CONCENTRATED ONE-POINTED DETERMINATION. SCATTERED AND ENDLESS ARE THE THOUGHTS OF THE IRRESOLUTE OR THE UNDECIDED.

In this Karma Yoga, even the highest achievement of Self-realization is possible because the man works with single-pointed determination with concentrated mind. Those who perform actions with endless desires for results get their inner personality disintegrated and dissipated. With the scattered minds they are not able to apply themselves to the tasks involved and therefore their attempts invariably end in failure.

Karma yoga is the path in which the seeker with concentrated resolution strives hard to reach his goal while in the Karma Kanda, the seeker, to satisfy his unending desires, performs various rituals as instructed in the Vedas meditating upon the prescribed Devata. As this process is more desire prompted there is always an inner agitation.

NO WISDOM FOR THE WORLDLY MINDED

yaam imaam pushpitaam vaacham pravadantyavipashchitah
vedavaadarataah paartha naanyad asteeti vaadinah // 2.42 //

kaamaatmaanah swargaparaa janmakarmaphalaprdaam
kriyaavisheshabahulaam bhogaishwaryagatim prati // 2.43 //

bhogaishwarya prasaktaanaam tayaapahritachetasaam
vyavasaayaatmika buddhih samaadhau na vidheeyate // 2.44 //

ARJUNA, THOSE WHO ARE OBSESSED BY DESIRES, WHO LOOK UPON HEAVEN AS THE SUPREME GOAL AND ARGUE THAT THERE IS NOTHING BEYOND HEAVEN AND ITS PLEASURES AND WHO ARE DEVOTED TO THE LETTER OF THE VEDAS ARE UNWISE. THEY MAKE THIS TYPE OF FLOWERY SPEECHES RECOMMENDING MANY ACTS OF VARIOUS KINDS, FOR THE ATTAINMENT OF PLEASURE AND PROSPERITY AND WITH REBIRTH AS THEIR MOTIVE. THOSE WHOSE MINDS ARE CARRIED AWAY BY SUCH FLOWERY WORDS (WHO ARE ATTRACTED BY AND ATTACHED TO PLEASURES AND PROSPERITY) ARE NOT WELL-ESTABLISHED IN THE SELF (IN CONCENTRATION).

Here the reference is to the Karma Kanda or the ritualistic portion of the Vedas, which lays down specific rules for specific actions for attaining specific results. Those who give too much importance to this section of the Vedas are called as unwise and lacking in discrimination.

These people are highly enamored about such Vedic passages which prescribe ways for attaining heavenly enjoyments. They say that there is nothing else than the sensual enjoyments and power here and happiness in heaven hereafter which can be achieved by performing the rites of the Karma Kanda of the Vedas. They regard such attainments as the ultimate object of human existence. Hence ordinary individuals are attracted towards their flattering talk. They ignore the philosophical section of the Vedas dealing with the knowledge of the soul and which alone leads to liberation.

Life in heaven is also transitory. After the fruits of one's good actions have been exhausted, one has to return to this earth-plane and liberation can be attained only through knowledge of the Self.

Although it is stated here that the Karma Kanda of the Vedas cannot give us final liberation and a declaration is made that such persons tossed by desires shall never experience any tranquility in their inner lives, we have to keep in mind that if these rituals when performed without desire for results purify the mind which is also an initial step in the Jnana Yoga. The point to note is that the results of the rites and sacrifices performed with desires are ephemeral for they are limited by time, space and the law of causation.

PRACTICE OF VEDIC RITES DOES NOT LEAD TO LIBERATION

traigunyavishayaa vedaa nistraigunyo bhavaarjuna
nirdwandwo nityasatwastho niryogakshema aatmavaan // 2.45 //

THE VEDAS DEAL WITH THREE ATTRIBUTES (OF NATURE); YOU BE ABOVE THESE THREE ATTRIBUTES, O ARJUNA.

FREE YOURSELF FROM THE PAIRS OF OPPOSITES AND EVER REMAIN IN THE QUALITY OF SATTVA (GOODNESS), FREED FROM ALL THOUGHTS OF ACQUISITION (OF WHAT YOU LACK) AND PRESERVATION (OF WHAT YOU HAVE) AND BE ESTABLISHED IN THE SELF.

After advising Arjuna about the ineffectiveness of the blind obedience to the Karma Kanda, Sri Krishna tells him to transcend himself from the triple Gunas. Guna means attribute or quality. Nature is made of three Gunas viz., Sattva - purity, light, harmony; Rajas - passion, restlessness, motion; and Tamas - inertia, and darkness. These three Gunas remain in all the living creatures in varying degrees. The mind and intellect are constituted with these qualities. Going above these temperaments means going beyond the mind and intellect to re-discover one to be the Supreme Self. How such transportation from imperfection to perfection can take place is explained here.

Pairs of opposites like heat and cold, pleasure and pain, victory and defeat, honor and dishonor, praise and censure etc. are the experiences of man in his life. To ever remain in the quality of Sattva means to keep oneself least agitated in one's perceptions of objects and persons and in the assessment of their true nature.

Every activity in this world is guided by two prime motives viz. acquisition for purposes of possession and preservation of possessions acquired. These two motives in all actions indicate our selfish desire to acquire and hoard. Renouncing these two temperaments implies getting away from the source of restlessness and sorrows in life.

Sri Krishna advises Arjuna the practical method to be free from all the pairs of opposites and from the thought of acquisition and preservation and ever remaining in the quality of Sattva by establishing himself in the Self by remaining on guard and not yielding to the objects of the senses. The sorrows of the pairs of the opposites, the temptation to be impure and the desire for acquiring and preserving all belong to the ego-centre arising out of the Self identifying with not-Self i.e. body, mind and intellect.

To keep ourselves detached from these ego-centric ideas through constant awareness of our pure divine nature is the path shown by The Lord to establish oneself in the Self when the individual ego finds itself free from all anxieties of the world. Necessarily then one will be beyond the three Gunas free from the pairs of opposites, remaining always in the Sattwic quality. This attitude implies that one should be balanced and not swayed by either extremes. Sattva enables an aspiring soul to go beyond the Gunas and attain freedom.

Arjuna is asked to follow these injunctions while engaged in the performance of his duty.

WHAT IS THE USE OF THE VEDAS?

yaavaanartha udapaane sarvatah samplutodake
taavaan sarveshu vedeshu braahmanasya vijaanatah // 2.46 //

TO THE BRAHMANA WHO HAS KNOWN THE SELF, ALL THE VEDAS ARE OF AS MUCH USE AS IS A RESERVOIR OF WATER IN A PLACE WHERE THERE IS A FLOOD.

Only for a sage who has realized the Self or truth concerning the Absolute Reality, the Vedas (Karma Kanda) are of no use because he is already in possession of the highest knowledge of the Self. This however does not imply ridiculing or ignoring the Karma Kanda of the Vedas. They are certainly a useful means for achieving the goal by the aspirants who just started their spiritual journey and serve the purpose of the unenlightened. Through the performance of the works prescribed by the Vedas one becomes fit for the path of knowledge.

As all the transient pleasures derived from the proper performance of rituals enjoined in the Karma Kanda of the Vedas are comprehended in the Infinite Bliss of Self Knowledge, Karma Kanda is as much useful as the utility of a reservoir in a place having floods. All kinds of limited bliss are included in the Infinite Bliss. A knower of the Self does not need to follow the Vedic injunctions.

WORK WITHOUT CONCERN FOR THE RESULTS

karmanyevaadhikaaraste maa phaleshu kadaachana
maa karmaphalahetur bhoor maa te sango'stwakarmani // 2.47 //

YOUR RIGHT IS TO WORK ONLY, BUT NEVER TO CLAIM ITS FRUITS. DO NOT BECOME AN INSTRUMENT FOR MAKING YOUR ACTIONS YIELD FRUIT, NOR LET YOUR ATTACHMENT BE TO INACTION.

This is one of the most quoted verses of the Gita. This famous verse contains the essential principle of disinterestedness in action. When we do our work we will be sidetracked from disinterestedness if we think of name, fame, income or any such extraneous consideration. Nothing should matter except the willing fulfillment of the purpose of God, keeping in mind that success or failure depends upon other forces as well.

Sri Krishna's advice here is a call to the man not to waste his present time in imaginary fears about the future but to bring out the best in him and live fruitfully every present moment of his life. Thereby the future will take care of itself and provide the Karma Yogins with supreme achievement.

Arjuna is advised that all that is given to him is to act and having known the cause of action to be noble, bring into that activity all that is the best in him and immerse himself in performing that activity. That will be the inspired action and its fruits will be such action itself.

This verse gives the following four guidelines to a Karma Yogin:

1. His concern is with the action alone
2. He has no concern with the results
3. He should not become a tool for gaining a desired result of a given action since such desired-result-oriented-action produces bondage and
4. The above mentioned ideas should not be taken to mean advocating inaction.

The advice is to make the worker release himself from his mental anxieties and make him aware of the divinity through work alone. The work itself is his reward -- satisfaction of the job well done is the end in itself.

By performing actions in this manner one gets peace and his vasanas get reduced. Freed from the bondage of expectations he becomes purified for realizing the knowledge of the Self and attain God-Realization or Salvation. Through this knowledge one is freed from the wheel of births and deaths.

Bhagavan, however, warns that one should be careful not to lapse into inaction thinking that there is no use performing actions without expecting any rewards.

Various meanings are attached to the word Karma. The followers of Karma Kanda mean it as rituals and sacrifices. Another meaning is one's duty as per the caste or station in life. Karma also means action. But a deeper meaning of the word is destiny or the tendencies, impulses, characteristics and habits-Vasanas-which determine his next birth and environment. But Karma in the present verse means action or performing one's duty.

IF A MAN HAS TO WORK WITHOUT ANY DESIRE FOR ITS RESULTS, HOW, THEN, SHOULD HE GO ABOUT IT?

yogasthah kuru karmani sangam tyaktwaa dhananjaya
siddhyasiddhyoh samo bhootwaa samatwam yoga uchyate // 2.48 //

PERFORM YOUR ACTIONS, O DHANANJAYA (ARJUNA), BEING ESTABLISHED IN OR INTEGRATED WITH YOGA, ABANDONING ATTACHMENT AND REMAINING EVEN-MINDED BOTH IN SUCCESS AND FAILURE. THIS EVENNESS OF MIND IS CALLED YOGA.

From here the technique of Karma Yoga is discussed exhaustively wherein Yoga means evenness of mind through work. In this path towards progress, a complete erasure of individuality and its false sense of values are essential.

Evenness of mind, tranquility of mental composure in all pairs of opposites, is Yoga. In this context the term Yoga indicates a special condition of mind in which it comes to a neutral equilibrium in all the ups and downs of life's situations. It is a state of being an instrument in the hands of God, having given up even the desire that through our action we shall please Him. Only thus one can remain unconcerned as to success and failure.

Attachment is the notion that arises when a man regards himself not as an instrument but as a doer of an action. It is necessary for the true worker not only to have equanimity and poise in his behavior but he should reinforce it with a total renunciation of his attachment to the anxieties for the results. By this way he may transform even his ordinary chores as inspired actions. During the performance of such inspired actions, the performer becomes self-forgetful and would not care for success or failure for his venture. This equilibrium is Yoga.

The attainment of knowledge of the Self through purity of heart obtained by performing actions without the expectation of the fruits is success - Siddhi. Failure is the non-attainment of such knowledge by doing actions with the expectation of fruits.

The secret of Karma Yoga is the complete effacement of one's individuality and total identification with God's will. Thus alone does the worker become free from the joy or grief that results from the success or failure of his works; this alone ensures that he enjoys peace while performing his duties.

AN ACTION PERFORMED AIMING AT THE RESULT IS INFERIOR.

doorena hyavaram karma buddhiyogaad dhananjaya
buddhau sharanamanwiccha kripanaah phalahetavah // 2.49 //

O ARJUNA, FAR INFERIOR, INDEED, IS MERE ACTION, TO ACTION PERFORMED WITH EVENNESS OF MIND. SEEK REFUGE IN THIS EVENNESS. WRETCHED ARE THEY WHO WORK FOR RESULTS.

Actions performed to gain a result are the cause of future birth and death and hence create bondage. Such actions are referred to here as inferior. The state of not being exalted or depressed by success or failure is called evenness. It is not callousness or indifference but a total devotion of the worker to his duty, whereby he regards himself as an instrument of God. One attains true evenness only as a result of the Knowledge of the Supreme Reality. This Knowledge alone, not any incidental result, should be the goal of work.

Wretched indeed are they who busy themselves with calculation of the gains or losses resulting from their actions and thus depart from the world without realizing the Supreme Reality.

RESULT OF PERFORMING DUTY WITH EVENNESS OF MIND.

buddhiyukto jahaateeha ubhe sukrita dushkrite
tasmaad yogaaya yujyaswa yogah karmasu kaushalam // 2.50 //

ENDOWED WITH EVENNESS OF MIND, ONE CASTS OFF IN THIS VERY LIFE BOTH GOOD AND EVIL DEEDS. THEREFORE, DEVOTE YOURSELF TO YOGA (OF EQUANIMITY); SKILL IN ACTION LIES IN THE PRACTICE OF THIS YOGA.

A person, endowed with equanimity, becomes free from virtue and vice. In such a state while living in the world, he detaches himself from the trappings of the world and remains untouched by virtue and sin. Virtue and vice accrue to a person when he identifies himself with the body, the unreal. If he does not so identify himself, virtue and vice have no effect on him.

Therefore, Krishna says 'devote yourself to the yoga of equanimity' i.e. remain continuously even-minded through realization of God. If a man performs his duties, maintaining this evenness, then his mind rests on God all the while. Work that otherwise enslaves, becomes a means to freedom when performed with evenness of mind. Work becomes worship. Skill in action, therefore, lies in the practice of this equanimity (of yoga) in success and failure. It should be noted that here Krishna does not define Yoga as skill in action but explains the importance of Yoga (equanimity) in action. Otherwise, the action of a thief carried out skillfully also can come within the meaning of the Yoga which will be obviously ridiculous.

HOW DOES ACTION LEAD TO LIBERATION?

karmajam buddhiyuktaa hi phalam tyaktwaa maneeshinah
janmabandha vinirmuktaah padam gacchantyanaamayam
// 2.51 //

THE WISE, POSSESSED OF EQUANIMITY, HAVING ABANDONED THE FRUITS OF THEIR ACTIONS AND BEING FREED FROM THE FETTERS OF BIRTH, ATTAIN THE STATE THAT IS BEYOND ALL EVIL (REACHES THE BLISSFUL SUPREME STATE).

Clinging to the fruits of actions creates vasanas to exhaust which one has to get into the cycle of births and deaths. If actions are performed as a dedication to the God in fulfillment of his purpose, without desire for the fruits, one is released from the bonds of birth and death and attains bliss. Birth and death is called bondage because it is the result of action in a previous life.

The wise i.e those who know the art of true living undertake all work with evenness of mind (renouncement of ego) and abandoning the anxiety for the fruits of their actions (renouncement of ego-motivated desires). Thereby, they have no occasion to enter into the cycle of birth and death as there are no vasanas left in them for fulfillment.

Such an entity who is called a Karma Yogin will attain bliss i,e, the state which is beyond all evils. As knowledge is superior to action, the implication is that selfless actions purify the mind and prepare the individual for higher meditations through which he ultimately discovers himself as the Self which lies beyond all blemish. This is also called as Buddhi Yoga.

WHEN DOES ONE ATTAIN THE WISDOM THAT IS THE RESULT OF THE PURITY OF MIND INDUCED BY KARMA YOGA?

yadaa te mohakalilam buddhir vyatitarishyati
tadaa gantaasi nirvedam shrotavyasya shrutasya cha // 2.52 //

WHEN YOUR MIND CROSSES BEYOND THE MIRE OF DELUSION, THEN YOU SHALL ACHIEVE INDIFFERENCE REGARDING THINGS ALREADY HEARD AND THINGS YET TO BE HEARD (ABOUT ENJOYMENTS OF THIS WORLD OR THE NEXT).

Delusion is the non-discrimination between the Self and the non-Self or ego and it turns the mind towards the sense objects. This is the state which favors egoism in this body and attachment for the body, family, kinsmen and objects. When the man gets entangled in this slough of delusion, he is perplexed and therefore cannot think properly.

When the intellect crosses over this delusion and attains purity of mind one develops disgust and indifference regarding things heard (enjoyed) and those yet to be heard (to be enjoyed in future). The things known and yet to be known being finite in nature are considered futile. The means to achieve this goal are by discrimination between the real and the unreal and selfless service.

The words 'things heard and yet to be heard' mean all the sense-organs oriented experiences already undergone and those that are yet to be experienced. Logically when the intellect becomes purer, it loses all its infatuation, fascination and attraction for the sense experiences that it had before and that may arise in future.

A question may arise how long this process of attaining freedom will take? The answer is that it is not a question of time. Freedom refers to the experience which can be attained at any moment, the only condition being the desirelessness of the aspirant or absence of attachment to objects attained or attainable.

WHEN DOES ONE ATTAIN THE TRUE YOGA OR KNOWLEDGE OF THE SUPREME TRUTH?

shrutivipratipannaa te yadaa sthaasyati nishchalaa
samaadhaavachalaa buddhistadaa yogam avaapsyasi // 2.53 //

WHEN YOUR MIND, NOW PERPLEXED BY WHAT YOU HAVE HEARD, STANDS FIRM AND STEADY IN THE SELF, THEN YOU WILL HAVE ATTAINED YOGA OR SELF-REALIZATION.

The mind gets agitated due to the continuous stimuli it receives from the external world through the sense organs. When an individual in spite of such disturbances and agitations of the mind does not lose his cool, inner serenity and equipoise, and remains concentrated in the knowledge of the Self, he is considered as having attained Yoga or Samadhi or Self Realization (God-Consciousness).

Samadhi is not the loss of consciousness but the highest kind of consciousness wherein the object with which the mind is in communion is the Divine Self which is the result of the discrimination between the Self and the Non-Self, the Real and the Unreal.

We must act with equanimity which is more important than the action itself. The question is not what shall we do but how shall we do and with what spirit shall we do? While Karma implies action, Buddhi implies how to act. Buddhiyoga is the method by which we go beyond Vedic Ritualsim and do our duty without any attachment for the results of our actions.

Sri Krishna's advice made so far reduces the dejection in Arjuna and induces him to seek clarifications from Him as to what are the characteristics of the man who has attained wisdom through Samadhi. This is dealt with next.

The Lord told Arjuna that when his mind would have crossed the mire of delusion and would develop indifference towards the enjoyment of this world and the next and when his mind would rest steady and undistracted in meditation on God, he would realize God or attain union with Him. With reference to this advice, Arjuna desires to know the marks and conduct of the perfect Yogi, possessed of a stable mind who is termed as a *sthita prajna*. He asks Krishna to describe the nature of such an enlightened Soul. Viz. How would he express himself in the world? What happens to him internally? How does he contact the external world?

Krishna answers, "Reveling in the bliss of the Self, the enlightened one stays free from all egocentric attachments and desires. In the state of absolute fulfillment, all worldly enjoyments fall into insignificance and fail to have any impact on him. He is like a river which has entered the ocean. Having reached that supreme state he has merged with eternity. He is liberated, attained *Moksha,* the ultimate *Purushartha* and the goal of life".

The last eighteen verses of this chapter give a brilliant exposition of a Self-realized soul, a perfect personification of a stress-free complete man. These verses can be easily taken as a dissertation on Stress Management Technique from a spiritual angle eliminating the necessity to use anti-depressant drugs.

CHARACTERISTICS OF A PERSON WHO HAS ATTAINED WISDOM THROUGH SAMADHI.

arjuna uvaacha
sthitaprajnasya kaa bhaashaa samaadhisthasya keshava
sthitadheeh kim prabhaasheta kimaaseeta vrajeta kim // 2.54 //

ARJUNA SAID
O KESHAVA, WHAT IS THE DESCRIPTION OF HIM WHO HAS STEADY WISDOM AND IS MERGED IN THE SUPER

CONSCIOUS STATE (SAMADHI)? HOW DOES ONE OF STEADY WISDOM SPEAK? HOW DOES HE SIT? HOW DOES HE WALK?

With the advice thus far given, Arjuna seems to have got a better understanding and a doubt appears to have crept in his mind as to whether a person after gaining the goal of life through Buddhi Yoga may yet have a vigorous life at all in the outside world. This doubt is because of the common notion that a perfected individual is ill-suited to lead a normal day-to-day life.

'The man of steady wisdom" means the one who, through direct realization, has the settled knowledge of his identification with Brahman, the Self. He is the one who realizes that he is Brahman.

The two questions asked by Arjuna are:
1. How is a man of steady wisdom described by others?
2. How does the influence of wisdom manifest itself in his actions in the outer world when he comes out of Samadhi?

The answers to these questions occupy the rest of this Chapter. They comprise of the characteristic attributes of a man of steady wisdom and also the means of attaining such wisdom. These attributes apply equally to Jnana Yogis and Karma Yogis.

Arjuna's questions mean

- How does a wise person respond to the daily situations in life?
- What are the distinguishing marks or characteristics of a wise person?

The characteristics of a wise person are also the characteristics of one who wants to be wise. In the case of a wise person, such characteristics are natural to that person; but, in the case of one who is not yet wise – but wants to become one– such characteristics need to be cultivated by proper attitude, discipline and practice.

In the next 18 verses, Sri Krishna responds to the question of Arjuna. Sri Krishna does not say how a wise person talks, sits or walks. Appreciating the spirit of Arjuna's question, Sri Krishna tells Arjuna – and indeed all humanity, the characteristics of a wise person, and also, what makes a person wise.

These verses are of extraordinary significance for two reasons - they tell precisely what wisdom means in practical every day life. They are also a do-it-yourself road-map for spiritual self-help and self-development. These 18 verses are therefore the best known and extensively commented in the entire Bhagavad Gita.

sri bhagavaan uvaacha
prajahaati yadaa kaamaan sarvaan paartha manogataan
atmanyevaatmanaa tushtah sthitaprajnastadochyate // 2.55 //

SRI BHAGAVAN SAID
O PARTHA, WHEN A MAN COMPLETELY CASTS OFF ALL THE DESIRES OF THE MIND, HIS SELF FINDING SATISFACTION IN ITSELF ALONE, THEN HE IS CALLED A MAN OF STEADY WISDOM.

An exhaustive exposition of the inner and outer life of the 'man of steady wisdom' or the 'man of Self-realization' follows now. This section of the Gita enumerates the guidelines that should be followed as to what types of values and mental attitudes should be developed during one's spiritual practices in order that he may come to realize the Divinity in himself.

The man of steady wisdom does not long for external possessions for he enjoys the Supreme Bliss of Self-Knowledge. Such a man of wisdom has renounced all cravings like progeny, wealth and attainment of heaven etc. and enjoys the bliss of communion with the Self. This is what is meant by the self finding satisfaction in itself alone.

Man is a bundle of desires. They may be strong or weak and have an origin and a locus in his mind for whatever cause it may be. Therefore when the mind along with the intellect rests stable in God, all the desires will vanish. After the cessation of all the desires, when a seeker perceives the Supreme Self and rests in the perpetual calm, he is known as 'satisfied in the self through the self'.

A spiritually ignorant or immature person hangs on to desires, because that person depends on the fulfillment of such desires for his happiness. When a person grows into maturity and completely casts off his dependence on the fulfillment of desires for happiness, he then becomes a wise person.

When can this happen? Bhagavan says that when one discovers happiness in oneself by oneself - then one is called - a wise person.

When one recognizes that one's very nature is *"ananda"*- one's very nature is happiness, there is no need for one to depend on the external objects for fulfillment of one's happiness. When one recognizes that one's very nature is *sat-chit-ananda-svarupa-atma* - one discovers that one has nothing to gain from outside to be happy - and also, one realizes that one has already gained everlasting happiness in the form of Vision of oneself everywhere and in everything including oneself.

The happiness arising from such vision is called "one discovering Happiness in oneself, by one self in the wake of self knowledge". When that knowledge takes place, there is no craving for any object or experience external to ones own self, to be happy. At that time all desires have no hold on oneself and they naturally fall from one's mind and buddhi, which is the same as telling that one naturally and completely grows out of one's dependence on the fulfillment of one's desires for one's happiness. Discovering happiness as one's own very self, one has no need to go after something else to be happy. Such discovery is indeed the mark of a wise person.

Negatively, this state is one of freedom from selfish desires and positively, it is one of concentration on the Supreme. This verse answers the first part of Arjuna's question.

duhkheshwanudwignamanaah sukheshu vigatasprihah
veetaraagabhayakrodhah sthitadheer munir uchyate // 2.56 //

HE WHOSE MIND IS NOT SHAKEN BY ADVERSITY, WHO DOES NOT HANKER AFTER PLEASURES AND WHO IS FREE FROM ATTACHMENT, FEAR AND ANGER, IS CALLED A SAGE OF STEADY WISDOM.

Verses 56 - 58 answer the second part of Arjuna's question as to the conduct of the man of steady wisdom.

Times of pain and sorrow hit everybody and a wise man is no exception; but his mind does not get weighed down by them. His pain is localized, and it stops there. Similarly, in times of pleasure, the one who has no craving has no thirst for more of that pleasure. Thus the one who does not feel depressed in times of pain and sorrow, and who in times of pleasure has no craving for more of that pleasure is a wise man.

The one whose mind and intellect are totally free from intense longing or passion for anything outside of oneself, free from fear of any kind and devoid of anger or temporary madness about anything is called one who is steady and well rooted in self knowledge. Such a person is also called one who is capable of reflection, analysis and proper judgment at all times being always immersed in God Consciousness. He is called the wise person.

In this world there is no end to sorrow and unfavorable situations. Here a man of steady wisdom is described as the one who maintains equanimity in pleasure and pain. An individual who remains undisturbed in sorrow or in joy, unattached, fearless and without anger is described here as a *muni* - a sage, a man of steady wisdom.

It may be noted of all the emotions that must be absent in the perfected individual only three have been emphasized here viz., attachment -Raga, fear -Bhaya and anger -Krodha because attachment to things is the root cause for the fear of non-winning the desired object. If it is won then there is fear of losing it and therefore anxiety to keep it safe and secure is equally strong. Attachment and fear lead to anger against those who create obstacles between the person infatuated with the object and the desired object. It is self-mastery, conquest of desire and passion that is insisted upon.

yah sarvatraanabhisnehas tattat praapya shubhaashubham
naabhinandati na dweshti tasya prajnaa pratishthitaa // 2.57 //

HE WHO IS NOT ATTACHED TO ANYTHING, WHO NEITHER REJOICES NOR IS, VEXED WHEN HE OBTAINS GOOD OR EVIL - HIS WISDOM IS FIRMLY FIXED.

The ideas expressed in the previous verses are repeated:

- The enlightened sage or the Perfected one has evenness of mind.
- He does not rejoice in pleasure nor is he averse to any pain.
- He has no attachment to any worldly object.
- He does not get disturbed when praised or censured.
- He is always identified with the Self.

A mere detachment from life and retiring to the jungles is not implied here. Such aimless detachment cannot lead a man to any higher level of existence and it is merely an escapist view of life. The detachment from the outside world should be coupled with capacity to face all challenges in life - auspicious and inauspicious - with a balanced mind in both. Life by its very nature is a mixture of good and bad. The perfected one experiences both of them with equal detachment because he is ever established in the Self.

Since the perfect man of wisdom has neither aversion for the sorrows nor attraction for the pleasures of life he neither compliments nor condemns anything in the world. For him everything is fine. He looks at the world through the plain glass and not through colored glasses. Flowers bloom and they also whither away. There is no need to praise the former and condemn the latter. We must accept whatever comes without excitement, pain or revolt.

This verse is in reply to Arjuna's query about the speech of a perfect master. His speech has for its background the mental state as described above.

yadaa samharate chaayam koormo'ngaaneeva sarvashah
indriyaaneendriyaarthebhyas tasya prajnaa pratishthitaa // 2.58 //

WHEN LIKE THE TORTOISE WHICH WITHDRAWS ITS LIMBS ON ALL SIDES, HE WITHDRAWS HIS SENSES FROM THE SENSE OBJECTS, THEN HIS WISDOM BECOMES STEADY.

So far a man of steady wisdom has been described as the one who (a) is ever satisfied in the Self (b) lives in perfect equanimity in pleasure and pain and (c) in whom there is complete lack of attachment for feelings of joy or aversion. Now it is mentioned in this verse that a man of steady wisdom has the capacity to withdraw his sense organs from the fields of their objects just like a tortoise can draw back its limbs from all sides within its shell when apprehending danger.

The sense organs receive the stimuli from the objects of the external world which are passed on to the mind. The mind has got a natural tendency to run after such worldly objects. The yogi withdraws the mind again and again from the objects of the senses and fixes it on the Self and makes himself free from the disturbances of life.

DISTINCTION BETWEEN THE SENSE-CONTROL BY AN ORDINARY PERSON AND A REALIZED SOUL

vishayaa vinivartante niraahaarasya dehinah
rasavarjam raso'pyasya param drishtwaa nivartate // 2.59 //

THE OBJECTS OF THE SENSES FALL AWAY FROM THE ABSTINENT MAN BUT NOT THE TASTE FOR THEM. BUT EVEN THE TASTE FALLS AWAY WHEN THE SUPREME IS SEEN.

The sense objects reach out to only those who is badly in need of them and not to those who do not want them. Even then, the sense objects are capable of leaving their taste behind even in an abstinent seeker who may find it difficult to erase them completely from his mind. Sri Krishna says here that all such longings created even at the mental level because of ego will be made ineffective when the seeker transcends ego and comes to experience the Self - attains wisdom. But the reverse i.e. with the disappearance of the taste a striver attains steadfast wisdom is not true.

Sri Krishna is explaining the difference between outer abstention and inner renunciation. We may reject the object but the desire for it may remain. Even the desire is lost when the Supreme is seen. The control should be both at the body and mental levels. Liberation from the tyranny of the body is not enough; we must be liberated from the tyranny of desires also which presupposes realization of the Supreme.

Thus in the restraint of the senses evinced by a man of realization, not only the sense objects turn away from him but also attachment itself with its roots vanish.

WHAT IS THE HARM IF ATTACHMENT DOES NOT DISAPPEAR?

yatato hyapi kaunteya purushasya vipashchitah
indriyaani pramaatheeni haranti prasabham manah // 2.60 //

THE TURBULENT SENSES, O SON OF KUNTI, DO VIOLENTLY CARRY AWAY THE MIND EVEN OF A WISE MAN THOUGH HE MAY BE STRIVING TO CONTROL THEM.

Sri Krishna has so far emphasized that a perfect master is the one who has a complete control over his sense-cravings. Sense cravings are like turbulent horses. If these horses are kept under control destination can be reached with safety; otherwise the rider gets thrown out.

Even a man of discrimination falls prey to the temptations of the world. Therefore, the aspirant must not relax his effort for self-control. He should bring all the senses under his control; otherwise his mind will be dragged into the field of sense objects leading to a sorrowful experience. This is more likely to happen even to a highly evolved seeker whereby he will not be able to reach his spiritual destination of final liberation. This is an advice of caution to the seeker.

SENSE CONTROL IS A MEANS OF GOD-REALIZATION FOR A PERSON OF STABLE MIND

taani sarvaani samyamya yukta aaseeta matparah
vashe hi yasyendriyaani tasya prajnaa pratishthitaa // 2.61 //

HAVING RESTRAINED ALL THE SENSES HE SHOULD SIT STEADFAST, INTENT ON ME; HIS WISDOM IS STEADY WHOSE SENSES ARE UNDER CONTROL.

Sri Krishna warns Arjuna here that as a seeker of Self-perfection he should control his mind by withdrawing all his sense organs from their wanderings and should concentrate his entire attention on 'me' i.e. The Lord, The Supreme. The idea is that the mind should be made completely calm to meditate on Him, the Supreme Lord.

Such a Yogi, having brought under control all his senses, is called a person of steady wisdom and established in the Self. Self-discipline is not a matter of intelligence. It is a matter of will of the mind and vision of the Highest. This is a technique of Self-Development.

THE VERY THOUGHT OF SENSE-OBJECTS CAUSES FUTURE MISFORTUNE

dhyaayato vishayaan pumsah sangas teshoopajaayate
sangaat sanjaayate kaamah kaamaat krodho'bhijaayate// 2.62 //

WHEN A MAN THINKS OF OBJECTS, ATTACHMENT FOR THEM ARISES; FROM ATTACHMENT DESIRE IS BORN; FROM DESIRE ARISES ANGER.

krodhaad bhavati sammohah sammohaat smriti vibhramah
smritibhramshaad buddhinaasho buddhinaashaat pranashyati // 2.63 //

FROM ANGER COMES DELUSION, FROM DELUSION THE LOSS OF MEMORY, FROM THE LOSS OF MEMORY THE DESTRUCTION OF INTELLIGENCE; FROM THE DESTRUCTION OF INTELLIGENCE HE PERISHES.

From here onwards Sri Krishna explains the theory of fall of man from God-hood to sense-entanglements. The source of all evils is wrong thinking and false perceptions. When a man constantly thinks upon the alluring features of the sense objects the consistency of such thought creates an attachment in him for the objects of his thought. When similar thoughts come to play on his mind continuously they become strong desire for possessing and enjoying the objects of attachment.

He tries his level best to obtain them. When this motive energy encounters with forces creating obstacles in the way of fulfillment of his desires it is called anger. He starts hating the people who come in the way of satisfying his wants, fights with them and develops hostility towards them. When a person is afflicted with anger, his mind gets confused casting a shadow on the lessons of wisdom learnt by him through past experience. Thus deprived of the moral strength, he loses his power of discrimination between right and wrong which is called destruction of intelligence.

Failing in discrimination, he acts irrationally on the impulse of passions and emotions and thereby he is unable to attain the spiritual goal paving the way for self-destruction. Here Krishna traces moral degradation to those first breaths of thought that come softly and almost unconsciously to the mind.

Desires may prove to be as rebellious and challenging as the most powerful external forces. They may lift us into glory or hurl us into disgrace. Kalidasa in Kumarasambhavam says that they are really brave whose minds are not disturbed when the sources of disturbance are face to face with them

What is called for is not a forced isolation from the world or destruction of sense life but an inward withdrawal. To hate the senses is as wrong as to love them. The horses of the senses are not to be unyoked from the chariot but controlled by the reins of the mind.

The movement from desire to destruction can be illustrated as under:

Brooding on the objects of senses ▶attachment ▶desire ▶anger ▶delusion ▶loss of memory ▶loss of reason ▶utter ruin.

HOW A PERSON OF STABLE MIND MOVES AMONG SENSE OBJECTS AND WHAT IS HIS REWARD?

raagadwesha viyuktaistu vishayaanindriyaishcharan
aatmavashyair vidheyaatmaa prasaadamadhigacchati // 2.64 //

BUT THE SELF-CONTROLLED MAN, MOVING AMONG OBJECTS WITH HIS SENSES UNDER RESTRAINT AND FREE FROM BOTH ATTRACTION AND REPULSION, ATTAINS PEACE.

The mind and the senses are endowed with the two natural currents of attraction and repulsion - liking some objects and disliking certain others. But a man with mental discipline approaches these sense objects with a mind free from attraction or repulsion thereby attaining the peace of the Eternal. The senses and the mind are his servants but not the masters; he is the Master of wisdom. Running away from the sense objects cannot ensure mental tranquility because mind's agitations for getting the desired objects or to get rid of the undesired ones will persist.

When the mind is trained in these two aspects viz., (a) to live in self-control and (b) to move among the sense objects with neither attachment nor hatred towards them, its agitations caused by the charm of such objects are brought under control. This condition of the mind, which has the least sense disturbances because of the ineffectiveness of the sense objects upon it, is called tranquility or peace or 'Prasada'.

This verse answers Arjuna's question as to how does the man of steady wisdom move about?

WHAT DOES ONE ATTAIN THROUGH SERENITY?

prasaade sarvaduhkhaanaam haanirasyopajaayate
prasannachetaso hyaashu buddhih paryavatishthate// 2.65 //

IN THAT SERENITY THERE IS AN END OF ALL SORROWS; FOR THE INTELLIGENCE OF THE MAN OF SERENE MIND SOON BECOMES STEADY.

What happens when peace is attained is explained here. Sri Krishna says that when mental peace is attained there is no hankering after sense-objects. The Yogi has perfect mastery over his reason and sense of discrimination. The intellect abides in the Self. It is quite serene and steady. The miseries of the body and mind come to an end.

Peaceful mind is a condition- precedent for happiness. Peace is happiness; happiness is peace. The least agitated mind is the proof of absence of sorrows and sorrows are the proof of the state of mental disturbance. Destruction of sorrows or pain indicates the elimination of vasanas in as much as vasanas are the cause for delusion which creates all sorrows. Keeping the mind under tranquil atmosphere through a life of self-control is the secret for the elimination of vasanas.

PEACE OF MIND ALONE LEADS TO HAPPINESS

naasti buddhir ayuktasya na chaayuktasya bhaavanaa
na chaabhaavayatah shaantir ashaantasya kutah sukham
// 2.66 //

THE MAN WHOSE MIND IS NOT UNDER HIS CONTROL HAS NO SELF-KNOWLEDGE AND TO THE UNSTEADY NO MEDITATION IS POSSIBLE AND TO THE UNMEDITATIVE THERE CAN BE NO PEACE AND TO THE MAN WHO HAS NO PEACE HOW CAN THERE BE ANY HAPPINESS?

The necessity for the quietness of mind for practicing the technique of Self-perfection is explained here. The unsteady mind cannot practice meditation. The mind which cannot be focused on meditation cannot acquire the knowledge of the Self.

Such a person will not have intense devotion and longing either to Self-knowledge or to liberation. A person with these negative qualities cannot have peace of mind. How can a man who has no peace of mind enjoy happiness? Insatiable thirst for sense-objects is the enemy of peace and there cannot be even an iota of happiness for a man with no peace. His mind is always restless and runs after worldly objects. Only when this thirst dies down a man can enjoy a real and abiding peace when he will be able to meditate and rest in the Self.

True happiness is not in the thirst for objects but in the restraint of the senses from thirst for enjoyment. Thirst is misery indeed.

WHY IS THE UNSTEADY MAN INCAPABLE OF KNOWLEDGE?

indriyaanaam hi charataam yanmano'nuvidheeyate
tadasya harati prajnaam vaayur naavam ivaambhasi // 2.67 //

WHEN THE MIND RUNS AFTER THE WANDERING SENSES, IT CARRIES AWAY HIS DISCRIMINATION AS THE WIND CARRIES AWAY A BOAT ON THE WATERS.

The mind which constantly thinks about the sense objects and moves only in pursuit of such objects destroys altogether the discriminatory faculty in man. Just as a gale carries away a rudderless ship from its charted course and drives her away from reaching its destination, so too the unsteady mind carries away the aspirant from his spiritual path and turns him towards the worldly objects by taking away his discrimination.

CONDITION OF THE SEEKER WHO CONTROLLED HIS SENSES

tasmaad yasya mahaabaaho nigriheetaani sarvashah
indriyaaneendriyaarthebhyas tasya prajnaa pratishthitaa // 2.68 //

THEREFORE, O MIGHTY ARMED ARJUNA, HIS WISDOM IS STEADY WHOSE SENSES ARE COMPLETELY RESTRAINED FROM THEIR OBJECTS.

The man of steady wisdom can, at his will, withdraw the senses, from their objects and enter into communion with the Self.

DIFFERENCE BETWEEN THE WISE AND THE IGNORANT

yaanishaa sarvabhootaanaam tasyam jaagarti samyamee
yasyaam jaagrati bhootani saa nishaa pashyato muneh // 2.69 //

IN THAT WHICH IS NIGHT TO ALL BEINGS, THE SELF-CONTROLLED MAN IS AWAKE AND WHERE ALL BEINGS ARE AWAKE, THAT IS THE NIGHT FOR THE MAN WHO SEES (HAS VISION).

To the ignorant the Supreme reality is like the night. They see in it confusion and darkness. But the man of steady wisdom is fully awake with regard to reality.

Again, the multiplicity of the world of time and space is as clear as a day to the ignorant. But the man of wisdom sees in it the confusion of a night.

Ignorance creates the idea of multiplicity and duty while the wise never deviates from the knowledge of the Self. Error stands in the same relation to truth as sleeping to waking.

IF THE WORLD IS DARK TO A SEER, THEN HOW DOES HE LIVE IN THE WORLD?

aapooryamaanam achalapratishtham
samudram aapah pravishanti yadwat
tadwat kaamaa yam pravishanti sarve
sa shaantim aapnoti na kaamakaami // 2.70 //

HE ATTAINS PEACE INTO WHOM ALL DESIRES ENTER AS THE WATERS ENTER THE OCEAN, WHICH IS FULL TO THE BRIM AND GROUNDED IN STILLNESS, BUT NOT THE MAN WHO IS THE DESIRER OF DESIRES.

Just as the ocean is not at all affected by the waters flowing into it continuously from all sides an enlightened person, who rests in his essential nature or Self is not in the least disturbed by desires produced by the objects of enjoyment which he happens to come across during his sojourn on earth. Such an individual who maintains true peace in spite of being a target for the stimuli conveyed through his sense organs by innumerable sense objects is called a man of perfection, a true saint. A man attains such a state through constant awareness of the unchangeable Reality that constitutes his innermost Self. He who looks outside for enjoyments never attains peace. The principle behind this phenomenon is that the insentient cannot satisfy the sentient; the sentient can be satisfied by the sentient alone.

vihaaya kaamaan yah sarvaan pumaamshcharati nihsprihah
nirmamo nirahankaarah sa shaantim adhigacchati // 2.71 //

THAT MAN ATTAINS PEACE WHO, ABANDONING ALL DESIRES, MOVES ABOUT WITHOUT LONGING, DEVOID OF THE SENSE OF 'I'-NESS AND 'MY'-NESS.

This verse explains the mental condition of such a one who finds peace in himself. Such a sage renounces all desires and is without any longings or attachments. Affinity for the world exists only because of desires. If desires are given up, no affinity for the world remains. Such a person's intellect is without any sense of 'I'-ness or 'my'-ness i.e. without any ego which is the cause for the sense of attachment.

All the sufferings in the world are caused by our egocentric misconception and consequent eruption of endless wants. He is a genuine *Sanyasin* who leads a life of constant inspiration gained through an intelligent renunciation of his egocentric misconceptions.

The well-known Upanishadic saying is "The human mind is of two kinds, pure and impure. That which is intent on securing the desires is impure; that which is free from attachment to desires is pure".

This verse answers Arjuna's question 'how a man of steadfast mind walks or what is his mode of conduct?

ULTIMATE STATE OF A PERSON OF STEADY WISDOM

eshaa braahmee sthitih paartha nainaam praapya vimuhyati
sthitwaasyaamantakaale'pi brahmanirvaanamricchati // 2.72 //

Where ego ends and the individuality is completely wiped out, a state of Selfhood, the state of Brahman - Existence, Knowledge, Bliss Absolute - Sat Chit Ananda - dawns. Renouncing every thing and living in the Self is the Brahmi state or the state of God-realized soul. If the aspirant attains this state he never falls into delusion again; never again deluded by the world. It is the highest state of happiness. This experience needs to take place at an early age. But if it is attained even at the time of death he attains liberation. Hence what doubt can there be about liberation of a man who practices the discipline of renunciation from an early age and dwells on Brahman throughout life?

"Wisdom is the supreme means of liberation, but this wisdom is not exclusive of devotion to God and desireless work. Even while alive, the sage rests in Brahman and is released from the unrest of the world. The sage of steady wisdom lives a life of disinterested service. The descriptions of the ideal man, the *jnani,* the *sthitaprajna*, the *yogarudha*, the *gunatita* or the *bhakta* agree in all essentials. (Ref. 6.4-32; 10.9-10; 12.13-20; 13.7-11; 14.21-35; 16.1-3; 18.50-60)". - Dr. S.Radhakrishnan.

Working without attachment and desires, egoism and vanity, always equanimous with pairs of opposites is to control the ego and experience the Self. This technique of Karma Yoga is not different from the technique of meditation or knowledge or devotion. Such a sage of steady wisdom lives a life of disinterested action. But Arjuna remains confused and so The Lord explains Karma Yoga further in the next chapter.

om tat sat iti srimad bhagavadgeetaasu upanishatsu brahma vidyaayaam yogashaastre sri krishnaarjuna samvaade saankhya yogo naama dvitiyo'dhyaayah ||

THUS IN THE UPANISHADS OF THE GLORIOUS BHAGAVAD GITA, THE SCIENCE OF THE ETERNAL, THE SCRIPTURE OF YOGA, THE DIALOGUE BETWEEN SRI KRISHNA AND ARJUNA ENDS THE SECOND DISCOURSE ENTITLED THE YOGA OF KNOWLEDGE.

AN OUTLINE VIEW OF THIS CHAPTER

The second chapter contains 72 verses. It is entitled Sankhya Yoga, the Yoga of Knowledge, because the chapter expounds in great detail the knowledge of the Self. Arjuna seeks refuge in Lord Krishna, imploring him to remove the intense grief that burns him from within. But Arjuna is in no condition to receive any advice for the reasons that 1. He is mentally distraught. 2. He considers Krishna only as a friend and not as a wise man or Guru.

This mental state prevents him from taking any help from Krishna. Krishna finds the need to wait until Arjuna recovers from his deep depression. Also, Arjuna must first become convinced of Krishna's ability to help. Therefore, Krishna iniates his sermon in Verse 11 with the highest philosophy not so much to impart that particular knowledge as to overwhelm him with his staggering wisdom. In the process of realising the profundity of Krishna's wisdom Arjuna wakes up from his stupor and asks Krishna several practical questions.

I - ARJUNA'S DESPONDENT CONDITION - VERSES 1-10

Arjuna continues in his state of dejection. His personality is destroyed by his overwhelming emotions erupting at the sight of his near and dear ones on the battlefront. Assuming a false sense of renunciation, he argues that he would rather live on alms than slay noble elders like Bhishma and Drona and that even an undisputed sovereignty over all the worlds would not drive away his grief. Arguing thus, he expresses his unwillingness to fight and thus completely burnt out he becomes silent.

II - INDESTRUCTIBILITY OF THE EMBODIED - VERSES 11 – 30

Krishna starts the Sermon on the Battlkefield by stating that

- The wise grieve neither for the living nor for the dead.
- The Self within is eternal, indestructible.
- The bodies enveloping the Self are ephemeral. They have a beginning and an end.
- Death is certain for the born and birth for the dead.
- Beings constantly pass through the repeated stages of unmanifest, manifest and again unmanifest. So why grieve over the inevitable?
- The indwelling Self remains eternally the same.

III - YOUR DUTY TO ACT - VERSES 31 – 40

Krishna explains to Arjuna the importance of performing his duty. A kshatriya (warrior) is fortunate to find an opportunity to fight a righteous battle. Abandoning such an opportunity will only incur infamy and sin. In victory a Kshatriya enjoys sovereignty over the worls. If slain in battle he will gain heaven. Therefore, Krishna advises Arjuna to arise from his paralysed state and fight the battle without concern for the results. The knowledge imparted upto verse 38 in this chapter is Sankhya. Thereafter Krishna turns towards Karma Yoga, the practice of which will eradicate the deepest fear in Arjuna.

IV - DESIRE RIDDEN ACTIONS - VERSES 41 – 44

Those who fanatically adhere to mechanical rituals are the irresolute whose desires dissipate their minds. They eulogize the ritualistic portion of the Vedas and declare in flowery speech that there is nothing beyond these rituals. Despite regular performance of the rituals their attention in life remains focused on enjoying the pleasures and power in the world. Such people possess a vacillating mind unable to concentrate and meditate on the Suprem Self.

V - DESIRELESS ACTIONS LEAD TO SELF-REALISATION - VERSES 45 – 53

The Vedas deal with three gunas – sattwa, rajas and tamas. They explain the process of evolution from tamas to rajas and from rajas to sattwa. Krishna advises Arjuna to free himself from the endless pairs of opposites that plague this world and rise to the state of sattwa and to be liberated from the mania of acquiring and preserving and then slowly merge with the Self. An enlightened soul remains ever in supreme peace and bliss. In that state he will find even the Vedas as redundant to him as a pond would be in a flooded village.

Krishna induces Arjuna to act steadfastly towards the goal of Realisation without worldlty attachments and remain balanced in success or failure. and to keep the mind calm and composed while the body acts dynamically towards the higher ideal. The process of pursuing the supreme goal steadfastly with an equanimous mind is Yoga. Continuing on the path of yoga one sheds vasanas / desires and the mind turns introvert. An introverted mind alone can meditate and realise the supreme Self.

VI - DESCRIPTION OF AN ENLIGHTENED SOUL - VERSES 54 – 72

Arjuna asks Krishna to describe the nature of enlightened Soul. How would he express himself in the world? What happens to him internally? How does he contact the external world? The last eighteen verses of this chapter give a brilliant expostioin of a Self-realised soul. Revelling in the bliss of the Self the enlightened one stays free from all egocentric attachments and desires. In the state of absolute fulfilment all worldly enjoyments fall into insignificance. He is like a river which has entered the ocean. Having reached that supreme state he has merged with eternity.

<<<000>>>

Chapter 3

Karma Yogah:

Yoga of Action

PREAMBLE

This Chapter analyses from various points of view and establishes the fact that the performance of prescribed duties is obligatory for everyone. Lord Krishna comprehensively explains how it is the duty of the members of society to carry out their responsibilities in their respective stages of life according to the rules and regulations of the society in which they live. Further, He explains in detail why such duties must be performed, what benefit is gained by performing them, what harm is caused by not performing them, what actions lead to bondage and what actions lead to salvation. Hence this chapter is entitled "Karma Yogah: Yoga of Action".

In the previous Chapter Bhagavan advised Arjuna that his duty was to work without pre-occupying himself with its result and at the same time suggested that he should not be attached to inaction. He concluded His advice with the advocacy of the path of attaining the state of steady wisdom or Brahmi state by knowledge and renunciation.

Arjuna feels confused by the Lord's praise of righteous war (2.31-38) and the Buddhi Yoga i.e. equanimity of mind (2.49 & 50) as also about the man of steady wisdom in conclusion. These apparently conflicting views seem to have perplexed Arjuna as to which path he has to take for his self-development i.e. whether it is knowledge or action or either together or total renunciation of both. The Lord's advice to Arjuna is that selfless action performed in a spirit of dedication and surrender and with pure motive is the right path.

THE TEXT

WHY THEN WORK AT ALL?

arjuna uvaacha
jyaayasee chet karmanaste mataa buddhir janaardana
tat kim karmani ghore maam niyojayasi keshava // 3.1 //

ARJUNA SAID
IF YOU THINK THAT KNOWLEDGE IS SUPERIOR TO ACTION, O JANARDANA, WHY THEN DO YOU ASK ME TO ENGAGE IN THIS TERRIBLE ACTION, O KESAVA?

vyaamishreneva vaakyena buddhim mohayaseeva me
tadekam vada nishchitya yena shreyo'ham aapnuyaam // 3.2 //

WITH THESE APPARENTLY PERPLEXING WORDS YOU CONFUSE MY UNDERSTANDING, AS IT WERE; THEREFORE, TELL ME DEFINITELY THAT ONE THING BY WHICH I MAY ATTAIN THE HIGHEST GOAL.

Arjuna misunderstands the teaching that work for reward is less excellent than work without attachment and desire and believes that Sri Krishna is of the view that knowledge without action is better than work. If Sankhya method of gaining wisdom is superior, then action is an irrelevance. In this confusion he asks Sri Krishna as to which of the paths he has to follow for his self-development since he still believed that to fight against his people was a terrible action. Hence, Arjuna requests Sri Krishna to teach him for certain either of the two – knowledge or action - in accordance with the state and power of his understanding by which he could attain the highest good i.e. complete eradication of grief and infatuation and attainment of that imperishable. The confusion only seems. It is not the intention of the Lord to confuse Arjuna but yet Arjuna is confused.

LIFE IS WORK BUT THE NEED IS UNCONCERN FOR RESULTS

sri bhagavaan uvaacha
loke'smin dwividha nishthaa puraa proktaa mayaanagha
jnaanayogena saankhyaanaam karmayogena yoginaam // 3.3 //

SRI BHAGAVAN SAID

IN THIS WORLD THERE IS A TWO-FOLD PATH, AS I SAID BEFORE, O BLAMELESS ONE (ARJUNA), THE PATH OF KNOWLEDGE FOR MEN OF CONTEMPLATION AND THE PATH OF WORK FOR MEN OF ACTION.

The words 'As I said before' indicate the beginning of the created world. Even at the very beginning of the cycle of time, two classes of people, those with contemplative and those with active temperaments, were in existence.

Those of contemplative mind are born with a clear knowledge of the Self and the non-Self. They easily renounce the world even at the early age of their lives and concentrate their thoughts on Brahman always. For them the path of knowledge is prescribed so that their ideas can mature and blend with Brahman.

The understanding of those who believe in external action as a means of self-unfoldment is still colored by the stain of duality. The performance of unselfish action purifies their souls and enables them to practice knowledge and contemplation.

The path of knowledge (Gnana Yoga) was described by The Lord in verses 11-38 and the path of action (Karma Yoga) in verses 40-53 of the Second Chapter which created confusion in the mind of Arjuna although never intended by The Lord.

To consider the path of action and the path of knowledge as competitive is to understand neither of them, they being complementary. Selfless activity enables the mind to exhaust many of its existing mental impressions and thus purified it prepares the man for the reception of knowledge of the Absolute through meditation or contemplation. There cannot be any knowledge of Brahman unless the mind is pure.

The Lord distinguishes two main types of seekers viz., the active and the contemplative. Because temperamentally these two categories are so wide apart that a common technique for spiritual development cannot yield results. So Sri Krishna explains the two-fold path of Self-development Viz. the Path of knowledge for the introverts whose natural tendency is to explore the inner life of the Spirit and the Path of action for the extroverts who have a natural bias for work in the outer world.

Those who are endowed with discrimination, dispassion, six-fold virtues, and longing for liberation and who have a sharp, subtle intellect and bold understanding are fit for Gnana Yoga or the Path of Knowledge. The six-fold virtues are control of the mind, control of the senses, fortitude, turning away from the objects of the world; faith and tranquility. Those who have tendency for work are fit for Karma Yoga or the Path of Action.

But this distinction cannot be absolute because all men are in different degrees both introverts and extroverts. For the Gita, the path of action is a means of liberation as efficient as that of knowledge and these are intended for two types of people. The practice of a particular spiritual discipline is determined by the competence of the aspirant. Both the active and the contemplative have one goal viz. the realization of Brahman. The path of action, however, does not directly lead to the realization.

WHAT IS ACTIONLESSNESS?

na karmanaam anaarambhaan naishkarmyam purusho'shnute
na cha sannyaasanaad eva siddhim samadhigacchati // 3.4 //

NOT BY ABSTENTION FROM WORK DOES A MAN REACH ACTIONLESSNESS, NOR BY MERE RENUNCIATION DOES HE ATTAIN TO PERFECTION.

Action as it is generally understood is the outcome of want and desire. Actionlessness does not mean mere idling or abandoning of all actions. Although one can while away his time doing nothing, his mind will be full of thoughts scheming, speculating and planning over several matters. Desires generate thoughts at the mental level which when expressed in the outer world become actions. Thus thought is the real action. If one is free from thoughts, wishes, likes and dislikes and has knowledge of the Self he can be said to have reached the state of actionlessness.

The one who has reached such a state of actionlessness has neither the necessity nor the desire for action as a means to the end. He has a perfect satisfaction in the Self. Thus actionlessness and perfection are synonymous terms meaning, becoming one with the Infinite and free from all ideas of want and desire.

Mere renunciation or abandonment of action or running away from life does not lead to perfection. Through selfless dedicated action, purification of mind is achieved and the purified mind helps in attaining the Knowledge of the Self which is the ultimate Bliss. The natural law is that every action has its reaction and hence the result of the action is a source of bondage preventing the man from his union with the Supreme. What is needed is not renunciation of works but renunciation of selfish desires. This is *naishkarmya*, a state where one is unaffected by work.

WHY RENUNCIATION OF ACTION UNACCOMPANIED BY KNOWLEDGE DOES NOT LEAD TO PERFECTION?

na hi kashchit kshanamapi jaatu tishthatyakarmakrit
kaaryate hyavashah karma sarvah prakritjair gunaih // 3.5 //

VERILY NONE CAN EVER REMAIN EVEN FOR A MOMENT WITHOUT PERFORMING ACTION; FOR EVERYONE IS MADE TO ACT BY THE GUNAS OR QUALITIES BORN OF PRAKRITI (NATURE), IN SPITE OF HIMSELF.

Man is always under the influence of triple tendencies viz., unactivity- based on his Sattwic quality, activity- based on Rajasic quality and inactivity- based on Tamasic quality. Even for a single moment nobody can ever remain without any activity; even if one remains inactive physically his mind and intellect will always be active. Sattwic actions help a man to attain liberation. Rajasic and Tamasic actions bind a man to worldliness.

So long as we lead embodied lives we remain under the influence of these three Gunas or mental tendencies and we cannot escape from action. Without work life cannot be sustained. But these Gunas cannot affect a man who has the knowledge of the Self, for he has gone beyond them. He has become a *Gunatita* - one who has transcended the qualities of nature and for him the work ceases. The man who has no knowledge of the Self who is called un-illumined, will be swayed by ignorance and will be driven to action by the Gunas.

While life remains, action is inevitable. Thinking is an act. Living is an act. These acts cause many effects. To be free from desire, from the illusion of personal interest, is the true renunciation and not the physical abstention from activity.

When it is said that work ceases for a man who is liberated, all that it means is that he has no further personal necessity for work which however does not mean that he goes into masterly inactivity. He works, but without egoism or any binding necessity. Even in performing work he is not involved. When his egoism is removed, his actions are governed by the Supreme Self seated in his heart. Free from desire and attachment, one with all beings, he is released from the bondage of actions. Such actions do not bear fruit in the same way as a roasted or boiled seed loses its potency to sprout.

karmendriyaani samyamya ya aaste manasaa smaran
indriyaarthaan vimoodhaatma mithyaachaarah sa uchyate
// 3.6 //

HE WHO RESTRAINS HIS ORGANS OF ACTION, BUT CONTINUES TO DWELL IN HIS MIND ON THE OBJECTS OF THE SENSES, DELUDES HIMSELF AND IS CALLED A HYPOCRITE.

The five organs of action - the Karma Indriyas - are the organs of speech, hands, feet, genitals and anus. They are born of the Rajasic portion of the subtle elements viz. organ of speech is born of ether element, hands of air, feet of fire, genitals of water and anus of earth. Despite restraining these organs if one sits revolving in his mind the thoughts regarding the objects of these sense organs in order to give an impression that he is meditating on God, he is called a self-deluded hypocrite and a man of sinful conduct.

True renunciation is not just the control of the organs of action or abstention from physical movement. It is the control of the mind and the organs of perception. It is the absence of longing for the activity. An active mind and an actionless body do not indicate the life of *sanyasa*. We may control outwardly our activities but if we do not restrain the desires which impel them, we have failed to grasp the true meaning of restraint.

yastwindriyaani manasaa niyamyaarabhate'rjuna
karmendriyaih Karma Yogam asaktah sa vishishyate // 3.7 //

BUT HE WHO RESTRAINS HIS SENSES WITH HIS MIND AND DIRECTS HIS ORGANS OF ACTION TO WORK, WITH NO FEELING OF ATTACHMENT - HE, O ARJUNA, IS INDEED SUPERIOR.

The science of right action and the art of right living are explained in this verse. Mind gets its inputs through five organs of perception which are also called sense-organs or organs of knowledge (Gnana Indriyas) from the outer world of sense objects. These five sense organs are the eye (sense of sight), ear (sense of hearing), nose (sense of smell), skin (sense of touch), and tongue (sense of taste). Mind perceives the sense objects by interacting with the sense organs and if that interaction is absent, perception of objects by the mind is not possible even though the objects might be within the range of the sense organs. This verse asks the seeker to control the sense organs by the mind. This implies substitution of sense objects by nobler and diviner alternatives for the mind to dwell upon.

When the sense organs are thus controlled, a huge quantity of energy gets stored up which unless properly directed will disturb the inner equilibrium of an individual. This verse says that the pent up energies must be spent by directing the seeker's organs of action (explained in the previous verse) to the appropriate fields of activities. Even when so acting it is advised not to have attachment arising out of doership and enjoyership so that instead of gathering new mental impressions one may use such activities for exhausting the existing vasanas. Thus the very field of activity becomes a ground for liberation. In the previous verse mere outer renunciation is condemned and in this verse true spirit of inward detachment is commended.

IMPORTANCE OF PERFORMING ALLOTTED DUTY

niyatam kuru karma twam karma jyaayo hyakarmanah
shareerayaatraa pi cha te na prasiddhyed akarmanah // 3.8 //

DO YOUR ALLOTTED WORK; FOR ACTION IS SUPERIOR TO INACTION. EVEN THE BARE MAINTENANCE OF THE BODY WOULD NOT BE POSSIBLE IF YOU REMAIN INACTIVE.

Allotted action is one's own duty as laid down in the scriptures to different persons in accordance with their inherited tendencies, the stage in life and the order in society. Non-performance of such bounden duties would mean inaction. The very fact of living involves several natural and unavoidable actions which have to be performed by all. Even bodily healthy existence is just not possible if one has to live in complete inertia and inaction.

UNSELFISH ACTION DOES NOT CREATE BONDAGE

yajnaarthaat karmano'nyatra loko'yam karmabandhanah
tadartham karma kaunteya muktasangah samaachara // 3.9 //

THE WORLD IS IN BONDAGE TO WORK UNLESS THEY ARE PERFORMED FOR THE SAKE OF YAJNA (SACRIFICE). THEREFORE, O SON OF KUNTI, GIVE UP ATTACHMENT AND DO YOUR WORK AS A SACRIFICE.

All work is to be done in a spirit of sacrifice, for the sake of the Divine. Yajna here means any unselfish action done with a pure motive. It is a self-sacrificing work undertaken in a spirit of self-dedication for the good of all. Such actions cannot be self-serving but self-liberating and do not bind the performer. An action which is not governed by the spirit of unselfishness binds one to worldliness, however glorious it may be.

WHAT IS SACRIFICE?

sahayajnaah prajaah srishtwaa purovaacha prajaapatih
anena prasavishyadhwam esha vo'stvishtakaamadhuk // 3.10 //

THE CREATOR (PRAJAPATI), HAVING IN THE BEGINNING CREATED MANKIND TOGETHER WITH YAJNA, SAID 'BY THIS YOU MULTIPLY'; THIS SHALL BE THE MILCH COW OF YOUR DESIRES'.

When the Universe was created by the Creator - Prajapati - he simultaneously created Yajna also, the spirit of self-dedicated activities which is seen everywhere, e.g. shining of the sun and the moon, flowing of rivers, tolerance of the Earth etc., All these activities show the spirit of sacrifice without any selfish motives. The second part of the verse means that no achievement is impossible for man if he knows how to act in the spirit of self-effacement and self-sacrifice with the required amount of non-attachment.

HOW CAN WELFARE BE ACHIEVED BY SACRIFICE?

devaan bhaavayataanena te devaa bhaavayantu vah
parasparam bhaavayantah shreyah param avaapsyatha // 3.11 //

CHERISH THE DEVAS WITH THIS AND MAY THOSE DEVAS CHERISH YOU, THUS CHERISHING ONE ANOTHER YOU SHALL GAIN THE HIGHEST GOOD.

ishtaan bhogaan hi vo devaa daasyante yajnabhaavitaah
tair dattaan apradaayaibhyo yo bhungkte stena eva sah // 3.12 //

DEVAS, CHERISHED BY THE SACRIFICE, WILL GIVE YOU THE DESIRED OBJECTS. INDEED, HE WHO ENJOYS

OBJECTS GIVEN BY THE DEVAS WITHOUT OFFERING IN RETURN TO THEM IS VERILY A THIEF.

By performing actions as Yajna, as dedication to the Self, recognize and express your sense of appreciation and gratitude to all the Devas, the presiding functionaries of natural laws such as wind, fire etc.

By worshipping the various Devas in a spirit of sacrifice, by being grateful to all the presiding deities of the unchanging laws of nature, you recognize the Self behind all the Devas, behind all the laws of nature and natural phenomenon in this creation. Thus, through the Yajnam - by propitiating the Devas, you propitiate the Self itself.

In any sacrifice or ceremonial ritual we propitiate the Devas by offering oblations to them. It is a simple way of expressing our deep sense of appreciation and gratitude to them for the roles that they play in this creation. Whether one is grateful or not, the sun rises, the rain rains and the wind blow. By recognizing their functions in this creation, and by expressing one's deep appreciation and gratitude to them, man recognizes the significance of his part in this universe. He, then, progressively identifies himself with the creation and the creator - The Self, Brahman.

When you express your appreciation and gratitude to the Devas, what do they do to you? Having been properly propitiated, the Devas will protect you; nourish you by their functions. Thus, all the laws of nature, by their own natural functions, uplift you by being an asset to you in your endeavors for gaining your overriding goal of life, namely liberation.

By doing work as a sacrifice totally dedicated to the Self, everything in this creation becomes an asset to you for your own upliftment in life, for your own true progress in life, for a life of non-binding, everlasting prosperity, success and happiness, leading ultimately to *Shreyas*, total fulfillment in life. Therefore, mutually interacting with each other, man reaps the supreme good. He gains *moksha*.

What about the person who never says a prayer, who has no sense of gratitude, but only wants to enjoy whatever he can get out of this world? The one who enjoys all the blessings of daily life without even a sincere expression of gratitude to the Self (Devas) who made all such enjoyments possible, is indeed a thief, says the Gita.

Thus in the Vedic view, every human being is meant for action as a participant in this creation. Every one's destination is the same, namely *shreyas, moksha*. One reaches this destination by doing one's Karma with the attitude of Karma Yoga - as an act of sacrifice dedicated to the Self.

In this relative world, man and Devas are interdependent. They are nourished by one another. Men offer oblations to the gods; gods in return ensure men's welfare by creating ecological balance. Thus, a chain of mutual obligation binds together all created beings.

THOSE WHO ACT IN A SPIRIT OF SACRIFICE ARE SUPERIOR PERSONS

yajnashishtaashinah santo muchyante sarva kilbishaih
bhunjate te twagham paapaa ye pachantyaatma kaaranaat // 3.13 //

THE RIGHTEOUS WHO EAT THE REMNANTS OF THE SACRIFICE ARE FREED FROM ALL SINS; BUT THOSE SINFUL ONES WHO COOK FOOD ONLY FOR THEIR OWN SAKE, VERILY EAT SIN.

Sins of the past are the cause for the present pains and the present sins are the cause for future sorrows. All the causes for the sorrows in social life can be removed if the members of the community find happiness in enjoying the results of their efforts performed in true Yajna spirit. As a contrast to this, it is pointed out that those who cook for themselves only meaning those who perform actions only with selfish motives are eating nothing but sin. By doing the work in yajna spirit, the selfish life is transformed into an unselfish one and the individual becomes aware of the interdependence of all beings.

ACTION SETS THE WHEELS OF THE COSMOS GOING

annaad bhavanti bhootani parjanyaad anna sambhavah
yajnaad bhavati parjanyo yajnah karma samudbhavah // 3.14 //

FROM FOOD, ALL CREATURES ARE BORN; FROM RAIN, FOOD IS PRODUCED; FROM SACRIFICE COMES RAIN; SACRIFICE IS BORN OF ACTION.

karma brahmodbhavam viddhi brahmaakshara samudbhavam
tasmaat sarvagatam brahma nityam yajne pratishthitam // 3.15 //

KNOW THAT ACTION ARISES FROM THE VEDAS, AND THE VEDAS FROM THE IMPERISHABLE. THEREFORE, THE ALL-PERVADING VEDAS EVER REST IN SACRIFICE.

The cosmic wheel of co-operative and complementary action is painted here. The living creatures are born out of food and nourished by food. The mineral wealth of the world becomes assimilable food because of the action of the rain upon it. Rain is the cause for the conversion of mineral raw material into nutritive food in life. Similarly, in all fields of activity profit can be gathered only when the field comes under conditions favorable for it to produce those profits. Self-dedicated activity - Yajna - when performed in any field of endeavor will create conditions-rains- for the field to yield profit - Annam-enjoyable by the society.

This wheel of action is connected with and includes the Supreme. The principle of right action has come out of the Creator himself who is none other than the Imperishable Supreme Reality expressed through the Vedas. Therefore, the all-pervading Supreme is ever centered in all efforts undertaken with an honest spirit of self-dedication for the common good. He who lives in unison with this wheel of action is contributing to the harmony of life.

evam pravartitam chakram naanuvartayateeha yah
aghaayur indriyaaraamo mogham paartha sa jeevati // 3.16 //

HE WHO DOES NOT FOLLOW THE WHEEL THUS SET-IN MOTION, BUT TAKES DELIGHT IN THE SENSES, HE LIVES IN VAIN, O ARJUNA.

Every member of the Universe follows the principle of Yajna and contributes to the smooth running of the Universal Wheel of Action. But among all the living creatures only man has been endowed with the option of freedom of action - to contribute to the harmonious working of the cosmic mechanism or strike a discordant note.

While a majority of the people live abiding in the Law of Harmony, some do not believe in this Eternal Law and revolt against it. During such dark periods nobody works with the spirit of Yajna without which no favorable circumstances can be created (rain) for the productive potential to manifest. Such seekers of selfish pleasures bring about discordance in the Wheel of Action. They are considered to be living in sin and that too in vain by the Gita.

In these verses (10 to 16), the Vedic conception of sacrifice as an inter-link between God and man is set in the larger context of the inter-dependence of beings in the cosmos. He who works for himself alone lives in vain.

TO THE ONE WHO REMAINS SATISFIED IN THE SELF, THERE IS NOTHING TO WORK FOR

yastwaatmaratir eva syaad aatmatriptashcha maanavah
aatmanyeva cha santushtas tasya kaaryam na vidyate // 3.17 //

BUT FOR THAT MAN WHO REJOICES ONLY IN THE SELF, WHO IS SATISFIED IN THE SELF, WHO IS CONTENT IN THE SELF ALONE, VERILY THERE IS NOTHING TO DO.

The motivation for any human action in the outer world is to achieve better satisfaction and contentment. The man of perfection does not depend on external objects for his happiness. He finds his joy, bliss and contentment in his own Divine experience. When he has already achieved satisfaction and contentment, no more desires arise in him. Where there are no desires there is no action. Such a realized man is a person endowed with Self-Knowledge. He has no worldly duties to perform. He is the knower of Brahman.

naiva tasya kritenaartho naakriteneha kashchana
na chaasya sarvabhooteshu kashchidartha vyapaashrayah // 3.18 //

HE HAS NOTHING TO GAIN BY WHAT HE DOES IN THIS WORLD, NOR ANYTHING TO LOSE BY WHAT HE LEAVES UNDONE; NOR IS THERE ANYONE, AMONG ALL BEINGS, ON WHOM HE NEED TO DEPEND FOR ANY THING.

An ordinary man is required to act for earning profit or avoiding loss. But for a man who discovered eternal satisfaction in his own Self and reached perfect contentment therein no purpose is served by engaging himself in any action because there is neither anticipation of gain nor fear of loss for him. Such a person does not depend upon for his joy on any being or on any object from the Creator Brahma to a blade of grass.

PERFORM ACTION WITHOUT ATTACHMENT

tasmaad asaktah satatam kaaryam karma samaachara
asakto hyaacharan karma param aapnoti poorushah // 3.19 //

THEREFORE, ALWAYS DO WITHOUT ATTACHMENT THE WORK YOU HAVE TO DO; FOR BY PERFORMING ACTION WITHOUT ATTACHMENT A MAN REACHES THE SUPREME.

After explaining the wheel of action Sri Krishna concludes His dissertation by asking Arjuna to perform actions which are obligatory on his part in his present status in life. Even here

The Lord warns him to keep his mind away from the pitfalls of attachments.

Though the liberated man has nothing to gain by action or non-action and is perfectly happy in the enjoyment of the Self, there is such a thing called desireless action which he undertakes for the welfare of the world. The work done without attachment is superior to the work done in a spirit of sacrifice which is itself higher than the work done with selfish aims. While this verse says that the man reaches the Supreme performing actions without attachment, Sankara holds that karma yoga helps us to attain purity of mind which leads to salvation. It takes us to perfection indirectly through the attainment of purity of mind.

EXAMPLES SET BY THE WISE

karmanaiva hi samsiddhim aasthitaa janakaadayah
lokasangraham evaapi sampashyan kartum arhasi // 3.20 //

JANAKA AND OTHERS ATTAINED PERFECTION VERILY BY ACTION ONLY; EVEN WITH A VIEW TO THE PROTECTION OF THE MASSES YOU SHOULD PERFORM ACTION.

Ancient kings like Janaka and others attained perfection or liberation - *samsiddhi* - by the path of action, performing right actions in a spirit of detachment and self-dedication. They set an example to the world by their lives of service and achievement. They attained purity of mind through the performance of duty and then realized Brahman.

Sri Krishna means Arjuna too, belonging to a princely class, who has the responsibility to protect his people, should act diligently and perform his duties as a Kshatriya without running away from the battle as he intended earlier.

We may sense the modern leadership principle here. Born as a king Arjuna has got a greater commitment towards his subjects. He is a leader of men and their welfare depends on him and his activities. Therefore, it is his bounden obligation to keep his post and discharge his duties diligently, risking all dangers and fighting enemies for achieving *Lokasangraha.*

Lokasangraha stands for the unity of the world, the inter-connectedness of society, protection and maintenance by each other. If the world is not to sink into physical misery and moral degradation, if the common life is to be decent and dignified, religious ethics must control social action. The aim of religion is to spiritualize everyday life for establishing universal brotherhood on earth and maintenance of the world order.

HOW WORLD ORDER CAN BE MAINTAINED BY PERFORMING ONE'S OWN DUTIES?

yad yad aacharati shreshthas tattadevetaro janah
sa yat pramaanam kurute lokas tad anuvartate // 3. 21 //

WHATEVER A GREAT MAN DOES, THAT, OTHERS FOLLOW; WHATEVER HE SETS UP AS THE STANDARD, THAT, THE WORLD FOLLOWS.

Common people are more influenced by the living examples of great men than by the abstract teaching of the scriptures. Man is a social animal. He is also an imitating creature with a herd-instinct.. He takes his ideas of right and wrong from those whom he considers his superiors. The examples set by the leaders are implemented by the followers. As is the quality of leaders, so will be the quality of the followers. Whatever the persons in authority do, the subordinates emulate.

Sri Krishna implies that if Arjuna were to abandon his duty to act, then the entire community will follow the low standard of retreating from action set up by him which will lead to general social decadence. The Lord cites Himself as an example for Arjuna to act.

na me paarthaasti kartavyam trishu lokeshu kinchana
naanavaaptam avaaptavyam varta eva cha karmani // 3.22 //

THERE IS NOTHING IN THE THREE WORLDS, O PARTHA THAT HAS TO BE DONE BY ME, OR IS THERE ANYTHING UNATTAINED THAT SHOULD BE ATTAINED BY ME, YET, I CONTINUE TO ENGAGE MYSELF IN WORK.

Being a Perfect man and a Yogi, Sri Krishna had nothing to gain in this world. His entire life is an example of a perfect life of complete detachment. Even though He had nothing that He did not gain nor had anything further to gain, He was engaging Himself constantly in activity.

Here Krishna speaks of Himself as the Godhead. Though He transcends all claims of duty, yet He acts according to the scriptural injunctions to set an example to others.

yadi hyaham na varteyam jaatu karmanyatandritah
mama vartmaanuvartante manushyaah paartha sarvashah // 3.23 //

FOR, SHOULD I NOT EVER ENGAGE IN ACTION, WITHOUT RELAXATION, MEN WOULD IN EVERY WAY FOLLOW MY PATH, O SON OF PRITHA.

If The Lord remains inactive the people also will imitate Him and sink themselves in inertia and unproductive existence and great harm will come in the world. The entire Universe survives and sustains itself by activity alone. In these verses the word 'I' implies Atman or the Self-realized man of perfection. The God principle serves the pluralistic phenomenal world as a substratum for its existence.

utseedeyur ime lokaa na kuryaam karma ched aham
sankarasya cha kartaa syaamupahanyaam imaah prajaah // 3.24 //

IF I SHOULD CEASE TO WORK, THESE WORLDS WOULD PERISH. I SHOULD THEN BE THE CAUSE OF CONFUSION AND DESTRUCTION OF THESE PEOPLE.

If The Lord does not work it will not be conducive to the progress of the Universe. The Universe is not a chaos but a cosmos. Nowhere chaotic conditions are observed in the working of the cosmic forces. Movement of planets, occurring of seasons, laws of the oceans, various social orders and disiplines etc., always obey the law of nature or God. Just imagine the turmoil that may follow if these elements don't follow their natual laws!

The Lord represents not only the law governing the outer world of things but also the law that governs the inner world of thoughts and emotions. Human society is divided into four castes on the basis of individual mental temperaments.

In case the law governing the inner temperaments does not function there will be confusion in behavior and instability in the character of people bringing about their own destruction.

We had seen in the previous verses that by citing His own example The Lord described the consequences of not doing any action and proved that for the sake of the world order it is necessary for all of us to perform our allotted duties. Bhagavan continues his sermon and advises that it is incumbent upon even the man of knowledge to perform action for the sake of world amity.

saktaah karmanyavidwaamso yathaa kurvanti bhaarata
kuryad vidwaam stathaa saktash chikeershur lokasangraham // 3.25 //

AS THE IGNORANT MEN ACT FROM ATTACHMENT TO WORK, O BHARATA (ARJUNA), SO SHOULD THE WISE ACT WITHOUT ATTACHMENT, WISHING THE WELFARE OF THE WORLD.

It is well known that every member of the society by and large always keeps himself busy through out his life time performing actions in his chosen field. A man of Self-realization also works in the world with the same enthusiasm and sincerity as an average man of the society with the difference that the actions of the ignorant are motivated by attachments and anxieties for the fruits of actions while the man of perfection will work without attachment and for the purpose of the welfare of the world at large.

Attachment becomes an obstruction only when it is ego-centric. But to the extent the attachment envelopes the welfare of a larger section of the community it gathers ethical value. Hence the advice to Arjuna is that he must fight as a warrior who is called upon to protect the higher values of living unattached to his ego-centric conception of himself and his people.

The idea is that an ignorant person acts zealously for his personal happiness; but a wise man should act, with the same zeal, for the welfare of others.

na buddhibedam janayed ajnaanaam karmasanginaam
joshayet sarva karmaani vidwaan yuktah samaacharan // 3.26 //

LET NO ENLIGHTENED MAN UNSETTLE THE UNDERSTANDING OF THE IGNORANT PEOPLE WHO ARE ATTACHED TO ACTION; HE SHOULD ENGAGE THEM IN ACTION, HIMSELF PERFORMING IT WITH DEVOTION.

This verse is a sort of caution to those who are over-zealous in the art of giving guidance to others. A society functioning in a particular way should not be suddenly asked to stop and change its direction by a leader. On the contrary the leader should fall in line with the generation and slowly and steadily guide and help them to act in the right direction through his own example. When a man of equipoise works in the society at large, the chances are that he will start advising on abstract ideologies and ethics which may make the ordinary people to conclude that renunciation of all activities is the direct path to Self-development and thus give up prematurely all work. The men of wisdom are warned not to go against the spirit of the times.

No wise man should unsettle his generation's firm faith in their actions. He should perform even the ordinary actions in a diviner and better way and set an example to the world in performing actions without any selfish motive or attachment so that the lesser folk may follow his example.

DIFFERENCE BETWEEN THE MAN OF KNOWLEDGE AND THE MAN ATTACHED TO ACTION

prakriteh kriyamaanaani gunaih karmaani sarvashah
ahamkaara vimoodhaatmaa kartaa'hamiti manyate // 3.27 //

ALL ACTIONS ARE BEING PERFORMED BY THE GUNAS OF PRAKRITI. BUT HE, WHOSE MIND IS DELUDED BY EGOISM, THINKS 'I AM THE DOER'.

Earlier it was explained how ignorance leads to desires, desires to thoughts and how thoughts in conjunction with mental tendencies i.e.Gunas viz. Sattva, Rajas and Tamas - manifest themselves in the outer world as actions of different qualities. Nobler the thought, nobler the action and meaner the thought, meaner the action and so on.

Thus the Gunas modify themselves into the outside world, the body and the senses which are called the modes of Prakriti. They are classified into twenty three categories viz. intellect, ego, mind, the five subtle elements of ether etc., the ten organs of perception and action, and the five objects of senses viz. sound, touch, sight, taste and smell. These are the performers of all action. The word 'action' includes all the functions of the organs of perception and action *(jnana indriyas and karma indriyas).* The self looks on without participating in any way in the action done by the body and the senses. Whatever actions take place in this world are nothing but the operations of the aforesaid modes of Prakriti and the absolute and formless Atma or the Self has really nothing to do with them.

An ignorant man, however, identifies the Self with the aggregate of the body and the senses and calls it as 'I 'and thinks that the Self is the doer.

Even though the Self or the soul has no relation with actions, the unwise man identifying himself with the body and the senses associates himself with the different actions of the body and thus assumes himself to be the doer of those actions. In other words he thinks it is he who resolves, he who reflects, he who hears, he who sees, he who eats, he who drinks, sleeps, walks and so on and thus traces every action to himself. Thus he ascribes to the Self all the characteristics that really belong to the Gunas. That is why action becomes the cause of bondage to him. It is the reason for him to go through the process of repeated births and deaths to reap the fruits of those actions

BUT THE ENLIGHTENED MAN FEELS DIFFERENTLY

tattwavittu mahaabaaho gunakarma vibhaagayoh
gunaa guneshu vartanta iti matwaa na sajjate // 3.28 //

BUT HE WHO HAS TRUE INSIGHT INTO THE RESPECTIVE SPHERES OF GUNAS AND THEIR ACTIONS, HOLDING THAT IT IS THE GUNAS (IN THE FORM OF SENSES, MIND ETC.) THAT MOVE AMONG THE GUNAS (OBJECTS OF PERCEPTION) DOES NOT GET ATTACHED TO THEM, O MIGHTY ARJUNA.

As a contrast to the attitude of the ignorant man explained in the previous verse, Sri Krishna here explains the attitude of the wise man who knows that the Self is entirely distinct from the Gunas, their classification and functions.

The enlightened man who has obtained insight into the categories of the gunas and actions, attributes every action of the mind, intellect, senses and the body to the fact that it is the product of these gunas in the shape of all instruments of perception such as the mind, intellect and senses that are moving within the sphere of their respective objects, which are also products of the gunas and that he has no relation with either. Therefore, he does not get attached to either any action or to their fruits in the shape of agreeable or disagreeable experiences.

The difference between the active enlightened man and the active ignorant man is that the former is beyond the influence of the gunas and considers himself as a non-doer while the latter is controlled by the gunas and feels that everything is being done by him.

prakriter gunasammoodhaah sajjante gunakarmasu
taan akritsnavido mandaan kritsnavin na vichaalayet // 3.29 //

THE MAN OF PERFECT KNOWLEDGE SHOULD NOT UNSETTLE (THE UNDERSTANDING OF) THE FOOLISH WHO IS OF IMPERFECT KNOWLEDGE, WHO DELUDED BY THE GUNAS OF NATURE, ATTACH THEMSELVES TO THE FUNCTIONS OF THE GUNAS.

Ignorant people perform actions with the expectation of results. The wise, who have knowledge of the Self, should not disturb the conviction of such ignorant persons (people of insufficient knowledge, or men of meager intelligence) because if their minds are unsettled they will give up actions themselves and plunge themselves into inertia.

Therefore, in the beginning they should be encouraged to perform actions irrespective of their attachment to its fruits and gradually they should be taught the goal of selfless activities for the attainment of Self-realization.

HOW SUCH PERSONS OF IMPERFECT UNDERSTANDING SHOULD PERFORM ACTIONS?

mayi sarvaani karmaani sannyasyaadhyaatma chetasaa
niraasheer nirmamo bhootwaa yudhyaswa vigatajwarah // 3.30 //

SURRENDERING ALL ACTIONS TO ME, WITH THE MIND INTENT ON THE SELF, FREEING YOURSELF FROM THE LONGING AND SELFISHNESS, FIGHT UNPERTURBED BY GRIEF.

THIS VERSE IS THE HEART OF THIS CHAPTER CONVEYING ITS CENTRAL THEME. THE LORD REVEALS TO ARJUNA THE DEFINITE DISCIPLINE THAT WOULD LEAD HIM TO HIS HIGHEST GOAL.

Here the word 'me' means not Sri Krishna, the person but the Supreme Self, the Divine Being, the Supreme Lord, the Eternal and the Omniscient, the Self of all. The Lord asks Arjuna to fight on surrendering all activities unto Him, with the mind always concentrated on the Self. Surrendering all actions does not mean inactivity but acting without attachment and the sense of possession with regard to them. Actions performed with egocentric and selfish motives become bondage. Actions performed without attachment and desires are not actions at all in as much as they are not capable of producing any painful reactions.

It also means giving up of wrong motives behind actions. Purification of motives is possible only when the mind is made to concentrate on the Self and the Divine glory. Actions performed with such mind cannot be ordinary actions but they will be activities performed for the sake of The Lord and are the expressions of the Supreme Will through an individual.

The Lord further advises action without longing, ego and mental perturbance. Longing is an expectation of a happening at a future point of time. Ego is one's own self-estimation based on his past. To act without ego and longing thus means acting without the memories of the past or the anxieties about the future but to live in the present. Even in the present there is a chance for the man of action to waste his time and energy in unnecessarily worrying about his activities through his inborn nature. This anxiety and worry is what is called here as mental fever or perturbance.

The idea is that we must engage in work by self-surrender to the Lord who presides over cosmic existence and activity. "Thy will be done" should be our attitude in all work. We must do the work with the sense that we are the servants of The Lord. The word 'fight' indicates individual's confrontation with circumstances and situations in daily life.

RESULT OF SUCH ACTION BASED ON SURRENDERING IT TO THE SUPREME

ye me matam idam nityam anutishthanti maanavaah
shraddhaavanto'nasooyanto muchyante te'pi karmabhih // 3.31 //

THOSE MEN WHO CONSTANTLY PRACTICE THIS TEACHING OF MINE WITH FAITH AND WITHOUT

FINDING FAULT ARE ALSO FREED FROM THE BONDAGE OF ALL ACTIONS.

Shraddha -faith- is a mental attitude. It is faith in one's own Self, in the Scriptures and in the teachings of the spiritual preceptor. It is a combination of the higher emotions of reverence and humility. It is the sincerity of purpose.

Sri Krishna advocates Karma Yoga as a path that takes one ultimately to the Supreme because through desireless activity alone when performed with full faith and without criticism and questioning we will be able to bring about Vasana-exhaustion and thus make the mind purer for its meditative purposes.

The words 'they too are freed from the bondage of all actions' are intended to show that when by pursuing this discipline it is possible even for an ordinary person to get over the binding effects of action by surrendering the results of action to the Supreme, it should be much easier for Arjuna to attain that state.

WHAT IS THE HARM IF THIS ADVICE OF THE LORD IS NOT FOLLOWED?

ye twetad abhyasooyanto naanutishthanti me matam
sarvajnaanavimoodham staan viddhi nashtaan achetasah
// 3.32 //

BUT THOSE WHO FIND FAULT WITH MY TEACHING AND DO NOT PRACTICE IT, DELUDED IN ALL KNOWLEDGE AND DEVOID OF DISCRIMINATION, KNOW THEM TO BE DOOMED TO DESTRUCTION.

Sri Krishna warns here that those who are obstinate in finding fault with His teachings without practicing them are doomed for destruction. Such people will be more and more deluded and will lose their discrimination.

Karma Yoga is a way of life and one has to live it if one wants to receive His grace. The path of work is a process of elimination of desires in us. When egoism and egocentric desires are eliminated the work done through such pure mind is a divine action which will have enduring achievements. To the extent an individual does not practice this efficient way of work he loses his discriminative capacity and ultimately will meet his destruction.

ACTION IS DRIVEN BY ONE'S OWN NATURE

sadrisham cheshtate swasyaah prakriter jnaanavaan api
prakritim yaanti bhootani nigrahah kim karishyati // 3.33 //

EVEN A WISE MAN ACTS IN ACCORDANCE WITH HIS OWN NATURE; BEINGS WILL FOLLOW NATURE; WHAT CAN RESTRAINT DO?

The question as to why some people do not follow the teachings of The Lord and instead act on their own is answered in this verse; the reason is that their lower nature proves too strong for them. Every one is conditioned by his thoughts which in turn are influenced by his nature (tendency) or *prakriti*. Even an honest person finds it difficult to practice the technique in life shown by The Lord because of his own mental conditioning being overwhelmed by his incapacity to pursue the path of action.

Prakriti is the mental equipment with which one is born as the result of the past acts performed in a previous life. This nature is the mainspring of the man's action. This must run its course; there is no escape from this and even God cannot prevent its operation (Shankara). Even He ordains that past deeds produce their natural effects.

Restraint or forcible repression of senses for renouncing activities cannot be of much avail since actions flow inevitably from the workings of Prakriti and the Self is only an important witness. This indicates the omnipotence of the nature over the Self which makes us to act according to our nature, the law of our being. However, this is not a statement of despair to the effect that there is no scope for personal exertion to reach the highest goal and that the teachings of Sri Krishna are all purposeless. On the other hand it is a call to find out our true being and give expression to it as explained in the next verse.

ROLE FOR PERSONAL EXERTION

indriyasye'ndriyasyaarthe raagadweshau vyavasthitau
tayor na vasham aagacchet tau hyasya paripanthinau // 3.34 //

THE LOVE AND HATRED THAT THE SENSES FEEL FOR THEIR OBJECTS ARE INEVITABLE. BUT LET NONE COME UNDER THEIR SWAY; FOR, THEY ARE HIS ENEMIES.

Attachment and aversion of the sense organs to sense objects are natural to every one. Although the sense objects as such are not capable of attraction or repulsion it is the mind which produces such agitations because of its being conditioned by vasanas. Thus mind develops attachment for the agreeable objects and aversion for disagreeable ones. Sri Krishna does not advise running away from the sense objects but emphatically says 'Let none come under its sway' meaning that one should be a master of the senses and not their victim.

If we do not interfere attachments and aversions will determine our acts. So long as we act in certain ways because we like them and abstain from some others because we dislike them we will be bound by our actions.
But if we overcome these impulses from our egocentric ideas and act from a sense of duty, we cannot be the victims of the play of Prakriti. Thus in the process of controlling the mind - stopping it from running after the objects of attachment and aversion - lies the personal exertion for the seeker. That is his Purushartha.

Linking this advice to the previous verse it can be understood that it is not possible for anybody to renounce all his activities forcibly. But man can by changing the aim of his life, turn the course of life from one direction to the other. In other words, avoiding likes and dislikes he can convert his actions as aids to God-realization.

DANGER IN PERCEIVING OTHER'S DUTIES AS BETTER THAN ONE'S OWN

shreyaan swadharmo vigunah paradharmaat swanushthitaat
swadharme nidhanam shreyah paradharmo bhayaavahah
// 3.35 //

BETTER IS ONE'S OWN DUTY, THOUGH IMPERFECTLY PERFORMED, THAN THE DUTY OF ANOTHER WELL PERFORMED. BETTER IS DEATH IN THE DOING OF ONE'S

OWN DUTY; THE DUTY OF ANOTHER IS FRAUGHT WITH PERIL.

Although the word Dharma is meant here as duty, in a special sense it is one's own basic nature or vasana. Swadharma is the type of vasanas one finds in his mind. To act according to one's taste, inborn and natural, is the only method to live in peace and joy. To act against one's vasanas is to act in terms of Paradharma which is fraught with danger.

Here the Swadharma of Arjuna is that of a prince and not that of Brahmana. He wanted to take up the latter abandoning the former. In this verse Sri Krishna reminds him that to act according to his own vasanas or Dharma, even though imperfect, is the right path for his development. It is dangerous to suppress one's own personality expression and imitate the activities of others, however divinely they may be. There is more happiness in doing one's own work even without excellence than in doing another's duty well. We must play our part, manfully, be it great or small.

The implication is that Arjuna's thought of desisting from fight and going in for the calm and peaceful life of a Brahmana is prompted by man's natural desire to shun what is disagreeable and adopt what is momentarily agreeable to the senses. He should on no account yield to such weakness. It is indeed much better for a person to die while discharging his own duty, though it may not have any merit, than doing the duty of another, though it may be performed in a perfect manner, because the duty of another has many pitfalls.

THE ENEMY IS DESIRE AND ANGER

arjuna uvaacha
atha kena prayukto'yam paapam charati poorushah
anicchannapi vaarshneya balaad iva niyojitah // 3.36 //

ARJUNA SAID
BUT UNDER WHAT COMPULSION DOES A MAN COMMIT SIN, IN SPITE OF HIMSELF, O VARSHNEYA, AND DRIVEN, AS IT WERE, BY FORCE?

This question raised by Arjuna is illustrative of our daily situations. Everybody knows what is right and what is not right, what is good and what is bad. Yet when it comes to action people are invariably tempted to commit the wrong.

Arjuna's query is why this paradoxical confusion between one's ideology and one's own actions. The Divine in us wants us to achieve great things but the animal in us wants us to do most abominable things many times much against our will. We seem to be constrained by an outside force. Arjuna wants to know the cause for this peculiar paradox.

sri bhagavaan uvaacha
kaama esha krodha esha rajoguna samudbhavah
mahaashano mahaapaapmaa viddhyenam iha vairinam // 3.37 //

SRI BHAGAVAN SAID
IT IS DESIRE, IT IS ANGER BORN OUT OF THE QUALITY OF RAJAS, ALL SINFUL AND ALL DEVOURING; KNOW THIS AS THE FOE HERE (IN THIS WORLD).

The cause of all sins and wrong actions in this world is desire. Anger is also a desire expressed in another form. When a man's desire is not gratified he becomes angry with those who stand as obstacles in the way of their fulfillment. When a desire arises the quality of Rajas in a man urges him to work for its satisfaction.

The desire-anger-emotion combination of the three-in-one is the root cause which makes an individual to compromise with higher values of existence. Once the virus of desire enters the intellectual computer the results are bound to be chaotic, blocking out the entire wisdom because desire is never satiated by its gratification. One gets rid of desire only through the constant practice of detachment. Therefore Sri Krishna says desire is the man's greatest enemy on the earth because man commits sin only at the command of desire against his will and better judgment which lands him in terrible suffering in the form of repeated birth and death.

HOW DOES DESIRE AFFECT MAN?

dhoomenaavriyate vahnir yathaadarsho malena cha
yatho'lbenaavrito garbhas tathaa tenedam aavritam // 3.38 //

AS FIRE IS ENVELOPED BY SMOKE, AS A MIRROR BY DUST AND AS AN EMBRYO BY THE WOMB, SO IS THIS (KNOWLEDGE) ENVELOPED BY THAT (DESIRE).

'This' means true knowledge or wisdom and 'that' means desire which is clearly stated in the next verse. The three different examples refer to the different degrees to which desire in the form of ignorance envelopes and conceals the inner Light in man and deludes his capacity to think rationally.

Discrimination is blocked by the sense of attachment in the mind for the worldly objects. Desires fall under three categories depending upon the quality of attachments - Tamasic - inert, Rajasic - active, and Sattwic -divine.

Even Sattwic desires veil the discrimination just as smoke envelopes fire where rise of the slightest wind of discrimination can dispel the smoke of desire. The veiling is thin and hence it requires only a little effort to remove it.

For the Rajasic where intellect is covered by desire prompted agitations, the example is of wiping out of dust on a mirror. Here the covering by the impurities is complete as compared to the Sattwic. In the case of smoke fire can be at least perceived while dust completely blocks the reflection in a mirror. Hence, in this case the efforts for the removal of the dirt of desires require more time and effort.

In the case of a Tamasic, diviner aspects are completely shut out from the view by base animal instincts. The case of a foetus covered with amnion fluid in the womb is given as an illustration. Here there is no method of removing the covering until a definite period of time is elapsed. Similarly the low desires can be removed only after a longer period of spiritual evolution a Tamasic has to undergo.

aavritam jnaanam etena jnaanino nityavairinaa
kaamaroopena kaunteya dushpoorenaanalena cha // 3.39 //

O SON OF KUNTI, WISDOM IS ENVELOPED BY THIS CONSTANT ENEMY OF THE WISE IN THE FORM OF DESIRE, WHICH IS UNAPPEASABLE AS THE FIRE.

Desires are insatiable. They are never satisfied by the enjoyments of the objects of the desires. They grow more and more as does the fire to which fuel is added. Desire screens off our capacity to discriminate right from the wrong, reál from the unreal. The ignorant man considers desire as his friend because his senses are gratified. The wise man knows by experience that desire will bring nothing but suffering to him. He knows that the enemy in the form of desire does not allow the ideas of discrimination, dispassion and disinterestedness to get a hold in the mind of a seeker and presents obstacles in the path of his spiritual progress. Hence it is said to be the constant enemy of the wise but not the ignorant.

SEAT OF DESIRE

indriyaani mano buddhir asyaadhishthaanam uchyate
etair vimohayatyesha jnaanamaavritya dehinam // 3.40 //

THE SENSES, THE MIND AND THE INTELLECT ARE SAID TO BE ITS SEAT; THROUGH THESE IT DELUDES THE EMBODIED BY VEILING HIS WISDOM.

If the enemy's hide-outs are known it is easy to capture him. Similarly Sri Krishna gives the clues to Arjuna as to where the enemies of wisdom lurk so that he can locate and eliminate them. The Lord says the senses, the mind and the intellect are seats of action for the desire to play havoc with the inner serenity and equipoise of a man. The sense organs transmit the stimuli received from the objects of enjoyment to the mind which working in close collaboration with the intellect starts living in the experience of sense enjoyments. To eliminate the inner enemy of desire at its source - sense-organs, mind and intellect- is the crux of the problem. How it is to be achieved is explained in the following verses.

CONTROL THE SENSES AND DESTROY THE DESIRE

tasmaat twam indriyaanyaadau niyamya bharatarshabha
paapmaanam prajahi hyenam jnaana vijnaana naashanam
// 3.41 //

THEREFORE, O THE BEST OF THE BHARATAS, CONTROLLING THE SENSES FIRST, YOU KILL THIS SINFUL THING, THE DESTROYER OF KNOWLEDGE AND WISDOM.

Sri Krishna states that the first step to kill desire is to control the senses. Desire is referred to here as a sinful thing posing a threat to both knowledge and wisdom. Desire is a sinful thing because it leads us to live a life of lowly nature.

Adi Sankara defines Knowledge - *Jnana* - as the knowledge of the Self acquired through a study of the scriptures and from a teacher. This is an indirect knowledge or *Paroksha Jnana*. *Vijnana* or wisdom is the direct knowledge or the personal experience, *anubhava,* of the things so taught or Self-realization - *Aparoksha Jnana*. Thus desire oriented agitations are not only an impediment to our direct personal spiritual experiences but also to our indirect way of acquiring knowledge through the study of scriptures.

indriyaani paraanyaahur indriyebhyah param manah
manasastu paraa buddhir yo buddheh paratastu sah // 3.42 //

THEY SAY THAT THE SENSES ARE SUPERIOR TO THE BODY; SUPERIOR TO THE SENSES IS THE MIND; SUPERIOR TO THE MIND IS INTELLECT; AND ONE WHO IS SUPERIOR EVEN TO THE INTELLECT IS HE - THE SELF.

evam buddheh param buddhwaa samstabhyaatmaanam aatmanaa jahi shatrum mahaabaaho kaamaroopam duraasadam // 3.43 //

THUS KNOWING HIM WHO IS SUPERIOR TO THE INTELLECT AND RESTRAINING THE SELF BY THE SELF, O MIGHTY ARMED, DESTROY THE ENEMY IN THE FORM OF DESIRE, NO DOUBT HARD INDEED TO CONQUER.

These two verses conclude the third chapter of The Gita giving the seeker a technique to conquer desire, the inner enemy. The Upanishadic method of meditation for the withdrawal of ego from the outer world of sense objects to the inner world of the Self for the purposes of curbing desire oriented tendencies and thereby achieving Self-discovery is commended here. These verses give us the hierarchy of levels of consciousness.

The physical body is gross, external and limited. As compared to this the senses are superior because they are subtler and more internal and have a wider range of activity. Superior to the senses is the mind as it can direct the function of the senses (as it can undertake the work of the senses also). Superior to the mind is the intellect because it is endowed with the faculty of discrimination and finality; when the mind doubts, the intellect decides. But The Self is superior to even the intellect because the intellect draws its power to illuminate from the Self alone. The Self is the indweller in the body, the Witness of the activities of the body, senses, mind and intellect.

Sri Krishna advises Arjuna to conquer desire with this understanding of the superior power of the Self, though it is difficult to achieve. The Lord points out that a man of discrimination and dispassion will be able to achieve this by increasing his Sattwic quality and by appealing to the indwelling Presence, The Self, through meditation. This controlling of the lower self i.e. the mind with the knowledge of the Higher Self is termed here as 'restraining the self by the Self'.

The technique of meditation is a conscious withdrawal of all our identifications with our body, mind and intellect and thereby turning our awareness or desire-faculty towards our diviner existence where the ego is under the perfect control of the Self with no desires to agitate the mind any more. Thus a constructive re-organization of life is taught here by the Gita without the suppression or rejection of the life's situations. "This Chapter expounds the necessity for the performance of work without any selfish attachment to results, with a view to securing the welfare of the world, with the realization that agency belongs to the modes of *prakriti* or to God himself." - Dr.S.Radhakrishnan.

om tat sat iti srimad bhagavadgeetaasu upanishatsu brahma vidyaayaam yogashaastre sri krishnaarjuna samvaade karmayogo naama tritiyo'dhyaayah ||

THUS IN THE UPANISHADS OF THE GLORIOUS BHAGAVAD GITA, THE SCIENCE OF THE ETERNAL, THE SCRIPTURE OF YOGA, THE DIALOGUE BETWEEN SRI KRISHNA AND ARJUNA, ENDS THE THIRD DISCOURSE ENTITLED THE YOGA OF ACTION.

AN OUTLINE VIEW OF THIS CHAPTER

The third chapter entitled Karma Yoga, the path of action, contains 43 verses. In the previous chapter Krishna provided sufficient time and knowledge to Arjuna to recover from his despondent state on the battlefield. The dialogue between them in this chapter indicates Arjuna's emergence from the mood of despondency.

I - INTRODUCING THE PATH OF ACTION - VERSES 1 – 3

Krishna introduces the idea of action to Arjuna. Human beings fall under two classifications, introverts and extroverts. The introverts, being contemplative, follow jnana yoga, the path of knowledge. The extroverts, naturally inclined to action, take up karma yoga, the path of action.

II - AN INTELLECTUAL APPEAL FOR ACTION - VERSES 4 – 19

This portion gives the logic and reason for performing action. Arjuna collapses emotionally on seeing his elders, relatives and friends on the battleground. Incapacitated to fight the battle, he ceases to act. Krishna tries to convince him intellectually on the importance of action. He gives a new meaning to the age-old term 'Yajna'. According to The Lord Yajna means performing one's obligatory duties without indulging in ego and egocentric desires. The idea is performing of selfless actions dedicated to a higher and noble ideal.

III - EMOTIONAL APPEALS FOR ACTION - VERSES 20 -24

Arjuna does not respond to the intellectual appeal made earlier. Krishna now tries to reach him emotionally. He makes six different psychological appeals to support his intellectual reasoning for inducing him to action. They are devotion, persuasion, vanity, personal appeal, fear and threat. Arjuna appears to be responding to this plea.

IV - THE TECHNIQUE OF RIGHT ACTION - VERSES 25 – 35

This topic gives the prescription for right action. For the most part people live their lives selfishly, acting merely to fulfill their egocentric desires and craving for the fruits of their actions. They cling to actions for their own personal ends. Instead they must direct their actions to a greater cause, a higher ideal. The highest ideal one can aspire for is Self-realization. To work towards it, first choose a field of activity according to your basic nature. Fix the highest goal, take care that your personal likes and dislikes do not interfere with your higher pursuit. Do not waste your energies in brooding over the past and worrying about the future. Act in the present in a spirit of service and sacrifice for the achievement of your ideal.

V - IMPEDIMENTS TO RIGHT ACTION - VERSES 36 – 39

Arjuna asks Krishna why people abandon virtue and court vice, while knowing it to be wrong and wishing to remain virtuous. What forces them to commit such sins? A person who knows right from wrong and wishes to tread right path and yet he feels constrained to take the wrong direction by some inner compelling force. Arjuna wants that force to be identified. Krishna replies that the underlying force behind such sinful actions is desire and its modification, anger. Desire is your greatest foe which, unchecked, ultimately destroys you. Desires are insatiable like fire. They conceal the Self and cause mental agitation, suffering and sorrow.

VI - WAY TO OVERCOME THE IMPEDIMENTS - VERSES 40 – 43

The last topic provides the method of overcoming desire, since desire impedes right action. Desire can be physical, emotional or intellectual. It veils the wisdom in an individual and deludes him. In the concluding verse Krishna advises the practice of self-restraint and pursuit of Self-Knowledge to destroy this enemy.

<<<000>>>

CHAPTER 4

Jnaana Karma Sanyaasa Yogah:

Yoga of Renunciation of Action in Knowledge

PREAMBLE

In the previous Chapter Sri Krishna advocated the path of Karma Yoga as a method to realize the Self. Fearing that Arjuna may misunderstand this advice as the only way for the self-development Lord Krishna reveals in this chapter how spiritual knowledge is received by successive disciples and the reason and nature of His descent into the material worlds. He also explains the paths of action and knowledge as well as the wisdom regarding the supreme knowledge which results at the culmination of the two paths. Thus this chapter dealing with the paths of action and knowledge is entitled: 'The Yoga of Renunciation of Action in Knowledge'. In a way this Chapter can be considered as an Appendix to the Third Chapter.

In this Chapter we can observe Sri Krishna talking to Arjuna not as his friend or charioteer but as an omnipotent and omniscient God probably to instill in his mind the necessary reverence and respect for Him and His teachings.

THE TEXT

TRADITION OF JNAANA YOGA

sri bhagavaan uvaacha
imam vivaswate yogam proktavan aham avyayam
vivaswaan manave praaha manur ikshwaakave'braveet // 4.1 //

SRI BHAGAVAN SAID
I TAUGHT THIS ETERNAL YOGA TO VIVASVAN; HE TAUGHT IT TO MANU AND MANU PROCLAIMED IT TO IKSHVAKU.

This eternal yoga means the yoga taught in the Second and Third Chapters. The fruit of this yoga is liberation, which transcends time, space and causality. Hence it is eternal. Vivasvan is the Sun-God. Manu is the ancient law-giver. Ikshvaku is the ancestor of Kshatriyas whose lineage goes back to the Sun-God.

Jnaana Yoga, discussed in the 2nd and 3rd Chapters, is based on renunciation and is attained through the performance of duty. Thus it comprehends both the life of activity *(pravritti)* and the life of retirement *(nivritti)* as taught in the Vedas. The path of knowledge has been described in the Gita as leading directly to liberation. Therefore, it is extolled here by pointing out its antiquity.

evam paramparaa praaptam imam raajarshayo viduh
sa kaaleneha mahataa yogo nashtah parantapa // 4.2 //

THIS KNOWLEDGE, HANDED DOWN THUS IN REGULAR SUCCESSION, THE ROYAL SAGES KNEW. THIS YOGA BY LONG LAPSE OF TIME HAS BEEN LOST TO THE WORLD, O PARANTAPA (ARJUNA).

The royal sages, men like Rama and Janaka, who were kings and at the same time sages also were well versed in this Yoga because of their austerities and wisdom. If the leaders of a country possess the knowledge of Yoga i.e. moral values of life, they will percolate down the line into the entire society.

The teachings of this yoga were lost by falling into the hands of selfish and unrighteous people. It is the intention of the Lord to revive it through the Gita.

sa evaayam mayaa te'dya yogah proktah puraatanah
bhakto'si me sakhaa cheti rahasyam hyetad uttamam // 4.3 //

THAT SAME ANCIENT YOGA HAS BEEN TAUGHT TO YOU BY ME TODAY, FOR YOU ARE MY DEVOTEE AND MY FRIEND AND IT IS A SUPREME SECRET

The yoga mentioned here is considered secret because it is not commonly known to everybody and that it should be revealed only to those who are worthy to receive it.

ARJUNA'S DOUBT

arjuna uvaacha
aparam bhavato janma param janma vivaswatah
katham etadvijaaneeyaam twam aadau proktavaan iti // 4.4 //

ARJUNA SAID
LATER WAS YOUR BIRTH AND EARLIER WAS THE BIRTH OF VIVASVAN; HOW, THEN, AM I TO UNDERSTAND THAT YOU TAUGHT THIS YOGA IN THE BEGINNING?

The birth of Sri Krishna was later than that of The Sun. Arjuna wants to know how he should believe that the former taught this yoga to the latter.

THEORY OF AVATARS

sri bhagavaan uvaacha
bahooni me vyateetaani janmaani tava chaarjuna
taanyaham veda sarvaani na twam vettha parantapa // 4.5 //

SRI BHAGAVAN SAID
MANY BIRTHS OF MINE HAVE PASSED AS WELL AS OF YOURS, O ARJUNA; I KNOW THEM ALL BUT YOU KNOW THEM NOT, O PARANTAPA.

Arjuna with a limited knowledge thinks that Sri Krishna is an ordinary man and not the omnipotent and omniscient Lord. This doubt is cleared here. Sri Krishna knows the past and future because He is the Lord Himself. He is unobstructed in His power of vision.

SECRET OF LORD'S BIRTH

ajo'pi sannavyayaatmaa bhootaanaam eeshwaro'pi san
prakritim swaam adhishthaaya sambhavaamy aatmamaayayaa // 4.6 //

THOUGH I AM UNBORN, AND ETERNAL BY NATURE, AND THOUGH I AM THE LORD OF ALL BEINGS, YET SUBJUGATING MY OWN NATURE, I COME INTO BEING BY MY OWN MAYA.

The Lord is eternal because Existence-Knowledge-Bliss Absolute, which forms His nature, is eternal and changeless. 'My own nature' means His inherent power of Maya. Maya inheres in Brahman, but Brahman remains unaffected by it in the same way as the poison of a cobra which is in the cobra does not injure it. This power of Maya which is made up of the three Gunas, deludes the embodied being from recognizing the Lord who is his true Self. 'I come into being by my own Maya' means that it is through Maya the Lord appears to be born. His embodiment is not real as are the embodiments of other beings.

The embodiments of human beings (birth in the human form) are not voluntary. Driven by nature or prakriti, through ignorance, they are born again and again. The Lord controls nature and assumes embodiment through His own free will. The ordinary birth of creatures is determined by the force of nature while The Lord takes birth through His own power. He uses His nature in such a way which is free from subjection to karma. Yogamaya refers to the free will of God, His incomprehensible power.

To put it differently, the embodiment of the Lord is only an appearance. A created being is under the control of Maya but the Lord is the controller of Maya. The birth and death of the Lord depends upon His own will. But the birth and death of an embodied being are due to the law of Karma. This is the difference between an embodied being and the incarnate Lord.

THE LORD'S INCARNATION

yadaa yadaa hi dharmasya glaanir bhavati bhaarata
abhyutthaanam adharmasya tadaa'tmaanam srijaamyaham // 4.7 //

WHENEVER THERE IS A DECLINE OF DHARMA (RIGHTEOUSNESS), O BHARATA, AND RISE OF ADHARMA (UNRIGHTEOUSNESS), THEN I MANIFEST MYSELF.

FOR WHAT PURPOSE?

paritraanaaya saadhoonaam vinaashaaya cha dushkritam
dharma samsthaapanaarthaaya sambhavaami yuge yuge // 4.8 //

FOR THE PROTECTION OF THE GOOD, FOR THE DESTRUCTION OF THE WICKED AND FOR THE ESTABLISHMENT OF RIGHTEOUSNESS, I AM BORN IN EVERY AGE.

Whenever there is a serious tension in life, when the all-pervasive materialism invades the hearts of human souls, to preserve the equilibrium, a responsive manifestation of wisdom and righteousness is essential. The Supreme, though unborn and undying, becomes manifest in human embodiment to overthrow the forces of ignorance and selfishness.

Avatara means descent, one who has descended. The Divine comes down to the earthly plane to raise it to a higher status. The purpose of Avatar is to inaugurate a new world, a new Dharma. By His teaching and example, He shows how a human being can raise himself to a higher grade of life.

The issue between right and wrong is the most crucial one. The Lord works on the side of the right. Love and mercy are more powerful than hatred and cruelty.

Dharma will conquer Adharma, truth wins over falsehood and power behind death will be overthrown by the Reality, Sat Chit Ananda - Being, Intelligence and Bliss.

Dharma means the mode of the being. It is the essential nature of a being that determines its mode of behavior. So long as our conduct is in conformity with our essential nature, we are acting in the right way. Adharma is nonconformity to our nature. Harmony of the world is on account of conformity of all beings to their respective natures; disharmony of the world is due to their nonconformity.

When the freedom given to humans is abused causing disequilibrium The Lord does not merely stand aside and allow the things to drift. He, through His manifestation, sets the matter on the right track and lets it jog along by itself while His loving hand is steering it all the time.

Sri Krishna says that His manifestations in this world in every age are for the following purposes:

- for the protection of the good: To protect those who lead a life of truth and righteousness, who utilize their bodies in the service of the community, who are free from selfishness, anger, hatred, lust and greed and who devote their life to divine contemplation.
- for the destruction of the evil-doers: For the elimination of wrong tendencies in those who lead a life of unrighteousness, who break the laws of the society, who are vain, dishonest and greedy, who injure others, who take possession of other's property by force and who commit all sorts of crimes and

- for the establishment of dharma: When dharma is protected and wickedness destroyed, society lives according to dharma and affords opportunities to its members to lead a spiritual life. It connotes cosmic and moral order.

janma karma cha me divyam evam yo vetti tattwatah
tyaktwaa deham punarjanma naiti maameti so'rjuna // 4.9 //

HE WHO THUS KNOWS IN TRUE LIGHT MY DIVINE BIRTH AND ACTION, WILL NOT BE BORN AGAIN WHEN HE LEAVES HIS BODY: HE WILL ATTAIN ME, O ARJUNA.

After explaining the reasons for His incarnations in this world Sri Krishna declares that he, who knows the great truth that the Lord though apparently born is ever beyond birth and death, though apparently active in the cause of righteousness, is ever beyond all action - becomes illumined with Self-knowledge, has realized the ultimate truth. Thus he transcends birth and death in the relative world and attains Brahman.

veetaraagabhayakrodhaa manmayaa maam upaashritaah
bahavo jnaana tapasaa pootaa madbhaavamaagataah // 4.10 //

FREED FROM ATTACHMENT, FEAR AND ANGER, ABSORBED IN ME, TAKING REFUGE IN ME, PURIFIED BY THE FIRE OF KNOWLEDGE, MANY HAVE ATTAINED MY BEING.

The purpose of incarnation is not merely to uphold the world order but to help the human beings to become perfected in their nature.

The steps required to be undertaken by beings in this regard are:

- renouncing attachments to sense objects
- becoming desireless
- getting free from selfishness
- realizing that he is constant, indestructible, eternal Self and that change is merely a quality of the body.

When an individual has reached this stage of self-development he becomes fearless and sees the Self everywhere and in such a state anger cannot arise in him. He is absorbed in Him and becomes fully devoted to Him. He thus takes absolute refuge in The Lord after getting purified with the fire of this knowledge.

The wisdom is referred to here as fire. Just as fire burns everything the wisdom burns down or completely removes all latent tendencies, impressions, cravings etc in an individual and thus makes him pure.

IS THE LORD PARTIAL TOWARDS SOME?

ye yathaa maam prapadyante taamstathaiva bhajaamyaham
mama vartmaanuvartante manushyaah paartha sarvashah // 4.11 //

IN WHATEVER WAY MEN WORSHIP ME, IN THE SAME WAY I REWARD THEM; IT IS MY PATH, THAT MEN FOLLOW IN ALL THINGS, O SON OF PRITHA.

This verse brings out the wide catholicity of the Gita religion. God meets every aspirant with favor and grants to each his heart's desire. He does not extinguish the hope of any but helps all hopes to grow according to their nature. The Lord bestows pleasure to those who seek pleasure, rewards those who aim liberation, and rescues them from distresses who pray to Him, and so on. In whatever form man worships the Lord, the Lord appears to him in that form. The various deities and cosmic forces, the angels, the prophets, the incarnations, are only different manifestations of the Lord Himself.

As there are innumerable ideals cherished by men, so there are innumerable forms of the Lord corresponding to those ideals. It is to Him alone that man offers worship under different names and forms, through different symbols and rites. Likewise, from Him alone comes the fulfillment of all desires, whether they are secular or spiritual. As the Self within He brings to fruition all wishes when the necessary conditions are fulfilled. The Atharva Veda says "*ekam jyoti bahudha vibhati*' - the one light manifests itself in various forms. (XIII.3.17)

"The spiritually immature are unwilling to recognize other Gods than their own. Their attachment to their creed makes them blind to the larger unity of Godhead. This is the result of egotism in the religious ideas. The Gita on the other hand affirms though beliefs and practices may be many and varied, spiritual realization to which these are the means is one". Dr.S.Radhakrishnan.

WHY DO PEOPLE NOT DESIRE LIBERATION?

kaangkshantah karmanaam siddhim yajanta iha devataah
kshipram hi maanushe loke siddhirbhavati karmajaa // 4.12 //

THOSE WHO LONG FOR SUCCESS IN ACTION IN THIS WORLD WORSHIP THE GODS, BECAUSE SUCCESS IS QUICKLY ATTAINED BY MEN THROUGH ACTION.

Men worship God in this world because they want immediate fruits in terms of pleasures from their activities. Worldly success is much easier of attainment than Self-knowledge which demands perfect renunciation.

ALL ARE NOT BORN EQUAL

chaaturvarnyam mayaa srishtam gunakarma vibhaagashah
tasya kartaaram api maam viddhyakartaaram avyayam // 4.13 //

THE FOURFOLD CASTE HAS BEEN CREATED BY ME ACCORDING TO THE DIFFERENTIATION OF GUNA AND KARMA; THOUGH I AM THE AUTHOR THEREOF KNOW ME AS NON-DOER AND CHANGELESS.

This verse explains the diversity of human temperaments and tendencies. All men are not of the same nature because of the preponderance of the different Gunas in them. The caste system was originally meant to make the growth of human society perfect. But this principle later on came to be abused and misused by the society which gave it a totally wrong meaning based on the accident of birth.

On the basis of the temperamental distinctions and the quality of thoughts entertained by the individuals, the entire mankind has been, for the purpose of spiritual study, classified as the four castes or Varnas just as people are divided as professionals, merchants, agriculturists and laborers etc on the basis of activities or vocation pursued by them. For the well being of the society in general each class of people is as important and essential as the other.

Accordingly the four castes are:

- Brahmana - where Sattva (purity, goodness etc.) predominates in thoughts and action.
- Kshatriya - where Rajas (courage, valor etc.) predominates in thoughts and deeds.
- Vaishya - where Rajas and Tamas (indolence, ignorance etc.) predominate
- Sudra - where Tamas alone predominates.

The Lord is the Creator of the four castes only from the standpoint of maya. Maya is the immediate cause of everything that happens in the relative world. But since maya has no existence independent of the Lord, He is said to be the Creator.

The Lord with reference to the mind and intellect is the creator of the temperaments although in His essential nature He is not the Doer or the Creator because He is the changeless and all-pervading irrespective of what happens in the creation.

ACTION WITHOUT ATTACHMENT DOES NOT LEAD TO BONDAGE

na maam karmaani limpanti na me karmaphale sprihaa
iti maam yo'bhijaanaati karmabhir na sa badhyate // 4.14 //

ACTIONS DO NOT TAINT ME, NOR HAVE I A DESIRE FOR THE FRUITS OF ACTIONS. HE WHO KNOWS ME THUS IS NOT BOUND BY ACTIONS.

Actions do not taint the Lord because He is totally free from egoism. Since He is unselfish, He is not taking rebirths as men to reap the fruit of His actions. Anyone who knows his own inmost Self to be the Lord, unattached to action and its result, is not bound by action and will not be reborn in the world of maya.

Taint and desire can come only to an Ego which is the Self functioning through a given state of mind and intellect. The one who has renounced his identification with his limited ego and rediscovered himself as none other than the Self is no more affected by his actions in the outer world.

evam jnaatwaa kritam karma poorvair api mumukshubhih
kuru karmaiva tasmaat twam poorvaih poorvataram kritam // 4.15 //

HAVING KNOWN THIS, THE ANCIENT SEEKERS AFTER LIBERATION PERFORMED ACTION; THEREFORE, YOU TOO PERFORM ACTION, AS DID THE ANCIENTS IN THE OLDEN TIMES.

Knowing that the Self can have no desire for the fruits of actions and cannot be tainted or soiled by them and knowing that no one can be tainted if he works without egoism, attachment and expectation of fruits, Arjuna is called upon to do his duty as the ancients like King Janaka and others did in the days of yore. The idea is that the ignorant perform action for self purification, and the wise perform action for the maintenance of the world.

DOCTRINE OF ACTION AND INACTION

kim karma kim akarmeti kavayo'pyatra mohitaah
tat te karma pravakshyaami yajjnaatwaa mokshyase'shubhaat // 4.16 //

WHAT IS ACTION? WHAT IS INACTION? AS TO THIS EVEN THE WISE ARE PERPLEXED. THEREFORE, I SHALL TELL YOU WHAT ACTION IS BY KNOWING WHICH YOU SHALL BE FREED FROM THE EVIL (OF SAMSARA - THE WHEEL OF BIRTH AND DEATH).

The Lord thus instructed Arjuna to perform action in a disinterested spirit. But one cannot duly perform one's duty without knowing in reality what constitutes action and what inaction is. Therefore the Lord promises to reveal to Arjuna the truth about action showing its intricate nature and the value of its knowledge in order that Arjuna may really understand the truth about transcendent actions, which are free from the feeling of possession, the sense of doership, attachment and the desire for fruit. Thus the mystery of action is extremely difficult to unravel.

karmano hyapi boddhavyam boddhavyam cha vikarmanah
akarmanashcha boddhavyam gahanaa karmano gatih // 4.17 //

ONE HAS TO UNDERSTAND WHAT ACTION REALLY IS AND LIKEWISE ONE HAS TO UNDERSTAND WHAT IS FORBIDDEN ACTION AND ALSO WHAT INACTION IS. INDEED HARD TO UNDERSTAND IS THE WAY OF ACTION.

One must not oversimplify action and inaction by thinking that the former means the activity of the body and the latter its idleness. The definition of these three terms is as under:

- Action: That which is prescribed in the scriptures and not merely approved by men.
- Forbidden action: That which is forbidden by the scriptures.
- Inaction: Renunciation of action.

Activity is the very essence of life. The great Seers of ancient days evaluated the life on the basis of the quality of activities.

Life is constituted of moments of activity (Karma) and inactivity (Akarma). Through inactivity neither progress nor deterioration is ever possible. Periods of activity alone create man. Such creation of man depends upon what type of activity he undertakes. Activity or Karma need not imply only ritualism but it encompasses all dedicated actions. It is known to all that action means movement of the body etc., and inaction means absence of such movements or to sit quiet. But these two terms imply much more than these familiar ideas.

Activity can be broadly classified as constructive and destructive. Constructive activities are termed here as Karma (i.e. actions to be done) which contribute towards the evolution of an individual. Destructive activities are those which debase the individual and hence totally condemned by the Sastras; these are referred to here as Vikarma (actions to be avoided).

Karma (Constructive activity) can be of three types:

- Nitya Karma: constant duties
- Naimittika Karma: special duties on special occasions and
- Kamya Karma: duties done expecting rewards.

Sri Krishna advises Arjuna to avoid prohibited actions (Vikarma) and to pursue the constructive and creative activities of self-development (Karma) and to totally reject inactivity (Akarma). It is essential that a true seeker should know the triple classification of activities constituting life. Sri Bhagavan admits that it is not easy to understand these concepts of activities implying that for evaluating actions one should go beyond the actions as such and look into the motive or desire or intention behind such actions. If motives are pure actions will be noble and if motives are impure so also actions will be mean.

karmanyakarma yah pashyed akarmani cha karma yah
sa buddhimaan manushyeshu sa yuktah kritsnakarmakrit // 4.18 //

HE WHO RECOGNIZES INACTION IN ACTION AND ACTION IN INACTION IS WISE AMONG MEN; HE IS A YOGI AND A TRUE PERFORMER OF ALL ACTIONS.

This verse conveys the central theme of this Chapter. Sri Krishna describes the nature of action and inaction by introducing the concepts of seeing inaction in action and action in inaction. Bhagavan asserts that he who so recognizes is a wise person, a Yogi and is deemed to have preformed all actions.

Although these terms are common and familiar they are used in the Gita with special meaning and implications. They are examined hereunder.

Inaction in action:
It is only the ignorant that regard the Self as active. But the wise person regards the Self as actionless even when he himself is engaged in action. Activity belongs to the senses, the body and the mind. It is a function of the Gunas.

Action in inaction:
The body, the senses and the mind, regarded by the ignorant as actionless, are perceived by the wise to be active. Hence he sees action in what the ignorant think to be inaction.

Performed all actions:
A wise person devoid of the idea of agency is really a free soul, though he participates in action. Action does not bind him.

The terms 'action' and 'inaction' are not rightly understood; the one is mistaken for the other. The Lord tries to remove this misunderstanding. The Self of man is actionless. Action pertains to the physical body, the senses and the mind. But ignorant people falsely attribute action to the Self and say to themselves that 'I am the doer, mine is the action, and by me is the fruit of action reaped' and so on.

Similarly, he falsely imputes to the Self the cessation of activity, which really pertains to the body, the senses and the mind. So he says to himself 'I shall be quiet, I may be free from work and worry and be happy' and so on.

Through right knowledge a man sees inaction in action; he sees that action commonly associated with the Self really belongs to the body, the senses and the mind and that the Self is actionless. Likewise, a man with right knowledge sees action in inaction; he knows that inaction is also a kind of action. Inaction is a correlative of action and pertains to the body. The Self is beyond action and inaction.

Sankara explains that in *atman* there is no action; in the body, however, there is no rest, even when there seems to be rest.

He who knows the meaning of action and inaction as explained above is wise among men; he is a Yogi. He does all action without being bound; he is free from the evil result of action. He has achieved everything.

yasya sarve samaarambhaah kaamasankalpa varjitaah
jnaanaagni dagdhakarmaanam tam aahuh panditam budhaah
// 4.19 //

WHOSE UNDERTAKINGS ARE ALL DEVOID OF DESIRES AND SELF-WILL AND WHOSE ACTIONS HAVE BEEN BURNT BY THE FIRE OF KNOWLEDGE, THE WISE WILL CALL HIM THE SAGE.

Realization of 'inaction in action' and 'action in inaction' is praised here. Sri Krishna says that he is a perfect sage whose actions in the outside world are without desires or the thoughts which cause such desires. Such actions performed are mere movements without any attachment for the actions and for their results because of the absence of any selfish purpose.

They are undertaken for preventing people from going astray or merely for the maintenance of the body or to set an example to others. When a sage performs these actions in the community such a learned person really does no action and his action is equivalent to inaction since all his actions are consumed by the fire of wisdom in having known the truth about action and inaction through the knowledge of Self.

The Self knowledge is a spiritual fire which consumes the results of all kinds of actions, good or bad, making the enlightened sage free from the bonds of action. Even when such a saint works in the world outside he is only expressing the will of the Divine and not his own desires and therefore, it is said that his actions are burnt by the fire of knowledge.

tyaktwaa karmaphalaasangam nityatripto niraashrayah
karmany abhipravritto'pi naiva kinchit karoti sah // 4.20 //

GIVING UP ATTACHMENT TO THE FRUITS OF ACTIONS, EVER CONTENT, DEPENDING UPON NOTHING, HE DOES NOT DO ANYTHING THOUGH ENGAGED IN ACTIONS.

A man of wisdom is described here. He who has abandoned all concern for actions and has also renounced all his attachments for their fruits is a perfect worker. This, however, does not mean that the Path of Action is to act without an eye upon the fruits of activities. It only means that we should avoid our mental dependence and intellectual attachment to the desired or expected results of our activities. Only when one gets pre-occupied with the expected fruits of actions, he gets worried and anxious and thereby becomes ineffective. Hence we are advised to work for the happiness and welfare of the society by forsaking (Tyaktwaa) our clinging (Sangam) to the fruits of action (Karma phalam).

If an attitude of non-attachment to fruits of actions is developed one becomes anxiety-free and his intellect can have no more desires because anxiety is the direct result of desires. He thus becomes ever content (Nitya-Tripta) in his experience of the Self acting in the world not seeking any fulfillment for himself.

An ordinary man lives entirely depending on the fruits of his actions and derives joy out of such fruits. In the case of a sage, he expects no fruits of his activities and his very actions are by themselves a reward for him. Hence he depends on nothing (Niraashraya).

The weaknesses of anxiety for the fruits of action, a sense of discontentment and a feeling of dependency on things and beings of the world, belong to the Ego. When the seeker ends his ego and realizes his identity with the Self, he though seemingly engaged in activity does not do anything. He is an emancipated soul who sees inaction in action and action in inaction.

niraasheer yatachittaatmaa tyaktasarvaparigrahah
shaareeram kevalam karma kurvannaapnoti kilbisham // 4.21 //

FREE FROM DESIRE, WITH THE BODY AND THE MIND CONTROLLED, AND SURRENDERING ALL POSSESSIONS HE INCURS NO SIN THROUGH MERE BODILY ACTIVITY.

A knower of Brahman is always absorbed in his communion with the Absolute and no outside activity is possible for him. However, actions for the bare maintenance of the body are done by him without any real identification with the body. The question whether such a person commits any sin accruing from failure to perform one's prescribed duties is answered now.

When an individual

- completely renounces desire
- brings his body and mind under perfect control and
- relinquishes all possessions, his ego ends.

When the ego has ended his actions do not leave any impressions on his mind and intellect and hence they are not capable of bringing about any consequences.

Such a saint's activities do not bind him since he is not the performer of actions but the actions merely flow through him. He is not a doer of actions but only an instrument for the Lord's will to express itself. The human soul becomes the pure channel of Divine power.

yadricchaalaabhasantushto dwandwaateeto vimatsarah
samah siddhaavasiddhau cha kritwaapi na nibadhyate // 4.22 //

CONTENT WITH WHAT COMES TO HIM WITHOUT ANY EFFORT ON HIS PART, FREE FROM THE PAIRS OF OPPOSITES AND ENVY, EVEN MINDED IN SUCCESS AND FAILURE, THOUGH ACTING HE IS NOT BOUND.

An individual who has gone beyond ego cannot perform any desire-prompted and result-motivated activity. So he will be happy with whatever gain spontaneously accrues to him out of his actions. This is called 'without any effort'.

The state of egolessness indicates perfect victory over mind and intellect and so the pairs of opposites - heat and cold, success and failure, good and bad, joy and sorrow, gain and loss etc., cannot affect him because they are only the interpretation of the world of objects by the mind. Such an individual who has conquered his egocentric misconceptions about himself, though acting is not bound by the consequences of the actions performed (Karma-Phalam) because he realizes that the gunas act upon the gunas and is ever steady in the true knowledge of the Self. From the standpoint of the world such a man may appear to be working or engaged in action, but from his own point of view he is not the agent of any action. The egoistic motive of action has been consumed, in his case, in the fire of knowledge.

The Cosmos is a manifestation of the Supreme and what binds is not the act but the selfish attitude to action, born of ignorance which makes us imagine that we are many separate individuals with our likes and dislikes.

In the following verses Sri Krishna proceeds to point out how the actor, the act and the action are all different manifestations of the one Supreme and action offered as a sacrifice to the Supreme does not bind.

SACRIFICE AND ITS SYMBOLIC VALUE

gatasangasya muktasya jnaanaavasthitachetasah
yajnaayaacharatah karma samagram pravileeyate // 4.23 //

FOR THE ONE WHO IS DEVOID OF ATTACHMENT, WHO IS LIBERATED, WHOSE MIND IS ESTABLISHED IN KNOWLEDGE, WHO ACTS FOR THE SAKE OF SACRIFICE ALONE, THE WHOLE ACTION DISSOLVES AWAY.

The qualities of a man of wisdom are enumerated in this verse which explains the path to perfection.

They are:
Devoid of attachment - Divinity attained by man is not something that is newly acquired by him but it is only a rediscovery of perfection already existing in him which is veiled from him because of his attachment to the finite world of objects. The wise man is he for whom attachment with the world of objects has ceased.

Liberated - Bondages created around the personality of a man are his own creation due to his attachments with things. His ego feels fulfilled only through the material world of objects and it develops a sense of clinging to these objects. Thus his body gets itself attached to the world of sense-objects, his mind gets itself enslaved in the world of emotions and his intellect gets entangled in its own ideas and he feels bound and fettered.

It is only when one goes beyond these attachments and handcuffs he becomes liberated.

Mind established in knowledge - Perfect detachment and complete liberation can be accomplished only when the seeker's mind gets focused on the discriminative knowledge of knowing the difference between the permanent and impermanent. Mind's attachment to the worldly objects is because of its delusion. If, however, the mind were to concentrate on the discriminative knowledge with the support of the intellect all the false attachments will drop off.

Acting for the sake of sacrifice (Yagna) - 'Yagna' does not mean only the rituals performed in an attitude of Dedication to God for achieving freedom from the cycle of mortal existence; it means all actions performed without ego and without the motivation of egocentric desires in a spirit of service.

When a man of perfect wisdom with the qualities as stated above performs actions in a spirit of sacrifice (Yagna), such actions dissolve away of themselves i.e. they do not leave any impressions upon his mind and cannot produce any reaction of newly formed vasanas.

Yagna ritual, the holiest act known to man, is used in the following verses as a symbol standing for the outlook of an illumined man on all his work. It is interpreted in a larger spiritual way.

brahmaarpanam brahmahavirbrahmaagnau brahmanaa hutam
brahmaiva tena gantavyam brahmakarmasamaadhinaa // 4.24 //

BRAHMAN IS THE ACT OF OFFERING; BRAHMAN IS THE CLARIFIED BUTTER ETC. CONSTITUTING THE

OFFERINGS; BY BRAHMAN IT IS OFFERED INTO THE FIRE OF BRAHMAN; BRAHMAN IS THAT WHICH IS TO BE REACHED BY HIM WHO ALWAYS SEES BRAHMAN IN ALL HIS WORKS.

This is a famous verse which is generally recited before taking food. This verse is a capsule of the entire Vedanta.

Brahman is the Infinite Reality which is changeless substratum behind the changing phenomenal world in contrast with that aspect of Brahman which functions in and through a body termed as the Atman.

When the waves of the ocean dash against each other nothing new happens because all waves are nothing but the ocean and by their act of dashing against each other the ocean rises over the ocean itself and becomes one with the ocean. Similarly when a Yagna is performed by a sage for whom there is no plurality of the world, Brahman the Truth is the performer, offering Brahman the sacrificial materials to the sacred fire, which is also Brahman, invoking Brahman only.

In the previous verse it was stated that performing actions for the sake of sacrifice, Yagna, alone melts away all his actions. It is explained here that after attaining the true knowledge the seeker's whole life becomes an act of Yagna, in which the process of offering, the objects offered, the fire, the doer of the sacrifice, the work itself and the goal are all Brahman.

After attaining the Knowledge of Brahman, a man sees Brahman in everything. He sees Brahman in every part of the action: the instrument, the doer, the result and the action itself. These have no existence apart from Brahman just as the mirage has no existence apart from the desert. What appears to be water to the ignorant is nothing but the desert. Likewise, what appears to the unenlightened as the instrument of action, the doer, and so on, is realized by one who is endowed with the knowledge of Brahman as Brahman Itself. To him everything is Brahman.

Thus the action performed by the knower of Brahman to set an example to the world is in reality no action, since all the accessories of action are consumed, as it were, in the fire of Brahman. The knowledge of Brahman removes all duality. Therefore action performed by a knower of Brahman melts away with its result and cannot bind its performer.

The significance of reciting this verse before taking food is that eating food is an unavoidable necessity for existence. When one is hungry he enjoys any type of food that comes to him. Even at this moment of enjoyment he should not forget the truth that it is Brahman eating Brahman, and that during meals he is offering to Brahman the food that is Brahman invoking nothing but the grace of Brahman.

After describing the Knowledge sacrifice and the faculty of seeing everything as Brahman the Lord proceeds to enumerate other kinds of sacrifices (Yajnas) and extols the Knowledge sacrifice as the highest. When a seeker constantly practices the different types of Yajnas suggested in this section he gains wisdom. With the dawn of wisdom he begins to develop renunciation and perceives the identity of the *atman* and *brahman*.

Yajna in the ancient past merely meant the ritual of fire worship by kindling the flames with the offerings therein by the people.

Krishna gives a new interpretation to the word Yajna to mean the conversion of human day to day activities into worship. The cycle of human activity starts with the receipt of stimuli from the world at large by the organs of perception, which turn them into reaction in mind and intellect, and which are returned as a response into the world through the organs of action. This entire cycle has been split into twelve main activities; each of them turned into a ritual, worship, a Yajna. Those who understand this and turn their daily activities into a practice of these yajnas will free themselves from the vasanas / desires.

This concept of viewing daily activities as a Yajna can be further explained in simpler terms. Take for instance the most common activities of eating and reading. This can be stated in the Gita language as *"People offer the sense of hunger as sacrifice in the fire of food; others offer the sense of ignorance as sacrifice in the fire of the knowledge"*. What does this mean? It simply means that food satisfies hunger or hunger is burnt in the *Yajnakund* of food or hunger is burnt by food or just hunger is satiated by consuming food. Similarly, knowledge removes ignorance or ignorance is burnt in the sacrificial fire of knowledge or ignorance is burnt (removed) by knowledge or just ignorance disappears when knowledge dawns.

By converting activities into Yajna (worship) a seeker drops his vasanas and gradually gains knowledge of the Self. The supermost of all yajnas is *jnana yajna*, the yajna of Wisdom. A seeker should prepare himself for the yajna through devotion, enquiry and service. With such preparation he will attract a perfect Guru to teach him the knowledge of the Self. This knowledge of the Self destroys all desires and agitations and removes forever his delusion that the world is real.

The knowledge of Self purifies the mind of all agitations and gives supreme Peace. Those devoted to Self control their senses and pursue the Self with consistency until they reach it. The ignorant, ever doubtful of the Self, lack steadiness of purpose. They will not achieve anything in this world or the next nor will they find any enduring happiness. Krishna, therefore, advises Arjuna to gain knowledge and remove all doubts and delusion and thus become established in the Supreme Self.

daivamevaapare yajnam yoginah paryupaasate
brahmaagnaavapare yajnam yajnenaivopajuhwati // 4.25 //

SOME YOGIS OFFER OBLATIONS OR PERFORM SACRIFICE TO DEVAS ALONE (DEVA-YAGNA); WHILE OTHERS OFFER THE SELF AS SACRIFICE BY THE SELF INTO THE FIRE OF BRAHMAN (BRAHMA YAGNA).

Sri Krishna explains the mental attitude of a saint when he comes in contact with the world and functions in it. The Lord is enumerating in these verses twelve different types of Yagnas, each one apparently meaning ritualism but in fact suggesting different patterns of life wherein by the necessary adjustments in the mind we can effectively change the entire reactions of the world upon us.

Deva Yagna - Some Yogis perform sacrifice to Devas alone: According to ritualism this means invoking the grace of a specific deity and offering oblations to it in the sacred fire for gaining its blessings. But here it means that the perfect masters (Yogis) when they move in the world do perceive objects but their understanding and experience of the perception is of such a nature that the world of objects was subservient to the five sense organs which are Devas. When this mental attitude is entertained by the seeker, he feels detached from the sense experience and is able to have a sense of inner equanimity. It is surrendering individual consciousness to Cosmic Consciousness.

Brahma Yagna - Offering the Self as a sacrifice by the Self in the fire of Brahman: The outer world by itself is incapable of giving us sorrow or joy; but it is our attitude towards the objects and situations of the outer world that brings us such feelings. The perfect masters understand that the sense organs are mere instruments of perception and tune them to sacrifice themselves in the knowledge of the Brahman. When an individual's organs of perception and action are to function not for satisfying his selfish needs but for the sake of serving the society at large, then although he lives in the world of objects he will not have any attachment to them.

The limiting accessories such as body, mind and intellect which are super imposed on the Self through ignorance are subordinated and the identity of the individual soul with the Supreme Soul is realized. The offering of the Self in the Brahman is to know that the Self which is associated with the limiting adjuncts is identical with the unconditioned Supreme Brahman. This is called Brahma Yagna wherein the Self is divested of Its Upadhis or limiting adjuncts so that it is recognized as the Supreme Self or Brahman.

Brahman is described in the scriptures as Consciousness, Knowledge and Bliss and as the innermost Self of all. It is devoid of all limitations imposed by time, space and causality. The individual self is in reality Brahman, but appears as the individual through association with the body, mind, intelligence and senses. To know the conditioned self as one with the unconditioned Brahman is to sacrifice the self in the fire of Brahman. This sacrifice is performed by those who have renounced all action and are devoted to the Knowledge of Brahman.

shrotraadeeneendriyaanyanye samyamaagnishu juhwati
shabdaadeen vishayaananya indriyaagnishu juhwati // 4.26 //

SOME AGAIN OFFER HEARING AND OTHER SENSES AS SACRIFICE IN THE FIRE OF RESTRAINT; OTHERS OFFER SOUND AND OTHER OBJECTS OF THE SENSES AS SACRIFICE IN THE FIRE OF THE SENSES.

To offer hearing and other senses in the fire of restraint: Some masters live constantly offering the senses into the fire of self-control so that the senses, of their own accord, get burnt up giving them inner joy. The more we satisfy the sense organs, the more they demand and this process goes on endlessly. Hence self-control of the sense organs is the only way to tame them for experiencing inner peace. This is the path of self control which is also an act of Yagna. Every form of self control, where we surrender the egocentric enjoyment for the higher delight, where we give up lower impulses, is said to be a sacrifice.

To offer sound and other objects of sense in the fire of the senses: Others direct their senses towards pure and unforbidden objects of the senses and in so doing regard themselves as performing acts of sacrifice. Under this method the senses are made the best use of for the adoration of the Almighty. In the fire of the senses, sense objects are offered as oblation. The sensual is transformed into spiritual.

Two diametrically opposite types of Yagnas are mentioned here. One makes the senses ineffective and the other makes the senses super-effective. The method of self control is negative (which is given to the few) while sense-sublimation is positive (which is given to the aspiring many); but both achieve the same objective i.e. purification of the mind.

sarvaaneendriya karmaani praanakarmaani chaapare
aatmasamyamayogaagnau juhwati jnaanadeepite // 4.27 //

OTHERS AGAIN SACRIFICE ALL THE FUNCTIONS OF THE SENSES AND THE FUNCTIONS OF THE BREATH (VITAL ENERGY) IN THE FIRE OF THE YOGA OF SELF-RESTRAINT KINDLED BY KNOWLEDGE.

Control of the ego by better understanding of the Divine behind it is called *atma-samyama-yoga* i.e. the Yoga of self-restraint. All the activities of sense organs and the organs of action as well as the objects of the senses together with the functions of the *prana* are offered into the knowledge-kindled fire of right understanding i.e. meditation which is one-pointed discriminative wisdom. The idea conveyed here is that by stopping all activities, the masters concentrate the mind on the Self.

dravyayajnaas tapoyajnaa yogayajnaastathaa'pare
swaadhyaaya jnaanayajnaashcha yatayah samshitavrataah // 4.28 //

OTHERS AGAIN OFFER WEALTH, AUSTERITY AND YOGA AS SACRIFICE, WHILE THE ASCETICS OF SELF-RESTRAINT AND RIGID VOWS OFFER STUDY OF SCRIPTURES AND KNOWLEDGE AS SACRIFICE.

Dravya Yagna: Charity and distribution of honestly acquired wealth in a spirit of devotion in the service of the community is called Dravya yagna. Wealth includes love, kindness, sympathy and affection also.

Tapo Yagna: Offering of a life of austerity to The Lord in a spirit of dedication so that the seeker may attain a little self-control.

Yoga Yagna: Yoga is an attempt to grow from the lower in us to the higher standard of divine living; it comprises such practices as breath-control and the withdrawal of the mind from the objects of the world.

Swadhyaya Yagna: This means study and understanding of the scriptures without which no progress in spiritual practices is possible. It also implies introspection.

Jnana Yagna: It is that activity in man by which he renounces all his ignorance into the fire of knowledge kindled by him in him. This has two aspects - negation of the false and assertion of the real nature of the Self. These two activities are undertaken during the seeker's meditation.

All these five methods of self-development can be practiced only by him who is sincere and consistent in his practices.

apaane juhwati praanam praane'paanam tathaa'pare
praanaapaana gatee ruddhwaa praanaayaamaparaayanaah
// 4.29 //

OTHERS OFFER AS SACRIFICE THE OUT-GOING BREATH IN THE IN-COMING AND THE IN-COMING IN THE

OUT-GOING, RESTRAINING THE COURSES OF THE OUT-GOING AND IN-COMING BREATHS, SOLELY ABSORBED IN THE RESTRAINT OF BREATH.

Sri Krishna explains here Pranayama as another technique for self-control. Pranayama consists of three processes viz.

- Puraka: process of filling in the breath
- Rechaka: process of blowing out the breath
- Kumbhaka: process of holding the breath for some time.

Puraka and Rechaka are alternated by an interval of Kumbhaka. This process of Puraka-Kumbhaka-Rechaka-Kumbhaka-Puraka when practiced in the prescribed manner becomes the method of Pranayama. Pranayama is referred to here as a Yagna where the practitioner offers all the five subsidiary Pranas into the main Prana. Prana does not merely mean breath. It indicates the various manifested activities of life in a living body.

Generally five different Pranas are enumerated corresponding to different functions in every living body viz.

- function of perception - prana
- function of excretion - apana
- function of digestion and assimilation - samana
- circulatory system which distributes food to all parts of the body - vyana and
- capacity of a living creature to improve himself in his mental outlook and intellectual life - udana.

These activities of life are brought under the perfect control of the individual through the process of Pranayama so that a seeker can gain capacity to withdraw completely all his perceptions of the outer world for gaining the knowledge of the Self.

apare niyataahaaraah praanaan praaneshu juhwati
sarve'pyete yajnavido yajnakshapita kalmashaah // 4.30 //

OTHERS, HAVING THEIR FOOD REGULATED, OFFER THE VITAL FORCES IN THE VITAL FORCES. ALL OF THEM ARE KNOWERS OF THE SACRIFICE, WHOSE SINS ARE DESTROYED BY SACRIFICE.

In the series of techniques enumerated by Sri Krishna this is the last method. There are some, who through systematic regulation of their diet, come to gain complete mastery over themselves.

Those, who know the art of living these techniques, weaken the functions of the organs of action and thereby control their passions and appetites leading to purification of the mind and destruction of sins for achieving the goal of Self-knowledge.

In the above mentioned twelve different types of Yagna techniques self-effort is a common factor. The yajnas are only the means to enable the mind-intellect equipment to adjust itself better for meditation. Meditation is the only path through which the ego withdraws from false evaluation of itself for achieving spiritual growth.

yajnashishtaamritabhujo yaanti brahma sanaatanam
naayam loko'styayajnasya kuto'nyah kurusattama // 4.31 //

THE EATERS OF THE NECTAR - THE REMNANT OF THE SACRIFICE - GO TO THE ETERNAL BRAHMAN. THIS WORLD

IS NOT FOR THE NON-PERFORMER OF THE SACRIFICE; HOW THEN THE OTHER WORLD, O BEST OF THE KURUS?

'Eating the nectar - the remnant of the sacrifice' means the result of the above mentioned twelve types of Yagnas. The result of performing any one of the above Yagnas is a greater amount of self-control and the consequent inner integration of the individual personality for the purpose of intense meditation. Such an integrated person will have greater inner poise in his meditations through which he comes to experience the Infinite and the Eternal indicated by the term 'Brahman'.

Self-development and inner growth cannot be had without sincere self-effort. Therefore, Sri Krishna exclaims how one could hope to achieve the highest without sincere effort when even in this world nothing great can be obtained without selfless and dedicated activity.

evam bahuvidhaa yajnaa vitataa brahmano mukhe
karmajaan viddhi taan sarvaan evam jnaatwaa vimokshyase // 4.32 //

THUS INNUMERABLE SACRIFICES LIE SPREAD OUT BEFORE BRAHMAN - LITERALLY AT THE MOUTH OR FACE OF BRAHMAN - KNOW THEM ALL AS BORN OF ACTION AND THUS KNOWING, YOU SHALL BE LIBERATED.

When twelve different Yagnas differing from one another have been described a doubt arises as to whether these different paths lead to the same goal or produce different effects. It is clarified here that all of them lead to the same goal - innumerable sacrifices lie spread out before Brahman.

Another doubt as to the origin of the theory of Yagnas is clarified by interpreting the same line of the verse to mean the various Yagnas lie strewn about at the door of the Vedas giving authenticity to the idea.

It is also urged that the paths prescribed are to be achieved through self effort and hence the inevitability of right action accomplished through the activities of the body, speech and mind.

These activities cannot be attributed to the Self as the Self is actionless. Thus if one realizes that these are not my (Self) actions and I (Self) am actionless and detached he will be freed from the worldly bondage.

As compared with these sacrifices which are the means to attain inner integration, knowledge (considered as a sacrifice) is being extolled in the next verse.

WISDOM AND WORK

shreyan dravyamayaadyajnaaj jnaanayajnah parantapa
sarvam karmaakhilam paartha jnaane parisamaapyate // 4.33 //

SUPERIOR IS THE KNOWLEDGE-SACRIFICE TO ALL MATERIAL SACRIFICES, O PARANTAPA. ALL ACTIONS IN THEIR ENTIRETY, O PARTHA, CULMINATE IN WISDOM.

Sri Krishna explains that Gnana Yagna, the offering of our ignorance into the Fire of Knowledge - acquired and experienced- is the noblest of all the activities. Compared with the formalistic ritualism with material offerings (Dravya Yagna), Gnana Yagna - destroying the misunderstanding in the fire of right understanding - is superior because sacrifices with material objects produce only material results while the Knowledge of the Self, Brahman, ends desire, the source of all activity and therefore all actions get themselves fulfilled. Hence Sri Krishna says 'all actions in their entirety culminate in Knowledge'. The goal is the life giving wisdom, which gives us freedom of action and liberation from the bondage of work.

HOW DOES ONE GAIN THAT EXALTED KNOWLEDGE?

tadviddhi pranipaatena pariprashnena sevayaa
upadekshyanti te jnaanam jnaaninas tattwadarshinah // 4.34 //

LEARN IT BY PROSTRATION, BY INQUIRY AND BY SERVICE. THE WISE WHO HAVE REALIZED THE TRUTH WILL TEACH YOU IN THAT KNOWLEDGE.

The method of gaining the Knowledge by which all actions get exhausted is told here. The verse explains the qualities of a teacher who alone can give guidance on the Path of Knowledge. It also prescribes the mental attitude and intellectual approach that a student should possess for having an effective and rewarding Guru-Sishya relationship.

The student acquires knowledge of the Self by:

- Prostration: It is not only the show of physical surrender by prostration before the Master by the student but an intellectual attitude of humility, reverence and obedience when he approaches the teacher for receiving instructions. The student should exhibit readiness to understand, grasp and follow the Master's instructions.

- Inquiry: The student should be ever ready to raise doubts about bondage and liberation and about knowledge and ignorance etc. and have them clarified from the Teacher within the limits of devotion and respect. Discussions between the teacher and the taught bring forth the best from the teacher which gets transferred to the student.
- Service: Service does not imply any physical service or offering of material objects but it means the attunement of the student to the principles of life advised to him by the Master.

The qualifications of a fully useful teacher are:

- perfect knowledge of the Scriptures and
- a subjective experience of the Infinite Reality.

Sri Krishna means to say that mere theoretical knowledge, however perfect, does not qualify a person to be a Guru. The Truth or Brahman must be realized before one can claim that most elevated position. That knowledge alone which is imparted by those who have full personal enlightenment can prove effective and not any other because he who has no subjective experience of what is taught cannot understand the inner meaning of the scriptures just as a spoon cannot have any idea of the soup. This verse makes out that in spiritual life faith comes first, then knowledge and then experience.

RESULT OF KNOWLEDGE

yajjnaatwaa na punarmoham evam yaasyasi paandava
yena bhootaanyasheshena drakshyasyaatmanyatho mayi // 4.35 //

KNOWING THAT, O PANDAVA, YOU WILL NOT AGAIN GET DELUDED LIKE THIS: AND BY THAT YOU WILL SEE ALL BEINGS IN YOUR OWN SELF AND ALSO IN ME.

Sri Krishna declares that after gaining the Knowledge of Brahman (referred to in the previous verse, to be learnt from the Guru) one will be able to recognize the entire creation, constituted of the world of objects, emotions and ideas, as nothing but the Self which is none other than 'Me', The Lord, The Paramatman, just as having recognized the ocean, all the waves are recognized as nothing but the ocean itself. The Self and the Lord are identical. All beings too are identical with the immortal Self; through ignorance they appear as separate.

Meaning thereby, that having received the true knowledge from a teacher one will realize the identity of the individual Self and God and he will not be subject to any confusion again like Arjuna. Here the confusion of Arjuna refers to his despondency about killing of his kith and kin assembled on the battlefield.

api chedasi paapebhyah sarvebhyah paapakrittamah
sarvam jnaanaplavenaiva vrijinam santarishyasi // 4.36 //

EVEN IF YOU ARE THE MOST SINFUL OF ALL SINNERS, YET YOU SHALL VERILY CROSS ALL SINS BY THE RAFT OF KNOWLEDGE.

Gita, being a scripture for living, says here that even if one is the most sinful among the entire sinful, one can attain salvation and cross the world of imperfections through the Knowledge of the Self.

Sin is an act of ego forgetting its own divine nature. It is an act indulged in by man in his delusion catering to his baser instincts with the hope of achieving bliss. To rediscover that our ego is nothing other than the Self in us and to live thereafter as the Self of all is called true wisdom - Jnana. Having thus realized one's own true nature, the material objects do not have any attraction to such an individual.

HOW DOES KNOWLEDGE DESTROY SIN?

yathaidhaamsi samiddho'gnir bhasmasaat kurute'rjuna
jnaanaagnih sarvakarmaani bhasmasaat kurute tathaa // 4.37 //

AS THE BLAZING FIRE REDUCES PIECES OF WOOD TO ASHES, O ARJUNA, SO DOES THE FIRE OF KNOWLEDGE REDUCES ALL ACTIONS TO ASHES.

As the fuel pieces, irrespective of their quality, shape, size etc., will be reduced to one homogeneous mass of ash in the Yagna fire, all Karmas, good, bad or indifferent, get burnt up in the Fire of Knowledge and will become something different from what they were in their cause and effect condition. When the Knowledge of the Self dawns, all actions and their results cannot bring man into this world again for the enjoyment of fruits of his actions. This is reducing actions to ashes. When there is full enlightenment i.e. no idea of agency or doership and no desire for the fruits of actions, then action is no action at all as it loses all its potency.

Actions leave reactions in the form of residual impressions which mature at different periods of time depending upon the quality and intensity of the action. There are three kinds of Karmas or actions or fructification of past actions Viz.

- Prarabhdha - so much of the past actions that have given rise to the present birth (operative).
- Sanchita - the balance of past actions that will give rise to future births (not yet operative)
- Agami - the actions done in the present life (to be operative in the future).

The Fire of Knowledge cannot bring about the results of all actions except the Prarabdha which have already started producing effects.

na hi jnaanena sadrisham pavitram iha vidyate
tat swayam yogasamsiddhah kaalenaatmani vindati // 4.38 //

CERTAINLY, THERE IS NO PURIFIER IN THIS WORLD LIKE KNOWLEDGE. A MAN WHO HAS BECOME PERFECT IN YOGA FINDS IT WITHIN HIMSELF IN COURSE OF TIME.

There exists no purifier equal to knowledge of the Self. He who has attained perfection by the constant practice of Karma Yoga and Meditation will find knowledge of the Self in himself after some time. The surest means of acquiring this knowledge or wisdom is taught in the next verse.

MEANS OF ACQUIRING KNOWLEDGE

shraddhaavaan labhate jnaanam tatparah samyatendriyah
jnaanam labdhvaa paraam shaantim achirenaadhigacchati // 4.39 //

THE MAN WHO IS FULL OF FAITH, WHO IS DEVOTED TO IT AND WHO HAS SUBDUED ALL THE SENSES, OBTAINS THIS

KNOWLEDGE; AND HAVING OBTAINED KNOWLEDGE HE GOES AT ONCE TO THE SUPREME PEACE.

The three qualities that are necessary for an individual to be assured of the Knowledge Divine are enumerated here. Faith, devotion and self-control are the three imperative necessities to be acquired before one hopes to evolve to a diviner stature.

Faith (Sraddha): This is not blind belief or unquestioned acceptance of any declaration said to be divine. Faith indicates that by which an individual understands readily the exact import of the scriptural text as well as the words of advice of the teacher.

Devotion (Tatparah): The seeker must give his undivided attention to the path of self-development chosen by him and must on all occasions maintain in his mind a continuous consciousness of the Divine.

Self-control (Samyatendriyah): It is the sense organs that cause mental agitations and come in the way of maintaining oneself quietly in the higher values of life. Therefore, a seeker should learn to live in steady and constant sense-control.

The seeker who follows the above agenda of life reaches the state of Knowledge having attained which he soon reaches the Supreme Peace or the Supreme Joy, the goal of life. All activities in this world are undertaken to achieve better happiness or joy. So the goal of life is absolute happiness where all strife ends, all desires fulfilled and agitations exhausted. Sri Krishna indicates here that such a state of Supreme Peace is attained by acquiring the Divine Knowledge.

ajnashchaashraddhaadhaanashcha samshayaatmaa vinashyati
naayam loko'sti na paro na sukham samshayaatmanah // 4.40 //

THE IGNORANT, THE FAITHLESS, THE DOUBTING SELF GOES TO DESTRUCTION; THERE IS NEITHER THIS WORLD NOR THE OTHER NOR HAPPINESS FOR THE DOUBTING SOUL.

In the previous verse it was said that those who have faith and knowledge would soon reach the Supreme Peace. Sri Krishna repeats the same idea through a negative statement in this verse. Those who do not have these qualities will get themselves ultimately destroyed and completely ruined. He who has no Knowledge of the Self (ignorant), who has no faith in his own self, in the scriptures and in the teachings of his Guru (faithless) and who is of a doubting disposition because of which fails to enjoy this world on account of his suspicion about the people and things around him and who has innumerable doubts as regards the other world will not find any joy anywhere - neither here nor in the hereafter.

yogasannyasta karmaanam jnaanasamchhinnasamshayam
aatmavantam na karmaani nibadhnanti dhananjaya // 4.41 //

ACTIONS DO NOT BIND THE ONE, WHO HAS RENOUNCED THEM THROUGH YOGA, WHOSE DOUBTS HAVE BEEN FULLY DISPELLED BY KNOWLEDGE AND WHO IS POISED IN THE SELF, O DHANANJAYA.

This verse is the summary of all the main secrets of life explained in this Chapter. It is only egoistic activities, motivated by egocentric desires that leave gross impressions in the inner personalities of men and bind them to reap their reactions.

When an individual learns to renounce his attachments to the fruits of his actions, righteous or unrighteous, through Yoga and yet works on in perfect detachment and when all his doubts about the goal of life have been removed through Self-Knowledge, the ego comes to realize that it is none other than Atman, the Self. When such a person works, his actions do not bind him. The mutual relationship of true work, wisdom and self-discipline is brought out here.

Tasmaad ajnaanasambhootam hritstham jnaanaasinaatmanah
chhittwainam samshayam yogamaatishthottishtha bhaarata // 4.42 //

THEREFORE, WITH THE SWORD OF KNOWLEDGE (OF THE HE SELF) CUT ASUNDER THE DOUBT ABOUT THE SELF BORN OF IGNORANCE, RESIDING IN YOUR HEART AND TAKE REFUGE IN YOGA, ARISE O BHARATA!

Sri Krishna advises Arjuna in this last verse of the Chapter to perform action with the help of knowledge and concentration. The knowledge referred to here is the knowledge by which one discriminates between the body and the Self and which consequently destroys grief and delusion.

The doubt in his heart whether it is better to fight or abstain is the product of ignorance. It will be destroyed by wisdom. Then he will know what is right for him to do. It is a call to every seeker to get up and act well in the spirit of Yagna and gain inner purity, so that he can experience the Supreme Peace which is the final goal of evolution.

om tat sat iti srimad bhagavadgeetaasu upanishatsu brahma vidyaayaam yogashaastre sri krishnaarjuna samvaade jnaana karma sanyaasa yogo naama chaturtho'dhyaayah ||

THUS IN THE UPANISHADS OF THE GLORIOUS BHAGAVAD GITA, THE SCIENCE OF THE ETERNAL, THE SCRIPTURE OF YOGA, THE DIALOGUE BETWEEN SRI KRISHNA AND ARJUNA, ENDS THE FOURTH DISCOURSE ENTITLED THE YOGA OF RENUNCIATION OF ACTION IN KNOWLEDGE

AN OUTLINE VIEW OF THIS CHAPTER

The fourth chapter shows the state of development in a seeker after having followed the course of Karma Yoga prescribed in the last chapter. When a seeker constantly practices the different types of Yajnas suggested in this chapter he gains wisdom. With the dawn of wisdom a seeker begins to develop renunciation. The next chapter covers this aspect of spiritual progress and connects it to Chapter 6 in which meditation and realization of the Self have been expounded.

I - SELF IS ETERNAL TEACHER - VERSES 1 – 10

A Guru can impart the knowledge of the Self to the extent that he has unfolded the Self within. Only a fully enlightened person becomes the real spiritual master. Krishna was one such master. He declares that the Self-realized souls have been emerging periodically from time immemorial whenever dharma (righteousness) declined and adharma (un-righteousness) prevailed in the world. These great masters protect the virtuous, destroy the wicked and re-establish dharma. The maintenance of dharma had been lost by efflux of time.

II - HOW SELF RELATES TO ACTION? - VERSES 11 -18

The Self is the primeval cause of all actions. No being can act without Self. Nevertheless, the Self remains immaculate, untainted by the actions which it enlivens. Though the Self causes all beings to act, It does not interfere with the mode and quality of actions performed. Nor is It affected in any way by the result of actions. The wise regard the Self as the inactive principle catalyzing all sorts of actions, be they good or evil, secular or spiritual. Realizing the true nature of the Self thus, they become one with It.

III - ACTIONS OF ENLIGHTENED NOT BINDING - VERSES 19 – 24

The enlightened sages, having merged with the Self, become free from desire and expectation. Ever content, never depending on anything, expecting nothing, they live a life of perfect detachment, totally liberated from all worldly entanglements. Even as these perfected souls keep acting, their actions do not bind them to this world. They are free from sin, suffering and sorrow.

IV - THE TWELVE YAJNAS (SACRIFICES) - VERSES 25 – 30

Yajna in the ancient past merely meant the ritual of fire worship by kindling the flames with the offerings of the people. Krishna gives a new interpretation to the word Yajna to mean the conversion of human day to day activities into worship. The cycle of human activity starts with the receipt of stimuli from the world at large by the organs of perception, which turn into reaction in mind and intellect, and returns as a response back into the world through the organs of action. This entire cycle has been split into twelve main activities, each of them turned into a ritual, worship, a Yajna. Those who understand this and make their daily activities a practice of these yajnas will free themselves of the vasanas / desires.

V - ALL YAJNAS CULMINATE IN WISDOM - VERSES 31 – 37

By converting activities into Yajna (worship) a seeker drops his vasanas and gradually gains knowledge of the Self. The uppermost of all yajnas is jnana yajna, the yajna of Wisdom. A seeker should prepare himself to obtain the knowledge of the Self from a Guru through devotion, enquiry and service. This knowledge destroys all desires and agitations and removes forever his delusion that the world is real.

VI - KRISHNA'S ADVICE TO GAIN WISDOM - Verses 38 – 42

The knowledge of Self purifies the mind of all agitations and gives supreme Peace. Those devoted to Self, control their senses and pursue the knowledge of Self with consistency until they reach it. The ignorant, ever doubtful of the Self, lack steadiness of purpose. They will not achieve anything in this world or the next nor will they find any enduring happiness. Krishna, therefore, advises Arjuna to gain knowledge and remove all doubts and delusion and thus become established in the supreme Self.

<<<000>>>

CHAPTER 5

Karma Sannyaasa Yogah:

Yoga of Renunciation of Action

PREAMBLE

Arjuna doubts which of the two ways - whether renunciation of action or participation in action - is the nobler and the greater. To Arjuna action meant ritualism and renunciation meant a total retirement from everything and running away to a place of solitude. Sri Krishna attempts here to give deeper insights to these oft misunderstood terms. The Lord propounds the theory of self-development in three stages viz. through desire-prompted activities, through desireless activities and through pure meditation.

Having practiced the Yajnas prescribed in the preceding chapter and gained wisdom, a seeker sheds his vasanas / desires and develops a dispassion for the world. He enters into a state of renunciation, an essential pre-requisite for practicing meditation. This chapter elucidates this stage of development preliminary to meditation and realization.

This Chapter answers the questions: What is the spirit of renunciation? How the Yoga of renunciation of action can be practiced? What are its effects on the human personality? Thus this Chapter deals with both Action and Knowledge and is therefore a link between Karma Yoga and Pure Meditation.

In the opening verse of the chapter Arjuna asks Krishna to advise him conclusively as to which is better of the two – the path of action or the path of renunciation. Krishna clarifies the doubt by explaining the three distinct stages of spiritual growth. A seeker embarking on his spiritual journey with vasanas / desires is termed Yogi. Through Karma Yoga, the path of action, he sheds the bulk of his vasanas. As he does so, he becomes dispassionate towards the world and becomes an ascetic, a Sanyasi. A Sanyasi following the path of knowledge practices contemplation and meditation until he reaches the ultimate state of realization to become a Jnani, an enlightened soul. Both Karma Yogi and Sanyasi reach the supreme goal. Thus, one takes up either the path of action or the path of renunciation according to one's basic nature.

The above three types of individuals (Karma Yogi, Sanyasi, Jnani) relate differently to action. The enlightened one, the Jnani, having merged with the Self, realizes that the Self does not act at all. In and through all actions, external and internal, the Jnani remains a silent witness while the senses contact the sense objects. The Sanyasi, in his state of dispassion, dedicates all his actions to Brahman. He acts without any attachment. Consequently, his actions are not sinful and do not leave a residue of vasanas / desires. Such a person, like a lotus leaf in water, remains in the world, but detached from and unaffected by it. The Karma Yogi, the one at the beginning of the spiritual journey, detaches himself from worldly entanglements and directs all his physical, mental and intellectual activities towards his own self purification.

THE TEXT

arjuna uvaacha
sannyaasam karmanaam krishna punar yogam cha shamsasi
yacchreya etayorekam tanme broohi sunishchitam // 5.1 //

ARJUNA SAID
RENUNCIATION OF ACTIONS, O KRISHNA, YOU PRAISE AND AGAIN YOGA, PERFORMANCE OF ACTIONS. TELL ME CONCLUSIVELY THAT WHICH IS BETTER OF THE TWO.

In Chapter IV, verses 18, 19, 21, 22, 24, 32, 33, 37 and 41 The Lord has spoken of the renunciation of all actions and in the verse 42 He exhorted Arjuna to engage in Yoga, the performance of action. Owing to the mutual contradiction between these two injunctions, action or renunciation, as they cannot be followed by the same individual at the same time, Arjuna asks Sri Krishna to indicate decisively that one path which will lead to spiritual welfare.

sri bhagavaan uvaacha
sannyaasaah Karma Yogashcha nihshreyasakaraa vubhau
tayostu karmasannyaasaat karmayogo vishishyate // 5.2 //

SRI BHAGAVAN SAID
RENUNCIATION OF ACTION AND YOGA OF ACTION BOTH LEAD TO THE HIGHEST GOOD; BUT OF THE TWO, PERFORMANCE OF ACTION IS SUPERIOR TO THE RENUNCIATION OF ACTION.

Man is essentially prone to be inert and inactive. He prefers to get the maximum benefit from the outside world with the minimum exertion. From this stage of utter inactivity he goes to the first stage where he works because of the promptings of his desires; the second stage of his evolution is from the desire motivated activities to dedicated activities in the service of others with the least ego. In this stage when the ego is subordinated his vasanas get exhausted and mind becomes pure. With the purity of mind he reaches the third stage where he meditates for realizing the ultimate goal of joy and peace.

Thus the spiritual path of self-evolution falls into three stages viz. a) desire prompted activities b) selfless dedicated activities and c) meditation.

The first - Karma Yoga - was dealt with in Chapters III and IV while the technique of Meditation will be taken up in Chapter VI.

This Chapter deals with as to how one can renounce the desire oriented ego-centric actions and take up selfless dedicated activities. In this Chapter, Yoga means Karma Yoga and Sankhya means the intellectual way with renunciation of works.

The Lord says renunciation of action (Karma Sanyas) and performance of action (Karma Yoga) both lead to the liberation or the highest bliss. Yet of these, performance of action is much better than renunciation of action without the knowledge of the Self. However, it will be seen later that renunciation of action with the knowledge of the Self is decidedly superior to performance of action without such knowledge.

jneyah sa nityasannyaasi yo na dweshti na kaangkshati
nirdwandwo hi mahaabaaho sukham bandhaat pramuchyate
// 5.3 //

HE SHOULD BE KNOWN AS A PERPETUAL SANYASI (AS CONSTANTLY PRACTICING RENUNCIATION) WHO NEITHER HATES NOR DESIRES; FOR, FREE FROM THE PAIRS OF OPPOSITES, O MIGHTY ARMED, HE IS EASILY SET FREE FROM BONDAGE.

According to The Lord he is a true Sanyasi who 'neither likes nor dislikes'. Likes and dislikes, gain and loss, honor and dishonor, praise and censure, success and failure, joy and sorrow and similar other pairs of opposites are the attitudes of mind by which it gains life's experiences.

The Karma Yogi, a true worker, is known as a *nitya sanyasi* or a true renouncer, for he does his work in a detached spirit without being influenced by the pairs of opposites. A man does not become a Sanyasi merely by giving up actions for whatever reason. One need not take Sanyasa formally; if he has the mental frame of renunciation of egoism and desires he is a true Sanyasi. Mere physical renunciation of objects is no renunciation at all.

KNOWLEDGE AND ACTION ARE ONE

saankhyayogau prithagbaalaah pravadanti na panditaah
ekam apyaasthitah samyag ubhayor vindate phalam //5. 4 //

CHILDREN, NOT THE WISE, SPEAK OF SANKHYA (KNOWLEDGE) AND YOGA (YOGA OF ACTION) AS DISTINCT; HE WHO IS TRULY ESTABLISHED IN ONE OBTAINS THE FRUITS OF BOTH.

This verse clarifies that there is no contradiction between the paths of Sankhya (knowledge) and Yoga (action).

There are two ways of making an ordinary action into a divine action of dedication and worship viz.

1. By renouncing the idea of agency or doership in every action or
2. By performing actions without any anxiety for their fruits and maintaining equanimity in success and failure.

The former is called Sankhya method and the latter is Karma Yoga.

The Lord says that only the ignorant people (here referred to as children) who have no knowledge of the Self find a contradiction between the two methods. But the wise who have lived through either of the paths say that both the paths lead to the same goal viz. liberation or God consciousness.

HOW TO OBTAIN THE RESULTS OF BOTH BY FOLLOWING ONE PATH?

yatsaankhyaih praapyate sthaanam tad yogair api gamyate
ekam saankhyam cha yogam cha yah pashyati sa pashyati // 5.5 //

THE STATE (OF LIBERATION) REACHED BY THE SANKHYAS (GNANIS) IS REACHED BY THE YOGINS (KARMA YOGINS). HE TRULY 'SEES', WHO 'SEES' SANKHYA (KNOWLEDGE) AND YOGA (PERFORMANCE OF ACTION) AS ONE.

Sri Krishna emphasizes that the goal reached by the Sankhya method is also reached by those who practice Karma technique. Those who have renounced the world and immersed themselves in the knowledge are the Sankhyas. Through *Sravana* (hearing of Vedantic texts). *Manana* (reflecting on what is heard) and *Nidhidhyasana* (profound meditation) they attain liberation directly. The Karma Yogis who engage in selfless service, who perform their actions as offerings to The Lord, also reach the same state as is attained by the Sankhyas indirectly through purification of the heart, renunciation and the consequent realization of the knowledge of the Self.

He who sees that Sankhya and Yoga are one and that both lead to the same goal, is the one who really understands the Truth of the Vedas.

It is to be noted that Karma Yogins perform actions, surrendering the result to God, attain purity of mind and thus qualify themselves for the path of knowledge i.e. Sankhya, the path of knowledge, through which the final experience of Bliss is achieved. Thus both ultimately produce the same result, viz. liberation through Self-Knowledge.

RENUNCIATION SUCCEEDS ACTION

sannyaasastu mahaabaaho duhkham aaptumayogatah
yogayukto munir brahma na chirenaadhigacchati // 5.6 //

BUT RENUNCIATION OF ACTION, O MIGHTY ARMED, IS HARD TO ATTAIN WITHOUT PERFORMANCE OF ACTION (YOGA); THE SAGE PURIFIED BY DEVOTION TO ACTION, QUICKLY REACHES BRAHMAN.

The Lord means that the method of performance of action is easier for a beginner and qualifies him for the higher path by purifying his mind. Hence it is the proper and therefore the superior course, specifically for such beginners. Without performing action the renunciation of action is impossible.

Mind gets purified by performing right actions which enables one to have a deeper meditation leading to renunciation of all activities. If this process is cut short and activities are renounced in the beginning itself it will amount to physical inactivity where the purity of mind and meditative power cannot be gained.

One who is engaged in selfless and unattached activities develops single pointed meditative power. He is called a Muni (sage) who will reach the Supreme experience of the Self in him before long. A sage, purified by the performance of selfless action, soon attains Brahman.

The true renouncer is not he who remains completely inactive but he whose work is done in a spirit of detachment. Renunciation is a mental attitude, the casting off of desire in work; true work is work with all desire renounced.

yogayukto vishuddhaatmaa vijitaatmaa jitendriyah
sarvabhootaatmabhootaatmaa kurvannapi na lipyate // 5.7 //

WITH THE MIND PURIFIED BY DEVOTION TO PERFORMANCE OF ACTION, AND THE BODY CONQUERED AND SENSES SUBDUED, HE WHO REALIZES HIS SELF, AS THE SELF OF ALL BEINGS, IS NOT TAINTED THOUGH HE IS ACTING.

Sri Krishna explains the different stages of development and change that would take place in an individual through Karma Yoga. One who is established in Karma Yoga gets his intellect purified which reduces agitations caused by desires or emotions from within. With the selfless action and no anxiety for the fruits, his intellect becomes immune from disturbances which are reflected in his mind.

When a man gains inward peace at intellectual and mental levels, it becomes easy for him to control his sense organs from their tendency to run after sense objects. A seeker who controls his body, mind and intellect in this manner is qualified for the highest meditation because all the stumbling blocks for purposeful meditation arise from desire-motivation and emotional agitation. If these obstacles are removed, meditation becomes natural and the rediscovery of the Self is easier to achieve.

This realization of the Self is complete and not partial. He sees the divinity of the Self as all pervading. He finds divinity everywhere at all times. Hence The Lord says 'realizes one's own self as the Self in all beings'.

When an individual after achieving the inner change comes to realize the Infinite Divinity and performs actions in the world, his actions cannot have any reactions on him because no sense of ego is left in him. This verse highlights that it is the desire motivated egocentric activities alone that create vasanas in the intellect which block the discriminative power to experience one's own essential nature of Eternal Divinity.

naiva kinchit karomeeti yukto manyeta tattwavit
pashyan shrunvan sprishan jighrann ashnan gacchan swapan shwasan / 5.8/

pralapan visrijan grihnan nunmishan nimishannapi
indriyaaneendriyaartheshu vartanta iti dhaarayan // 5.9 //

THE KNOWER OF THE TRUTH, BEING CENTERED IN THE SELF, THINKS 'I DO NOTHING AT ALL' - THOUGH SEEING, HEARING, TOUCHING, SMELLING, EATING, GOING, SLEEPING, BREATHING, SPEAKING, LETTING GO, SEIZING, OPENING AND CLOSING THE EYES - CONVINCED THAT IT IS THE SENSES THAT MOVE AMONG THE SENSE OBJECTS.

It is explained that a man of wisdom will not have any egoism even in the common, natural and unavoidable activities of the world, where he happens to live like eating, sleeping, breathing, speaking, closing and opening of eyes etc.

He remains as a witness to all the activities of the senses, endowed with the knowledge of the actionless Self, with an 'I do nothing at all' feeling. He identifies himself with the Self and sees inaction in action for he realizes that in all works the senses occupy themselves with their objects and the Self remains inactive. He may be said to have renounced action, for he sees no action as performed by himself.

brahmanyaadhaaya karmaani sangam tyaktwaa karoti yah
lipyate na sa paapena padmapatram ivaambhasaa // 5.10 //

HE WHO PERFORMS ACTIONS, OFFERING THEM TO BRAHMAN, ABANDONING ATTACHMENT IS NOT TAINTED BY SIN, JUST AS A LOTUS LEAF REMAINS UNAFFECTED BY THE WATER ON IT.

A life of detachment where one renounces the sense of doership is not easy to attain. This verse instructs us how to live the Gita way rather than talk about it i.e. how to lead a life of intelligent detachment. One should be clear that total detachment is impossible for the human mind. So long as there is a mind it has to attach itself with something because that is its very nature. The only practical way of achieving detachment therefore is to disassociate the mind from the false and attach it to the Real.

The advice given is to surrender the sense of Agency and do the actions without egoism and attachment to their fruits, considering all actions as offerings to The Lord. The more the thoughts on The Lord the less will be the attention on one's own ego. Once this is realized, the actions of the body, mind and intellect will not leave any impression on the Self. Such a yogi has no attachment even for liberation.

Having thus realized the Self the Yogi lives in the world of objects with perfect detachment like the lotus leaf existing in the water without getting itself moistened. The sage lives in the world of objects detaching himself from his own perceptions of the world, likes and dislikes etc.

kaayena manasaa buddhyaa kevalair indriyairapi
yoginah karma kurvanti sangam tyaktwaatmashuddhaye // 5.11 //

YOGIS PERFORM ACTIONS ONLY WITH THE BODY, MIND, INTELLECT AND THE SENSES WITHOUT ATTACHMENT, FOR THE PURIFICATION OF THE HEART.

The Karma Yogis always utilize their organs of action, knowledge, mind and intellect renouncing all attachments. The sage remains as if he were a mere observer of all that is happening around him.

The Karma yogis are those who are devoted to the path of action, free from egoism and selfishness, who work for the purification of their hearts without any attachment to the results of their actions and who dedicate all their actions to The Lord as their offering.

yuktah karmaphalam tyaktwaa shaantim aapnoti naishthikeem
ayuktah kaamakaarena phale sakto nibadhyate // 5.12 //

A SELFLESS MAN WHO HAS RENOUNCED THE FRUIT OF HIS ACTION ATTAINS PEACE, BORN OF STEADFASTNESS; BUT THE ONE, WHO IS NOT SELFLESS, LED BY DESIRE, IS ATTACHED TO THE FRUIT OF ACTION AND THEREFORE BOUND.

The harmonious man who does actions for the sake of The Lord without expectation of the results and who considers all his actions as offerings to The Lord only and not for any personal gain or profit attains peace arising out of steadfastness or devotion. Steadfastness is achieved through the following four stages of development viz.

- purity of mind
- gaining of knowledge
- renunciation of action
- steadiness in wisdom.

Peace is not a product of external origin but it is a mental condition in an individual when he is not agitated by any kind of disturbing thoughts. Peace is an unbroken feeling of joy and a symbol of an integrated personality. Sri Bhagavan says that this can be brought about through selfless actions undertaken in a spirit of Yagna. When a worker renounces his egocentric sense of agency and desire for the fruits of his actions he immediately becomes an integrated personality and experiences peace.

The one who is unbalanced or unharmonised, who is motivated by desire and attachment to the fruits of actions and who is full of egoism and sense of agency gets himself bound and tortured by the reactions of his own actions.

Sri Krishna explains the spirit of renunciation and the state of Supreme Being in more details. The Self, Atman, though the primeval cause of all actions, is not at all liable for either the merit or demerit accruing from them. Though the Self enlivens the actions of all beings, it is neither the actor nor the action nor is it responsible for the fruits of action. Those ignorant of this relationship remain deluded in the world. But he whose ignorance has been removed by knowledge of the Self reaches the Supreme state from where there is no return. Thereafter, he maintains a universal vision of oneness and evenness towards everything he comes across in the world. Having reached that eternal state he has forever transcended the cycle of birth and death.

The Lord advises that renunciation precedes meditation and realization. Sensual enjoyments arising out of external contacts have a diminishing value and they culminate in sorrow. The very sight of sense objects inflames desires in people. Then they lose control and succumb to the lure of the sense objects. The wise understand the ephemeral nature of contact-born enjoyments and prevent any desire from developing into an uncontrollable force of momentum. Instead of indulging in such temporary bouts of sensual pleasure they divert their attention and interest to the Self within. Thus they free themselves gradually from desires, subdue their mind and turn introvert. They begin to revel in the bliss of the Self. When the mind is subdued and relatively peaceful it becomes fit for meditation. This chapter concludes with a few procedural details for practicing meditation and realizing the ultimate Self in oneself.

THE ENLIGHTENED SELF

sarvakarmaani manasaa sannyasyaaste sukham vashee
navadwaare pure dehee naiva kurvan na kaarayan // 5.13 //

MENTALLY RENOUNCING ALL ACTIONS AND FULLY SUBDUING HIS SENSES, THE EMBODIED SOUL DWELLS HAPPILY IN THE CITY OF NINE-GATES, NEITHER ACTING NOR CAUSING OTHERS (BODY AND THE SENSES) TO ACT.

Sanyas is not a mere physical escapism but a mental withdrawal from things which have no real significance. It is a state of mind and not an external symbol. Therefore one who has brought all his sense cravings under perfect control and renounced all his egocentric and desire prompted actions comes to live in peace, joy and contentment in the city of nine gates. City of nine gates means the body which has nine apertures in its physical form viz. two eyes, two ears, two nostrils, one mouth, the genital and the excretory outlet without which life cannot be sustained. The Self within this physical structure activates the instruments of action and perception governing the life of all of them though by itself it does not perform any actions. Krishna says that such an individual, always identifying with the Self, observes the activities around him unaffected, unattached and without any agitations. Hence he neither acts nor causes others to act.

All actions in life (Karma) can be categorized as under.

- Nitya Karma - Obligatory duties such as daily prayers.
- Naimittika Karma - Actions to be performed on special occasions such as on birth of a child.

- Kamya Karma - Works intended for securing special ends such as for curing illness etc.
- Nishiddha Karma - Actions forbidden by scriptures like stealing and other crimes.

The enlightened soul refrains from all these actions and lives only for the sake of exhausting the *prarabdha karma* which has caused his present body. He lives happily established in Self-Knowledge. Unlike the ignorant, he does not identify himself with the body which is termed here as the city of nine gates. He neither acts nor causes others to act means that he is totally free from consciousness of 'I' 'me' or 'mine' and is free from the idea of acting or causing action. After the exhaustion of *prarabdha karma* his soul merges in Brahman.

IDEAS OF ACTION, ACTOR ETC, ARE DUE TO MAYA

na kartritwam na karmaani lokasya srijati prabhuh
na karmaphala samyogam swabhaavas tu pravartate // 5.14 //

THE LORD CREATES NEITHER AGENCY NOR ACTIONS FOR THE WORLD, NOR DOES HE BRING ABOUT THE UNION WITH THE FRUITS OF ACTIONS; BUT IT IS NATURE THAT DOES ALL THIS.

This verse gives a general definition of the concept of God. But the principle stated here is not that described in the ritualistic portion of the Vedas but a description of the relationship between the Self and the not-Self, the Atman and the matter.

The Supreme Self *(Prabhuh)* neither creates any sense of agency nor does it initiate any action. It does not match every action with its corresponding fruit.

However when the Self functions through the equipments - physical, mental and causal bodies - It becomes a conditioned Self and gathers to itself all the egocentric attitudes of agency, action and fruits etc.

Thus the beneficiary of the fruits and the performer of actions in us is the ego and not the Atman or the Self. The Self becomes an actor performing all actions only when it gets conditioned by *'Swabhava'*- nature or the Divine Maya made up of the three Gunas. The Self comes under the control of maya and regards itself as acting and enjoying the fruits of action. As long as the Self remains identified with maya it is bound. But when it detaches itself from maya it becomes free. Thus such ideas as those of duty, work and the result belong to the relative world. They have no relevance from the standpoint of the Supreme Lord. It is the Prakriti or nature that does everything.

naadatte kasyachit paapam na chaiva sukritam vibhuh
ajnaanenaavritam jnaanam tena muhyanti jantavah // 5.15 //

NOR DOES THE ALL-PERVADING SPIRIT TAKE ON THE MERIT OR DEMERIT OF ANY. KNOWLEDGE IS ENVELOPED IN IGNORANCE AND HENCE BEINGS GET DELUDED.

The Supreme who is all-pervading (Vibhu) and underlying in all the lives' activities cannot be considered to take note of all the activities that are happening in the finite world. From the point of view of the Infinite, the finite does not exist.

When the sun light passes through a plane glass it comes out clearly but if it passes through a prism it emerges as seven colors which are part and parcel of the same sun light. Similarly the Self passing through Knowledge emerges out as the Self which is all-pervading. But when the same Self passes through ignorance i.e. body, mind and intellect it gets itself split up into the unending world of plurality.

As there is neither day or night from the stand point of the sun, so there is neither virtue nor vice from the standpoint of the Supreme whose nature is Existence-Knowledge - Bliss absolute, *Sat-Chit-Ananda*. Through ignorance man separates himself from the Lord and comes under the spell of ego. Thus he thinks of himself as the agent of various works, good or evil and experiences pleasure and pain accordingly. The law of Karma applies only to the embodied beings in the relative world. When the aspirant becomes free from ignorance and realizes his identity with the Lord, he goes beyond virtue and vice and is not affected by the results of his actions.

Where there is knowledge there is no place for ignorance and where there is ignorance knowledge cannot exist. So the statement that knowledge is enveloped by ignorance means that unveiling of truth is a process of removal of ignorance and not creation of knowledge and therefore it is only a re-discovery.

jnaanena tu tadajnaanam yeshaam naashitamaatmanah
teshaam aadityavajjnaanam prakaashayati tatparam // 5.16 //

BUT TO THOSE WHOSE IGNORANCE IS DESTROYED BY THE KNOWLEDGE OF THE SELF, THAT KNOWLEDGE, LIKE THE SUN, REVEALS THE SUPREME (BRAHMAN).

In the case of ordinary mortals the Self is screened of by ignorance or Avidya whereas the man of realization is the one in whom the ignorance is removed by Knowledge. Ignorance creates the egocentric concept which thrives in the body, mind and intellect and is the root cause of all sufferings. When this ignorance is destroyed by knowledge of the Self, the ego ends and the Self becomes manifest just as the sun illuminates and reveals all the objects of the physical universe when the clouds surrounding it move away.

Knowledge is the very faculty of knowing. So when the ego re-discovers the Self it becomes the Self. Therefore, the Self is awareness, consciousness or the Atman.

RESULT OF KNOWLEDGE OF THE SUPREME

tadbuddhayas tadaatmaanas tannishthaas tatparaayanaah
gacchantyapunaraavrittim jnaana nirdhoota kalmashaah
// 5.17 //

FIXING THEIR MINDS ON HIM, AT ONE WITH HIM, ABIDING IN HIM, REALIZING HIM ALONE AS THE SUPREME GOAL, THEY REACH A STATE, FROM WHICH THERE IS NO RETURN, THEIR SINS HAVING BEEN DESTROYED BY THEIR KNOWLEDGE.

They fix their intellect on the Supreme Self. They feel and realize their identity with the Self. By constant meditation they get established in the Self. The whole world of names and forms cease to exist for them. They live in the Self alone. They have the Self alone as their goal. They rejoice in the Self alone. They are satisfied in the Self alone. Such men never return to this world as their sins or impurities (vasanas) are removed by knowledge.

The import of this verse is that Self-Realization is the final experience in the process of evolution whereby the Soul of an illumined person does not return to the relative world to assume a physical body. He does not come again under the sway of maya.

CHARACTERISTICS OF KNOWLEDGE

vidyaavinaya sampanne braahmane gavi hastini
shuni chaiva shvapaake cha panditaah samadarshinah // 5.18 //

THE WISE SEE THE SAME IN ALL - WHETHER IT BE A BRAHMANA ENDOWED WITH LEARNING AND HUMILITY, OR A COW, OR AN ELEPHANT OR A DOG OR AN OUTCASTE.

The wise see divinity everywhere just as the ocean does not differenciate waves. He finds no distinction in the world of names and forms. The liberated sage has equal vision as he recognizes the Self everywhere.

The Self is not affected by any limiting factors as it is subtle, pure, formless and attributeless just as the sun's rays fall on the river Ganga, on the ocean and on the dirty canal and yet the sun's purity and splendor are not spoilt by the quality of water on which its rays fall. The limiting adjuncts do not affect the Supreme Self just as the outer space is not affected by the pot, cloud etc. The Brahmin is Sattwic, the cow is Rajasic, the elephant, the dog and the down trodden are Tamasic. But the wise see in all of them one homogeneous immortal Self that is not affected by any of the three Gunas. This is the quality of equal mindedness of the wise.

ihaiva tairjitah sargo yeshaam saamye sthitam manah
nirdosham hi samam brahma tasmaad brahmani te sthitaah // 5.19 //

EVEN HERE (ON EARTH) THE CREATED WORLD IS OVERCOME BY THOSE WHOSE MIND IS ESTABLISHED IN UNITY. BRAHMAN IS FLAWLESS AND THE SAME IN ALL. THEREFORE THESE PERSONS ARE INDEED ESTABLISHED IN BRAHMAN.

Created or relative world means all bondages of birth, death etc. All possibilities of bondage are destroyed when the mind attains perfect evenness which in other words means becoming Brahman.

Perfection is not an idealism that has to be realized in the heavens after death. Contrary to this vague expectation, Sri Krishna asserts that the relative existence of bondage can be ended and the imperfect individual can be made to live in the Consciousness of God and can come out of one's ego sense in this life itself, in this very body and among the very same worldly objects.

The method of achieving this goal is stated in the verse as the one whose mind rests in evenness and gains the Divine tranquility. Where the thought flow is arrested there the mind ends. Where the mind ends, which is the instrument through which life expresses itself as ego, the sense of separate existence also ends and the egocentric slavery of *samsar* ceases. The ego, devoid of samsaric sorrows, rediscovers itself to be none other than the Self Itself.

Such persons who have conquered their minds and live in perfect harmony in all conditions of life and its relationships are indeed aware of their identity with Brahman who is even, ever-perfect and uncontaminated though indwelling in all pure and impure bodies.

Brahman is all pervading and homogeneous. Everything happens in it and nothing happens to it. Thus the Truth is changeless just as a river-bed remains motionless though water flowing on it is ever changing. The substratum is changeless and remains the same but the superimpositions and manifestations will change by their very nature. An individual with his identification with body, mind and intellect is changing factor but the Substratum, the Self, remains the same.

The Lord says that a mortal who can maintain his equanimity under all conditions is indeed the one who rests in Brahman i.e. aware of Brahman.

CHARACTERISTICS OF A MAN OF PERFECTION OR A KNOWER OF BRAHMAN

na prahrishyet priyam praapya nodwijet praapya chaapriyam
sthirabuddhir asammoodho brahmavid brahmani sthitah // 5.20 //

RESTING IN BRAHMAN, WITH INTELLECT STEADY AND WITHOUT DELUSION, THE KNOWER OF BRAHMAN NEITHER REJOICES ON OBTAINING WHAT IS PLEASANT NOR GRIEVES ON OBTAINING WHAT IS UNPLEASANT.

From this verse onwards the characteristics of a man of perfection are given.

The Lord describes him as having always a balanced intellect because of the absence of egocentric influences. He is never deluded. He has abandoned all actions as he rests in the Self.

He is neither exhilarated when he gets pleasant objects nor feels disappointed when he obtains unpleasant ones. This does not mean that he has no reactions at all but it means that he remains balanced always with a sense of equipoise which cannot be shattered easily.

baahyasparsheshwasaktaatmaa vindatyaatmani yatsukham
sa brahma yoga yuktaatmaa sukham akshayamashnute // 5.21 //

WITH THE HEART UNATTACHED TO EXTERNAL CONTACTS HE DISCOVERS HAPPINESS IN THE SELF; WITH THE HEART ENGAGED IN THE MEDITATION OF BRAHMAN HE ATTAINS ENDLESS BLISS.

The happiness from the enjoyment of outer objects is transitory while the Bliss of Brahman is eternal. When the mind is not attached to the external objects of the senses, when one is deeply and constantly engaged in the contemplation of the Self, one finds eternal peace within. If one wishes to enjoy the imperishable happiness of the Self within, one has to withdraw the senses from their respective objects and enter in deep meditation on the Self within. It is to be noted that through self-control a void is created in the mind and heart which will have to be filled in with bliss through contemplation of Brahman.

ye hi samsparshajaa bhogaa duhkhayonaya eva te
aadyantavantah kaunteya na teshu ramate budhah // 5.22 //

THE ENJOYMENTS THAT ARE BORN OF CONTACTS WITH OBJECTS ARE GENERATORS OF PAIN ONLY, FOR THEY HAVE A BEGINNING AND AN END, O SON OF KUNTI, AND THE WISE DO NOT FIND DELIGHT IN THEM.

Man goes in search of happiness among the external and perishable objects. He finds no permanent joy in them but receives a load of sorrows instead. One should, therefore, withdraw the senses from the sense objects which are not at all a source of permanent joy. One should fix the mind on the immortal, blissful Self within. The sense objects have a beginning and an end. The pleasure out of them is therefore momentary and fleeting during the interval between the contact of the senses with the objects and their separation. One who has discrimination or knowledge of the Self will never rejoice in the objects of the senses.

LUST AND ANGER ARE THE GREATEST ENEMIES

shaknoteehaiva yah sodhum praak shareera vimokshanaat
kaamakrodhodbhavam vegam sa yuktah sa sukhee narah // 5.23 //

HE WHO IS ABLE TO WITHSTAND THE MIGHT OF LUST AND ANGER EVEN BEFORE HE QUITS THE BODY - HE IS A YOGI, A HAPPY MAN.

Desire (lust) and anger are powerful enemies of peace. It is extremely difficult to annihilate them. One has to make strong efforts to destroy these enemies. He who has controlled desire and anger is the happiest man in the world.

Desire is longing for a pleasant and agreeable object which gives pleasure when it is seen, heard or remembered. Anger is the feeling one gets when he finds obstacles in the way of getting the desired objects. The greater the desire for an object the greater will be the anger against any obstacle that comes between the desirer and the objects desired. Lust and anger create an agitation of mind accompanied by appropriate physical symbols.

A Yogi is the one who controls the impulses of desire and anger, destroys likes and dislikes and attains equanimity of mind by resting in the Self. He is always happy because there is neither desire nor hatred in him. The implication of what Sri Krishna says is that in this very world and in this very life one can be perfectly happy if one learns to withstand the avalanche of desire and anger.

WHAT KIND OF YOGI ATTAINS BRAHMAN?

yo'ntah sukho'ntaraaraamas tathaantarjyotireva yah
sa yogee brahma nirvaanam brahma bhooto'dhigacchati // 5.24 //

HE WHO IS HAPPY WITHIN, WHO REJOICES WITHIN, WHO IS ILLUMINED WITHIN, SUCH A YOGI ATTAINS ABSOLUTE FREEDOM OR MOKSHA, HIMSELF BECOMING A BRAHMAN.

It will be seen from the above three verses that the man of perfection does not attain joy in the ordinary sensual objects of the world. Renouncing all these he reaches a state of bliss where there is no place for desire or anger, love or hatred. The Lord says such a man alone can be said to be happy. Such an individual who lives in the Self is the one who has known Brahman. He becomes a Jivanmukta. The next verse clarifies that this state is not annihilation but the positive one full of knowledge and Self-possession.

labhante brahma nirvaanam rishayah ksheena kalmashaah
chinnadwaidhaa yataatmaanah sarvabhootahite rataah // 5.25 //

WITH SINS DESTROYED, DOUBTS DISPELLED, SENSES CONTROLLED, AND DEVOTING THEMSELVES TO THE

WELFARE OF ALL BEINGS, THE SAGES ATTAIN FREEDOM IN BRAHMAN.

When a man of perfection brings his senses under control, his sinful mental impressions are cleared which were blocking his vision of the Self behind several doubts about the Reality. Knowledge of his real nature comes to dawn on him and he comes to rediscover himself as the Self.

Having thus reached the goal of all evolution his duties till he leaves his mortal body will be to engage himself in the good of all beings. Thus *loka-seva* becomes his obsession. To overcome the world is not to become other-worldly. It is not to evade social responsibilities. His body, mind and intellect are offered to the sacred fire of activity for the common welfare while remaining at rest with himself and living in an unbroken consciousness of the Divine, the Eternal.

The two sides of religion viz. personal and social are emphasized here.

kaamakrodha viyuktaanaam yateenaam yatachetasaam
abhito brahma nirvaanam vartate viditaatmanaam // 5.26 //

RELEASED FROM DESIRE AND ANGER, THE MIND CONTROLLED, THE SELF REALIZED, ABSOLUTE FREEDOM EXISTS FOR SUCH YOGINS BOTH HERE AND HEREAFTER.

When the seeker conquers his lust and anger and can face all the threats coming from within and without, he knows the Self and gains the Bliss of Perfection both here and hereafter.

The import of this verse is that those who renounce all actions and do intense *Sravana, Manana and Nididhyasana,* who are established in the Self and who are steadily devoted to knowledge of the Self, attain liberation instantly (Sankhya Yoga). But Karma Yoga in which action is performed in complete devotion to The Lord and as dedication to Him, leads to liberation step by step; first the purification of the mind, then knowledge, then renunciation of all action and lastly liberation.

To enunciate the Dhyana Yoga, which is the nearest and effective means to right knowledge, The Lord teaches the path of meditation in the following two verses.

sparshaan kritwaa bahir baahyaamshchakshus chaivaantare bhruvoh praanaapaanau samau kritwaa naasaabhyantara chaarinau // 5.27 //

yatendriya manobuddhir munir mokshaparaayanah
vigatecchaabhayakrodho yah sadaa mukta eva sah // 5.28 //

SHUTTING OUT ALL EXTERNAL CONTACTS, STEADYING THE GAZE OF HIS EYES BETWEEN THE EYEBROWS, REGULATING THE OUTWARD AND INWARD BREATHS FLOWING WITHIN HIS NOSTRILS, THE SENSES, MIND AND INTELLECT CONTROLLED, WITH MOKSHA (LIBERATION) AS THE SUPREME GOAL, FREED FROM DESIRE, FEAR AND ANGER, SUCH A MAN OF MEDITATION IS VERILY LIBERATED FOR EVER.

In these two verses The Lord has given a pre-view of the next Chapter. Sri Krishna gives a scheme of practice by which one can gain in himself a complete integration.

The external world of objects by itself cannot bring any disturbances unless one remains in contact with them through body, mind or intellect. But if we shut out external objects - not physically- but through discreet intellectual detachment at the mental plane, we shall discover in ourselves the necessary tranquility for starting meditation.

Then the gaze should be fixed in between the eye brows so that the eye balls remain steady. This is followed by rhythmical breathing which makes the mind quiet and perfect harmony is developed in the system. These instructions relate to physical adjustments.

The instructions relating to mental and intellectual adjustments are then given. The seeker is asked to be free from desire, fear and anger to attain perfect peace of mind. When the senses, mind and intellect are subjugated by dedicating all his outer and inner activities to achieve the goal of realizing the Self he attains liberation. The mind gets restless because of the agitations caused by desire, fear and anger. When it is desireless, it proceeds towards the Self spontaneously and Liberation becomes one's highest goal. When an individual follows these steps he can remain in the contemplation of Truth without any distractions. Such a man of meditation comes to experience the freedom of the God-hood before long.

The question as to what a person of balanced mind has to know and on what to meditate upon in the Dhyana Yoga is discussed in the following last verse of this Chapter.

bhoktaaram yajnatapasaam sarvaloka maheshwaram
suhridam sarvabhootaanaam jnaatwaa maam shaantim ricchati
// 5.29 //

HE WHO KNOWS ME AS THE ENJOYER OF ALL SACRIFICES AND AUSTERITIES, THE SUPREME LORD OF ALL THE WORLDS AND THE FRIEND OF ALL BEINGS, ATTAINS PEACE.

The words 'knowing Me' do not mean Sri Krishna in the bodily figure but indicate knowing that the Self in the individual is the real illuminator behind the ego (Jiva).

Yajna is the dedicated selfless work in any field of activity. Tapas means all self-denial and practice of self-control which the ego undertakes to seek identity with the eternal. Self is the Lord of all Lords- the Maheshwara. Iswara is the controller of all activities of perception and action -individual faculties illuminating the respective organs. The Self is the Lord of all these individual Lords governing the various fields, *Sarva Loka Maheswara.*

The gist of this verse is that spiritual experience is to realize that the Self is the one great ruler within, who presides over all the activities within the body-politic and before whom the ego surrenders. Knowing Him to be none other than Sri Krishna, the individual reaches the goal of peace, the eternal Perfection.

om tat sat iti srimad bhagavadgeetaasu upanishatsu brahma vidyaayaam yogashaastre sri krishnaarjuna samvaade karma sannyaasa yogo naama panchamo'dhyaayah||

THUS IN THE UPANISHADS OF THE GLORIOUS BHAGAVAD GITA, THE SCIENCE OF THE ETERNAL, THE SCRIPTURE OF YOGA, THE DIALOGUE BETWEEN SRI KRISHNA AND ARJUNA, ENDS THE FIFTH DISCOURSE ENTITLED: THE YOGA OF RENUNCIATION OF ACTION

AN OUTLINE VIEW OF THIS CHAPTER

Having practised the Yajnas prescribed in the preceding chapter and gained wisdom, a seeker sheds his vasanas / desires and develops a dispassion for the world. He enters into a state of renunciation, an essential pre-requisite for practicing meditation. This chapter elucidates this stage of development preliminary to meditation and realization.

I - *YOGI* (active), *SANYASI* (ascetic) AND *JNANI* (enlightened) - VERSES 1 – 7

In the opening verse of the chapter Arjuna asks Krishna to advise him conclusively as to which is better of the two – the path of action or the path of renunciation. Krishna clarifies the doubt by explaining the three distinct stages of spiritual growth. A seeker embarking on his spiritual journey with vasanas / desires is termed Yogi. Through Karma Yoga, the path of action, he sheds the bulk of his vasanas. As he does so, he becomes dispassionate towards the world and becomes an ascetic, a Sanyasi. A Sanyasi following the path of knowledge practices contemplation and meditation until he reaches the ultimate state of realization to become a Jnanai, an enlightened soul. Both Yogi and Sanyasi reach the supreme goal. Thus, one takes up either the path of action or the path of renunciation according to one's basic nature.

II - HOW THEY RELATE TO ACTION - VERSES 8 – 12

The above three types of individuals relate differently to action. The enlightened one, the Jnani, having merged with the Self, realizes that the Self does not act at all. In and through all actions, external and internal, the Jnani remains a silent witness while the senses contact the sense objects. The Sanyasi, in his state of dispassion, dedicates all his actions to Brahman. He acts without any attachment. Consequently, his actions are not sinful and do not leave a residue of vasanas / desires. Such a person, like a lotus leaf in water, remains in the world, but detached from and unaffected by it. The Yogi, the one at the beginning of the spiritual journey, detaches himself from worldly entanglements and directs all his physical, mental and intellectual activities towards his own self-purification.

III - STATE OF SUPREME BEING - VERSES 13 – 19

The Self, Atman, though the primeval cause of all actions, is not at all liable for either the merit or demerit accruing from them. Though the Self enlivens the actions of all beings, It is neither the actor nor the action nor is It responsible for the fruits of action. Those ignorant of this relationship remain deluded in the world. But he whose ignorance has been removed by knowledge of the Self reaches the supreme state of Being from where there is no return. Thereafter, he maintains a universal vision of oneness and evenness towards everything he comes across in the world. Having reached that eternal state he has forever transcended the cycle of birth and death.

IV-RENUNCIATION PRECEDES MEDITATION AND REALISATION -VERSES 20 -29

Sensual enjoyments arising out of external contacts have a diminishing value and they culminate in sorrow. The very sight of sense objects inflames desires in people. Then they lose control and succumb to the lure of the sense objects. The wise understand the ephemeral nature of contact-born enjoyments and prevent any desire from developing into an uncontrollable force of momentum. Instead of indulging in such temporary bouts of sensual pleasure they divert their attention and interest to the Self within. Thus they free themselves gradually from desires, subdue their mind and turn introvert. They begin to revel in the bliss of the Self. When the mind is subdued and relatively peaceful it becomes fit for meditation. This chapter concludes with a few procedural details for practicing meditation and realizing the ultimate Being in oneself.

<<<000>>>

CHAPTER 6

Dhyaana Yogah:

Yoga of Meditation

PREAMBLE

The Gita has been described as an elaborate commentary on the *mahavakya* of the Chhandogya Upanishad, *'tat tvam asi* - that thou art'. The first six chapters elucidate the word 'thou' which stands for the individual self. It is called the *Twam-pada*. The second set of six chapters deals with the word 'that' which denotes *brahman*. This is called the *Tat-pada*. The last set of six chapters establishes the identity of the individual self and Brahman. It is called the *Asi-pada*, which establishes the identity of the individual soul with the Supreme Soul.

Another way of looking at these three sets of six chapters each is to consider the first six chapters as emphasizing *Karma Yoga*, the second six *bhaktiyoga* and the last six *jnanayoga*. The term 'yoga' here stands for 'path'. Thus we have the three paths of karma, bhakti and jnana. These three paths are, however, not independent of one another, but they together form a synthetic whole. None of these paths can be practiced without the help of the other two; only the emphasis varies according to the temperament and level of spiritual development of the aspirant.

Chapter 2 described the sage of perfection, his mental equipoise and the methods of self-evolution to guide us in pure meditation and detached thinking. Chapter 3 gave a scientific treatment of the Karma Yoga - the path of action. The principle of 'Renunciation of action in knowledge' had been propounded in Chapter 4. As there was confusion in Arjuna between the ideas of 'action' and 'renunciation of action', Chapter 5 explained the 'way of renunciation of action' under two methods Viz. 1. Renunciation of the sense of doership and 2. Abandoning attachment and anxiety about the fruits of actions. A person who has followed the teachings of The Lord thus far would have got rid off his doubts. He would be fit for the higher purposes of meditation and Self-contemplation. How this is done is the theme of the present Chapter 6. This chapter concludes one of the sections in the thought-flow of the Gita as already explained.

This Chapter elucidates how one can give up one's weaknesses and positively grow into a healthier, stronger and integrated personality. This technique is called "*Dhyana Yoga*" or 'Path of meditation'. It discusses this path as auxiliary to the practice of both Karma Yoga and Sankhya Yoga.

Control over the body, senses, mind and intellect is extremely necessary in Dhyana Yoga. These instruments are collectively called as "Atma" and hence this Chapter is also called 'The Yoga of Self-Control'. Many classical commentators, particularly Madhusudan Saraswati, have therefore associated this Chapter with the *Ashtanga Yoga* of Patanjali's *Yoga Sutras*.

The first nine verses of this Chapter reiterate the three stages of spiritual development as described in the previous chapter. A yogi with worldly vasanas needs karma yoga, the path of action, to evolve spiritually. Through action he sheds his vasanas and becomes a Sanyasi. A Sanyasi, in a state of renunciation, needs meditation and quietitude to reach the ultimate state of Jnani. Both Karma Yogi and Sanyasi aim at the same goal of Self realization but their *sadhanas* (spiritual practices) differ. Whatever be the *sadhana*, every seeker has to put in his own effort to raise himself.

Though the Yogi and Sanyasi are both on the spiritual path, the Sanyasi alone, having developed a dispassion for the world, is capable for meditation and realization. Details of the environmental, physical, mental and intellectual preparations necessary to take the seat of meditation are elaborated here. When a seeker follows all these preparations he will become freed from desire, possessiveness, and the consequent sorrow. He will then become established in Yoga and be fully prepared to enter into meditation.

THE TEXT

RENUNCIATION AND ACTION ARE ONE

sri bhagavaan uvaacha
anaashritah karmaphalam kaaryam karma karoti yah
sa sannyaasi cha yogee cha na niragnirna chaakriyah // 6.1 //

SRI BHAGAVAN SAID
HE WHO PERFORMS HIS BOUNDEN DUTY WITHOUT DEPENDING ON THE FRUITS OF HIS ACTIONS - HE IS A SANNYASIN AND A YOGIN, NOT HE WHO HAS MERELY RENOUNCED THE SACRED FIRE; EVEN SO HE IS NO YOGI, WHO HAS MERELY GIVEN UP ALL ACTION.

So far, two currents of thought were discussed viz. 1. 'Renunciation of the sense of agency' (Sanyas) and 2. 'Renunciation of attachment to the fruits of actions' (Yoga).

The Sanyasi is himself the Yogi and the seekers must therefore engage themselves in noble works renouncing both their sense of doership and attachment to the fruits of their actions. Sanyasa or renunciation has little to do with outward works. It is an inward attitude. It is mental purity and intellectual equipoise.

Arjuna thought Sanyasa as mere abandonment of all activities, symbolized here by the word 'fire'. To become a Sanyasi, it is not necessary to give up the daily sacrificial fire and other rituals. To abstain from these without the spirit of renunciation is futile.

yam sannyaasamiti praahuryogam tam viddhi paandava
na hyasannyastasankalpo yogee bhavati kashchana // 6.2 //

O PANDAVA, PLEASE KNOW WHAT THEY CALL RENUNCIATION TO BE DISCIPLINED ACTIVITY, FOR NONE BECOMES A YOGI WHO HAS NOT RENOUNCED HIS SELFISH DESIRE.

The word *'Sankalpa'* means the mental faculty that makes plans for the future expecting the results of the plans so made. No one can become a Karma Yogi who plans future actions and expects the fruits of such actions. Only a devotee who renounced the thoughts of fruits of his actions can become a Yogi of steady mind because the thoughts of fruits of actions always cause mental disturbances.

Sanyasa i.e. renunciation consists in the accomplishment of the necessary action without an inward striving for reward. This is true yoga, firm control over oneself, complete self-possession. This verse says that disciplined activity (Yoga) is just as good as renunciation or Sanyasa.

Karma Yoga practiced without regard to the fruit of actions forms a stepping stone and an external aid to Dhyana Yoga or meditation. How Karma Yoga is a means to a better and greater meditation is explained in the following verses.

PATH AND THE GOAL

aarurukshormuner yogam karma kaaranamuchyate
yogaaroodhasya tasyaiva shamah kaaranamuchyate // 6.3 //

FOR A SAGE WHO WISHES TO ATTAIN TO YOGA, ACTION IS SAID TO BE THE MEANS; FOR THE SAME SAGE WHO HAS ATTAINED TO YOGA SERENITY IS SAID TO BE THE MEANS.

For a man who cannot practice meditation for a prolonged period and who is not able to keep his mind steady in meditation, action or work is a means of establishing himself in concentration and self-improvement. By working in the world with no egocentric concept of agency and desire for the fruits of actions, the mind gets purified and makes it fit for the practice of steady meditation.

When the required amount of concentration is achieved and his mind conquered, his agitations get well under control. In that state of mental growth his mind thoroughly gets fixed in the Self. These two means are not contradictory. Selfless work is necessary for a beginner; but a developed seeker needs more calmness and self-withdrawal for deep meditation to realize the Self. All his actions are then performed with perfect equanimity,

yadaa hi nendriyaartheshu na karmaswanushajjate
sarvasankalpasannyaasee yogaaroodhas tadochyate // 6.4 //

WHEN A MAN IS NOT ATTACHED TO SENSE OBJECTS OR TO ACTIONS, HAVING RENOUNCED ALL THOUGHTS, HE IS SAID TO HAVE ATTAINED YOGA.

Sri Krishna explains the physical and mental condition of the *Yogarudha* - the one who is established in Yoga. The Lord says that when one is without mental attachment to sense-objects or actions in the outer world, he is said to have obtained mastery over the mind.

When the mind is without even traces of attachment either to the sense-objects or to the fields of activity, even then it is possible that it will get distracted by its own power of longing and desiring. Such disturbances caused by the inner forces of the mind (Sankalpa) are more devastating than the ones caused by the external world of objects.

Sri Krishna indicates that the one who is said to have gained a complete mastery over his mind is he who has not only withdrawn himself from all sense-contacts and activities in the outer world but has also conquered all the Sankalpa-disturbances arising in his own mind. Such an individual, at the moment of meditation, in that inward state, is termed Yogarudha.

uddharedaatmanaatmaanam naatmaanamavasaadayet
atmaiva hyaatmano bandhuraatmaiva ripuraatmanah // 6.5 //

LET A MAN LIFT HIMSELF BY HIMSELF; LET HIM NOT DEGRADE HIMSELF; FOR, HE HIMSELF IS HIS FRIEND AND HE HIMSELF IS HIS ENEMY.

Sri Krishna declares that 'man should lift himself by himself'. Man, if he wants to raise himself from an animal existence to a noble life with all cultural and spiritual possibilities which lie dormant in him, has to convert the lower instincts in him to a higher level of perfection which is his essential nature.

Man is basically a plural personality - he thinks he ought to be a morally strong, ethically perfect, physically loving and socially disciplined ideal personality but in actual practice he is always a victim of his own attachments and aversions, likes and dislikes, love and hatred etc. So long as he does not realize his own duality, there cannot be any religion for him. But if he wants to make the lower in him as bright as the higher, he has to adopt the technique called Religion. The processes by which the lower is brought under the control and discipline of the higher are called spiritual practices.

This process of self-rehabilitation cannot be executed with any outside help but has to be done all by himself unto himself, all alone, all the way. Teachers, scriptures and temples etc. are all guides only and the actual achievement depends on the seeker's ability to come out of his misunderstandings.

The step suggested so far goes only half way and the other half as suggested by The Lord, is to see that the self thereafter does not fall down to its old level of mundane existence. When the lower allows itself to be corrected by the higher, the higher is called his friend. But when the lower does not allow itself to be controlled by the higher, the latter is considered to be his enemy.

"The Supreme is within us. It is the consciousness underlying the individualized consciousness of every day life but not proportionate to it. The two are different in kind, though the Supreme is realizable by one who is prepared to lose his life in order to save it. For the most part we are unaware of the Self in us because our attention is engaged by objects which we like or dislike. We must get away from them, to become aware of the Divine in us. If we do not realize the pointlessness, the irrelevance and the squalor of our ordinary life, the true Self becomes the enemy of our ordinary life.

The Universal Self and the personal self are not antagonistic to each other. The Universal Self can be the friend or the foe of the personal self. If we subdue our pretty cravings and desires, if we do not exert our selfish will, we become the channel of the Universal Self. If our impulses are under control and if our personal self offers itself to the Universal Self, the latter becomes our guide and teacher. Every one of us has the freedom to rise or fall and our future is in our own hands". Dr.S.Radhakrishnan.

IDEA OF FRIENDSHIP AND ENMITY CLARIFIED

bandhuraatmaatmanastasya yenaatmaivaatmanaa jitah
anaatmanastu shatrutwe vartetaatmaiva shatruvat // 6.6 //

TO HIM WHO HAS CONQUERED HIMSELF BY HIMSELF, HIS OWN SELF IS A FRIEND, BUT TO HIM WHO HAS NOT CONQUERED HIMSELF, HIS OWN SELF IS HOSTILE LIKE AN EXTERNAL ENEMY.

To the extent that the lower in us withdraws itself from its identifications with the body and sense-organs, feelings and emotions to that extent it (the ego) is said to have come under the influence of the nobler in us.

To such an ego the Self is the friend. But where the ego rebels against the higher, to that unconquered self or uncontrolled ego the Diviner Self is as inimical as an external foe.

The higher Self becomes a friend to the lower if the latter allows itself to be influenced by the former. The Diviner becomes inimical to the lower limited ego when the latter resists nobler aspirations. We are therefore called upon to master the lower self by the higher. The point is that the lower self is not to be destroyed. It can be used as a helper, if it is held in check.

jitaatmanah prashaantasya paramaatmaa samaahitah
sheetoshna sukha duhkheshu tathaa maanaapamaanayoh // 6.7 //

WHEN ONE HAS CONQUERED ONE'S (LOWER)SELF AND HAS ATTAINED IN THE REALM OF SELF-MASTERY, HIS SUPREME SELF ABIDES EVER FOCUSED; HE IS AT PEACE IN COLD AND HEAT, IN PLEASURE AND PAIN, IN HONOR AND DISHONOR.

This verse explains what exactly is achieved in the state of mental equipoise called 'Yogarudha'. When the stage of Yogarudha or the state of mental equipoise is reached, the mind is held steadfast in the contemplation of the Supreme and the seeker is capable of maintaining consistency of meditation in all circumstances, favorable and unfavorable.

Sri Krishna enumerates all possible threats that an individual may come across against his maintaining mental tranquility. These impediments fall into three categories viz.

- relating to body - heat and cold,
- relating to mind - pleasure and pain
- relating to intellect - honor and dishonor.

The Lord says that in spite of all these obstacles in man's life the Supreme Self is to be the focal point for constant realization. The man of serenity remains unruffled in all circumstances, in all environments and in all companies.

"This is the state of blessedness of the person who has established himself in unity with the Universal Self. He is a *jitatman* whose calm and serenity are not disturbed by the pairs of the opposites. The self in the body is generally absorbed by the world of dualities, heat and cold, pain and pleasure but when it controls the senses and masters the world, the self becomes free. The Supreme Self is not different from the self in the body. When the self is bound by the modes of prakriti or nature, it is called *kshetrajna*; when it is freed from them, the same self is called the Supreme Self". - Dr.S.Radhakrishnan

jnaana vijnaana triptaatmaa kootastho vijitendriyah
yuktah ityuchyate yogee samaloshtaashmakaanchanah // 6.8 //

HE IS SAID TO BE A STEADFAST YOGI WHO IS SATISFIED WITH KNOWLEDGE AND WISDOM, WHO REMAINS UNSHAKEN, WHO HAS CONQUERED THE SENSES, AND TO WHOM A LUMP OF EARTH, A STONE AND GOLD ARE THE SAME.

Sri Krishna says that an individual, self-controlled and serene, who contemplates constantly on the nature of the Self in all circumstances in life, soon gets full divine satisfaction and becomes an unshakeable Yogi.

Knowledge gained by study of Sastras is Gnana and one's own experience of the teachings of Sastras is Vignana. Kootastha is the anvil. Red hot iron pieces are hammered on the anvil for giving proper shape to them but the anvil itself remains unchanged in spite of receiving repeated hammerings. So too, the seeker is called changeless-Kootastha- whose heart remains unchanged in spite of it being surrounded by the worldly objects. He is unperturbed by things and happenings of the world and is therefore said to be equal-minded to the events of this changing world. Such a saint remains tranquil with equal mental vision in all conditions of life. To him a clod of mud, a stone and gold are all the same. Thus equanimity of mind is the touchstone for spiritual evolution.

suhrinmitraaryudaaseena madhyastha dweshya bandhushu
saadhushwapi cha paapeshu samabuddhirvishishyate // 6.9 //

HE WHO HAS EQUAL REGARD FOR WELL-WISHERS, FRIENDS, ENEMIES, THE INDIFFERENT, THE NEUTRAL, THE HATEFUL, RELATIVES, THE RIGHTEOUS AND THE UNRIGHTEOUS, EXCELS.

In the previous verse it was stated that the man of perfection develops equal vision to all the things of the outside world. Here the nature of relationship of a man of perfect equipoise with the other living beings of the world is discussed.

The Lord says that such a man of excellence regards all relationships with equal love and consideration irrespective of whether they are friends or foes or the indifferent or the neutral or the hateful or the nearest relations. He does not make any distinction between the righteous and unrighteous, the good and the bad.

In realizing the Self in him, he sees unity in all diversities and observes a rhythm in the world outside. To him, who has realized himself to be the Self which is all pervading, the entire universe becomes his own Self and therefore his relationship with other parts of the universe is equal and the same.

The method by which one can attain this highest goal with an assured result is called Meditation which is explained exhaustively in the following verses.

DIRECTIONS FOR THE PRACTICE OF YOGA

yogee yunjeeta satatamaatmaanam rahasi sthitah
ekaakee yatachittatmaa niraasheeraparigrahah // 6.10 //

A YOGI SHOULD TRY CONSTANTLY TO CONCENTRATE HIS MIND (ON THE SUPREME SELF), REMAINING IN SOLITUDE, LIVING ALONE WITH THE MIND AND BODY CONTROLLED, FREE FROM DESIRES AND POSSESSIONS.

In the previous verses Arjuna wanted to know the ways and means of achieving the constant experience of inward equilibrium. Sri Krishna explains the methods of self-development and the technique of self-perfection which can be attained by all. The method taught by The Lord requires the seekers to exert themselves by constantly practicing concentration which is called meditation.

The pre-requisites for practicing meditation are:

- Rahasi Sthitah - Remaining in solitude: Sitting in solitude one should practice meditation. This does not mean that meditation can be practiced only in jungles or in lonely caves. It means that even in one's own home one should try to withdraw himself mentally and physically from the normal preoccupations and retire to a secluded spot for practicing meditation. Solitude can be gained only when there is mental withdrawal from the world outside. One who is full of desires and constantly thinking about sense-objects cannot gain solitude even in a remote forest. Solitude lifts our hearts and exalts our minds. In a world which is daily growing noisier, the duty of the civilized man is to have moments of thoughtful stillness. Retiring to a quiet place, we should keep off all external distractions.

- Ekaki – Alone: For the purposes of meditation one has to be physically alone. His success depends upon the amount of self-control he is adopting in his daily life.
- Yatachittatmana - Self-controlled. He must not be excited, strained or anxious. There should be no restlessness or turbulence. The heart must become clean if it is to reflect God who is to be seen and known only by the pure in heart.
- Niraasheer - Free from desires: Worry about daily needs, about earning and spending, disturbs meditation and takes us away from the life of the spirit. So we must be free from desire and anxiety born of it, from greed and fear. We should expect nothing, insist on nothing.
- Aparigrahah - Free from longing for possessions: This is a spiritual state and not a material condition. We must control the appetite for possessions; free ourselves from the tyranny of belongings. One cannot hear God's voice, if one is restless and self-centered,

if one is dominated by feelings of pride, jealousy or possessiveness.

"The Gita points out our happiness is inward. It invites our attention to the manner of our life, the state of human consciousness, which does not depend upon the outward machinery of life. The body may die and the world pass away but the life in spirit endures. Our treasures are the things of the world that perish but the knowledge and love of God endure. We must get out of the slavery to things to gain the glad freedom of spirit.

Here the Lord develops the technique of mental discipline on the lines of Patanjali's Yoga Sutras. When one starts meditating upon the Truth within these parameters, he is considered to be the true seeker trying to achieve the highest in life. The main purpose of this exercise is to raise our consciousness from its ordinary waking condition to higher levels until it attains Union with the Supreme. The human mind is ordinarily turned outwards. Absorption in the mechanical and material sides of life leads to misbalanced condition of consciousness.

Yoga attempts to explore the inner world of consciousness and helps to integrate the conscious and the sub-conscious. We must divest our minds of all sensual desires, abstract our attention from all external objects and absorb it in the object of meditation. By summoning all the energies of the mind and fixing them on one point, we raise the level of reference from the empirical to the real, from observation to vision and let the spirit take possession of our whole being. The practice must be constant. It is no use to taking to meditation by fits and starts. A continuous creative effort is necessary for developing the higher, the intenser form of consciousness". - Dr. S.Radhakrishnan.

OTHER AIDS TO MEDITATION

The Lord now explains the other aids to meditation like modes of sitting, eating, recreation etc. in the following verses.

shuchau deshe pratishthaapya sthiramaasanamaatmanah
naatyucchritam naatineecham chailaajinakushottaram // 6.11 //

HAVING ESTABLISHED IN A CLEAN SPOT HIS FIRM SEAT, NEITHER TOO HIGH NOR TOO LOW, MADE OF A CLOTH, A SKIN AND KUSA GRASS, ONE OVER THE OTHER.

tatraikaagram manah kritwaa yatachittendriyakriyah
upavishyaasane yunjyaadyogamaatmavishuddhaye // 6.12 //

THERE, HAVING MADE THE MIND ONE-POINTED, WITH ACTIONS OF THE MIND AND SENSE CONTROLLED, LET HIM, SEATED ON THE SEAT, PRACTICE YOGA FOR THE PURIFICATION OF THE SELF.

Sri Krishna now gives a complete and exhaustive explanation of the technique of meditation. The seat for practice of meditation should be in a clean place. The external conditions have a direct bearing on the human mind. The chances for the seeker to maintain a pure mental condition are more in a clean place. A tidy atmosphere causes the least mental disturbances.

The meditator should sit steady (sthiram) in his seat without moving his body in any direction since physical movements destroy the mental concentration and inner equipoise. In order to get established in a firm posture, it would be advisable to sit in any comfortable seat with the vertebral column erect, fingers interlocked and hands thrown in front.

The seat of meditation should not be too high or too low. Too high a seat causes a sense of insecurity and a seat too low may cause bodily pains. During meditation the heart becomes slightly slow causing even a slight fall in blood pressure and to that extent one gets withdrawn in himself. At such a time of low resistance, the position of the seat plays a vital part.

The mattress of Kusa Grass on the ground covered by a deer skin and a piece of cloth on top of it protects one from dampness, cold and heat.

Sitting properly by itself is not Yoga. While proper physical condition is necessary for inducing right mental attitude for spiritual practices, by itself it cannot assure any spiritual self development. Hence Sri Krishna tells here what a seeker should do in the seat of meditation having brought his body in a steady condition and how his mind and intellect should be kept engaged.

These instructions of The Lord are: One should make the mind single pointed by subduing the faculty of imagination and activities of the sense organs. Although single pointedness is the nature of the mind, by virtue of its capacity for imagination or wishful thinking and on account of the pulls and pressures of the external sense objects on the sense organs, it gets wild and scattered. The Lord says that if these two sources of dissipation are closed, the mind will get automatically single pointed. Keeping the mind contemplating on the Ultimate Self constantly is the inner Yoga suggested here.

The effect of such meditation is inner purification. A purified mind is the one wherein there are no agitations and when the mind becomes thus steady and pure, it discovers its own Real

Nature just like one understands himself by looking at his own image in a mirror. The purification of the heart, *chittasuddhi,* is a matter of discipline. It is a disciplined disinterestedness. Blessed are the pure in heart for they shall see God. Wisdom is a condition in a being at rest.

samam kaayashirogreevam dhaarayannachalam sthirah
samprekshya naasikaagram swam dishashchaanavalokayan
// 6.13 //

LET HIM FIRMLY HOLD HIS BODY, HEAD AND NECK ERECT AND STILL, GAZING AT THE TIP OF HIS NOSE WITHOUT LOOKING AROUND.

The Lord tells that the meditator should firmly hold his body in such a way that his vertebral column is completely erect - the head, neck and the spinal column should be vertical to the horizontal seat. Holding the body firmly means that it should not be moved in any direction although it has to be kept relaxed.

Patanjali points out that the posture should be steady and pleasing so as to aid concentration. A right posture gives serenity of body. The body must be kept clean if the living image of God is to be installed in it.

His gaze should be fixed at the tip of his nose. If this is followed literally there is a possibility of the seeker getting headache, giddiness etc. Adi Sankara says that the term means that the meditator should have his attention as though turned towards the tip of his own nose. The meditator is advised not to look around so that his attention may not get distracted.

prashaantaatmaa vigatabheer brahmachaarivrate sthitah
manah samyamya macchitto yukta aaseeta matparah // 6.14 //

SERENE MINDED, FEARLESS, FIRM IN THE VOW OF BRAHMACHARYA, HAVING CONTROLLED THE MIND, THINKING ON ME AND BALANCED, LET HIM SIT IN YOGA, HAVING ME AS THE SUPREME GOAL.

The word Prashaanta means inward peace. This is the inner joy in which the meditator will find himself as a result of regular practice. Fear is the quality in a person who cannot believe that there is something beyond himself which is the Supreme.

The very process of turning towards the Supreme makes him afraid of nothingness. The seeker should therefore be fearless since it is the deadliest enemy for spiritual progress.

Even after the mind becomes peaceful and joyous and fearlessness achieved after a continuous practice of meditation and study of scriptures, no progress towards the goal can be possible unless the seeker gets established himself in perfect Brahmacharya. Brahmacharya implies the observance of celibacy as well as the practice of self control in all fields of sense-stimulations and sense-gratifications.

Without self control the mind will become chaotic due to the pressures of the world of objects. Unless the mind is provided with another target to concentrate upon it cannot retreat from its usual pre-occupations with the external world. This alternative is the inner field of the Self.

When the body, mind and intellect are controlled through the above process, the seeker gains mental energy and experiences an increasing capacity to withdraw within himself and fix all his thoughts on 'Me', the Self. After taming the mind and stopping it from its external wanderings, it should be kept focused upon the Divine seeking nothing but the Supreme. The mind becomes still but not vacant for it is fixed on the Supreme. *Ishvara Pranidhana* is a recognized way in yoga discipline. They act in the world but the passionless tranquility of the spirit remains undisturbed. They are like lotus in the lake which is unruffled by the tide.

yunjannevam sadaa'tmaanam yogee niyatamaanasah
shaantim nirvaanaparamaam matsamsthaam adhigacchati
// 6.15 //

THUS, ALWAYS KEEPING THE MIND BALANCED, WITH HIS MIND CONTROLLED, THE YOGI ATTAINS TO THE PEACE ABIDING IN ME - THE PEACE THAT CULMINATES IN TOTAL LIBERATION - NIRVANA OR MOKSHA.

After explaining 1. The physical pose 2. Mental stability and 3. The consequent intellectual self-application, The Lord gives out the last step in the technique of meditation. When all the above stages of meditation have been gone through the seeker becomes an unwavering person in his physical and subtler existence. Such a person who constantly keeps his mind free from agitations surely reaches the Supreme. The word 'constantly' does not mean at the cost of his duty to his home and the society. It means a consistent inner silence during meditation. At the peak of meditation the mind becomes completely 'still' and comes to a 'halt'.

The individual comes to experience an infinite peace when his mind is calmed. This is the peace that always resides in the seeker. Thus when there is no mental, intellectual and bodily disturbances and agitations, the seeker attains the peace unknown in the outside world that ultimately ends in the Supreme Liberation i.e. Nirvana-Paramam. In brief, the meditator awakens to his own status of Selfhood which is the achievement of the meditation.

MODERATION IS ESSENTIAL

naatyashnatastu yogo'sti na chaikaantamanashnatah
na chaati swapnasheelasya jaagrato naiva chaarjuna // 6.16 //

VERILY, YOGA IS NOT POSSIBLE FOR HIM, WHO EATS TOO MUCH, OR FOR HIM WHO DOES NOT EAT AT ALL; OR FOR HIM WHO SLEEPS TOO MUCH, OR FOR HIM WHO IS ALWAYS AWAKE, O ARJUNA.

The Lord gives guidelines in this verse and the following ones on the possible pitfalls that have to be guarded against while pursuing meditation. The central theme of His guidance is that moderation in all activities at all levels is the precondition for achieving success in Meditation. Intemperateness in any field of behavior and activity brings about mental agitations which are not conducive to the development of an integrated personality. Therefore moderation in food, sleep and recreation is directed.

Yoga is not possible for him who eats too much nor for him who does not eat at all. Eating means not only the process of consuming food but includes enjoyments gained through all means of sense perceptions and inward experiences. Similarly, neither too much sleep which erodes the faculties nor lack of sleep which disturbs the body rhythm is advised for spiritual life. Everything in moderation is the rule.

yuktaahaaravihaarasya yuktacheshtasya karmasu
yuktaswapnaavabodhasya yogo bhavati duhkhahaa // 6.17 //

YOGA PUTS AN END TO ALL SORROWS FOR HIM WHO IS MODERATE IN FOOD AND RECREATION, WHO IS MODERATE IN HIS EXERTION AT WORK, WHO IS MODERATE IN SLEEP AND WAKEFULNESS.

Moderation but not complete self-denial in all activities of life like eating, recreation, sleep and exertion in working is the basic principle stated here. The important guideline in this verse is that the amount of effort put in for all work, including selfless divine work, should be moderate as otherwise such work instead of redeeming the seeker would enslave him and make his life miserable. What is required is restraint but not abstinence.

We have seen Sri Bhgavan describing the process of meditation. He continues the discussion in the following verses pointing out that the controlled mind remains peaceful and explaining the process by which the seeker can gain the experience of the Essential Self through such disciplined mind. By training the mind, one must give up its preoccupation with the world and direct it to the Self within and make it introvert. As soon as the mind tastes the bliss of the Self it will realize that there is no greater enjoyment. Being established therein, even the greatest of the sorrows in the world cannot disturb its equanimity and peace. One practices Yoga (union with the Self) through complete control of the senses and the thought flow which are the source-point of all desires. This sets the stage for practicing meditation and the realization of the Self.

The mind in the state of meditation thinks of the Self. The intellect holds the mind single pointedly upon the Self without allowing it to slip into any other thought. Whenever the mind wanders away the intellect brings it back through supervision and control. By maintaining single pointed thought of the Self, the mind becomes absolutely tranquil and quiet. The Jnani then experiences the infinite bliss of Brahman. Thereafter, he sees the Self in all beings and all beings in the Self. He sees the Supreme Being everywhere.

When he heard the exposition on how to discipline and control the mind, Arjuna raises a doubt as to whether the mind is such a thing which can be controlled at all. He wonders how the mind, a restless, turbulent, strong and obstinate entity, can be brought under control. And even if forcefully brought under control, how can the mind continue to remain steady and calm? Krishna assures Arjuna that the intellect can control the mind through sustained practice and dispassion.

Arjuna wonders as to what will happen to a seeker and his efforts if he fails to attain Self-realization in his lifetime. Will he not be denied the benefits of both the material and spiritual worlds? Krishna allays Arjuna's logical and natural concern and assures him that no seeker falling short of Realization in his life time will ever suffer either here or hereafter. Such a person will gain a heavenly bliss and reincarnate in a pure and pious home or in a family of wise yogis, which will provide him with an ideal environment for pursuing spiritual goal of Realization in his new life. Therefore, Krishna advises Arjuna to practice yoga with devotion and determination until he merges with the Supreme Brahman.

WHO IS A YOGI

yadaa viniyatam chittamaatmanyevavatishthate
nihsprihah sarvakaamebhyo yukta ityuchyate tadaa // 6.18 //

WHEN THE WELL-CONTROLLED MIND RESTS IN THE SELF ALONE, FREE FROM LONGING FOR OBJECTS OF DESIRES, THEN ONE IS SAID TO HAVE ATTAINED YOGA.

When the mind is completely under control it rests peacefully in the Self alone. Uncontrolled mind is the one which wanders in search of satisfaction among the sense objects. To make the mind withdraw from its nomadic nature for contemplating continuously on the Self, which is the substratum that illumines all perceptions and experiences, one has to make it free from desires. While desires by themselves are not unhealthy, Gita advises us to renounce our cravings for all objects of desires seen or unseen, belonging to this world or the next.

When the mind is withdrawn from sense objects, it becomes capable of contemplating on the Self as it is free from agitations. The finite and limited sense objects disturb the mind, while the unlimited and infinite Self brings peace and joy to it. This condition of replacing sense oriented thoughts with contemplation on the Self is called steadfastness. The steadfast mind of a Yogi is described in the next verse.

yathaa deepo nivaatastho nengate sopamaa smritaa
yogino yatachittasya yunjato yogamaatmanah // 6.19 //

"LIKE A LAMP KEPT IN A WINDLESS PLACE WHICH DOES NOT FLICKER" - THAT IS THE FIGURE (USED BY THE WISE)

FOR THE DISCIPLINED MIND OF A YOGI PRACTICING CONCENTRATION ON THE SELF.

Mind is as unstable as a flickering flame of a lamp. But when the same mind is made to concentrate in the Self by the meditator its vacillations and wanderings are stopped. It becomes brilliant just as a flickering lamp when placed in a windless spot.

yatroparamate chittam niruddham yogasevayaa
yatra chaivaatmanaatmaanam pashyannaatmani tushyati // 6.20 //

WHEN THE MIND, RESTRAINED BY THE PRACTICE OF YOGA, ATTAINS QUIETITUDE AND WHEN SEEING THE SELF BY THE SELF, HE IS REJOICED IN HIS OWN SELF.

sukhamaatyantikam yattad buddhi graahyamateendriyam
vetti yatra na chaivaayam sthitashchalati tattwatah // 6.21 //

WHEN HE (THE YOGI) FEELS THAT INFINITE BLISS - WHICH CAN BE GRASPED BY THE (PURE) INTELLECT AND WHICH TRANSCENDS THE SENSES, WHEREIN ESTABLISHED, HE NEVER MOVES FROM THE REALITY.

yam labdhwaa chaaparam laabham manyate naadhikam tatah
yasminsthito na duhkhena gurunaapi vichaalyate // 6.22 //

WHICH HAVING OBTAINED, HE THINKS THERE IS NO OTHER GAIN SUPERIOR TO IT; WHEREIN ESTABLISHED, HE IS NOT MOVED EVEN BY THE HEAVIEST OF SORROWS –

tam vidyaad duhkhasamyogaviyogam yogasamjnitam
sa nishchayena yoktavyo yogo'nirvinna chetasaa // 6.23 //

LET THAT BE KNOWN AS YOGA WHICH IS SEVERANCE FROM THE CONTACT OF PAIN. THIS YOGA SHOULD BE PRACTICED WITH PERSEVERANCE AND WITH AN UNDAUNTED MIND.

All these four Verses (20 - 23) should be taken together which give a complete picture of Yoga and explain the stages that a Yogi passes through whose mind has become single pointed by meditation. They end with a call given by The Lord to all mankind to practice this Yoga of Meditation and self development.

The goal of the meditator is attaining serene quietitude when his mind becomes completely restrained and gains an experience of the Self, not as an entity separate from himself but as his own true nature. This self discovery of the mind is nothing other than the process by which ego's identification with body, mind and intellect is replaced by the principle of Divine Consciousness. The experience of the self is an enduring state from which there is no return.

Sri Krishna says that having gained this Infinite Bliss, no one can come to the worldly sorrows and feel the urge to go after the worldly objects and pursuits. The Yogi who attained the state of Supreme Truth will consider no other gain as equal to it and worth comparable. Thus Sri Krishna defines Yoga as a state of "*DISUNION FROM EVERY UNION WITH PAIN*".

The term yoga means contact. Man is always in contact with finite worldly objects through the instruments of body, mind and intellect and gets finite joy only. When this temporary joy ends on account of the cessation of the instrumentality of the senses, sorrow begins. Therefore it is said that life through these matter instruments is called the life of union-with-pain.

Detachment from this union is the process in which we disassociate ourselves from the fields of objects and their experiences. As mind cannot exist without any attachment, once it is detached from the unreal and pain giving world of objects, it has to get itself attached to the Real and Permanent Bliss, which is called meditation. In deep meditation, the senses do not function; they are resolved into their cause i.e. the mind. And when the mind becomes steady and cognition alone functions, then the indescribable Self is realized.

Thus Yoga is nothing but a man's renunciation of contacts with sorrows and turning towards Bliss which is his real nature. Sri Krishna says that this Yoga is to be practiced with an eager and decisive mind. Success in meditation is possible only when it is carried out with firm conviction, perseverance and an undespairing heart as the Yoga or connection with the Real can be gained only with Viyoga or disconnection from the Unreal. There should be no relaxation of effort even though there is no quick result and the practice appears difficult. If living among the finite objects with its limited joys is sorrow, then to get away from it all is to enter the realm of Bliss which is the Self. This is Yoga.

Patanjali Yoga Sutras declare that the root of sorrow in the form of repeated births and deaths lies in the contact between the subject and the object or in the liaison due to ignorance between the soul and the objective world. With the termination of this contact, sorrows and sufferings also come to an end for all time.

Patanjali says "The great sorrow in the form of future births and deaths is called 'Heya'- that which ought to be avoided (2.16). The cause of 'Heya' or suffering is the contact between the subject and the object (2.17). Ignorance is the root of that contact (2.24). The termination of that contact between the subject and the object through the eradication of the ignorance is known as 'Hana' - shutting out the 'Heya'. This represents the aloofness of the subject - Kaivalya (2.25)

This state of God realization is termed 'Yoga' in the Gita. Further instructions on yoga are continued in the following verses.

sankalpaprabhavaan kaamaanstyaktwaa sarvaan asheshatah
manasaivendriyagraamam viniyamya samantatah // 6.24 //

ABANDONING WITHOUT RESERVE ALL DESIRES BORN OF SANKALPA AND COMPLETELY RESTRAINING THE WHOLE GROUP OF SENSES BY THE MIND FROM ALL SIDES...

shanaih shanairuparamed budddhyaa dhritigriheetayaa
aatmasamstham manah kritwaa na kinchidapi chintayet // 6.25 //

LITTLE BY LITTLE LET HIM ATTAIN QUIETITUDE BY THE INTELLECT HELD IN FIRMNESS; HAVING MADE THE MIND ESTABLISHED IN THE SELF, LET HIM NOT THINK OF ANYTHING.

The goal of Yoga was to accomplish that state wherein the mind, through the practice of concentration, comes to get it absolutely restrained and achieves perfection or bliss. The way of attaining single pointedness of mind, what the single pointed mind should then do, how to approach and ultimately realize the Truth have all been exhaustively dealt with here. The various stages to be undergone in this regard are:

Renounce all desires fully by controlling the mind and restrain all the sense organs from their fields of sense objects. This mind-quietening process cannot be achieved at one go. It is clearly advised that mind should achieve quietitude as a result of withdrawal from sense objects by degrees - slowly and slowly.

Thereafter, patiently, the mind should be made to contemplate on the Self with the aid of the intellect. A mind that continuously contemplates on the Self becomes still and gets pervaded by the divine quietitude. This is the last stage of the journey that conscious and deliberate action can take any seeker.

Sri Krishna warns that the meditator after reaching the last stage of inner peace should not think of anything else. Undisturbed by any new thought waves he should maintain inner silence and come to live it more and more deeply.

yato yato nishcharati manashchanchalamasthiram
tatastato niyamyai tadaatmanyeva vasham nayet // 6.26 //

FROM WHATEVER CAUSE THE RESTLESS AND THE UNSTEADY MIND WANDERS AWAY, FROM THAT LET HIM RESTRAIN IT AND BRING IT BACK TO BE UNDER THE CONTROL OF THE SELF ALONE.

Mind by its very nature is unsteady and restless; it always wanders away from the point of concentration. The true seeker on the path of meditation will therefore get despaired at his inability to fix his mind on a focal point, contemplating on the Self. During the practice of meditation although the sense organs are controlled, the chasing of the sense objects by the mind will continue and cause dejection in the seeker.

The reasons for this roving mind may be many such as memories of the past, proximity of the tempting sense objects, attachments etc. Sri Krishna directs that whatever be the reason for the restlessness of the mind, the seeker is not to lose hope. On the contrary he should understand that these tendencies are the very characteristics of the mind and the process of meditation is the technique to eliminate them.

The means of bringing under control the restless mind are the realization of the illusoriness of sense-objects and the cultivation of indifference to them. Through practice of discrimination and detachment the mind gradually attains inner peace.

The Lord advises the seeker to bring back the mind that has gone out on a roaming mission. As soon as the mind is withdrawn through will power it will go out again because mind means flow of thoughts and it can never be steady without any motion. Therefore in the meditation when the mind is withdrawn from the sense objects it should be provided with an alternative to keep it busy. That alternative is its application towards contemplating on the Self alone.

RESULT OF THE YOGA OF MEDITATION

prashaantamanasam hyenam yoginam sukhamuttamam
upaiti shaantarajasam brahmabhootamakalmasham // 6.27 //

SUPREME BLISS VERILY COMES TO THIS YOGI WHOSE MIND IS COMPLETELY TRANQUIL, WHOSE PASSIONS ARE QUIETENED, WHO IS FREE FROM SIN AND HAS BECOME ONE WITH BRAHMAN.

yunjannevam sadaa'tmaanam yogee vigatakalmashah
sukhena brahmasamsparsham atyantam sukham ashnute // 6.28 //

THE YOGI ALWAYS ENGAGING THE MIND THUS (IN THE PRACTICE OF YOGA) FREED FROM SINS EASILY ENJOYS THE INFINITE BLISS OF CONTACT WITH BRAHMAN.

In these two verses the Lord describes the benefits of Yoga. During meditation when the mind is withdrawn from the world of objects and is concentrated on the Self, it acquires quietitude and the thought flow ceases. Where there is no thought flow there is no mind. Where the mind has ended, there the seeker experiences the Infinite nature of the Self and the meditator reaches to the Supreme Bliss by ending all his mental agitations.

The ego discovers that it is none other than the Self and hence there is no dualism at this stage. Such a man of self-realization himself becomes Brahman. The meditator *(Upasaka)* becomes one with the object of meditation *(Upasya).*

A meditator step by step grows out of his own ignorance and imperfection represented by his ego and merges with the Supreme. He loses contact with the objects of the senses and comes into contact with the Self within - Brahman. This means that the seeker becomes Brahman and comes to experience the Infinite Bliss as against contact with the world of objects ('not-Self') whose joys are always finite. He becomes a *Jivanmukta*, liberated while living in a body.

Chandogya Upanishad (VII-xxiii.I) says "That which is infinite or great beyond all, is true happiness. There is no joy in that which is finite. Happiness lies in infinity. Efforts should be made in particular to know the Infinite alone". It continues "The Infinite represents that plane of consciousness in which no other is cognized and the state in which another is seen, another is heard and another is cognized represents the finite. That which is infinite is immortal. That which is finite is mortal". (VII-xxiv.I)

PURPOSE OF YOGA IS ACHIEVED

sarvabhootasthamaatmaanam sarvabhotani chaatmani
eekshate yogayuktaatma sarvatra samadarshanah // 6.29 //

WITH THE MIND HARMONIZED BY YOGA HE SEES THE SELF ABIDING IN ALL BEINGS AND ALL BEINGS IN THE SELF; HE SEES THE SAME EVERYWHERE.

That the perfect man of Self-knowledge or God-Realization is not merely the one who realized his own divinity but is also one who has equally understood and has come to live in the knowledge of divinity inherent in all creatures without any distinction. He sees the same spirit dwelling in all objects. He sees the identity of Atman, the inmost reality of himself, and Brahman, the inmost reality of the universe.

The essence in all names and forms is the same Self which is the substratum in the world of objects just like the clay in all the pots, gold in all the ornaments, ocean in all the waves and electricity in all the gadgets. The Yogi observes oneness or unity of the Self everywhere.

Isa Upanishad says "But he who sees all beings in the Self and the self in all beings, no longer hates anyone". (6)

yo maam pashyati sarvatra sarvam cha mayi pashyati
tasyaaham na pranashyaami sa cha me na pranashyati // 6.30 //

HE WHO SEES ME EVERYWHERE AND SEES EVERYTHING IN ME, NEVER GETS SEPARATED FROM ME (BY TIME, SPACE OR ANYTHING INTERVENING) NOR DO I GET SEPARATED FROM HIM.

Here the words 'I' and 'Me" mean the Self. On rediscovering the Self the ego becomes the Self and there is no distinction between the ego and the Self just as the dreamer becomes the waker and the waker is not separate from the dreamer. When we are one with the Divine in us, we become one with the whole stream of life.

sarvabhootasthitam yo maam bhajatyekatwamaasthitah
sarvathaa vartamaano pi sa yogee mayivartate // 6.31 //

HE WHO, BEING ESTABLISHED IN ONENESS, WORSHIPS ME, WHO DWELLS IN ALL BEINGS - THAT YOGI, IN WHATEVER WAY LEADS HIS LIFE, LIVES IN ME.

The Lord dwells in all beings as their inmost Self irrespective of their forms. The Yogi who sees the Lord in all beings and worships him through all beings has attained liberation. No matter how he lives and acts, he is always free. He is no longer under the control of scriptural injunctions.

aatmaupamyena sarvatra samam pashyati yo'rjuna
sukham vaa yadi vaa duhkham sa yogee paramo matah // 6.32 //

I HOLD HIM TO BE A SUPREME YOGI, O ARJUNA, WHO LOOKS ON THE PLEASURE AND PAIN OF ALL BEINGS AS HE LOOKS UPON THEM IN HIMSELF.

This verse is the golden rule of Hinduism. The highest yogi sees that whatever is pleasant to him is pleasant to all others, including subhuman beings and that whatever is painful to him is painful to all others. Therefore he cannot cause pain to any. He leads a life of complete non-violence. The true Yogi is one who feels the pains and joys of others as if they were his own. He feels the entire universe as his own form.

CONTROL OF MIND IS DIFFICULT BUT POSSIBLE

arjuna uvaacha
yo'yam yogastwayaa proktah saamyena madhusoodana
etasyaaham na pashyaami chanchalatwaat stithim sthiraam // 6.33 //

ARJUNA SAID
THIS YOGA OF EQUANIMITY, TAUGHT BY YOU, O SLAYER OF MADUSUDANA (KRISHNA), I DO NOT SEE HOW IT CAN LONG ENDURE, BECAUSE OF THE RESTLESSNESS OF THE MIND.

Perfect equanimity, a mind free from torpidity and restlessness, in all circumstances, conditions and challenges of life seemed an uphill task and impracticable to Arjuna. He says that achieving evenness of mind is day dreaming because the human mind, by its very nature, is restless in its own excitements.

chanchalam hi manah krishna pramaathi balavad dridham
tasyaaham nigraham manye vaayor iva sudushkaram // 6.34 //

THE MIND VERILY IS RESTLESS, TURBULENT, POWERFUL AND UNYIELDING, O KRISHNA; IT SEEMS TO ME, TO CONTROL IT IS AS HARD AS TO CONTROL THE WIND.

Arjuna argues that the mind is without doubt restless, turbulent, strong and unyielding and is as difficult to control it as the wind.

The characteristics of the mind described in this verse are:

- Restless - Because the mind constantly changes its focus from one object to another.
- Turbulent - Because of the speed in the flow of thoughts and consequent agitations it creates in the body and the senses by bringing them under the control of the sense objects.
- Strong - Because once it gets attached to any sense object, it gains strength in the same attachment and sticks to that object despite logical reasoning to the contrary.
- Unyielding - Because of the impossibility of an individual to pull it back from its fast journey into the world of sense objects and to make it steady on a predetermined focus.

sri bhagavaan uvaacha
asamshayam mahaabaaho mano durnigraham chalam
abhyaasena tu kaunteya vairaagyena cha grihyate // 6.35 //

SRI BHAGAVAN SAID
UNDOUBTEDLY, O MIGHTY ARMED, THE MIND IS DIFFICULT TO CONTROL AND RESTLESS, BUT, BY PRACTICE AND DETACHMENT, O SON OF KUNTI, IT IS RESTRAINED.

Sri Krishna agrees that mind is unsteady and restless and therefore difficult to control and that the goal cannot be easily reached. But through practice and detachment mind can be brought under control.

Practice is the effort of the mind towards calmness. Practice becomes firmly grounded when it is followed for a long time and unremittingly with devotion. The end is easily achieved with the help of austerity, continence, discrimination and faith. The aspirant must not lose courage in the face of repeated failures.

Detachment is freedom from thirst for any pleasure seen or heard of. It is acquired through a constant perception of evil in sensuous happiness, either of this life or hereafter.

Patanjali Yoga Sutra 1.12 says *"abhyasavairagyabhyam tan nirodhaha"* meaning that the restless mind, accustomed to act on impulse, can be controlled only by non-attachment and practice. Of these two methods, the attempt to make the mind steady is called practice. (Sutra 1.13)

Bhagavatam explains non-attachment (vairagya) as "When there is earth to lie upon, why trouble about bed? When one's arm is readily available, why need pillows? When there is the palm of one's hand, why seek for plates and utensils? When there is the atmosphere, the bark of trees etc., what need is there of silks?"

Yoga Sutra (1.16) says "Supreme or the highest form of dispassion represents absence of thirst for all the three Gunas or modes of Prakriti. It is attained through the Knowledge of Purusha or Spirit, who is altogether different from Prakriti."

asamyataatmanaa yogo dushpraapa iti me matih
vashyaatmanaa tu yatataa shakyo'vaaptumupaayatah // 6.36 //

YOGA, I THINK, IS HARD TO ATTAIN BY ONE WHO IS NOT SELF-CONTROLLED BUT BY THE SELF-CONTROLLED IT IS ATTAINABLE THROUGH PROPER MEANS.

An uncontrolled mind cannot progress in spiritual path unless it discovers the Self. The discovery of the Self is possible by self-control achieved through the withdrawal of sense organs from their respective objects. Yoga can be attained by striving hard to utilize the conserved energies for the Divine purposes.

Yoga is the science of religion. The test of its validity lies in one's seeing results through actual experimentation. Hence the teachers of yoga emphasize self-control and other disciplines.

arjuna uvaacha
ayatih shraddhayopeto yogaacchalitamaanasah
apraapya yogasamsiddhim kaam gatim krishna gacchati // 6.37 //

ARJUNA SAID
HE WHO IS ENDOWED WITH FAITH, BUT NOT WITH SELF-CONTROL, AND WHOSE MIND WANDERS AWAY FROM YOGA - TO WHAT END DOES HE GO, O KRISHNA, HAVING FAILED TO ATTAIN PERFECTION IN YOGA?

This verse relates to a seeker who has faith in the efficacy of Yoga but who is unable to control the senses and the mind. Arjuna asks what happens to such a person for he may lose both the joys of the sense objects and the Absolute Bliss hereafter. The word Sraddha does not mean blind faith but an intellectual understanding of the deeper significance of what the teachers teach and scriptures declare.

kacchinnobhayavibhrashtash chhinnaabhramiva nashyati
apratishtho mahaabaaho vimoodho brahmanah pathi // 6.38 //

FALLEN FROM BOTH, DOES HE NOT, O MIGHTY ARMED, PERISH LIKE A RENT CLOUD, SUPPORTLESS AND DELUDED IN THE PATH OF BRAHMAN?

Arjuna wonders as to what will happen to the seeker who though full of faith but for want of mental restraint fails to achieve success having fallen from both. Fallen from both means achieving no success in the path of worldly success as also in the path of Yoga.

Rent cloud is that very small portion of the large cloud which gets detached from the latter on account of heavy winds and as a consequence moves about without any set direction hit by every passing breeze. Arjuna enquires whether such unsuccessful seekers will meander about the universe as the rented clouds and get lost.

etanme samshayam krishna chhettumarhasyasheshatah
twadanyah samshayasyaasya chhettaa na hyupapadyate // 6.39 //

O KRISHNA, PLEASE DISPEL THIS DOUBT OF MINE COMPLETELY FOR, IT IS NOT POSSIBLE FOR ANYONE BUT YOU TO DISPEL THIS DOUBT.

CLARIFICATION REGARDING PARTIAL SPIRITUAL EFFORTS

sri bhagavaan uvaacha
paartha naiveha naamutra vinaashastasya vidyate
nahi kalyaankrit kaschid durgatim taatagacchati // 6.40 //

SRI BHAGAVAN SAID
O PARTHA, THERE IS NO DESTRUCTION FOR HIM EITHER IN THIS WORLD, OR IN THE NEXT WORLD; NONE VERILY, WHO DOES GOOD, O MY SON, EVER COMES TO GRIEF.

In the following five verses Sri Krishna elucidates the path of progress of a seeker whose spiritual endeavors have not been met with any success either on account of death or due to any other temptation. The Lord assures him that he who does not achieve perfection in Yoga in this birth will not be destroyed either in this world or in the next. No destruction means that surely he will not take a birth lower than the present one in his next life. Doing good means striving for Self-realization.

WHAT HAPPENS TO HIM IS AS FOLLOWS.

praapya punyakritaam lokaanushitwaa shaashwateeh samaah
shucheenaam shreemataaam gehe yogabhrashto'bhijaayate // 6.41 //

HE WHO HAS FALLEN FROM YOGA GOES TO THE WORLD OF THE RIGHTEOUS AND HAVING LIVED THERE FOR LONG YEARS, HE IS BORN AGAIN IN THE HOUSE OF THE PURE AND THE PROSPEROUS.

The Lord says that the one who was not able to attain perfection in Yoga or the one who achieved some progress in Yoga but had fallen due to lack of dispassion or on account of turbulent senses, attains the worlds inhabited by those pious souls who performed great religious sacrifices while living on this earth. Having lived there as long as the merit of his past spiritual life lasts he is born again in the house of those whose conduct is governed by religion where he can continue his spiritual journey from the point where he had left in the previous birth.

athavaa yoginaameva kule bhavati dheemataam
etaddhi durlabhataram loke janma yadeedrisham // 6.42 //

OR HE IS BORN IN A FAMILY OF YOGIS RICH IN WISDOM; VERILY SUCH A BIRTH IS VERY DIFFICULT TO OBTAIN IN THIS WORLD.

Sri Krishna says that those who are possessed of genuine dispassion but yet fail to achieve success in Yoga are born in the family of enlightened yogis poor in resources but rich in wisdom. A birth in such families is rare to obtain than the one mentioned in the preceding verse. It is rare because he is placed right from the beginning of his life in an environment which is conducive for the practice of Yoga so that he could start his spiritual journey from a very early stage. Considering the greatness of the illumined souls, a birth in their families is stated to be very difficult to obtain.

Mundaka Upanishad (III-ii-9) says "In the family of a Knower of Brahman, none remains ignorant of Brahman. Transcending both grief and sin, and freed from the knot of ignorance in the heart, the member of such a family becomes immortal, i.e. attains freedom for all time from birth and death".

tatra tam buddhisamyogam labhate paurvadehikam
yatate cha tato bhooyah samsiddhau kurunandana // 6.43 //

THERE HE COMES IN TOUCH WITH THE KNOWLEDGE ACQUIRED IN HIS FORMER BODY AND STRIVES MORE THAN BEFORE FOR PERFECTION, O SON OF THE KURUS.

When he takes a human body again in this world, his previous efforts and practice of Yoga do not go in vain. They bear fruit in this birth and hasten his moral and spiritual evolution. Our thoughts, actions and experiences are left in our subconscious mind in the form of subtle impressions. These impressions of the present and the past births will be re-energized in the next birth. The impressions of the yogic tendencies will compel the seeker to work with greater vigor than in his former birth. Whatever progress a man makes in the path of yoga he retains. He again starts from there when the next opportunity arises.

poorvaabhyaasena tenaiva hriyate hyavasho'pi sah
jijnaasurapi yogasya shabdabrahmaativartate // 6.44 //

BY THAT FORMER PRACTICE ALONE HE IS BORNE ON IN SPITE OF HIMSELF. EVEN HE WHO MERELY WISHES TO KNOW YOGA GOES BEYOND THE WORLD OF VEDIC RITES.

The man who had failed in yoga is carried to the goal, which he intended to reach in the previous birth, by the force of impressions of his past yogic practices, though he may not be aware of it. If he had not done that many evil deeds as to overcome his yogic tendencies, he will certainly continue his yogic practices in this birth with great vigor by force of the impressions of the previous birth.

If the force of evil actions is very strong, the yogic tendencies would be overpowered or suppressed by them temporarily. As soon as the fruits of evil actions are exhausted the yogic vasanas will again manifest themselves and he will eventually attain the final realization.

Sri Krishna says even a man of enquiry in whom there is a desire to know about Yoga goes beyond the Brahmic word i.e. beyond Vedas. He rises above the Vedic rituals and ceremonies. He is not satisfied with mere ritualism and yearns for a higher fulfillment. If this is the case of an aspirant without any spiritual inclinations of the previous birth, how much more exalted will be the state of a seeker who takes up the practice of Yoga in this birth after having fallen from that path in his previous birth?

What the Lord implies is that no effort in the practice of yoga goes waste. Even the least effort bears fruit either in this birth or in another and there is no cause for any disappointment for any one including the dullest seeker.

prayatnaadyatamaanastu yogee samshuddhakilbishah
aneka janma samsiddhastato yaati paraam gatim // 6.45 //

BUT THE YOGI, WHO STRIVES DILIGENTLY, PURIFIED FROM SINS AND PERFECTED THROUGH MANY BIRTHS, ATTAINS THE SUPREME GOAL.

Mind and intellect of an individual function through the body in the world outside as per the qualities they assume because of the actions performed in their earlier births. The wrong and negative qualities of the mind and intellect are sins in the language of Vedanta. After purifying the mind from these sins the aspirant practices meditation and ultimately the mind becomes devoid of impressions which is called the end of the mind since the mind is nothing but a flow of thoughts.

When there is no thought, there is no mind and where there is no mind there is no ego which is termed as 'reaching the highest goal' or Self-Rediscovery. Little by little acquiring, through many births, the knowledge of Reality, he ultimately attains perfection. The Gita thus gives us hopeful belief in the redemption of all.

Although this theory is explained here in one or two sentences, in actual implementation, it is an achievement of many life times – 'many births' as The Lord puts it.

THE PERFECT YOGI

tapaswibhyo'dhiko yogee jnaanibhyo'pi mato'dhikah
karmibhyashchaadhiko yogee tasmaad yogee bhavaarjuna // 6.46 //

THE YOGI IS THOUGHT TO BE SUPERIOR TO THE ASCETICS AND EVEN SUPERIOR TO MEN OF KNOWLEDGE (OBTAINED MERELY THROUGH THE STUDY OF SCRIPTURES); HE IS ALSO SUPERIOR TO MEN OF ACTION; THEREFORE, YOU STRIVE TO BE A YOGI, O ARJUNA.

Sri Krishna brings out here that meditation is more important than various other practices in the matter of Spiritual Development. He says that the meditator is nobler than the Tapaswi, the one who observes austerities of the body and physical self-denials. The meditator is nobler than the Gnani also who deeply studies the scriptures and acquires their knowledge. The meditator is nobler than Karmis who undertake actions like sacrifices and other rituals enjoined in the Vedas as also charitable activities for obtaining rewards.

Through austerities, study, Vedic rituals, and philanthropic action, one attains purity of heart and then follows the path of Self-Knowledge. But the practice of yoga which is said to be superior to jnana, tapas and karma has the best of all the three and includes devotion. Yoga or union with God which is attained through Bhakti is superior because it enables one to arrive directly at the Supreme Goal. Arjuna is therefore advised to strive to be a yogi. Jnana here means scriptural learning and not spiritual realization.

yoginaamapi sarveshaam madgatenaantaraatmanaa
shraddhaavaan bhajate yo maam sa me yuktatamo matah // 6.47 //

AND AMONG ALL THE YOGIS, THE ONE WHO WORSHIPS ME WITH FAITH, HIS INMOST SELF ABIDING IN ME, I HOLD HIM TO BE THE MOST CLOSELY UNITED WITH ME IN YOGA.

It has been told earlier that meditation is the best among all the paths of spirituality. Meditation is a deliberate act by which the seeker strives to keep his thoughts channelized into one pre-determined line of thinking by not allowing the mind to entertain any other thoughts. It is therefore an attempt to fix the mind upon some object of contemplation.

According to the chosen nature of the object of contemplation and the method of controlling the mind from its wanderings, the art of meditation is classified as meditation upon a symbol, on a god-principle with a form, on the teacher, on the Kundalini, on any of the Great Elements or on a chosen text in the scriptures. Accordingly, the practitioners may be considered as followers of different kinds of meditation.

Yoga or union with the God which is attained through Bhakti is the highest goal. It also means the science of concentration and stilling of the modes of the mind. After giving a long account of the yoga discipline, the obstacles to be overcome, the Lord concludes that the greatest among the yogins is the devotee or the Bhakta.

This verse, following the praise of yoga, tells that devotion to God which makes one to cling to The Lord in utter faith and self-surrender makes yoga all the more exalted.

Gita stresses the importance of love of God or Ishwara and devotion to Him which make spiritual discipline complete. It emphasizes the path of Bhakti (devotion) as the easiest and best form of Yoga.

om tat sat iti srimad bhagavadgeetaasu upanishatsu brahma vidyaayaam yogashaastre sri krishnaarjuna samvaade dhyaanayogo naama shashthodhyaayah ||

THUS IN THE UPANISHADS OF THE GLORIOUS BHAGAVAD GITA, THE SCIENCE OF THE ETERNAL, THE SCRIPTURE OF YOGA, THE DIALOGUE BETWEEN SRI KRISHNA AND ARJUNA, ENDS THE SIXTH DISCOURSE ENTITLED THE YOGA OF MEDITATION

AN OUTLINE VIEW OF THIS CHAPTER

Through proper service and sacrifice one develops sufficient renunciation to enable one to concentrate, meditate and realize the supreme Self. The preceding chapter helps the seeker to attain dispassion and thus prepare himself for meditation. This chapter continues with the process of spiritual development culminating in the practice of meditation and ultimate merging eith Brahman.

I - YOGI (ACTIVE) RISES TO JNANI (ENLIGHTEND) - Verses 1 – 9

The first nine verses reiterate the three stages of spiritual development as described in the previous chapter. A yogi with worldly vasanas, needs karma yoga, the path of action, to evolve spiritually. Through action he sheds his vasanas and becomes a sanyasi. A sanyasi, in a state of renunciation, needs meditation and quietness to reach the ultimate state of Jnani. Both yogi and sanyasi head towards the same goal of Self-realization but their sadhanas (spiritual practices) differ. Whatever the sadhana, every seeker must put in his own effort to raise himself by himself.

II - EXTERNAL AND INTERNAL DISCIPLINES FOR MEDITATION - VERSES 10 – 18

Yogi and Sanyasi are both on the spiritual path. However, the Sanyasi alone, having developed a dispassion for the world, qualifies for meditation and realization. This topic enumerates all the steps that one must take for practicing meditation. It also details the environmental, physical, mental and intellectual preparations necessary to take the seat of meditation. When a seeker follows all these preparations he will become freed from desire, possessiveness, and the consequent sorrow. He will then become established in Yoga and be fully prepared for plunging into meditation.

III - CONTROLLED MIND REMAINS PEACEFUL - VERSES 19 – 24

Through physical, mental and intellectual disciplines one must withdraw the mind from its preoccupation with the world and direct it to the Self within. Render the mind introvert. As soon as the mind tastes the bliss of the Self it will know that there is no greater enjoyment. Being established therein, the greatest sorrow in the world cannot disturb its equanimity and peace. One practices Yoga(union with the Self) through complete control of the senses and of the thought flow which produce desires. This sets the stage for the practice of meditation and realization of the Self.

IV - MEDITATION REVEALS SELF IN ONE AND ALL - VERSES 25 – 32

The mind in the state of meditation thinks of the Self. The intellect holds the mind single-pointedly upon the Self without allowing it to slip into any other thought. Whenever the mind wanders away the intellect brings it back through supervision and control. By maintaining single pointed thought of the Self the mind becomes absolutely tranquil and quiet. The Jnani then experiences the infinite bliss of Brahman. Thereafter, he sees the Self in all beings and all beings in the Self. He sees the Supreme Being everywhere.

V - CAN A RESTLESS MIND BE CONTROLLED? - VERSES 33 – 39

When he heard the exposition on how to discipline and control the mind, Arjuna raises a doubt as to whether the mind can be controlled at all. He wonders how the mind, a restless, turbulent, strong and obstinate entity can be brought under control. And even if forcefully brought under control, how can the mind continue to remain steady and calm? Krishna assures Arjuna that the intellect can control the mind through sustained practice and dispassion. Arjuna wonders as to what will happen to a seeker and his efforts if he fails to attain Self-realisation in his lifetime. Will he not be denied the benefits of both the material and spiritual worlds?

VI ~ YOGI UNITES WITH BRAHMAN ~ VERSE 40 -47

Krishna allays Arjuna's concern and assures him that no seeker falling short of Realisation in his life time will ever suffer either here or hereafter. Such a person will gain a heavenly bliss and reincarnate in a pure and wealthy home or in a family of wise yogis, which will provide him with an ideal environment for him to pursue his spiritual goal of Realization in his new life. Therefore, Krishna advises Arjuna to practise yoga with devotion and determination until he merges with the Supreme Brahman.

<<<000>>>

CHAPTER 7

Jnaana Vijnaana Yogah:

Yoga of Knowledge and Wisdom

PREAMBLE

The following are the four *Mahavakyas* (Great Truths) taken out from each of the four Vedas all indicating the same Truth.

Prajnanam Brahma	>>>	Consciousness is Brahman
Tat Twam Asi	>>>	That You Are
Ayam Atma Brahma	>>>	This Atman is Brahman
Aham Brahma Smi	>>>	I am Brahman

We have seen earlier that the eighteen chapters of Gita can be divided into 3 sets of 6 Chapters each explaining the Truth of the Mahavakya - 'You Are That'. This sentence summarizes the entire vedic law and philosophy. The first 6 Chapters of Gita explain the significance of the term 'You' (Twam). The next 6 Chapters from the 7th to 12th explain the term 'That' (Tat). The last 6 Chapters give the meaning of the term 'Are' (Asi) and explain the message of the entire Mahavakya i.e. how the individual can blend with Parabrahman or attain Liberation. This Division does not mean any compartmentalization but implies a close relationship between the verses as also a logical thoughtflow from one Chapter to another.

Sri Krishna ended the previous Chapter by describing the supreme yogi as one who, with his inmost self abiding in Him, adores the Lord. We were told about the technique of meditation for obtaining Self-Realization and that a meditator is superior to a Tapasvi or Gnani. It declared that the one who has successfully merged his mind in the nature of Pure Consciousness through single-pointed meditation is the highest and the dearest to The Lord.

Arjuna still doubts how a limited and mortal mind and intellect of a finite entity like man could ever understand the limitless Infinite with all its virtues and glory. Sri Krishna therefore clarifies this doubt in this Chapter by describing the nature of the Lord Himself, who is the point of concentration of the yogi's unwavering devotion.

Sri Krishna uses the first person singular pronoun 'ME' to mean the supreme Reality or *brahman* or God. He tells Arjuna that the supreme Godhead has to be realized in both its transcendent and immanent aspects. The Yogi who has reached this summit has nothing more to know.

This complete union with the Lord is difficult to attain. Among many thousands of human beings, very few aspire for this union, and even among those who aspire for it, few ever reach the pinnacle of spiritual realization.

The Lord gives a clear description of the all-pervading static and infinite state of His Being. He then proceeds to explain His manifestations as the universe and the power behind it.

He speaks of these manifestations as His lower and higher Prakritis. The lower Prakriti is made up of the five elements, mind, ego and intellect. The higher Prakriti is the life-element which upholds the universe, activates it and causes its appearance and final dissolution.

Krishna says that whatever exists is nothing but Himself. He is the cause of the appearance of the universe and all things in it. Everything is strung on Him like clusters of gems on a string. He is the essence, substance and substratum of everything, whether visible or invisible. Although everything is in Him, yet He transcends everything as the actionless Self.

Prakriti or nature is made up of the three Gunas or qualities—Sattva, Rajas and Tamas. These three qualities delude the soul and make it forget its true nature, which is one with God. This delusion, termed Maya, can only be removed by the Grace of the Lord Himself.

'Jnana' means consummate knowledge of the formless and attributeless aspect of the Lord. 'Vijnana' means experiencing that knowledge. Awareness of the Lord comprises of both such knowledge and experience. The present Chapter deals with such Integral Divinity, the practices which lead to its knowledge and the fortunate souls who possess such knowledge. In simple terms the Chapter tells us about

- the concept of God or Brahman or Soul
- examples of manifestation of God in the universe and
- how to perceive God within oneself.

It is therefore named as 'The Yoga of Jnana and Vijnana', Yoga of Knowledge and Wisdom.

THE TEXT

sri bhagavaan uvaacha
mayyaasaktamanaah paartha yogam yunjanmadaashrayah
asamshayam samagram maam yathaa jnaasyasi tacchrinu // 7.1 //

SRI BHAGAVAN SAID
HEAR, O PARTHA, HOW, WITH YOUR MIND INTENT ON ME, AND TAKING REFUGE IN ME AND PRACTICING YOGA, YOU WILL WITHOUT DOUBT KNOW ME IN FULL.

A Yogi's mind is attached to the Lord alone setting aside all the other disciplines. It worships the Lord with complete concentration. The Lord alone is the whole basis of the yogi's being and the goal of his action. Practicing yoga means being united with the Lord in contemplation. Knowing the Lord in full implies knowing all His six attributes viz., infinite greatness, strength, power, grace, knowledge and detachment. As Arjuna has the necessary qualifications, Sri Krishna assures that He will give him a complete or integral knowledge of the Divine, not merely the abstract Pure Self but also its manifestations in the world.

jnaanam te'ham savijnaanam idam vakshyaamyasheshatah
yajjnaatwaa neha bhooyo'nyaj jnaatavyamavashishyate // 7.2 //

I SHALL TEACH YOU IN FULL BOTH KNOWLEDGE AND EXPERIENCE, WHICH HAVING BEEN KNOWN, NOTHING MORE REMAINS TO BE KNOWN BY YOU.

Jnana means knowledge, the direct spiritual illumination and Vijnana is the detailed rational knowledge of the principles of existence. We must have not merely the knowledge of the relationless Absolute but also of its varied manifestations.

The awareness that the Lord exists and that He is the inmost spirit of all is knowledge. This knowledge can be acquired by study of the scriptures, and reasoning about their contents. But to realize the Lord in oneself and in all other beings and to act according to that realization is experience, *vijnana*. For example, to know that one can obtain fire from wood is knowledge. But to kindle fire in the wood and feel its heat and light in a dark winter night is experience, *Vijnana*. In Hinduism knowledge of God is inseparable from experience.

Because the Lord is everything, when He is fully known everything else is automatically known. The Lord as *Sat-chit-ananda* (existence-knowledge-bliss absolute) forms the real essence of all objects. Names and forms are mere illusory superimposition.

manushyaanaam sahasreshu kaschidyatati siddhaye
yatataamapi siddhaanaam kaschinmaam vetti tattwatah // 7.3 //

AMONG THOUSANDS OF PEOPLE, ONE BY CHANCE ASPIRES FOR PERFECTION; EVEN AMONG THOSE SUCCESSFUL ASPIRANTS, ONE BY CHANCE KNOWS ME IN ESSENCE.

The question why the Self-Realized masters are so rare and why such a realization is not within the reach of everyone is answered.

'Knowing Me in essence' - The Being of the Lord and His diverse manifestations are incomprehensible to the human mind. He is the Impersonal Reality, the Personal God, and many other things besides. Of all living beings on earth, man alone can inquire about his self and its relationship with the Lord. Among innumerable human beings, only a few develop a desire for such an inquiry. Among those who show such desire, only a few know the means of attaining knowledge and strive after it. Among those who strive, only a fortunate few succeed in acquiring the true knowledge of the Lord. Hence knowledge of God is rare on this earth.

Thus far Ajuna has been taught the highest form of devotion, which leads to union with God in its static aspect as also with His dynamic Prakriti. Krishna tells him that there are also other forms of devotion which are inferior as they are performed with various motives. The distressed, the seeker of divine wisdom, and he who desires wealth, worship Him, as also the wise. Of these the Lord deems the wise as dearest to Him. Such a devotee loves the Lord for the sake of pure love alone. Whatever form the devotee worships, the ultimate goal is the Lord Himself. The Lord accepts such worship, knowing that it is directed to Him only.

TWO KINDS OF NATURE OF THE LORD

bhoomiraaponalo vaayuh kham mano buddhireva cha
ahamkaara iteeyam me bhinnaa prakritirashtadhaa // 7.4 //

EARTH, WATER, FIRE, AIR, ETHER, MIND, REASON AND EGO - SUCH IS THE EIGHTFOLD DIVISION OF MY NATURE.

apareyamitastwanyaam prakritim viddhi me paraam
jeevabhootaam mahaabaaho yayedam dhaaryate jagat // 7.5 //

O MIGHTY ARMED, THIS IS MY LOWER NATURE. BUT DIFFERENT FROM IT, YOU KNOW MY HIGHER NATURE,

THE INDWELLING SPIRIT BY WHICH THE UNIVERSE IS SUSTAINED.

The relationship between spirit and matter which is the source of creation is explained here. The vedantic technical terms for these words are *'Purusha'* for the indwelling spirit and *'Prakriti'* for the matter. Matter is inert, insentient while spirit is sentient, dynamic. A combination of these two ingredients causes things to be born and function. In a steam engine, steam is the spirit-factor which makes the iron and steel assemblage of the engine which are matter-envelopments to function. The iron and steel components which are manufactured by somebody cannot function by themselves unless steam is made to pass through them. When the steam passes through the iron and steel assemblage we say that a steam engine is born or created.

CREATION

Let us understand the process of creation from the Vedantic angle in more details.

First before understanding the topic of creation, we should clearly know that the very word creation is a misnomer because nothing can be created on account of the law of conservation of matter and energy. Then if at all we use the word Creation, it only refers to the manifestation of something which was potentially, un-manifestly existent. So only that which is un-manifestly, potentially existent in dormant form can come to manifestation.

MANIFEST VS UNMANIFEST

What is meant by the words manifest and unmanifest? By the word unmanifest, we mean *Pramanam Agocharam*. Unmanifest is that which is existent but is not available for perception or transaction like the butter in the milk. Butter is there in the milk, but we cannot see it in the milk. But we know that milk has butter. So what can we say about butter being existent or not? It is existent technically but for all practical purposes, since it is neither available for perception nor available for transaction we assume that butter is non-existent. But we know butter is there.

We can extend this analogy to everything in the creation. Nothing in the creation is non existent. It was existent in potential manner. Later it becomes manifest, which means it is available for transaction. The scriptures point out, before the origination of this cosmos, it should have existed because of this simple law of conservation. And if this creation existed before, it should have existed in un-differentiated and unmanifest form or potential form or dormant form which we can call as the seed of the creation. In Sanskrit we use the word *Bījam* for this Causal form of matter.

Matter in its causal form is the source of all forms of energy and all forms of matter. The causal matter is called *Maya*. This means that before the creation originated, one thing was there which is called Maya.

We have to include one more thing that existed before creation. That is *Atma* which is the consciousness principle, the non-material spirit. It does not come under matter and therefore it does not come within time and space. This means that as consciousness is beyond time and space it has to be eternal which implies that before the creation, consciousness also existed.

So now we had arrived at two things that were existing before creation -

- Principle 1: Consciousness which is called Atma which is unconditioned, un-influenced, un-circumscribed by the time and space.
- Principle 2: Whole creation in causal matter form called Maya

To put it in simple words, we can now conclude that Consciousness and Maya existed in causal form before creation.

In the context of cosmology or creation, consciousness is given another name. At the Micro level i.e., with reference to an individual, consciousness is given the name of Atma. The very same consciousness at the Macro level is called Brahman. Therefore Atma and Brahman are synonymous meaning the same thing i.e., consciousness.

Atma means *Apnoti Sarvam Iti Atma* – the boundless all pervading one. The word Brahman means infinite derived from the root Bruh – to be big – therefore Brahman means the Big One, the Absolutely Big One.

Thus the study of cosmology begins with two beginning-less principles known as
Brahman and Maya or Consciousness (Spirit) + Matter.

DIFFERENCE BETWEEN MAYA AND BRAHMAN

The common features of Brahman and Maya are both have no beginning, no origin. But differences are several as given below.

BRAHMAN

1. Non-material Principle called Consciousness.
2. Does not have physical properties. It is called *Nirguna*, propertyless principle because it is non-material in nature.
3. It is beyond Time & Space. It is never subject to change. It is changeless.
4. It is *nirvikalpa*, not subject to spatial division. Consciousness is one and not many. It is divisionless.

MAYA

1. Material principle.
2. It is full of potential properties because it is matter. Hence it is called *saguna*.
3. Because it is matter principle, it can never remain the same.
4. Maya, the material, is subject to multiplication and division.

These are the basic similarities and differences between Brahman and Maya and out of their blending alone this universe comes into manifestation for our recognition like we churn and bring out the butter which is then available tangibly for our transaction.

STAGES OF MANIFESTATION

In the scriptures the evolution or manifestation of the cosmos is presented in two stages. Like a seed becoming a plant in the middle stage, and then the plant becoming a full fledged tree in the final stage.

Therefore Maya is a seed stage containing the causal universe which comes to the level of subtle universe comparable to that of a plant and then the subtle universe evolves or manifests to become the gross universe fully available for all forms of transactions and engagement.

If you have to understand the difference between the subtle and gross creation you can compare your body and mind. Mind is also a creation or manifestation. Body is also a manifestation. But mind is a subtle manifestation not available for a physical vision because it is not tangible. But the body is gross and visible to the eye.

SUBTLE AND GROSS ELEMENTS

The scriptures point out that first, out of the causal universe five subtle elements is born. These are called *Pancha Bhuta.* These are 1.*Akasa* or space 2.*Vayu* or air 3.*Agni* or fire 4.*Jalam* or water 5.*Bhumi or Prithvi*: the earth. In the initial stages, they are in subtle form, which means they are not available for our transaction. They are not even visible.

Māyā is defined as *Tri Gunatmika* i.e endowed with threefold feature which is seen in the universe. They are *Sattva Guna, Rajo Guna and Tamo Guna.* These three Gunas or features or attributes inhere the five elements also. Thus we have got Sāttvika component of space, Rājasik a component of space and Tāmasik component of space. Similarly we have Sāttvika component of air, Rājasik component of air and Tāmasik component of air. Same applies for Fire, Water and Earth. Therefore we have fifteen items. Hence the first form of creation is *Sūkshma Bhūta Srushti* – the creation or manifestation of the subtle elements.

STAGE 1 – SATTVA GUNA AS GENERATOR:

From the Satvic portion of subtle elements are born the organs of perception *(jnana indriyas)*, Ear is born from the Satvic aspect of Space, Skin from Air, Eye from fire, Tongue from water and Nose from earth.

From the total Satvic content of the five elements are born the *Anthahkarana* or inner instrument. Antahkarana consists of four aspects, *manas,* Mind (doubting nature), *buddhi,* intellect (deciding nature), *ahankar,* ego ("I am the doer" nature) and *chitta,* memory (thinking faculty)

STAGE 2 – RAJO GUNA AS GENERATOR

From the Rajasic portion of subtle elements are born the organs of action *(karma indriyas)*. From the rajasic aspect of space is born the speech, hands from air, legs from fire, genitals from water and anus from earth.

From the total Rajasic content of the five elements are born the five vital airs or *pancha prana*..

Each of the subtle elements is endowed with the property of its own. Space *(akasa)* has the property of producing sound; air *(vayu)* of producing touch; fire *(agni)* of visibility; water *(ap)* of flavor; and earth *(bhumi)* producing smell *(sabda, sparsa, rupa, rasa, gandha)*. These are the five ways in which a man, through his five sense organs becomes aware of the *prakriti* or matter. Hence Hindu philosophers have divided matter into five elements. It is to be noted that mind or *manas* (the inner organ that creates doubt), intellect or *buddhi* (the inner organ that decides) and I-Consciousness or Ego belong to the realm of *prakriti* or matter.

The entire *Sūkshma Shariram* is born out of Sattva Guna and Rajo Guna of the five subtle elements. Therefore we have seen *Sukshma Bhuta Srushti* and *Sukshma Sharira Srushti* – in short the entire subtle universe.

STAGE 3 –TAMO GUNA AS GENERATOR

From the Tamasic portion of the subtle elements are born the gross elements. The gross elements are formed through combination of tamasic portion of subtle elements in which each of the subtle elements combines with the remaining four subtle elements under a peculiar formula to produce a gross element. This process of combination is called *panchikaranam.*

Thus the gross elements of ether, air, fire, water and earth are produced which we are able to see with our eyes. The five subtle elements are therefore the causes for the five gross elements. The scriptures point out that the Tamas components of the five elements alone get grossified to become the five gross elements – *Pancha Sthula Bhuta.*

The scriptures say that until grossification, each element was isolated and pure. One element was not adulterated or mixed with others. But when grossification takes place, the Tamo Guna of these five elements gets intermixed. This is just like eating a salad. *Sukshma Prapancha* is like eating grapes separately, bananas separately etc. Grossification means eating all together. Once we come to five grossified elements, each element has got a mixture of all the five. So Earth has got five elements, space has got five elements. Same way for Air, Fire and Water. This process of "salad making" is called Panchi Karanam or Grossification.

Once the five gross elements are born, out of that the entire cosmos including all our physical bodies are created. This is called *Sthula Srushti or Sthula Abhivyakti.*

Thus Maya is causal universe. And out of that comes subtle universe called *Sukshma Abhivyakti.* And out of that comes gross universe which is called *Sthula Abhivyakti.* Thus the entire creation comes out.

Therefore causal universe to subtle universe to Gross universe. This is the creation. Of these, the causal universe is beginningless, but the subtle and gross have a beginning and an end.

Once it has become fully gross and moved about for some time, what happens to the whole creation? Again it collapses, condenses or contracts; evolution will later end up in involution or dissolution. The gross becomes subtle and subtle again becomes gross. Thus unmanifest to manifest and manifest to Unmanifest, the universe undergoes this cycle always. But the Universe will always be there. The difference is only a question of degree but not substance. There is no increase or decrease in matter but there is only change in its condition or state – manifest condition to unmanifest condition and unmanifest to manifest.

Avyaktadini Bhuaani Vyaktamadhyani Bharata
Avyakta Nidhananyeva Tatra Ka Paridevana

Krishna will tell us in the Bhagavad Gita later – why are you talking about death? Death is nothing but body going out of shape. Nothing is lost, Arjuna, but for whom are you crying? The problem is that we have got attached to shape and lost sight of the substance.

The creation will last for some time and again collapse to Maya. What will be Brahman doing? Consciousness remains. When the appropriate conditions come forth, it manifests in the form of life. When the manifesting conditions are not there, consciousness remains unmanifest. This is Vedic Cosmology". *(Adopted from Swami Paramarthananda's Discourses on 'Tattva Bhodha')*

Let us turn back to the Gita.

Once the individual understands the distinction between matter and spirit, he will know that the cause of all our sufferings is due to spirit identifying with matter. When spirit is detached from all its identifications, it rediscovers for itself its own essential nature as Perfection and Bliss Absolute. The spirit identifying with matter or *apara prakriti* is called ego. This is also called super imposition on the Truth through ignorance. It is *apara prakriti* which is the cause of the world and by which the ego or Jiva gets bound. It is the ego that rediscovers itself to be nothing other than the spirit or *para prakriti* that presides over the matter. In order to make it clear Sri Krishna tells that the matter-aspect is distinct from the spirit-aspect in each individual.

The five elements are represented by the sense-organs by which the individual lives and gathers experiences in the world of sense objects as we have seen above. The sense organs are the channels through which the world of stimuli reaches the mind. The impulses received in the mind are classified and systematized as knowledge by the intellect. During all these assimilation the ego falsely identifies the body with the Spirit and the sense of 'I' or 'My' is produced.

Sri Krishna says that the equipments referred to in Verse 4 are not all that the Self possesses. The Self has, besides them, equipments of a higher nature which are Pure Consciousness or Awareness i.e., *para prakriti* (Verse 5). It is this spiritual aspect in everybody that makes it possible for the body, mind and intellect which are inert matters to function as if they are very cognizant and intelligent.

The spiritual factor is the entity with whose contact the body equipment works and without which it becomes dull and insentient. Without this spiritual spark man will be no more than a stone and he will not be able to experience the world outside or within him. The world of objects, the world of feelings and the world of ideas that we experience constitute in their totality the *Jagat* or universe which is supported by the principle of consciousness.

etadyoneeni bhootaani sarvaaneetyupadhaaraya
aham kritsnasya jagatah prabhavah pralayastathaa // 7.6 //

KNOW THESE TWO - MY HIGHER AND LOWER NATURES - FORM THE WOMB OF ALL BEINGS. THEREFORE, I AM THE ORIGIN AND DISSOLUTION OF THE WHOLE UNIVERSE.

The above mentioned higher and lower natures together cause the manifestation of the world of plurality. If there is no matter, the latent dynamic energy of the Spirit will not have a field for its expression. The matter by itself is dormant and it cannot function unless the Spirit is there to activate it, to enliven it. An example of this principle is electricity and the bulb. The bulb is the inert matter and the electricity is the dynamic spirit. It is obvious that one is of no use without the other. When the spirit functions through the five layers of the matter it finds a place to express itself.

The combination of the higher and lower natures (prakritis) is the womb of all beings i.e., these two are the cause for the origin of all creatures or manifestation. The lower nature manifests itself as the material body and the higher nature as the enlivening soul, the experiencer.

At the time of evolution, names, forms and life arise from prakriti and at the time of dissolution they go back into it. But prakriti, independent of the Lord (Consciousness or Brahman or Spirit) cannot generate anything. Prakriti is the Lord's instrument of creation, preservation and dissolution. Hence the Lord is the ultimate cause of the Universe; as we have seen under the topic "Creation" above. Brahman (the Lord) + Maya or Consciousness (Spirit) + Matter is the ultimate cause of the evolution and dissolution of the Universe or Creation or Manifestation.

These ideas constitute the nucleus of the knowledge about Brahman, Maya, Manifestation or Creation all of which are dealt with elaborately in the subsequent Chapters of the Gita especially in Chapters 8, 9, 13, 14 and 15. Hence these concepts and ideas should be thoroughly grasped and kept in mind for a fruitful study of the latter Chapters of the Gita.

mattah parataram naanyat kinchidasti dhananjaya
mayi sarvamidam protam sootre maniganaa iva // 7.7 //

THERE EXISTS NOTHING WHATSOEVER HIGHER THAN ME, O DHANANJAYA. ALL THIS IS STRUNG ON ME, AS A ROW OF GEMS ON A THREAD.

There exists no other cause of the universe except the Lord. To show that the Self is one and the same in all created beings on the earth it is stated here that The Lord is the supporter of the Universe just as the string is the supporter of gems in a garland. Without the string the gems will be scattered. Without the Lord, the planets, the stars and all else will be dispersed. The Lord, manifesting Himself through the physical and moral laws, sustains the relative world. He is also the Unity that underlies the diversity of names and forms.

The substance with which gems and thread are made is different. Similarly the world is constituted of infinite variety of names and forms which are held together by the Spiritual Truth into a complete whole. Even in an individual, the body, mind and intellect are different from one another but they work in harmony and in unity because of the same spiritual Truth, the principle of consciousness. Hence Sri Krishna says that there is no other cause of the Universe but Him; He alone is the cause of the Universe.

ILLUSTRATIONS OF THE LORD'S MANIFESTATIONS

raso'hamapsu kaunteya prabhaasmi shashisooryayoh
pranavah sarva vedeshu shabdah khe paurusham nrishu // 7.8 //

O SON OF KUNTI, I AM THE SAVOR OF WATERS, THE RADIANCE OF THE SUN AND MOON, THE SYLLABLE OM IN ALL THE VEDAS, THE SOUND IN ETHER AND THE MANLINESS IN MAN.

punyo gandhah prithivyaam cha tejashcha'smi vibhaavasau
jeevanam sarvabhooteshu tapashchaasmi tapaswishu // 7.9 //

I AM THE SWEET FRAGRANCE IN EARTH AND BRILLIANCE IN THE FIRE, THE LIFE IN ALL BEINGS AND I AM THE AUSTERITY IN THE ASCETICS.

In these two verses the doubt as to what is the eternal factor which is common in all and yet not readily perceptible to anybody is cleared.

That which remains always from beginning to end and without which the thing cannot be identified as such is declared to be its essence, its Dharma - the law of its being. All examples given here by The Lord like savor in water, radiance in the sun and the moon, syllable OM in the Vedas, the principle of sound in Space, manliness in man, brilliance in the fire, life in all beings etc. indicate that the Lord is that factor or subtle principle which gives the individual creatures different characteristics of their own..

beejam maam sarvabhootaanaam viddhi paartha sanaatanam
buddhir buddhimataamasmi tejastejaswinaamaham // 7.10 //

KNOW ME, O PARTHA, AS THE ETERNAL SEED OF ALL BEINGS THAT EXIST; I AM THE INTELLIGENCE OF THE INTELLIGENT AND THE SPLENDOR OF THE SPLENDID (THINGS AND BEINGS).

balam balavataamasmi kaamaraagavivarjitam
dharmaaviruddho bhooteshu kaamo'smi bharatarshabha // 7.11 //

OF THE STRONG, I AM THE STRENGTH - DEVOID OF DESIRE AND ATTACHMENT AND IN ALL BEINGS, I AM THE DESIRE UNOPPOSED TO DHARMA, O BEST AMONG THE BHARATAS.

The Lord continues to indicate the same truth by means of some more analogies. Sri Krishna tells that He is the strength among the strong but devoid of desire and attachment.

The terms desire and attachment are not synonymous. Desire is for what is absent at present in the scheme of life and attachment or affection is for what one has already obtained. These two emotions are generally the cause of conflict between individuals, communities and countries assisted by their respective strength.

Another concept is brought in here - Desire unopposed to Dharma. All actions, thoughts and ideas entertained by an individual which are not contrary to his own nature of Divinity make up his Dharma. Such actions, thoughts etc. which lead him to discover his nature of Divinity are considered righteous actions. Those actions which remove him from his inherent nature of Divinity are called unrighteous implying that The Lord is all the desires that are not wrongful to a living being.

ye chaiva saatvikaa bhaavaa raajasaas taamasaashcha ye
matta eveti taanviddhi natwaham teshu te mayi // 7.12 //

WHATEVER THINGS THERE BE THAT ARE PURE (PERTAINING TO SATTVA), ACTIVE (PERTAINING TO RAJAS) AND INERT (PERTAINING TO TAMAS), KNOW THEM TO PROCEED FROM ME ALONE; YET I AM NOT IN THEM, THEY ARE IN ME.

This verse concludes the discussion started with the statement "all this is strung in Me as a row of pearls on a thread". All things (including the different states of mind) are in The Lord but He is not in them just as all waves are in the ocean but the ocean is not in them. The universe is only an appearance superimposed by illusion (Maya) on the Lord. It is like a mirage in the desert. From the standpoint of the onlooker, the illusory water exists in the desert; but the desert does not depend upon or exist in the mirage. Likewise this universe, apparently superimposed on the Lord, exists in the Lord, but the Lord is not in the universe. None of the properties of the universe touches the Lord, just as the waters of the mirage cannot soak a single grain of the desert sand.

The gunas constitute prakriti or nature which is the lower manifestation of the Lord. Therefore the Lord is their ultimate cause. But the Lord is not, as in the case of worldly men, under the control of the gunas. The gunas, on the contrary, are subject to Him.

GUNAS

A reference to the gunas was made by Krishna in the Gita earlier vide Chapter 2 verse 45. In the beginning of this Chapter we have seen the Lord is of two kinds of nature viz, Purusha and Prakriti. The former denotes the Soul or Consciousness and the latter Nature or matter, which is dull and insentient. Prakriti consists of three gunas namely, sattva, rajas, and tamas. Rajas denotes restlessness or active principle. Tamas is the principle of inertia and Sattva, serenity and harmony, is the equilibrium between rajas and tamas. As prakriti consists of the three gunas, every object in prakriti is compounded of these three gunas. Samsara is the realm of the gunas. Freedom is beyond these gunas.

Prakriti is not independent of the Lord. Everything constituted by the three gunas is in no sense a self-dependent essence independent of God but springs from Him alone. While He contains and comprehends all, they do not contain and comprehend Him. This is the distinction between God and His creatures. They undergo changes because of the divine but their changes do not touch the integrity of the Divine. The lord is not subject to any one else, while all things are subject to Him.

Matter exists because of Spirit and Spirit is never restrained or regulated by the finite matter. The three Gunas - Sattva, Rajas and Tamas - which are temperaments or nature of the head and heart, by which the instruments of feeling, thinking and action come to play their role everywhere, rise from the Self.

MODES OF NATURE CONFUSE MEN

tribhirgunamayair bhaavairebhih sarvamidam jagat
mohitam naabhijaanaati maamebhyah paramavyayam // 7.13 //

DELUDED BY THESE THREEFOLD GUNAS (MODES OF NATURE) OF PRAKRITI THE WHOLE WORLD DOES NOT RECOGNIZE ME AS DISTINCT FROM THEM AND IMPERISHABLE.

The people of this world are deluded by the three gunas or qualities of nature. Affection, attachment and infatuated love, hatred are all the characteristics of the gunas. On account of delusion created by these qualities they are not able to break worldly ties and turn their minds towards the Supreme Lord though the Lord is the inmost Self of all beings and the object of direct and immediate perception.

The Lord in His purest essence is untouched by the gunas which belong only to His prakriti. The Self is the essence which does not have the six modifications of the body viz. birth, growth, existence, old age, decay and death.

This verse answers the question as to why the ordinary mortals are not able to understand at least the presence of the great truth about the spirit and matter. The answer in short is that deluded by the modifications of the three Gunas the living beings become blind to the divine possibilities in themselves. So long as a ghost is seen in the post, the vision of the post will not be available to the perceiver. Thus deluded, the ego does not realize the Supreme as different from it.

Dr.S.Radhakrishnan comments: "According to Sankara the Supreme expresses His regret that the world does not know Him, the Supreme Lord who is, by nature, eternal, pure, enlightened and free, the Self of all beings, devoid of attributes *(gunatheetha)* by knowing whom the seed of the evil of *samsara* is burnt up. We see the changing forms and not the Eternal Being of which the forms are the manifestations. We see the moving shadows on the wall whereas we must see the Light from which the shadows emanate".

WHO CAN REALIZE THE SUPREME?

daivee hyeshaa gunamayee mama maayaa duratyayaa
maameva ye prapadyante maayaametaam taranti te // 7.14 //

VERILY, THIS DIVINE ILLUSION OF MINE (MAYA), CONSISTING OF THE GUNAS, IS HARD TO OVERCOME. BUT THOSE WHO TAKE REFUGE IN ME ALONE SHALL CROSS OVER THIS ILLUSION.

Maya or illusion is divine because it is a part of the Lord's nature and inscrutable to human reason as we have seen earlier. It is hard to overcome by self-effort if unaided by divine grace. Although Sri Krishna Himself admits that it is not easy for any egocentric individual to transcend this illusion which is caused by His Maya, the Lord says that those who devote themselves to Him alone can overcome this obstacle which creates sorrows and imperfections in the objective world.

How to do this was already explained under 'Meditation' in the previous Chapter.

IF MAYA CAN BE OVERCOME BY DEVOTION WHY DO NOT ALL WORSHIP HIM?

na maam dushkritino moodhaah prapadyante naraadhamaah
maayayaapahritajnaanaa aasuraam bhaavamaashritaah // 7.15 //

THE EVIL-DOERS AND THE DELUDED AND THE VILEST AMONG MEN, DEPRIVED OF KNOWLEDGE BY MAYA AND FOLLOWING THE WAYS OF DEMONS DO NOT WORSHIP ME.

In the previous verse Sri Krishna talked of those who can successfully transcend their own subjective delusion. In this verse He gives the negative nature in those who cannot overcome this delusion for realizing the Divinity in themselves.

He says that low men because of their delusion and indulgence in evil actions, follow the path of the devil *(Asura)* and get themselves deprived of their discrimination. The difference between man and animal is his rational intellect by which he can distinguish between the good and the evil, the high and the low, the moral and the immoral etc. This rational discriminative capacity alone helps the man to cast off his imperfections and become aware of his essential nature of Absolute Divinity.

The evil doers cannot attain to the Supreme, for their mind and will are not instruments of the Spirit but of the ego. They do not seek to master their crude impulses but are a prey to the Rajas and Tamas in them. If they control their crude tendencies by the Sattva in them, their action becomes orderly and enlightened and ceases to be the outcome of passion and ignorance.

To go beyond the three gunas, first, we have to submit ourselves to the rule of Sattva. We have to become ethical, before we can become spiritual. At the spiritual level, we cross the dualities and act in the light and strength of the Spirit in us. We do not act then to gain any personal interest or avoid personal suffering but only as instrument of the Divine.

Thus far Ajuna has been taught the highest form of devotion, which leads to union with God in its static aspect as also with His dynamic Prakriti. Krishna tells him that there are also other forms of devotion which are at a lower level as they are performed with various motives.

Four kinds of virtuous people worship God. They are seekers of wealth, the distressed, seekers of knowledge, and jnani or the wise. The first three approach God only for gaining limited goals in the world. Distinct from these three types of worshippers, the jnani stands out with his self-oblivious, non-utilitarian worship. He has no desires for any worldly reward. His worship is wholly directed to Self-Realization, to reach Brahman. Krishna expresses His deep love and admiration for the Jnani. Whatever form the devotee worships, the ultimate goal is the Lord Himself. The Lord accepts such worship, knowing that it is directed to Him only.

The deluded, having lost sight of the transcendental Reality, entertain a variety of desires in this world. They seek and earn the fruits of their desires. The Reality, personified as Lord Krishna (Vasudeva) functions in every being as Atman. Atman enlivens all activities, be they material or spiritual. Hence Krishna says that He supports all actions of individuals pursuing their manifold desires.

Speaking as Brahman, the pure Consciousness, Krishna declares that He knows the past, present and future. Living Beings, deluded by the pairs of opposites which bind this world, do not recognize the underlying Reality. The wise, striving for liberation, free themselves from this delusion and reach the supreme Brahman. They realize the whole truth – the play of Brahman, the individual soul and the world, *jiva, jagat and jagadeesvara*

DIFFERENT KINDS OF DEVOTION

chaturvidhaa bhajante maam janaah sukritino'rjuna
aarto jijnaasurarthaarthee jnaanee cha bharatarshabha // 7.16 //

FOUR TYPES OF VIRTUOUS MEN WORSHIP ME, O ARJUNA; THE MAN IN DISTRESS, THE SEEKERS OF KNOWLEDGE, THE SEEKERS OF ENJOYMENT AND THOSE ENDOWED WITH WISDOM, O THE BEST AMONG THE BHARATAS.

Prayer is the effort of man to reach God. It assumes that there is an answering Presence in the world to whom the prayer is addressed. Through the exercise of Prayer, we kindle a light in our consciousness which shows up our pride, greed, fears and hopes. It is a means to build up an integrated personality, a harmony of the body, mind and Spirit.

The previous verse stated that sinful men possessed of demonic nature do not worship God. The question then who actually worships God is answered in this verse.

The Lord calls all the persons who offer prayers to Him as virtuous and classifies them in the following four categories. They are virtuous because anyone seeking the Lord, whatever be his motive, is a fortunate and righteous soul.

1. The distressed - They pray for fighting against and gaining total relief from the distress that is troubling them.
2. The seekers of knowledge – They pray for understanding the knowledge of the Self or the knowledge of God.
3. The seeker of enjoyment- They pray for satisfying their desires and attain enjoyment here and hereafter.
4. The Wise - They pray demanding nothing, expecting nothing. They carry with them as their offerings only themselves. They offer themselves in total surrender. Their only demand is that they should become one with The Lord. Their attitude is one of self-oblivious non-utilitarian worship of God for His own sake. He is the one who has renounced all desires born of maya.

It is to be noted that not all people belonging to the first three categories stated above worship the Lord; only those who are fortunate among them take refuge in Him although they are desirous of rewards *(phalakama).*

teshaam jnaanee nityayukta eka bhaktirvishishyate
priyo hi jnaanino'tyarthamaham sa cha mama priyah // 7.17 //

OF THEM THE WISE MAN, EVER IN CONSTANT UNION WITH THE DIVINE, WHOSE DEVOTION IS SINGLE MINDED, EXCELS; FOR I AM EXCEEDINGLY DEAR TO THE WISE AND HE IS DEAR TO ME.

The wise (Gnani) who with a single pointed mind surrenders himself to the Self with an integrated devotion, which is not distracted by other compelling desires represents the Best. The unbroken aspirations of the Seeker to reach his own real nature of the Self are called single pointed devotion or steadfast mind - *Ekabhakti.*

Single pointedness of the mind is possible only when one withdraws oneself totally from all other extrovert demands of the lower nature in him. In the case of a Gnani the spirit is invoked not for acquisition of any sensual enjoyments but for elimination of all the self-destructive desires. Therefore, Sri Krishna who is the personification of the Self says the wise are the best and the highest in the category of those who invoke Him.

Such a Gnani because of his selfless love is dear to The Lord and in turn He is dear to him. The Lord is regarded as the very Self of the wise. So long as we are seekers, we are still in the world of duality but when we have attained wisdom, there is no duality. The sage unites himself with the One Self in all.

udaaraah sarva evaite jnaanee twaatmaiva me matam
aasthitah sa hi yuktaatma maamevaanuttamaam gatim // 7.18 //

NOBLE INDEED ARE ALL THESE; BUT I DEEM THE WISE MAN AS MY VERY SELF, FOR STEADFAST IN MIND, HE IS ESTABLISHED IN ME ALONE AS THE SUPREME GOAL.

All devotees are noble because of the very fact that they are approaching the Self. But the wise is exceedingly dear to Him because he has a steady mind, with a single pointed concentration on Him. He does not desire any worldly objects except the Supreme Being. He seeks Him alone as the goal. He practices meditation on Him as the Self of all. He tries to realize that he is identical with the Supreme Self. So The Lord regards him as His very Self.

While the first three types attempt to use God according to their ideas, the Wise belong to God to be used according to His will. Therefore they are the best among them all.

By calling the man of wisdom His own self, the Lord shows that there is no difference between Himself and the man of wisdom. Such a devotee is the same as God, and God is the same as the devotee. There is perfect identity between the two.

bahoonaam janmanaamante jnaanavaanmaam prapadyate
vaasudevah sarvamiti sa mahaatmaa sudurlabhah // 7.19 //

AT THE END OF MANY BIRTHS THE WISE-MAN TAKES REFUGE IN ME, REALIZING THAT VAASUDEVA (THE INNERMOST SELF) IS ALL; SUCH A GREAT SOUL (MAHATMA) IS VERY DIFFICULT TO FIND.

It is rare to find in a community of men people of rational thinking and diviner emotions. Even among those who have fully developed mental and intellectual capacities it is only a rare few that take up study of scriptures seriously. All those who study scriptures do not try to live up to them, but feel satisfied in understanding their contents. Only the rarest of the few reach the goal of their evolution and discover their true nature of divine perfection.

This process of evolution takes place during several lives in different births. However, it does not mean those who strive hard in this birth have no chance of realizing the goal of life. The very fact that the seeker has found disappointment with his present state of existence and finds attracted towards Upanishadic literature itself means that he has reached the threshold of the Self.

A little more faithful pursuit of the higher life will take him to the highest state of evolution. At the end of his efforts spread over several births the seeker attains the Inner Self and realizes that everything is Vaasudeva (Self) only in the ultimate analysis. 'All' implies that the whole Universe with its sentient and insentient beings is nothing but the manifestation of Vaasudeva and that there is nothing apart from Him.

It is indeed very difficult to find such a great soul. None is equal to him. "Association with great souls is not only rare but hard to obtain, though unfailing in its effect". *Narada Bhakti Sutra.*

N.B.V<u>aa</u>sudeva means the Lord, the innermost Self of all beings, Sri Krishna.
Vasudeva means Sri Krishna's father and husband of Devaki.

TOLERATION

kaamaistaistairhritajnaanaah prapadyante'nyadevataah
tam tam niyamamaasthaaya prakrityaa niyataah swayaa // 7.20 //

THOSE, WHOSE DISCRIMINATION HAS BEEN DESTORTED BY DESIRES, RESORT TO OTHER GODS, OBSERVING VARIOUS RITUALS, LED BY THEIR OWN NATURES.

Desire for sense objects and their gratification is the greatest cause which separates the discriminating faculty from human intellect. It is discrimination which makes man conscious of his Self. But when the discriminative capacity is deprived of, the deluded individuals engage themselves in some ritualism, dictated by their inborn tendencies to propitiate some Deity or the other. The Deity referred to here means various joys contained in the different sensuous fields which are sought due to intense desires for getting complete satisfaction from them.

The chain of 'Desires - Thoughts - Actions' disturbs the mental equanimity resulting in loss of discrimination. With the loss of discrimination he propitiates the productive potential of the given fields of activity which is called a Devata. As the invocation is required to be done in a particular manner to achieve specific results he follows ritualistic practices. In this process each man follows his own way because each individual acts according to his mental impressions gathered in his earlier moments of activity and thought.

In short this verse implies that a deluded entity strives hard through various rituals, goes after the mirage of sensuality hoping to gain satisfaction therein that it will be everlasting while a man of discrimination finds out the pointlessness of sensuous pursuits and withdraws himself from all the unprofitable fields and seeks the path of the Real.

yo yo yaam yaam tanum bhaktah shraddhayaarchitum icchati
tasya tasyaachalaam shraddhaam taameva vidadhaamyaham
// 7.21 //

WHATEVER MAY BE THE FORM A DEVOTEE SEEKS TO WORSHIP WITH SRADDHA (FAITH), IN THAT FORM ALONE I MAKE HIS FAITH UNWAVERING.

Sri Krishna declares that wherever and in whatever form any devotee seeks to worship with belief, He makes that faith unshakable. Faith here implies unmitigated belief in the existence of divine intelligence, in their glory and virtues and in the methods of their worship and its rewards. The more we think in a particular fashion the more we become so. Faith alone brings success in worship. All deities are only minor forms of the all pervading Supreme Lord.

The deepening of the devotee's faith in every form of worship comes only from the Lord. Through this intense faith the devotee obtains the result of his worship, even though he has set before himself a limited goal. It is the Lord alone who bestows the fruit of worship.

"All worship elevates. No matter what we revere, so long as our reverence is serious, it helps progress. Every surface derives its soil from the depths even as every shadow reflects the nature of the substance". - Dr.S.Radhakrishnan.

sa tayaa shraddhayaa yuktastasyaaraadhanameehate
labhate cha tatah kaamaan mayaiva vihitam hi taan // 7.22 //

ENDOWED WITH THAT FAITH, HE WORSHIPS THAT FORM AND FROM IT ATTAINS HIS DESIRES, WHICH ARE IN REALITY, GRANTED BY ME (ALONE).

The seeker, equipped with that kind of faith as described in the previous verse, invokes the Devata of his choice and gains his desires. These desires are all nourished by Him alone. The Self is the source of all activities. The sense of joy or sorrow out of these activities is a mental-wave. We will not be aware of this experience of joy or sorrow but for the principle of consciousness.

Faithful activity in any field of action brings about success. But the capacity to act, the existence of the field of action, the consistency and zeal with which action is performed, are all due to the Self alone. Sri Krishna identifies Himself with this Spiritual Centre - The Self- and declares that He alone is the One who confers faith in all activities and when the actions are over He alone provides the results thereof.

The Supreme and Omniscient Lord alone knows the precise relationship between an action and its rewards. He is the dispenser of the fruit of action.

All forms are forms of the One Supreme; their worship is the worship of the Supreme; the giver of all rewards is the Supreme - Sridhara Swami.

antavat tu phalam teshaam tadbhavatyalpamedhasaam
devaan devayajo yaanti madbhaktaa yaanti maamapi // 7.23 //

VERILY, THE FRUIT THAT ACCRUES TO THOSE MEN OF SMALL MINDS IS FINITE. THE WORSHIPERS OF THE

DEITIES GO TO THE DEITIES, BUT MY DEVOTEES COME TO ME.

Since the deluded ones desire for finite sense objects they do not come to the all-satisfying peace and hence their results are also temporary and finite. They are called men of small minds because they take petty objects of enjoyment as the Supreme Goal.

Even if satisfaction is achieved after attaining the desired sensuous objects, it is ineffectual because after some time such satisfaction will end followed by sorrows. Any enjoyment in the world of time and space invariably has to come to an end.

The statement worshippers of Deities go to the Deities means that those who invoke a desired manifestation of the Lord in the relative world or aspect of the Supreme, gain only that particular result sought for and nothing else, for the Supreme accepts our prayers and answers them at the level we approach Him. No devotion goes in vain.

As against this those who devote themselves to The Lord go to Him since people through right living come to discover their identity with the Eternal Absolute and realize the transcendental and eternal aspect of the spirit. Those who rise to the worship of the Transcendental Godhead which embraces and transcends all aspects realize and attain the highest state, integral in being, perfect in knowledge, absolute in love and complete in will. All other deities are only partial and limited and have a meaning only at lower level of development.

The same exertion is needed either for the worship of the Lord or the minor deities; but the results are totally different.

Yet men, deluded by transitory desires, do not seek the Lord Himself, who is the source of all peace, happiness and knowledge.

POWER OF IGNORANCE

avyaktam vyaktimaapannam manyante maamabuddhayah
param bhaavamajaananto mamaavyayamanuttamam // *7.24* //

THE FOOLISH THINK OF ME, THE UNMANIFEST, AS ENDOWED WITH MANIFEST FORM, NOT KNOWING MY SUPREME, IMMUTABLE AND TRANSCENDENT NATURE.

That which is available for the perception of the sense organs or for the feelings of the mind or for the understanding of the intellect is called the 'manifest'. That which is not available for any one of these instruments of cognition, feeling or understanding is considered as 'unmanifest'.

The ignorant think that the Lord, too, like an ordinary mortal, comes down from the unmanifested state and assumes a body, impelled by His past karma. This belief is due to their ignorance of His real nature, which is unchanging and ever luminous. Thus disregarding the Lord, the foolish worship the minor deities for the fulfillment of their selfish desires.

The misunderstood men come to the conclusion that physical glory of an incarnation is all the eternal truth. Although the form of an incarnation can be the focus of concentration, it cannot by itself be the Truth. The forms we impose on the Formless are due to our limitations. We turn away from the contemplation of the Ultimate Reality to concentrate upon imaginative reconstructions.

All Gods except the One Unmanifest Eternal are forms imposed on Him. God is not one among many. He is the One behind the ever changing many, who stands beyond all forms, the immutable centre of mobility.

CAUSE OF IGNORANCE

naaham prakaashah sarvasya yogamaayaasamaavritah
moodho'yam naabhijaanaati loko maamajamavyayam // 7.25 //

VEILED BY MY MAYA BORN OF THE GUNAS, I AM NOT REVEALED TO ALL. THIS DELUDED WORLD DOES NOT KNOW ME AS THE UNBORN AND ETERNAL.

The Lord says this deluded world does not know Me, the Unborn and the Immortal because of their own illusion, born out of the three Gunas which veil Me from them. Maya is the illusion born out of the three Gunas through which the Non-dual expresses itself. The principle of Maya functioning in an individual is termed ignorance. By the play of the three Gunas or temperaments one gets confused and hence the Self is not available for direct experience.

For a person without any knowledge of electricity, it is unmanifest in a glowing bulb. Once he comes to have the knowledge of the principle of electricity, it becomes manifest to him in the very same bulb. Similarly, when through self-control, listening, reflection and meditation, the agitations of the mind are controlled and quietened and thereby when the veiling is removed, the seeker rediscovers 'Me, the unmanifest, the unborn, the Immutable'.

As long as the agitations of the mind veil the intellect from its awareness of the Self, the limited ego will continue to wander about among the sensual desires and cannot experience Pure Consciousness even for a moment. Hence The Lord says 'the deluded world knows Me not as they are steeped in the illusion born out of threefold Gunas' just as the waves shield the ocean from the visionary perception.

vedaaham samateetaani vartamaanaani chaarjuna
bhavishyaani cha bhootani maam tu veda na kashchana // 7.26 //

I KNOW O ARJUNA, THE BEINGS OF THE PAST, THE PRESENT AND THE FUTURE BUT NO ONE KNOWS ME.

Because of the Consciousness Principle, only the living beings are aware of the entire field of the mind and the intellect. Consciousness or the Self is the same everywhere which illumines the respective thoughts and ideas of the individual. Thus The Lord or the Self is omniscient i.e. all-knowing. Hence He says 'I know the beings of the whole past, of the present and of the future.'

The concept of awareness is eternal because It illumined the objects before, is illumining now and will be doing so in future. It is beginningless and endless. Although the Self activates the mind and the intellect neither of them can perceive, feel or comprehend the Self. Hence The Lord says although He knows everything and everyone at all times and places 'none knows Him.'

REASONS FOR ILLUSION

icchaadweshasamutthena dwandwamohena bhaarata
sarvabhootani sammoham sarge yaanti parantapa // 7.27 //

BY THE DELUSION OF THE PAIRS OF OPPOSITES ARISING FROM DESIRE AND AVERSION, O BHARATA, ALL BEINGS ARE SUBJECT TO ILLUSION RIGHT FROM BIRTH, O PARANTHAPA (SCORCHERER OF FOES).

Every individual, due to the instinct of self-preservation, has desire for things that contribute to existence and aversion for things that obstruct the attainment of such things desired. He suffers because of the conflict between desires and aversion and his mind and intellect are pre-occupied with chasing of objects desired as also running away from objects of aversion. This agitation due to the pairs of opposites is that which veils the truth from being grasped by an individual. In these circumstances no knowledge of the Self can be possible.

Therefore the only way we can discover our equipoise and tranquility as the eternal Self is to strike at the root i.e. to control the agitations. All spiritual practices in all religions are techniques - emotional, intellectual, and physical - that bring about mental poise at least for a moment. Such a moment of calmness is the moment of perfect mental illumination, fulfillment of re-union.

The Lord says that all beings fall into this delusion right at their very birth. To get out of this delusion and to gain right knowledge is the goal of life and the Gita provides such knowledge to the erring souls guiding them to come out of confusions and reach Perfection.

THE FORTUNATE SOULS

yeshaam twantagatam paapam janaanaam punyakarmanaam
te dwandwamohanirmuktaa bhajante maam dridhavrataah
// 7.28 //

BUT THOSE MEN OF VIRTUOUS DEEDS WHOSE SINS HAVE COME TO AN END, WHO ARE FREED FROM THE DELUSION OF THE PAIRS OF OPPOSITES, WORSHIP ME WITH FIRM RESOLVE.

The word 'sin' means an error of judgment in man which veils the Self from him. When the sins are renounced, when the ignorance is overcome, our life is spent in the service of the Lord, the One in all. In the process, devotion deepens and knowledge of God increases until it reaches the vision of the One Self everywhere. They are said to be free from delusion in the form of pairs of opposites who do not lose their balance of mind either in joy or sorrow. That is the life eternal, release from the cycle of birth and death.

jaraamaranamokshaaya maamaashritya yatanti ye
te brahma tadviduh kritsnamadhyaatmam karma chaakhilam // 7.29 //

THOSE WHO STRIVE FOR DELIVERANCE FROM OLD AGE AND DEATH, TAKING REFUGE IN ME, REALIZE IN FULL THE BRAHMAN - THE WHOLE KNOWLEDGE OF THE SELF AND ALL ABOUT ACTION AS WELL.

Those who aim for purifying themselves from all negative tendencies for contemplating on the Self do so to gain the freedom from old age and death. This, however, does not mean physical continuity of existence in the world. Birth, growth, disease, decay and death are necessary modifications for all living creatures on the earth. What is implied here is that a spiritual seeker in his meditation on the Self is to get over all his identifications with change which is indicated by the terms 'old age and death.'

Such a meditator, concentrating on the Self, realizes his oneness with the Consciousness Principle or the Self in him. To realize the Self is to become Brahman since Self in the individual is the One Self everywhere. This non-duality of the Truth is implied in the statement that those who meditate upon Me, the Self, come to know the Brahman.

A man of realization need not lead a life away from the society in which he lives. The Perfected One not only realizes the All-Pervading Self but comprehends the working of the psychological forces *(Adhyatma)* in him and becomes proficient in all activities (Karma). He becomes a well-integrated personality, dynamic and efficient in all activities, understanding the innermost Self.

saadhibhootaadhidaivam maam saadhiyajnam cha ye viduh
prayaanakaale'pi cha maam te viduryuktachetasah // 7.30 //

THOSE WHO KNOW ME 1. AS THE ONE THAT UNDERLIES ALL THE ELEMENTS (ADHI BHOOTAM) 2. AS THE ONE THAT UNDERLIES ALL THE GODS (ADHI DAIVAM) AND 3. AS THE ONE THAT SUSTAINS ALL THE SACRIFICES (ADHI YAJNAM), WILL WITH STEADFAST MIND, KNOW ME EVEN IN THE HOUR OF DEATH.

The man of perfection is he who is steadfast in mind, who has taken refuge in Him, who knows Him. We are not asked to remember at the time of death certain speculative doctrines, but to know Him in all aspects viz as that which underlies all elements, gods and sacrifices and trust Him and worship Him.

The terms used here mean that the Supreme is to be known not only in itself but also in its manifestations in nature, in objective and subjective phenomena, in the principle of works and sacrifice. The teacher explains all these terms in the next Chapter. In this connection a reference may also be made to Verses 7, 12 and 19 of this Chapter.

om tat sat iti srimadbhagavadgeetaasu upanishatsu brahma vidyaayaam yogashaastre sri krishnaarjuna samvaade jnaana vijnaana yogo naama saptamo'dhyaayah ||

THUS IN THE UPANISHADS OF THE GLORIOUS BHAGAVAD GITA, THE SCIENCE OF THE ETERNAL, THE SCRIPTURE OF YOGA, THE DIALOGUE BETWEEN SRI KRISHNA AND ARJUNA, ENDS THE SEVENTH DISCOURSE ENTITLED THE YOGA OF KNOWLEDGE AND WISDOM

AN OUTLINE VIEW OF THIS CHAPTER

In this chapter Krishna uses the first person singular pronoun 'ME' to mean the supreme Reality, BRAHMAN, God. He explains the immanence and transcendence of Brahman. The vicious do not know or seek God while the virtuous worship Him in four different ways. Those deluded from the vision of the supreme Reality seek and gain limited goals in the world, whereas those freed from delusion strive for liberation and merge with Brahman.

I - TWO ASPECTS OF BRAHMAN - VERSES 1 – 6

In the first three verses Krishna encourages spiritual seekers on the path of yoga and assures that He will give them knowledge and wisdom essential to reach the ultimate state of Brahman. The vast majority of human beings give in to the enchantments of the material and sensual world. A rare one among the deluded masses emerges to strive for spiritual enlightenment. Among those few who strive, rarer still is the one who actually achieves spiritual enlightenment. The lower and higher natures of Brahman are manifest in this world. Transcending these two lies the unmanifest Reality.

II - HOW BRAHMAN MANIFESTS ITSELF - VERSES 7 -11

Krishna declares Himself as Brahman manifesting as the quintessence of all sentient beings and insentient objects everywhere. He suggests subtly that one can locate Him in one's own ardent desire for the Supreme.

III - THE VICIOUS DO NOT KNOW OR SEEK BRAHMAN - VERSES 12 – 15

The three Gunas (qualities) – sattwa (pure), rajas (passionate), and tamas (indolent) – emanate from Brahman. But Brahman has no gunas. The Gunas merely project an illusion on Brahman. The deluded, caught up in this illusion, have lost sight of the Reality. They do not seek Brahman. Instead, they follow the demoniac ways of life.

IV - THE FOUR VIRTUOUS TYPES WHO WORSHIP GOD - 16 -19

Four kinds of virtuous people worship God. They are artharthi (seeker of wealth), arta (distressed), jijnasu (seeker of knowledge), and jnani (wise). The first three approach God only for gaining limited goals in the world. Distinct from these three types of worshippers, the jnani stands out with his self-oblivious, non utilitarian worship. He has no desires for any worldly reward. His worship is wholly directed to

Self-Realization, to reach Brahman. Krishna expresses His deep love and admiration for the Jnani.

V - THE DELUDED SEEK AND GAIN FINITE FRUIT - VERSES 20 -25

The deluded, having lost sight of the transcendental Reality, entertain a variety of desires in this world. They seek and earn the fruits of their desires. The Reality, personified as Lord Krishna (Vaasudeva) functions in every being as atman. Atman enlivens all activities, be they material or spiritual. Hence Krishna says that He supports all actions of individuals pursuing their manifold desires.

VI - THE WISE SEEK AND GAIN BRAHMAN - VERSE 26 – 30

Speaking as Brahman, Krishna declares that He knows the past, present and future. Beings, deluded by the pairs of opposites which bind this world, do not recognize the underlying Reality. The wise, striving for liberation, free themselves from this delusion and realize the whole truth-the play of Brahman, the individual soul and the world.

<<<000>>>

CHAPTER 8

Akshara Brahma Yogah:

Yoga of Imperishable Brahman

PREAMBLE

In the preceding Chapter Bhagavan explained about His integral Self and spoke of the deluded ones seeking finite fruit while the wise seek *Brahman* along with knowing *Adhyatma, Karma, Adhibhuta, Adhidaiva and Adhiyajna.* Arjuna could not grasp the implications of these terms and the secret of knowing God. Hence he puts seven questions to the Lord to know about these six terms and how to realize God. The 'Akshara' means indestructible or imperishable. As this Chapter deals with the imperishable and absolute nature of God and the Pranava Mantra 'OM', which symbolizes it, it is entitled Akshara Brahma Yoga.

In this chapter Bhagavan elucidates about the methodology to gain Brahman - how one can reach Brahman through concentrated yoga and single-pointed meditation. This is the path which leads one to the supreme abode wherefrom there is no return. The chapter also mentions the path of return, a realm of temporary bliss, to which one is transported, only to be brought back to the world of limitation.

The imperishable Brahman whose nature is transcendental and immanent pervades this perishable world of things and beings. Whatever one pursues in this world one gains that alone. By pursuing the Self one realizes the Self. Krishna advises mankind to surrender the mind and intellect to the Self while the body is engaged in action which will lead the seeker to the ultimate state of Brahman.

He further advices to turn the attention from the mundane world to the Supreme Self within and to control the senses and mind through spiritual practices and thereafter to let the intellect direct such controlled mind to single-pointed meditation upon the *pranava mantra* OM. By continuous and sustained meditation one will reach the supreme abode of Brahman.

THE TEXT

arjuna uvaacha
kim tadbrahma kimadhyaatman kim karma purushottama
adhibhootam cha kim proktamadhidaivam kimuchyate // 8.1 //

ARJUNA SAID
WHAT IS BRAHMAN? WHAT IS THE INDIVIDUAL SOUL? WHAT IS ACTION, O THE SUPREME PERSON? WHAT IS IT THAT IS SAID TO UNDERLIE ALL THE ELEMENTS?

adhiyajnah katham kotra dehesmin madhusoodhana
prayaanakaale cha katham jneyosi niyataatmabhih // 8.2 //

AND WHAT IS IT THAT IS SAID TO UNDERLIE ALL THE GODS? AND WHO SUSTAINS ALL THE SACRIFICES HERE IN THE BODY, O MADHUSUDANA? AND IN WHAT WAY? AND

HOW, AGAIN, ARE YOU TO BE KNOWN AT THE TIME OF DEATH BY THOSE WHO HAVE PRACTICED SELF-CONTROL?

Arjuna seeks the explanation of certain terms used by the Lord at the end of the Seventh Chapter.

SRI KRISHNA ANSWERS

sri bhagavaan uvaacha
aksharam brahma paramam swabhaavodhyaatmamuchyate
***bhootabhaavodbhavakaro visargah karma samjnitah** // 8.3 //*

SRI BHAGAVAN SAID
BRAHMAN IS THE IMPERISHABLE, THE SUPREME. DWELLING IN EACH BODY, BRAHMAN IS CALLED THE INDIVIDUAL SOUL. THE OFFERING OF THE OBLATION, WHICH, BRINGS INTO EXISTENCE ALL BEINGS AND SUPPORTS THEM, IS CALLED ACTION.

IMPERISHABLE IS THE SUPREME BRAHMAN:

Brahman indicates the one changeless and imperishable Essence behind the phenomenal world. It is the Self or the Principle of Consciousness which illumines the body, mind and intellect. Its presence in each individual body is called *Adhyatma*, the individual soul. "At the command of this Imperishable, O Gargi, heaven and earth are held in their proper places". Brihadaranyaka Upanishad (III.viii.9). The Supreme Brahman alone exists in every individual body as the *pratyagatman*, the ego, the inmost Self and is known as the Adhyatma. At the culmination of the spiritual discipline, the inmost Self is realized as one with Brahman. Though the Self is formless and subtle and therefore all pervading, its power is felt by every living embodiment. The Self expressing through a given embodiment, as though conditioned by it, is called the Adhyatma.

ACTION (KARMA):

According to the Vedas, the offering of oblations to the gods brings about the birth of all creatures; the oblations cause rain and the rain causes food, and food causes created beings. The offering of oblations in sacrifice is called *karma* or action.

adhibhootam ksharo bhaavah purushashchaadhidaivatam
adhiyajno 'hamevaatra dehe dehabhritaam vara // 8.4 //

THAT WHICH UNDERLIES ALL THE ELEMENTS IS THE PERISHABLE ENTITY (ADHIBHOOTA); AND THAT WHICH UNDERLIES ALL THE DEVATAS IS THE PURUSHA, THE COSMIC SPIRIT (ADHIDAIVATA). AND HE WHO SUSTAINS ALL THE SACRIFICES IS MYSELF, HERE IN THE BODY (ADHIYAJNA), O THE BEST OF MEN.

Adhibhootha is the perishable existence. It comprises all material objects, everything that comes into existence.

Adhidaivata is that which underlies all the Devatas, the presiding deities of the sense organs, mind and intellect.

Adhiyajna: As oblations are poured in the Yajnas, the sense objects are offered into the act of perception, feeling and thought when the Devata or the particular faculty in it is invoked and as a blessing of this act we gain the fruit thereof viz. the knowledge of the perception. That which underlies the Devatas is Purusha, the Cosmic Spirit, *Adhidaivata.*

The implication of these definitions is that the Eternal Self alone is the Real and all the rest is delusory and super-impositions upon It. Thus to know the Self is to know everything and having known It as one's own real nature one is free to act or not to act in any of the fields of Not-Self.

As the Inner Controller of the body - *antaryamin* - Sri Krishna is the presiding Deity directing the various physical functions which are described as acts of sacrifice. Though He rests in the body, He is not attached to it and is completely different from the senses.

One who is aware of this play of the Self at all levels of his personality - physical, mental and intellectual - experiences himself as a Witness of the process of his relations with the Not-Self.

antakaale cha maam eva smaran muktwaa kalevaram
yah prayaati sa madbhaavam yaati naastyatra samshayah // 8.5 //

WHOSOEVER AT THE TIME OF DEATH LEAVES HIS BODY REMEMBERING ME ALONE AND GOES FORTH - HE ATTAINS MY BEING; THERE IS NO DOUBT ABOUT THIS.

yam yam vaapi smaran bhaavam tyajatyante kalevaram
tam tamevaiti kaunteya sadaa tadbhaavabhaavitah // 8.6 //

FOR WHATEVER OBJECT A MAN THINKS OF AT THE FINAL MOMENT, WHEN HE LEAVES HIS BODY - THAT ALONE DOES HE ATTAIN, O SON OF KUNTI, BEING EVER ABSORBED IN THE THOUGHT THEREOF.

The most prominent thought of one's life occupies the mind at the time of death. The last thoughts of a dying person determine the quality of his next birth. The soul goes to that on which its mind is set during the last moments. What we think we become. Our past thoughts determine our present birth and our present ones will determine the future.

Therefore, Sri Krishna tells that one who leaves the body with his mind completely turned towards the Self will naturally reach the Eternal and the Immortal - the Supreme abode, reaching which there is no return. We can think of God in the last moments only if we are devoted to Him previously also.

The Lord explains that whatever object one remembers while leaving the body, he reaches that alone because of his constant thought of that object. It is not the casual fancy of the last moment but a persistent endeavor of the whole life that determines the future birth.

tasmaat sarveshu kaaleshu maamanusmara yudhya cha
mayyarpitamanobuddhir maamevaishyasyasamshayah // 8.7 //

THEREFORE, AT ALL TIMES, CONSTANTLY REMEMBER ME AND FIGHT. WITH YOUR MIND AND INTELLECT ABSORBED IN ME, YOU SHALL DOUBTLESS COME TO ME ALONE.

Sri Krishna, advises Arjuna to constantly keep his mind fixed on Him and at the same time perform his Swadharma (to fight). The mind is purified when a man performs his own dharma, regarding himself as an instrument of God. Only a pure mind can constantly remember God.

CONSTANT PRACTICE IS NECESSARY TO REALIZE GOD

abhyaasayogayuktena chetasaa naanyagaaminaa
paramam purusham divyam yaati paarthaanuchintayan // 8.8 //

ENGAGED IN THE YOGA OF CONSTANT PRACTICE AND NOT ALLOWING THE MIND TO WANDER AWAY TO ANYTHING ELSE, HE WHO MEDITATES ON THE SUPREME, RESPLENDENT PURUSHA, REACHES HIM, O SON OF PRITHA.

Constant practice is the uninterrupted repetition of one and the same idea, with reference to the Lord as the sole object of meditation. Such practice by which one surrenders his heart and soul to the Lord alone is known as Yoga.

Resplendent Purusha means the presiding deity of the solar orb which is considered as the manifestation of the Absolute as the Cosmic Spirit. He is also known as *Saguna Brahman.*

MEDITATING AND ATTAINING PURUSHA

kavim puraanam anushaasitaaram
anoraneeyaamsam anusmaredyah
sarvasya dhaataaram achintyaroopam
aadityavarnam tamasah parastaat //8.9//

WHOSOEVER MEDITATES UPON THE OMNISCIENT, THE ANCIENT, THE RULER (OF THE WHOLE WORLD), WHO IS SUBTLER THAN THE SUBTLE, THE SUPPORTER OF ALL, WHOSE FORM IS INCONCEIVABLE, EFFULGENT LIKE THE SUN AND BEYOND THE DARKNESS (OF IGNORANCE),

prayaanakaale manasaa'chalena
bhaktyaa yukto yogabalena chaiva
bhruvormadhye praanamaaveshya samyak
sa tam param purushamupaiti divyam // 8.10 //

AT THE TIME OF DEATH, WITH AN UNSHAKEN MIND FULL OF DEVOTION, BY THE POWER OF *'YOGA'* FIXING THE WHOLE *'PRANA'* (BREATH) BETWEEN THE TWO EYEBROWS, HE (THE SEEKER) REACHES THE SUPREME RESPLENDENT *'PURUSHA.'*

In these two verses Sri Krishna gives Arjuna exhaustive guidance that will help in undertaking meditation by all. The meaning of the various terms used here is as follows.

Verse - 9

Omniscient (*Kavi*) - Just as the sun is said to be seeing everything because it illuminates all the objects of the world, so too is the Principle of Awareness without which no knowledge whatsoever is possible. Thus, in terms of the limited knowledge we presently experience, the Self is considered as the Supreme Knower who knows everything i.e. Omniscient and without whom no knowledge is ever possible.

Ancient (*Puranam*) - The Self is considered as the most ancient because the Eternal Truth which was there before all creation remains the same always.

The ruler of the whole world *(Anushaasitaaram)* - It indicates that if the principle of awareness were not present in our faculties of perception, feeling and comprehension, harmonization of our physical, mental and intellectual experiences would not have been possible to lead a meaningful existence. Hence the Knowing Principle or Consciousness is the very essence of life just as without the mud the mud-pot cannot exist. The mud is the ruler in the world of mud pots so too is the Self the over-ruler of the Universe.

Minuter than the Atom *(Anoraneeyaam)* - The smallest divisible particle of any element maintaining the properties of that element is called its atom. It indicates that the Self is the subtlest of the subtle.

The more a thing is subtle the more is its pervasiveness. Water is subtler than the ice and hence water is said to be more pervasive than the ice and similarly steam is more pervasive than water. So also, the Self is the subtlest of the subtle which pervades all but nothing pervades it.

The nourisher of all (*Sarvasya Dhaataram*) - Nourishment here means the support which sustains everything. Just like the canvas supports ever so many different paintings of an artist, the Consciousness illuminates constantly the ever changing things and happenings, around and within us, from birth to death, through all situations which results in homogeneous oneness of life.

Of inconceivable form (*Achintyaroopam*) - Various descriptions of the Self given above should not lead to the wrong conclusion that It can be thought about and understood as any finite object or idea. We should be clear that the Infinite cannot be comprehended by the finite instruments of perception, feeling or understanding. Although the Self is in the form inconceivable, It is not inexperienceable since an individual can apprehend It to be of his own real nature during the process of Divine awakening.

Effulgent like the sun (*Aadityavarnam*) - So long as a man identifies himself with his limited auxiliaries in his body he lives in the external world of multiplicities wherein the Self is inconceivable, inexperienceable and incomprehensible. Once these auxiliaries are crossed through a process of contemplation of the Self, he realizes his own nature of Pure Being.

To see the sun no other light is necessary or a dreamer cannot know the waker, because to know the waker the dreamer has to end his dream state and become the waker. So too, on ending the egocentric existence during spiritual awakening, one realizes that he is nothing but the Self at all times.

Beyond all the darkness (*Tamasah parastaat*) - The sun is variable in nature like its brightness during the day with various degrees of intensity and its total absence during the night. It may be erroneously concluded that the Self is also variable in its intensity or there are times when It is totally absent. To remove this possible misunderstanding The Lord says that the Self is beyond darkness of ignorance.

Thus, the one who meditates upon the Self as omniscient, ancient, over-ruler, subtlest of the subtle, nourisher of all, of in-conceivable form, self illuminating as the sun and beyond all ---

Verse - 10

At the time of death (*Prayaanakaale*) - These words do not mean 'the physical death' but they are to be understood as 'at the moment of the death of the ego' when all identifications with the body, mind and intellect are consciously withdrawn during meditation.

Endowed with full devotion (*Bhakti*) - It means selfless love for the Divine without any expectation which implies identification of the ego with its real nature. The idea is that the meditation should be accompanied by the meditator's readiness to identify himself with the principle of awareness as earlier indicated.

By the power of Yoga (*Yogabalena*) - This is the inward strength that grows in the mind of the meditator when he meditates upon the Supreme for long periods of time when the mind is withdrawn from its agitations and the intellect rests on contemplation of the Absolute. When one is thus engaged in meditation, all his *pranas* get concentrated at the point of his concentration between the eyebrows which represents the seat of steady thought.

Fixing the whole *prana* between the eyebrows - This is the process of controlling the breath. Life expressing itself at the various functions in a living body is called the Prana which can be classified under five categories viz. *Prana*: faculty of sense perception, *Apana*: the excretory system, *Vyana*: the digestive system, *Samaana*: the circulatory system and *Udana*: capacity to visualize some greater concepts beyond the present world of knowledge. When an individual gets himself merged with the Self, at that moment all these faculties are temporarily arrested.

Reaches the resplendent Supreme person - Such a person in whom the mind becomes completely silent and calm, all manifestations of life's presence through his body are halted. At this stage he goes to the Supreme Resplendent Self (*Purusha*) i.e. completely identifies himself with his point of contemplation, the Self.

MEDITATION ON THE SUPREME PERSON THROUGH 'OM'

yadaksharam vedavido vadanti
vishanti yadyatayo veetaraagaah
yadicchanto brahmacharyam charanti
tatte padam samgrahena pravakshye // 8.11 //

WHAT THE KNOWERS OF THE VEDAS SPEAK OF AS IMPERISHABLE, WHAT THE SELF-CONTROLLED (SANNYAASINS) FREED FROM ATTACHMENT ENTER AND TO GAIN WHICH GOAL THEY LIVE THE LIFE OF A BRAHMACHARI, THAT STATE I SHALL DECLARE TO YOU IN BRIEF.

Sri Krishna now starts giving guidance for meditating upon the monosyllable 'OM' or the Pranava which is the ultimate goal for man. Worship of the syllable OM is advised in almost all the Upanishads as a prelude to the meditation for an easier concentration of the mind. OM is considered as an expression of the Supreme Self or Its symbol like an idol.

Freed from attachment means detachment from the world of objects with full understanding of the goal of life. Men of least desires will have the maximum success in traveling the Path of Knowledge. Brahmachari is a religious student who takes the vow of continence etc. Every moment of this stage is one of hard discipline and asceticism.

sarvadwaaraani samyamya mano hridi nirudhya cha
moordhnyaadhaayaatmanah praanamaasthito yogadhaaranaam
// 8.12 //

HAVING CLOSED ALL THE GATES (CONTROLLED ALL THE SENSES), HAVING CONFINED THE MIND IN THE HEART, HAVING FIXED THE LIFE-BREATH IN THE 'HEAD', ENGAGED IN THE PRACTICE OF CONCENTRATION,

Omityekaaksharam brahma vyaaharan maamanusmaran
yah prayaati tyajan deham sa yaati paramaam gatim // 8.13 //

UTTERING THE MONOSYLLABLE OM-THE BRAHMAN-AND REMEMBERING ME, HE WHO SO DEPARTS, LEAVING THE BODY, ATTAINS THE SUPREME GOAL.

The conditions to be fulfilled in the meditator for achieving effective concentration are narrated in these verses in the same order in which they are to be practiced.

Closing all the gates - The sense organs Viz. skin, ear, nose, eyes and the tongue are the five entry points through which the external stimuli reach the mind and cause agitations in it. To close these five entrances through discrimination and detachment means controlling all the senses.

Confining the mind in the heart - Although external stimuli can be prevented through controlling senses, it is always possible for the mind to get disturbed on account of the accumulation of past impressions gathered from the external world of change and pleasure. It is therefore advised that the mind which is the tool for emotion and feeling should be confined to the heart. Here heart does not mean the physical part of the body but an imaginary centre of the mind from which all positive thoughts like love, kindness, devotion, surrender etc. emanate which means the mind whose functions are checked.

Drawing Prana into the Head and occupied in the practice of concentration - The mental condition wherein the intellect is withdrawn from its identification with all the perceptions and engaging it in the total contemplation of the Self. In this condition of mental and intellectual equipoise the seeker is fit for meditating upon the monosyllable OM.

He who departs, leaving the body - This does not mean 'at the time of death'. While chanting and meditating on OM, the seeker gets so much detached from his identification with the world of objects that the ego gets tuned towards a higher objective. This is called death - leaving the body - when he attains the Supreme goal.

WHO CAN EASILY ATTAIN THE LORD?

ananyachetaah satatam yo maam smarati nityashah
tasyaaham sulabhah paartha nityayuktasya yoginah // 8.14 //
I AM EASILY ATTAINABLE BY THAT EVER-STEADFAST YOGI WHO CONSTANTLY AND DAILY REMEMBERS ME NOT THINKING OF ANYTHING ELSE, O PARTHA.

Ever-steadfast, Constantly: One who does not allow his mind wander freely among sense objects. The meditator who constantly keeps himself aware of the Self is the successful practitioner.

Daily: One has to remember The Lord daily till the end of his life and not merely at fixed times of the day or on fixed days of the week. No part-time behaviorism or weekly engagements in religion are advised. Divine consciousness must be maintained by the seeker constantly and continuously like a 24 hour TV channel.

Not thinking of anything else: One is not to think of any other object except his Deity. If these conditions are negated none can hope for an easy success in Meditation

Every individual being remains as vasanas, unmanifest desires, in deep sleep at night. His vasanas manifest at daybreak upon awakening. This cycle of dissolution and emanation continues until the individual completely exhausts his vasanas, reaching the state of Self-realization. A similar phenomenon takes place at the macrocosmic level. The entire macrocosm manifests during the day of Lord Brahma (a God of Hindu Trinity as distinguished from Brahman, the Supreme Reality). Brahama's celestial day consists of 4.32 billion terrestrial years. Similarly, the macrocosm folds back into the unmanifest state during the night of Lord Brahma, covering an equal period as his day. Beyond this unmanifest lies the Supreme Unmanifest, Brahman. Humans reach Brahman through spiritual disciplines culminating in single-pointed meditation.

The Path of Sun, Uttarayana and the Path of Moon, Dakshinayana are discussed. The Path of Sun takes a seeker to Brahmaloka, the heaven of Lord Brahma wherefrom he goes to the supreme Brahman. Whereas the Path of Moon takes the individual to pitrloka, only to enjoy heavenly pleasures and return to the cycle of birth and death in this world. The latter path provides only temporary pleasures of heaven for meritorious deeds done here. The former, however, takes the seeker to Brahman, through heaven because of having mixed meritorious deeds with his spiritual practice. But the true yogi, through his determined effort on the path of yoga of meditation goes directly from here to the abode of supreme Brahman.

RESULT OF THE ACCESSIBILITY OF THE LORD

maamupetya punarjanma duhkhaalayamashaashwatam
naapnuvanti mahaatmaanah samsiddhim paramaam gataah // 8.15 //

HAVING ATTAINED ME, THESE GREAT SOULS ARE NO MORE SUBJECT TO REBIRTH (IN THIS MORTAL WORLD) WHICH IS TRANSITORY AND THE ABODE OF PAIN, FOR THEY HAVE REACHED THE HIGHEST PERFECTION (LIBERATION).

The question why should one struggle so hard to realize the Self is answered. The benefit accruing on realization of the Self is that having attained Me, The Lord, the Mahatmas are no more subject to rebirth because the world of rebirth is impermanent and the starting point for all pains and miseries.

Those who die without realizing the Lord come back again to the earth. Life on earth, in spite of many moments of happiness, is intrinsically painful. On account of the intense love of God, the devotees do not experience suffering on earth and after death they attain Him.

aabrahmabhuvanaanllokaah punaraavartino'rjuna
maamupetya tu kaunteya punarjanma na vidyate // 8.16 //

THE DWELLERS IN ALL THE WORLDS, O ARJUNA, INCLUDING THE REALM OF BRAHMA, ARE SUBJECT TO RETURN TO REBIRTH, BUT FOR THOSE WHO REACH ME, O SON OF KUNTI, THERE IS NO REBIRTH.

Even after reaching the Brahmaloka, the realm of the Creator, all cannot achieve total liberation because of their remaining Vasanas for exhausting which they have to take rebirth. But to those who rediscovered their Essential Eternal Nature and realized themselves to be the One, All Pervading Self (after attaining Me) there is no rebirth in the *Samsar*, the plane of limited existence.

Complete liberation, attended by cessation of birth and death, is possible only for a man who has realized his identity with Brahman. All other worlds, whether sub-human or super-human, are places of transitory enjoyments, where men departing from earth, experience the fruit of their actions and after exhausting such fruits are re-born on this earth.

But one can directly attain liberation from re-birth through love of God alone without waiting till the end of the cosmic cycle.

ALL THESE WORLDS ARE LIMITED BY TIME

sahasrayugaparyantam aharyad brahmano viduh
raatrim yugasahasraantaam te'horaatravido janaah // 8.17 //

THOSE WHO KNOW THAT THE DAY OF BRAHMA LASTS FOR THOUSAND YUGAS (AGES) AND THAT THE NIGHT OF BRAHMA LASTS THOUSAND YUGAS AGAIN, ARE INDEED PEOPLE WHO KNOW DAY AND NIGHT.

Brahma is the first manifestation of the Absolute, Brahman in time and space. He is also known as Prajapati and Viraj.

Day means evolution or projection of the universe. It is the period of cosmic manifestation. Night means cosmic involution or dissolution of the universe. It is the period of non-manifestation. According to the Hindu philosophy time is the measurement of interval between two different experiences.

In a given single experience there is no perception of time just as in one point there is no concept of distance for distances arise between two points only.

The worlds are conditioned by time and hence they manifest again and again although the duration of their cycles vary and are very long - each cycle lasting for crores of years (in terms of our present understanding of 365 days in a year). A thousand such cycles makes a day of Brahma and another such cycle is the night of Brahma. Those who can see and live through the day and night of Brahma can really know what a day is and what a night is meaning thereby that such yogis can visualize many Brahmas arising and disintegrating in the Ocean of great Cause. Thus they do not feel any attachment even to the happiness of the highest heaven, how much less to that of earth.

In this and the following two verses Gita points out the life of the Cosmic Man and his concept of time. It points out the non-distinction between microcosm (vyashti) and macrocosm (samashti).

The God principle (Hiranyagarbha - the source of all objects) is a concept which represents the total mind and intellect of all the living creatures living at any given point of time in the world. To understand the ways of the mind projecting the world of its own objects is to understand not only the all powerful nature but also the limitations of God-principle as conceived to be a Creator, Sustainer and Annihilator. Sri Krishna brings out this subtle idea clearly in the mind of Arjuna in these three verses.

WHAT HAPPENS DURING BRAHMA'S DAY AND NIGHT?

avyaktaadvyaktayah sarvaah prabhavantyaharaagame
raaatryaagame praleeyante tatraivaavyaktasamjnake // 8.18 //

AT THE APPROACH OF THE DAY ALL MANIFEST OBJECTS COME FORTH FROM THE UNMANIFESTED AND AT THE APPROACH OF THE NIGHT THEY MERGE AGAIN INTO THAT WHICH IS CALLED THE UNAMANIFEST.

bhootagraamah sa evaayaam bhootwaa bhootwaa praleeyate
raatryaagamevashah paartha prabhavatyaharaagame // 8.19 //

THE SAME MULTITUDE OF BEINGS, COMING FORTH AGAIN AND AGAIN, MERGE IN SPITE OF THEMSELVES, O PARTHA, AT THE APPROACH OF THE NIGHT AND REMANIFEST THEMSELVES AT THE APPROACH OF THE DAY.

How the Creator keeps Himself occupied during His day and night each of which is of long duration is explained. It is indicated that the Creator creates during His day and the entire creation ends during His night by merging itself in the unmanifested. Creation is the crystallization of the unmanifested dormant existence into the manifested existence with names, forms and qualities. That is, creation is only the production of a name, form with some specific qualities, out of the raw material in which the same name, form and quality are already existing in an unmanifested condition. When a pot is created out of the mud the potness is already prevalent in the mud because no other thing than a pot can be created out of mud.

The thought impressions in the mind (vasanas) which lie unmanifested to the sense-organs and the mental and intellectual perceptions become manifested as gross actions, thoughts and words making the life either tough or smooth depending on the quality of the thoughts manifested. A doctor, advocate and a criminal are all same as human beings while thy are asleep which is their unmanifested state (Pralaya) but when they wake up their respective qualities as a doctor, advocate or criminal get manifested which in philosophy is called creation.

In the cosmic process of creation and dissolution the Creator or the total mind during the waking hours of long ages project out the already existing vasanas and at the night they merge into the unmanifested. The declaration that the very same beings are born again and again and merge in spite of themselves shows that Hinduism does not believe in a creation preceded by the condition of absolute non-existence.

The same multitude meant that which comprised of the moving and non-moving who existed in the preceding cycle or age and who did not attain liberation. They repeatedly come forth and dissolve by the effect of their own karma. "In spite of themselves" implies the law of karma is inexorable. In this world of Maya there is no freedom as long as one is caught in the wheel of karma. The only way of liberation is to free oneself from Maya.

parastasmaat tu bhavo'nyo'vyakto'vyaktaatsanaatanah
yah sa sarveshu bhooteshu nashyatsu na vinashyati // 8.20 //

BUT BEYOND THIS UNMANIFESTED, THERE IS YET ANOTHER UNMANIFESTED ETERNAL BEING, WHO DOES NOT PERISH WHEN ALL BEINGS PERISH.

This unmanifested means the seed state of the whole multitude of created things; the night of Brahma. Another unmanifested eternal Being refers to the imperishable Brahman, which is imperceptible to senses and which is altogether of a different kind, It is supra-cosmic and beyond ignorance. It does not perish because it is beyond time, space and causality. All beings perish implies that everything from Brahma downwards all beings.

That which is The Truth, the ignorance of which projects the manifested, is the factor that is changeless substratum. The idea is that the Ultimate Reality, the Self, is that which lies beyond the delusory experiences of creation, dissolution and repeated re-creations.

avyaktokshara ityuktastamaahuh paramaam gatim
yam praapya na nivartante taddhaama paramam mama // 8.21 //

THE UNMANIFESTED IS CALLED THE IMPERISHABLE; IT IS SAID TO BE THE ULTIMATE GOAL FROM WHICH THOSE WHO REACH IT NEVER COME BACK. THAT IS MY SUPREME ABODE.

What has been indicated in the previous verse as 'the other Unmanifest - which is the Eternal Existence - which does not persish' is explained here as the Imperishable mentioned in

Verses 3 & 13 of this Chapter. The Imperishable was defined therein as the Brahman, the substratum for the entire universe and that we should meditate on 'OM' as the symbol of this Imperishable.

The Self which is Pure Awareness gives existence and dynamism to the unmanifested vasanas and makes them to project out to form the manifested world of activities and behaviors. This eternal Unmanifested Factor, the Imperishable Self, is the highest goal for man to achieve.

The knower of such Imperishable, Eternal Brahman never again falls under the spell of Maya or ignorance (never comes back). The abode of Brahman is called Supreme because the relative universe is the inferior manifestation of Brahman.

The ultimate goal referred to in the text does not indicate any state or condition but the Imperishable Brahman Itself, Existence-Knowledge-Bliss absolute, *sat-chit-ananda.*

MEANS TO ATTAIN THAT SUPREME ABODE

purushaha sa parah paartha bhaktya labhyastwananyayaa
yasyaanthahsthaani bhootaani yena sarvamidam tatam // 8.22 //

THAT SUPREME PURUSHA, IN WHOM ALL BEINGS ABIDE AND BY WHOM THE ENTIRE UNIVERSE IS PERVADED, CAN BE ATTAINED, O PARTHA, BY UNDISTRACTED DEVOTION DIRECTED TO HIM ALONE.

The technique by which the Unmanifest, the Imperishable - the Supreme Purusha is attainable is explained. Single pointed devotion with the total detachment from the world of body, mind and intellect is the means to achieve the Supreme Purusha. The detachment from the false is achieved by the growing attachment with the Real. Total Identification of oneself with the experience of the Self or the realization that nothing exists except the Lord, is undistracted devotion.

In whom all beings abide - All the beings (which are the effects) dwell within the Purusha, the Supreme Person (which is the cause) because every effect rests in its cause just as all mud pots (which are the effects) exist in the mud (which is the cause). The mud pervades all mud-pots irrespective of their size and shape. The essential nature of the mud-pot is nothing but the mud from which it is born. So also all beings and the world rest within their cause, the Purusha and hence the whole world is pervaded by the Purusha.

But for the cotton the beauty of the design woven in the cloth made out of that cotton cannot get projected. When Pure Awareness acts through vasanas It becomes the multiple worlds of names and forms. Therefore when one realizes the Self, he understands the very core out of which the world of multiplicity called *Samsar* has arisen.

Brahman is called Purusha (Person) because It dwells in every body *(pura)* or It is full *(poornam)*.

THE TWO PATHS

yatra kale twanaavrittim aavrittim chaiva yoginah
prayaataa yaanti tam kaalam vakshyaami bharatarshabha // 8.23 //

NOW I WILL TELL YOU, O CHIEF OF BHARATAS, THE TIME IN WHICH THE YOGIS DEPART NEVER TO RETURN AND ALSO THE TIME IN WHICH THEY DEPART TO RETURN.

Sri Krishna now tells about the routes taken by the seekers to reach the two different destinations viz. the one from which there is a return and the other from which there is no return. The former is a Divine Mission seeking the Imperishable by ending the ego and re-discovering ones own Real Nature as none other than the Eternal Consciousness, the Changeless Substratum of the whole universe. The latter path is the life of satisfying the ego by gaining the experiences of joy among sense objects each of which ultimately brings forth sorrow.

These two worlds differ from each other since the one leads to a return again and again to a finite embodiment for living a life of limitations and the other assures a goal, having reached which, there is no return and where one enjoys Absolute Bliss.

If there are two different destinations there will be two separate routes guiding the respective types of seekers to reach their correct places. The Lord promises Arjuna that He will explain both the 'Path of return' and the 'Path of no return'. Here, the word *'Kale'* means the time of departure as well as the path pursued by different types of seekers at the end of their present manifestations.

agnirjyotirahah shuklah shanmaasaa uttaraayanam
tatra prayaataa gacchanti brahma brahmavido janaah // 8.24 //

FIRE, FLAME, DAY-TIME, THE BRIGHT FORTNIGHT, THE SIX MONTHS OF THE NORTHERN PASSAGE OF THE SUN, DEPARTING WHEN THE MEN WHO KNOW BRAHMAN GO TO BRAHMAN.

dhoomo raatristathaa krishnah shanmaasaa dakshinaayanam
tatra chaandramasam jyotir yogee praapya nivartate // 8.25 //

ATTAINING TO THE LUNAR LIGHT BY SMOKE, NIGHT-TIME, THE DARK FORTNIGHT, OR THE SIX MONTHS OF THE SOUTHERN PASSAGE OF THE SUN, THE YOGI RETURNS.

The verses 24 and 25 have been commented upon differently by different commentators. Fire, flame, day-time, the bright fortnight, the six months of the northern passage of the sun - all these indicate the path of the Gods presided over by the sun while the path of the ancestors is described in the verse 25 which is presided over by the moon. The path of Gods is the path of illumination that leads to liberation from where there is no return for the departed souls. On the other hand the path of ancestors is the path of darkness which leads to rebirth.

These two verses indicate that a seeker trying to raise himself above the various matter-envelopments and his identifications with them, can reach the higher spiritual realms of the Ultimate in his life time itself. But in case he happens to run after pleasure and sensuality, he comes back again to the field of action here wherein he can again make or unmake himself.

shuklakrishne gatee hyete jagatah shaashwate mate
ekayaa yaatyanaavrittim anyayaavartate punah // 8.26 //

TRULY THESE BRIGHT AND DARK PATHS OF THE WORLD ARE CONSIDERED ETERNAL; ONE LEADS TO NON-RETURN, AND THE OTHER ONE RETURNS.

Both these paths are eternal because worldly existence of finitude and change or Samsara is eternal. But as per Vedanta the Samsara can be ended for the individual through sincere meditation.

Life is a conflict between light and darkness. The former makes for release and the latter for rebirth. The Lord here uses the ancient belief to illustrate the great spiritual truth that those who are lost in the darkness of ignorance go by the path of the ancestors and are subject to rebirth and those who live in the day of illumination and walk on the path of knowledge obtain release from rebirth. This attainment of liberation through Self-Knowledge, while living in a physical body, is the goal of human life. The other courses, paths etc. are described in order to spur men to strive for Self-Knowledge and for attainment of liberation here on earth.

naite sruti paartha jaanan yogee muhyati kashchana
tasmaat sarveshu kaaleshu yogayukto bhavaarjuna //8.27 //

O SON OF PRTHA, NO YOGI IS DELUDED AFTER KNOWING THESE PATHS. THEREFORE ARJUNA, AT ALL TIMES YOU BE STEADFAST IN YOGA.

Knowing that one of the paths leads to Samsara and the other to Moksha, the Yogi takes up the one leading to illumination and rejects the other. Here Yogi is the one who has withdrawn himself from his false-identifications and entered into contemplation of the Self with single-pointed mind.

In short, this entire Chapter is Krishna's advice to Arjuna that he should, even while acting in this world, strive constantly to be the one living in the awareness of the Divine, through selfless identification with the Eternal, the Imperishable Purusha. The guiding principle is that whatever work one undertakes, he should not lose sight of the Eternal.

GLORY OF YOGA

vedeshu yajneshu tapahsu chaiva
daaneshu yat punyaphalam pradishtam
atyeti tatsarvam idam viditwaa
yogee param sthaanamupaiti chaadyam // 8.28 //

THE YOGI WHO KNOWS THIS TRANSCENDS ALL REWARDS LAID DOWN FOR THE STUDY OF THE VEDAS, FOR SACRIFICES, FOR AUSTERITIES, FOR MAKING CHARITIES; HE REACHES THE SUPREME, PRIMAL ABODE.

Sri Krishna means a true Yogi - a sincere meditator - goes beyond whatever meritorious results are promised in the Scriptures from the study of Vedas, performance of yajnas, practice of austerities and from charities to reach the final goal, the Primeval, Supreme Abode

The word 'this' in the verse means the answers given by the Lord to the seven questions of Arjuna. One should not only understand but also follow the teachings contained in these answers of the Lord.

(To recapitulate:
Arjuna asks Sri Krishna seven questions with a view to understand the technical and philosophical terms used by Him in the previous Chapter. Arjuna's Questions and Sri Krishna's Answers are as under:

1. What is Brahman?
Brahman is that which is Supreme, Imperishable, Unchanging and all-pervading. It is the cause for all effects. It is a causeless cause.

2. What is Adhyatma?
One's own individual Self or essential nature or individual consciousness is called Adhyatma. It is that part of Supreme Consciousness together with limiting ancillaries viz. time, space, name and form.

3. What is Karma?
It is the creative force which is the cause of existence, manifestation and sustenance of all beings

4. What is Adhibhuta?
It means all perishable things - the five elements of the Universe with all its objects, all things that have a beginning and an end, the intellect, mind, senses and body.

5. What is Adhidaiva?
The Universal Soul or the Divine Intelligence which is the controller of all. He is the vital energy or life-force behind all movable and immovable objects of the entire Universe.

6. What is Adhiyajna?
It is the presiding Deity of all sacrifices and the witnessing consciousness i.e. who dwells in the body

6. How the Lord is to be known by the self-controlled one at the time of death?
He who dies with his last thought fixed on God will reach God alone.)

om tat sat iti srimadbhagavadgeetaasu upanishatsu brahma vidyaayaam yogashaastre sri krishnaarjuna samvaade akshara brahma yogo naama ashtamo'dhyaayah ||

Thus in the Upanishads of the glorious Bhagavad Gita, the science of the Eternal, the scripture of Yoga, the dialogue between Sri Krishna and Arjuna, ends the eighth discourse entitled: The Yoga of Imperishable Brahman.

AN OUTLINE VIEW OF THIS CHAPTER

The preceding chapter spoke of the deluded seeking finite fruit while the wise seek Brahman. Herein we will find procedure to gain Brahman - how one can reach Brahman through concentrated yoga and single-pointed meditation, a path which leads one to the supreme abode wherefrom there is no return. The chapter also mentions the path of return, a realm of temporary bliss, to which one is transported, only to be brought back to the world of limitation.

I - BRAHMAN AND THE WORLD – ONE GAINS WHAT ONE PURSUES - VERSES 1 – 7

The topic covers the transcendental and immanent nature of Brahman - how the imperishable Brahman pervades this perishable world of things and beings. Whatever you pursue in this world you gain that alone. By pursuing the Self you realize the Self. Krishna advises mankind to surrender the mind and intellect to the Self while the body is engaged in action. This will lead the seeker to the ultimate state of Brahman.

II - STEADFAST IN YOGA AND MEDITATION YOU REACH BRAHMAN - VERSES 8 – 14

Turn your attention from the world to the supreme Self within. Control your senses and mind through spiritual practices. Then let your intellect direct the controlled mind to single-pointed meditation upon the mantra OM. By sustained meditation you will reach the supreme abode of Brahman.

III - BRAHMAN BEYOND THE MANIFEST AND UNMANIFEST WORLD - VERSES 15 – 22

Every individual being remains as vasanas, unmanifest desires, in deep sleep at night. His vasanas manifest at daybreak upon awakening. This cycle of dissolution and emanation continues until the individual completely exhausts his vasanas, reaching the state of Self-realization. Similar phenomenon takes place at the macrocosmic level. The entire macrocosm manifests during the day of Lord Brahma (a God of Hindu Trinity as distinguished from Brahman, the Supreme Reality). Brahama's celestial day consists of 4.32 billion terrestrial years. Similarly, the macrocosm folds back into the unmanifest state during the night of Lord Brahma, covering an equal period as his day. Beyond this unmanifest lies the Supreme Unmanifest, Brahman. Humans reach Brahman through spiritual disciplines of single-pointed meditation.

IV - PATHS OF RETURN AND NON-RETURN - VERSES 23 – 28

This topic covers the Path of Sun, Uttarayana and the Path of Moon, Dakshinayana. The Path of Sun takes a seeker to Brahmaloka, the heaven of Lord Brahma wherefrom he goes to the supreme Brahman. Whereas the Path of Moon takes the individual to pitrloka, only to enjoy heavenly pleasures and return to the cycle of birth and death in this world. The latter path provides only temporary pleasures of heaven for meritorious deeds done here. The former, however, takes the seeker to Brahman, through heaven because of having mixed meritorious deeds with his spiritual practice. But the true yogi, through his determined effort on the path of yoga of meditation goes directly from here to the abode of supreme Brahman.

<<<000>>>

CHAPTER 9

Raajavidyaa Raajaguhya Yogah:

Yoga of Royal Knowledge and Royal Secret

PREAMBLE

This chapter explains how the Self - *Atman* - pervades the entire world. The wise seek the Self while the ignorant, disregarding the Self, lead an empty life with vain hopes and unfulfilled aspirations. They go through the endless cycle of birth and death. Confirming the truth behind the saying that whatever one strives for, be it material or spiritual, one attains that particular goal, the ignorant gain their limited, mundane ends but never find accomplishment in their lives, whereas, the wise pursue the ultimate goal of Realization and find absolute peace and bliss in their own Self. Sri Krishna, therefore, advises Arjuna to seek the Self, to subsume all worldly activities to the Self until Spiritual Enlightenment is reached.

Krishna begins the chapter by offering to impart the knowledge of Reality that pervades the world and also as to the means of achieving this supreme knowledge and thereby free oneself from all agitations and sorrows.

The previous Chapter of the Gita dealt with liberation by stages through the process of meditation. But this way is not the only means of emancipation. A direct way is described in this Chapter. This knowledge being unknown to the mankind at large, Krishna terms it as a supreme secret and hence this Chapter is called 'Yoga of Royal Knowledge and Royal Secret'.

All living beings and inert things arise from the supreme Reality, exist in the Reality and ultimately merge into the Reality. The periods of manifestation of the world and its dissolution run into billions of years. The supreme Reality acts as the disinterested Self, witnessing the entire creation and dissolution. Those who fail to pursue this knowledge remain bound to the world of mortality. Krishna, therefore, appeals to the seekers to free themselves from the manifest world and reach the unmanifest Reality and to discover the Divinity that supports the pluralistic phenomenal existence.

THE TEXT

SOVEREIGN MYSTERY

sri bhagavaan uvaacha
idam tu te guhyatamam pravakshyaamyanasooyave
jnaanam vijnaanasahitam yajjnaataa mokshyase'shubhaat // 9.1 //

SRI BHAGAVAN SAID
TO YOU, O ARJUNA, WHO DO NOT CRITICIZE, I WILL PROPOUND THIS, THE GREATEST MYSTERY OF KNOWLEDGE COMBINED WITH REALIZATION, BY UNDERSTANDING WHICH YOU WILL BEE RELEASED FROM EVIL.

In this opening verse Sri Krishna assures Arjuna that He will reveal the theoretical knowledge of the Self combined with Its intuitive perception. Such knowledge is the direct means of attaining liberation. This knowledge about the Self dwelling in the body, and about the identity of the individual self and the Supreme Self, is considered most profound mystery because it has only to be realized through one's own experience or spiritual intuition and cannot be expressed in any words.

Arjuna is considered to be the most suitable candidate to know this deep mystery because he is free from jealousy and does not belong to the category of those who always find fault with whatever others do or say. Only jealousy-free mind can absorb deep knowledge, for jealousy is another form of ignorance.

Sri Bhagavan says that the one who receives this knowledge (a realized person) shall be free from all irksome problems of life, can rule over circumstances and face adversities with a smile. Krishna assures that by understanding that knowledge one will be released from the evil i.e. bondage of the world.

GREATNESS OF THAT KNOWLEDGE

raajavidyaa raajaguhyam pavitramidamuttamam
pratyakshaavagamam dharmyam susukham kartumavyayam // 9.2 //

IT IS THE ROYAL SCIENCE, ROYAL MYSTERY, AND THE SUPREME PURIFIER. IT IS PERCEIVED BY DIRECT EXPERIENCE. IT ACCORDS WITH DHARMA, IT IS EASY TO PRACTICE AND IT IS IMPERISHABLE.

In order to develop enthusiasm in the pursuit of Self, perfection is praised in this verse. Here the word secret or mystery means that which is too deep and striking and hence Vedanta is a secret for the uninitiated which has to be unraveled by a person endowed with scriptural knowledge.

Sri Krishna says that Vedanta, the science of life which is sovereign in its import, deep in its substance and supreme in its purifying effects, is clearly comprehensible since it can be verified by direct experience. It is knowledge by acquaintance and not by description. The truth is waiting to be seen by us, if the obstructing veils are removed. The Supreme is to be seen by one as one's own Self, through one's developed and purified intuition. The gains obtained by pursuit of this Royal Science are of imperishable nature.

As a lamp, when lighted in a room, instantly destroys the accumulated darkness of the ages, so the knowledge of Brahman, when realized in the heart, reduces to ashes the accumulated karma of all the past ages. Hence it is called supreme purifier.

The Bliss of Brahman is as directly perceived as the feelings of pleasure and pain. An object endowed with great qualities can also be against Dharma; but such is not the case with the knowledge of Brahman which is easily acquired when taught by a qualified teacher. It is always in accordance with Dharma. The Bliss arising out of the knowledge of Brahman, though easily acquired, is eternal. Therefore the knowledge of Brahman should be pursued by all who desire peace and happiness.

ashraddhadhaanaah purushaa dharmasyaasya parantapa
apraapya maam nivartante mrityusamsaaravartmani // 9.3 //

THOSE WHO HAVE NO FAITH IN THIS KNOWLEDGE OF THE SELF AND REGARD PHYSICAL BODY ITSELF AS THE SELF, O PARANTAPA, RETURN TO THE PATH OF MORTAL LIVING.

Faith or unswerving conviction of the existence of God, the soul and immortality is the prerequisite of spiritual life. Those without faith mean those who regard the physical body as the self and do not believe in the indestructibility and immortality of the soul.

ELUCIDATION OF THE SOVEREIGN WISDOM

mayaa tatamidam sarvam jagadavyaktamoortinaa
matstaani sarvabhootani na chaaham teshvavasthitah // 9.4 //

ALL THINGS IN THIS UNIVERSE ARE PERVADED BY ME IN MY UNMANIFEST ASPECT; ALL BEINGS EXIST IN ME BUT I DO NOT EXIST IN THEM.

na cha matsthaani bhootaani pashya me yogamaishwaram
bhootabhrinna cha bhootastho mamaatmaa bhootabhaavanah // 9.5 //

AND YET THE BEINGS DO NOT EXIST IN ME; BEHOLD, THAT IS MY DIVINE MYSTERY. MY SPIRIT WHICH IS THE SUPPORT OF ALL BEINGS AND THE SOURCE OF ALL THINGS DOES NOT DWELL IN THEM.

These two verse are very popular but yet difficult for easy comprehension. They require considerable reflection.

As we have seen earlier whenever Bhagavan uses the word 'ME' it does not refer to him as any individual but it means the Supreme Lord, the Ultimate Cause of All, the Uncaused Cause. His unmanifested form is Consciousness, Atman which is imperceptible to the senses. All things in the universe denote from the highest Brahma, the cosmic Spirit, to a blade of grass. Nothing can exist in this world unless the Lord, the Spirit, forms its substratum. Upanishads declare that the Lord, after creating the objects entered them as their indwelling consciousness to enliven them. Brahman, God, exists as the unmanifest Reality and pervades everywhere. Nothing exists other than Brahman. Yet because of delusion we see only the manifested world of beings and not it's underlying Reality. We superimpose the illusory world on the eternal Reality, Brahman.

This is like a deluded person misunderstanding a post as a ghost in darkness. He is said to superimpose the figure of ghost on the post on account of his wrong perception. The post is the substratum of the ghost; the post pervades every part of the ghost; the ghost cannot exist unless there is the post but the post can survive in spite of the absence of the ghost. Similarly Brahman exists without the world, but the world's existence depends upon Brahman.

Hence Krishna declares this truth in Verse 4 above that All things in this universe are pervaded by Him in His unmanifest aspect and that all beings exist in Him but He does not exist in them. This is just like saying that the ghost exists in the post but the post does not exist in the ghost. The post remains the source of the ghost. There can be no ghost without the post, but the post can remain without the ghost.

A thing devoid of inner reality cannot exist or be an object of experience. The Lord is the inner reality of everything. The reality of the Lord makes real everything in this world. But the reality of the Lord does not depend upon the world. He always exists whether the universe of names and forms exists or not.

The Lord is incorporeal and therefore has no real contact with the material world. He cannot be contained in any object. He is self-existent and self-luminous. Only a fraction of His majesty illumines the sun, the moon and the universe. But He himself is transcendental.

Having said that, the Lord further declares in the Verse 5 that "All beings do not dwell in Me; My spirit which is the support of all beings and the source of all things, does not dwell in them". On the face of it, this verse seems to contradict what was stated in the previous verse. Verse 4 admits the existence of beings in Brahman while Verse 5 denies the existence of beings in Brahman. A little critical analysis will remove this apparent mismatch of ideas.

Applying the same previous example of the post and the ghost to this verse, it is like the post telling that 'The ghost is not in me nor I am in the ghost. In fact, there never was a ghost. The ghost you perceive is only your imagination and not based on any fact or reality. The only reality is I, the post. I was, I am and I will be (the post only). This is the only truth from my standpoint'.

Thus the contradiction between these two verses is reconciled if we understand that there is no real existence of the universe and the beings. The existence of beings admitted in Verse 4 has only an illusory appearance to the eyes of the deluded. Beings do not actually exist, Brahman alone exists. Those who are fortunate to have wisdom clearly perceive and experience this truth. They see Brahman alone supporting the illusory phenomenon of this universe.

While in dream state we do not see the connection between the dream world and our mind. Only on waking up we understand such connection. Our mind alone projected the dream world which on waking up disappeared. Similarly, on tuning to God-consciousness, upon realizing the Self, we see the relation between the universe and God, Brahman.

What is this relation? The infinite Lord cannot be contained in a finite universe. Then why cannot the universe and the beings dwell in Him? The Lord, in reality, is neither the container nor the contained. In Him there is not the slightest trace of duality. In His purest essence He is above the law of cause and effect. In the final realization, the object and the subject become one; the whole universe merges in the Lord. In that state the Lord remains as One without a second, a homogeneous concentration of consciousness. The concepts of container and contained, cause and effect, apply to the realm of manifestation or maya. Through maya even though the Lord manifests in the tangible, relative universe, and appears to be its cause and support, yet He is always One without a second, transcendental, incorporeal and unattached. This is His eternal mystery - 'My Divine Mystery' as the Lord puts it in the Verse 5.

HOW THE LORD SUPPORTS THE WORLD?

yathaakaashasthito nityam vaayuh sarvatrago mahaan
tathaa sarvaani bhootani matsthaaneetyupadhaaraya // 9.6 //

AS THE MIGHTY WIND MOVING EVERYWHERE RESTS ALWAYS IN SPACE (THE AKASA), EVEN SO YOU KNOW THAT ALL BEINGS REST IN ME.

It is really difficult for the ordinary intellect to comprehend the idea that a substance which exists everywhere, allowing everything to exist in it, but at the same time it in itself does not get conditioned by the things existing in it.

Although the wind moves everywhere in the space, exists in the space and is supported by the space yet the wind does not put any limitation on the space. Space holds them all but is touched by none. This illustrates the relationship between the Self and the Not-Self. When the wind moves the space does not move. None of the qualities of the wind is the quality of the space. So also, the Real supports the unreal which seemingly lives in the Real and yet the unreal full of misery and sorrow can never condition the Real.

On the same analogy, without affecting the Lord in any way, good and evil, pain and pleasure, and the other traits of this universe do not touch the Lord because from His point of view they are illusory. He can never be touched by anything happening in time and space. As a light cannot be affected by the good or evil deed done with its help, so the soul, which in its essence is one with the Lord, cannot be affected by the good and evil action of the body and mind.

MAYA IS THE CAUSE FOR CREATION & DISSOLUTION

sarvabhootaani kaunteya prakritim yaanti maamikaam
kalpakshaye punastaani kalpaadau visrijaamyaham // 9.7 //

O SON OF KUNTI, ALL BEINGS, GO BACK TO MY NATURE AT THE END OF A TIME-CYCLE (KALPA); I SEND THEM FORTH AGAIN AT THE BEGINNING OF THE NEXT CYCLE.

prakritim swaamavashtabhya visrijaami punah punah
bhootagraamamimam kritsnamavasham prakritervashaat // 9.8 //

CONTROLLING MY OWN NATURE, I AGAIN AND AGAIN SEND FORTH ALL THIS MULTITUDE OF BEINGS, HELPLESS UNDER THE SWAY OF MAYA.

In these two verses Sri Krishna describes how His power of maya is instrumental in the process of creation and dissolution of the universe.

The whole process of creation, preservation and dissolution is due to the Lord's maya, His lower *prakriti* or nature consisting of the three gunas in their undifferentiated state and yet He is unaffected by it. Vedanta while recognizing the fact of creation does not approve of the act of creation. The Lord does not create the universe from nothing or void, for nothing only can come out from nothing. Therefore Vedanta believes that the Lord, because of His power of lower nature, maya, projects out of Himself (manifests) all the names and forms at the time of creation. Consciousness or His higher nature endows them with life.

At the end of the time-cycle, the names and forms of the manifested universe go back into the seed state and remain merged in Prakriti. At this state the three gunas of Prakriti remain in equilibrium. When this symmetry is disturbed, again creation takes place. This process of creation and dissolution is without beginning. Thus the better terms to indicate creation and dissolution are manifestation or evolution and merger or involution. The Lord, in His pure essence, remains unaffected by the activities of His maya, though the insentient maya is activated because of its proximity to the Lord.

Verse 8 says that the Lord, with the help of Prakriti manifests the universe. Because of His very proximity, insentient Nature acts. Maya or Prakriti is under His control. But Jiva or the created being is under the control of maya.

Living beings come out of Prakriti which remains dormant at the end of the previous cycle. Dissolution or the state in which the three gunas remain at perfect steadiness is called the sleep (dormant state) of Prakriti.

The beings at the end of the previous cycle merged in Prakriti are still under the influence of maya or ignorance. As Prakriti becomes active at the beginning of the next cycle, the beings also assume appropriate births according to their past karma.

Since the creation is falsely superimposed upon the Lord, what is perceived to be the universe existing in time and space is, from the point of Reality, nothing but the Lord Himself. Just as in the illusion of a rope appearing as a snake, the falsely perceived snake is in reality nothing but the rope.

IS THE LORD PARTIAL?

na cha maam taani karmaani nibadhnanti dhananjaya
udaaseenavadaaseenamasaktam teshu karmasu // 9.9 //

THESE ACTS DO NOT BIND ME, O DHANAJAYA, FOR I REMAIN UNATTACHED TO THEM AS ONE UNCONCERNED.

Because the Lord is responsible for the manifestation of heterogeneous beings of unequal conditions, a question arises whether He is guilty of partiality as we normally presume. This issue is answered here. The Lord says that He is unconcerned about fruit of His action relating to the creation of unequal and diverse beings.

It is attachment to the fruit that binds. He is unconcerned because He is totally devoid of the feeling of "I do". The creation belongs to the realm of maya and the Lord is beyond maya. There is no relationship between the Lord and creation just as there is no contact between the desert and the mirage. He is totally free from any desire, purpose, motive or agency so far as the creation is concerned.

Wherever and whenever egocentric actions are performed with selfish desires, they leave behind their impressions either pleasant or unpleasant. However, in the case of the Self which is Eternal there is neither attraction nor aversion in these actions i.e. in the creation and dissolution of the Universe. It is unmindful of what type of world is projected or what kind of activities take place therein.

The Self is neutral or indifferent to everything. It does nothing nor does It cause anything to be done. The Self has no attachment to the fruits of Its actions nor has It any egocentric feeling of agency or doership just as an Umpire is not interested in the results of the game he is umpiring. Therefore, the actions involved in creation and dissolution do not bind The Lord.

The absence of egocentric feelings of doership and attachment to fruits of actions is the cause for freedom from Dharma and Adharma or virtue and vice. The ignorant man who works with egoism and with a desire for the rewards of his actions is bound by his own actions.

mayaadhyakshena prakritih sooyate sacharaacharam
hetunaanena kaunteya jagadwiparivartate // 9.10 //

BY REASON OF MY PROXIMITY, PRAKRITI PRODUCES ALL THINGS, THE MOVING AND THE UNMOVING; BECAUSE OF THIS, O KAUNTEYA THE WORLD REVOLVES.

The finite acts because of the Infinite and yet the Infinite is said to be neutral. This strange relationship between the finite and the Infinite is explained here. The Lord presides over only as a witness; nature does everything. By reason of His proximity or presence, nature sends forth the moving and the unmoving. The prime cause of this creation is nature or prakriti.

Although all actions are done with the help of the light of the sun, yet the sun cannot become the doer of all actions. Similarly, the Lord cannot become the doer of actions eventhough nature does all actions with the help of the light of the Lord.

As the Self illumines ignorance or maya, which is the material cause of this world, the Self is regarded as the cause of this world. The magnet is indifferent although it makes the iron pieces move on account its proximity.

Similarly, The Lord remains indifferent although He makes the nature-Prakriti- create the world. He presides over the world which consists of moving and unmoving objects as a witness. By His presence the wheel of the manifested and unmanifested beings revolves round and round.

The question why The Lord created the world when He is a mere witness is a mystic one. We cannot say that the purpose of creation is meant for the enjoyment of the Supreme; for the Supreme is devoid of desire and does not enjoy. It is pure consciousness, a mere witness. And there is no other enjoyer for there is no other consciousness; A question arises whether creation is intended to secure heaven for it is opposed to heaven. Thus the question regarding the purpose of creation cannot be asked if one remembers that creation is maya or an illusion.

In Verses 7 to 10 The Lord defines His position through easy steps leading to a subtle concept which may appear contradictory. He begins by saying that He projects all beings at the beginning of evolution; Prakriti is only an instrument in His hands. Next, He says, He is not affected by the act, since He sits by, as the one neutral, perfectly unattached. Lastly, He tells the final truth that He really does nothing, that it is Prakriti, activated by His proximity produces the universe. It is His light that lights up the Prakriti and makes it live and act. This is the only relation between the Lord and His Prakriti.

The important point for us to note in these Verses 7 to 10 is that Sri Krishna imparts the subtle knowledge that Brahman, being neutral, remains apart as a silent witness of all that happens in the phenomenal world of the animate and inanimate.

DEVOTION TO THE SUPREME BRINGS ITS GREAT REWARDS

avajaananti maam moodhaah maanusheem tanumaashritam
param bhaavamajaanantomama bhootamaheshwaram // 9.11 //

UNAWARE OF MY HIGHER NATURE AS THE SUPREME LORD OF ALL BEINGS, FOOLS DISREGARD ME, WHEN I ASSUME A HUMAN FORM.

From time to time the Lord assumes a human form so that men may attain a godly nature. In that state the Lord acts outwardly like a human being though always remaining in full possession of the knowledge that He is unattached to anything material and that He is the very Self of all beings. The deluded only see Him acting as a man and therefore disregard Him as an ordinary human being while the wise understand Him as the Supreme Self.

moghaashaa moghakarmaano moghajnaanaa vichetasah
raakshaseemaasureem chaiva prakritim mohineem shritaah // 9.12 //

Of vain hopes, of vain actions, of vain knowledge and senseless, they definitely are possessed of the delusive nature of Rakshasas and Asuras.

'They' refers to those described in the previous verse. Rakshasas are those having Tamasic nature who indulge in acts of cruelty. Asuras are those having Rajasic nature with qualities of ambition, greed, and the like. They cling to the world of transient forms with the hope of finding peace and happiness and are victims of their own deceitful nature and disregard the Lord, who dwells in them as their underlying Reality.

mahaatmaanastu maam paartha daiveem prakritimaashritaah
bhajantyananyamanaso jnaatwaa bhootaadimavyayam // 9.13 //

BUT THE MAHATMAS (GREAT SOULS) O PARTHA, POSSESSING THE DIVINE NATURE WORSHIP ME WITH UNDISTURBED MINDS KNOWING ME AS THE IMPERISHABLE ORIGIN OF ALL BEINGS.

Deceitful nature mentioned above is contrasted with Divine nature. People of Demoniac nature live in their ego consciousness making it as a centre of their activities and get lost in the fruitless Samsara missing their true destiny. On the other hand people of wisdom who possess divine or saatwic nature and are endowed with self-restraint, mercy, faith, purity etc., know Him as the origin of all beings just as those who know the mud to be the origin of all mud pots will see the mud in all pots. They worship Him with single minded devotion. Their whole life becomes a continuous adoration of the Supreme and hence they are Mahatmas.

satatam keertayanto maam yatantashcha dridhavrataah
namasyantashcha maam bhaktyaa nityayuktaa upaasate // 9.14 //

ALWAYS GLORIFYING ME, STRIVING WITH FIRM RESOLVE, BOWING DOWN TO ME IN DEVOTION, ALWAYS STEADFAST, THEY WORSHIP ME.

These great souls always sing His glory, committed to lead a spiritual life of self-redemption with determination to reject the False and to pursue the path of the Real. They prostrate before The Lord with total detachment and surrender of all false identifications with their own matter-envelopments. They worship Him with great faith and devotion keeping in mind the nature of the Self as the substratum of the entire Universe and the essence of all beings. They represent the highest perfection of a combination of knowledge, devotion and work.

jnaanayajnena chaapyanye yajanto maamupaasate
ekatwena prithaktwena bahudhaa vishwatomukham // 9.15 //

OTHERS AGAIN OFFER THE OBLATION OF KNOWLEDGE AND WORSHIP ME EITHER AS THE ONE WITH THEM OR AS THE DISTINCT FROM THEM AND STILL OTHERS IN VARIOUS WAYS WORSHIP ME WHOSE FORM IS THE WHOLE UNIVERSE.

Oblation of knowledge implies that the knowledge of the Lord is itself a Yajna. The destruction of ignorance with fires of knowledge is called Gnana Yagna - Wisdom Sacrifice It implies that for the purpose of invoking Right Knowledge false ideas in us must be thrown into the flames of Right Knowledge. The Gnana Yagna has no ritualism. It is a constant attempt on the part of the performer to see the Consciousness Principle in every familiar name and form in all conditions and situations. It means an understanding that the Immutable Self pervades all, holding together the phenomenal multiplicities.

They offer their worship from the non-dualistic view or from the dualistic view. The man of realization identifies himself with the All-formed which is the view of Advaita. Some worship Him by making a distinction between The Lord and themselves which is the Dualistic view (Dvaita).

Some worship Him with the knowledge that He exists as the various Divinities like Brahma, Vishnu and Rudra etc (Vishishtaadvaita).

aham kraturaham yajnah swadhaahamahamaushadham
mantro'hamahamevajyam ahamagniraham hutam // 9.16 //

I AM THE KRATU, I AM THE YAJNA - THE SACRIFICE, I AM THE SVADHA - THE OFFERING (FOOD) TO THE ANCESTORS, I AM THE AUSHADHA - THE MEDICINAL PLANTS AND HERBS, I AM THE MANTRA, I AM THE AJYA - THE MELTED BUTTER (GHEE), I AM THE FIRE, AND I AM THE OBLATION.

Verses 16 - 19 explain how all the different types of worship performed in variety of forms become the worship of the one Self - the essence behind the seeming plurality of the world which is nothing but a superimposition gaining its existence from the Reality behind it. In this verse the existence of Self everywhere is explained giving the example of ritualistic worship widely prevalent in Arjuna's time. He is told that all the methods of worship are nothing but the worship of the Self.

Not only the different ritualistic prescriptions (Yajna) are presided over by the Self but all the vegetable food and medicinal herbs used in the sacrifice (Aushadha), the ghee poured into the altar of fire (Ajya), the oblations (Hutam) offered, the fire that is invoked (Agni), the mantras chanted with which oblation is offered, the food offered to the ancestors (Svadha) and the Kratu- a kind of Vedic rite are all nothing but the Self expressed in different ways and through different fields.

The Vedic sacrifice is interpreted as an offering of our whole nature, an entire self giving to the Universal Self. What we receive from Him we give back to Him. The gift and surrender are both His.

Through the symbol of sacrifice the Lord suggests that He alone forms all the accessories of worship and also the act and the result of the sacrifice.

pitaahamasya jagato maataa dhaataa pitaamahah
vedyam pavitramonkara rik saama yajureva cha // 9.17 //

I AM THE FATHER OF THIS UNIVERSE - THE MOTHER, THE SUSTAINER, THE GRANDFATHER, THE PURIFIER, THE KNOWABLE, THE SACRED MONO-SYLLABLE OM AND ALSO THE RIG, SAMA AND THE YAJUR VEDAS.

In order to show that the Self permeates everywhere The Lord says that He is the father, the mother, the sustainer, the grandfather and the purifier of the worlds. He is the one thing to be known because the Self is that which having known, everything becomes known. The Self, the substratum of the entire living universe, is symbolized by the Vedic mantra called OM. Life, which is the flow of constant experiences, implies the sum-total of all experiences in each one of us during the waking, dreaming and deep-sleep states.

The substratum for these three states and their experiences must be something other than the super-impositions on it just as the container is different from the contained. The fourth state supporting the ordinary states of consciousness in every one of us is termed Turiya. The sacred symbol OM represents all these four states. Therefore the Ultimate indicated by OM is the Self. This Absolute Reality is the theme of all the Vedas and therefore it is said that 'I am also the Rik, Sama and Yajus.'

gatirbhartaa prabhuh saakshee nivaasah sharanam suhrit
prabhavah pralayah sthaanam nidhaanam beejamavyayam
// 9.18 //

I AM THE GOAL, THE SUPPORTER, THE LORD, THE WITNESS, THE ABODE, THE SHELTER, THE FRIEND, THE ORIGIN, THE DISSOLUTION, THE FOUNDATION, THE TREASURE-HOUSE AND THE SEED WHICH IS IMPERISHABLE.

The Lord continues the enumeration of Brahman's various manifestations. He is:

The Goal (Gati): The Self is the goal because when the imperfections of the world of multiplicities are crossed over, the Absolute abode of Reality is experienced.

The Supporter (Bharta): Just as the desert supports the mirage, the Self lends a semblance of reality to the varied perceptions of the sense organs and thus holding together the ever-so-many changes into a consistent pattern which is called life.

The Lord (Prabhu): The Self, as the Pure Awareness. is beyond the sorrows and joys of the apparent and delusory universe just as electric energy is beyond the characteristics of its own manifestation through varied equipments.

The Witness (Saakshee): The Self is a mere witness and not a participant as It is an uninterested illuminator of what is happening in the body, mind and intellect as well as in the world outside.

The Abode (Nivasah): When different minds on different occasions project different forms and moods of a ghost on the same lamp post, the post is said to be the abode of different ghosts. So too, whenever our sense organs experience the pluralistic phenomena of the world, the Self or the Awareness is their abode.

The Shelter (Sharanam): The Self is the refuge or the harbor of tranquility which protects the confused ego from the sorrows and pains of Samsar.

The Friend (Suhrith): the Infinite is always the friend of the finite giving the latter security and well-being.

The Origin and Dissolution, the Substratum and the Store-house: As mud is in all pots, gold is in all ornaments, the Self is in the universe. Therefore, all things can come to manifestation and dissolve into the unmanifest only on the basis of a substratum. Hence the substratum, the Self, is the store-house of all names, forms and qualities that constitute the world.

The Immutable Seed (Beejam Avyayam): In contrast with the other seeds which undergo changes when they germinate, although the Self is the origin of all beings, It remains imperishable or unchanged even after beings arise out of it. It is therefore Immutable i.e. It endures so long as the Samsara endures.

tapaamyahamaham varsham nigrihnaamyutsrijaami cha
amritam chaiva mrityushcha sadasacchaaham arjuna // 9.19 //

AS THE SUN I GIVE HEAT; I WITHHOLD AND SEND FORTH THE RAIN; I AM IMMORTALITY AND ALSO DEATH; BOTH BEING AND NON-BEING, O ARJUNA.

This verse explains that the Self is the essence and the ruling factor behind all phenomenal objects and happenings in the universe.

I give heat: Just as electricity conditioned through various equipments expresses itself as heat in a heater, light in a bulb and cold in a fridge, the Self, the Existence itself, identifying with the phenomenon called the sun becomes the source of heat for the entire universe.

I withhold and send forth rain: The sun influences the climatic conditions of the universe thereby causing rainfall or drought.

I am immortality and also death: Self being the spark of life, It gives realistic experiences of existence in the world including to the phenomenon called death. Once it is realized that the Self is Immutable and Eternal, the state of immortality is reached. Change is what is called death and therefore the Self is the illuminator of change, Itself ever changeless.

I am the Being and Non-Being: Sat (existence) and Asat (non-existence) are the terms used in Vedanta to indicate cause and effect, the manifest and unmanifest. The Self being that Illuminating factor without which neither manifest nor unmanifest can be experienced, the Self is conceived of as the

Essence in both the manifest and unmanifest. He is being when manifested and non-being when the world is unmanifested.

The main idea is that the devotees regard the Lord in various ways and follow different methods of worship. The Supreme Lord grants our prayers in whatever form we worship Him.

The variety of human pursuits and how each gains its particular objective in life are described now. These pursuits fall under three distinct types of activities in the world. The persons belonging to the first type act with self-centered interests in this world. They go about their activities merely fulfilling their ego and egocentric desires. Consequently they suffer from mental agitations and sorrow *(papa)*.

Others in the second category work unselfishly for higher and nobler goals in life. They serve and sacrifice for their chosen ideal. They gain the joys of heaven *(punya)*.

The third variety seeks spiritual Enlightenment. They strive for liberation through their devout offerings to the Supreme Being. They surrender their actions, feelings and thoughts at their altar of Self-realization. Such seekers become liberated from their mundane existence and gain the ultimate bliss of Realization.

A seeker's direction in the spiritual path matters more than his spiritual status. A righteous person may move towards worldly attractions and devolve spiritually, whereas an unrighteous person may take to the spiritual path and evolve. Therefore, in the spiritual life what really matters is not where you are but what direction you choose to take – the path of evolution or devolution.

The discussion in this Chapter concludes with the encouraging words that anyone can attain Enlightenment through devotion and dedicated effort towards the Supreme Self.

NON-WORSHIPPERS ARE CAUGHT IN THE WHEEL OF BIRTH & DEATH

traividyaa maam somapaah pootapaapaa yajnairishtwaa swargatim praarthayante te punyamaasaadya surendralokamashnanti divyaandivi devabhogaan/9.20 /

THE KNOWERS OF THE THREE VEDAS, THE DRINKERS OF SOMA, PURIFIED OF ALL SINS, WORSHIPPING ME BY SACRIFICES, PRAY FOR THE WAY TO HEAVEN: THEY REACH THE HOLY WORLD OF THE LORD OF THE GODS (INDRA) AND ENJOY IN HEAVEN THE DIVINE PLEASURES OF THE GODS.

te tam bhuktwaa swargalokam vishaalam ksheene punye martyalokam vishanti evam trayeedharmamanuprapannaa gataagatam kaamakaamaa labhante /9.21 /

THEY HAVING ENJOYED THE VAST HEAVEN, RETURN TO THE WORLD OF MORTALS WHEN THEIR MERITS ARE EXHAUSTED; THUS ABIDING BY THE INJUNCTIONS OF THE THREE VEDAS AND DESIROUS OF ENJOYMENTS, THEY ARE SUBJECT TO BIRTH AND DEATH.

The Lord refers to the Vedic Theory that those who perform rituals gain heavenly enjoyments after death and points out how it cannot be regarded as the highest goal. Such men are bound by the law of karma as they are still lured by desire and they will return to this cosmic procession since they act from an ego-centre and since their ignorance is not destroyed.

If we seek rewards in heaven, we will gain them but we return to mortal existence so long as we do not gain the true aim of life. Human life is an opportunity to develop soul's divine nature from the imperfect material we are composed of. We operate from the ego-centered consciousness, whether we seek the pleasures of this world or a future paradise and therefore do not gain liberation from the ever running wheel of birth and death.

ananyaashchintayanto maam ye janaah paryupaasate
teshaam nityaabhiyuktaanaam yogakshemam vahaamyaham // 9.22 //

TO THESE MEN WHO WORSHIP ME ALONE, THINKING OF NO OTHER, TO THOSE EVER SELF-CONTROLLED, I SECURE WHICH IS NOT ALREADY POSSESSED (YOGA) AND PRESERVE WHAT THEY ALREADY POSSESS (KSHEMA).

The case of those who worship the Eternal (with love free from any desire) as the Substratum for the entire Universe is illustrated here. They meditate upon The Lord as the one and the only reality behind the entire universe. Sri Krishna promises them *Yoga* - more and more spiritual enlightenment and *Kshema* - the final liberation resulting from the Yoga.

This verse can be interpreted to mean that The Lord takes up all the cares and burdens of His devotees. To become conscious of divine love, all other love must be abandoned. If we cast ourselves entirely on the mercy of God, He bears all our sorrows. We can depend on His saving grace and energizing care. The Lord promises complete protection or final merger with His Immortal Being to those who love Him with all their body, heart and soul.

This Verse conveys the central theme of the Gita and is very famous.

WORSHIPPING OF OTHER GODS

yepyanyadevataa bhaktaa yajante shraddhaya'anvitaah
te'pi maameva kaunteya yajantyavidhipoorvakam // 9.23 //

EVEN THOSE DEVOTEES, WHO ENDOWED WITH FAITH, WORSHIP OTHER GODS, WORSHIP ME ALONE, O SON OF KUNTI, BY THE WRONG METHOD.

All do not worship at the same altar since tastes differ from person to person. Although they worship at the different altars, they adore the same Vitality that is the substratum for all the created world of change. Thus even when they worship different deities with perfect faith, all of them invoke nothing but the One Eternal Truth expressed through different forms of worship.

Once it is agreed that the Infinite Reality is the One without a second, which remains the same in the past, present and future, it will be clear that the Self as Consciousness expressed through the instruments of different saints, sages, prophets and incarnations is one and the same wherever and whenever they are born and functioned among the people of their times. Hence Sri Krishna declares that they too worship Me alone, eventhough by wrong methods.

The term other Gods referred to in this verse means different forms or aspects of the single God-hood like Indra, Varuna etc., which the man assumes in his different Gunas. Such worshipers are said to follow wrong methods because while worshipping when there is a possibility of achieving the Highest - Realization of the Self, Liberation - they pray for ordinary things of life like health, wealth etc. Because of this ignorance they come back to the world to satisfy their unfulfilled desires.

aham hi sarvayajnaanaam bhoktaa cha prabhur eva cha
na tu maamabhijaananti tattwenaatashchyavanti te // 9.24 //

(FOR) I ALONE AM THE ENJOYER IN AND THE LORD OF ALL SACRIFICES; BUT THEY DO NOT KNOW ME IN ESSENCE AND HENCE THEY FALL (RETURN TO THIS MORTAL WORLD).

This verse explains why these methods are wrong and why the pursuers of these wrong methods return to the mortal world when they have finished enjoying the joys of heaven which were the rewards for their merits acquired through ritualism.

These methods are wrong because only a limited potentiality of the Supreme is invoked and Its infinite glory is not realized. Hence they fall into the delusory mundane world again and again.

The Lord alone is the enjoyer of all sacrifices and the lord of all sacrifices. As a result of their sacrifices they attain a higher plane to enjoy their merits. However as they perform the worship without recognizing the Supreme and as they do not consecrate their actions to Him, they return to the mortal world after their merits have been exhausted.

yaanti devavrataa devaan pitreenyaanti pitrivrataah
bhutaani yaanti bhutejyaa yaanti madyaajino'pi maam // 9.25 //

THE WORSHIPPERS OF THE DEVAS OR GODS GO TO THE DEVAS; TO THE PITRIS OR ANCESTORS GO THE ANCESTOR-WORSHIPPERS; TO THE BHUTAS OR THE ELEMENTS GO THE WORSHIPPERS OF THE BHUTAS; BUT THOSE WHO WORSHIP ME COME TO ME.

'Devas' represent the various sense-organs by the activities of which the world is experienced. In other words the word 'Devas' means the entire field of all physical experiences. Those who solicit the external world of joys and successes consistently and with the required amount of devotion, come to gain such enjoyments. The worshippers of ancestors mean those who strive to live up to the cultural purity and traditions of their ancients. Such an individual gains the beauty and perfection of a pure life. The worshippers of the Bhutas reach the Bhutas indicate that even for those who diligently pursue the understanding of nature success is assured to the extent of their efforts made.

But these are the limited forms of the Supreme and cannot give the aspiring soul the peace that is beyond all understanding. The result of worship is assimilation to the form worshipped and these limited forms give limited results. But devotion to the Supreme brings the supreme reward of merging with the Self and such persons become on with Brahman.

DEVOTION AND ITS EFFECTS

patram pushpam phalam toyam yo me bhaktyaa prayacchati
tadaham bhaktyupahritamashnaami prayataatmanah // 9.26 //

WHOEVER OFFERS ME WITH DEVOTION AND A PURE MIND, A LEAF, A FLOWER, A FRUIT OR A LITTLE WATER - THAT I ACCEPT (THE DEVOUT GIFT OF THE PURE MINDED).

A gift, however small, is accepted by The Lord when it is offered with profound faith and devotion. He is satisfied even with a leaf, a flower, a fruit or a little water when it is offered with single-minded devotion and pure heart. What is offered is not as important as how it is offered. Although all the objects of the world belong to Him only and not to the devotee, yet if they are offered to Him by a devotee they become the conveyors of the latter's love and dedication unto The Lord.

Therefore the offerings serve their purpose only if they are accompanied by (a) devotion and (b) pure mind and heart. If these qualities are absent they are mere economic waste, vanity and false belief breeding superstition. On the other hand, if properly done, they are the means of transport in the spiritual path of self-development.

The way to the Highest is not by way of subtle metaphysics or complicated ritual. It is by sheer self-giving, which is symbolized by the offer of a leaf, a flower, a fruit or water.

WHY AT ALL THE LORD REQUIRES OFFERING FROM A SEEKER?

yatkaroshi yadashnaasi yajjuhoshi dadaasi yat
yattapasyasi kaunteya tatkurushva madarpanam // 9.27 //

WHATEVER YOU DO, WHATEVER YOU EAT, WHATEVER YOU OFFER IN SACRIFICE, WHATEVER YOU GIVE AWAY,

WHATEVER YOU PRACTICE AS AUSTERITY, O KAUNTEYA, DO IT AS AN OFFERING TO ME.

This verse explains how through all activities of life one can constantly live in the spirit of 'devout offering' unto the Supreme. It is repeatedly said in the Gita that mental attitude is of utmost importance than the mere physical act and this fact is generally overlooked by the seekers.

The Lord being the creator and sustainer of all objects needs nothing from anybody. All that is required by Him is the devotion expressed through the spirit of offering. Sri Krishna therefore says that even simple common tasks of daily life like what we eat, what we offer in sacrifices, what we give as gifts and what we practice as austerity, can be done as a sacred offering unto the Eternal and thereby a constant remembrance of the Supreme can be maintained although undergoing the vagaries of life.

When all the activities of life are performed with a spirit of offering, not only our love to the Supreme increases in us but also our entire life becomes sanctified with a nobler and diviner focus. A devotee who constantly remembers the Substratum behind everything in life can give to life the respect and reverence that it deserves and in turn the life bestows its rewards on him. Love of God is not an escape from harshness of life but a dedication for service. Karma Yoga or the way of works which starts with the duty of performance of prescribed rites concludes with the position that all tasks are sanctified when done with disinterestedness and dedication.

The message is when all actions are consecrated unto Him with disinterestedness and dedication they become sanctified by which one is freed from the bondage of Karma with no re-birth to him. The individual becomes one with the Cosmic Will.

It is appropriate to quote here a verse from Adi Sankara's *"Siva Manasa Pooja"* which reads:

Aatmaa tvam girijaa matih sahacharaah praanaah shariiram griham |
Poojaa te vishhayopabhogarachanaa nidraa samaadhisthitih |
Sajnchaarah padayoh pradakshinavidhih stotraani sarvaagiro |
Yadyat karma karomi tat tad akhilam shambho tavaaraadhanam||

You are my self, Parvati is my understanding. My five *praanaas* are your attendants. My body is your house, and all the pleasures of my senses are objects to use for your worship. My sleep is your state of *samaadhii.* Wherever I walk I am walking around you *(pradakshina)*, everything I say is a prayer in praise of you. Whatever act is done by me, every one of them, O Lord, is worship unto You.

Dedication of all our activities to the Supreme is the corner-stone for spiritual awakening.

RESULT OF SUCH DEDICATION OF ACTIVITIES

shubhaashubhaphalairevam mokshyase karmabandhanaih
sannyaasa yogayuktaatmaa vimukto maamupaishyasi // 9.28 //

YOU SHALL THUS BE FREED FROM THE BONDAGE OF ACTIONS YIELDING GOOD AND EVIL RESULTS. WITH YOUR MIND FIRMLY SET ON THE YOGA OF RENUNCIATION YOU SHALL BECOME FREE AND COME TO ME.

Sri Krishna continues the theme how by living the life in a spirit of surrendering the fruit of all actions to the Lord, an individual achieves the highest perfection. When actions are undertaken by an individual without ego, their reactions, good or bad, cannot bind him because the vasanas in him were already eliminated due to egoless actions and absence of egocentric desires and the mind already got purified.

The next stage is to live a life of Sanyasa and Yoga. The word Sanyasa does not mean physical rejection of the world. It is a renunciation of all egocentric activities and all cravings for fruits of actions. The offering of all works to the Lord constitutes the yoga of renunciation.

Such a life would be possible for those who dedicate all the end results of their actions unto The Lord. To the one who thus lives the life of Sanyasa, Yoga is natural as through out all of his activities he remembers only The Lord, the Self, the Infinite. Such a seeker discovers the futility of his earlier identification with the false and realizes his own Divine Nature. Hence the seeker is promised that he will go to the Supreme and even while living in the body one will be free from the bondage of action.

samo'ham sarvabhooteshu na me dweshyosti na priyah
ye bhajanti tu maam bhaktyaa mayi te teshu chaapyaham // 9.29 //

I AM THE SAME TOWARD ALL BEINGS; TO ME THERE IS NONE HATEFUL OR DEAR. BUT THOSE WHO WORSHIP ME WITH DEVOTION, ARE IN ME AND I AM ALSO IN THEM.

I am in all beings: The self is one in all beings; the same Consciousness Principle illumines the emotions and thoughts in all living creatures just as the same sun illuminates all objects in the world and its rays get reflected on all surfaces whether polished or rough.

To Me there is none hateful or dear: The Self is always the same everywhere and It neither bears distinction between the good and bad nor does It entertain love or hatred for any living being just as the same sunlight reflects on the surfaces of different types of objects, the quality of reflections being different on account of the varying quality of the respective surfaces. On the same analogy if some people show better spiritual development as compared to others it cannot be presumed that the Self is partial towards or showing any special preference to the former or having any prejudice against the latter.

But those who worship Me with devotion are in Me and I too am in them: Having said that the Self has neither love nor hatred towards anybody The Lord says that those who worship the Self with devotion rediscover that they themselves are none other than the Self that is worshipped by them.

The idea is that the Eternal Self does not choose any individual for bestowing Its grace but the individuals themselves create such environment in themselves that they rediscover the Self in themselves. A mind pre-occupied with egocentric attachments with the non-Self cannot realize the Bliss while the same mind if it is made to detach itself from all the extrovert diversions it realizes its identity with the Self. From this sense we can say that the worshipper with devotion is 'blessed' by The Lord and so he is in Him and He too is in the worshipper.

api chet suduraachaaro bhajate maamananyabhaak
saadhureva samantavyah samyagvyavasito hi sah // 9.30 //

EVEN IF THE MOST SINFUL MAN WORSHIPS ME WITH UNSWERVING DEVOTION, HE MUST BE REGARDED AS RIGHTEOUS, FOR HE HAS FORMED THE RIGHT RESOLUTION.

Bhakti is selfless contemplation with a single-pointed mind upon the non-dual Brahman who is none other than the essence of the devotee himself. A constant attempt to live upto one's own Real Nature is called single-pointed devotion. If a vicious sinner changes his evil thoughts his behavioral pattern gets transformed. If such a person worships The Lord with undivided devotion he is to be regarded as righteous and thoroughly rehabilitated.

From the moment contemplation on the Supreme is taken up with devotion, the sinner becomes a saint because he has formed a resolution to abandon the evil ways of his early life. He will soon grow out of himself into the spiritual glory. The evil of the past cannot be washed away except by his turning to God with undivided heart.

This verse does not mean that there is an easy escape from the consequences of our deeds. We cannot prevent the cause from producing its effect. Any arbitrary interference with the order of the world is not suggested. When the sinner turns to God with undistracted devotion, a new cause is introduced.

His redemption is conditional on his repentance. Repentance is a genuine change of heart and includes regret for the past sin and a decision to prevent a repetition of it in the future. When once the resolution is adopted, the transformation of the lower into higher is steadily effected.

If only human effort is to be depended upon for this change, it may be hard, erroneous, imperfect and difficult to overcome the ego. By surrendering the ego when one opens himself to the Divine, The Lord takes up the burden of changeover and lifts the soul to the spiritual plane from its contamination. A peace of charcoal loses its blackness only when it is charged with fire.

kshipram bhavati dharmaatmaa shashwacchaantim nigacchati
kaunteya pratijaaneehi na me bhaktah pranashyati // 9.31 //

HE SOON BECOMES RIGHTEOUS AND ATTAINS TO ETERNAL PEACE; O KAUNTEYA, KNOW YOU FOR CERTAIN THAT MY DEVOTEE NEVER PERISHES.

The effect of single-pointed devotion to The Lord is stated here. Sri Krishna says that such a person soon becomes righteous - he realizes the Divine Atman in himself. He attains eternal peace - an inward peace which is beyond the tumults of the daily living. He lives in tranquility free from agitations and excitements. He rediscovers in himself his own real nature which is Supreme Peace. Such a devotee never perishes or is destroyed. The seeker of the nobler values shall have no failures if his resolve is firm and his application is sincere.

The import of this and the previous verses is that the constant awareness of the Divine Principle protects the human personality from the destructive nature of its negative tendencies. Once we place ourselves in the hands of the Divine we cannot fall into the chasm of darkness.

maam hi paartha vyapaashritya ye'pi syuh paapayonayah
striyo vaishyaastathaa shoodraaste'pi yaanti paraam gatim // 9.32 //

FOR, TAKING REFUGE IN ME, THEY ALSO O PARTHA, WHO MIGHT BE OF INFERIOR BIRTH - WOMEN, VAISHYAS AND SUDRAS - ATTAIN THE SUPREME GOAL.

This verse requires a little careful understanding. The words 'persons of inferior birth- women, vaishyas and sudras- should not be regarded as justifying the customs prevailing then debarring these segments of the society from Vedic Study. Hinduism does not restrict salvation to any one group or section of the community nor does it regard any class of people as inferior by birth. More so, when the Gita, the Universal Scripture, is addressed to the humanity in general without distinction of race, gender or caste. This verse merely refers to the view prevalent in those historical times and does not attribute any sanction or mandate to the social practices then prevailing. These terms are to be understood as indicating some unique and varying qualities of the human mind and intellect obtained in different individuals at different points of time in history and not as denoting any caste or gender.

This verse says that through constant remembrance of The Lord and meditation upon the Divine Self with single pointed mind and devotion not only men of evil ways are redeemed but even those who cannot attune themselves to spirituality due to some impediments in them can also achieve progress. Sri Krishna means that when the peculiar shortcomings are removed such people also attain the Supreme Goal.

kim punarbraahmanaah punyaa bhaktaa raajarshayastathaa
anityamasukham lokamimam praapya bhajaswa maam // 9.33 //

HOW MUCH MORE EASILY THEN THE HOLY BRAHMANAS AND DEVOTED ROYAL SAINTS ATTAIN THE GOAL; HAVING

COME TO THIS TRANSITORY AND JOYLESS WORLD, YOU DO WORSHIP ME.

As compared to those who were referred to in the previous verse, Sri Krishna says how much easier and natural it would be for the Rajarishis (kings who have attained saintliness even while continuing to discharge their duties as kings) and holy Brahmanas who are bestowed with purity of mind to achieve Self-Realization.

The world is described by The Lord here as transient and joyless. The most characteristic feature of the world of experiences is that no experience is permanent at any period of time or place. Again no experience can be entirely satisfactory to any one. The world is lived by men in a field consisting of objects, instruments of perception and mental moods. As all these three factors are always in a state of variableness, the joys that come to us through these variable entities must also be transient. When the joys are broken, it becomes a joyless world and not merely a world of sorrows. Hence Sri Krishna advises Arjuna that he must engage himself constantly in the worship of the Self, having taken birth in this world which is *anityam* and *asukham.* This path alone can bring about imperishable happiness. The Gitacharya shows us the way out of this world of transitoriness and the curse of joylessness by asking us to take refuge in Him, the Divine.

manmanaa bhava madbhakto madyaajee maam namaskuru
maamevaishyasi yuktwaivamaatmaanam matparaayanah // 9.34 //

FIX YOUR MIND ON ME; BE DEVOTED TO ME; SACRIFICE TO ME; BOW DOWN TO ME. HAVING THUS DISCIPLINED YOURSELF AND REGARDING ME AS THE SUPREME GOAL, YOU SHALL COME TO ME.

This verse summarizes the ideas enunciated in the entire Chapter. The technique for self-development and self-perfection through right knowledge and meditation is 'contemplation on That, talking on That, discussing That, and to live on the bliss-concept of the Reality'. This is called the pursuit of Brahman or Brahma Vidya. This thought is expounded here by Sri Krishna. The Lord says 'with the mind ever filled with Me, My devotee makes all sacrifices and offers all salutations to Me at all times in whatever activity he is engaged in'.

"It is not the personal Krishna to whom we have to give ourselves up utterly but the Unborn, Beginningless, Eternal who speaks through Krishna. The way to rise out of our ego-centered consciousness to the divine plane is through the focusing of all our energies, intellectual, emotional and volitional, on God. Then our whole being is transformed and lifted up into the unity and universality of spirit. Knowledge, love and power get fused in a supreme unification. Joy and peace are the result of self-oblivion, of utter abandonment, of absolute acceptance". Dr.S.Radhakrishnan.

Sri Krishna promises Arjuna 'taking Me as the supreme goal you shall come to Me'. When one surrenders to The Lord without reservation, his whole life undergoes a wonderful transformation. His mind becomes one with the Divine Consciousness. Such a sage gets rid of ignorance and all limiting adjuncts through direct realization of the Self and becomes one with the Para Brahman. He attains *Jivanmukti* or liberation in this very life.

om tat sat iti srimadbhagavad geetaasu upanishatsu brahma vidyaayaam yogashaastre sri krishnaarjuna samvaade raajavidyaa raajaguhyayogo naama navamodhyaayah ||

THUS IN THE UPANISHADS OF THE GLORIOUS BHAGAVAD GITA, THE SCIENCE OF THE ETERNAL, THE SCRIPTURE OF YOGA, THE DIALOGUE BETWEEN SRI KRISHNA AND ARJUNA, ENDS THE NINTH DISCOURSE ENTITLED: THE YOGA OF ROYAL KNOWLEDGE AND ROYAL SECRET.

To recapitulate, the Lord's enumeration of His different manifestations (as Described in Verses 16 – 19) is summarized below for easy reference.

Kratuh - Vedic ritual
Gatih - Supreme goal
Yajnah - Sacrifice
Bhartaa - Supporter
Svadhaa -Offering to the departed
Prabhuh -Lord
Aushadham - Herbage & food grains
Saakshee - Witness
Mantrah - Sacred chanting
Nivaasah - Abode
Ajyam - Clarified butter
Sharanam - Shelter
Agnih - Sacred fire
Suhrit - Well-wisher
Hutam - Offering oblations in fire
Prabhavah - Origin
Pita - Father
Pralayah - Dissolution
Maataa- Mother
Sthaanam - Resting place
Dhaataa - Sustainer
Nidhaanam - Store-house
Pitaamaha - Grandsire

Avyayambeejam - Imperishable seed
Vedyam - The one worth knowing
Tapaamy - Radiate heat as the Sun
Pavitram - Purifier
Varsham- Rainfall
Omkara - Sacred syllable OM
Amritam - Immortality
Rik - Rg Veda
Mrityuh - Death
Saama - Sama Veda
Sat- Being
Yajuh-Yajurveda
Asat- Non-being

AN OUTLINE VIEW OF THIS CHAPTER

This chapter explains how the Self - Atman, pervades the entire world. The wise seek the Self while the ignorant, disregarding the Self, live a senseless life with vain hopes and aspirations. They go through the endless cycle of birth and death. Whatever one strives for, be it material or spiritual, one attains that particular goal. The ignorant gain their limited, mundane ends but never find fulfillment in their lives, whereas, the wise pursue the ultimate goal of Realization and find absolute peace and bliss in their own Self. Krishna, therefore, advises Arjuna and all mankind to seek the Self, to oblate all worldly activities to the Self until they reach spiritual Enlightenment.

I - SELF PERVADES THE WORLD - VERSES 1 – 10

Krishna begins the chapter by offering to impart the knowledge of Reality that pervades the world and also as to the means of achieving this supreme knowledge and thereby free oneself from all agitations and sorrow. This knowledge being unknown to the mankind at large, Krishna terms it as a supreme secret. Those who fail to pursue this knowledge remain bound to the world of mortality. Krishna, therefore, appeals to the seekers to free themselves from the manifest world and reach the unmanifest Reality and to discover the Divinity that supports the pluralistic phenomenon. All living beings and inert things arise from the supreme Reality, exist in the Reality and ultimately merge into the Reality. The periods of manifestation of the world and its dissolution run into billions of years. The supreme Reality acts as the disinterested Self, witnessing entire creation and dissolution.

II - THE DELUDED DISREGARD SELF, THE WISE GLORIFY AND SEEK SELF- VERSES 11 – 19

People remain ignorant of the Self within. They do not recognize the supreme architect of the cosmic phenomenon. Deluded of the Self, they sink into the quagmire of perceptions; emotions and thoughts. These deluded people live a purposeless life of vain hopes and aspirations in this world. The wise perceive the Self as the source of the world. They glorify and pursue the Self. Firm in their vows, deep in their devotion, they strive all their lives until they realize the Self. Krishna describes the manifestation of the Self in the world as the one Divinity pervading the infinite range of beings and things everywhere.

III - ONE ATTAINS WHAT ONE STRIVES FOR - VERSES 20 -28

The variety of human pursuits and how each gains its particular objective in life are described now. These pursuits fall under three distinct types of activities in the world. The persons belonging to the first type act with self-centered interests in this world. They go about their activities merely fulfilling their ego and egocentric desires. Consequently they suffer from mental agitations and sorrow (papa). Others in the second category work unselfishly for higher and nobler goals in life. They serve and sacrifice for their chosen ideal. They gain the joys of heaven (punya). The third variety seek spiritual Enlightenment. They strive for liberation through their devout offerings to the Supreme Being. They oblate their actions, feelings and thoughts to their altar of Self-realization. Such seekers become liberated from their mundane existence and gain the ultimate bliss of Realization.

IV - DEDICATED EFFORT LEADS SEEKERS, EVEN THE UNRIGHTEOUS, TO SELF-REALISATION - VERSES 29 -34

A seeker's direction in the spiritual path matters more than his spiritual status. A righteous person may move towards worldly attractions and devolve spiritually. Whereas an unrighteous person may take to the spiritual path and evolve. Therefore, in the spiritual life what really matters is not where you are but what direction you choose to take – the path of evolution or devolution. The topic concludes with encouraging words that anyone can attain Enlightenment through devotion and dedicated effort towards the Supreme Self.

<<<000>>>

CHAPTER 10

Vibhooti Yogah:

Yoga of the Divine Manifestations

PREAMBLE

In Chapters 7 to 9 Bhagavan Sri Krishna made an elaborate exposition of Jnana and Vijnana (Knowledge and Wisdom) about Brahman wherein He dealt with predominantly its *nirguna* aspects (characteristics without any attributes or manifestations). But for an ordinary person these discourses would be very much perplexing. Therefore, the Lord introduces this Chapter dealing with the same subject in a more easy to comprehend way by describing Brahman in Its *saguna* aspects (characteristics with attributes or manifestations). In the next Chapter He physically demonstrates to Arjuna what He has been talking about.

Chapters 7 to 9 may be taken as the pure science of Brahman, Chapter 10 as its applied science and Chapter 11 as the practical demonstration of what had been stated in these Chapters. Thus the Bhagavad Gita gives us an integrated and complete data about the Absolute, Supreme Being.

Vibhooti Yoga means the yoga of Supreme Manifestation of God – revealing Brahman as the source of the material world. Even highly evolved persons do not know the origin of Brahman. The wise, however, pursue Brahman with devotion and steadfastness until they become one with Brahman.

Arjuna stands bewildered at the astounding knowledge and personality of Krishna. He asks how Krishna (Brahman) manifests Himself in the world. Krishna responds by detailing His (Brahman's) manifested expressions analytically and tells how Brahman permeates the whole universe (Verses 20 to 39). Reiterating the fact that the range of His divine manifestations is infinite, He winds up this topic by pointing out to Arjuna that the entire universe is an insignificant, minuscule fraction of Him (Brahman).

This is Yoga because by meditating over the glories of The Lord as described in this Chapter one can discover the Infinite in the finite world of pluralities. The Self conditioned by or functioning through the individual mind and intellect is the Ego (Jiva), limited by its imperfections. While the same Eternal Self conditioned by or functioning through the total (cosmic) mind and intellect is the God-principle or Ishwara unlimited by any imperfections. This concept of the Self as seen through an individual mind and the cosmic mind is explained in this and the next Chapters.

THE TEXT

THE IMMANENCE AND TRANSCENDENCE OF GOD

sri bhagavaan uvaacha
bhooya eva mahaabaaho shrinu me paramam vachah
yatteham preeyamaanaaya vakshyaami hitakaamyayaa // 10.1 //

SRI BHAGAVAN SAID
AGAIN, O MIGHTY ARMED, LISTEN TO MY SUPREME WORD, WHICH I, WISHING YOUR WELFARE, WILL DECLARE TO YOU, WHO ARE DELIGHTED TO HEAR ME.

Encouraged by the keen interest shown by Arjuna in the discourses so far and the resultant satisfaction visible in him, The Lord comes forward to repeat what He had told in the previous discourses (Ch.7 to 9) about His essential nature, manifestations and Divine glories. He does this because He desires Arjuna's welfare who is also delighted to hear Him.

na me viduh suraganaah prabhavam na maharshayah
ahamaadirhi devaanaam maharsheenaam cha sarvashah // 10.2 //

NEITHER THE HOSTS OF THE DEVAS NOR THE GREAT RISHIS KNOW MY ORIGIN; FOR IN ALL RESPECTS I AM THE SOURCE OF ALL THE DEVAS AND RISHIS.

The Lord is without a cause. He is changeless and immutable. Yet He manifests His glories in the Universe in various ways. The mystery of these manifestations is not known even to the Devas and sages much less to the ordinary mortals. Human reasoning cannot know His nature. He reveals Himself out of His infinite compassion in the pure hearts of His devotees.

The Supreme is unborn and eternal and He is also the Lord of the world. Though He has no birth, all existence derives from Him. The teacher announces that He is in truth the Eternal God Himself, more ancient than all else and that all manifested glory is from Him.

yo maamajamanaadim cha vetti lokamaheshwaram
asammoodhah sa martyeshu sarvapaapaih pramuchyate // 10.3 //

HE WHO KNOWS ME AS UNBORN AND WITHOUT A BEGINNING, AND AS THE SUPREME LORD OF THE WORLDS, HE, AMONG THE MORTALS, IS UNDELUDED AND IS LIBERATED FROM ALL SINS.

Knows Me: Knowing not merely by emotion but by spiritual understanding achieved through one's identification with the Self.

Unborn: The Infinite cannot be born because It never expresses Itself in any finite manifestation. The ghost is born and hence it has to die; but the post cannot be said to have given birth to the ghost nor it has taken birth from the ghost. The post was, is and shall always be a post only. Similarly, The Self is eternal and therefore It is birthless.

Beginningless: Everything is born in the Self, exists in the Self and ends in the Self. Waves are born but ocean is birthless. Every wave - every manifestation- has a beginning and an end but the ocean has none. Hence the Self is beginningless.

Supreme Lord of the Worlds: 'World' includes not only the objective world perceived by our physical senses but also the world of feelings and emotions experienced by us. Experiences of the body, mind and intellect cannot be ours unless we are constantly aware of them. This awareness or Consciousness or Self is that which rules our 'world' which is called the 'Supreme Lord of the worlds'.

When we learn to look at things as derived from the One Transcendent Reality, we are delivered from all gropings and bewilderment.

buddhirjnaanamasammohah kshamaa satyam damah shamah
sukham duhkham bhavo'bhaavo bhayam chaabhayameva cha //
10.4 //

INTELLIGENCE, KNOWLEDGE, NON-DELUSION, FORGIVENESS, TRUTH, SELF-CONTROL, CALMNESS, HAPPINESS, MISERY, BIRTH OR DEATH, FEAR AND ALSO FEARLESSNESS;

ahimsaa samataa tushtistapo daanam yasho'yashah
bhavanti bhaavaa bhootaanaam matta eva prithagvidhaah
// 10.5 //

NON-INJURY, EQUANIMITY, CONTENTMENT, AUSTERITY, CHARITY, FAME, ILL FAME (ALL THESE) DIFFERENT ATTRIBUTES OF BEINGS ARISE FROM ME ALONE.

Continuing the idea that The Lord is the cause for the world of plurality within an individual and for the world outside, Sri Krishna enumerates the qualities of head and heart emanating from Him.

The Lord alone is the cause and the basis of the universe and all its beings. Created beings are endowed with different attributes according to their karma. The law of karma functions in the relative world through the power of the Lord and thus the Divine is indirectly responsible for the pain and sufferings of the world. He is the lord of the world and guides it, though He is unaffected by its oppositions of duality.

maharshayah sapta poorve chatwaaro manavastathaa
madbhaavaa maanasaa jaataa yeshaam loka imaah prajaah
// 10. 6 //

THE SEVEN GREAT SAGES AND ALSO THE FOUR ANCIENT MANUS, POSSESSED OF POWERS LIKE ME (ON ACCOUNT OF THEIR MINDS BEING FIXED ON ME), WERE BORN OF (MY) MIND; FROM THEM ARE THESE CREATURES IN THE WORLD ORIGINATED AND SUSTAINED.

According to the theory of creation found in Puranas Brahman in association with *maya* projected the universe. The first manifestation of Brhman in space and time is called Hiranyagarbha or *prana* or *sutratma* which pervades the universe as a thread runs through a garland. The process of creation further down the line is as under.

Hiranyagarbha

-

From the mind of Hiranyagarbha

-

The first four created beings were Sanaka, Sanandana, Sanatana and Sanatkumara. They withdrew from the world, devoted themselves in austerities and did not participate in creation. Hence, seven sages and four Manus were produced who were ordered to populate the world with animate and inanimate beings.

These seven *rishis* were the original teachers of spiritual wisdom and the four Manus were the original rulers of the world. The present inhabitants of the world according the Puranas have descended from these primeval personages.

etaam vibhootim yogam cha mama yo vetti tattwatah
so'vikampena yogena yujyate naatra samshayah // 10.7 //

HE WHO KNOWS IN TRUTH THIS GLORY AND POWER OF MINE ACQUIRES UNSHAKABLE DEVOTION; OF THIS THERE IS NO DOUBT.

One who knows the immanent pervading power of The Lord and the diverse manifestations caused thereby gets united with Him in firm and unalterable Yoga and attains eternal Bliss and harmony (unshakable yoga). The Yogi realizes that the Lord and his manifestations are one. He is aware of his oneness with Him. The knowledge of the determinate Brahman (manifestations) is the way to the knowledge of the indeterminate (unmanifest Absolute) Brahman.

KNOWLEDGE AND DEVOTION

aham sarvasya prabhavo mattah sarvam pravartate
iti matwaa bhajante maam budhaa bhaavasamanvitaah // 10.8 //

I AM THE ORIGIN OF ALL, FROM ME EVERYTHING EVOLVES, UNDERSTANDING THUS, THE WISE WORSHIP ME WITH ALL THEIR HEART.

The technique by which we can get ourselves established permanently in the continuous experience of the Supreme is explained by Sri Krishna who now speaks as The Lord, Ishwara. God is the material and efficient cause of the world. The seeker is not deluded by passing forms but knowing that the Supreme is the source of all the forms, he worships the Supreme with all his heart.

matchittaa madgatapraanaa bodhayantah parasparam
kathayantashcha maam nityam tushyanti cha ramanti cha
// 10.9 //

WITH THEIR THOUGHTS FIXED ON ME, WITH THEIR LIFE ABSORBED IN ME, ENLIGHTENING ONE ANOTHER ABOUT ME, AND ALWAYS SPEAKING ABOUT ME, THEY DERIVE SATISFACTION AND DELIGHT.

The characteristics of a devotee who has attained the realization of oneness with the divine are described in this verse.

With their minds wholly in Me (Matchittah): Once a person's intellect is convinced that the essence behind the God principle (Ishwara) and the individual ego (Jiva) is one and the same, any agitating feelings in the mind and disturbing thoughts in the intellect will not upset him and he will constantly be aware of the Conscious principle or the Self behind them all.

With their senses absorbed in Me (Mat-gata-praanaah): Here Prana indicates the five sense organs. The implication is not to run away from the sense objects but to have discrimination through which one can regulate and train his thoughts so that in any situation in life he will always be reminded of the Eternal Consciousness without which any sense object could not have been illumined for the mind to experience it.

Discussing with one another: Mutual discussion about Brahma Vidya enables crystallization of ideas and attaining deeper insight into the amount of knowledge gained.

A true seeker is the one who remembers constantly the Consciousness principle. They ultimately lead him to be free from external circumstances and inner dissatisfactions. He experiences a sense of contentment and delight which provide an ideal backdrop for the spiritual progress.

teshaam satatayuktaanaam bhajataam preetipoorvakam
dadaami buddhiyogam tam yena maamupayaanti te // 10.10 //

TO THEM, EVER DEVOTED TO ME, WORSHIP ME WITH LOVE, I GIVE THE YOGA 'BUDDHI' BY WHICH THEY COME TO ME.

The devotees who have dedicated themselves to The Lord, who are ever harmonious and self-abiding, who are ever devout and who adore Him with intense love and with no selfish motives obtain the divine grace. The Lord gives them *'buddhiyoga'* or the Yoga of understanding by which they gain the wisdom which sees the One in all the forms which constantly change and pass.

teshaam evaanukampaartham aham ajnaanajam tamah
naashyaamyaatmabhaavastho jnaanadeepena bhaaswataa // 10.11 //

SOLELY OUT OF COMPASSION FOR THEM, I, DWELLING WITHIN THEIR HEARTS, DESTROY THE DARKNESS BORN OF IGNORANCE BY THE SHINING LAMP OF KNOWLEDGE.

The purpose of imparting the Buddhi Yoga is given here.

Darkness born of ignorance - The veil which prevents one from recognizing the Self which is already within him due to the absence of the knowledge of Right Discrimination. Even in darkness the Self is abiding in us but It is only not available for subjective experience by the seeker due to ignorance.

Destroy by the shining lamp of knowledge - Seekers who established themselves in the constant awareness of the Supreme, with the aid of Buddhi Yoga, experience their real identity with the Self. This act of Self-revelation is performed by The Lord (The Self) who always abides in the hearts of the devotees out of the spirit of compassion.

The Lord makes out how Bhakti or devotion leads to the destruction of ignorance and the rise of illumination. When ignorance is destroyed God stands revealed in the human spirit. When love and wisdom arise, the eternal is fulfilled in the individual. Bhakti is also a means to Jnana. Through it we obtain Divine Grace and the power of understanding, buddhiyoga. Intellectual knowledge is rendered luminous and certain by the direct intuition of the Buddhi.

LORD IS THE SEED AND PERFECTION OF ALL THAT IS

arjuna uvaacha
param brahma param dhaama pavitram paramam bhavaan
purusham shaashvatam divyamaadidevamajam vibhum // 10.12 //

ARJUNA SAID
YOU ARE THE SUPREME BRAHMAN, THE SUPREME ABODE (OR THE SUPREME LIGHT), THE SUPREME PURIFIER, THE ETERNAL, DIVINE PERSON, THE PRIMEVAL GOD, UNBORN AND OMNIPRESENT.

aahustwaam rushayah sarve devarshinaaradastathaa
asito devalo vyaasah swayam chaiva braveeshi me // 10.13 //

ALL THE SAGES HAVE THUS DECLARED YOU AS ALSO THE DEVARSHI NARADA; SO ALSO ASITA, DEVALA AND VYASA AND NOW THE SAME YOU YOURSELF ARE TELLING ME.

Arjuna tells Sri Krishna that he was taught much earlier the same ideas as He has been telling him now such as Supreme Brahman, Supreme Abode, Supreme Purifier, Eternal, Self-luminous Purusha, First Deva, Birthless and All Pervading. These were also declared by the ancient Rishis like Asita, Devala and Vyasa and by the Deva Rishi Narada. Hence he wonders how Sri Krishna who is standing before him be Himself the Infinite, the Supreme, the Birthless and the All pervading.

Param Brahman - The highest Self, the pure and attributeless Absolute completely free from the limiting adjuncts. Param Dhama - The Supreme Light, the Supreme Abode, the substratum. Pavitram Paramam - He who destroys ignorance which is the very cause for all dualities.

sarvametadritam manye yanmaam vadasi keshava
na hi te bhagavan vyaktim vidurdevaa na daanavaah // 10.14 //

I BELIEVE ALL THIS THAT YOU SAY TO ME AS TRUE, O KESHAVA, VERILY O BHAGAVAN, NEITHER THE DEVAS NOR THE DANAVAS KNOW YOUR MANIFESTATION (IDENTITY).

All wisdom, dispassion, lordship, virtue, wealth and omnipotence exist in full in Bhagavan. He also knows the origin, dissolution and the future of all beings. He is omniscient.

Arjuna admits the truth of what has been declared and proclaims his conviction that Sri Krishna who is speaking to him is the Supreme Godhead, the Absolute. He confirms by his own experience to the truth revealed by the seers who have seen It and become one with It. Abstract truths uttered by the sages become now luminous intuitions and glowing experiences of one's own being.

swayamevaaatmanaa'tmaanam vettha twam purushottama
bhootabhaavana bhootesha devadeva jagatpate // 10.15 //

VERILY, YOU YOURSELF KNOW YOURSELF BY YOURSELF, O PURUSHOTTAMA (SUPREME PERSON), O SOURCE AND LORD OF ALL BEINGS, O GOD OF GODS, O RULER OF THE WORLD.

The Self cannot be known as an object through the instruments of knowing. It cannot be understood as an object either by the best or the worst in us. The Self being itself Awareness or Knowledge no other knowledge is required to know It. Thus Arjuna says 'You Yourself know Yourself by Yourself'.

Purushottama: The best or the most glorious among the Purushas who is the source of beings, The Lord of the beings, God of the gods and the ruler of the world. It means the Self of all the selves, the one without any second, the Supreme Self.

vaktumarhasyasheshena divyaa hyaatmavibhootayah
yaabhir vibhootibhir lokaanimaamstwam vyaapya tishthasi // 10.16 //

YOU SHOULD INDEED TELL, WITHOUT RESERVE, OF YOUR DIVINE GLORIES BY WHICH YOU EXIST, PERVADING ALL THESE WORLDS.

katham vidyaamaham yogimstwaam sadaa parichintayan
keshu keshu cha bhaaveshu chintyo'si bhagavan mayaa // 10.17 //

HOW SHALL I, EVER MEDITATING, KNOW YOU O YOGIN? IN WHAT ASPECTS, O BLESSED LORD, ARE YOU TO BE THOUGHT OF BY ME.

vistarenaaatmano yogam vibhootim cha janaardana
bhooyah kathaya triptirhi shrinvato naasti me'mritam // 10.18 //

TELL ME AGAIN IN DETAIL, O JANARDANA, OF YOUR YOGA-POWER AND IMMANENT GLORY; FOR I AM NOT SATISFIED IN HEARING YOUR NECTAR-LIKE SPEECH.

After expressing his wonder on what Sri Krishna was telling him all along Arjuna now directly asks The Lord: What exactly are The Lord's divine manifestations in the world of plurality? In what aspects of nature where The Lord's presence is more clearly manifest? In what various aspects he should think of Him to help his meditation?

Arjuna, full of anxiety to listen (Jigyasa), tells The Lord that he is not satisfied with His invigorating nectar-like words of Discourses and requests Him to tell him in detail His Yogic power and eminent glory. This shows that Arjuna has come to realize that the whole creation is nothing but the manifestation of the Lord's powers and no one but the Lord himself knows their mystery. So he desires to learn about those powers from the Lord Himself.

By divine glory or manifestation or Vibhooti is meant the formative forces or spiritual powers which give to each object its essential nature. The Gita does not set up an opposition between Brahman and the world, between the Ineffable Reality and its inadequate expression. It gives a comprehensive spiritual view. Worship of the Absolute is difficult for embodied beings. It is easier to approach the Supreme through Its relations with the world and this method is more natural. The nature of the Supreme in man and the universe is veiled by the series of becomings. Man has to discover his spiritual unity with God and so with all His creatures.

sri bhagavaan uvaacha
hanta te kathayishyaami divyaa hyaatmavibhootayah
praadhaanyatah kurushreshtha naastyanto vistarasya me // 10.19 //

SRI BHAGAVAN SAID
VERY WELL, NOW I WILL DECLARE TO YOU MY DIVINE GLORIES BUT ONLY OF THOSE WHICH ARE PROMINENT, O THE BEST OF KURUS. THERE IS NO END TO THEIR DETAILED DESCRIPTION.

Sri Krishna in the rest of this Chapter explains to Arjuna exhaustively the identity of the Self (i.e. His identity) in individual beings and things and in their combinations. The Lord makes it clear His supreme importance in individual beings and things and emphasizes the fact that without Him none of the constituent members of a community will have any organized existence.

God is infinite and His manifestation is infinite. He manifests Himself in the universe through innumerable forms. Each form is a symbol of an attribute of the Lord. The true seer finds each finite form carrying in it its own revelation of the infinite.

ahamaatmaa gudaakesha sarvabhootaashayasthitah
ahamaadishcha madhyam cha bhootaanaamanta eve cha // 10.20 //

I AM THE SELF, O GUDAKESA, SEATED IN THE HEARTS OF ALL BEINGS; I AM THE BEGINNING, THE MIDDLE AND ALSO THE END OF ALL BEINGS.

The Lord tells Arjuna 'I am the Self that exists in the heart of all beings'. This general statement is the sum and substance of His entire talk in Gita. He specifically tells that He is the birth, life and death of all beings. The world is a living whole, a vast inter connectedness, a cosmic harmony inspired and sustained by the One Supreme.

If one is unable to meditate on the Lord as the Self, then one should think of Him in the various beings and things enumerated in the following verses as a special manifestation of the Godhead, for the Lord is the essence of all the things

aadityaanaamaham vishnur jyotishaam raviramshumaan
mareechirmarutaamasmi nakshatraanaamaham shashee // 10.21 //

AMONG THE (TWELVE) ADITYAS I AM THE VISHNU; AMONG THE LUMINARIES, THE RADIANT SUN; I AM MARICHI AMONG THE WINDS; AMONG THE STARS I AM THE MOON.

Adityas are Gods representing the twelve months of the year. Vishnu is considered the most important among them. Maruts are the gods controlling the winds. The twelve Adityas, luminaries like Agni, Lightning, the Maruts, the Stars etc. are the ordinary manifestations of The Lord. Vishnu, Marichi, the sun and the moon are his special manifestations and hence they have greater splendor in them.

While the Supreme is in all things, He is more prominent in some than in others. There is an ascending order in the world. God is more revealed in life than in matter, in consciousness than in life and in saints and sages than in others. Within the same order, He is most revealed in the pre-eminent individuals.

In all these verses of this Chapter Sri Krishna supplies the seekers with various items of thought (names and forms) over which The Lord can be superimposed for deeper and single-pointed meditation.

vedaanaam saamavedo'smi devaanaamasmi vaasavah
indriyaanaam manashchaasmi bhootaanaamasmi chetanaa // 10.22 //

AMONG THE VEDAS I AM THE SAMA VEDA; I AM VAASAVA AMONG THE GODS; AMONG THE SENSES I AM THE MIND AND I AM THE INTELLIGENCE AMONG LIVING BEINGS.

Sama Veda - It is the essence of Rig Veda which is the most important of all the four Vedas. Sama Veda has the additional characteristic of musical beauty with tunes, melody and rhythm. Sri Krishna is the Infinite Essence tuned to music as Rig Veda mantras are in Sama Veda.

Vaasava - The king of gods, Indra. The Self is as Indra among the Gods, ruling over the others, controlling, directing and organizing the lives.

Mind - Indra also means the king of sense organs, the latter being the Devas. Mind is the controller without which sense organs cannot have the power of functioning.

Intelligence - Of all the creations in the world intelligence is the mysterious power which is still beyond comprehension. It is that which illumines all from the intellect down to the grossest physical object.

rudraanaam shankarashchaasmi vittesho yaksharakshasaam
vasoonaam paavakashchaasmi meruh shikharinaamaham // 10.23 //

AND AMONG THE RUDRAS I AM SANKARA; AMONG THE YAKSHAS AND RAKSHASAS KUBERA, THE LORD OF WEALTH; AMONG THE VASUS I AM PAVAKA, AGNI; AND AMONG THE MOUNTAINS I AM THE MERU.

Rudras - Deities of destruction. Destruction is a necessary precedent for construction just as the seed must perish to enable the plant to come out. Sankara is the deity for creative destruction.

Pavaka - Vasus are the deities presiding over the seasons. The six external seasons get colored by two internal seasons viz. joy and sorrow and all of these can be experienced only through Consciousness within.

Meru - A mythological mountain believed to be the centre of the Universe from which Ganga (Spiritual Knowledge) flows in all four directions to bless the humanity.

purodhasaam cha mukhyam maam viddhi paartha brihaspatim
senaaneenaamaham skandah sarasaamasmi saagarah // 10.24 //

AND, AMONG THE HOUSEHOLD PRIESTS, O PARTHA, KNOW ME THE CHIEF, BRIHASPATI; AMONG THE GENERALS, I AM SKANDA; AMONG THE LAKES, I AM THE OCEAN.

Brihaspati - The spiritual teacher for the celestials. Skanda- Son of Siva the peacock rider and the wielder of the spear. Ocean - It is the source of all rivers because from it the evaporation of water takes place to flood the rivers. Similarly the sentient and insentient things and beings of the world cannot exist but for the Infinite Ocean of Truth, The Lord.

maharsheenaam bhriguraham giraamasmyekamaksharam
yajnaanaam japayajno'smi sthaavaraanaam himaalayah // 10.25 //

AMONG THE GREAT SAGES I AM BHRIGU; AMONG WORDS I AM THE ONE SYLLABLE "OM"; AMONG SACRIFICES I AM THE SACRIFICE OF SILENT REPETITION (JAPA YOGA); AMONG IMMOVABLE THINGS THE HIMALAYAS.

Bhrigu - He is the chief of the seven rishis. One syllable 'OM' - It indicates the Eternal and Infinite. Japa Yoga - It is the repetition of the mantra or divine name by maintaining the same divine thoughts. Japa Yagna is regarded as the best of all Yagnas because it involves the unbroken remembrance of the Self. The Himalayas - It is great because it is the highest in the world and helps in spiritual advancement to the seekers.

ashwatthah sarvavrikshaanaam devarsheenaam cha naaradah
gandharvaanaam chitrarathah siddhaanaam kapilo munih // 10.26 //

AMONG ALL TREES I AM THE PEEPUL; AMONG THE DIVINE RISHIS, NARADA; AMONG GANDHARVAS CHITRARATHA; AMONG THE PERFECTED ONES, THE SAGE KAPILA.

Peepul - Both in magnitude and life span it is the largest and hence considered immortal. It has divinity attached to it and therefore worshipped. As per Upanishads and Gita itself it represents pluralistic phenomenal world. Narada - He is a great devotee of Narayana. He is the greatest sage because he guides the deluded. He has the missionary zeal and enthusiasm. Gandharvas - Celestial beings famous for their art and music. Chitraratha is the most brilliant among them noted for his singing.

Siddhas - Those who at their very birth attained virtue, wisdom and dispassion. They are great thinkers and perfected ones. Sage Kapila is the author of Sankhyan Philosophy and is the greatest thinker.

ucchaihshravasamashwaanaam viddhi maamamritodbhavam
airaavatam gajendraanaam naraanaam cha naraadhipam // 10.27 //

KNOW ME AMONG HORSES AS UCCHAISRAVAS, BORN OF NECTAR, AMONG LORDLY ELEPHANTS THE AIRAVATA AND AMONG MEN, THE KING.

Ucchaisravas, Airavata - The winged horse, mighty and powerful and the white elephant came up during the churning of the Milky ocean which were presented to Indra. King - Leader among men.

aayudhaanaamaham vajram dhenoonaamasmi kaamadhuk
prajanashchaasmi kandarpah sarpaanaamasmi vaasukih // 10.28 //

AMONG THE WEAPONS I AM THE THUNDERBOLT; AMONG COWS I AM KAMADHUK; I AM KANDARPA THE CAUSE FOR OFF-SPRINGS; AMONG SERPENTS I AM VASUKI.

Vajra - An item in the divine artillery which can never be destroyed. Kamadhuk - The cow 'Kamadhenu' which yields all the desired objects. Kandarpa - The Cupid, the God of Love. Vasuki - Mythological serpent living on Siva's ring finger as an ornament. This serpent served as a rope for churning the milky ocean. Sarpa is single-hooded serpent.

anantashchaasmi naagaanaam varuno yaadasaamaham
pitreenaamaryamaa chaasmi yamah samyamataamaham // 10.29 //

I AM ANANTA AMONG NAGAS; I AM VARUNA OF WATER-DEITIES; ARYAMAN OF PITRIS OR ANCESTORS I AM; AMONG CONTROLLERS I AM YAMA.

Nagas - Many hooded serpents among which Sesha Naga is the mightiest and the most divine because he is the substratum upon which Vishnu, the sustainer and Brahma, the creator of the multiple worlds function. Varuna - He is the ruler of the oceans, the Lord of all waters. Aryaman - Ruler of the world of ancestors. Yama - The Lord of Death who controls life. The principle of creation has to be preceded by the principle of death. Death serves the purpose of orderly existence in the world.

prahlaadashchaasmi daityaanaam kaalah kalayataamaham mrigaanaam cha mrigendro'ham vainateyashcha pakshinaam // 10.30 //

I AM PRAHLADA AMONG DAITYAS (DEMONS); AMONG MEASURERS I AM TIME; AMONG BEASTS I AM THEIR KING, THE LION; AND GARUDA AMONG BIRDS AM I.

Prahlad - Though the son of a demon king, Hiranyakashipu, Prahlad was a great devotee of Sri Krishna. Time - Time is an Eternal Factor which is divided into past, present and future by the play of mind and intellect. The Lord is thus an Infinite Substratum supporting the finite multiplicity. The Lion - Noted for its majesty, manliness and dignity among the animals. Garuda - Noted for its flight, powers of perception and the heights upto which it can soar among the birds.

pavanah pavataamasmi raamah shastrabhritaamaham jhashaanaam makarashchaasmi srotasaamasmi jaahnavee // 10.31 //

AMONG PURIFIERS I AM THE WIND; AMONG WARRIORS RAMA AM I; AMONG THE FISHES I AM THE SHARK; AMONG THE RIVERS I AM THE GANGA.

Wind - Sweeps clean every thing. Rama - A Perfect man in all aspects of life: as a son, husband, brother, friend, warrior, teacher, ruler and even as a father.

Shark - The largest and most powerful fish. Jahnavi - Most sacred river Ganga.

sargaanaamaadirantashcha madhyam chaivaham arjuna
adhyaatmavidyaa vidyaanaam vaadah pravadataamaham
// 10.32 //

AMONG CREATIONS I AM THE BEGINNING, THE MIDDLE AND ALSO THE END, O ARJUNA; AMONG SCIENCES I AM THE SCIENCE OF THE SELF AND I AM THE LOGIC IN ALL ARGUMENTS.

In verse 20 of this Chapter The Lord said that He is the beginning, middle and also the end of all individual beings (movable and immovable). Here He says that He is the essence of the entire creation.

The science of Self is the way to beatitude or salvation. It is not an intellectual exercise or a social adventure. It is a way to saving wisdom and so is pursued with deep conviction. Philosophy as the science of Self helps us to overcome the ignorance which hides from us the vision of Reality. Without it the sciences of objective elements become misleading.

Logic - There are various types of argumentations in logic such as vada, jalpa and vitanda. Vada (Logic) is a way of arguing by which one gets at the truth of a question without any attraction, repulsion or jealousy or for scoring victory over the other. Jalpa means assertion of one's own opinion through vehement criticism of the other's while vitanda means harping upon one's own views without caring for the opposite side. In jalpa and vitanda the aim is to gain victory over the other side.

aksharaanaamakaaro'smi dwandwah saamaasikasya cha
ahamevaakshayah kaalo dhaataaham vishwatomukah // 10.33 //

AMONG THE LETTERS OF THE ALPHABET, THE LETTER 'A' I AM AND THE DUAL (CO-ORDINATES) AMONG ALL COMPOUNDS, I AM VERILY, THE INEXHAUSTIBLE OR THE EVERLASTING TIME; I AM THE (ALL-FACED) DISPENSER (OF FRUITS OF ACTIONS) HAVING FACES IN ALL DIRECTIONS.

The letter 'A' - In Sanskrit the sound of the letter 'A' preponderates in every letter which makes the pronunciation of the words very sweet and rhythmical. This letter also occupies the first place among the alphabets in all languages.

Dual- One of the Sanskrit forms of compounds is Dwandwa in which the essential elements in the components co-ordinate with each other in the newly formed compound word. Similarly the Self and the Not-Self look mixed up together constituting the world of perceptions experienced by us, but to a discriminative mind the component parts are clear.

Everlasting Time - The 'Time' mentioned earlier in verse 30 is finite time while here it is mentioned as infinite. These put together mean that the Self is the substratum for both the absolute concept of Pure Time and the finite experience of each Moment. But for the awareness of each fraction of time the total concept of Time is impossible. Hence The Lord is immanent in each unit of time and also the substratum for the total time.

Dispenser - He is the sustainer of the mental impressions in every individual which determine as to how he will react with the outside world.

Facing all directions - As the Supreme Being is all pervading He is said to face all directions. In all perceptions whether physical, mental or intellectual there is the grace of Consciousness which is the Self and hence It is said to see in all directions.

mrityuh sarvaharashashchaaham udbhavashcha bhavishyataam keertih shreervaakcha naareenaam smritirmedhaadhritih kshamaa // 10.34//

AND I AM ALL DEVOURING DEATH AND THE SOURCE OF ALL THAT IS TO BE; AMONG THE FEMININE QUALITIES (I AM) FAME, PROSPERITY, SPEECH, MEMORY, INTELLIGENCE, FIRMNESS AND FORGIVENESS.

Death - It is the supreme leveler. Separateness and individuality are maintained only during life time due to one's relationship with other than oneself. After death all individualities vanish and all beings wise and ignorant, rich and poor, noble and ignoble, strong and weak etc. are reduced to the same dust wherein no distinction can be identified.

Source of all that is to be - The Lord is the source of all new creations that will have to come in future. In the scheme of life destruction is only a modification of the existing form into another new one to come in the future. The idea is that the Infinite, through the continuous process of destruction and creation, is in fact the finite Universe.

Fame, prosperity etc. - These qualities are such that through them one can visualize the Divine more clearly.

brihatsaama tathaa saamnaam gaayatree chhandasaamaham maasaanam maargasheersho'ham ritoonaam kusumaakarah // 10.35 //

AMONG THE HYMNS ALSO I AM THE BRIHAT SAMAN; AMONG THE METRES GAYATRI AM I; AMONG MONTHS I AM MARGASHIRSHA (DECEMBER-JANUARY); AMONG SEASONS (I AM) THE FLOWERY SPRING.

Brihatsama - Songs of Sama Veda, consisting of various tunes and meters which require long and enduring practice to sing. Of all the meters in Sama Veda, the meter called 'Brihati' is the most difficult one and the songs composed in this meter are called 'Brihatsama'.

Gayatri - This meter is the most divine and powerful. The hymn composed in this meter (Om Gayatri Mantra) which glorifies the sun is recited every morning and evening by all. The Supreme is indicated in the Gayatri Mantra as All-pervading, Omniscient and Eternal. He who understands Gayatri in this way attains full and unending prosperity.

Margashirsha - End of hot season and beginning of cold.
Spring - Flowery season with all colors, beauty and charm around.

dyootaam chhalayataamasmi tejastejaswinaamaham
jayo'smi vyavasaayo'smi Sattvam Sattvavataamaham // 10.36 //

I AM THE GAMBLING OF THE DECEITFUL; I AM THE SPLENDOR OF THE SPLENDID; I AM VICTORY, I AM DETERMINATION (OF THOSE WHO ARE DETERMINED); I AM THE GOODNESS OF THE GOOD.

Gambling - Most deceptive game of that time on account of which Pandavas had to undergo extreme sufferings. Splendor -It is the most satisfying experience. Victory, effort and goodness - Great qualities in an individual.

vrishneenaam vaasudevo'smi paandavaanaam dhananjayah
muneenaamapyaham vyaasah kaveenaamushanaa kavih
// 10.37 //

AMONG THE VRISHNIS I AM VAASUDEVA; AMONG THE PANDAVAS (I AM) DHANANJAYA; ALSO AMONG THE MUNIS I AM VYASA; AND AMONG THE POETS I AM USHANA, THE GREAT SEER.

Vrishni - Yadva clan, Vaasudeva - Sri Krishna whose father's name was Vasudeva. Dhananjaya - Arjuna, the winner of wealth, the focal point among the five Pandava brothers but for whom nothing could have been achieved by them. Vyasa- Of all the men of reflection, The Lord is he who is behind all the Puranas, Vedas and Upanishads, sage Vyasa. Ushana - Sukracharya, the preceptor of demons.

dando damayataamasmi neetirasmi jigeeshataam
maunam chaivaasmi guhyaanaam jnaanam jnaanavataamaham
// 10.38 //

AMONG THOSE WHO CHASTISE I AM THE SCEPTER (ROD OF CHASTISEMENT); AMONG THOSE WHO SEEK VICTORY I AM STATESMANSHIP; AND ALSO AMONG THE SECRETS I AM SILENCE; THE WISDOM AMONG KNOWERS AM I.

Scepter - Symbol of the royal power to punish the guilty. Statesmanship - Finesse, skill, tact etc. in administration. Secret - Secret if expressed in any form, subtle or overt, remains no more a secret. Silence is therefore the best form of maintaining secrecy. Wisdom - The knowledge in the knower or the wisdom in the wise are the expressions of Divinity through individuals.

yacchaapi sarvabhootaanaam beejam tadahamarjuna
na tadasti vinaa yatsyaanmayaa bhootam charaacharam // 10.39 //

AND WHATSOEVER IS THE SEED OF ALL BEINGS, THAT ALSO AM I, O ARJUNA; THERE IS NO BEING, WHETHER MOVING OR UNMOVING THAT CAN EXIST WITHOUT ME.

Self is the source of all creation just as the seed is the source of all trees. This idea is repeated in several ways. When the seed germinates it dies to become a tree. But this is not the case with the Self. Hence Sri Krishna says that He is the seed of the Universe and even after its germination and growth the tree (universe) is sustained by the seed (Self) just as all the waves during their appearance and disappearance are sustained by the ocean and without which waves cannot exist. Nothing can exist without the Self, which is the essence of everything like saying all cloth has come out of cotton and no cloth can exist without cotton.

naanto'sti mama divyaanaam vibhooteenaam parantapa
esha too'ddeshatah prokto vibhootervistaro mayaa // 10.40 //

THERE IS NO END TO MY DIVINE GLORIES, O PARANTAPA; BUT THIS IS A BRIEF STATEMENT BY ME OF THE PARTICULARS OF MY DIVINE GLORIES.

As the Lord is infinite so are His manifestations. Although there is no end to narrate all His glories the Lord has provided Arjuna with some specific examples in order to teach him the Art of seeing the Unseen through the Seen.

The implication is that one should meditate upon these ideas or examples and try to discover the Infinite Resplendency of The Lord in every finite shape and name.

yadyad vibhootimat Sattvam shreemadoorjitameva vaa
tattadevaavagaccha twam mama tejom'shasambhavam // 10.41 //

WHATEVER THAT IS GLORIOUS, PROSPEROUS OR POWERFUL IN ANY BEING, YOU KNOW THAT TO BE A MANIFESTATION OF A PART OF MY SPLENDOR.

The above examples illustrate clearly that The Lord is present in all names and forms revealing Himself as the glorious or the great or the mighty aspect in all beings and things. Sri Krishna summarizes his discourse on His several glories by saying whatever that is great or glorious or mighty is nothing but the expression of a ray of His infinite splendor. Each one of the examples given by The Lord indicates as either the great one in the whole species or the noblest and the most glorious thing or happening or the mightiest among the powerful. This indication is useful to the seekers to perceive the play of the Infinite among the finite and ever changing world of names and forms. "While all things are supported by God, things of beauty and splendor reveal Him more than others. Every deed of heroism, every life of sacrifice, every work of genius, is a revelation of the Divine. The epic moments of man's life are inexplicably beyond the finite mind of man". Dr.S.Radhakrishnan

athavaa bahunaitena kim jnaatena tavaarjuna
vishtabhyaahamidam kritsnamekaamshena sthito jagat // 10.42 //

BUT OF WHAT USE TO YOU IS THE KNOWLEDGE OF ALL THESE DETAILS, O ARJUNA? I EXIST SUPPORTING THIS WHOLE WORLD BY ONE PART OF MYSELF.

Jagat - The sum total the world perceived by the sense organs and the worlds of ideas and emotions i.e. the entire field comprehended by the sense organs, the mind and intellect. Sri Krishna declares that the total world is supported and nourished by a fraction of Him or His glory. Not that the Divine glory is broken into fragments. This cosmos is but a partial revelation of the Infinite, is illumined by one ray of His shining light. The transcendent light of the Supreme dwells beyond all this cosmos, beyond time and space. *Purusha Suktam* makes out that all this is only a description of His greatness; the Purusha Himself is much greater than this.

The long list of the divine manifestations described in the Verses 20-39 has been tabulated below for easy reference.

Sri Krishna says that He is the

1. UNIVERSAL SELF SEATED IN THE HEARTS OF ALL BEINGS
2. Beginning, middle and end of all beings and that

AMONG	*HE IS*
3. Twelve sons of Aditi	Vishnu
4. Lights	Radiant Sun
5. Maruts	Marichi
6. Stars	Moon
7. Vedas	Sama
8. Gods	Indra

9. Organs of perception	Mind
10. Living Beings	Consciousness
11. Eleven Rudras	Siva
12. Yakshas & Rakshasas	Kubera
13. Eight Vasus	God of Fire
14. Mountains	Meru
15. Household Priests	Brihaspati
16. Generals	Skanda
17. Lakes	Ocean
18. Great Sages	Bhrigu
19. Words	Sacred syllable 'OM'
20. Sacrifices	Japa Yagna
21. Immovable Things	Himalayas
22. Trees	Holy Aswattha
23. Celestial Sages	Narada
24. Gandharvas	Chitraratha
25. Siddhas	Sage Kapila
26. Horses	Ucchaisravaa
27. Mighty Elephants	Airavata
28. Men	King
29. Weapons	Thunderbolt
30. Cows	Kamadhenu
31. Kandarpa	The progenitor
32. Serpents (Sarpa)	Vasuki
33. Snakes	Sesha (Ananta Nag)
34. Deities of water	Varuna
35. Pitris (Forefathers)	Aryama,
36. Controllers	Yama, Lord of Death
37. Daityas	Prahlada
38. Reckoners	Time
39. Beasts	Lion
40. Birds	Garuda
41. Purifiers	Wind

42. Warriors	Rama
43. Fishes	Shark
44. Rivers	Ganga
45. Creation	Beginning, middle, end
46. Sciences	Science of Self
47. Discussions	Logic
48. Alphabet	The letter 'A'
49. Compounds in grammar	The Dual
50. The Lord is	The imperishable Time
51. Creator facing all around	
52. Death and prosperity	
53. Feminine Qualities	Fame, prosperity, speech, memory, intelligence, firmness and forgiveness
54. Hymns	Brihatsaman
55. Metres	Gayatri
56. Twelve Months	Margashirsha
57. Six Seasons	Spring, flowering season
58. Deceitful Practices	Gambling
59. Splendid	Splendour
60. Victorious	Victory
61. Resolute	Determination
62. Good	Determination, goodness
63. Vrishnis	Vaasudeva (Krishna)
64. Pandavas	Arjuna
65. Sages	Vyasa
66. Wise or Poets	Ushanas (Sukracharya)
67. Rulers	Subduing Power
68. Those who seek victory	Statesmanship
69. Secrets	Silence
70. Wise	Wisdom
71. All Beings	Seed

Sri Krishna concludes that nothing can exist without Him, that there is no limit to His divine manifestations and that He supports the entire Universe by a fraction of His power.

om tat sat iti srimadbhagavadgeetaasu upanishatsu brahma vidyaayaam yogashaastre sri krishnaarjuna samvaade vibhootiyogo naama dashamo'dhyaayah ||

THUS IN THE UPANISHADS OF THE GLORIOUS BHAGAVAD GITA, THE SCIENCE OF THE ETERNAL, THE SCRIPTURE OF YOGA, THE DIALOGUE BETWEEN SRI KRISHNA AND ARJUNA, ENDS THE TENTH DISCOURSE ENTITLED: THE YOGA OF THE DIVINE MANIFESTATIONS.

AN OUTLINE VIEW OF THIS CHAPTER

Vibhuti Yoga means the yoga of Supreme Manifestation – revealing Brahman as the source of the material world. Even highly evolved persons do not know the origin of Brahman. The wise, however, pursue Brahman with devotion and steadfastness until they become one with Brahman.

Arjuna stands bewildered at the astounding knowledge and personality of Krishna. He asks how Krishna (Brahman) manifests Himself in the world.

Krishna responds by detailing His (Brahman's) manifested expressions analytically and tells how Brahman permeates the whole universe. At the end, He points out to Arjuna that the entire universe is an insignificant, minuscule fraction of Brahman.

I - KNOWING ITS SUPREME NATURE THE WISE ATTAIN BRAHMAN - VERSES 1 – 11

Brahman reins supreme. The entire universe arises from Brahman – things, beings and all their characteristics. Even the sages and Gods do not know the origin of Brahman. But the wise, undeluded by this world, understand Brahman's absolute nature and Its expression, Its transcendence and Its immanence. Identifying with Brahman they maintain this supreme knowledge of Brahman until they become one with Brahman. The preparation, the Sadhana (spiritual practice) and the meditation required for a seeker to realize Brahman are also outlined here.

II - HOW BRAHMAN PERVADES THE WORLD, HOW DOES ONE KNOW BRAHMAN - VERSES 12 –18

Arjuna acclaims Krishna as the supreme Brahman, the primeval God, eternal and all-pervading. The divine sages acknowledged Krishna as supreme. Arjuna pleads to Krishna saying "Neither the gods nor demons know your divine manifestations. You alone know your real Self – the source of all beings, the God of gods, the Lord of the universe. You should now speak to me of your divine glories in your countless manifestations. How am I to contemplate and meditate on your existence? How am I to unite with the supreme Self through this manifested world? Krishna remains silent as Arjuna goes on speaking.

III - BRAHMAN'S SUPREME MANIFESTATION SHOWN ANALYTICALLY - VERSES 19 – 38

In this section Krishna enumerates some of His divine glories. He begins by declaring Himself as the Self in all beings. Beings emerge from Him, exist in Him and ultimately merge into Him. He is the essence in everything, and every being like the mind is the essence in the dream, clay in the clay pots, and gold in all gold ornaments. While declaring Himself as the quintessence of every being and everything, Krishna chooses Himself as the very best among all species and objects. By using the superlatives Krishna made it possible for even the less evolved people to recognize His latent glories of His countless manifestations.

IV - BRAHMAN TRANSCENDS THE WORLD, A MERE FRAGMENT OF ITS BEING - VERSES 39 – 42

After describing the grand glories, Krishna claims these glorious, prosperous and powerful manifestations as a fragment of His original splendor. He emphasizes that they form only an insignificant part of His infinite Being, implying thereby that one should not miss the essential Reality behind these non-essential details of His manifestation.

<<<000>>>

CHAPTER 11

Vishwaroopa Darshana Yogah:

Yoga of the Vision of the Universal Form

PREAMBLE:

In the previous Chapter the Lord explained His presence in all things and beings in His different manifestations indicating that the Self is the substratum for the world of multiplicities. In this Chapter He provides Arjuna with a practical demonstration to show that everything exists in the Self. It is easier to see the Self in finite objects than to cognize the entire Universe in one Reality, the Self.

The concept of space divides the individual objects from one another. If there is no space in between them all objects will come together so closely that they become one single entity. In this mass of things there will certainly be different shapes and forms of all things at one and the same place and time. This is the picture of the Universal or Cosmic Man, the vision of the world viewed from a mind wherein there is no concept of time and space.

Sri Krishna removes the concept of space from Arjuna's mind and assumes Himself the form of one universal structure to demonstrate that everything in the Universe is in Him. Having seen this form of The Lord, Arjuna re-visits his faith and understanding. In this Chapter we see Arjuna full of emotions of wonder, amazement, fear, reverence, devotion etc. In its concept and description, this Chapter is considered as one of the highest philosophical poems in all the sacred books of the world.

A major part of this Chapter is soleley devoted to a description of the Cosmic Body and praises offered by Arjuna to the Lord manifested in that form; hence it has been given the title Vishwaroopa Darshana Yogah: Yoga of the Vision of the Universal Form.

THE TEXT

On hearing the Lord declaring that the entire universe is held in a mere fraction of His being, Arjuna is desirous of seeing with his own eyes the form of the Lord that so sustains the world system. Therefore, extolling the Lord and His teachings, Arjuna requests Him to grant him a direct vision of His Cosmic Body.

arjuna uvaacha
madanugrahaaya paramam guhyamadhyaatmasamjnitam
yattwayoktam vachastena moho'yam vigato mama // 11.1 //

ARJUNA SAID
OUT OF COMPASSION TOWARDS ME, YOU HAVE SPOKEN WORDS OF ULTIMATE PROFUNDITY CONCERNING THE SELF AND THEY HAVE DISPELLED MY DELUSION.

Removal of delusion or misunderstanding is not equivalent to acquiring knowledge of the Real. The illusion that things of the world exist in themselves and maintain themselves, that they live and move apart from God and hence he is responsible for his relatives being killed and that he would be committing sin etc., have disappeared from Arjuna but he was yet to experience the Unity in diversity.

bhavaapyayau hi bhootaanaam shrutau vistarasho mayaa
twattah kamalapatraaksha maahaatmyamapi chaa'vyayam // 11.2 //

I HAVE LEARNT FROM YOU AT LENGTH, O LOTUS-EYED LORD, OF THE ORIGIN AND DISSOLUTION OF BEINGS, AND ALSO YOUR INEXHAUSTIBLE GREATNESS.

Although Arjuna says that he has understood that The Lord is immanent in all names and forms still some doubts linger in his mind which could be removed only through practical demonstration. This verse is preparing him to demand such a proof. In this Chapter the Lord out of His sheer kindness shows His Cosmic form to Arjuna just because he asked for it.

Kamalapatraksha: Lotus-eyed, having eyes like lotus leaves. It also means knowledge of the Self. He who can be obtained by the knowledge of the Self is Kamalapatraksha.

evametadyathaattha twamaatmaanam parameshwara
drahstumicchaami te roopamaishwaram purushottama // 11.3 //

(NOW) O SUPREME LORD, AS YOU HAVE THUS DESCRIBED YOURSELF, IN THAT WAY, O SUPREME PURUSHA, I WISH TO SEE ACTUALLY YOUR ISHWARA FORM.

Ishwara Form: As possessed of omnipotence, omnipresence, omniscience, infinite strength, infinite virtue and infinite splendor. These are the six qualities which characterize the God - Principle. Arjuna tells the Lord that he desires to see that Ishwara or Divine or Cosmic Form of His.

manyase yadi tacchakyam mayaa drashtumiti prabho
yogeshwara tato me twam darshayaa'tmaanamavyayam // 11.4 //

O LORD, IF YOU THINK IT POSSIBLE FOR ME TO SEE IT, THEN YOU PLEASE, O LORD OF YOGIS, REVEAL TO ME YOUR FORM OF IMPERISHABLE SELF.

It is one thing to know that the Eternal Spirit dwells in all things and another to have the vision of it. Arjuna now wishes to see the Cosmic Form of The Lord, the visible embodiment of the Unseen Divine, how He is the 'birth and passing away of all beings'. The idea is that the abstract metaphysical truth should be given a visible reality.

Yogeshwara: Lord of Yogis - A yogi is one who is endowed with the eight psychic powers. A Yogeshwara is the Lord of such Yogis. Yoga is the identification of the individual soul with the Self. He who bestows this realization of identity on the deserving spiritual aspirant is a Yogeswara.

THE REVELATION OF THE LORD

sri bhagavaan uvaacha
pashya me paartha roopaani shatasho'tha sahasrashah
naanaavidhaani divyaani naanaavarnaakriteeni cha // 11.5 //

SRI BHAGAVAN SAID
BEHOLD, O PARTHA, BY HUNDREDS AND THOUSANDS, MY DIFFERENT FORMS CELESTIAL, VARIED IN COLORS AND SHAPES.

To see gold in different types of ornaments is easy because it involves mere physical perception. But to see different types of ornaments in total gold is comparatively difficult because it requires the vision of the intellect. Similarly, Sri Krishna helped Arjuna to gain the necessary insight to enable him to perceive The Lord, who is already in front of him, in the form he desired. Sri Krishna did not transform Himself in the cosmic form but only bestowed His grace on Arjuna to enable him to perceive the Divine form of The Lord and hence Sri Krishna says 'Behold'. The stupendous self-revelation of Divine power is manifested to Arjuna who understands the true meaning of the cosmic process and destiny. The vision is not a myth or a legend but spiritual experience.

pashyaadityaan vasoon rudraan ashwinau marutas thathaa
bahoonyadrishtapoorvaani pashyaa'shcharyaani bhaarata // 11.6 //

BEHOLD THE ADITYAS, THE VASUS, THE RUDRAS, THE (TWO) ASHWINS AND ALSO THE MARUTS; BEHOLD MANY WONDERS NEVER SEEN BEFORE, O BHARATA.

The Lord enumerates the most important and striking factors to be seen in His Cosmic Form. The various forms mentioned here were already explained in the previous Chapter except the term Ashwins. There are various interpretations about the twins, Ashwini Kumars. They are called Dawn and Dusk or Morning and Evening stars.

ihai'kastham jagatkritsnam pashyaadya sacharaacharam
mama dehe gudaakesha yacchaanyad drashtumicchasi // 11.7 //

NOW BEHOLD TODAY, O GUDAKESA, THE WHOLE UNIVERSE OF THE MOVING AND THE UNMOVING AND WHATEVER ELSE YOU DESIRE TO SEE, ALL CONCENTRATED IN MY BODY.

The entire universe comprising of both moving and static objects and beings is being shown by Sri Krishna as compressed within the frame work of His own physical structure. As explained earlier the concept of space as a divider between objects is being removed from Arjuna's mind by The Lord leaving in him the concept of 'total space' which is equivalent to Sri Krishna's own physical dimensions. It is the vision of all in the One.

na tu maam shakyase drashtum anenaiva swachakshushaa
divyam dadaami te chakshuh pashya me yogamaishwaram // 11.8 //

BUT WITH THESE YOUR OWN EYES YOU CANNOT SEE ME; I GIVE YOU THE DIVINE EYE; BEHOLD NOW MY SOVEREIGN YOGA POWER.

It was already explained under verse 5 that to see many in the one requires right intellectual power through philosophical understanding. The Lord says that Arjuna cannot see Him in the Cosmic Form with his own fleshy eyes *(Mamsa Chakshu)* and hence gives him the divine eye *(Divya Chakshu).* Human eyes can see only the outward forms, the inner soul is perceived by the eye of the Spirit.

There is a type of knowledge that we can acquire by our own efforts, knowledge based on the perceptions by the senses and intellectual activity. Another kind of knowledge is possible when we are under the influence of grace, a direct knowledge of spiritual realities. The god-vision is a gift of God. All these indicate the unity of the cosmic manifold in the Divine nature.

The vision is not a mental construction but the disclosure of a truth from beyond the finite mind. The spontaneity and directness of the experience is highlighted here.

SANJAYA DESCRIBES THE FORM

sanjaya uvaacha
evam uktwaa tato raajan mahaa yogeshwaro harih
darshayaamaasa paarthaaya paramam roopamaishwaram // 11.9 //

SANJAYA SAID
HAVING SPOKEN THUS, O KING, THE GREAT LORD OF YOGA, HARI REVEALED TO PARTHA HIS SUPREME AND DIVINE FORM.

King: This verse is addressed to Dhritarashtra by Sanjaya. Hari: The one who maintains the champions of Truth by destroying the powers of falsehood. Sanjaya now starts describing the list of things that were visible within the frame work of The Lord.

anekavaktra nayanam anekaadbhuta darshanam
anekadivyaabharanam divyaanekodyataayudham // 11.10 //

WITH MANY FACES AND EYES, WITH MANY WONDERFUL SIGHTS, WITH MANY DIVINE ORNAMENTS, WITH MANY DIVINE WEAPONS UPLIFTED (SUCH A FORM HE SHOWED)

divyamaalyaambaradharam divyagandhaanulepanam
sarvaashcharyamayam devam anantam vishwatomukham // 11.11 //

WEARING DIVINE GARLANDS AND APPAREL ANOINTED WITH DIVINE PERFUMES AND CREAMS THE ALL-WONDERFUL, RESPLENDENT, ENDLESS, WITH FACE TURNED EVERYWHERE.

Total cosmos is not a subject matter that is amenable for easy mental comprehension. Sanjaya therefore stumbles for words to give its description. He means to say that Arjuna looked at this Cosmic Form in all its magnificence and saw The Lord everywhere, at all times and in every thing indicating that He is beyond the three limitations of place, time and thing. The Self is everywhere as it is all pervading. It exists in the past, present and future. It dwells in all parts. It is therefore endless.

divi sooryasahasrasya bhavedyugapadutthitaa
yadi bhaah sadrishee saa syaadbhaasastasya mahaatmanah // 11.12 //

IF THE RADIANCE OF A THOUSAND SUNS WERE TO BURST FORTH AT ONCE IN THE SKY, THAT WOULD BE LIKE THE SPLENDOR OF THAT MIGHTY ONE. (THE COSMIC OR THE UNIVERSAL FORM).

The splendor of the Cosmic Form excels all others; it is indeed beyond comparison.

tatraikastham jagatkritsnam pravibhaktamanekadhaa
apashyaddevadevasya shareere paandavastadaa // 11.13 //

THERE, IN THE BODY OF THE GOD OF GODS, ARJUNA THEN SAW THE WHOLE UNIVERSE WITH ITS MANIFOLD DIVISIONS ALL GATHERED TOGETHER IN ONE.

In the Cosmic Form of The Lord, Arjuna perceived the entire world of multiple varieties brought together and made to rest at one and the same place. This does not mean that the Universe has shrunk into the physical structure of Sri Krishna. It means that Arjuna could intellectually comprehend the sense of oneness in the world of matter. He could see many in the one and the One in the many. The vision is a revelation of the potential divinity of all earthly life.

ARJUNA ADDRESSES THE LORD

tatah sa vismayaavishto hrishtaromaa dhananjayah
pranamya shirasaa devam kritaanjalirabhaashata // 11.14 //

THEN, DHANANJAYA, OVERCOME WITH WONDER, WITH HIS HAIR STANDING ON END, BOWED DOWN HIS HEAD TO THE LORD, JOINED HIS HANDS IN SALUTATION AND THUS ADDRESSED HIM.

Sanjaya tells the blind King about the strong emotions and humility passing through Arjuna on seeing the Cosmic Form of The Lord. Arjuna was struck with wonder causing his hairs to stand on end. He bent his head low and with folded hands spoke as under.

arjuna uvaacha
pashyaami devaamstava deva dehe
sarvaamstathaa bhootavisheshasangaan

brahmaanameesham kamalaasanastham
risheemshcha sarvaanuraagaamshcha divyaan // 11.15 //

ARJUNA SAID
I SEE ALL THE GODS, O LORD, IN YOUR BODY AND HOSTS OF VARIOUS CLASSES OF BEINGS; LORD BRAHMA SEATED ON THE LOTUS, ALL THE SAGES AND THE CELESTIAL SERPENTS.

These descriptions indicate not only the things of this world but also the Devas are represented in the Cosmic Form. Even the creator, Brahma, the annihilator, Siva and the sustainer, Vishnu could be seen by Arjuna. These names belong to 'Samashti' (Macrocosm). The things of microcosm (Vyashti) like serpents and sages also were seen.

"The vision of God widens our horizon and takes us beyond the earthly tumults and sorrows which so easily obsess us. God's creation is not limited to this small planet, which is only an insignificant part of the cosmos. Arjuna sees the great and various companies of spirits filling the Universe". - Dr.S.Radhakrishnan.

anekabaahoodaravaktranetram
pashyaami twaam sarvato'nantaroopam
naantam na madhyam na punastavaaadim
pashyami vishweshwara vishwaroopa // 11.16 //

I BEHOLD YOU INFINITE IN FORM ON ALL SIDES WITH MANIFOLD ARMS, STOMACHS, FACES AND EYES; NEITHER YOUR END NOR YOUR MIDDLE NOR ALSO YOUR BEGINNING DO I SEE, O LORD OF THE UNIVERSE, O COSMIC FORM.

Various organs of the body mentioned here should not be taken literally. They only indicate the Truth from which all names and forms emanate, in which they exist and into which they merge back at the end of their temporary play on the earth. These verses show the oneness that runs through mortal beings and finite things of the world making a single entity of them all.

kireetinam gadinam chakrinam cha
tejoraashim sarvato deeptimantam
pashyaami twaam durnireekshyam samantaad
deeptaanalaarka dyutimaprameyam // 11.17 //

I SEE YOU WITH YOUR CROWN, MACE AND DISCUS; A MASS OF RADIANCE SHINING EVERYWHERE, VERY HARD TO LOOK AT, ALL AROUND BLAZING LIKE BURNING FIRE AND SUN AND IMMEASURABLE.

Arjuna is giving more and more details of what he is seeing in that Cosmic Form. The items mentioned here are the symbolic insignia of Lord Vishnu.

The reference to radiance shining everywhere like blazing sun and fire does not mean tremendous amount of light in its physical sense but it indicates the glory of Pure Awareness. Consciousness is the light through which we see our own thoughts and emotions. It is the light which illumines for us various objects, sounds etc. Hence Sri Krishna who Himself is Infinite Awareness is described as resplendent light immeasurable. Although the Universal Form is painted here in an objective manner it is only a subjective experience and is not an object of even intellect.

twamaksharam paramam veditavyam
twamasya vishwasya param nidhaanam
twamavyayah shaashwatadharmagoptaa
sanaatanastwam prusho mato me // 11.18 //

YOU ARE THE IMPERISHABLE, THE SUPREME BEING TO BE REALIZED. YOU ARE THE SUPREME SUPPORT OF THE UNIVERSE; YOU ARE THE IMPERISHABLE PROTECTOR OF THE ETERNAL DHARMA; IN MY OPINION YOU ARE THE PRIMAL PERSON, PURUSHA.

Imperishable, Supreme Being: Arjuna states that the Supreme is Brahman and Isvara, Absolute and God. He is the eternal Truth and Supreme worthy to be known because He is the substratum from which the pluralistic world rises up, exists in and merges into. He is the sum total of experiences of every one at their physical, mental and intellectual levels. He is the changeless 'knowing principle' through which all changes are perceived.

Protector of eternal Dharma: For Hindus the protector of Dharma is The Lord Himself and not any mortal. He is the guardian of the *sattvata dharma.*

Purusha: That which dwells in the body is Purusha; the Consciousness principle is the presiding deity which rules the body and hence it is the Purusha.

anaadimadhyaantamanantaveeryam
anantabaahum shashisooryanetram
pashyaami twaam deeptahutaashavaktram
swatejasaa vishwamidam tapantam // 11.19 //

I SEE YOU AS ONE WITHOUT BEGINNING, MIDDLE OR END, INFINITE IN POWER, OF ENDLESS ARMS, THE SUN AND THE MOON BEING YOUR EYES, THE BURNING FIRE YOUR FACE, WHOSE RADIANCE BURNS UP THIS UNIVERSE.

The Supreme Self is the one essential strength behind every thing.
Sun and Moon: sources of entire light energy, the oneness of the individual and the Cosmic Form.
Burning fire your face: power of speech and taste.
Heating the whole Universe with your radiance: The light of Consciousness not only illumines but gives warmth to life. The light here is its own light and not that of any external source.

dyaavaaprithivyoridamantaram hi
vyaaptam twayaikena dishashcha sarvaah
drishtwaa'dbhutam roopamugram tavedam
lokatrayam pravyathitam mahaatman // 11.20 //

THE SPACE BETWEEN THE EARTH AND THE HEAVEN AND ALL THE QUARTERS ARE FILLED BY YOU ALONE; HAVING SEEN THIS, YOUR WONDERFUL AND TERRIBLE FORM, THE THREE WORLDS ARE TREMBLING WITH FEAR, O EXALTED ONE.

As the Lord is eternal and infinite He fills the whole universe with innumerable objects, animate and inanimate. The all-pervading, omnipresent Being penetrates and inter-penetrates the entire creation. As the Cosmic Form is of unusual nature Arjuna says everybody is wonder-struck and trembling to look at it.

amee hi twaam surasanghaah vishanti
kechid bheetaah praanjalayo grinanti
swasteetyuktwaa maharshisiddhasanghaah
stuvanti twaam stutibhih pushkalaabhih // 11.21 //

VERILY, INTO YOU ENTER THESE HOSTS OF DEVAS; SOME EXTOL YOU IN FEAR WITH JOINED PALMS; 'MAY THERE BE PEACE' THUS SAYING, BANDS OF GREAT RISHIS AND SIDDHAS PRAISE YOU WITH SUBLIME HYMNS.

So far Arjuna described the Cosmic Form in Its static state. Now he describes it in its active state. He says some are entering and disappearing in His Form, some are praying with fear and some more praise Him singing hymns of His glory and lost in ecstatic worship.

rudraadityaa vasavo ye cha saadhyaa
vishwe'shvinau marutashchoshmapaashcha
gandharvayakshaasura siddhasanghaa
veekshante twaam vismitaashchaiva sarve // 11.22 //

THE RUDRAS, ADITYAS, VASUS, SADHYAS, VISHWA DEVAS, THE TWO ASHWINS, MARUTS, USHMAPAS AND HOSTS OF GANDHARVAS, YAKSHAS, ASURAS AND SIDDHAS - THEY ARE ALL LOOKING AT YOU, ALL QUITE ASTONISHED.

The terms used here were already explained in the previous Chapter. They are all of the Vedic concepts.

roopam mahat te bahuvaktranetram
mahaabaaho bahubaahoorupaadam
bahoodaram bahudamshtraakaraalam
drishtwa lokaah pravyathitaastathaa'ham // 11.23//

HAVING SEEN YOUR IMMEASURABLE FORM WITH MANY MOUTHS AND EYES, O MIGHTY-ARMED, WITH MANY ARMS, THIGHS AND FEET, WITH MANY STOMACHS AND FEARFUL WITH MANY TUSKS, THE WORLDS ARE FRIGHTENED AND SO AM I.

These terms of poetic description bring about the universality and omnipresence of the Supreme. The Universal form of the Lord reveals to Arjuna the malevolent and benevolent aspects of the creation both of which are necessary to complete the picture and understand the whole containing the pairs of opposites.

nabhahsprisham deeptamanekavarnam
vyaattaananam deeptavishaalanetram
drishtwaa hi twaam pravyathitaantaraaatmaa
dhritim na vindaami shamam cha vishno // 11.24 //

ON SEEING YOU (YOUR FORM) TOUCHING THE SKY, SHINING IN MANY COLORS, WITH MOUTHS WIDE OPEN, WITH LARGE FIERY EYES, I AM TERRIFIED AT HEART AND FIND NEITHER COURAGE NOR PEACE, O VISHNU!

The vision experienced by Arjuna here is not actually a physical appearance but a wide, all pervading manifestation of the Lord signifying the omnipotence of the Supreme. Arjuna feels that His Universal Form has a definite shape and color which is so uncommon and terrifying that he has no courage to face it.

damshtraakaraalaani cha te mukhaani
drishtwaiva kaalaanalasannibhaani
disho na jaane na labhe cha sharma
praseeda devesha jagannivaasa // 11.25 //

WHEN I BEHOLD YOUR MOUTHS STRIKING TERROR WITH THEIR TUSKS, LIKE TIME'S ALL-CONSUMING FIRE, I AM DISORIENTED AND FIND NO PEACE; BE GRACIOUS, O LORD OF THE DEVAS, O ABODE OF THE UNIVERSE.

Pralaya Fires: The fires which consume the worlds during the final dissolution of the universe. Time (Kala) is the consumer of all that is manifested. The tremendous experience has in it elements of astonishment, terror and rapture. In this condition of extreme wonder an individual loses his vanity and stands before the Cosmic Power with utter humility and self-surrender.

amee cha twaam dhritaraashtrasya putraah
sarve sahaivaavanipaalasanghaih
bheeshmo dronah sootaputraastathaa'sau
sahaasmadeeyairapi yodhamukhyaih // 11.26 //

vaktraani te twaramaanaa vishanti
damshtraakaraalaani bhayaanakaani
kechidwilagnaa dashanaanthareshu
sandhrishyante choornitairuttamaangaih // 11.27 //

ALL THE SONS OF DHRITARASHTRA WITH HOSTS OF KINGS OF THE EARTH, BHISHMA, DRONA AND KARNA, ALONG WITH THE CHIEF WARRIORS ON OUR SIDE TOO - ENTER, HURRIEDLY, YOUR MOUTHS WITH TERRIBLE TEETH AND FEARFUL TO BEHOLD. SOME ARE FOUND STICKING IN THE GAPS BETWEEN THE TEETH WITH THEIR HEADS CRUSHED TO POWDER.

These strange descriptions of The Lord or the Cosmic Form are to reassure Arjuna as to how the forces are entering into the inescapable mouth of time 'kala' and disappear. Destruction always precedes construction. Here the power of destruction of the Supreme as well as His ugly and bitter forms are given.

The Multiplicity that has risen from the Totality, after its play upon the surface of Truth, must necessarily rush back in all hurry into the very whole from which it had risen up. Arjuna thus observes Bhishma, Karna etc entering into the mouth of the principle of destruction as represented by the Cosmic Form. This sight not only frightens Arjuna but generates in him self-confidence to face the events of future.

In the Universal Form of The Lord wherein He expresses Himself as the entire world of phenomena indicating the principle of oneness, the concepts of space and time disappear. Therefore, when the whole Universe is brought together at the same time and place Arjuna could see the past, present and the future.

yathaa nadeenaam bahavo'mbuvegaah
samudramevaabhimukhaah dravanti
tathaa tawaamee naraloka veeraa
vishanti vaktraanyabhivijwalanti // 11.28 //

VERILY, AS MANY TORRENTS OF RIVERS FLOW TOWARDS THE OCEAN, SO THESE HEROES IN THE WORLD OF MEN ENTER YOUR FIERCELY FLAMING MOUTHS.

yathaa pradeeptam jwalanam patangaa
vishanti naashaaya samriddhavegaah
tathai va naashaaya vishanti lokaas
tavaapi vaktraani samriddhavegaah // 11.29 //

AS MOTHS HURRIEDLY RUSH INTO A BLAZING FIRE FOR THEIR OWN DESTRUCTION, SO ALSO THESE CREATURES HURRIEDLY RUSH INTO YOUR MOUTHS FOR DESTRUCTION.

The essential oneness between the manifest (river) that has come out of the unmanifest (ocean) and the very unmanifest which is the source of all manifestation has been illustrated in this verse. It is also to be noted that the manifest looses its name and form and becomes one with the unmanifest at the end of its journey. The projection of unmanifest to the manifest-condition is the process of creation and that the manifest merging back to its own sanctuary of the unmanifest is destruction or death.

These two verses vividly illustrate how the assembled warriors rush to destruction, out of their own uncontrollable nature, with or without discrimination.

As the rivers flow towards the ocean, as the moths fly into the fire, so too all names and forms must, that too willingly, rush towards the unmanifest. If anyone realizes this, he can live without fear of death with the full understanding that life is nothing but a process of continuous change.

"These beings blinded by their own ignorance are rushing to their destruction and the Divine Controller permits it, as they are carrying out the effects of their own deeds. When we will a deed, we will its consequences also. The free activities subject us to their results. As the law of cause and consequence is an expression of the Divine mind, the Divine may be said to execute the law. While we think consecutively, Divine mind knows all as one. There is no past or future to It". Dr.S.Radhakrishnan.

lelihyase grasamaanah samantaal
lokaan samagraan vadanair jwaladbhih
tejobhiraapoorya jagatsamagram
bhaasastavograah pratapanti vishno // 11.30 //

SWALLOWING ALL THE WORLDS ON EVERY SIDE WITH YOUR FLAMING MOUTHS, YOU ARE LICKING (IN ENJOYMENT) YOUR LIPS. YOUR FIERCE RAYS, FILLING THE WHOLE WORLD WITH RADIANCE, ARE BURNING, O VISHNU!

The principle of destruction is never ending. Hence Arjuna exclaims 'You are swallowing the entire world and licking Your lips in enjoyment'. This verse gives us an idea about the Trinity viz. Brahma, Vishnu and Maheswara. Death, birth, sustenance and again death is the continuous process of existence which is revealed in the Cosmic Form. Arjuna thus notices Its resplendency and wonders about the fiery radiance of the fierce rays of The Lord.

aakhyaahi me ko bhavaanugraroopo
namo'stu te devavara praseeda
vijnaatumicchaami bhavantamaadyam
na hi prajaanaami tava pravrittim // 11.31 //

TELL ME WHO YOU ARE SO FIERCE IN FORM. SALUTATIONS TO YOU, O GOD SUPREME, HAVE MERCY. I DESIRE TO KNOW YOU, THE PRIMEVAL ONE. I KNOW NOT INDEED YOUR PURPOSE.

The disciple seeks for deeper knowledge. Arjuna, realizing the sanctity and divinity of The Lord's power, bows down and humbly requests Him to tell him who He is. He refers to The Lord as Primeval One (Original Being). He asks Him His purpose or His mission in taking such a terrible form and presenting Himself before him exhibiting how the Kaurava forces are going in all hurry towards their destruction.

GOD AS THE JUDGE

sri bhagavan uvaacha
kaalo'smi lokakshayakrit pravriddho
lokaan samaahartumiha pravrittah
ritepi twaam na bhavishyanti sarve
ye'wasthitaah pratyaneekeshu yodhaah // 11.32 //

SRI BHAGAVAN SAID
I AM THE MIGHTY WORLD-DESTROYING TIME NOW ENGAGED IN SUBDUING THE WORLD. EVEN WITHOUT YOU, NONE OF THE WARRIORS ARRAYED IN THE OPPOSITE ARMIES SHALL LIVE.

The power that is behind destruction and construction is that which rules over things and governs the lives of beings. Sri Krishna declares that this power is the all destroying 'Kala'. Kala or Time is the prime mover of the Universe. If God is thought of as time, then He is perpetually creating and destroying. Time is the streaming flux which moves unceasingly. Time absorbs in its womb of oblivion all names and forms.

The Supreme Being takes up the responsibility for both creation and destruction. The doctrine that God is responsible for all that is good and Devil is responsible for all that is evil is a clumsy device. If God is responsible for mortal existence, then He is responsible for all that it includes - life and creation, anguish and death, pain and pleasure and so on. The Gita teaches us to see Reality as a whole. God, the bountiful and prodigal Creator and Preserver is also the God, the Destroyer and Devourer.

God has control over time because He is outside of it. As the force behind this, He sees farther than us, knows how all events are controlled and so tells Arjuna that causes have been at work for years and are moving towards their natural effects which we cannot prevent by anything we know of. The destruction of the enemies is decided irrevocably by acts committed by themselves long ago. There is an impersonal fate, a general cosmic necessity, the will of the Sovereign Personality, which pursues its own unrecognizable agenda. All protestations, abstentions, non-interventions of the individuals against it are of no avail before the divine will. On the contrary such complaints increase confusion.

tasmaat twam uttishtha yasho labhaswa
jitwaa shatroon bhungkshwa raajyam samriddham
mayaivaite nihataah poorvameva
nimittamaatram bhava savyasaachin // 11.33 //

THEREFORE, STAND UP AND WIN GLORY. CONQUER YOUR ENEMIES AND ENJOY AN OPULENT KINGDOM. VERILY, BY ME AND NONE OTHER THEY HAVE BEEN ALREADY SLAIN; YOU BE A MERE INSTRUMENT, O ARJUNA!

Savyasaachin: Arjuna, the one who could shoot arrows with his left hand as well as his right.

dronam cha bheeshmam cha jayadratham cha
karnam tathaa'nyaanapi yodhaveeraan

mayaa hataamstwam jahi maa vyathishthaa
yudhyaswa jetaasi rane sapatnaan // 11.34 //

DO SLAY DRONA, BHISHMA, JAYADRATHA, KARNA AND OTHER GREAT WARRIORS AS WELL WHO HAVE ALREADY BEEN SLAIN BY ME; BE NOT DISTRESSED WITH FEAR; FIGHT AND YOU SHALL CONQUER YOUR ENEMIES IN THE BATTLE.

Sri Krishna says whatever be the strength of the negative forces they have already been destroyed by the all powerful 'Time' and Arjuna has only to act as an instrument in their ruin and claim victory to himself. In fact during all actions in our lives we are merely the instruments in the hands of The Lord. The concept of self surrender for serving the world in the constant awareness of The Lord is the only way for claiming glory in our lives. The God of destiny decides and ordains all things and Arjuna is to be the instrument, the flute under the fingers of the Omnipotent One who works out the mighty evolution. Arjuna is self-deceived if he believes that he should act according to his own imperfect judgment. No individual soul can encroach on the prerogative of God. In refusing to take up arms, Arjuna is guilty of such mischievous presumption.

The doctrine of Divine Predetermination is upheld here that indicates utter helplessness and insignificance of the individual and the futility of his will and efforts. The decision is made already and Arjuna can do nothing to change it. This however does not mean that the cosmic process is a mere unveiling of a ready made scenario. It only affirms the meaning of eternity in which all moments of the whole of time, past, present and future, are contemporary to the Divine Spirit. Each moment of evolution in time has no novelty in it nor does it project any inconsistency in the Divine Eternity.

The ideas of God are worked out through human instrumentality. Nothing exists save the Lord's will. He alone is the doer and we are only the instruments. Judged from the human standards the consequences of war are abhorrent and hence none should encourage it. But once the purpose of the Almighty behind the war is revealed Arjuna acquiesces in it. What he desires or what he gains do not count any more. Behind this world of space-time, inter-penetrating it, is the creative purpose of God. We must understand that Supreme Design and be content to serve it. The consciousness of the divine agency and its constant application in all works release man from responsibility.

Every act is a symbol of something beyond itself. Sri Krishna specifically mentioned the names of the four great warriors because they were considered invincible and even then they were eliminated by the Principle of Destruction and therefore He advises Arjuna not to be afraid of incurring sin by killing them and others though they are venerable to him.

When Krishna tells Arjuna that he will conquer his enemies in the battle we have to understand it as the divine will and that Arjuna is not permitted to take credit for his victory.

Seeing the Lord's cosmic form Arjuna is struck with awe and wonder. He sees the entire universe in a single immeasurable form as also His destructive, all-devouring expression. Fraught with fear and overwhelmed with adoration, Arjuna surrenders completely to that colossal form. He bows; he prostrates and begs forgiveness for his lack of reverence towards Krishna in their relationship.

The vision of the Lord's cosmic form terrifies Arjuna. He pleads with Krishna to resume His original form, the form of Vishnu. Krishna assumes His gentle form. Arjuna regains his composure when Krishna explains the difficulty in gaining the state of God-realization. He points out the way to reach the Supreme Being. The Lord tells him that all spiritual practices like study of scriptures, austerities, charity, performing sacrifices etc. by themselves cannot lead one to the Supreme. They will at the most make one an introvert. Thereafter, deep meditation only is the means to become one with the Absolute.

sanjaya uvaacha
etacchrutwaa vachanam keshavasya
kritaanjalirvepamaanah kireetee
namaskritwaa bhooya evaaha krishnam
sagadgadam bheetabheetah pranamya // 11.35 //

SANJAYA SAID
HAVING HEARD THESE WORDS OF KESAVA, THE CROWNED-ONE (ARJUNA), WITH JOINED PALMS, TREMBLING, PROSTRATING HIMSELF, AGAIN ADDRESSED KRISHNA, IN A CHOKED VOICE, BOWING DOWN, OVERWHELMED WITH FEAR.

Arjuna was extremely terrified on seeing the Cosmic Form and so he spoke in a choked and stammering voice. These words of Sanjaya are very significant because he thought that at this late moment (after knowing fully well the impending destruction of all in the Kaurava side) King Dhritarashtra would halt the war and call for peace to save at least his own son from being killed. But the blind king was obstinate and did not consider Sanjaya's indirect advice worthy.

ARJUNA'S HYMN OF PRAISE

arjuna uvaacha
sthaane hrisheekesha tava prakeertyaa
jagat prahrishyatyanurajyate cha
rakshaamsi bheetaani disho dravanti
sarve namasyanti cha siddhasanghaah // 11.36 //

O HRISHIKESHA! IT IS PROPER THAT THE WORLD DELIGHTS AND REJOICES IN YOUR PRAISE; RAKSHASAS FLEE IN FEAR IN ALL DIRECTIONS AND ALL THE HOSTS OF SIDDHAS BOW TO YOU.

In an ecstasy of adoration and anguish, Arjuna praises The Lord. He sees not only the destructive power of Time but also the spiritual presence and law governing the cosmos. While the former produces terror, the latter gives rise to a sense of peace.

kasmaaccha te na nameran mahaatman
gareeyase brahmano'pyaadikartre
ananta devesha jagannivaasa
twamaksharam sadasattatparam yat // 11.37 //

AND WHY SHOULD THEY NOT BOW TO YOU, O MIGHTY BEING, GREATER THAN ALL ELSE, THE PRIMAL CAUSE EVEN OF BRAHMA, O INFINITE BEING, O LORD OF LORDS, O ABODE OF THE UNIVERSE, YOU ARE THE IMPERISHABLE, THE MANIFEST AND THE UNMANIFEST, THAT WHICH IS SUPREME (THAT WHICH IS BEYOND THE BEING AND NON-BEING).

Arjuna clarifies as to why the great men of knowledge bow down before Sri Krishna by enumerating the majestic and divine qualities of The Lord.

twamaadidevah purushah puraanas
twamasya vishwasya param nidhaanam
vettaasi vedyam cha param cha dhaama
twayaa tatam vishwamananta roopa // 11.38 //

YOU ARE THE PRIMAL GOD, THE ANCIENT PURUSHA, YOU ARE THE SUPREME REFUGE OF THIS UNIVERSE, YOU ARE THE KNOWER, THE KNOWABLE AND THE SUPREME GOAL. THE UNIVERSE IS PERVADED BY YOU, O BEING OF INFINITE FORMS.

Param Dhaama: Just as the rope (the substratum for the superimposed snake) pervades the snake, so also the Self, through its nature of Existence, Knowledge and Bliss absolute, pervades this entire Universe.

vaayuryamo'gnirvarunah shashaankah
prajaapatistwam prapitaamahashcha
namo namaste'stu sahasrakritwah
punascha bhooyo'pi namo namaste // 11.39 //

YOU ARE VAYU, YAMA, AGNI, VARUNA, THE MOON, PRAJAPATI, AND THE GREAT GRANDFATHER, SALUTATIONS! SALUTATIONS! UNTO YOU, A THOUSAND TIMES AND AGAIN SALUTATIONS, SALUTATIONS UNTO YOU.

Great Grandfather: The Creator of even Brahma who is known as the Grandfather.

namah purastaadatha prishthataste
namostu te sarvata eva sarva
anantaveeryaamitavikramastwam
sarvam samaapnoshi tato'si sarvah // 11.40 //

SALUTATIONS TO YOU, IN FRONT AND BEHIND; SALUTATIONS TO YOU ON EVERY SIDE! O ALL! YOU, INFINITE IN POWER AND INFINITE IN PROWESS, PERVADE ALL; THEREFORE YOU ARE THE ALL.

The Supreme dwells everywhere within, without, above, below and around. There is no place where He is not. He is the all pervading essence like space in the Universe and also the source of all potentiality, power and capability. Since nothing can exist without Him He is Pure Existence. Hence He is the All and He alone is the All. (Ocean alone is all the waves or mud alone is all the pots).

sakheti matwaa prasabham yaduktam
he krishna he yaadava he sakheti
ajaanataa mahimaanam tavedam
mayaa pramaadaat pranayena vaapi // 11.41 //

WHATEVER I HAVE RASHLY SAID FROM CARELESSNESS OR LOVE, ADDRESSING YOU AS O KRISHNA, O YADAVA, O FRIEND, REGARDING YOU MERELY AS A FRIEND, UNKNOWING OF THIS FACT OF YOUR GREATNESS....

yacchaavahaasaartham asatkrit' si
vihaarashayyaasanabhojaneshu
eko' thavaapyachyuta tatsamaksham
tat kshaamaye twaamaham aprameyam // 11.42 //

IN WHATEVER WAY I MAY HAVE INSULTED YOU FOR THE SAKE OF FUN, WHILE AT PLAY, REPOSING, SITTING OR AT MEALS, WHEN ALONE (WITH YOU), O ACHYUTA OR IN COMPANY - THAT I PRAY TO YOU, IMMEASURABLE ONE, TO FORGIVE.

The vision of God produces a deep sense of unworthiness and sin. Arjuna, beholding the Cosmic Form of The Lord, seeks forgiveness for his past familiar conduct with Him. He says he was treating Him with casualness and intimacy not knowing His greatness and glory. He asks The Lord for forgiveness for his misconception of His powers. So long, Arjuna was thinking of Sri Krishna as a mere cowherd boy with whom he, a prince, made patronizing friendship. But when he realized His true nature, Arjuna bows down before Him in adoration and pleads for His mercy and forgiveness for whatever impropriety he might have committed either knowingly or unknowingly.

pitaasi lokasya characharasya
twamasya poojyashcha gururgareeyaan
na twatsamostyabhyadhikah kuto'nyo
lokatraye'pyapratimaprabhaava // 11.43 //

YOU ARE THE FATHER OF THIS WORLD, MOVING AND UNMOVING; THE OBJECT OF THEIR WORSHIP; YOU, THE GREATEST GURU, FOR THERE EXISTS NONE WHO IS EQUAL TO YOU; FOR HOW CAN THERE BE ANOTHER, SUPERIOR TO YOU IN THE THREE WORLDS, O BEING OF INCOMPARABLE GREATNESS.

Our experiences in the three states of existence - waking, dream and deep sleep - are the interpretations of the same Eternal from the levels of gross, subtle and the causal bodies. The

Truth that illumines these experiences is everywhere one and the same. Hence there cannot be anything superior to That.

tasmaatpranamya pranidhaaya kaayam
prasaadaye twaamahameeshameedyam
piteva putrasya sakheva sakhyuh
priyah priyaayaarhasi deva sodhum // 11.44 //

THEREFORE, BOWING DOWN, PROSTRATING MY BODY BEFORE YOU, I CRAVE YOUR FORGIVENESS, ADORABLE LORD! AS A FATHER FORGIVES HIS SON, A FRIEND HIS FRIEND, A LOVER HIS BELOVED, EVEN SO SHOULD YOU FORGIVE ME, O DEVA.

God as a father is a familiar conception in all religions. The Supreme is not to be regarded as a transcendent mystery but as close to us as a father to the son, a friend to the friend or as a lover to the beloved. These human relations find in God their fullest realization.

adrishtapoorvam hrishito'smi drishtwaa
bhayena cha pravyathitam mano me
tadeva me darshaya deva roopam
praseeda devesha jagannivaasa // 11.45 //

I AM DELIGHTED HAVING SEEN WHAT WAS NEVER SEEN BEFORE; AND YET MY MIND IS DISTRESSED WITH FEAR. SHOW ME THAT PREVIOUS FORM ONLY, O GOD; HAVE MERCY, O GOD OF GODS, O ABODE OF THE UNIVERSE.

Eventhough Arjuna experienced immense joy on seeing the Cosmic Form of The Lord yet the sudden expansion of consciousness caused in him great fear and distress. Hence he prays to Sri Krishna to resume His usual form and give up the terrifying aspects of the transcendent and the universal.

kireetinam gadinam chakrahastam
icchaami twaam drashtumaham tathaiva
tenaiva roopena chaturbhujena
sahasrabaaho bhava vishwamoorte // 11.46 //

I DESIRE TO SEE YOU AS BEFORE, CROWNED, BEARING A MACE, WITH A DISCUS IN THE HAND, IN YOUR FORMER FORM ONLY, HAVING FOUR ARMS, O THOUSAND ARMED COSMIC BEING!

Arjuna describes the exact form in which he wants Sri Krishna to appear before him. The four hands of God represent the four facets of the inner instruments in Man Viz. mind, intellect, *chitta* and the ego-sense. Blue color represents the Infinite. Yellow clothes mean the earth. Thus the Infinite clothed in the finite leading the life through four inner instruments is the symbolism of Lord Vishnu. In short Arjuna wants The Lord to appear before him in a serene form with quiet attitude.

THE LORD'S GRACE AND ASSURANCE

sri bhagavan uvaacha
mayaa prasannena tavaarjunedam
roopam param darshitamaatmayogaat
tejomayam vishwamanantamaadhyam
yanme twadanyena na drishtapoorvam // 11.47 //

SRI BHAGAVAN SAID

O ARJUNA, BY MY GRACE, THROUGH MY OWN YOGA POWER, I HAVE SHOWN YOU THIS SUPREME FORM,

RESPLENDENT, UNIVERSAL, INFINITE AND PRIMEVAL, WHICH NONE BUT YOU HAVE EVER SEEN.

The revelation of the Lord depends upon His grace alone, besides His lordly power in the Godhead; man cannot force it by his efforts. The Lord has shown His grace on Arjuna because he is His beloved devotee.

na vedayajnaadhyayanairna daanair
na cha kriyaabhirna tapobhirugraih
evam roopah shakya aham nriloke
drashtum twadanyena krupraveera // 11.48 //

NEITHER BY THE STUDY OF THE VEDAS AND SACRIFICES, NOR BY GIFTS, NOR BY RITUALS, NOR BY SEVERE AUSTERITIES, CAN I BE SEEN IN THIS FORM (UNIVERSAL FORM) IN THE WORLD OF MEN BY ANY ONE ELSE BUT YOU, O GREAT HERO OF THE KURUS.

By human endeavor through knowledge, austerities, sacrifices etc., one can see a particular aspect of Godhead. But Arjuna has seen the Lord in His Universal Form, reconciling all the aspects of divinity at one and the same time and in one and the same vision.

In an indescribable oneness are revealed all the facets of the Godhead - spirit and matter, being and becoming, creation and destruction, infinite and finite, space and time, past and future. This vision is granted only to the devotee who adores the Lord with single-minded, all-consuming, and unswerving love.

maa te vyathaa maa cha vimoodhabhaavo
drishtwaa roopam ghorameedringmamedam
vyapetabheeh preetamanaah punastwam
tadeva me roopamidam prapashya // 11.49 //

BE NOT AFRAID NOR BEWILDERED ON SEEING SUCH A TERRIBLE FORM OF MINE AS THIS; WITH YOUR FEAR DISPELLED AND WITH GLADDENED HEART, NOW BEHOLD AGAIN THIS FORMER FORM OF MINE.

The Lord saw Arjuna in a state of distress and terror. Therefore, He withdrew the Cosmic Form and assumed once more His usual gentle form. He consoled Arjuna and spoke to him with kindness. The microcosmic representation of Truth in the form of gentle and smiling Sri Krishna is macrocosmic Universal Form representing the essence in all forms and names.

sanjaya uvaacha
ityarjunam vaasudevastathoktwaa
swakam roopam darshayaamaasa bhooyah
aashwaasayaamaasa cha bheetamenam
bhootwaa punah saumyavapurmahaatmaa // 11.50 //

SANJAYA SAID
HAVING THUS SPOKEN TO ARJUNA, VAASUDEVA AGAIN REVEALED TO HIM HIS OWN FORM. THE EXALTED ONE (SRI KRISHNA) HAVING ASSUMED AGAIN THE FORM OF GRACE, COMFORTED THE TERRIFIED ARJUNA.

Sanjaya confirms to Dhritarashtra that Sri Krishna came back to is usual form i.e. the very form in which He was born in the house of Vasudeva.

arjuna uvaacha
drishtwedam maanusham roopam tava saumyam janaardana
idaaneemasmi samvrittah sachetaah prakritim gatah // 11.51 //

ARJUNA SAID
HAVING SEEN THIS YOUR GENTLE HUMAN FORM, O SRI KRISHNA, NOW I AM COMPOSED AND RESTORED TO MY NORMAL NATURE.

Arjuna admits that when he sees the normal and gentle form of Sri Krishna he feels relieved from his inner tensions and agitations.

sri bhagavan uvaacha
sudurdarshamidam roopam drishtwaanasi yanmama
devaaapyasya roopasya nityam darshanakaangkshinah // 11.52 //

SRI BHAGAVAN SAID
VERY HARD INDEED IT IS TO SEE THIS FORM OF MINE WHICH YOU HAVE SEEN. EVEN THE GODS ARE EVER EAGER TO SEE THIS FORM.

Sri Krishna says that even the Gods are eager to see the Universal Form but their wishes do not materialize even in their dreams. Such is the marvelous vision seen by Arjuna so easily.

naa ham vedairna tapasaa na daanena na chejyayaa
shakya evamvidho drashtum drishtavaanasi maam yathaa // 11.53 //

NEITHER BY THE VEDAS NOR BY AUSTERITY NOR BY CHARITY NOR BY SACRIFICE CAN I BE SEEN IN THIS FORM AS YOU HAVE NOW SEEN ME.

This is a repetition of Verse-48.

bhaktyaa twananyayaa shakyamaham evamvidho'rjuna
jnaatum drashtum cha tattwena praveshtum cha parantapa
// 11.54 //

BUT BY THE SINGLE-MINDED DEVOTION, CAN I, OF THIS FORM (COSMIC FORM) BE KNOWN AND SEEN IN REALITY AND ALSO ENTERED INTO, O ARJUNA.

The reason why The Lord has shown the Cosmic Form to Arjuna only and to none else is given here. Devotion is the sole means to the realization of the Cosmic Form. In unbroken devotion which seeks none but The Lord alone, nothing other than The Lord is experienced by the sense organs wherein egoism and dualism totally vanish. Such experience by means of direct and immediate perception is what is called seeing in reality. 'Entered into' means that the devotee attains final liberation in the Lord after giving up the body. Thus the fulfilled seeker becomes the very essence of the sought.

matkarmakrinmatparamo madbhaktah sangavarjitah
nirvairah sarvabhooteshu yah sa maameti paandava // 11.55 //

HE WHO DOES ALL ACTIONS FOR ME, WHO LOOKS UPON ME AS THE SUPREME GOAL, WHO IS DEVOTED TO ME, WHO IS FREE FROM ATTACHMENT, WHO BEARS ENMITY TOWARDS NONE, HE COMES TO ME, O PANDAVA.

This verse is the substance of the whole teaching of the Gita. He who practices this teaching will attain supreme bliss and immortality.

He who dedicates all works to the Lord, seeking no rewards to himself, who serves Him with all his heart and soul, who regards Him as his supreme goal, who lives for Him alone, who works for Him alone, who sees Him in everything, who sees the whole world as His Cosmic Form, cherishing no feeling of hatred or enmity towards anyone, who has no attachment to worldly objects, who seeks nothing but The Lord - such a one realizes Him and becomes completely one with Him. He enjoys eternal Bliss, peace and immortality. Thus the art of right living consists of the following five ingredients viz.

1. Dedication of work to The Lord
2. Keeping The Lord as the goal
3. Devotion to The Lord
4. Freedom from all worldly attachments and
5. Absence of enmity towards anyone.

Whatever be our vacation and character, whether we are creative thinkers or contemplative poets or humble men and women with no special gifts, if we possess the one great gift of the love of God, we become God's tools, the channels of His love and purpose. When this vast world of living spirits becomes attuned to God and exists only to do His will, the purpose of life is achieved.

"The Gita does not end after the tremendous experience of the celestial vision. The great secret of the Transcendental Atman, the source of all that is and yet itself unmoved for ever is seen. The Supreme is the background for the never ending procession of finite things. Arjuna has seen this truth but he has to live in it by transmuting his whole nature into the willing acceptance of the Divine. A fleeting vision however vivid and permanent its effects may be, is not complete attainment. The search for abiding reality, the quest of final truth cannot end, in emotional satisfaction or experience". Dr.S.Radhakrishnan. Hence the Lord continues his advice to Arjuna in the following chapters of the Gita till Arjuna exclaims that all his delusions and confusions are cleared.

Omtatsatiti srimadbhagavadgeetaasu upanishatsu brahma vidyaayaam yogashaastre sri krishnaarjuna samvaade vishwaroopa darshanayogo naama ekaadasho'dhyaayah ||

THUS IN THE UPANISHADS OF THE GLORIOUS BHAGAVAD GITA, THE SCIENCE OF THE ETERNAL, THE SCRIPTURE OF YOGA, THE DIALOGUE BETWEEN SRI KRISHNA AND ARJUNA, ENDS THE ELEVENTH DISCOURSE ENTITLED: THE YOGA OF THE VISION OF THE UNIVERSAL FORM

AN OUTLINE VIEW OF THIS CHAPTER

The preceding chapter described the omnipresence of Lord Krishna, Brahman. It presented analytically His endless manifestations everywhere. In this chapter Arjuna requests Krishna to show His divine manifestations synthetically in one form. Krishna grants his prayer.

Seeing the Lord's cosmic form Arjuna is struck with awe and wonder. He sees the entire universe in a single immeasurable form as also His destrctive, all-devouring expression. Fraught with fear and overwhelmed with adoration, Arjuna surrenders completely to that colossal form. He bows; he prostrates and begs forgiveness for his lack of reverence towards Krishna in their past association.

The vision of the Lord's cosmic form terrifies Arjuna. He pleads with Krishna to resume His original form, the form of Vishnu. Krishna assumes His gentle form. Arjuna regains hiis composure when Krishna explains the difficulty in gaining the divine vision. He points out the way to reach the supreme Being.

I - COSMIC FORM OF THE LORD-VERSES 1 – 12

Satisfied with Krishna's presentation of endless glories of His universal manifestation in the preceding chapter, Arjuna now requests the Lord to show him all that infinite magnificence in one unified form. While acceding to Arjuna's request Krishna points out the limitation of his eyes to see that colosaal form. The Lord therefore grants Arjuna a divine vision and displays His cosmic form. Arjuna needs some time to adjust to this spectacular vision. Sanjaya's six verses cover that period describing the splendour of the exalted Being – wonderful sights, divine ornaments, divine garlands, divine unguents, resplendent and brilliant like a thousand suns ablaze.

II - STRUCK WITH WONDER ARJUNA DESCRIBES THE COSMIC FORM - VERSES 13 – 25

Wonderstruck by the Lord's cosmic form, Arjuna bends over in utter reverence. He then begins to describe that form. He sees the entire macrocosm and microcosm – all the gods and demons, everything conceivable and inconceivable, the hosts of beings therein and Arjuna himself standing aghast, trembling at that terrible form.

III - THE ALL-CONSUMING DESTRUCTIVE EXPRESSION OF THE SUPREME BEING - VERSES 26 -34

Arjuna describes the destructive aspect of the Lord's terrible form – how He pulverises everything and everybody. The worlds enter His devastating form and get consumed like a moth plunging into a flame. Terrified at that sight, Arjuna salutes the mighty form and queries "Who are you so fierce? What is your original being? Have mercy and tell me your purpose." The Lord replies "I am the world-destroyer. I have already slain these warriors. You are only an instrument for that purpose. Fear not. Now slay them and obtain fame."

IV - OVERWHELMED WITH FEAR AND ADORATION ARJUNA SURRENDERS TO THE COSMIC FORM - VERSES 35 – 45

Arjuna seeing and hearing Krishna in that cosmic form, trembles with fear.
He prostrates to Krishna with joined palms. In a choked voice he utters words, epithets and praises glorifying the supernatural form. Arjuna then remembers his close friendship with Krishna and expresses regrets that he could have behaved in an indifferent manner lacking due reverence and respect towards Krishna and begs Him to forgive his past immoderate behaviour. Imploring thus, Arjuna surrenders with reverence to that divine form.

V - ARJUNA APPEASED UPON SEEING THE LORD'S GENTLE FORM - VERSES 46 – 51

Trembling at that terrible revelation, Arjuna could no longer perceive the cosmic form. He begs krishna to rsume the form of Vshnu with the lotus, conch, mace and disc in His four hands. Krishna explains to Arjuna the enormous effort required to gain that vision and that rarely one gets such an experience despite severe penance, rituals and study etc. The Lord tells him that he is an exception in receivng His grace and hence assumes the congenial form to console the terrified Arjuna. Arjuna feels composed and restored to his normal mood on seeing the gentle form of the Lord.

VI - THE WAY TO REACH THE SUPREME BEING - VERSES 52 – 55

Krishna reiterates the difficulty in reaching the state of God-realisation. All spiritual practices like study of scriptures, austerities, charity, performing sacrifices etc. by themselves cannot lead one to the Supreme. They will at the most make one an introvert. Thereafter, deep meditation only is the means to become one with the Absolute.

<<<000>>>

Chapter 12

Bhakti Yogah:

Yoga of Devotion

PREAMBLE

Bhagavan Sri Krishna has in many places laid stress on the importance of the worship of the formless and attributeless Brahman. In the end of the last Chapter, He declared God-Realisation as the reward of exclusive devotion to God with form and attributes and that through single-minded devotion, the Cosmic Form can be known, seen and entered into by anyone.

On hearing this advice a doubt has arisen in the mind of the Pandava hero Arjuna as to which of the two methods is better to attain the spiritual realisation. He seeks the precise knowledge regarding the techniques of devotion. He begins the chapter with the perennial question that confuses mankind. Should one worship God with a form or as a formless Reality i.e., whether the Truth is to be meditated upon as unmanifested Absolute or in its manifested form?

Sri Krishna answers by explaining the importance of both types of worship to spiritual development, one catering to the devotional while the other to the intellectual predisposition of the seekers.

Krishna then presents the most pragmatic approach to God Realisation. For seekers who find it difficult to practise various spiritual disciplines *(sadhanas)*, He provides a series of alternatives which cater to the needs of diverse kinds of aspirants. He concludes the chapter by enumerating thirty five qualities of a devotee *(bhakta)* of God. He emphasises that those who possess these qualities are dear to Him.

This Chapter thus deals mainly with devotion to God along with various forms of spiritual disciplines and discusses the marks of a true devotee. As the Chapter begins and ends with devotion it is titled the Yoga of Devotion.

THE TEXT

DEVOTION AND CONTEMPLATION

arjuna uvaacha
evam satatayuktaa ye bhaktaas twaam paryupaasate
ye chaapyaksharamavyaktam teshaam ke yogavittamaah // 12.1 //

ARJUNA SAID

THOSE DEVOTEES WHO, EVER STEADFAST, THUS WORSHIP YOU AND THOSE WHO WORSHIP THE IMPERISHABLE AND THE UNMANIFESTED - WHICH OF THEM HAVE THE GREATER KNOWLEDGE OF YOGA?

In the last Chapter the Lord assured that any seeker can realise the glory of the Cosmic Form if he has unfaltering devotion.

Arjuna now enquires whether one should meditate upon the manifested form of the Infinite or upon the unmanifested form of the Supreme. Unmanifested is that which is not directly perceptible for the sense organs. The objects that can be perceptible to the sense organs are the manifested.

There are those who seek oneness with the Absolute, one impersonal and unrelated to the universe and others who seek unity with the Personal God manifested in the world of men and nature. The question is which of these have the better knowledge of Yoga - the one who devotes himself to the Lord manifest, Personal God, or the one who meditates on the unmanifested Infinite with complete detachment from all the external stimuli? Are we to turn our back on all manifestations and strain after the Unchanging Unmanifest or are we to be devoted to the Manifested Form and work to its service? Is it Absolute or the Personal God, Brahman or Ishwara that we should worship? That is the question.

The difference between the devotion to the 'Absolute or Brahman or the Unmanifest' and devotion to the 'Personal God or Ishwara or the Manifest' is explained in the following table.

Sr.No.	Devotion to the Unmanifest, the one without form, Impersonal, Brahman, the Absolute.	Devotion to the manifest, the one with form, Ishwara, the Personal God.
1	Regards the object of worship or Godhead as the incomprehensible, indefinable, formless, relationless, actionless, featureless, attributeless and transcendental Absolute.	Regards the Godhead as the Lord of the universe, the Supreme Person, the Creator, Preserver and Destroyer, the omniscient and omnipresent Lord, endowed with the Universal Form and possessed of the great powers of Yoga.

2	The Absolute never puts on any form, abstains from all actions, enters into no relation with the universe and is eternally silent and immutable.	The Personal god is our Lord and Master, the source and Origin of all beings, immanent in all things, manifest in both nature and living beings as their inmost Self

Both these aspects of the Godhead have been described by Krishna in the Gita, though with an emphasis on the Impersonal aspect in Chapters 2 through 10. The 11th Chapter deals with the Universal form of Godhead and ends with an exhortation to Arjuna to worship It as the Lord of the universe. Now Arjuna asks which of the two methods of worship is better; meditation on the Impersonal or worship of the Lord through work and love. However the Bhagavan will show us later on that there exists no real contrast between these two types of devotees.

sri bhagavan uvaacha
mayyaaveshya mano ye maam nityayuktaa upaasate
shraddhayaa parayopetaaste me yuktaatmaa mataah // 12.2 //

SRI BHAGAVAN SAID

THOSE WHO, FIXING THEIR MINDS ON ME, WORSHIP ME, EVER EARNEST AND ENDOWED WITH SUPREME FAITH, THESE IN MY OPINION ARE PERFECT IN YOGA.

Sri Krishna starts His discourse explaining the path of meditation on a form representing the Divine (Idol or Symbol). He emphasises three important conditions to be fulfilled by a seeker to enable his devotion to The Lord bear fruit.

Fixing mind on Me: 'Me' means the Universal form, which reveals the Godhead as the Supreme Lord of the universe.

Thought is the source of activity for the mind and intellect. Thought should not only revolve around the concept of The Lord but it should be of so much depth that it is able to merge itself with and dissolve into the ideal of perfection represented by The Lord.

Ever-steadfast and worship Me: One should have sufficient self-balance while worshipping The Lord. Mind by its very nature will try to wander away from the object of meditation and hence self-control is necessary to keep it focussed on the point of contemplation. 'Worship Me' means devotion to the Lord as the omniscient, free from attachment, aversion and other evil passions. This has a reference to the last verse of the 11th Chapter.

Supreme faith: Faith is not blind belief. It is that by which one understands the exact import of the scriptural text and the advice of the teacher and by which alone the reality of things i.e., seeing God in all beings and all beings in God. can become clear to him.

If these conditions are accomplished by any one he is considered as the sincere devotee by The Lord because such a devotee spends his whole time in the uninterrupted thought of the Lord.

FEATURES OF THE UNMANIFEST

ye twaksharamanirdeshyamavyaktam paryupasate
sarvatragamachintyam cha kootasthamachalam dhruvam
// 12.3 //

THOSE WHO WORSHIP THE IMPERISHABLE, THE INDEFINABLE, THE UNMANIFEST, THE OMNIPRESENT,

THE UNTHINKABLE, THE UNCHANGEABLE, THE IMMOVABLE AND THE ETERNAL

samniyamyendriyagraamam sarvatra samabuddhaya
te praapnuvanti maameva sarvabhootahite rataah // 12. 4 //

HAVING RESTRAINED ALL THE SENSES, EVEN MINDED IN ALL CONDITIONS, REJOICING EVER IN THE WELFARE OF ALL BEINGS - INDEED THEY ALSO COME TO ME (JUST LIKE THE OTHERS).

The nature of the Unmanifest specified in the Verse 3 and their explanations are given in the following table.

Sr. No.	Nature of the Unmanifest	Meaning
1	Imperishable	All those which have forms and qualities are substances and all substances are perishable. That which has no quality or form cannot be perceived by sense organs and hence It is imperishable.
2	Indefinable	Definitions are always in terms of what is perceived. That which cannot be perceived is indefinable
3	Omnipresent	All pervading. The Infinite that has no qualities, that is not manifest and therefore that is not definable should necessarily be everywhere and all pervading.
4	Unthinkable	That which can be conceived by mind and intellect will become objects of feelings and thoughts which will always be perishable. That which cannot be conceived or comprehensible will naturally be imperishable.
5	Unchangeable	The Self or Consciousness remains unchanged although It is the substratum on which all changes takes place.

6	Immovable	Motion is a change in time-space mechanism. Movement is a change of a thing from one place and time to another place and at a different time where it was not there. As the Infinite is all pervading there cannot be a place or time where It is not there and hence It is immovable.
7	Eternal	That which has a change is conditioned by time and space. The Supreme being the substratum for all, at all times and all places, supports the very time and space and hence eternal

The seeker who meditates upon the unmanifest which is of the above mentioned nature has to fulfil the following three conditions mentioned in the Verse 4.

1. Having restrained all the senses - He has to avoid dissipation of his energies through the sense organs and redirect his energies so conserved in pursuit of higher thoughts. The senses are to be restrained but not rejected.
2. Even-minded in all conditions or Always equanimous - Intellectual equanimity in all conditions and situations while living in the world is a fundamental requisite for successful meditation. Maintenance of one's own balance in spite of his favourable and unfavourable experiences while living in contact with world is called equanimity.
3. Intent on the welfare of all - He should be the one who is ever ready to serve others to the best of his abilities.

Sri Krishna says that they also who meditate on the unmanifest in the aforesaid manner reach Him; they too reach the same goal, the Supreme Self. But the Lord adds a rider here.

CONCENTRATION ON THE UNMANIFEST, A DIFFICULT TASK FOR THE WORLDLY

klesho'dhikatarasteshaam avyaktaasaktachetasaam
avyaktaa hi gatirduhkham dehavadbhiravaapyate // 12.5 //

GREATER IS THEIR TROUBLE WHOSE MINDS ARE SET ON THE UNMANIFESTED; FOR, THE GOAL - THE UNMANIFESTED - IS VERY HARD FOR THE EMBODIED TO REACH.

The embodied: Those who identify themselves with or attached to their bodies *(Dehabhimana).*

Those who seek the Manifested Lord and those who seek the Unmanifested Lord reach the same goal. But the path taken up by the latter is arduous because the aspirant has to practise utmost self-control, renounce the world outwardly and inwardly, wipe out all human emotions and desires and still the mind in the contemplation of the Absolute. It is also extremely difficult to fix the restless mind on the formless and attributeless Self. Such a method of contemplation demands a sharp, one pointed and subtle intellect. The Immutable does not offer an easy hold to the mind and the path is more arduous.

For a majority of the seekers meditation upon The Lord as expressed in the Universe, a Personal God (manifested form) is easier because they have a tangible ideal of the Lord to whom they can direct their feelings, emotion, love, will, energies and knowledge.

WORSHIP OF THE QUALIFIED ASPECT OF THE LORD IS EASIER

ye tu sarvaani karmaani mayi sannyasya matparaah
ananyenaiva yogena maam dhyaayanta upaasate // 12.6 //

BUT THOSE WHO WORSHIP ME, RENOUNCING ALL ACTIONS IN ME, REGARDING ME AS THE SUPREME GOAL, MEDITATING ON ME WITH UNSWERVING DEVOTION;

teshaamaham samuddhartaa mrtyusamsaarasaagaraat
bhavaami nachiraat paartha mayyaaveshitachetasaam // 12.7 //

FOR THEM WHOSE MINDS ARE SET ON ME, VERILY I BECOME ERE LONG, O PARTHA, THE SAVIOUR OUT OF THE OCEAN OF FINITE EXPERIENCES, THE SAMSARA.

Later on in this Chapter the way of life prescribed for the worshippers of the unmanifest Lord has been dealt with. Now the discipline in life for a seeker through his devotion on the manifest lord is described.

Sri Krishna lays down certain conditions to be followed by those who want to meditate upon the Form of The Lord and concludes that those who follow these instructions fully and sincerely will be saved from their mortal limitations by Himself on whose form they have been contemplating. These instructions are:

1. Renouncing all actions in Him - renouncing one's individual ego and limitations and identifying oneself with Him by complete surrender before The Lord.
2. Regarding Him as the supreme goal - directing one's energy and dealings for achieving the goal of self perfection symbolised in the form of The Lord.

3. Meditating on Him with unswerving devotion - Lifting the mind from agitation prone thoughts to a greater goal with single-pointed attention.

Thus Upasana is not merely meditation upon the goal but becoming one with the goal contemplated upon. Sri Krishna assures such a devotee that He will be his saviour from all imperfections, agitations and sorrows of the mortal life and that too ere long.

For the one whose nature is not steeped in *vairagya* or renunciation, for the one who is neither very tired of nor very attached to the world, the path of devotion is the most suitable one *(Bhagavata XI.20.7)*. It is a matter of temperament whether we adopt the *pravritti dharma*, the path of works or *nivritti dharma*, the path of renunciation. Then what should Arjuna do? He should take up the worship of god with attributes.

mayyeva mana aadhatswa mayi buddhim niveshaya
nivasishyasi mayyeva ata oordhwam na samshayah // 12.8 //

FIX YOUR MIND ON ME ALONE, PLACE YOUR INTELLECT IN ME; THEREAFTER YOU SHALL, NO DOUBT, LIVE IN ME ALONE.

Fix your mind on Me - By meditation, mind can be made to concentrate on the form of The Lord giving up all thoughts of sense objects.

Place your intellect in Me - Also the intellect, which discriminates and determines, should be made to focus itself on The Lord.

Live in Me alone - If the mind rests on The Lord and the intellect understands the Infinite, the individuality ends and one merges with the Infinite, the All Pervading. There is no doubt about this says Sri Krishna.

IF THAT IS NOT POSSIBLE WHAT ARE THE OPTIONS OPEN? THE LORD EXPLAINS:

atha chittam samaadhaatum na shaknoshi mayi sthiram
abhyaasayogena tato maamicchaaptum dhananjaya // 12.9 //

IF YOU ARE UNABLE TO FIX YOUR MIND STEADILY ON ME, THEN BY THE YOGA OF CONSTANT PRACTICE YOU DO SEEK TO REACH ME, O DHANANJAYA.

If one is not able to fix his mind and intellect wholly on the Lord without any break then Sri Krishna advises that by constant practice to steady the mind and fix it on one point one can achieve realisation. The practice of withdrawing the mind from all sorts of sensual objects and fixing it again and again on one particular ideal or a tangible symbol or the Self with the help of discriminative intellect which rules over and directs the mental energies is known as *Abhyasa*. By such constant practice, Divinity takes gradual possession of our nature.

abhyaase'pyasamartho'si matkarmaparamo bhava
madarthamapi karmaani kurvansiddhimavaapyasi // 12.10 //

IF YOU ARE UNABLE EVEN TO SEEK BY PRACTICE, THEN YOU BE INTENT ON DOING ACTIONS FOR MY SAKE; EVEN BY PERFORMING ACTIONS FOR MY SAKE, YOU SHALL ATTAIN PERFECTION.

If concentration is found difficult on account of the outward wandering tendencies of the mind or external circumstances, then do all actions for the sake of The Lord. Thus the individual with the purity of mind achieved becomes aware of the Eternal Reality.

athaitadapyashakto'si kartum madyogamaashritah
sarvakarmaphalatyaagam tatah kuru yataatmavaan // 12.11 //

IF YOU ARE UNABLE TO DO EVEN THIS, TAKING REFUGE IN ME, SELF CONTROLLED, SURRENDER THE FRUITS OF ALL ACTIONS.

Renouncing the fruits of action - Every action culminates in a result or fruit at a future date. Generally individuals waste their energies in worrying about the future results of their present actions. Sri Krishna urges here to curb these wasteful anxieties and fears about the future and do the work without desire of the fruit by surrendering all the fruits of actions to Him. He says that even this act can integrate one's personality and make him single pointed and strong.

In the preceding four verses, the concentration of the mind on The Lord is enjoined first; in case of inability to do that, three alternatives have been put forward to achieve the same goal. They are:

1. Abhyasa Yoga, constant practice to still the mind.
2. Performance of actions for the sake of The Lord alone.
3. Giving up the fruits of actions to The Lord i.e. the Yoga of desireless action, *nishkamakarma.*

YOGA OF DESIRELESS ACTION IS COMMENDED

shreyo hi jnaanamabhyaasaat jnaanaaddhyaanam vishishyate dhyaanaat karmaphalatyaagas tyaagaadcchaantir anantaram // 12.12 //

BETTER INDEED IS KNOWLEDGE THAN PRACTICE; MEDITATION IS BETTER THAN KNOWLEDGE; BETTER THAN MEDITATION IS THE RENUNCIATION OF THE FRUITS OF ACTION; PEACE IMMEDIATELY FOLLOWS SUCH RENUNCIATION.

The order of importance given in this Verse is as under: Renunciation of the fruits of action> Meditation > Knowledge > Practice.

Knowledge is better than practice - Spiritual practices mean listening to discourses on scriptures, performing rituals etc in a routine manner without understanding the significance behind them. Knowledge means acquiring discrimination and discipline at mental and intellectual levels. A correct knowledge of the implications of the spiritual practices and the scriptures is necessary to make them fruitful.

Meditation is better than knowledge - More important is the meditation on the knowledge so acquired than the mere knowledge. This means long pondering over the meaning of spiritual terms and declarations which can take place only through meditation. Meditation based on knowledge is considered superior to mere knowledge.

Renunciation of fruits of action is better than meditation - Meditation is an attempt by the intellect towards a better understanding of the knowledge acquired. Anxiety about the future causes agitation in mind. An agitated mind is not suitable for meditation. Renunciation of the fruits of actions while practising self-control and seeking refuge in the Lord destroys the desire in the seeker which is the source of unrest and brings about the inner calm and peace. For one tranquil in heart the cessation of ignorance comes without delay.

We have seen two methods of worship viz., the one of the manifested form and the other of the unmanifested Absolute in the foregoing verses.

ATTRIBUTES OF THE GOD-REALIZED DEVOTEE

In the following eight Verses (from 13 to 20) Sri Krishna paints the picture of a true devotee and his relationship with the world around him. These verses answer the question posed by Arjuna in the opening verse of this Chapter.

adweshtaa sarvabhootaanaam maitrah karuna eva cha
nirmamo nirahankaarah samaduhkhasukhah kshamee // 12.13 //

HE WHO HAS NO ILL WILL TO ANY BEING, WHO IS FRIENDLY AND COMPASSIONATE TO ALL, WHO IS FREE FROM ATTACHMENT AND EGOISM (FEELING OF 'I' - NESS AND 'MY' - NESS) EVEN-MINDED IN PAIN AND PLEASURE AND FORGIVING,

santushtah satatam yogee yataatmaa dridhanishchayah
mayyarpitamanobuddhiryo madbhaktah sa me priyah // 12.14 //

EVER CONTENT, STEADY IN MEDITATION, POSSESSED OF FIRM CONVICTION, SELF-CONTROLLED, WITH THE MIND AND INTELLECT DEDICATED TO ME - HE, WHO IS THUS DEVOTED TO ME, IS DEAR TO ME.

These two verses give 10 noble qualities of a true devotee viz.

1. Hatred towards none
2. Friendly and compassionate to all
3. Freedom from attachment and egoism
4. Balanced in the pairs of opposites
5. Forgiving nature
6. Always with contentment
7. Steadfast in meditation
8. Self-controlled
9. Firm in conviction and
10. Mind and intellect always cantered on the Lord.

yasmaannodwijate loko lokannodwijate cha yah
harshaamarshabhayodwegairmukto yah sa cha me priyah
// 12.15 //

HE BY WHOM THE WORLD IS NOT AGITATED AND WHO CANNOT BE AGITATED BY THE WORLD, WHO IS FREED FROM JOY, ANGER, ENVY, FEAR AND ANXIETY - HE TOO IS DEAR TO ME.

Three more characteristics of a real devotee are enumerated.

11. He by whom the world is not agitated - where there is sun there can be no darkness; similarly where there is a man of equanimity and perfection an atmosphere of divinity, serenity, joy and peace prevails.

12. Who cannot be agitated by the world - not only serenity is spread around him but such a devotee cannot also be agitated or his inner equipoise disturbed by the chaotic conditions of the world around him.
13. He who is completely freed from joy, anger, envy, fear and anxiety which are all the causes for inner agitations.

Such a devotee, who is ever peaceful with himself and the world, is not a source of grief to any and none can make him feel grief.

anapekshah suchirdaksha udaaseeno gatavyathah
sarvaarambhaparityaagee yo madbhaktah sa me priyah // 12.16 //

HE WHO IS FREE FROM EXPECTATION, PURE, SKILFUL IN ACTION, UNCONCERNED AND UNTROUBLED, RENOUNCING ALL UNDERTAKINGS - HE WHO IS THUS DEVOTED TO ME, IS DEAR TO ME.

In this verse six more subtle qualities of a perfect devotee are added. They are:

14. Free from expectation - A true devotee is independent of the world outside drawing equanimity from within himself.
15. Who is pure - pure externally and internally – External purity is cleanliness of physical body and things around. Internal purity is friendship, compassion, nobility and virtuous dealings with others.
16. Skilful - swiftness and enthusiasm in all actions and in decision making.

17. Unconcerned - It means not squandering away the mental energies by avoiding exaggeration of small difficulties in life and being impartial.
18. Untroubled - who never allows himself to be disturbed by agitations caused by desire.
19. Renouncing all undertakings - This does not mean abandoning all undertakings or productive efforts. It means renouncing the egoistic sense of self importance in undertaking any venture. All our undertakings are controlled by many external factors and our role is thus limited. Hence there is no place for self-importance in any work we undertake.

The devotee who has all these six qualities is dear to The Lord.

Yo na hrishyati na dweshti na shochati na kaangkshati
shubhaashubhaparityaagee bhaktimaan yah sa me priyah
// 12.17 //

HE WHO NEITHER REJOICES NOR HATES, NOR GRIEVES, NOR DESIRES, AND WHO HAS RENOUNCED GOOD AND EVIL, HE WHO IS THUS DEVOTED IS DEAR TO ME.

The ideas spelt out in verse 13 are dealt with in more details. The devotee who does not

20. Rejoice when he attains desirable objects,
21. Hate or fret and fume on getting undesirable objects,
22. Grieve over parting with beloved and cherished objects and

23. Who has a complete sense of fulfilment and has no desire for anything that he has not attained, (he having attained the Self, attained everything).
24. Renounces good and evil - none of the dualistic experiences can be of any consequence to him and
25. Who is of full devotion to the Lord, is dear to Him.

The import of this verse is that when a devotee has awakened to the God-consciousness and evaluates life from his new experience, he cannot rejoice at or hate, grieve at or desire anything in this world and he comes to renounce totally the very concepts of good and evil.

samah shatrau cha mitre cha tathaa maanaapamaanayoh
sheetoshnasukhaduhkheshu samah sangavivarjitah // 12.18 //

HE WHO IS THE SAME TO FRIEND AND FOE, IN HONOUR AND DISHONOUR, IN COLD AND HEAT, IN PLEASURE AND PAIN, WHO IS FREE FROM ATTACHMENT,

tulyanindaastutirmaunee santushto yena kenachit
aniketah sthiramatirbhaktimaan me priyo narah // 12.19 //

TO WHOM CENSURE AND PRAISE ARE EQUAL, WHO IS SILENT (RESTRAINED IN SPEECH), CONTENT WITH ANYTHING THAT COMES, HAS NO FIXED ABODE, STEADY MINDED, FULL OF DEVOTION - THAT MAN IS DEAR TO ME.

26. That man who is Equal to friend and foe,
27. In honour and dishonour,
28. In heat and cold,
29. In pleasure and pain -

30. Equal to censure and praise - To a true devotee the worldly praise or censure has no meaning and significance because of his experiences of the Divine.
31. Who is silent - He is a man of few words both physically and mentally.
32. Content with anything - Contentment in anything that reaches him unasked for and unexpected of. Entertaining demands and to strive for their satisfaction is the never ending game of life. The policy of contentment is the only way to seek and achieve the divine goal of life.
33. Homeless - Home indicates a sense of possession and belonging. Homeless means the absence of such sense. As these souls exist not for any family or social group but live for mankind as a whole, they do not have a settled home. They are not chained to one place or community. They are free to move wherever their inspiration takes them.
34. Steadfast in understanding of the goal and
35. Always with full devotion to The Lord,

is dear to The Lord.

These terminologies indicate the entire possibilities in life at physical, mental and intellectual levels. In all of these situations a true devotee remains unagitated because he is free from attachment which is the cause for all agitations,

Sri Krishna has thus given the complete picture of a Man of Perfection, his relationship with the outside world, his psychological life and intellectual evaluation of the world of beings and happenings. This enumeration concludes the various moral, ethical and spiritual qualities of a true devotee.

CONCLUSION AS TO WHO IS EXTREMELY DEAR TO THE LORD

ye tu dharmyaamritamidam yathoktam paryupaasate
shraddhadhaanaah matparamaa bhaktaaste'teeva me priyaah
// 12.20 //

BUT THOSE WITH FAITH, HOLDING ME AS THEIR SUPREME AIM, FOLLOW THIS NECTAR OF PIOUS WISDOM, THOSE DEVOTEES ARE EXCEEDINGLY DEAR TO ME.

The Sanatana Dharma is summarised in the Verses 13 through 19 above. To realise the Self and live in that wisdom at all levels - physical, mental and intellectual - is the fulfilment of human existence. By following the ideal set in the above seven Verses the devotee is freed forever from the grasp of the cycle of birth and death and succeeds in realizing God who is immortality itself. It is in order to bring out this idea that the marks of a true devotee described above are spoken as '*Dharmyamrita*' or the nectar of pious wisdom.

It is not enough that one gets the knowledge of Dharma (Law of Life) but such knowledge should be lived. He should be able to digest it properly and become perfect in life. Therefore Sri Krishna says he must be endowed with faith - the capacity to assimilate spiritual ideas through subjective personal experience. Such devotees are supremely dear to The Lord.

When we see the One Self in all things, virtues like equal mindedness, freedom from selfish desires, surrender of our whole nature to the Indwelling Spirit and love for all sprout in us. When these qualities are manifested, our devotion is perfect and we are God's own men. Our life then is guided not by forces of attraction and repulsion, friendship and hostility, pleasure and pain, but by the single urge to give oneself to God and therefore to the service of the world which is one with God.

om tat sat iti srimadbhagavadgeetaasu upanishatsu brahma vidyaayaam yogashaastre sri krishnaarjuna samvaade bhakti yogo naama dwaadasho'dhyaayah ||

THUS IN THE UPANISHADS OF THE GLORIOUS BHAGAVAD GITA, THE SCIENCE OF THE ETERNAL, THE SCRIPTURE OF YOGA, THE DIALOGUE BETWEEN SRI KRISHNA AND ARJUNA, ENDS THE TWELFTH DISCOURSE ENTITLED: THE YOGA OF DEVOTION

AN OUTLINE VIEW OF THIS CHAPTER

Arjuna begins the chapter with the perennial question that baffles mankind. Should one worship God with a form or as a formless Reality? Bhagavan answers by giving the relevance of both types of worship to spiritual development. One caters to the devotional while the other to the intellectual seekers. Krishna then presents the most pragmatic approach to God. For seekers who find it difficult to practise various spiritual disciplines (sadhanas), He provides a series of alternatives which cater to the needs of different levels of aspirants. He concludes the chapter by enumerating the quality of a devotee (bhakta) of God. He emphasises that those who possess these qualities are His true devotees.

I - FORM AND FORMLESS WORSHIP - VERSES 1 – 5

Arjuna expresses his doubt to Krishna regarding the mode of worship. Does one worship God with a form? Or the unmanifest Reality? Which of the two is more suitable for appraoaching God and better designed for a seeker's spiritual evolution? Krishna considers Arjuna to be more devotional. He therefore declares worshipping Him as the better approach. But, he follows up His declaration by affirming that worshippers of the Unmanifest also reach God. The devotional need a form, an idol for worship. They lack the capacity to focus their concentration on the Unmanifest Ideal without the help of an idol whereas the intellectual, the introvert, can concentrate on the all pervading formless Reality. Either way, a seeker finally uses single pointed concentration and meditation to gain Enlightenment.

II - PROGRESSIVE WAYS TO REACH GOD - VERSES 6 – 12

A spiritual seeker must reach an advanced state of concentration before he can actually meditate and attain Godhood - Self-Realization. In deep meditation the mind is set on the Self with the intellect supporting it. A seeker maintains this state of single-pointedness before merging with the Self. This being the most advanced and ultimate spiritual practice few can directly relate to it. To those less-evolved Krishna advises self-purification through constant practice of spiritual disciplines. Practicing these helps one to to withdraw the mind from the world and concentrate upon te Self. If one cannot practise even spiritual disciplines he can, then, surrender all his actions to the Lord. He can perform actions for His sake and not merely to satisfy his own personal desires. If this is also not possible, one should keep the goal of Realization in mind while acting in the world. He may satisfy his desires but renounce the attachment to the fruits of his actions. Four facets of spiritual practices were dealt with. Any spiritual practice must be backed by knowledge. A seeker must practice a discipline with full understanding of its significance and purpose. It then leads him to concentrate and meditate upon the supreme Goal. He must then meditate without any anxiety for the result. In the spirit of renunciation the meditator attains the absolute state of peace and bliss.

III - THIRTYFIVE QUALITIES OF A DEVOTEE OF GOD - VERSES 13 – 20

Thirtyfive qualities of a Bhakta – devotee of God are enumerated. Devotion to God is not blind faith, a mere prayer or routine ritual. True devotion comprises these outstanding qualities enumerated. The Lord declares that those who possess them are dear to Him.

<<<000>>>

CHAPTER 13

Kshetra Kshetrajna Vibhaaga Yogah:

Yoga of Distinction between
The Field and the Knower of the Field

PREAMBLE

This is one of the most well-known Chapters in the Gita which provides guidance to experience the Self. It is an extension of the previous Chapter in as much as it gives exhaustive instructions for meditation upon the Imperishable Formless Spirit (Unmanifest). This Chapter continues the discussion of the theme started in Chapter 7 entitled 'Yoga of Knowledge and Wisdom' and Chapter 8 entitled 'Yoga of Imperishable Brahman'. The intervening four Chapters (9-12) are a slight detour in order to clarify the doubts raised by Arjuna.

As earlier stated each group of six Chapters of the Gita explains the sacred words of the Great Declaration *(Mahavakya) -Tat Twam Asi* - That Thou Art. The terms 'Thou' and 'That' were dealt with in Chapters 1-6 (Path of action or Karma Yoga) and 7-12 (Path of devotion or Bhakti Yoga) respectively. The closing group of six Chapters beginning with this Chapter explains the term 'Art' (Path of knowledge or Jnana Yoga) which establishes the identity of the individual soul with the Supreme Soul.

A living organism is the Spirit functioning through the covering of matter. 'That' (Spirit) covered by matter is 'Thou' (Man). Therefore, man without matter covering him is the Eternal, Infinite Spirit.

One should know what constitutes this matter envelopment in order to discard it and reach the 'Man' (Spirit). This discrimination between matter, which is inert, and Spirit, which is the spark of life, is the focus of discussion in this Chapter. The body called the Field *(Kshetra)*, the soul called the Knower of the Field *(Kshetrajna)* and the difference between them are the subject matter of this Chapter.

The process of discarding or getting rid of the matter is nothing but the process of meditation. The techniques of meditation were explained in Chapters 5 & 6. This Chapter tells us as to what the disciplined mind and intellect have to do during meditation and how to draw ourselves from ourselves to reach our identity with the Infinite.

The matter equipments and the world of objects perceived by them is the Field. The Knower of the Field is the Supreme Consciousness which illumines the Field and therefore apparently functions within the Field. It is obvious that one can be knower only so long as one is in the field of knowable. A driver is one so long as he is driving a vehicle. Once he is out of the vehicle he is no more a driver although he, as a person, remains the same.

Similarly the Pure Consciousness when it perceives the world of plurality becomes the knower of the field (Driver). As the driver experiences the pains and pleasures of driving while performing the act of driving, the knower of the field (Consciousness) experiences the joys and sorrows of the pluralistic world while perceiving such world of multiplicity through the body equipments. Thus the joys and miseries of the *samsara* are the features of the knower of the field, the Jiva.

If the field and the knower of the field can be understood as separate entities through the process of meditation, one can get himself detached from the sheath of matter and consequently from the joys and sorrows associated with it. Thereby, the knower of the field who was the experiencer of the sorrows and joys of the material world himself becomes the experiencer of the Absolute Bliss just as the driver himself becomes an ordinary person without any designation when he is enjoying the pleasure of being with his family. The knower minus the field of the known becomes the Pure Knowledge, Itself being always perfect.

This Chapter, therefore, leads us to deep spiritual insights enabling us to realize the Imperishable and the Eternal within ourselves. When the knower of the field understands his real nature which is apart from the field, he rediscovers his own Divine nature. He realizes that he is the Self which, when enveloped by the field, becomes the knower of the field full of agitations.

Krishna answers the query of Arjuna through the entire chapter. A significant contribution of this chapter is the enumeration of twenty two qualities of a *jnani* (enlightened person) on the lines of the listing of thirty five qualities of a *bhakta* in the previous chapter. This chapter concludes by showing the way towards realization of the Self and how with the Eye of Wisdom one can liberate himself.

In the last Chapter the glory and the means to realize the Absolute was not elaborately dealt with. Hence this aspect which is the subject of *jnana yoga* is taken up for detailed discussion in this Chapter. The *kshetra,* the body and the *kshetrajna*, the soul are entirely different from each other. It is due to ignorance that they are being identified as one and the same. In the present Chapter both these terms are differentiated for explanation and hence the title of this Chapter is Kshetra Kshetrajna Vibhaaga Yogah: Yoga of Distinction between The Field and the Knower of the Field. Some editions of the Gita omit the first verse of this chapter containing Arjuna's query seeking clarification on certain philosophic terms on the ground that it is a later interpolation in the text like the commentator sage Madhusudana Saraswati. But its inclusion appears appropriate in view of the context of the question raised by Arjuna.

THE TEXT

arjuna uvaacha
prakritim purusham chaiva kshetram kshetrajnam eva cha
etadveditumicchaami jnaanam jneyam cha keshava // 13.1 //

ARJUNA SAID
PRAKRITI (MATTER) AND PURUSHA (SPIRIT) ALSO THE KSHETRA (THE FIELD) AND THE KSHETRAJNA (THE KNOWER OF THE FIELD), KNOWLEDGE AND THAT WHICH IS TO BE KNOWN, ALL THESE I WISH TO LEARN, O KESAVA.

PRAKRITI AND PURUSHA:

Prakriti is matter, inert equipments. Purusha is the Spirit, the vital sentient truth. The spirit in itself has no expression except when it functions through matter. When Purusha joins Prakriti experiences - good or bad - take place. Electricity by itself is unmanifest but when it functions through different gadgets it is manifested as light or heat or cold etc.

THE FIELD AND THE KNOWER OF THE FIELD:

The knower of the field is the knowing principle when it functions in the knowable. Without knowable the knower himself becomes nothing but Pure Knowledge in which the functions of knowing are absent. Arjuna desires to learn the implications of these concepts.

sri bhagavaan uvaacha
idam shareeram kaunteya kshetramityabhidheeyate
etadyo vetti tam praahuh kshetrajna iti tadvidah // 13.2 //

SRI BHAGAVAN SAID
THIS BODY, O KAUNTEYA, IS CALLED THE FIELD; HE WHO KNOWS IT (BODY) IS CALLED THE KNOWER OF THE FIELD BY THOSE WHO KNOW OF THEM I.E. BY THE SAGES.

THIS BODY IS THE FIELD:

The use of the demonstrative pronoun 'this' while referring to the body suggests that this body is different from the one who perceives or knows it. The word *'kshetra'* signifies both 'body' and matter. The body is called 'field' because the fruits of action are reaped in it as in the field. It is the body in which events happen; all growth, decline and death take place in it. Just as seeds sown in a field yield the corresponding crops in course of time, even so seeds of karma sown in this body yield their fruit at the appropriate time. Hence the body is called the field, the object.

KNOWER OF THE FIELD:

The word *'kshetrajna'* or knower of the field means the individual soul, which is, in reality one with the Supreme Soul who is the Subject. The entire range of objective reality, the *prakriti*, the matter, which is open to knowledge through the equipments of mind, intellect and senses, are material in their constitution, perishable in their nature and mutable in their essence.

The conscious Self is wholly different from the aforesaid material world of objective reality. It is the knower of the matter consisting of perceptions, feelings and thoughts. *Prakriti* is unconscious activity and *purusha* is inactive consciousness. The conscious principle, inactive and detached, which lies behind all active states as witness, is the Knower of the Field. It is the Lord of the matter and runs through it. This is the distinction between consciousness and the objects which that consciousness observes. Kshetrajna is the light of awareness, the Knower of all objects and He is neither the embodied mind nor an object in the world. He is the Supreme Lord, calm and eternal and does not need the use of the senses and the mind for His witnessing. It is the *'para prakriti'* or the higher nature referred to in the 7th Chapter of the Gita wherein Sri krishna described the two prakritis of the Lord. The lower, *apara prakriti,* or the field, consists of three *gunas* and the higher *prakriti* (the soul or *Jiva* when individualized) is the Knower of the Field.

The 13th Chapter proposes to describe the two prakritis- the Field and the Knower of the Field- in order to determine finally the nature of the Supreme Lord Himself i.e., the word *'tat'* in the *mahavakya 'Tat Twam Asi'*.

kshetrajnam chaapi maam viddhi sarvakshetreshu bhaarata
kshetrakshetrajnayor jnaanam yattajjnaanam matam mama // 13.3 //

YOU ALSO KNOW ME AS THE KNOWER OF THE FIELD IN ALL FIELDS, O BHARATA. ONLY THE KNOWLEDGE OF THE FIELD AND ITS KNOWER IS CONSIDERED BY ME AS TRUE KNOWLEDGE.

Sri Krishna declares that only the knowledge of the perishable and inert matter and the nature of the Infinite and Imperishable Spirit is the True Knowledge.

Kshetra or the field is the matter consisting of equipments of perception and what is perceived by them. Kshetrajna is the knower of what is perceived through the instruments of perception. To distinguish thus the worlds of the subject and the object is what the Lord tells as true knowledge.

SALIENT POINTS TO BE DISCUSSED

tat kshetram yaccha yaadrikcha yadvikaari yatashcha yat
sa cha yo yatprabhaavashcha tatsamaasena me shrinu // 13.4 //

HEAR BRIEFLY FROM ME WHAT THE FIELD IS, WHAT ITS PROPERTIES ARE, WHAT ITS MODIFICATIONS ARE, FROM WHERE IT COMES, WHO ITS KNOWER IS AND WHAT HIS POWERS ARE.

Sri Krishna says He is going to explain what constitutes the Field, its properties, its origin, its modifications i.e. what its by-products are when it changes its form, what is the knowing principle in the Field and what are powers of perception, feeling and thought of the Knower of the Field?

CITING THE AUTHORITIES

rishibhirbahudhaa geetam chhandobhirvividhaih prithak
brahmasootrapadaishchaiva hetumadbhirvinishchitaih // 13.5 //

ALL THIS HAS BEEN SUNG BY SAGES IN MANY AND DIFFERENT WAYS, IN VARIOUS DISTINCTIVE HYMNS, AND ALSO IN WELL REASONED AND CONVINCING PASSAGES INDICATIVE OF BRAHMAN.

Sri Krishna speaks very highly of the nature of the Field and the Knower of the Field in order to create interest in Arjuna. He says what He is going to explain are the very truths that are already contained in the Vedas, the Upanishads and the *Brahmasutras* or the aphorisms of Brahman, later systemized by Badarayana. The Veda hymns are called *cchandas* or rhythmical utterances. These revelations of the sages are not in the nature of any commandments but they are logical thoughts, full of reasoning which are highly convincing.

THE FIELD IS DESCRIBED

mahaabhootaanyahankaaro buddhiravyaktameva cha
indriyaani dashaikam cha pancha chendriyagocharaah // 13.6 //

THE GREAT ELEMENTS, EGOISM (I-CONSCIOUSNESS), INTELLECT AND ALSO THE UNMANIFESTED, THE TEN

SENSES AND THE MIND AND THE FIVE OBJECTS OF THE SENSES.

icchaa dweshah sukham duhkham sanghaatashchetanaa dhritih
etat kshetram samaasena savikaaramudaahritam // 13.7 //

DESIRE, HATRED, PLEASURE, PAIN, THE AGGREGATE (BODY), INTELLIGENCE, AND FORTITUDE - THIS BRIEFLY STATED, IS THE FIELD TOGETHER WITH ITS MODIFICATIONS.

From here onwards Sri Krishna starts explaining His promised themes one by one in great details. The above two verses explain various items constituting together as the Field which was earlier indicated as the body. A reference may be made to the Chapter 7 where a detailed discussion appears covering all these concepts.

Elements: Five in number viz. space, air, fire, water and earth. (Ref. Ch.7.4)

Egoism: The sense of 'I' ness and 'My' ness or the individuality that arises in our relationship with the world of objects.

Intellect: The determining faculty which thinks, discriminates and decides.

Unmanifested: They are the unseen cause, total vasanas (impressions) which rule the mind and intellect in determining their activities in the outside world. When these vasanas are manifested they are seen as the world of objects. (Ref. Ch.7.14)

Ten senses: Five sense organs of perception viz. ear, skin, eye, tongue and nose and five sense organs of action viz, hands, feet, mouth, anus and generative organs. These are the channels by which an individual perceives the stimuli and responds to them.

The one: This stands for the mind which thinks about the stimuli received from the sense organs and sends forth the responses after getting the judgment from the intellect.

Five objects of the senses: Each sense organ perceives only one type of sense object. They are ear -sound, skin - touch, eye - a form, tongue - taste and nose - smell.

The above 24 items constitute *kshetra*, the matter or the gross body or the Field.

Their modifications are enumerated now. They are desire, hatred, pleasure, pain, the assemblage of the body, intelligence, steadfastness etc. In short, not only the gross body, mind and intellect but also the perceptions experienced through them, the world of objects, emotions and thoughts are included in the term 'Field' - this body. All the world of objects, which includes emotions and thoughts, are 'knowable' put together in a bunch. This is called the Field, the object. The Knowing Principle or the Knower is the subject. Real knowledge consists in understanding the distinction between the object and the subject.

The following five verses enumerate the 22 qualities which together indicate the Knower of the Field.

THE KNOWER OF THE FIELD IS DESCRIBED

amaanitwam adambhitwam ahimsaa kshaantiraarjavam
aachaaryopaasanam shaucham sthairyamaatmavinigrahah
// 13.8 //

HUMILITY, MODESTY, NON-INJURY, FORGIVENESS, UPRIGHTNESS, SERVICE TO THE TEACHER, PURITY, STEADFASTNESS, SELF CONTROL

"The knower is the subject and the turning of it into an object or a thing means ignorance, *avidya*. Objectification is the ejection of the subject into the world of the objects. Nothing in the world of objects is an authentic reality. We can realize the subject in us only by overcoming the enslaving power of the object world, by refusing to be dissolved into it. This means resistance, suffering. Acquiescence in the surrounding world and its conventions diminishes suffering; refusal increases it. But suffering is the only process through which we fight for our true nature - *sat chit anand."* - Dr.S.Radhakrishnan.

The Lord therefore prescribes certain conditions necessary for understanding the Infinite Self by describing the elements of knowledge and practices conducive to spiritual enlightenment in the Verses 8 -12.

1. Humility - absence of self-esteem.
2. Modesty- Un-pretentiousness, not proclaiming one's own greatness.
3. Non-injury - not causing suffering to any other living being intentionally.
4. Forgiveness - forbearance and patience, capacity to put up with everything without getting disturbed.
5. Uprightness - straight forwardness in behavior.
6. Service to the teacher - not merely physical but seeking mental and intellectual identity with the teacher's heart and intellect.

7. Purity - external: cleanliness of body and environment; internal: taintless thoughts, emotions, intentions and motives.
8. Steadfastness - firmness and consistency of purpose, concentration of all efforts in achieving the spiritual goal.
9. Self control - self-restraint practiced in dealing with others.

indriyaartheshu vairaagyamanahankaara eva cha
janma mrityu jaraa vyaadhi duhkha doshaanu darshanam // 13.9 //

DISPASSION TO THE OBJECTS OF THE SENSES, ABSENCE OF EGOISM, PERCEPTION OF EVIL OF BIRTH, DEATH, OLD AGE, SICKNESS AND PAIN.

10. Dispassion or absence of attachment to objects - does not mean running away from objects of the world but detaching oneself from becoming a slave to the sensuous objects.
11. Absence of egoism - absence of the sense of superiority in oneself.
12. Perception of evil in birth, death, old age and sickness - every physical body goes through these changes and at each stage of life encounters sorrows and troubles which fact should be thoroughly understood by a seeker.
13. Pain - birth, death, old age and sickness are full of miseries and all miseries are always painful which one should be conscious of. Pain is of three types viz, those arising in one's own person, those produced by

external agents and those produced by God i.e. by circumstances beyond anybody's control. Unless the seeker is aware of the pain in existence there will not be any urge for spiritual enquiry. The sense of revolt against pain is the fuel which propels the seeker to run fast to reach the spiritual goal.

Reflection on the evils and miseries of birth, death, old age and sickness leads to indifference to sense-pleasures and the senses turn towards the Innermost self for knowledge. Birth, death etc. are not miseries by themselves but they produce misery in their aftermath.

asaktiranabhishwangah putradaaragrihaadishu
nityam cha samachittatwam ishtaanishtopapattishu // 13.10 //

NON-ATTACHMENT, NON-IDENTIFICATION OF SELF WITH SON, WIFE, HOME AND THE REST AND EVEN-MINDEDNESS TO ALL AGREEABLE AND DISAGREEABLE EVENTS.

14. Nonattachment - When a man thinks that an object is his, the idea of 'Mine'-ness is born in his mind. He identifies himself with that object, loves it and gets attached to it. Non-attachment is the absence of such identification with any object. Keeping the mind away from all attachments assures peaceful life.
15. Non-identification with son etc. - Excessive love towards all these is an intense form of attachment with them so much so one's own material happiness or otherwise is equated with the happiness or otherwise of the other.

16. Constant even-mindedness - Equanimity under all circumstances and conditions, desirable or undesirable, is a sign of knowledge.

mayi chaananyayogena bhaktiravyabhichaarinee
viviktadesha sevitwam aratir janasamsadi // 13.11 //

UNSWERVING DEVOTION UNTO ME THROUGH CONSTANT MEDITATION ON NON-SEPARATION, RESORTING TO SOLITUDE, AVERSION TO THE SOCIETY OF MEN

If one has developed the virtues mentioned in the previous verses, he would conserve in himself a vast energy which should be directed through proper channels for self-unfoldment. This is explained here.

17. Unswerving devotion to Me - Devotion to The Lord should be of single point concentration without any thought of other objects.
18. Yoga of non-separation - Undivided attention and enthusiasm in the mind of the devotee.
19. Such an integrated mind and steady contemplation is not possible unless there is a conducive environment which is suggested in two ways viz. a. To resort to solitary places and b. To develop a distaste for the crowded society life.

The implication is to live alone in oneself away from the maddening crowd. This is natural because whenever the mind is pre-occupied with an ideal it loses all its contacts with the outside world; thereafter the seeker lives in himself in a cave of his own experiences, as a solitary man walking alone in the world. He hates the crowd of other thoughts entering in his mind. However, these terms are not to be understood as physical aversion to the society in general and escapism into solitude.

adhyaatma jnaana nityatwam tattwa jnaanaartha darshanam
etajjnaanamiti proktam ajnaanam yadatonyathaa //13.12 //

CONSTANCY IN THE KNOWLEDGE OF THE SELF, INSIGHT INTO THE OBJECT OF THE KNOWLEDGE OF TRUTH; THIS IS DECLARED TO BE KNOWLEDGE AND WHAT IS OPPOSED TO IT IS IGNORANCE.

In this concluding verse of the section explaining the various essential qualifications in a seeker, the Lord adds two more items viz. constancy in Self knowledge and understanding the end of true knowledge.

20. Constancy in Self-knowledge: The knowledge of the Self is to be lived and not merely learnt. If the Self is everywhere and is real, then the seeker should try to live as the Self in his personality layers. This consistency of living the spiritual knowledge in all contacts with the world outside is one of the practices a seeker should always keep up. Knowledge includes practice of the moral virtues.
21. Understanding the end of True Knowledge: To keep the vision of the goal always before us adds enthusiasm in all our activities. Thus Liberation from all our imperfections and limitations is the goal to be aspired for by all spiritual seekers.

22. All that is contrary to it is ignorance: Qualities such as pride, hypocrisy, cruelty, impatience, insincerity and the like are all ignorance and therefore should be avoided as tending to the perpetuation of *samsara.*

These traits described from Verse 8 to Verse 12 are declared to be the true 'knowledge' because they are conducive to the realization of the Self. These qualities are said to be the 'knowledge' because once they have been fully developed the mind gets matured enough to reach the goal of Pure knowledge of the Self.

PURE KNOWLEDGE

jneyam yattat pravakshyaami yajjnaatwaamritam ashnute
anaadimatparam brahma na sattannaasaduchyate // 13.13 //

I WILL NOW DESCRIBE THAT WHICH HAS TO BE KNOWN; KNOWING WHICH ONE ATTAINS TO IMMORTALITY, THE BEGINNINGLESS SUPREME BRAHMAN, CALLED NEITHER EXISTENT NOR NON-EXISTENT.

After explaining in the previous five verses the various auxiliary causes of knowledge, The Lord promises here that He will explain what is to be known by this knowledge. Although He says He will explain what is to be known, He does not do so directly but gives an elaborate description of what the result would be of such knowledge. This is because the glorification of the result of the knowledge would instill greater desire in the seeker to realize it.

Knowledge by which one attains the Immortal: Mortality is related to matter. If the Immortal Spirit identifies itself with matter It suffers the imaginary sense of finitude and mortality. But if the real nature of the Spirit is discovered in itself the concept of finitude and death disappears and the sense of immortality dawns. To realize the Spiritual Nature is the goal and meditation with the qualities described above is the means.

Beginningless Supreme Brahman: Beginning can occur with reference to a particular time. If time itself is a created factor there cannot be any beginning. Therefore Brahman which is substratum for all must be existent even before time. Thus the Supreme, the Brahman, is always considered 'beginningless'.

Neither Existent nor Non-Existent: The Supreme Consciousness, being the very perceiving principle cannot be perceived. With reference to it everything is an object and It is the one subject. Since It cannot be perceived It is said to be non-existent, a Non-Being. But because Truth cannot be defined as non-existent, It can be defined only as neither Being nor Non-Being.

Sankara says the Brahman cannot be existent (Sat) as it belongs to no category or class such as man, animal etc., nor does it have any qualities such as whiteness, blackness etc. But at the same time It shows Itself to be not non-existent (asat) by manifesting itself through living bodies.

The concepts of being and non-being are the work of human intellectual judgment. The Consciousness that illumines these judgments is the Self. As the illuminator and the illumined cannot be one and the same, the one subject, Brahman, as opposed to all the objects cannot be either existent or non-existent because existence and non-existence are two types of thoughts both of which are illumined by the Self. Hence Brahman is neither 'being' nor 'non-being'.

The following verses describe this all pervading nature of the knower of the field.

sarvatah paanipaadam tat sarvato'kshishiromukham
sarvatah shrutimalloke sarvamaavritya tishtathi // 13.14 //

WITH HANDS AND FEET EVERYWHERE, WITH EYES, HEADS AND MOUTHS EVERYWHERE, WITH EARS EVERYWHERE HE EXISTS IN THE WORLD, ENVELOPING ALL.

Hands and feet etc everywhere suggest the Principle of Consciousness functioning behind them all. The functioning of all the parts of the body in every human being is based on the Life Principle. The functions of perception, feeling and thinking are carried out only so long as there is life in the body. Life is said to be everywhere and hence the Principle of Consciousness exists pervading all. This Consciousness behind every living being, that which is common to all, is *Paramatman, Para Brahman.*

As the one subject of all objects of experience, He is said to envelop all and have hands and feet, ears and eyes everywhere. Without the seeing light there is no experience at all. The Supreme has got two aspects. As for example so long as one is associated with an Organization while in service he is called a Manager or President or Director etc. Once he retires from service, although he loses all his designations he does not become a zero, but continues to remain a human being as he was earlier. Similarly, when the Self is associated with the modes of nature, it is called Kshetrajna; when It is released from these, It is called the Paramatman or the Supreme Self.

sarvendriyagunaabhaasam sarvendriyavivarjitam
asaktam sarvabhricchaiva nirgunam gunabhoktru cha // 13.15 //

SHINING BY THE FUNCTIONS OF ALL THE SENSES, YET WITHOUT THE SENSES, UNATTACHED, YET SUPPORTING ALL, DEVOID OF QUALITIES, YET THEIR EXPERIENCER.

The Self in us functioning through the sense organs looks as though It possesses all sense organs. But the sense organs decay and perish while the Consciousness which functions through them and which provides each of them with its own individual faculty is Eternal and Changeless just as electricity is not the light in the bulb and yet when it functions through the bulb it looks as if it were light.

The relationship of unattached support can be explained as follows. Waves are not the ocean but the ocean supports all the waves in as much as there can be no waves without the ocean. Cotton is in the cloth but cloth is not the cotton. But it is the cotton in the cloth that supports the cloth. Similarly the world of plurality is not the Consciousness but it is the Consciousness that supports the world of multiplicities.

The influences which govern the human minds are called Gunas or Qualities. They are Sattva (Unactivity), Rajas (Activity) and Tamas (Inactivity). A live mind alone can experience these influences. But Life is the illuminator of these influences. Thus Consciousness conditioned by the mind is Jiva, the Ego and that is the experiencer of the Gunas. Unconditioned by the mind, Consciousness in itself is 'Its own nature', 'It is the Absolute'.

Thus the Self, the Absolute, is beyond sense organs, mind and intellect, detached from everything and without any relation to the various Gunas. But the same Self conditioned by the sense organs looks as though It possess all these sense organs, It is the sustainer of them all and It is the experiencer of all the Gunas.

bahirantashcha bhootaanaam acharam charameva cha
sookshmatwaat tadavijneyam doorastham chaantike cha tat
// 13.16 //

'THAT' IS WITHOUT AND WITHIN (ALL) BEINGS, IS THE UNMOVING AND ALSO THE MOVING; IS TOO SUBTLE TO BE KNOWN; IS FAR AWAY AND YET IS NEAR.

The all pervasiveness of the Consciousness is indicated here.

Without and within all beings - Consciousness is present in body, mind and intellect and also outside these equipments just as sound waves converted into electric waves are present even where there are no radio sets to receive them.

Unmoving and moving - All that moves by itself is classified as alive and that which has no motion in itself is inert. As Consciousness is all pervasive and all encompassing it cannot move within itself and hence It is unmoving. Yet when Consciousness is conditioned by the equipments through which it functions it looks as if it were moving. Hence it is said to be moving. When we sit in a moving train we feel we are moving although we are only sitting i.e. when we are conditioned by a moving train we feel as if we were moving. So also Consciousness looks as if it were moving when conditioned by moving things.

Although without Consciousness no activity is ever possible none is able to perceive It, feel It or intellectually comprehend It. This is because of its subtle nature. Grosser the thing more it is perceptible. Subtle nature makes comprehension difficult.

Near and far: The concept of distance - nearness and farness - arises only in respect of conditioned things or those that which has limitations in terms of space or volume etc.

When a thing is all pervasive and exists everywhere the question of its being near or far does not arise; such things are both near and far. Consciousness is far because of its Absolute nature and yet it is near because of the existence of the living beings with shapes and forms through whom it functions.

avibhaktam cha bhooteshu vibhaktamiva cha sthitam
bhootabhartru cha tajjneyam grasishnu prabhavishnu cha // 13.17 //

HE IS UNDIVIDED, YET HE EXISTS AS IF DIVIDED AMONG BEINGS; HE IS TO BE KNOWN AS THE SUPPORTER OF BEINGS; HE DESTROYS THEM AND CREATES THEM AFRESH.

Undivided yet divided: Paramatman is all pervading and yet it individualizes as special manifestation only at points where equipments are available just as electricity manifests as light only at the point of filament in the bulb. Although space is one entity it looks divided as room space, pot space etc.

Supports all, destroys all and creates all: The Ocean is a supporter of waves, waves are born in the ocean and yet the same ocean destroys all waves. The Truth or Self is the substratum on which the world of plurality is projected by the deluded mind and intellect and when we go beyond the mind and intellect the vision of *samsar* gets swallowed up in the tranquility of the Self.

jyotishaamapi tajjyotistamasah paramuchyate
jnaanam jneyam jnaanagamyam hridi sarvasya vishthitam // 13.18 //

HE, THE LIGHT OF ALL LIGHTS, IS SAID TO BE BEYOND DARKNESS. AS KNOWLEDGE, THE OBJECT OF KNOWLEDGE, THE GOAL OF KNOWLEDGE HE IS SEATED IN THE HEARTS OF ALL.

Since the Consciousness in us brings our various experiences within our understanding, it is compared to light. To see an object it should be illumined by the light. Similarly to cognize the outer world experiences there must be light within us to illumine our emotions and thoughts that arise in us.

This light of wisdom by which we become aware of our own mental and intellectual conditions is called the Light of the Soul or the Self or the Consciousness. The Self is said to be the light of all lights because without Consciousness even the sun which has immeasurable light within itself cannot be perceived.

Beyond Darkness: If the sun were to shine in a location all the twenty four hours, the concept of day and night or brightness and darkness loses its meaning because the question of darkness appearing anytime does not arise and it is sunshine all throughout. In this situation the sun is said to know no darkness. Similarly, Consciousness is beyond the concept of darkness; it is the Light Absolute; where there is consciousness there cannot be any darkness or night. Moreover the principle of Consciousness makes us aware not only the light but also the darkness. That which illuminates both light and darkness must be beyond the experience of light and darkness. Hence the Self is said to transcend even darkness.

Knowledge *(Jnaanam),* the thing to be known (*Jneyam)* and the goal of all knowledge *(Jnaana gamyam):* This is the final experience to be gained for which groundwork has been done from verses 7 to 18. This is the point of concentration. It is the Consciousness that transcends all our experiences and illumines our life. It is the very goal of all spiritual endeavors at all times and at all places.

Dwelling in the hearts of all: The Lord says that Consciousness, the Infinite, dwells in the hearts of all. Heart does not mean the blood supplying physical part of the body. It means the mental area from where all noble thoughts emanate. In a tranquil and pious atmosphere when the intellect contemplates upon the 'Light' that is beyond darkness, all pervading, subtle, It can be realized and hence it is stated to dwell in everybody's heart.

Many of these passages are quotations from the Upanishads. Ref: *Svetasvatara Up.III.8 and 16; Isa Up. 5; Mundaka Up. III. 1. 7; Brihadaranyaka Up. IV.4.16.*

THE FRUITS OF KNOWLEDGE

iti kshetram tathaa jnaanam jneyam choktam samaasatah
madbhakta etadvijnaaya madbhaavaayopapadyate // 13.19 //

THUS THE FIELD AS WELL AS THE KNOWLEDGE AND THE OBJECT OF KNOWLEDGE HAVE BEEN STATED. MY DEVOTEE WHO UNDERSTANDS THIS ENTERS INTO MY BEING.

Sri Krishna concludes the theme of His discourse so far by saying those who seek the light through devotion to Him reach Him. Devotion here implies not only emotional surrender unto The Lord but intellectual apprehension of the Truth, the Self, through a correct understanding of the Field and the Knower of the Field. One who is able to recognize the one Sri Krishna as the vitalizing Consciousness Principle in all fields of matter envelopments, he is the true devotee who as The Lord says 'enters into His Being', attains liberation or release from birth and death.

The 'Field' is described in verses 6 & 7, 'Knowledge' is described in verses 8-12 and the 'Knowable' is described in verses 13-18. One who understands the Field, knowledge and the object of knowledge knows the whole doctrine of the Vedas and the Bhagavad Gita.

The two prakritis of the Lord, the higher and the lower, were discussed in the Seventh Chapter. It has been said that all created beings are born of them. (7.6). This topic dealing with Prakrti, matter and Purusha, spirit are elaborated in this section. Matter functions with several modifications and qualities while spirit functioning through them all is but one and the same. The union of spirit with matter produces a living being. The supreme Self, being the same, expresses differently in different individuals.

The path to Self-realization begins with action, passing through knowledge, it ends in meditation. Those who cannot pursue the path all by themselves can still reach the Self by surrendering to and following a spiritual master.

Spiritual growth is marked by recognizing the homogeneous principle in the heterogeneous variety of beings. Perceiving the Imperishable in the perishable world, the seeker realizes Brahman as the substratum in the diversified existence of all beings. He becomes one with Brahman.

The supreme Self within does not act; nor is It tainted by the actions of beings. It remains ever immaculate like space which is never polluted by the different objects occupying it. He who recognizes the supreme Self in the manifold beings is endowed with *jnanachakshu*, the Eye of Wisdom, with which he perceives the Supreme.

NATURE AND SPIRIT

prakritim purusham chaiva viddhyanaadee ubhaavapi
vikaaraamshcha gunaamshchaiva viddhi prakritisambhavaan
// 13.20 //

KNOW YOU THAT PRAKRITI AND PURUSHA ARE BOTH WITHOUT BEGINNING AND KNOW YOU ALSO THAT ALL FORMS AND GUNAS ARE BORN OF PRAKRITI.

In Chapter 7 Sri Krishna said that His Prakriti falls under two categories viz. the Higher and the Lower. In this Chapter both these are explained as the Knower of the Field (Kshetrajna, Purusha) and the Field (Kshetra, prakriti). It was also stated earlier that both the Higher and Lower Matter together constitute the source of creation. The same thought is repeated here as the Field and the Knower of the Field together form the origin of all beings.

Prakriti, Matter or nature is inert. Matter is that out of which all forms (from intelligence down to the gross body) and gunas (qualities such as sattva, rajas and tamas, which manifest themselves in the form of pleasure, pain delusion so on,) come into existence. All changes or modifications are related to Matter. Prakriti is maya, the sakti or power of the Lord. It is the cause of the manifestation of the relative universe.

Since Prakriti or maya is the eternal source of all forms and gunas, Brahman (Purusha) remains ever changeless and immutable. Purusha, Self, Soul, Spirit, is the changeless substratum in the presence of which all changes take place.

Matter (Prakriti) and Spirit (Purusha) are both beginningless. They are the two aspects of Iswara, the Lord. As the Lord is eternal so also is His two aspects Matter and Spirit. The play of Matter and Spirit causes the origin, preservation and dissolution of the Universe.

FUNCTIONS OF *PRAKRITI* AND *PURUSHA*

kaaryakaaranakartrutwe hetuh prakritiruchyate
purushah sukhaduhkhaanaam bhoktritwe heturuchyate // 13.21 //

PRAKRITI IS SAID TO BE THE CAUSE OF THE GENERATION OF THE BODY AND THE ORGANS AND PURUSHA IS SAID TO BE THE CAUSE OF THE EXPERIENCE OF PLEASURE AND PAIN.

Prakriti (nature) is the material from which the body and the sense organs are produced. The five elements out of which the body is made and the five sense-objects are included under the term 'body' or *'karya'* used in the Verse. The sense organs are thirteen namely five organs of perception, five organs of action, the mind, intellect (buddhi), and I-consciousness (ahamkara). Pleasure, pain, delusion and the rest, which are born of three gunas of prakriti, are included under the term organs or *'karana'* since they cannot exist independently of the sense-organs.

Purusha and Prakriti are stated to be the cause of samsara or phenomenal existence. Prakriti transforms itself into body and senses, as also into pleasure, pain and so on and Purusha experiences pleasure and pain. This union between Purusha and Prakriti makes relative life possible. Eventhough the Purusha, the Soul, identifies Himself with the body and appears to experience pleasure and pain, yet in reality He remains unchanging. It is this apparent experience which constitutes His illusory world or samsara and which makes Him a samsari or phenomenal being.

It should be clearly understood that although the term Purusha used here is synonymous with jiva, the individualized soul, or Kshetrajna, the Knower of the Field, or *bhokta*, the enjoyer, it should not be confused with the Paramatman or Brahman or the Highest Self. The term Purusha is used here merely as an intelligent principle and a conditioned being. Again, this should not be construed that there are two separate purushas; the same one purusha is seen from two different angles. In the Gita, no distinction is made between the knower of the Field and the Supreme Lord, Paramatman, Brahman. This has got relevance to Chapter 15 also.

HOW DOES IMMUTABLE ATMAN EXPERIENCE PLEASURE AND PAIN?

purushah prakritistho hi bhungte prakritijaan gunaan
kaaranam gunasango'sya sadasadyoni janmasu // 13.22 //

PURUSHA SEATED IN PRAKRITI, EXPERIENCES THE QUALITIES (GUNAS) BORN OF PRAKRITI. IT IS ATTACHMENT TO THESE QUALITIES IS THE CAUSE OF HIS BIRTH IN GOOD AND EVIL WOMBS.

Purusha seated in Prakriti: When the knower of the Field (Purusha) identifies himself with the Field (Prakriti), he becomes the experiencer.

He experiences the qualities born of Prakriti: Purusha identifies with the body and the senses which are the effects of Prakriti (Matter). Pleasure and pain, heat and cold etc. arise out of Matter envelopments. The experiences of Matter become the experiences of the Spirit because of the latter's contact with the former. Purusha not only experiences the sorrows and joys of life but develops attachment with them which is the cause of its birth in good or evil wombs.

Having identified with the Field (World of objects), the knower of the Field (Purusha) develops attachment to the Field, the delusory *samsar* and finds himself as though he has forgotten his real nature. Thus this ignorance (*Avidya*) and attachment to the Field are the two causes due to which the *Satchidananda* has become a miserable *Samsarin.* The re-discovery of the Self and realizing our real nature would therefore be through detachment from the Field. *Vairagya* and *Viveka* are the means for such rediscovery.

Avidya or ignorance and *kama* or attachment to the *gunas*, together constitute the cause of *samsara* or relative existence. The aspirant seeking liberation, should avoid them both. Ignorance is to be removed by knowledge, the knowledge of the Field and the Knower of the Field as imparted in the beginning of this Chapter. Attachment is to be destroyed by vairagya or dispassion. The injunction delivered in the Gita is to renounce the illusory world.

REAL NATURE OF PURUSHA

upadrashtaanumantaa cha bhartaa bhoktaa maheshwarah
paramaatmeti chaapyukto dehe'smin purushah parah // 13.23 //

THE SUPREME PURUSHA IN THIS BODY IS ALSO CALLED THE WITNESS, THE APPROVER, THE SUPPORTER, THE EXPERIENCER, THE SOVEREIGN LORD AND THE SUPREME SELF.

As a contrast to the deluded knower of the Field, Purusha, discussed in the previous Verse, there must be the Pure Spirit or unconditioned Purusha also. Hence there must be knowledge which is not conditioned by the field although it may look conditioned. Sri Krishna thus mentions here two Purushas viz. the Lower one and the Higher one. The Lower Purusha is the knower of the Field and the Higher one is Pure Consciousness unconditioned by the Prakriti. Both of these function in this body.

The Supreme Self, Pure Consciousness, is described as Spectator, a silent witness, *upadrashtaa,* when it sees evil actions performed. When noble actions take place it is referred to as the Approver, *anumantha*. When noble actions are done in a spirit of surrender to the Lord, the Supreme is referred to as *bharta*, the fulfiller. The individual in his Eternal Conscious state initiates all actions and reaps the fruit. Therefore, He is referred to as the Experiencer, *bhokta.*

Finally it is stated that the Higher Self, *paramaatma,* the Sovereign Lord, *maheshwarah,* is in this body itself. This theme will be again discussed in Chapter 15.17.

RESULT OF SELF-KNOWLEDGE

ya evam vetti purusham prakritim cha gunaih saha
sarvathaa vartamano'pi na sa bhooyobhijaayate // 13.24 //

HE WHO THUS KNOWS THE PURUSHA AND PRAKRITI ALONG WITH THE GUNAS IS NOT BORN AGAIN, IN WHATSOEVER CONDITION HE MAY BE.

He who has realized in himself

- that which is the matter, prakriti
- that which is the Spirit, purusha, and who understands
- how the Supreme Spirit gets identified with matter and behaves as Purusha, the knower of the Field
- as also the mysteries of the Gunas under the influence of which the body equipments function is the one called 'Man of Wisdom'. Such a person frees himself from the cycle of births and deaths whatever may be his conduct.

DIFFERENT ROADS TO SALVATION

dhyaanenaatmani pashyanti kechidaatmaanamaatmanaa
anye saankhyena yogena karmayogena chaapare // 13.25 //

SOME BY MEDITATION BEHOLD THE SELF IN THE SELF BY THE SELF, OTHERS BY THE PATH OF KNOWLEDGE (JNAANA YOGA) AND STILL OTHERS BY KARMA YOGA OR PATH OF WORKS.

Realization of the Self is the goal of the spiritual seeking and many paths are prescribed for the purpose keeping in view the differences in the mental and intellectual capabilities of the seekers.

By meditation some behold the Self: Meditation is defined as withdrawing the hearing, seeing, and the functioning of the other senses into the mind away from sound, form and other sense objects; next withdrawing the mind into the inmost Intelligence; and then contemplating the Intelligence with undeviating concentration. Meditation is continuous thinking and the mind of one absorbed in it dwells on the ideal uninterruptedly.

Through meditation the seeker directs his flow of thought of the Self in a continuous and unbroken manner like an unbroken stream of flowing oil when pouring from one vessel to another. Through concentration the senses are withdrawn into the mind and are not allowed to run after their respective sensual objects. Keeping it thus under control, the mind itself is made to abide in the Self through constant meditation on the Self.

The mind is purified by meditation. A pure mind will not have any attachment to sense objects and naturally moves towards the Self. The seekers of this type have a very high degree of detachment from sense objects (Vairagya) and sense of discrimination to distinguish the Permanent from the

Impermanent. (Viveka). This type of individuals belongs to the highest class.

Sankhya Yoga or Jnaana Yoga: The second path meant for those who do not have the steadiness of the mind and intellect is the study of the Shastras. The term 'Sankhya' means arriving at philosophical conclusions through logical thoughts. The study of Shastras and reflections upon them is called Yoga which will lead one to deeper conviction of the goal and steadiness of mind to realize it.

Karma Yoga: The third one is for those who cannot even study and reflect on shastras due to their inner limitations. Such a person surrenders his actions and their fruits to the Lord. This produces purity of mind which leads to the knowledge of the Self.

The paths of meditation, knowledge and work are prescribed to cater to the temperaments of different classes of people.

WHAT ABOUT PEOPLE OF LEAST UNDERSTANDING?

anye twevamajaanantah shrutwaanyebhya upaasate
te'pi chaa'titarantyeva mrityum shrutiparaayanaah // 13.26 //

OTHERS ALSO, IGNORANT OF THIS (THESE PATHS OF YOGA), WORSHIP HAVING HEARD OF IT FROM OTHERS; THEY TOO CROSS BEYOND DEATH, BY THEIR DEVOTION TO WHAT THEY HAVE HEARD AS THE SUPREME REFUGE.

Three main paths - Yoga of meditation, Yoga of knowledge and Yoga of action- were referred to in the previous verse. In this verse Yoga of worship is described. This path is shown to those who could not adopt any of the aforesaid three methods.

Some people listen with intense faith to the teachings of the spiritual preceptors regarding the Self. Solely depending upon their advice and worship according to their advice they attain immortality. Some study books and adhere with faith the teachings contained therein and live according to them. They also overcome death. Whichever path one follows, one eventually attains liberation from birth and death. The various paths exist only to suit the aspirants of different temperaments and equipments, the ultimate goal being the same.

Here death does not mean what happens to the physical body but the principle of change. When we identify with the body, the experiences can only be of the finite. To experience the Infinite is to enter the state of immortality which is beyond death.

yaavat sanjaayate kinchit Sattvam sthaavarajangamam
kshetrakshetrajnasamyogaat tadviddhi bharatarshabha // 13.27 //

WHEREVER ANY BEING IS BORN, THE UNMOVING OR THE MOVING, KNOW YOU, O BEST OF THE BHARATA, THAT IT IS FROM THE UNION BETWEEN THE FIELD AND THE KNOWER OF THE FIELD.

All life is commerce between Self and not-Self.
- Dr.S.Radhakrishnan.

The union between the Field and the Knower of the Field is not of any physical kind or of any material nature but it is of mutual superimposition. It is illusory, confounding the one with the other. In every superimposition a delusion is recognized upon the substratum just like a ghost on the post. Not only all the characteristics of a ghost are projected upon the post but the post lends its existence to the non-existent ghost. As a result of their mutual union we find that the non-existent ghost comes into existence and the existing post gives place to non-existent ghost.

This trick of the human mind is called mutual superimposition which is known in Vedanta as *adhyasa*. This means false superimposition of one thing upon the other. This superimposition is due to *maya* or absence of discrimination. This unreal relationship, created by ignorance, conjures up before our vision the manifold phenomenon of the relative material world. When this confusion is cleared, bondage terminates.

In the Pure Consciousness or Supreme Soul, Paramatman or Brahman, there is no Field of the Matter. But when the Spirit starts playing in the Field it becomes the Knower of the Field (Purusha). When Purusha works in Prakriti the combination brings forth the entire phenomenal universe consisting of the moving and the unmoving. The insentient body is mistaken for the sentient Self and vice versa. This illusion disappears when one realizes the real knowledge of the Self and when one knows the distinction between the Field and the Knower of the Field.

samam sarveshu bhooteshu tishthantam parameshwaram
vinashyatswavinashyantam yah pashyati sa pashyati // 13.28 //

HE SEES WHO SEES THE SUPREME LORD EXISTING EQUALLY IN ALL BEINGS, THE UNPERISHING WITHIN THE PERISHING.

The substratum that supports all is the Supreme Lord remaining the same in all beings. Everything in this phenomenal world is subject to change and modifications - birth, growth, decay and death. The Changeless Consciousness that supports all changes is the Principle that illumines the changing world of plurality just as gold is the changeless factor in different types of ornaments which are always made and destroyed to make new ones of different types. The shape and size of ornaments change but the changeless factor in them all is gold. He who recognizes the harmony of Universal Spirit in all things, from the highest deity to the grain of sand, sees and becomes universal. The same divine spirit dwells in all. The difference between one object and another from the relative standpoint lies in the degree of manifestation of the Spirit in it. In a Saint, the Spirit is highly manifested while in a lowly object the spirit is hidden.

samam pashyan hi sarvatra samavasthitameeshwaram
na hinastyaatmanaatmaanam tato yaati paraam gatim // 13.29 //

BECAUSE HE WHO SEES THE SAME LORD EVERYWHERE EQUALLY DWELLING, DOES NOT DESTROY THE SELF BY THE SELF; THEREFORE, HE GOES TO THE HIGHEST GOAL.

He does not destroy the Self by the self: In Chapter 6.5 & 6 it was explained as to when the self becomes the enemy of the Self. Whenever the lower egocentric personality is not available for guidance by the higher wisdom the lower becomes the enemy for the higher in us. Such an ignorant man destroys the Self by identifying himself with the body and the modifications of the mind and by not seeing the immortal Self in all beings.

In an individual who recognizes and experiences the one Parameswara everywhere the lower cannot overshadow the higher. Such a sage does not destroy the Self by the self. To rediscover the spiritual Reality, the Supreme Lord, in this world of change and sorrow is to end all agitations.

He goes to the highest goal: The mutual conflict between the lower and the higher personality is due to non-apprehension of the Reality or due to mis-apprehension arising out of non-apprehension. Because of this lack of understanding, we do not recognize the one Eternal Divine everywhere and identify ourselves with the body and the mind and thereby feel that they alone are real. Consequently, we come to the conclusion that sensuality, materialistic pursuits and selfish satisfactions are the only goals worth pursuing in life. Hence The Lord says that when both these non-apprehension and mis-apprehension are ended that Absolute experience is the experience of the highest goal and therefore, 'He goes to the highest'.

prakrityaiva cha karmaani kriyamaanaani sarvashah
yah pashyati tathaatmaanam akartaaram sa pashyati // 13.30 //

HE SEES WHO SEES THAT ALL ACTIONS ARE PERFORMED BY PRAKRITI ALONE AND LIKEWISE THAT THE SELF IS NOT THE DOER.

Prakriti alone performs all actions: Actions depend upon the quality of the matter. If the mind is evil, actions arising out of it cannot be good. The Self is perfect and there is no desire in it. Where there are no desires, there is no action. He who recognizes the Imperishable amidst the perishable is the right perceiver. He alone sees who sees. The true Self is not the doer but only the witness. It is the spectator, not the actor. Actions affect the mind and understanding and not the Self.

REALIZATION OF THE UNITY OF EXISTENCE LEADS TO THE ATTAINMENT OF BRAHMAN

yadaa bhootaprithagbhaavam ekastham anupashyati
tata eva cha vistaaram brahma sampadyate tadaa // 13.31 //

WHEN A MAN SEES THE WHOLE VARIETY OF BEINGS AS CENTERED IN THE ONE AND FROM THAT ONE ALONE THEY SPREAD OUT, HE THEN ATTAINS BRAHMAN.

To know that the Self is the ultimate Truth behind names and forms is only half knowledge. It can become complete only when we understand how the multiplicity of names and forms arise from the Self and spread to become the Universe. When the variety of nature and its development are traced to the Eternal One, we assume eternity. He realizes the all pervading nature of the Self, because the cause of all limitation has been destroyed by the knowledge of unity with Brahman.

The Chhandogya Upanishad (VII.xxvi.1) says "From the Self is life, from the Self is desire, from the Self is love, from the Self is *akasa,* from the Self is light, from the Self are the waters, from the Self is the manifestation and disappearance, from the Self is the soul".

anaaditwaan nirgunatwaat paramaatmaayam avyayah
shareerasthopi kaunteya na karoti na lipyate // 13.32 //

BEING WITHOUT BEGINNING AND BEING DEVOID OF QUALITIES, THE SUPREME SELF, IMPERISHABLE, THOUGH DWELLING IN THE BODY, O KAUNTEYA, NEITHER ACTS NOR IS TAINTED.

The Spirit identifying itself with the Field becomes the knower of the Field (Purusha) and it is this individualized ego that acts and accomplishes.

'Without beginning' means 'no cause'. Every cause itself becomes an effect and an effect is the cause in a changed form. Therefore all effects are liable to change and that which changes is perishable. The Supreme Self being an uncaused cause for all that has been created has no beginning.

Having no quality or guna: That which has no change cannot have any quality since that which has qualities are substances and all substances are perishable.

Imperishable: The process of change occurring in the properties and qualities of a thing is a phenomenon of its decay. That which has no quality cannot change and that which is changeless cannot perish. Paramatman is thus Imperishable. Therefore the Beginningless, Qualityless, Imperishable Supreme Self, Paraamatman, though lives in physical body and activates the inert matter (Field) around each embodied creature into life, by Itself and in Itself, It does not act.

Neither acts nor is tainted: As the Paramatman is not the doer of any action he is not affected by the fruit of action.

A question arises here that if the Spirit dwelling in the body does not act and is not affected by the result of action, then, who is the performer or doer or agent of action and the reaper of its fruit? The answer to this riddle is that it is Prakriti that acts (Chapter 5.14). Through illusion arises the idea of the action, the actor, and the result of action. No action really exists in the Supreme Lord. From the standpoint of Reality there exists neither good nor evil. When the knowledge of the unity of the Lord and the universe is veiled by ignorance, there arise the ideas of the pairs of opposites, and also the idea of action, characterized by agency, instrument and result. e.g. from the standpoint of the desert, there is neither mirage nor water as everything is desert only; from the standpoint of the ocean there are neither waves nor foam as everything is ocean only, from the standpoint of gold, there is neither a bangle nor a necklace as everything is gold only.

This is one of the most difficult concepts in Vedanta and the seeker must reflect on this deeply to grasp it. The Lord gives some examples to illustrate the actionlessness of the Self.

yataa sarvagatam saukshmyaadaakaasham nopalipyate
sarvatraavasthito dehe tathaatmaa nopalipyate // 13.33 //

AS THE ALL PERVADING ETHER IS NOT TAINTED, BECAUSE OF ITS SUBTLETY, SO TOO THE SELF THAT IS PRESENT IN EVERY BODY DOES NOT SUFFER ANY TAINT.

As the all pervading Akasa (ether, space) is not soiled: Akasa means the concept of pure space. It is the subtlest of all gross elements and hence pervades everything that is grosser than it. Space being subtle, it allows everything to remain in it and yet nothing that it contains can contaminate it. The Supreme Self which is the cause of the very Akasa and therefore is subtler than Akasa. Hence It pervades all and nothing pervades It. It cannot be contaminated by anything that exists or is happening in the world of plurality.

As the waters of the mirage cannot drench the desert, the world of plurality - the domain of matter and its activities - cannot contaminate the Eternal. The Self, though permeates and pervades the whole body, is not soiled by its virtuous or vicious actions just as space does not get dirtied by the things accommodated under it.

yathaa prakaashayatyekah kritsnam lokamimam ravih
kshetram kshetree tathaa kritsnam prakaashayati bhaarata // 13.34 //

JUST AS THE ONE SUN ILLUMINATES THE WHOLE WORLD, SO ALSO THE LORD OF THE FIELD (PARAMATMAN) ILLUMINES THE WHOLE WORLD, O BHARATA.

The exact relationship of Consciousness, the Eternal Principle of Life, with matter and its various expressions is explained here. The example given by The Lord for the purpose is the one sun which illumines the entire world at all times. Just as the sun, the Consciousness merely illumines the world of objects, the body, the mind and the intellect.

Lighting of the world by the sun is not an activity undertaken by him for achieving any purpose. On the other hand light itself is the very nature of the sun and in his light everything gets illumined. Similarly, the nature of Consciousness is awareness and in Its presence everything becomes known i.e., illumined. The sun illumines everything, good and bad, beautiful and ugly, virtue and vice etc. So too, in our inner life Consciousness functions through body equipments and illumines them but never gets contaminated by the actions of the body or by the emotions of the mind or by the thoughts of the intellect.

kshetrakshetrjnayorevamantaram jnaanachakshushaa
bhootaprakritimoksham cha ye vidur yaanti te param // 13.35 //

THEY, WHO BY THE EYE OF WISDOM PERCEIVE THE DISTINCTION BETWEEN KSHETRA AND KSHETRAJNA AND OF THE LIBERATION OF THE BEING FROM PRAKRITI, GO TO THE SUPREME.

It was explained that the Spirit is the illuminator. It cannot be tainted by the qualities of the illumined. Sri Krishna now concludes that man's life is fulfilled only when he with his discrimination meditates upon and realizes the constitution of and relationship between the Field, the Knower of the Field and the Supreme Self in himself. This can be achieved through the eye of wisdom or intuition which is opened up by meditation, study of scriptures or teachings of the preceptors. One who realizes this is liberated and attains eternal freedom.

Thus it has been very clearly and emphatically laid down in the Bhagavad Gita that the means of deliverance from maya or ignorance are meditation, renunciation and other spiritual disciplines.

om tat sat iti srimadbhagavadgeetaasu upanishatsu brahma vidyaayaam yogashaastre sri krishnaarjuna samvaade kshetra kshetrajna vibhaaga yogo naama trayodasho'dhyaayah ||

THUS IN THE UPANISHADS OF THE GLORIOUS BHAGAVAD GITA, THE SCIENCE OF THE ETERNAL, THE SCRIPTURE OF YOGA, THE DIALOGUE BETWEEN SRI KRISHNA AND ARJUNA, ENDS THE THIRTEENTH DISCOURSE ENTITLED "THE YOGA OF DISTINCTION BETWEEN THE FIELD AND THE KNOWER OF THE FIELD"

AN OUTLINE VIEW OF THIS CHAPTER

Some editions of Gita omit the first verse of this chapter containing Arjuna's query seeking clarification on certain philosophic terms on the ground that it is a later interpolation in the text. But its inclusion is more appropriate in view of the context of the question raised by Arjuna. Krishna answers the query of Arjuna through the entire chapter. A significant contribution of this chapter is the enumeration of twenty qualities of a jnani (enlightened peerson) on the lines of the listing of thirtyfive qualities of a Bhakta in the previous chapter. This chapter concludes by showing the way towards realisation of the Self and how with the Eye of Wisdom one can liberte himself.

I - KSHETRA (FIELD) AND KSHETRAJNA (KNOWER OF THE FIELD) - VERSES 1 – 7

Arjuna sought clarification on certain philosophic terms viz., *prakrti and purusha, kshetra and kshetrajna, jnana and jneya.* Krishna explains the meaning and significance of these terms one by one. The important point to note is that Kshetra is the field, seat, body in which Kshetrajna, the Knowing Principle, the supreme being functions. Krishna declares Himself the supreme, Godhead in all beings.

II - TWENTY QUALITIES OF A JNANI, ENLIGHTENED PERSON - VERSE 8 – 12

Twenty qualities of a jnani, the enlightened person, are enumerated now. After describing these qualities, the Lord concludes by stating that these qualities per se constitute jnana, pure knowledge. A person who lives these values is endowed with Knowledge.

III - JNEYA THAT WHICH IS TO BE KNOWN - VERSES 13 – 19

Krishna states the jneya, the supreme knowledge, the ultimate goal where all human pursuits culminate. Having gained that ultimate knowledge the seeker attains immortality and becomes one with brahman. The Lord describes the supreme Brahman in the language of contradictions.

IV - PRAKRTI, MATTER AND PURUSHA, SPIRIT - VERSES 20 – 24

Prakrti, matter and Purusha, spirit are elaborated in these verses. Matter functions with several modifications and qualities while spirit functioning through them all is but one and the same. The union of spirit with matter produces a living being. The supreme Self, being the same, expresses differently in different individuals. The Self assumes the position of a witness in evil-doers, whereas in a true seeker It seems to permit and fufil whatever he does. When he continues further on the spiritual path, the Self supports him to enjoy the world and command power. Utimately, the spirit reveals Iself as his supreme Self.

V - WAY TO REALISE THE SELF - VERSES 25 – 31

The path to Self-realisation begins with action, passing through knowledge, it ends in meditation. Those who cannot pursue the path all by themselves can still reach the Self by surrendering to and following a spiritual master. Spiritual growth is marked by recognising the homogeneous principle in the heterogeneous variety of beings. Perceivng the Imperishable in the perishable world, the seeker realises

Brahman as the substratum in the diversified existence of all beings. He becomes one eith Brahman.

VI - WITH EYE OF WISDOM LIBERATE YOURSELF - VERSES 32 – 35

The supreme Self within does not act; nor is It tainted by the actions of beings. It remains ever immaculate like space which is never polluted by the different objects occupying it. He who recognises the supreme Self in the manifold beings is endowed with jnanachakshu, the Eye of Wisdom, with which he perceives the Supreme.

<<<000>>>

CHAPTER 14

Gunatraya Vibhaaga Yogah:

Yoga of the Division of the three Gunas

PREAMBLE

This Chapter explains why the same Spirit when expressed through matter manifests itself in different ways. Although the same water is poured in different bottles, it will look different not because of the water but because of the color of the glass out of which the bottles were made. Similarly, the one Eternal Principle expresses itself differently in various matter equipments as different individuals even though the elements constituting matter are the same. This is due to *Gunas* born of *Prakriti.*

Gunas indicate not the properties of a material but the attitude with which the mind functions. These attitudes are three in number viz. *Sattva* - Unactivity, *Rajas* - Activity and *Tamas* - Inactivity. These three qualities influence the mind and intellect of every individual in different proportions at different times. Although all these three Gunas are always present in everybody their proportions differ from individual to individual. It is these diversities that differentiate one person from the other in character, conduct and behavior etc.

The three Gunas – *sattva, rajas* and *tamas* – together constitute every human being. Sattva is stainless, pure and brilliant. When this predominates over the other two Gunas, a person's wisdom shines in his expression. Rajas is of the nature of passion which creates a craving for what you do not have and attachment to what you possess. When this Guna dominates over the other two, the person develops greed, becomes involved in endless activity and suffers from mental unrest. Tamas arises out of ignorance which manifests as delusion, inertia and heedlessness. Sattva binds people through attachment to knowledge, and happiness. Rajas binds through attachment to action. Tamas binds through heedlessness, indolence and sleep.

This Chapter helps us to find out for ourselves the powerful tendencies that rule our minds (influence of Gunas) and take remedial measures wherever called for. A seeker who recognizes the influence under which he is forced to function at different times can take timely steps to arrest the wrong impulses, unethical urges and animal tendencies in order to keep himself fully under self-control and equanimous in all situations in life. The discussion is concluded with a description of the person who has risen above the Gunas and realized God. As this Chapter is entirely dealing with the nature and working of the Gunas as also the methods to give up all connections with them, it is entitled as "Yoga of the Division of the three Gunas".

In the previous Chapter the Lord stated that the attachment to the three Gunas alone was responsible for one's repeated birth in good and evil wombs (13.22). This statement will raise questions about diverse characteristics of the Gunas, how they bind the Jivatma to the body, the result of such attachment, the means of ridding oneself of the three Gunas and the marks and conduct of the soul who has given up such attachments.

Krishna personifying Brahman elucidates all these points. The Chapter concludes with a detailed exposition on the most important philosophic concept of the embodied transcending the Gunas and becoming Brahman.

Bhagawan Sri Krishna assures that a seeker can reach that exalted state through unswerving yoga of devotion to Him, thereby crossing the Gunas and reaching the Abode of the immortal, immutable Brahman. This is the state of eternal righteousness, absolute bliss.

THE TEXT

THE HIGHEST KNOWLEDGE

sri bhagavaan uvaacha
param bhooyah pravakshyaami jnaanaanaam jnaanamuttamam
yajjnaatwaa munayah sarve paraam siddhimito gataah // 14.1 //

SRI BHAGAVAN SAID
I WILL AGAIN EXPOUND THAT SUPREME KNOWLEDGE, THE MOST EXALTED OF ALL FORMS OF KNOWLEDGE, AND BY KNOWING WHICH ALL THE SAGES HAVE ATTAINED THE SUPREME PERFECTION AFTER PASSING FROM THIS WORLD.

The subject matter of this chapter is that supreme knowledge which is above all other knowledge. It deals with the behavior of man and the different influences that play on his subtle body in life. It is the highest knowledge in as much as without a correct understanding of this theme, self observation and analysis as also timely self-correction will be impossible on the spiritual path.

Having known which all the Munis have attained the highest perfection: On understanding this knowledge and learning about the real goal of life, men of reflection and contemplation have reached perfection. Reaching perfection indicates that with the aid of the exhaustive knowledge about the Gunas, men can foresee the obstacles and dangers on the way of spiritual attainment and prepare themselves to face them effectively.

After passing from this world: This does not mean that perfection can be attained only after death. It means that perfection can be gained here and now after shedding our egocentric misconceptions of life. Through right reflection and true understanding our false values of life end and in the newly found wisdom a better quality of life can be lived. Perfection out of imperfection all around is achieved through constant contemplation.

idam jnaanam upaashritya mama saadharmyamaagataah
sargepi nopajaayante pralaye na vyathanti cha // 14.2 //

THEY WHO, HAVING TAKEN REFUGE IN THIS KNOWLEDGE, HAVE ATTAINED TO MY BEING ARE NEITHER BORN AT THE TIME OF CREATION NOR ARE THEY DISTURBED AT THE TIME OF DISSOLUTION.

Sri Krishna says that he who has correctly understood the significance of this Chapter can reach the state of Perfection i.e. 'Attain My Being'. Perfection is a state of awakening to a different level of Consciousness. When we go to sleep we become one with the sleeper leaving aside the waking personality. Similarly, on realizing the Self we cross over the body, mind and intellect and become one with the Spiritual Nature.

The sorrows and joys of one plane of consciousness do not extend to another plane. A seeker who could control his mind and reach beyond the ordinary realms of consciousness through meditation cannot come back to his previous state of sorrows and joys when he used to identify himself with the body, the matter. An individual ego when it rises above its own conditions rediscovers itself to be the Omnipotent Reality which knows no creation and dissolution. Thus such a saved soul achieves the *samana dharmata* or similarity of the quality and not the *svarupata* or identity of the Supreme Lord.

Let us awake into that heaven of freedom from all agitations and imperfections, where the mind is free by realizing the divine in our outer consciousness with the help of the knowledge of the Gunas,

mama yonirmahadbrahma tasmin garbham dadhaamyaham
sambhavah sarvabhootaanaam tato bhavati bhaarata // 14.3 //

MY WOMB IS THE GREAT BRAHMAN (PRAKRITI); IN THAT I PLACE THE SEED; FROM THERE, O BHARATA, IS THE BIRTH OF ALL BEINGS.

The Field and the knower of the Field are the two aspects of Prakriti, Matter. Both of them function on the substratum, the Absolute. When the Supreme functions in the Field He becomes the enjoyer of the Field and therefore the Knower of the field. When detached from the Field, He becomes Pure Absolute Consciousness.

The Lord is the Father and the Mother of the universe. Matter and Spirit are His two aspects which are inherent in Him. As the Father or the Supreme Soul He casts the seed; as the Mother or nature, or matter or prakriti, He receives the seed. From the embryo thus formed, which is termed as *Hiranyagarbha,* are produced all created beings.

This verse affirms that all existence is a manifestation of the Divine. He is the cosmic seed. With reference to this world, He becomes Hiranyagarbha, the cosmic egg. The world is the play of the Infinite on the Finite. It is the development of the form on the non-being. The forms of all things which arise out of the abysmal void are derived from God. They are the seeds He casts into non-being.

sarvayonishu kaunteya moortayah sambhavanti yaah
taasaam brahma mahadyoniraham beejapradah pitaa // 14.4 //

WHATEVER FORMS ARE PRODUCED, O KAUNTEYA, IN ANY WOMB, THE GREAT BRAHMAN IS THEIR WOMB, I THE SEED GIVING FATHER.

In all wombs: In the whole Universe every second innumerable births are taking place. Birth of a new organism is the expression of Spirit through a given matter envelopment. Viewed thus, every matter particle is the womb which when dynamised by the Light of Consciousness becomes a potential living being. Thus every expression of life is matter combined with Spirit. Hence Sri Krishna, the Supreme Consciousness, says that He is the Father of the entire Universe. A Field in itself has no existence without the Knower of the Field vitalizing it. Body, mind and intellect are mere inert matter till Consciousness enlivens them.

GOODNESS, PASSION, AND DULLNESS

Sattvam rajastama iti Gunaah prakritisambhavaah
nibadhnanti mahaabaaho dehe dehinamavyayam // 14.5 //

THE THREE MODES (GUNAS) PURITY, PASSION AND DULLNESS BORN OF NATURE (PRAKRITI) BIND FAST IN THE BODY, O MIGHTY-ARMED, THE IMPERISHABLE DWELLER IN THE BODY (THE EMBODIED SOUL).

The main theme of the Chapter starts now wherein Sri Krishna explains what the Gunas are and how they bind the Spirit within matter to create individualized Ego sense in us. Sattva has the characteristic of effulgence. It is harmony, goodness or purity. Rajas is passion or activity. Tamas is inertia or dullness. These three qualities indicate the triple mentality which produces attachment in the individual Self, delude It and bind It down to the worldly life.

Just as childhood, youth and old age are found in the same body these three Gunas are found in the same mind. The individual Self gets identified with the body and the three qualities and thereby it feels the changes in the body as Its own changes. It becomes subject to sorrows and joys of the body till it realizes its identity with the Supreme Self. This delusion is on account of the influence of the Gunas. When the soul identifies itself with the modes of nature, it forgets its own reality and uses the mind, life and body for the egoistic satisfaction.

Gunas are not merely qualities but they are the primary constituents of nature. They are the base for all substances. They are the three different influences under which every human mind expresses itself in a variety of ways at different moments of changing environments.

If water in a vessel is stirred, the sun reflected in that water also appears to be agitated. So too, the pure Supreme Self appears to be bound by the three qualities of Nature through superimposition. In reality the Self is ever free and untainted and beyond them.

The Gunas depend for their existence on the Knower of the Field whom they bind very fast. The knowledge of Gunas is therefore necessary to come out of their clutches. These three Gunas are always present in all human beings and none is free from them. However, they are not always constant; every time any one of them will be predominant.

One should analyze all phenomena in terms of these three modes of nature and know their characteristics. One should stand as a witness of these qualities but must not identify with them. Rising above these Gunas one should become Gunatita and attain supreme peace, immortality and eternal bliss.

NATURE OF SATTVA, RAJAS & TAMAS AND THE WAY THEY BIND

tatra Sattvam nirmalatwaat prakaashakam anaamayam
sukhasangena badhnaati jnaanasangena chaanagha // 14.6 //

OF THESE, SATTVA, THE LUMINOUS, FREE FROM EVIL AND BECAUSE OF ITS UNBLEMISHNESS, BINDS, O SINLESS ONE, BY ATTACHMENT TO HAPPINESS AND BY ATTACHMENT TO KNOWLEDGE.

Gunas cannot be defined directly without explaining their symptoms and processes. In the following verses a description of the mind under the influence of each of the three Gunas is given by describing the type of emotions, thoughts and behavior that emanate from the mind-intellect equipment.

Luminous, free from evil and unblemished:

Under the influence of Sattva, it being pure and hence luminous and without any blemish, the mind is steady and will constantly reflect on the Self. Though Sattva is thus the most Divine mental attitude, still it binds us and limits our spiritual nature.

It binds us by attachment to happiness and knowledge:

When the mind is cleansed from all its agitations and evil thoughts the seeker achieves greater inward peace, happiness, better understanding and intellectual comprehension.

Sattva does not rid us of the ego-sense. It also causes desire though for noble objects. The Self which is free from all attachments is here attached to happiness and knowledge. Happiness and knowledge are attributes of mind, which is form of matter. They belong to the category of the object and pertain to the *kshetra*. The Self which is of the nature of freedom and totally unattached, becomes bound by identification with matter. This is how sattva binds a soul to the world.

rajo raagaatmakam viddhi trishnaasangasamudbhavam
tannibadhnaati kaunteya karmasangena dehinam // 14.7 //

KNOW RAJAS TO BE OF THE NATURE OF PASSION, GIVING RISE TO THIRST AND ATTACHMENT; IT BINDS FAST, O KAUNTEYA, THE EMBODIED ONE BY ATTACHMENT TO ACTION.

Now the characteristics of Rajas are described. When the influences of Rajo Guna predominate, the mind gets full of passions. Passion denotes urges, desires, emotions and feelings. These fall under two categories viz. desires and attachments which are said to be the very sources of passion.

Passion gives rise to thirst and attachment: Thirst means insatiable desire. A human personality longs for the satisfaction of any desire that grows in him. Satisfaction of one kind of desire leads to attachment to the object desired. Desire is the mental relationship towards the objects that have not been possessed and attachment is the mental dependence on the objects so acquired.

Bind by attachment to action: When the Rajas predominates innumerable desires originate for things not acquired and deepest attachment sets in for things already possessed.

To fulfill the demands made by these two, one should necessarily undertake endless actions earning, spending, saving, procuring, protecting and thirsting for more all the time. Goaded by anxiety to possess more and to prevent from losing what he already has he has to act in many spheres. Thus he enters into a whirlpool of successes and failures arising out of his own actions.

Actions emanate from passions and passions arise out of desires and attachments all of which are the symptoms of the predominance of Rajo Guna on the mind. If Sattva Guna binds one with anxieties for happiness and peace, wisdom and knowledge, Rajo Guna binds him to inexhaustible actions. Thus though the Self is not acting, Rajas makes him act with the idea that 'I am the doer'.

tamastwajnaanajam viddhi mohanam sarvadehinaam
pramaadaalasyanidraabhis tannibadhnaati bhaarata // 14.8 //

AND KNOW TAMAS TO BE BORN OF IGNORANCE, DELUDING ALL EMBODIED BEINGS, IT BINDS FAST, O BHARATA, BY MIS-COMPREHENSION, INDOLENCE AND SLEEP.

Now the discussion is about tamas.

Born out of ignorance: Under the influence of Tamo Guna a man's discriminatory capacity gets blunted and he gets deluded. The Lord says that Tamas in a human personality binds us to a lower nature with endless mis-comprehensions about the goal of life. In such a stupefied state one lives in indolence heedless of the higher purposes in life. Such a person practically lives in sleep; he has neither any goal in life nor any nobility in action.

So far the symptoms observable in the mind when it is influenced by these three Gunas have been described. They not only bring about different degrees of responses in an individual but also bind the Eternal Self to feel and act as if It were limited and conditioned by the matter envelopments.

Sattvam sukhe sanjayati rajah karmani bhaarata
jnaanamaavritya tu tamah pramaade sanjayatyuta // 14.9 //

SATTVA ATTACHES TO HAPPINESS AND RAJAS TO ACTION, O BHARATA, WHILE TAMAS, VERILY, SHROUDING KNOWLEDGE ATTACHES TO MIS-COMPREHENSION.

The ideas of previous 3 verses are summarized and repeated here. Sattva makes us attached to the inward happiness arising from life fully lived. Rajas makes one passionate, thirsty of desires and deep attachments in fulfilling of which one perforce has to undertake endless actions. Tamas conceals right judgment and knowledge of the Self in us. It results in indiscrimination and creates attachment to wrong comprehensions.

HOW THE GUNAS FUNCTION?

rajastamashchaabhibhooya Sattvam bhavati bhaarata
rajah Sattvam tamaishchaiva tamah Sattvam rajastathaa
// 14.10 //

O BHARATA, SATTVA ARISES PREDOMINATING OVER RAJAS AND TAMAS; LIKEWISE RAJAS (PREVAILS) OVERPOWERING SATTVA AND TAMAS; SO TAMAS (PREVAILS) OVER SATTVA AND RAJAS.

The question whether these three Gunas act on the mind all at a time or each separately at different points of time is answered here. The Lord says that these Gunas act at different times - each one of them becoming powerful at any one point of time. At a given time human personality works under the influence of one predominant Guna when the other two Gunas get subdued but not totally absent.

Thus when Sattva predominates over Rajas and Tamas it produces on the mind its own nature of happiness and knowledge; when Rajas predominates over the other two it produces passions, desires, attachments and actions. When Tamas is prominent over Sattva and Rajas it shrouds discrimination and makes the mind unaware of its nobler duties.

sarvadwaareshu dehesmin prakaasha upajaayate
jnaanam yadaa tadaa vidyaadvivriddham Sattvamityuta
// 14.11 //

WHEN THROUGH EVERY GATE (SENSE ORGANS) IN THIS BODY, THE LIGHT OF INTELLIGENCE SHINES, THEN IT MAY BE KNOWN THAT SATTVA IS PREDOMINANT.

In this and next two verses the symptoms are explained by understanding which their sources i.e. Gunas can be known. The sense organs through which the body receives the stimuli from the external world are termed the gates of the body. Through these gates the light of awareness illumines the objects of the world like power of vision from the eyes, power of hearing for the ears etc. Each beam of light emanating from each gate illumines one aspect of the world outside.

When there is

- unruffled peace of mind,
- inner harmony,
- perfect serenity and tranquility,
- clarity of vision and
- penetrative insight

then we should understand that Sattva predominates.

When Sattva predominates ears refuse to hear improper sounds, eyes will not see undesirable sights, tongue avoids anything not proper and mind is not attracted towards sensual objects. If there is increase of Sattva there is increase of knowledge.

lobhah pravrittir aarambhah karmanaamashamah sprihaa
rajasyetaani jayante vivriddhe bharatarshabha // 14.12 //

GREED, ACTIVITY, THE UNDERTAKING OF ACTIONS, RESTLESSNESS, LONGING - THESE ARISE WHEN RAJAS IS PREDOMINANT, O BEST OF THE BHARATAS.

Sri Krishna enumerates the important qualities of the mind when Rajas dominates it.

- Greed - desire to appropriate the property of another.
- Activity - all activities motivated by selfish desires.
- Restlessness - lack of enjoyment and quietitude.

These three are interconnected and one succeeds the other in their impact. Greed leads to selfish activity, activity leads to unrest over the results of such activities. When one is completely subjugated by Rajas he feels inexhaustible longing for objects.

Aprakaasho'pravrittishcha pramaado moha eva cha
tamasyetaani jaayante vivriddhe kurunandana // 14.13 //

DARKNESS, INERTNESS, MIS-COMPREHENSION AND DELUSION - THESE ARISE WHEN TAMAS IS PREDOMINANT, O DESCENDENT OF KURU.

The symptoms when Tamas predominates are given now.

- Darkness - a condition in which intellect is not capable of arriving at any decision.
- Inertness - sense of incapacity to undertake any endeavor and lack of enthusiasm to achieve anything in the world.

- Mis-comprehension - Incapacity to respond to good or bad and miscalculation of one's relationship with others around. Delusion - when such a person fails to understand the outside world he is always deluded.

EFFECTS OF GUNAS

yadaa sattwe pravriddhe tu pralayam yaati dehabrit
tadottamavidaam lokaan amalaan pratipadyate // 14.14 //

IF THE EMBODIED ONE MEETS DEATH WHEN SATTVA IS PREDOMINANT THEN HE ATTAINS TO THE SPOTLESS WORLDS OF THE KNOWERS OF THE HIGHEST.

Sri Krishna now gives an idea as to the direction in which the mental equipment of the dead would reach soon after death. There is always a continuity of thought in this life. Today's thoughts are an extension of yesterday's thinking and the thoughts of tomorrow will be conditioned by today's thinking. On the same analogy the type of thoughts entertained during one's life time will determine the type of thoughts that will follow after death also. So if the Sattva Guna is dominant at the time of death one attains the highest realm of abundant joy.

rajasi pralayam gatwaa karmasangishu jaayate
tathaa praleenastamasi moodha yonishu jaayate // 14.15 //

MEETING DEATH IN RAJAS, HE IS BORN AMONG THOSE ATTACHED TO ACTION; DYING IN TAMAS, HE IS BORN IN THE WOMB OF THE SENSELESS.

If the mind is under the influence of Rajas at the time it leaves the body, it takes the embodiment among those who are attached to action. It means that the mind will seek an appropriate field to exhaust the existing tendencies or vasanas at the time of death. Similarly, when one dies when Tamas is dominant one reaches the realm of irrational beings such as animal or vegetable kingdom.

karmanah sukritasyaahuh saattwikam nirmalam phalam
rajasastu phalam duhkham ajnaanam tamasah phalam // 14.16 //

THE FRUIT OF GOOD ACTION, THEY SAY, IS SATTVIC AND PURE; VERILY THE FRUIT OF RAJAS IS PAIN AND IGNORANCE IS THE FRUIT OF TAMAS.

In this verse The Lord summarizes what He told in the previous verses. The results obtained by living in the three Gunas are given here.

- Sattva: If one lives a quiet and good life of service, devotion, of love and kindness, of mercy and compassion, it indicates the Sattvic nature of his mind. He achieves inward purity.

- Rajas: Leading a life full of desires and continuous actions to satisfy them always results in sorrows and pain.

- Tamas: Dullness in actions, lack of discriminating capacity and absence of understanding leading to ignorance is the fruit of Tamas.

Sattvaat sanjaayate jnaanam rajaso lobha eva cha
pramaadamohau tamaso bhavato'jnaanameva cha // 14.17 //

FROM SATTVA ARISES WISDOM, FROM RAJAS GREED, MIS-CONCEPTION AND DELUSION AND FROM TAMAS IGNORANCE ARISE.

When Sattva is predominant the intellect is enlightened and knowledge awakened. Rajas creates insatiable cravings, makes one to ignore the feelings of others and breeds selfish acquisitiveness. Tamas brings forth incapacity to perceive rightly the world outside and eliminates the power to right judgment.

oordhwam gacchanti Sattvasthaa madhye tishthanti raajasaah
jaghanyaGunavrittisthaa adho gacchanti taamasaah // 14.18 //

THOSE WHO ARE ABIDING IN SATTVA GO UPWARDS, THE RAJASIC DWELL IN THE MIDDLE AND THE TAMASIC ABIDING IN THE FUNCTION OF THE LOWEST GUNAS GO DOWNWARDS.

- Go upwards: Those who are living a pure life of discrimination, clear thinking, right judgment and self-discipline cultivate more and more Sattva qualities in themselves. When the mind is thus quiet it evolves to a higher level.
- Dwell in the middle: Those of Rajasic nature, with all their desires and agitations, ambitions and achievements again and again manifest as human beings till they acquire the required purity.
- Go downwards: Those of Tamasic nature that are full of misconceptions and deluded in their own lust and passions devolve themselves into the lower natures.

This verse repeats the ideas expressed in the verse which explained the continuity of existence even after death. It is made clear that all the three Gunas bind man to attachment; including Sattva which binds us to knowledge and happiness. Then the question is when will man become free from the contacts of the pluralistic world to attain Godhood?

So far we were told the nature of the Gunas the symptoms from which the predominant Guna could be identified, their reactions on our life and how they affect our future etc. It was also told that we get the predominant Guna from our past which influences the present which in turn determines the future. All these are the causes for the bondage arising out of the Self in us getting identified with the matter vestures surrounding it.

There can be release from these bondages only when we transcend all the Gunas. The three Gunas may be in different proportions present in each one of us but the true release comes not only when all the Gunas are transcended but also when we are established in the Spiritual Experience. This process of escaping ourselves from the subjective shackles on our psychological and intellectual nature is called Liberation or Moksha.

In the subsequent verses the path of liberation is described and the Moksha gained from the right judgment of the world outside is explained.

TRANSCENDING ALL THE GUNAS, A *GUNATITA*

naanyam gunebhyah kartaaram yadaa drashtaanupashyati
gunebhyashcha param vetti madbhaavam so'dhigacchati
// 14.19 //

WHEN THE SEER BEHOLDS NO AGENT OTHER THAN THE GUNAS AND KNOWS THAT WHICH IS HIGHER THAN THE GUNAS, HE ATTAINS TO MY BEING.

The Spirit identifying itself with the mind-intellect equipment gets conditioned by the three Gunas. To stand apart from the mind, without our identification with it, is the freedom from our thought entanglement.

- When the seer beholds: The art of disentangling ourselves from our own thought process within is the very art of meditation. A meditator would experience subjectively the state of Pure Knowledge undisturbed by the thoughts. The word 'behold' does not mean that God can be seen in the physical sense. God is not an object of our perception or feeling or thought. He is the 'subject' that perceives, feels and thinks through us. Hence the word 'behold' indicates that the subjective experience will be total beyond any doubt.
- No agent other than the Gunas: The experiencer realizes that he is not only the Infinite but also the Gunas, which transform themselves into the bodies, senses and sense objects and which in all their modifications constitute the agent in all actions.
- Knows that which is higher than the Guans: The mind cannot function on its own accord since it is inert. The Consciousness that functions through the mind is the Principle other than the mind. The Consciousness reflecting on the mind is the 'agent', the individualized ego (Jiva) in us. He who has understood that what is reflected is something other than the mind and therefore something higher

than the Gunas is the one who crossed over all the limitations.

- He attains to My Being: An individual who has thus transcended his own mind and intellect and discovered himself to be that which is behind his mental delusion that man of wisdom becomes the Self – 'Attains to My Being'.

Gunaanetaanateetya treen dehee dehasamudbhavaan
janmamrityurjaraaduhkhair vimukto'mritamashnute // 14.20 //

THE EMBODIED ONE HAVING GONE BEYOND THESE THREE GUNAS, OUT OF WHICH THE BODY IS EVOLVED, IS FREED FROM BIRTH, DEATH, DECAY AND PAIN AND ATTAINS TO IMMORTALITY.

When we identify with Gunas we suffer the sorrows of life and when we transcend these we are free from sorrows because finitude, agitations, change are not in the Perfect Self.

Having gone beyond Gunas which comprise body: The three Gunas are the expressions of ignorance which constitute the causal body. We experience the pure causal body in deep sleep and this is nothing other than Gunas.

They emerge out from the causal body to express themselves first as subtle body, as thoughts and feelings and again as gross body to express themselves in actions. Each body (plant or animal or man) is the instrument available for the subtle body to express through. The nature and qualities of the subtle body are determined by the causal body comprising Gunas. Thus those who have gone beyond the Gunas are no more under the tragedies of the subtle and causal bodies.

The embodied one is freed from birth, death, decay and pain: Birth, growth, decay, disease and death are the qualities of the matter and they are common to all everywhere. These are the sorrows of the matter and not that of Consciousness which illumines them. One who has realized himself to be the Awareness goes beyond all the sorrows. As the sun illumines all, good and bad, Consciousness in us illumines the various changes in the matter envelopments. But these changes are not that of Spirit and therefore one who has realized oneself to be the Spirit goes beyond all these struggles.

Attains immortality: The man of realization not only experiences absence of sorrow but lives in perfection. In sleep we forget our sorrows and pain. Sleep is a temporary relief against the worldly sorrows. But the Bliss experienced at the time of realization of the Self is not temporary cessation of tragedies of matter but a positive re-awakening of our Changeless, Infinite nature. Hence it is said that one experiences the state of immortality even while living in this body embodiment.

CHARECTERISTICS OF A GUNATITA

arjuna uvaacha
kairlingaistreenGunaanetaan ateeto bhavati prabho
kimaachaarah katham chaitaamstreen Gunaanativartate // 14.21 //

ARJUNA SAID
WHAT ARE THE MARKS OF HIM WHO HAS CROSSED OVER THE THREE GUNAS O, LORD? WHAT IS HIS CONDUCT AND HOW DOES HE GO BEYOND THESE THREE GUNAS?

Arjuna asks here three specific questions.

- What are the marks by which a man who has gone beyond the influences of these three Gunas can be recognized?
- In that state of perfection what would be his relationship with the world outside and his behavior among those who are still under the influence of three Gunas?
- How does such a man of perfection conquer his inner confusions and entanglements and attains his spiritual glory?

The characteristics of perfection in whatever way it may be reached, are more or less the same as those of the Sthitaprajna (2.55..), of the Bhaktiman, devotee (12.13..).

sri bhagavaan uvaacha
prakaasham cha pravrittim cha mohameva cha paandava
na dweshti sampravrittaani na nivrittaani kangkshati // 14.22 //

SRI BHAGAVAN SAID
HE WHO DOES NOT HATE THE APPEARANCE OF LIGHT (THE EFFECT OF SATTVA), ACTIVITY (THE EFFECT OF RAJAS) AND DELUSION (THE EFFECT OF TAMAS) IN HIS OWN MIND, O PANDAVA, NOR LONGS FOR THEM WHEN ABSENT,

This answers Arjuna's first question. The man of right understanding does not hate the effects of the three Gunas when they are clearly present in his inner life; nor does he long after these when they are absent. Equanimity in all circumstances is his hallmark and inner peace independent of the environment is his strength.

Light, activity and illusion when present: These are the effects of the respective causes viz. Light - Sattva, Activity - Rajas and Illusion - Tamas. The presence or absence of these influences does not make any difference to him because he has risen above all of them. Such a man who has crossed over the mind and intellect equipment lives in the Infinite joy of the Self. He conquers the pure world of awareness and attains the state of Godhood.

Just as we pull out a thorn by a thorn, so renouncing worldly things, we must renounce renunciation. By means of Sattva we overcome Rajas and Tamas and then we get beyond Sattva itself.

udaaseenavadaaseeno Gunairyo na vichaalyate
Gunaa vartanta ityeva yo'vatishthati nengate // 14.23 //

HE WHO IS SEATED LIKE ONE UNCONCERNED, UNPERTURBED BY THE GUNAS, WHO STANDS APART, WITHOUT WAVERING, KNOWING THAT IT IS ONLY THE GUNAS THAT ACT.

Verses 23, 24 and 25 answer Arjuna's second question. They describe the one who has risen above all the Gunas. The real test of a perfect one is not in a secluded forest but in actual day to day life where he is faced with all sorts of temptations because the true nature of a man comes out only in adversities.

In all experiences in the world-good or bad- a man of steady wisdom will be as if he were unconcerned since he knows that all this is due to play of the mind and intellect. He is not agitated by anything that is happening around him. He understands that the changes in him are due to changes of the

Gunas and the world outside changes according to one's own mental conditions. He is thus fully aware of the reasons behind the changes in himself and the world around him.

In order to watch the play of Gunas in himself he should be an observer of them from something beyond the Gunas. So if he is established in Pure Spiritual Nature he will be able to observe the play of Gunas in him and surrounding him. As the observer is not affected by the thing he is observing, so too, the man of wisdom when observing the play of Gunas in himself does not get disturbed from his equanimity and ever remains in his own Divine Nature. He sees the mutations of nature but is not entangled in them. The Gunas are lifted up into pure illumination, divine activity and perfect calm.

samaduhkhasukhah swasthah samaloshtaashmakaanchanah
tulyapriyaapriyo dheeras tulyanindaatma samstutih // 14.24 //

ALIKE IN PLEASURE AND PAIN, WHO DWELLS IN THE SELF, TO WHOM A CLOD OF EARTH, STONE AND GOLD ARE ALIKE, TO WHOM THE PLEASANT AND THE UNPLEASANT ARE ALIKE, FIRM, THE SAME IN CENSURE AND PRAISE.

The equanimity and balanced personality of a Perfect Man in the midst of all situations in life is explained.

- Self-abiding: He lives in a world of his own. His mind does not react to the worldly situations.
- Alike in pairs of opposites: Pleasure and pain are the reactions of the mind and intellect to the things of the world. For the one who does not look at the world through the colored glasses of his mind every situation in life is alike.

- Earth, stone and gold: All possessions either full of value or completely valueless will have the same response. What is of value to an egocentric man is charmless to an Awakened Man.
- Pleasant and unpleasant: What is considered as dear and not dear i.e. things which are loved and things which are hated do not create any different reactions in a man of wisdom.
- Censure and praise: He is unconcerned about blame or praise. They leave no reactions in him.

These are the main conditions of life in which the ordinary man finds sorrow or joy. Pleasure and pain, good and bad possessions, agreeable and disagreeable experiences, joys and sorrows, praise and censure are the conditions of life which disturb the equanimity in man. A man of Wisdom is neutral to the influences of all these situations.

maanaapamaanayostulyastulyo mitraaripakshayoh
sarvaarambhaparityaagee Gunaateetah sa uchyate // 14.25 //

THE SAME IN HONOR AND DISHONOR, THE SAME TO FRIEND AND FOE, ABANDONING ALL UNDERTAKINGS HE IS SAID TO HAVE CROSSED BEYOND THE GUNAS.

- In honor and dishonor: One of the clear signs of perfection is equanimity in honor and dishonor. Honor and dishonor are the evaluations of the intellect that change from time to time and place to place. To the one who has crossed over the ordinary plane of egoism and vanity, roses and thorns are the same.
- Friend and foe: There is neither a friend nor an enemy to a man of wisdom. To him who has realized the

oneness of the Spirit all others are not separate but they are also in him.

Abandoning every enterprise: Desire motivated activity undertaken for one's own benefit is enterprise. Ego and egocentric desires are motivating forces behind all enterprises. The man of tranquility is not affected by ego and egocentric desires. There are no ego motivated activities for him and hence he is said to give up all initiative of action. These three verses lay down a rule of conduct for the seekers of Moksha.

HOW ONE IS FIT TO BECOME BRAHMAN?

maam cha yo'vyabhichaarena bhaktiyogena sevate
sa Gunaan samateetyai'taan brahmabhooyaaya kalpate // 14.26 //

AND HE WHO SERVES ME WITH UNSWERVING DEVOTION, HE, GOING BEYOND THE GUNAS, IS FIT FOR BECOMING BRAHMAN.

This answers Arjuna's third question. To contemplate steadily upon the Infinite Nature of the Self is to become the Self and thus end our mortal Egoism. Such a steady contemplation cannot be maintained always effectively. We are not capable of maintaining our mind in meditation all the time. Therefore Sri Krishna advises a practical method of maintaining a thought for a longer period of time through a process of dedicated service. If all the work is undertaken in a spirit of dedication and service, then work becomes worship.

This is an instance where Gita expects not only devotion to The Lord but that devotion should also be given to every day life's activities and their contacts with the others around. Such a practice of dedicated service and God-awareness stills the agitations of the mind and prepares it for intensive meditation.

Such a seeker is fit to become Brahman just as if a dreamer wants to realize the waker he becomes a waker.

brhmano hi pratishthaaham amritasya avyayasya cha
shaashwatasya cha dharmasya sukhasyaikaantikasya cha // 14.27 //

FOR, I AM THE ABODE OF BRAHMAN, THE IMMORTAL AND THE IMMUTABLE, OF EVERLASTING DHARMA AND OF ABSOLUTE BLISS.

Sri Krishna indicates in the last verse of this Chapter the nature of the state of God-consciousness; when a devotee enters this state he himself becomes the Brahman.

The Lord declares Himself as the ground of that imperishable Brahman indicating that the latter is not different from Him, who is the God, possessed of attributes and that He is not different from Brahman.

By realizing Brahman, man becomes immortal i.e., freed from the cycle of birth and death. By referring to Himself as the ground of immortality, the Lord shows that He is none other than that immortality and that attaining immortality means realizing the Lord Himself.

By declaring Himself to be the ground of eternal virtue, *shaashwatasya dharmasya,* He conveys that the reward for practicing these virtues is nothing other than the Lord Himself.

By speaking of Himself as the ground of that Bliss, the Lord shows that such everlasting supreme bliss is the same as Himself and nothing else than Him. Hence attainment of that Bliss is the same as realizing the Lord.

om tat sat iti srimadbhagavadgeetaasu upanishatsu brahma vidyaayaam yogashaastre sri krishnaarjuna samvaade Gunatraya vibhaaga yogo naama chaturdasho' dhyaayah ||

THUS IN THE UPANISHADS OF THE GLORIOUS BHAGAVAD GITA, THE SCIENCE OF THE ETERNAL, THE SCRIPTURE OF YOGA, THE DIALOGUE BETWEEN SRI KRISHNA AND ARJUNA, ENDS THE FOURTEENTH DISCOURSE ENTITLED THE YOGA OF THE DIVISION OF THE THREE GUNAS

AN OUTLINE VIEW OF THIS CHAPTER

This chapter describes how Brahman generates beings through the creator, Brahma. It explains the distinct nature of the three Gunas, qualities – sattva, rajas, and tamas. These Gunas bind beings to the world and project them into future incarnations. But the one who transcends the Gunas attains Enlightenment, becomes Brahman.

I-REALIZING BRAHMAN, SAGES TRANSCEND CREATION AND DISSOLUTION -VERSES 1 – 4

Krishna personifying Brahman promises to declare the supreme knowledge which sages have used to gain the ultimate perfection, having attained which they transcended birth and death. Brahman is the primeval source of creation. The non-apprehension of Brahman causes the birth of all beings.

II - NATURE OF SATTVA, RAJAS, AND TAMAS – GUNAS, QUALITIES. HOW THEY BIND BEINGS - VERSES 5 – 13

The three gunas – sattva, rajas and tamas – together constitute every human being. Sattva is stainless, pure and brilliant. When this predominates over the other two gunas, a person's wisdom shines in his expression. Rajas is of the nature of passion which creates a craving for what you do not have and attachment to what you possess. When this guna dominates over the other two, the person develops greed, becomes involved in endless activity and suffers from mental unrest. Tamas arises out of ignorance which manifests as delusion, inertia and heedlessness. Sattva binds people through attachment to knowledge, and happiness. Rajas binds through attachment to action. Tamas binds through heedlessness, indolence and sleep.

III - CONSEQUENT EFFECTS OF SATTVA, RAJAS AND TAMAS - VERSES 14 – 18

When a person leaves the body during the predominance of sattva, he reincarnates in a pure, clean world conducive for his further spiritual development. The mind turns pure, tranquil which adds to the promotion of sattva and by this way a seeker evolves spiritually till he gains the Absolute. When a person leaves the body during the predominance of rajas, he reincarnates in a world of frenzied action motivated by desire and enjoyment of material comforts which in turn lead him to endless sorrow and misery. Such a person does not evolve spiritually and remains entangled in the cycle of birth and death. A person dying in tamas is born in a senseless ignorant world. He becomes a slave to heedlessness and delusion falling into the depths of degradation.

IV - TRANSCENDING GUNAS THE EMBODIED BECOMES BRAHMAN - VERSES 19 – 27

Krishna declares that a seer attains the supreme Being when he transcends the gunas, thus becoming free from birth, growth, decay, disease and death. From that supreme state he keeps observing the play of gunas. Arjuna aks how a person crosses the three gunas and also wants to know how such a person conducts himself in the society thereafter. Krishna describes the one who has reached the supreme state beyond the three gunas. Rooted in the supreme Self, the Enlightened becomes a disinterested witness, sakshi, of the world. He dispassionately perceives the functioning of the gunas without any longing or aversion for any of them. He regards physical, emotional and intellectual experiences similar by maintaining perfect equanimity for all pairs of opposites. Krishna assures that a seeker can reach that exalted state through unswerving yoga of devotion to Him, thereby crossing the gunas and reaching the Abode of the immortal, immutable Brahman. This is the state of eternal righteousness, absolute bliss.

<<<000>>>

Chapter 15

Purushottama Yogah:

Yoga of the Supreme Spirit

PREAMBLE

The last six Chapters of Gita state that the ever changing finite world of multiplicity is nothing but a projection of the Infinite and that the endless painful experiences are all caused by our misapprehension of the Reality. The world of Matter and Spirit, the Field of experience and the Knower of the Field were discussed. It was proved that the Knower of the Field without the Field of experience is the Pure Consciousness, Pure Awareness which is infinite and permanent.

Upto the thirteenth chapter we get an idea that the world of matter - the Cosmos - is one homogeneous entity and the Spirit is nondual and infinite. The variations in the expressions of the same Spirit and Matter in different individuals are on account of the play of the three Gunas.

In this Chapter Sri Krishna discusses the nature of the Spirit in all its implications and explains the Unknown from the Known manifested objects of perception, emotion and thought. Infinite is defined as the Imperishable *(Akshara)* with reference to the perishable *(Kshara)* equipments of matter.

Speaking of the *Kshara Purusha (Kshetra)*, the *Akshara Purusha (Kshetrajna)* and the Supreme Person *(Brahman)*, it explains how Brahman is superior to both 'Kshara' and 'Akshara', why he is called the Supreme Person, what is the value of knowing him as the Supreme Person and how can He be realized. Hence this Chapter is entitled "Purushottama Yoga" or the Yoga of the Supreme Person or Supreme Spirit.

The previous Chapter ended with a note that to worship the Lord with undeviating love leads to liberation. But such love is not possible without detachment from the world. So the Lord begins the present discourse with a description of the World Tree in order to create in the aspirant an intense dispassion leading to love and knowledge of the Supreme Lord, Brahman.

THE TEXT

THE COSMIC TREE

sri bhagavaan uvaacha
oordhwamoolam adhahshaakham ashwattham praahur avyayam
chhandaamsi yasya parnaani yastam veda sa vedavit // 15.1 //

SRI BHAGAVAN SAID
THEY (THE SCRIPTURES) SPEAK OF THE IMPERISHABLE ASVATTA TREE (PEEPAL TREE) AS HAVING ITS ROOTS ABOVE AND BRANCHES BELOW, WHOSE LEAVES ARE THE VEDAS AND HE WHO KNOWS THIS IS THE KNOWER OF THE VEDAS.

With roots above and branches below, this world tree is eternal. It is *Samsaravriksha*, the cosmic tree. This tree of *samsara* or cosmic existence rests on a continuous series of births and deaths without beginning and end. This tree cannot be cut down except by the knowledge and experience of man's identity with Brahman.

The word 'Asvatta' means that which does not endure till the next day. The phenomenal world is compared to the Asvatta tree on account of its ever-changing nature. In an ordinary tree the roots extend downwards. But in the tree of the world the roots are stated to be above. This is because the roots are Brahman with maya (Saguna Brahman) since the Immortal Absolute (Nirguna Brahman) is beyond the category of causality and Brahman with maya is very subtle and very great and is supreme over all things.

The branches are the cosmic mind, egoism, five subtle elements and the other cosmic principles which are stated to extend downwards because as they go downward they become more and more gross.

Just as the leaves protect a tree, so the Vedas serve to protect the tree of the world. They formulate its *dharma* and *adharma* with their causes and effects and also show the way to prosperity and well-being in the relative world. The knowledge of the Vedas gives men knowledge of the gods and the cosmos and hence nothing else remains to be known beyond the tree of the world and Brahman.

adhashchordhwam prasritaastasya shaakhaa
gunapravriddhaa vishayapravaalaah
adhashcha moolaanyanusantataani
karmaanubandheeni manushyaloke // 15.2 //

ITS BRANCHES EXTEND BELOW AND ABOVE, NOURISHED BY THE GUNAS WITH SENSE OBJECTS FOR ITS TWIGS AND BELOW, IN THE WORLD OF MEN STRETCH FORTH THE ROOTS, GIVING RISE TO ACTIONS.

Upward and downward its branches spread: The flow of life in the individual is sometimes for a higher evolution but very often it is to satisfy animal nature i.e. towards a lower purpose. Thus the tree of life has its branches growing both upwards and downwards.

Nourished by the Gunas: The tendency to lead a higher or lower life is determined by the dominance of any of the three Gu nas.

Sense objects are twigs: Nodular twigs are potential branches. Sense objects *(shabda, sparsha, roopa, rasa, gandha)* are twigs because in the presence of these objects there is a tendency to throw away higher values to attain carnal satisfaction.

Downward the roots extend: When the main root of the tree is firmly fixed high above In the Absolute, the subsidiary roots grow all around including downwards in the world of men initiating action. These secondary roots are vasanas created in us as a result of our past deeds driving us for actions and reactions, good or evil, in the world. Just as the secondary roots bind the tree to the earth firmly; these actions and reactions bind the individual to the plane of likes and dislikes, gain and loss etc.

The following two verses explain how we can cut down the tree and thereby experience the pure source of the life's manifestation, the Infinite Life.

na roopamasyeha tathopalabhyate
naanto na chaadirna cha sampratishthaa
ashwatthamenam suviroodhamoolam
asangashastrena dhridhena chhitwaa // 15.3 //

ITS FORM IS NOT PERCEIVED HERE AS SUCH, NEITHER ITS END NOR ITS ORIGIN, NOR ITS EXISTENCE; HAVING CUT ASUNDER THIS FIRMLY ROOTED PEEPAL TREE WITH THE STRONG AXE OF NON-ATTACHMENT.

tatah padam tat parimaargitavyam
yasmin gataa na nivartanti bhooyah
tameva chaadyam purusham prapadye
yatah pravrittih prasritaa puraanee // 15.4 //

THEN THAT GOAL SHOULD BE SOUGHT FROM WHERE HAVING GONE NONE RETURNS AGAIN PRAYING "I SEEK REFUGE IN THAT PRIMEVAL PURUSHA FROM WHOM HAS COME FORTH THIS COSMIC PROCESS".

In order to avoid misunderstanding about the tree, The Lord says that its form is not perceived here as such. The tree of life mentioned in the previous verses represents the entire field of manifested life.

It (The Tree) starts from the ignorance of reality, ends on the realization of the Self and exists only so long as the desires function. Very few understand this implication. The strongly rooted manifested world can be cut only with non-attachment. The experience of life is known through Consciousness. If the Consciousness is withdrawn from the body, mind and intellect the perception, emotion and thought necessarily end. This removing of Consciousness from the inert body matter is detachment with which alone multiple experiences can be wiped out. Detachment from perception, emotion and thought will be nothingness.

To avoid the nothingness Sri Krishna adds that one should aspire for that goal from where there will be no return. The seeker of the Divine should withdraw more and more from the worldly perceptions, emotions and thoughts and meditate upon the Higher - the source from which the tree of life itself draws its sustenance. The method suggested to achieve this goal is to take refuge in the Primeval Purusha who is the source of all expressions of life. How one can visualize this Primeval Purusha is the theme of this chapter.

nirmaanamohaa jitasangadoshaa
adhyaatmanityaa vinivrittakaamaah
dwandwairvimuktaah sukhaduhkhasamjnair
gacchantyamoodhaah padamavyayam tat // 15.5 //

FREE FROM PRIDE AND DELUSION, VICTORIOUS OVER THE EVIL OF ATTACHMENT, DWELLING CONSTANTLY IN THE SELF, THEIR DESIRES HAVING COMPLETELY TURNED AWAY, FREED FROM THE PAIRS OF OPPOSITES KNOWN AS PLEASURE AND PAIN, THE UNDELUDED REACH THE ETERNAL GOAL.

Sri Krishna explains certain disciplines or conditions by following which one can reach the Divine experience and live a life of supreme fulfillment.

- Free from pride and delusion: Pride and erroneous judgment indicate a false sense of importance or arrogance. These qualities always create mental preoccupation to maintain them leaving no opportunity to think about the greater values.

- Evil of attachment conquered: Mere sensuous way of life is nothing but a life wasted without realizing its nobler purpose.
- Ever dwelling in the Self: Detachment from worldly objects is not possible without attachment to precious ideals as human equipment cannot function in a vacuum. However to avoid attachment to evil the seeker should divert his concentration to the Self.
- Desires completely at rest: Desire is the activity of the intellect. To discipline the intellect pleasures arising out of worldly objects should be discouraged. A mind without desire becomes calm and serene.
- Released from the pairs of opposites: Mind is the focal point at which pleasure or pain is contacted. Once the mind recognizes the pairs of opposites, it likes that which is agreeable and hates that which is disagreeable. This continuous process of liking and disliking destabilizes the mind. Hence it is advised that one should be equanimous towards the pairs of opposites.

The Lord assures that such a person reaches the eternal Goal.

MANIFESTED LIFE IS ONLY A PART

na tad bhaasayate sooryo na shashaangko na paavakah
yad gatwaa na nivartante taddhaama paramam mama // 15.6 //

NEITHER DOES THE SUN ILLUMINE THERE, NOR THE MOON, NOR THE FIRE; HAVING GONE THERE THEY NEVER RETURN; THAT IS MY SUPREME ABODE.

Neither sun nor moon nor fire illumine there: It is explained that the spiritual goal is the one having gone into which none returns. Perfection gained is never to be lost. The goal - the state of Perfection - is described here. Sun, moon and fire are sources of light by which eyes get vision. Light indicates the power of illumination for the sense organs like hearing by the ears, tasting by the tongue, feeling by the mind, thinking by the intellect etc. This is the light of Consciousness by which we become aware of all experiences.

This light of Consciousness cannot be illumined by any outside gross agents of light perceived in the world such as sun, moon and fire. In fact the very light of sun, moon and fire are the objects of consciousness. An object of perception cannot illumine the subject that perceives it since the subject and the object cannot be one and the same at any time. The awareness by which we experience our lives is the Eternal Self and to realize that Consciousness is the goal of life.

My Supreme Abode: On transcending the agitations of the mind and intellect one reaches the state of Consciousness which is the Abode of the Divine. Once this state is attained the seeker is assured by The Lord that there is no risk of sliding back to the world of plurality '(to which having gone none returns)'.

THE LORD AS THE LIFE OF THE UNIVERSE

mamaivaamsho jeevaloke jeevabhootah sanaatanah
manah shashthaaneendriyaani prakritisthaani karshati // 15.7 //

A FRAGMENT OF MY OWN SELF, HAVING BECOME A LIVING SOUL, ETERNAL, IN THE WORLD OF LIFE, DRAWS

TO ITSELF THE FIVE SENSES WITH THE MIND FOR THE SIXTH, THAT REST IN NATURE.

The nature of Jiva, ego, is explained in this verse.

A portion of Myself: Although the Infinite has no parts or divisions, the Infinite when expresses through a limited entity called body, is considered limited by the ignorant, just as pot space and total space.

The eternal Jiva suffers no limitation although it undergoes pain and pleasure when it is associated with the body. Hence the Self in man is eternal Jiva.

Attracts senses: The Consciousness gives life to the entire body and maintains the sense faculties and mental capacities around itself. The power of seeing, hearing etc. is really the power of Consciousness functioning through the sense organs. Hence It is referred to as functioning with the mind and five senses. The conditioned Self is experienced as the limited ego, Jiva, the mortal, or an imaginary part of the Indivisible Whole, because of our ignorance.

The Jiva or the individual soul is that aspect of the Supreme Self which manifests itself in every one as the doer and enjoyer. It is limited because of ignorance; but in reality both (individual soul and Supreme Soul) are one and the same. It is like pot space and outer space. The pot space is a portion of the outer space and becomes one with the latter on the destruction of the pot, the cause of the limitation.

shareeram yadavaapnoti yacchaapyutkraamateeshwarah
griheetwaitaani samyaati vaayurgandhaanivaashayaat // 15.8 //

WHEN THE LORD OBTAINS A BODY AND WHEN HE LEAVES IT, HE TAKES THESE (SENSES AND MIND) AND GOES WITH THEM AS THE WIND TAKES THE SCENTS FROM THEIR SEATS (FLOWERS ETC.)

When The Lord acquires the body and leaves it: The Infinite conditioned by mind and intellect is Jiva and the Jiva takes various bodies from time to time. From the time Jiva enters the body and till it leaves i.e. constantly it keeps the sense faculties and mental impression with itself.

At death the subtle body departs from the gross body and it is left inert. Although the dead body is found to maintain its physical frame it neither has the sense faculty nor mental and intellectual capacity which it had before death. These physical, mental and intellectual expressions gave the body its individual personality and they are called subtle body. The gross body is called dead in the absence of the subtle body.

It is stated here that at death the subtle body moves off taking with itself all faculties -senses, mind and intellect - as the wind takes away the scent from its source i.e. flowers. Thus the mind is a bunch of vasanas which can exist only in Consciousness. This light of Awareness illumining the vasanas is called the Individual Personality - Jiva.

The Jiva is called The Lord here because the Individual Personality is the ruler of the body regulating all actions, feelings and thoughts.

shrotram chakshuh sparshanam cha rasanam ghraanameva cha
adhishthaaya manashchaayam vishayaanupasevate // 15.9 //

PRESIDING OVER THE EAR, THE EYE, TOUCH, TASTE AND SMELL, AS WELL AS THE MIND, HE ENJOYS THE OBJECTS OF THE SENSES.

The subtle body is explained in more details. The Jiva enjoys the world of objects through sense organs and mind. Consciousness never directly illumines any object but when reflected upon mind and intellect It becomes Intelligence in which the sense objects become illumined. The Jiva, using the mind along with sense organs, enjoys the sense objects such as sound, touch, taste, smell etc.

utkraamantam sthitam vaapi bhunjaanam vaa gunaanvitam
vimoodhaa naanupashyanti pashyanti jnaanachakshushah // 15.10 //

THE DELUDED DO NOT SEE HIM WHO DEPARTS, STAYS AND ENJOYS, UNITED WITH THE GUNAS; BUT THEY WHO POSSESS THE EYE OF KNOWLEDGE BEHOLD HIM.

The Self is visible to the eye of knowledge only. Though the Self is the nearest and comes most easily within the range of their consciousness in a variety of functions, still the ignorant and deluded do not see Him because of their complete subservience to the sense-objects.

But those who are with intuitive vision could see the Self. Those with the inner eye of knowledge behold the Self as entirely distinct from the body.

yatanto yoginashchainam pashyantyaatmanyavasthitam
yatantopyakritaatmaano nainam pashyantyachetasah // 15.11 //

THE SEEKERS STRIVING FOR PERFECTION BEHOLD HIM DWELLING IN THE SELF; BUT THE UNREFINED AND UNINTELLIGENT, EVENTHOUGH STRIVING, DO NOT FIND HIM.

Two conditions are necessary if meditation is to yield results.

- The purification of the mind - removal of agitations created by attachments to sense objects.
- The intellect has to be tuned to the correct understanding of the Self and thus all doubts about its perception are removed through study, reflection and practice.

If these two requirements are not met through devotion (Bhakti) and service (Karma) all attempts at meditation in the Path of Knowledge will be futile. Those minds which are not purified despite sincere meditation have no chance of realizing the Divine because of attachment to sense objects.

So far the Self has been indicated as

- that which cannot be illumined by the known physical source of light like sun, moon and fire,
- that which, having reached, none returns from the state of perfection
- that of which the individual entity is Jiva.

To show that this goal is the essence of all and the reality behind all experiences Sri Krishna gives in the following four verses a summary of His manifestations. He is described as

- the illuminating light of the consciousness

- the all sustaining life
- the subjective warmth of life in all living organisms.
- the Self in all.

yadaadityagatam tejo jagad bhaasayate'khilam
yacchandramasi yacchaagnau tattejo viddhi maamakam
// 15.12 //

THAT LIGHT WHICH, RESIDING IN THE SUN, ILLUMINES THE WHOLE WORLD, THAT WHICH IS IN THE MOON AND IN THE FIRE - KNOW THAT LIGHT AS MINE.

Sri Krishna says that the very light emerging from the sun which illumines the whole world is the light that is emerging from Him, the Infinite Consciousness. Not only are this but even the light coming from the moon and the fire all expressions of the Infinite Reality expressing through the moon and the fire.

The manifestations are different because the equipments are different just as the same electrical energy manifests in a bulb, in a fan and in a heater in different ways. Consciousness expressed through the sun is sun-light, through the moon is moon-light and through the fuel is fire. Yet all these manifestations are nothing but one Infinite Reality. The Infinite manifests itself in various forms in order to create conducive environment for the world to exist.

gaamaavishya cha bhootani dhaarayaamyahamojasaa
pushnaami chaushadheeh sarvaah somo bhootwaa rasaatmakah
// 15.13 //

PERMEATING THE EARTH I SUPPORT ALL BEINGS BY MY ENERGY; AND HAVING BECOME THE WATERY MOON, I NOURISH ALL HERBS.

The Lord says that the capacity in the earth to sustain life and nourish it, are all His own vitality, meaning the same Consciousness expressing through the sun, the moon, the earth, the atmosphere provide nourishment to all living beings. The energy of The Lord holds the vast heaven and earth together. The sun, the moon and the fire are the sources of all energy in the world, but that which gives these phenomenal factors the capacity to give out energy from them is the Consciousness which is common to all of them. Moon is considered to be the repository of all fluids which nourish the living beings.

aham vaishwaanaro bhootwaa praaninaam dehamaashritah
praanaapaana samaayuktah pachaamyannam chaturvidham //
15.14 //

HAVING BECOME THE FIRE, VAISWANARA, I ABIDE IN THE BODY OF LIVING BEINGS AND ASSOCIATED WITH PRANA AND APANA, DIGEST THE FOURFOLD FOOD.

The same Supreme Consciousness is that which expresses itself as warmth of life in all living beings: if there is no warmth in the body it is considered as dead. Metabolism creates heat in the body and this process continues so long as there is life. That Eternal Reality which is indicated as Life manifests as Digestive Fire *(Vaishwaanara)* which assimilates food. This digestive power assimilates food in four ways through masticating, swallowing, sucking and licking. The power in the digestive system is nothing but a manifestation of the Principle of Life. Prana and Apana are the physiological functions of perception and excretion that are present in all living creatures. It is The Lord that helps us to swallow the food, assimilate it and eliminate the wasteful by-products.

sarvasya chaaham hridi sannivishto
mattah smritir jnaanam apohanam cha
vedaishcha sarvairahameva vedyo
vedaantakrid vedavideva chaaham // 15.15 //

AND I AM SEATED IN THE HEARTS OF ALL; FROM ME ARE MEMORY, KNOWLEDGE, AS WELL AS THEIR ABSENCE. I AM VERILY THAT WHICH HAS TO BE KNOWN BY ALL THE VEDAS; I AM INDEED THE AUTHOR OF THE VEDANTA AND THE KNOWER OF THE VEDAS AM I.

I am seated in the hearts of all: A peaceful joyous mind settled in tranquility capable of concentrating on the higher inspirations is what is called the heart. The Lord is self-evident during meditation in the heart of the meditator.

Memory, knowledge and their absence: From the Supreme Consciousness alone all memory, knowledge and forgetfulness come to us. A capacity to forget is an essential requisite for acquiring new knowledge because unless the imperfect knowledge is thrown out new knowledge cannot be assimilated.

To be known by all the Vedas: The Infinite Consciousness is the one common factor that has been glorified in all the Vedas and to realize this is the fulfillment of existence.

Author of Vedanta and the Knower of Vedas: Since the very essence of Vedas is that Consciousness which is the Ultimate Reality, everything else is a projection upon it. The seeker who listens to the Vedas, who reflects upon their wisdom and who finally experiences the fulfillment of his life is also considered as nothing other than Consciousness.

In short, the phenomenal powers, the material world, the matter and its functions are all the manifestations at different levels of the One Infinite Eternal Divinity. This is the very theme indicated in the Vedas as the Eternal Reality and to know and bring it under our experience is to know the Infinite.

Till now the glories of The Lord in manifested forms have been described. In the following verses The True Nature of the Infinite is pointed out as

1. The Unconditioned,
2. The All Pervading and
3. The Eternal

This Infinite reality is above all concepts such as Finite and the Infinite, the Perishable and the Imperishable. This section is the heart of this Chapter and is the basis for its nomenclature.

THE SUPREME PERSON, *PURUSHOTTAMA*

dwaavimau purushau loke ksharashchaakshara eva cha
ksharah sarvaani bhootani kootastho'kshara uchyate // 15.16 //

TWO PURUSHAS ARE THERE IN THIS WORLD, THE PERISHABLE AND THE IMPERISHABLE. ALL THESE EXISTENCES ARE THE PERISHABLE AND THE UNCHANGING IS THE IMPERISHABLE.

In the Thirteenth Chapter, Field of the Matter and Knower of the Field were elaborated. In this Chapter it was made clear that the sun, earth, plant kingdom and man and his capabilities etc, consisting of the Field of the matter are nothing other than the Supreme Self. Thus the Field of the matter is the Spirit, the Consciousness, the difference being that when the Spirit expresses as matter It looks as if It were subject to change and destruction. Thus the realm of the matter is described in this verse as *Kshara Purusha* - the Perishable. With reference to this Kshara Purusha the Spirit is the Imperishable, *Akshara Purusha.* With reference to the ever changing world of the matter, Consciousness is Imperishable and Changeless. This Consciousness Principle is referred to here as Akshara with reference to and contact with the Kshara.

The Self in the midst of changes remains changeless and all changes can take place only in contact with It just as an anvil *(Kootastham)* remaining changeless allows all the iron pieces kept and hammered on it to change their shapes.

uttamah purushastwanyah paramaatmetyudaahritah
yo lokatrayamaavishya bibhartyavyaya eeshwarah // 15.17 //

BUT OTHER THAN THESE, IS THE SUPREME PURUSHA CALLED THE HIGHEST SELF, THE INDESTRUCTIBLE LORD WHO, PERVADING THE THREE WORLDS (WAKING, DREAM AND DEEP SLEEP), SUSTAINS THEM.

The Imperishable is the quality attained by the Spirit with reference to the Field surrounding It. A man occupying a high position in an office acquires the dignity and the status of that position. Even if that position is removed the man never ceases to exist; he exists as an individual living being. When the Field of the matter is removed from the Knower of the Field what remains is the Knowing Principle, the Pure Knowledge.

Similarly, when the perishable is transcended what remains is not the Imperishable but that which played as the Perishable and Imperishable Purushas. This is the Pure Spirit, the Supreme Self which sustains the three worlds or the three states of experiences viz. waking, dreaming and deep sleep states of consciousness. The Self alone is the illuminator in all these three states of existence.

Thus there are no three types of Purushas - Perishable, Imperishable or Supreme. If a pot is kept in a room we feel that there are three different types of space, one completely differing from the other - Pot space, room space and the total space. But in fact there is only one space which can be understood if the factors conditioning or limiting the space are removed i.e. if the pot is broken and the room is dismantled. The unconditioned pot space and room space are nothing but the total space itself.

Thus the Consciousness is itself Perishable Field in another form and as the knower of the Field the same Consciousness is the Imperishable Reality in the perishable conditionings. But when these conditionings are transcended the same Self is experienced as the Supreme Self - the *Paramatman, Purushottama.*

yasmaat ksharam ateeto'hamaksharaadapi chottamah
ato'smi loke vede cha prathitah purushottamah // 15.18 //

AS I TRANSCEND THE PERISHABLE AND AM HIGHER EVEN THAN THE IMPERISHABLE, I AM CELEBRATED AS

THE SUPREME PERSON, PURUSHOTTAMA, IN THE WORLD AND IN THE VEDAS.

The Lord explains here how He is the Purushottama, the Supreme Person. He says that Pure Consciousness is higher than both the Perishable and the Imperishable. The Perishable can continue the process of change only against the Imperishable Truth as no change is perceptible without reference to a changeless factor. If the changes in the matte - body, mind and intellect - have to be recognized there must be something which is steady that illumines these changes. This constant factor among the perishable is called the Imperishable.

The illumining factor can be called Imperishable only when it is compared to the Perishable. Once the Perishable spheres are crossed over, the Imperishable Itself becomes the Pure Infinite which is Purushottama.

Since the Truth, Purushottama, is experienced only after transcending both Perishable and Imperishable, the Absolute Truth is known as the Highest Spirit, Purushottama. This term is used to indicate the Supreme Spirit both in the Vedas and by the men of the world.

FRUIT OF THAT KNOWLEDGE

yo maamevam asammoodho jaanaati purushottamam
sa sarvavidbhajati maam sarvabhaavena bhaarata // 15.19 //

HE, WHO UNDELUDED, KNOWS ME THUS AS THE HIGHEST PURUSHA, HE KNOWING ALL, WORSHIPS ME WITH HIS WHOLE BEING (HEART) O BHARATA.

The Lord tells the fruits gained by the one who realizes the Supreme Truth. Undeluded is the one who never looks upon the physical body as himself or as belonging to himself. To know means not only the intellectual comprehension but the subjective experience that he is the Purushottama-principle. Sri Krishna declares that such a seeker is the greatest of the devotees because such knowledge leads to devotion.

The Highest Spirit, Purushottama, being the Infinite Consciousness, is the all-knower because he knows that the principle of Consciousness is behind all perception, feeling and thought.

iti guhyatamam shaastram idamuktam mayaanagha
etadbuddhwaa buddhimaan syaat kritakrityashcha bhaarata // 15.20 //

THUS THIS MOST SECRET SCIENCE (TEACHING) HAS BEEN TAUGHT BY ME, O SINLESS ONE. ON KNOWING THIS, A MAN BECOMES WISE AND ALL HIS DUTIES ARE ACCOMPLISHED, O BHARATA.

In this concluding verse The Lord praises the Purushottama theme which gives liberation from all sorrows and agitations. He says that He taught this most secret science; secret because It (the spiritual science, Brahmavidya) is a knowledge that cannot come to any one of its own accord unless one is initiated into it by the Knower of Reality. The secret is also that Purushottama is the substratum of every thing. Sinless means the one with steady mind. The knowledge of the Self which gives emancipation from the cycle of births and deaths and freedom from the bonds of Karma is eulogized here.

He who has realized the Purushottama-state of Consciousness becomes wise in as much as he cannot thereafter make any error of judgment in his life creating confusion and sorrows all around. The second benefit is the enjoyment of a complete sense of fulfillment, the joy of accomplishing what is expected of him (achieving the goal of life which is realization of Brahman).

If this most profound teaching is understood it makes a man wise. After this there is nothing for him to learn or strive for. He has attained the goal of life and the aim of human existence. He has the complete knowledge of the Supreme Being and gets Brahma Jnana. He becomes Jivan Mukta, who is beyond body-consciousness, three Gunas, three states of consciousness - Waking, Dream and Deep Sleep - pairs of opposites and the cycle of births and deaths. There is no rebirth for him. When a person has realized the Self, he has discharged all the duties of his life.

THIS CHAPTER IS THE ESSENCE OF THE GITA, THE VEDAS AND THE UPANISHADS. IT IS GENERALLY RECITED BEFORE TAKING FOOD AS A MARK OF SACRED OFFERING TO THE LORD.

om tat sat iti srimadbhagavadgeetaasu upanishatsu brahma vidyaayaam yogashaastre sri krishnaarjuna samvaade purushottama yogo naama panchadasho'dhyaayah ||

THUS IN THE UPANISHADS OF THE GLORIOUS BHAGAVAD GITA, THE SCIENCE OF THE ETERNAL, THE SCRIPTURE OF YOGA, THE DIALOGUE BETWEEN SRI KRISHNA AND ARJUNA, ENDS THE FIFTEENTH DISCOURSE ENTITLED THE YOGA OF THE SUPREME SPIRIT

AN OUTLINE VIEW OF THIS CHAPTER

This chapter describes the immanence and transcendence of Brahman. Brahman manifests as macrocosm and microcosm together constituting the 'perishable', Kshara. Brahman also remains as the 'imperishable', Akshara, aspect of the perishable. Lastly, Brahman, transcending the Kshara and Akshara, pervades everywhere as the Supreme Being – Purushottama.

I - BRAHMAN IS MACROCOSM (KSHARA, PERISHABLE) - VERSES - 1 – 6

Brahman, supreme Reality, manifests as the pluralistic phenomenon of macrocosmic world. Krishna compares the macrocosmic expression to Asvattha, pipal, tree. He advises mankind to cut asunder the deep rooted Asvattha to reach Brahman. Detachment serves as the axe that cuts the firm-rooted tree. It liberates you from the pairs of opposites that constitute the world; it frees you from desire and delusion that shroud your knowledge. It leads you to reach the eternal goal of Brahman.

II - BRAHMAN IS MICROCOSM (AKSHARA, IMPERISHABLE) - VERSES - 7 – 11

The supreme Reality that manifests as the macrocosm also expresses as the microcosm. The wise sages, yogis, perceive a living being as Reality, Self, enlivening the gross, subtle and causal bodies. They understand that the Self uniting with gunas goes through the experience of life and departs to another body at the time of death. Others lack this wisdom of understanding. They are not able recognize the Self dwelling within. Macrocosm and Microcosm together form Kshara, perishable.

III - BRAHMAN IS ESSENCE IN BOTH (KSHARA & AKSHARA) - VERSES - 12 -15

Personifying as Brahman, Krishna declares that He resides in the sun and the moon, permeates the earth, enters vegetation and enlivens the body, mind and intellect. He is the ultimate goal pointed out in various ancient scriptures, Vedas. Brahman is the essence of macrocosm and microcosm, the Imperishable aspect of the perishable world of things and beings.

IV- BRAHMAN IS UTTAMAPURUSHA (SUPREME BEING BEYOND KSHARA AND AKSHARA) - VERSES - 16 – 20

The world consists of Kshara, perishable objects and beings as well as Akshara, Imperishable substratum of the perishable world. The Supreme Being, Purushottama, the Indestructible Lord pervades and sustains the Kshara and Akshara. He pervades the deep-sleep, dream and waking worlds and also exists beyond them all. The wise understand and worship Purushottama as that whole Being.

<<<000>>>

CHAPTER 16

Daivaasura Sampad Vibhhaaga Yogah:

Yoga of the Division between
The Divine and the Demoniacal Traits

PREAMBLE

In this Chapter the entire mankind has been classified as the divinely (Good-Deva) and the diabolical (Fallen-Asura). It enumerates their respective qualities and ways of conduct.

The demoniac always live contrary to scriptural injunctions in agitation, sorrow and bondage. With endless desires they go through the cycles of birth and death. The divine conquer their desires. They live in peace and happiness until they reach the goal of Enlightenment.

The purpose of this Chapter is that one may adopt the divine qualities and reject the demoniac qualities after fully understanding their nature in the journey towards God-realization. Hence this Chapter is designated as "Yoga of the Division between the Divine and the Demoniacal Traits". Lord Krishna brings out quite clearly the intimate connection between ethics and spirituality, between a life of virtue and God realization and liberation.

Listing two sets of qualities of opposite kinds, the Lord urges us to eradicate the evil and cultivate the divine qualities. What kind of nature should one develop? What conduct must one follow? What way should one live and act if one must attain God and obtain divine bliss? These questions are answered with perfect clarity.

THE TEXT

TRAITS OF DIVINE NATURE

sri bhagavaan uvaacha
abhayam Sattvasamshuddhih jnaanayogavyavasthitih
daanam damashcha yajnashcha swaadhyaayastapa aarjavam // 16.1 //

SRI BHAGAVAN SAID
FEARLESSNESS, PURITY OF HEART, STEADFASTNESS IN KNOWLEDGE AND YOGA, CHARITY, CONTROL OF THE SENSES, SACRIFICE, STUDY OF SCRIPTURES, AUSTERITY AND STRAIGHTFORWARDNESS,

The Lord had earlier described in Chapter 13 verses 7-11 twenty values of life. Here He enumerates the nobler traits in a cultured man who lives those twenty values of life.

Fearlessness - abhayaam - comes first in these Divine Qualities. Fear is the expression of ignorance and when there is knowledge there is fearlessness.

Purity of heart - honesty of intentions and purity of motives.

Steadfastness in Knowledge and Yoga - Ethical purity can not be brought about when the mind is turned outward. Only when it is turned inward it can renounce worldly desires. Devotion to knowledge is the positive way to persuade the mind to leave all low temptations and make it aware to the joys of the Self.

Charity, Restraint of the Senses and Sacrifice - These are the techniques by which steady devotion to knowledge is cultivated. Oneness between the giver and the recipient is the basis of real charity. It is the capacity to restrain one's instinct of acquisition and attachment to wealth and replacing it with the spirit of sacrifice and sharing. Charity can be at the level of head and heart also and need not be merely at the material level. Sharing with others our sympathy and kindness and to distribute one's knowledge are also charities. Restraint of the sense organs is the saving of energy for the higher purposes of meditation.

Study of the scriptures - It implies not only the regular study of scriptural texts but also the practice of their teachings.

Austerity - It means the denial of sensual requirements and concentrating on the divine.

Straightforwardness - Avoidance of crookedness in thoughts, words and actions.

These ethical qualities, if pursued sincerely, will contribute to the discovery of the Divine in oneself.

ahimsaa satyamakrodhas tyaagah shaantirapaishunam
dayaa bhooteshvaloluptwam maardavam hreerachaapalam
// 16.2 //

HARMLESSNESS, TRUTH, ABSENCE OF ANGER, RENUNCIATION, PEACEFULNESS, ABSENCE OF CROOKEDNESS, COMPASSION TOWARDS BEINGS, UNCOVETOUSNESS, GENTLENESS, MODESTY, ABSENCE OF FICKLENESS.

Harmlessness - This connotes not as much physical non-injury as avoidance of injury in the thought process itself because in the world of living physical injury in some form or the other to another can not be avoided. But in so living one can always maintain pure and clean motives in which case the harm caused is not an injury.

Truth is explained under straightforwardness in the previous verse.

Absence of anger - It is the capacity to check anger as it arises and manifests in actions under its influence.
Renunciation - Without renunciation an even temper can not be maintained.

Peacefulness - Keeping a balance in the midst of stormy conditions of life.

Absence of crookedness - Honesty of conviction and avoiding double-talk, full of devotion, love and sincerity to others.

Compassion towards beings - Recognising the imperfections in others and loving them.

Uncovetousness - Remaining in self-control over sense enjoyments.

Gentleness and modesty - This is the result of an individual's good training.

Absence of fickleness - Economy of physical energy in any activity.

tejah kshamaa dhritih shauchamadroho naatimaanitaa
bhavanti sampadam daiveem abhijaatasya bhaarata // 16.3 //

VIGOR, FORGIVENESS, FORTITUDE, PURITY, ABSENCE OF HATRED, AND ABSENCE OF PRIDE - THESE BELONG TO THE ONE BORN IN A DIVINE STATE, O BHARATA.

Vigor - This is not of the physical structure of the body but the brilliance of the seeker's intellect, his peaceful nature, quietitude in his activities and his love for all.

Forgiveness - It implies unruffled serenity even in the face of powerful oppositions and provoking situations in life.

Fortitude - Strength of faith, conviction of the goal, consistency of purpose, vivid perception of the ideal and the spirit of sacrifice in the task undertaken.

Purity - Purity of thoughts and motives, purity of environments, cleanliness of habits and personal belongings.

Non-hatred - It implies not only absence of hatred but also absence of even a vague desire to injure any living creature.

Absence of pride - Leaving the sense of one's own over exaggerated pride and notions of self honor and importance.

The twenty six qualities described above give a complete picture of the man of Divine State. They serve as a guide to all those who are in search of a right way of living and endeavor to become perfect.

Sri Krishna now starts the description of a man of demoniac (Asuric) nature in the following verses. It should, however, be born in mind that human race is not divided into two exclusive categories; many beings partake of the natures of both. Nothing is wholly good or wholly evil.

DEMONIAC TRAITS

dambho darpo'bhimaanashcha krodhah paarushyameva cha
ajnaanam chaabhijaatasya paartha sampadamaasureem // 16.4 //

HYPOCRISY, ARROGANCE, SELF-CONCEIT, ANGER AND ALSO HARSHNESS AND IGNORANCE, BELONG TO ONE WHO IS BORN IN A DEMONIACAL STATE, O PARTHA.

Hypocrisy - Pretending to be righteous but living in unrighteous way of life.

Arrogance - Pride in one's learning, wealth, social status or family connections thereby living in imagined self-importance. This leads to self-conceit.

Anger - When a person of self-conceit looks at the world and finds that its estimate of him is totally different from his own he becomes angry over everything around him which leads to audacity.

All these qualities arise from one's own self-assessment out of self-delusion and ignorance about the scheme of life in the world around him. This ignorance of oneself and his relationship with the world around is the cause of his revolt against his environment and the resultant eccentric actions. These types of people are called demoniac or asuric in contrast to the Daivic or Divinely described earlier. The effect of these two types is discussed now.

THEIR RESPECTIVE RESULTS

daivee sampadvimokshaaya nibhandhaayaasuree mataa
maa shuchah sampadam daiveem abhijaato'si paandava // 16.5 //

THE DIVINE NATURE LEADS TO LIBERATION AND THE DEMONIACAL FOR BONDAGE. GRIEVE NOT, O ARJUNA, FOR YOU ARE BORN WITH DIVINE PROPERTIES.

After hearing the features of the Divine and Demoniac natures Arjuna starts wondering where he stands. Hence The Lord assures him that he is born with Divine qualities.

He reiterates that Divine nature is for liberation - liberation from the psychological entanglements through living these healthy values of righteousness. As a contrast to this Demoniac nature leads to confusion and sorrow preventing one from rising high in the spiritual and moral fields.

Sri Krishna analyses the diabolically fallen or people of demoniac nature in more details in the following verses.

NATURE OF THE DEMONIAC PEOPLE

dwau bhootasargau loke'smin daiva aasura eva cha
daivo vistarashah proktah aasuram paartha me shrinu // 16.6 //

THERE ARE TWO TYPES OF BEINGS IN THIS WORLD - THE DIVINE AND THE DEMONIAC; THE DIVINE HAS BEEN DESCRIBED AT LENGTH; HEAR FROM ME, O ARJUNA, OF THE DEMONIAC.

pravrittim cha nivrittim cha janaa na viduraasurah
na shaucham naapi chaachaaro na satyam teshu vidyate // 16.7 //

THE DEMONIAC DO NOT KNOW ABOUT THE WAY OF ACTION OR THE WAY OF RENUNCIATION; NEITHER PURITY NOR RIGHT CONDUCT NOR TRUTH IS FOUND IN THEM.

asatyamapratishtham te jagadaahuraneeshwaram
aparasparasambhootam kimanyat kaamahaitukam // 16.8 //

THEY SAY 'THIS UNIVERSE IS WITHOUT TRUTH, WITHOUT A (MORAL) BASIS, WITHOUT A GOD, BROUGHT ABOUT BY MUTUAL UNION WITH LUST FOR ITS CAUSE, WHAT ELSE'?

The devilish personality is incapable of deciding about the actions to be pursued and those to be avoided. He does not possess outer cleanliness or inward harmony. Good conduct is absent in him. He can not maintain truthfulness in his words.

They fail to recognize the truth that upholds the Universe i.e. they do not recognize the eternal unchanging Reality behind the ever-changing flux of things. According to them there is no commanding intelligence that orders, regulates, determines and guides the happenings in the world. They believe that the universe is formed as a result of mutual combination of the elements and the driving force that determines the creation is nothing but lust.

etaam drishtimavashtabhya nashtaatmaano'lpabuddhayah
prabhavantyugrakarmaanah kshayaaya jagato'hitaah // 16.9 //

HOLDING THIS VIEW, THESE RUINED SOULS OF SMALL INTELLECTS AND FIERCE DEEDS, COME FORTH AS ENEMIES OF THE WORLD FOR ITS DESTRUCTION.

Believing that the world has no substratum, that there is no controlling power and that it exists and continues on the basis of lust, the devilish people with selfish sense-gratifying intellect and ruined soul i.e. ignorant of their own Divine nature perform fierce deeds. They carry out all sorts of licentious acts to the detriment of the world at large ultimately leading to the destruction of the world itself. They bring about a discordant note of disharmony in the community and plunge the world into disaster.

kaamamaashritya dushpooram dambhamaanamadaanvitaah
mohaadgriheetvaasadgraahaan pravartante shuchivrataah // 16.10 //

FILLED WITH INSATIABLE DESIRES, FULL OF HYPOCRISY, PRIDE AND ARROGANCE, HOLDING EVIL IDEAS THROUGH DELUSION, THEY WORK WITH IMPURE RESOLVES.

Given to desire - Yielding to desires devilish persons lead a life of perpetual suffering and endless disturbances in and around them as all their desires are insatiable. They are full of hypocrisy, pride and arrogance. They are the victims of their own delusion because they forget their divine nature by identifying themselves with the unreal things and values of life.

When all these negative tendencies rule over the demoniac people their actions in the world can not but be the cause for disaster and destruction to others.

chintaamaparimeyaam cha pralayaantaamupaashritaah
kaamopabhogaparamaa etaavaditi nishchitaah // 16.11 //

GIVING THEMSELVES OVER TO IMMEASURABLE CARES ENDING ONLY WITH DEATH, REGARDING GRATIFICATION OF LUST AS THEIR HIGHEST AIM AND FEELING SURE THAT IT IS ALL.

aashaapaashatairbaddhaah kaamakrodhaparaayanaah
eehante kaamabhogaartha manyaayenaarthasanchayaan // 16.12 //

BOUND BY HUNDREDS OF TIES OF DESIRE, GIVEN OVER TO LUST AND ANGER, THEY STRIVE TO AMASS BY UNJUST MEANS HOARDS OF WEALTH FOR SENSUAL ENJOYMENT.

This materialistic doctrine which states

"*yavad jivet sukham jivet rnam krtva ghrtam pibet* |
bhasmibhutasya dehasya punar aagamanam kutah ||

"Eat, drink and be merry, for death is certain and there is nothing beyond".

Such desperate men with all anxieties and cares lead a futile life. Struggling to acquire the desired objects and to be anxious for preserving what is acquired are all the cares of their lives. Satisfaction of lust is their highest goal. Their firm conviction is that there is nothing beyond this in life. They do not know what is peace, harmony and joy in life. According to them sorrows and cares alone are the contents of life. Ultimately they end in miserable death, exhausted and disappointed.

Entangled by insatiable desires, the energies of demoniac persons get dissipated. They become restless and impatient with their surroundings and lose their sense of judgment.

Irritated and constantly unhappy with their environment, they become angry over unfulfilled desires. They ceaselessly try to acquire more and more wealth to satisfy their sensual hunger losing sight of a diviner principle of existence.

idamadya mayaa labdhamimam praapsye manoratham
idamasteedamapi me bhavishyati punardhanam // 16.13 //

THIS HAS BEEN GAINED BY ME TODAY; THIS DESIRE I SHALL OBTAIN; THIS IS MINE AND THIS WEALTH SHALL ALSO BE MINE IN FUTURE.

asau mayaa hatah shatrur hanishye chaaparaanapi
eeshwarohamaham bhogee siddhoham balavaan sukhee // 16.14 //

THAT ENEMY HAS BEEN SLAIN BY ME AND OTHERS ALSO I SHALL SLAY. I AM THE LORD; I ENJOY; I AM PERFECT, POWERFUL AND HAPPY.

aadhyobhijanavaanasmi konyosti sadrisho mayaa
yakshye daasyaami modishya ityajnaanavimohitaah // 16.15 //

I AM RICH AND BORN IN A NOBLE FAMILY. WHO ELSE IS EQUAL TO ME? I WILL SACRIFICE. I WILL GIVE CHARITY. I WILL REJOICE - THUS DELUDED BY IGNORANCE.

anekachittavibhraantaah mohajaalasamaavritaah
prasaktaah kaamabhogeshu patanti narake'shuchau // 16.16 //

BEWILDERED BY MANY A FANCY, ENTANGLED IN THE MESHES OF DELUSION, ADDICTED TO THE GRATIFICATION OF LUST, THEY FALL INTO A FOUL HELL.

Such persons live in constant consciousness of what has been acquired and always exert to acquire more and more wealth of the world. As desires are insatiable, they remain in perpetual disappointment and thirst for unlimited possessions.

They always raise the cry of success claiming themselves to be the lord and victor of all their enemies. They boast themselves to be perfect, powerful, healthy, wealthy and happy.

They look down upon the world with conceit, vanity and contempt and entertain the hope of rejoicing in the world. Sri Krishna says that these people are deluded by their ignorance. In short, such people fall into hell because of a) their fanciful egocentric ideas b) their judgment and discrimination getting eclipsed by delusion and false values and c) their addiction to sense gratification.

aatmasambhaavitaah stabdhaa dhanamaanamadaanvitaah
yajante naamayajnaiste dambhenaavidhipoorvakam // 16.17 //

SELF-CONCEITED, STUBBORN, FILLED WITH THE PRIDE AND INTOXICATION OF WEALTH, THEY PERFORM SACRIFICES IN NAME, OUT OF OSTENTATION, CONTRARY TO SCRIPTURAL ORDINANCES.

ahankaaram balam darpam kaamam krodham cha samshritaah
mam aatmaparadeheshu pradwishanto'bhyasooyakaah // 16.18 //

GIVEN OVER TO EGOISM, POWER, AND PRIDE AND ALSO TO LUST AND ANGER, THESE MALICIOUS PEOPLE HATE ME IN THEIR OWN BODIES AND THOSE OF OTHERS.

taanaham dwishatah krooraan samsaareshu naraadhamaan
kshipaamyajastram ashubhaan aasureeshweva yonishu // 16.19 //

THESE CRUEL HATERS, THE WORST AMONG MEN IN THE WORLD - I HURL THESE EVIL DOERS FOR EVER INTO THE WOMBS OF DEMONS ONLY.

Sri Krishna describes the characteristics of the demoniac people. He states that the spirit of selfless effort in the service of mankind is the greatest Yagna i.e. work is to be considered as worship. The Demoniac people because of their very personality are incapable of selfless service and whatever they do as sacrifice is merely an act influenced by their sensuality, arrogance and false values of life. As a result of this sorrow only ensues. Such men continue to fall lower and lower each day. They are full of egoism, brute strength, arrogance, passion and anger. A person of this kind of attitude would ignore the sanctity of life, become malignant and because of egoism would hate The Lord Himself or the Paramatman in his own body and those of the others. They will hate to seek the Self.

These people are called as the worst among the men in the world. They are malicious against the dignity of themselves and cruel to the people around. Hence Sri Krishna assuming the role of the Law of Action and Reaction orders such people again and again to be born in the Asuric environments till such time as they realize their follies.

aasureem yonimaapannaa moodhaa janmani janmani
maamapraapyaiva kaunteya tato yaantyadhamaam gatim // 16.20 //

ENTERING INTO DEMONIACAL WOMBS AND DELUDED IN BIRTH AFTER BIRTH, NOT ATTAINING ME, THEY THUS FALL, O KAUNTEYA, INTO A CONDITION STILL LOWER THAN THAT.

THE TRIPLE GATE OF HELL

trividham narakasyedam dwaaram naashanamaatmanah
kaamah krodhastathaa lobhastasmaadetattrayam tyajet // 16.21 //

TRIPLE IS THE GATE OF THIS HELL, DESTRUCTIVE OF THE SELF -LUST, ANGER AND GREED- THEREFORE, ONE SHOULD ABANDON THESE THREE.

etairvimuktah kaunteya tamodwaaraistribhirnarah
aacharatyaatmanah shreyas tato yaati paraam gatim // 16.22 //

A MAN WHO IS LIBERATED FROM THESE THREE GATES TO DARKNESS, O KAUNTEYA, PRACTICES WHAT IS GOOD FOR HIM AND THUS GOES TO THE SUPREME GOAL.

Sri Krishna says that an individual having repeatedly reached the Asuric environments, life after life, fails to realize the Infinite Self. They never climb higher in their culture and sink to the bottom most level in their evolution and thus complete their fall.

The Lord advises how even the one who has fallen so hopelessly can improve his spiritual evolution. He says that there are three gateways to hell viz. desire, anger and greed. These characteristics are corollary to each other. He emphasizes that these three evils must be abandoned if one wants to rise up in the ladder of spirituality.

The Lord says that the one who has abandoned these three gateways to darkness will steadily progress towards the life's goal. He will be practicing what is good for him; good in the sense that which not only brings happiness to the practitioner but also contributes much to the well being of the others around him. Progressing thus in the right direction such an individual goes to the Supreme, reaches the goal of life.

SCRIPTURES, THE CANON FOR DUTY

yah shaastravidhimutsrijya vartate kaamakaaratah
na sa siddhimavaapnoti na sukham na paraam gatim // 16.23 //

HE, WHO HAS CAST ASIDE THE ORDINANCES OF THE SCRIPTURES, ACTS UNDER THE IMPULSE OF DESIRE, ATTAINS NEITHER PERFECTION NOR HAPPINESS NOR THE SUPREME GOAL.

Scriptures need not mean the ritualistic ones but they mean the texts discussing the theory of Truth - *Brahma Vidya*. A seeker should renounce desire, anger and greed. Anger is the result when fulfillment of desire is obstructed and greed is the consequence of satisfaction of one desire.

Sri Krishna warns that if one were not to obey the life advocated in the scriptures he will live a life of restless agitations and passions. Such a man cannot feel any happiness or attain any cultural development.

tasmaat shaastram pramaanam te kaaryaakaaryavyavasthitau
jnaatwaa shaastra vidhaanoktam karma kartumihaarhasi // 16.24 //

THEREFORE, LET THE SCRIPTURES BE THE AUTHORITY IN DETERMINING WHAT OUGHT TO BE DONE AND WHAT OUGHT NOT TO BE DONE. HAVING KNOWN WHAT IS SAID IN THE ORDINANCE OF THE SCRIPTURES YOU SHOULD ACT HERE IN THIS WORLD.

The seeker should therefore follow the authority of the scriptures in conducting his way of life as to what is to be pursued and what is to be avoided. Sri Krishna concludes with the command that having known the scriptural injunctions regarding the right way of living, one should act here and now without desire, anger or greed.

The drive of desire must be displaced by the knowledge of right action, but when the supreme end of the freedom of spirit is attained, the individual acts not from instinct, not from law but from a deep insight into the spirit of all life.

om tat sat iti srimadbhagavadgeetaasu upanishatsu brahma vidyaayaam yogashaastre sri krishnaarjuna samvaade daivaasura sampad vibhhaaga yogo naama shodasho'dhyaayah ||

THUS IN THE UPANISHADS OF THE GLORIOUS BHAGAVAD GITA, THE SCIENCE OF THE ETERNAL, THE SCRIPTURE OF YOGA, THE DIALOGUE BETWEEN SRI KRISHNA AND ARJUNA, ENDS THE SIXTEENTH DISCOURSE ENTITLED THE YOGA OF THE DIVISION BETWEEN THE DIVINE AND THE DEMONIACAL TRAITS.

AN OUTLINE VIEW OF THIS CHAPTER

This chapter describes the divine and demoniac class of human beings. It enumerates their respective qualities and ways of conduct. The demoniac always live contrary to scriptural injunctions in agitation and sorrow. With endless desires they go through the cycles of birth and death. The divine conquer their ignorance based desires. They live in peace and happiness until they reach the goal of Enlightenment.

I - QUALITIES OF THE DIVINE AND DEMONIAC - VERSES 1 – 6

A distinction is made between the divine, daivika and the demoniac, asurika types of people. It enumerates twenty six qualities of the divine and six qualities of the demoniac. Krishna heartens Arjuna assuring that he is born into the divne category.

II - DEMONIAC NATURE, CONDUCT AND END - VERSES 7 – 21

The demoniac class of people are deluded, impure, and fierce in their deeds. They do not know what action to take and what to abstain from. They consider the world as a product of lust and mutual enjoyment. Nothing else. There is no other truth, no God. They merely pursue their desires with hypocrisy, conceit and arrogance. They commit terrible deeds with impure resolve. Bound by insatiable lust and expectations they suffer from sorrow and misery through out their lives. Being ignorant of the Supreme they sink to the lowest state.

III - THE DIVINE RISE TO THE HIGHEST GOAL - VERSES 22 -24

The divne, daivika, getting freed from the triple gates of hell – lust, anger and greed - attain the state of perfection. Avoiding the blunders of the demoniac, they take to the spiritual path and reach the Supreme Goal.

<<<000>>>

Chapter 17

Shraddhaa Traya Vibhhaaga Yogah:

Yoga of the Division of the Threefold Faith

PREAMBLE

At the end of the previous Chapter it was stated that he who discards the scriptural injunctions and acts according to the promptings of his desires cannot attain the highest knowledge. Arjuna had a doubt about the fate of those who worship with faith but who do not know the scriptures or are indifferent to their rules. For an average man it is difficult to be proficient in the knowledge of scriptural codes to guide his living although he has sufficient faith or Shraddhaa to lead a nobler way of life as enunciated in the scriptures.

Hence this Chapter deals with the questions whether it is sufficient if one lives with faith for a life of good conduct or is it necessary that he must know the scriptures in order that his faith will be subservient to the injunctions laid down in the scriptures. In short, the question raised by Arjuna is whether even without the knowledge of the Sastras, blind faith alone can take the seeker far.

Shraddhaa is that powerful force from within propelled by which all the faculties of a person act in their respective fields. It gives direction to a man's determination and endows him with character.

Instead of giving a direct clarification to Arjuna's doubts, Sri Krishna gives an analysis of the concept of 'faith' as obtained in the various fields of man's endeavors viz.

1. his physical indulgence *(Ahara)*
2. his dedicated activities *(Yagna)*
3. his self-denial *(Tapas)*
4. his charity *(Dana)*

He explains that faith is of three different types depending upon the nature of temperaments (Gunas) which an individual entertains in him. He concludes that the actions of those who are devoid of faith are as good as not done.

Since three types of faith have been expounded in this chapter it is called "Yoga of the Division of the Threefold Faith".

THE TEXT

arjuna uvaacha
ye shaastravidhimutsrijya yajante shraddhaayaanvitaah
tesham nishthaa tu kaa krishna sattvamaaho rajas tamah // 17.1 //

Arjuna said
O Krishna, what is the condition of those who, neglecting the ordinances of the scriptures, perform sacrifices with faith? Is it that of Sattva, Rajas, or Tamas?

Neglecting the ordinances of the scriptures: To an ordinary man who is ever full of anxieties and confusions of daily activities, planning his life as directed in the scriptures is somewhat difficult. But a sincere seeker may have a faith in the higher way of life and devotion to ideals preached in the scriptures.

Perform sacrifice with faith: The word sacrifice includes all selfless activities undertaken by an individual for the general welfare of the society.

What Arjuna wants to know is whether these selfless activities undertaken with detachment and faith by those who do not willfully defy the rules of scriptures but are ignorant of them, come under the category of unactivity (Sattva) or of activity (Rajas) or of inactivity (Tamas).

The answer given by The Lord is an exhaustive analysis of the three types of faith involved in all human endeavors.

THREE KINDS OF FAITH

sri bhagavaan uvaacha
trividhaa bhavati shraddhaaa dehinaam saa swabhaavajaa
saatvikee raajasee chaiva taamasee cheti taam shrinu // 17.2 //

SRI BHAGAVAN SAID
THREEFOLD IS THE FAITH OF THE EMBODIED, WHICH IS INHERENT IN THEIR NATURE - THE SATTVIC, THE RAJASIC AND THE TAMASIC. HEAR NOW ABOUT IT.

Faith inherent in nature: The nature of man consists of his latent tendencies created by his actions, good or bad, in his previous lives. The faith of each man takes the shape, color, and quality given to it by his nature, *svabhava,* the stuff of his being, his innate substance. Man acts according to his nature; he cannot easily change it. One can transform a worldly nature into a spiritual nature only with the help of insight gained through the study of the scriptures with an indomitable determination. This faith is of three types viz., the Sattvic, the Rajasic and the Tamasic.

sattvaanuroopaa sarvasya shraddhaaa bhavati bhaarata
shraddhaaamayo'yam purusho yo yacchraddhah sa eva sah
// 17.3 //

THE FAITH OF EVERY INDIVIDUAL IS IN ACCORDANCE WITH HIS NATURE, O BHARATA. MAN IS THE NATURE OF HIS FAITH; AS A MAN'S FAITH IS, SO IS HE.

The Lord says that faith is of three kinds viz. Sattva - the divine, the good, Rajas - the undivine, the passionate and Tamas - the diabolic, the dull. Faith is not acceptance of a belief. It is striving after self-realization by concentrating the powers of the mind on a given ideal. It governs our view of life which in turn conditions our desires, thoughts and actions. It is the pressure of the Spirit on humanity. It is the force that urges humanity towards what is better, not only in the order of knowledge but in the whole order of spiritual life.

The goals which religions offer prove effective according to one's faith in them. Hence an individual's physical activities, psychological behavior and intellectual maturity are controlled by the kind of faith entertained by him. If one's faith is of wrong type the expressions of his personality would also be erroneous.

The word 'shraddhaaa' usually translated as 'faith' is not a mechanical belief or acceptance of the words of a holy man or a book. It is an affirmative and reverent attitude toward supersensuous truths. Through faith a man is intuitively convinced of the existence of the Reality underlying the universe and his capacity for realizing that Reality. It is not imposed from outside, but is produced by the tendencies that are the results of his past actions. The intensity of this faith accounts for the passion with which he pursues an undertaking. This faith is a man's appeal to himself or to something present and compelling in him or in universal reality for his way to fullness and perfection.

So a man is made of his faith; he is that faith and that faith is he. The truth he sees is determined for him by his faith. If a man's innate tendencies are characterized by sattva, then his faith will direct him to the pursuit of knowledge and happiness. If they are characterized by rajas, then his faith will direct him to the pursuit of action ending in pain and suffering. If it is characterized by tamas, then his faith will lead him to ignorance and delusion.

yajante saatwikaa devaanyaksharakshaamsi raajasaah
pretaan bhootaganaamshchaanye yajante taamasaa janaah
// 17.4 //

THE SATTVIC OR PURE MEN WORSHIP THE GODS; THE RAJASIC OR THE PASSIONATE WORSHIP THE YAKSHAS AND THE RAKSHASAS; THE OTHERS (THE TAMASIC OR THE DELUDED) WORSHIP THE GHOSTS AND THE HOSTS OF NATURE-SPIRITS.

Worship means offering one's devotion at some altar or the other and seeking a fulfillment from the benefit accrued from his invocations.

Men of Sattvic temperament, because of their serene composure and tranquil disposition seek their fulfillment at an altar of Divinity indicating their impulses.

Rajasic people who are men of action and ambition worship the demi-gods.

The Tamasic people worship the dead spirits to satisfy their lower urges.

Thus the choice of an altar depends upon the quality of urges or the kind of Shraddhaa in a devotee and this Shraddhaa is the effect of his own Guna or temperament predominating in him.

ashaastravihitam ghoram tapyante ye tapo janaah
dambhaahamkaarasamyuktaah kaama raaga balaanvitaah
// 17.5 //

THOSE MEN WHO PRACTICE TERRIFIC AUSTERITIES NOT ENJOINED BY THE SCRIPTURES, GIVEN TO HYPOCRISY AND EGOISM IMPELLED BY THE FORCE OF LUST AND ATTACHMENT,

karshayantah shareerastham bhootagraamamachetasah
maam chaivaantahshareerastham taanviddhyaasuranishchayaan
// 17.6 //

SENSELESS, TORTURING ALL THE ELEMENTS IN THE BODY AND ME ALSO, WHO DWELL IN THE BODY, YOU KNOW THESE TO BE OF DEMONIACAL RESOLVES.

The wrong way of worshipping at an altar is described here. No spiritual enlightenment can be expected in wasting one's energy in wrong channels in the name of religion. Sri Krishna says that physical persecution of one's own body and self-denial would not constitute an austerity following which one would expect spiritual unfoldment and inner personality development. Some people undertake severe austerities merely as a show out of egoism and hypocrisy with a view to satisfy their lustful desires and attachment to worldly objects.

Even if such people gain anything out of such austerities they will only misuse their new found strength for wrongful purposes and ultimately destroy themselves. These people belong to Asuric type. Such unintelligent practices oppress the bodily elements and also the Self or the Divine Lord within. Intelligent control is Tapas but not cruel self-torture.

THREE KINDS OF FOOD

aahaarastwapi sarvasya trividho bhavati priyah
yajnastapastathaa daanam teshaam bhedamimam shrinu // 17.7 //

THE FOOD ALSO WHICH IS DEAR TO EACH IS THREEFOLD, AS ALSO SACRIFICE, AUSTERITY AND ALMS GIVING. YOU HEAR THE DISTINCTION OF THESE.

The temperamental influences which govern the mind, thought and actions of a man are enumerated here. The Lord analyses one's inward nature and consequent outward expressions when one is under the influence of any one particular Guna.

The choice of food, friends, and types of emotions entertained and the view of life in general are all indicative of the type to which the seeker belongs. In the choice of one's food, in the type of sacrifices one will make, in the kind of Tapas one will indulge and in the quality of charity one will make, any one of the three types of faith can be discernible.

aayuh sattvabalaarogya sukha preeti vivardhanaah
rasyaah snigdhaah sthiraa hridyaa aahaarah saatwikapriyaah // 17.8 //

THE FOODS WHICH PROMOTE LIFE, PURITY, STRENGTH, HEALTH, JOY AND CHEERFULNESS, WHICH ARE SWEET, SOFT, NOURISHING AND AGREEABLE ARE DEAR TO THE SATTVIC PEOPLE.

Sattvic persons like the food which increases vitality, supplies energy, enhances strength to resist temptations from the sense objects, provides health, augments joy and inward cheerfulness.

katvamla lavanaatyushna teekshna rooksha vidaahinah
aahaaraah raajasasyeshtaa duhkhashokaamayapradaah // 17.9 //

THE FOODS THAT ARE BITTER, SOUR, SALTISH, EXCESSIVELY HOT, DRY, PUNGENT AND BURNING PRODUCING PAIN, GRIEF AND DISEASE ARE LIKED BY THE RAJASIC.

Rajasic men to fulfill their uncontrolled passions desire food that has strong qualities like bitterness, sourness, hot, pungent etc. Although such food produces good amount of energy ultimately it leads to a life full of pain, grief and disease.

yaatayaamam gatarasam pooti paryushitam cha yat
ucchishtamapi chaamedhyam bhojanam taamasapriyam // 17.10 //

THAT WHICH IS STALE, TASTELESS, PUTRID, ROTTEN, REFUSE AND IMPURE IS THE FOOD LIKED BY THE TAMASIC.

The kind of diet we take has its influence on our power of self control.

THREE KINDS OF SACRIFICE

aphalaakaangkhibhir yajno vidhidrishto ya ijyate
yashtavyameveti manah samaadhaaya sa saatwikah // 17.11 //

THAT SACRIFICE WHICH IS OFFERED BY MEN WITHOUT DESIRE FOR REWARD, AS ENJOINED BY THE ORDINANCE (SCRIPTURES), WITH A FIRM FAITH THAT SACRIFICE IS A DUTY, IS SATTVIC OR PURE.

"The Yajna of the Gita is not the same as the ceremonial sacrifice of the Vedas. It is sacrificial action without expectation of any reward by which man dedicates his wealth and deeds to the service of the One Life in all. People with such a sacrificial spirit will accept even death gladly, though unjustly meted out to them so that the world may grow through their sacrifice. Good people maintain the world through their suffering and sacrifice". Dr.S.Radhakrishnan.

abhisandhaaya tu phalam dambhaarthamapi chaiva yat
ijyate bharatashreshtha tam yajnam viddhi raajasam // 17.12 //

THE SACRIFICE WHICH IS OFFERED, O ARJUNA, SEEKING A REWARD AND FOR OSTENTATION, YOU KNOW THAT TO BE A RAJASIC YAJNA.

In order to get some chosen result some people perform actions, while some others do so merely for show and to satisfy their vanity. These acts do not constitute Divine act nor can they bring about inward cheer or peace. Such sacrifices are termed Rajasika.

vidhiheenam asrishtaannam mantraheenam adakshinam
shraddhaaavirahitam yajnam taamasam parichakshate // 17.13 //

THEY DECLARE THAT SACRIFICE TO BE TAMASIC, WHICH IS CONTRARY TO THE ORDINANCES OF THE SCRIPTURES, IN WHICH NO FOOD IS DISTRIBUTED, WHICH IS DEVOID OF MANTRAS AND GIFTS AND WHICH IS DEVOID OF FAITH.

Disregarding all the requirements laid down in the scriptures, acting against all Vedic injunctions i.e. acts which are against all the principles of right living belong to the lowest type. These actions in which food is not distributed i.e. where no sharing of wealth with others takes place, where rituals are conducted without Mantras and without Dakshina or distribution of reward are all Tamasika.

The distribution of food and the payment of the fee are symbolic of help to others without which all work is self-centered.

THREE KINDS OF PENANCE

devadwijagurupraajna poojanam shauchamarjavam
brahmacharyamahimsaa cha shaareeram tapa uchyate // 17.14 //

WORSHIP OF THE GODS, THE TWICE BORN, THE TEACHERS AND THE WISE, PURITY, STRAIGHTFORWARDNESS, CELIBACY AND NON-INJURY - THESE ARE CALLED THE AUSTERITIES OF THE BODY.

anudwegakaram vaakyam satyam priyahitam cha yat
swaadhyaayaabhyaasanam chaiva vaangmayam tapa uchyate
// 17.15 //

SPEECH WHICH GIVES NO OFFENCE, WHICH IS TRUTHFUL, PLEASANT AND BENEFICIAL, THE PRACTICE OF THE STUDY OF THE VEDAS IS CALLED AUSTERITY OF SPEECH.

manahprasaadah saumyatwam maunamaaatmavinigrahah
bhaavasamshuddhirityetat tapo maanasamuchyate // 17.16 //

SERENITY OF MIND, GOOD HEARTEDNESS, SILENCE, SELF-CONTROL, PURITY OF NATURE - THIS IS CALLED THE MENTAL AUSTERITY.

These three verses explain what Tapas really means and classify Tapas pursued by different types of people.

Devotion and reverence to the ideals represented in the Deva, the Deity, lived by the Twice-Born, Brahmanas and preached by the Gurus and recommended by the wise is an act of worship. Such acts of worship, external and inward purity, straightforwardness in the dealings with others, control of the mind from sense enjoyments in order to concentrate on the Supreme Brahman and avoiding all acts of injuring others are all called austerities of the body or bodily asceticism.

Here Tapas or austerity means not merely a life of self-denial but an intelligent method of living in the right relationship with the world of objects thereby avoiding wastage of energies and utilizing such energy in creative fields of spiritual enquiry.

Speech or the spoken words which cause no disturbances in others, which are true, sincere, agreeable and beneficial to others, careful study and reflection over the scriptures are all called austerity in speech. This implies the investing of the energies of speech in the study and reflection of the teachings of the scriptures.

The five noble values of life mentioned in verse 16 constitute austerity of the mind. They are:

- Serenity of mind - this is the result of one's healthy relationship with the world outside
- Kindness or good heartedness - a feeling of warmth towards all
- Silence - this is not only non-speaking but an inward noiseless calm wherein no passions and desires are generated
- Self control - controlling of lower nature within us
- Purity of nature or honesty of motive - the motivating factor for any action should be noble and divine.

Tapas pursued by people of different Gunas give different results. In the following verses the different kinds of Tapas based on the different Gunas of the Tapaswins are discussed.

shraddhaayaa parayaa taptam tapastattrividham naraih
aphalaakaangkshibhiryuktaih saattwikam parichakshate
// 17.17 //

THIS THREEFOLD AUSTERITY PRACTICED BY STEADFAST MEN WITH THE UTMOST FAITH, DESIRING NO REWARD, THEY CALL SATTVIC.

satkaaramaanapoojaartham tapo dambhena chaiva yat
kriyate tadiha proktam raajasam chalamadhruvam // 17.18 //

THE AUSTERITY WHICH IS PRACTICED WITH THE OBJECT OF GAINING RESPECT, HONOR AND REVERENCE AND WITH HYPOCRISY IS SAID TO BE RAJASIC, UNSTABLE AND TRANSITORY.

moodhagraahenaatmano yat peedayaa kriyate tapah
parasyotsaadanaartham vaa tattaamasamudaahritam // 17.19 //

THE AUSTERITY WHICH IS PRACTICED OUT OF A FOOLISH NOTION, WITH SELF-TORTURE OR FOR THE PURPOSE OF DESTROYING ANOTHER, IS DECLARED TO BE TAMASIC.

These three types of austerities viz. of body, speech, and mind if practiced by men of harmonious nature with no attachment for their rewards and with utmost faith and sincerity are called Sattvic type. If these austerities are practiced with a view to gain respect, honor and reverence and with vanity and ostentation they are called Rajasic. Sri Krishna says that such a kind of Tapas is unstable and transitory which will only result in unproductive and painful self denials. Tapas undertaken with a foolish obstinacy involving self torture and not knowing its aim and indulging in destroying others is of the lowest kind. These misconceived, wrongly practiced austerities undertaken by anyone for bringing about sorrow and discomfort to others and to himself is considered as Tamasic.

THREE KINDS OF CHARITY

daatavyamiti yad daanam deeyateanupakaarine
deshe kaale cha paatre cha tad daanam saatwikam smritam // 17.20 //

THAT GIFT WHICH IS GIVEN TO ONE WHO DOES NOTHING IN RETURN, KNOWING IT TO BE A DUTY TO GIVE, IN A FIT PLACE AND TIME, TO A WORTHY PERSON, THAT GIFT IS HELD TO BE SATTVIC.

yattu pratyupakaaraartham phalamuddishya vaa punah
deeyate cha pariklishtam taddaanam raajasam smritam // 17.21 //

AND THAT GIFT WHICH IS MADE WITH A VIEW TO RECEIVING SOMETHING IN RETURN OR LOOKING FOR A REWARD OR GIVEN RELUCTANTLY IS SAID TO BE RAJASIC.

adeshakaale yaddaanam apaatrebhyashcha deeyate
asatkritamavajnaatam tattaamasamudaahritam // 17.22 //

THE GIFT WHICH IS GIVEN AT THE WRONG PLACE AND TIME TO UNWORTHY PERSONS, WITHOUT RESPECT OR WITH INSULT, IS DECLARED TO BE TAMASIC.

Now three kinds of charity is discussed. That gift which is given to some one out of conviction that it is an act that has to be done is the right kind of charity. Even if the recipient of the charity does no service in return, the giver of charity does not to make any discrimination among the recipients. The gift is to be made with a right faith, to the worthy person, in the right time and in the right place. Charity must come from within and out of one's heart. This is of Sattvic type.

That gift which is given with the hope of getting some benefit in return or looking forward to some reward or given with reluctance is Rajasic type.

Gifts which are made at the wrong place and time to an unworthy person with contempt and with no respect are said to be of Tamasic type.

THE MYSTICAL UTTERENCE, *OM TAT SAT,* PURIFIES ALL ACTIONS

om tatsaditi nirdesho brahmanas trividhah smritah
braahmanaastena vedaashcha yajnaashcha vihitaah puraa // 17.23 //

'OM TAT SAT' - THIS IS CONSIDERED TO BE THE THREEFOLD SYMBOL OF BRAHMAN. BY THIS WERE ORDAINED OF OLD THE BRAHMANAS, THE VEDAS AND THE SACRIFICES.

Om Tat Sat is a sentence of three words, each denoting one of the aspects of the Reality.

- 'OM' represents the Transcendental and the Pure Self, Absolute and Unborn which is the substratum upon which the projections of the body, mind and intellect are maintained.
- 'Tat' indicates the Eternal Goal, the Changeless and the Ever-Perfect, that from which everything has come, in which everything exists and into which everything merges back in the end.
- 'Sat' means existence, the principle functioning through all things.

Invoking this sentence purifies all our activities and motives behind them. When invoked in ritualism it removes all defects in the worship, it being the name for Brahman.

The Eternal Reality indicated in the triple nomenclature of Brahman 'Om Tat Sat' is the source from which all castes, the Vedas and Sacrifices commenced. All super impositions arise from, exist on and disappear into that which is their own substratum, the Brahman.

tasmaadomityudaahritya yajnadaanatapahkriyaah
pravartante vidhaanoktaah satatam brahmavaadinaam // 17.24 //

THEREFORE, WITH THE UTTERANCE OF 'OM' THE ACTS OF GIFT, SACRIFICE AND AUSTERITY ENJOINED IN THE SCRIPTURES ARE ALWAYS BEGUN BY THE EXPOUNDERS OF BRAHMAN.

tadityanabhisandhaaya phalam yajnatapah kriyaah
daanakriyaashcha vividhaah kriyante mokshakaangkshibhih // 17.25 //

AND WITH THE UTTERANCE OF THE WORD 'TAT' THE ACTS OF SACRIFICE AND AUSTERITY AND THE VARIOUS ACTS OF GIVING ARE PERFORMED BY THE SEEKERS OF SALVATION WITHOUT AIMING AT ANY REWARD.

sadbhaave saadhubhaave cha sadityetatprayujyate
prashaste karmani tathaa sacchabdah paartha yujyate // 17.26 //

THE WORD 'SAT' IS USED IN THE SENSE OF REALITY AND OF GOODNESS AND SO ALSO, O PARTHA, IT IS USED IN THE SENSE OF AN AUSPICIOUS ACT.

The context in which the terms - Om, Tat, Sat - have to be used is explained here. Sri Krishna says that when the acts of sacrifice, gift and austerity are undertaken by the seekers the term OM is to be uttered to cherish in the mind the divine awareness of the supremacy of the Infinite. This adds purpose and meaning to all our acts of sacrifice, charity and austerity by freeing the mind from the egocentric attachments.

Liberation means liberation of our personality from its physical, emotional and intellectual attachments. Once liberated the human personality realizes the Divinity in itself. One who endeavors to liberate himself must perform all his activities in such a way that the causes that create the attachments -vasanas- are completely eliminated.

To work in the field of Yagna or Tapas or Dana by understanding the meaning of the term 'Tat' i.e. the universal oneness of the spiritual truth is to work with no ego and consequent freedom from attachments. With the utterance of 'Tat' alone which indicates the universal truth of oneness of all living creatures all acts of sacrifice, penance and gifts are undertaken by the seekers of liberation without expecting any reward. The word 'Sat' means both reality and goodness. It is also used for all praiseworthy actions.

In our daily contact with the world of objects we more often believe that this world, as physically observed, is the reality although it is only relatively real in comparison to the unchanging substratum, the 'Sat', the Absolute Reality.

yajne tapasi daane cha sthitih saditi chochyate
karma chaiva tadartheeyam sadityevaabhidheeyate // 17.27 //

STEADFASTNESS IN SACRIFICE, AUSTERITY AND GIFT, IS ALSO CALLED 'SAT' AND SO ALSO ANY ACTION FOR SUCH PURPOSES IS CALLED 'SAT'.

The term 'Sat' is used to indicate man's faith and devotion in sacrifice, austerity and gift. It indicates steadfastness in Yagna, Tapas and Dana. If these activities are undertaken with faith and sincerity with the chanting of OM - the Supreme, TAT - the Universal and SAT - the Real (the Infinite Brahman), the seeker's mind gives up all its selfishness, arrogance and ego. The principle behind this advice is that actions will create reactions depending upon the motive and attitude of the performer while undertaking such actions.

ashraddhaayaa hutam dattam tapastaptam kritam cha yat
asadityuchyate paartha na cha tatpretya no iha // 17.28 //

WHATEVER OFFERING OR GIFT IS MADE, WHATEVER SACRIFICE IS PERFORMED, WHATEVER RITE IS OBSERVED, WITHOUT FAITH, IT IS CALLED 'ASAT' O PARTHA; IT IS OF NO ACCOUNT HERE OR HEREAFTER.

Sri Krishna in this concluding verse of this Chapter emphasizes that faith is man and even if anyone performs most glorious acts without faith they are of no use either here or hereafter. Actions create effects depending on the faith behind the actions. The Lord states that whatever sacrifice is made, whatever penance is performed or whatever charity is given it is called 'Asat' if they are undertaken without faith; they are mere barren actions. Such faithless actions will produce no results.

The Lord thus indicates that the spirit of faith is unavoidable and that without faith no progress or evolution can ever take place. This is true in this life and the life after death. Both in the secular activities as well as in the sacred performances of the religion, the factor that determines the quality and quantity of the result is our faith in our own goodness and in the field of activity undertaken.

om tat sat iti srimadbhagavadgeetaasu upanishatsu brahma vidyaayaam yogashaastre sri krishnaarjuna samvaade shraddhaaa traya vibhhaaga yogo naama saptadasho'dhyaayah ||

THUS IN THE UPANISHADS OF THE GLORIOUS BHAGAVAD GITA, THE SCIENCE OF THE ETERNAL, THE SCRIPTURE OF YOGA, THE DIALOGUE BETWEEN SRI KRISHNA AND ARJUNA, ENDS THE SEVENTEENTH DISCOURSE ENTITLED THE YOGA OF THE DIVISION OF THE THREEFOLD FAITH

AN OUTLINE VIEW OF THIS CHAPTER

This chapter covers different types of persons who worship with faith. Some conduct their life contrary to scriptural injunction, yet worship with great Shraddha, faith. Arjuna is confused as to their spiritual status – whether they are of sattvic or rajasic or tamasic nature? Krishna clarifies with an analysis of the three types of Shraddha. How they relate to food intake, sacrifice, austerity and charity etc since the nature of these activities helps determine the quality of Shraddha. Towards the end of the chapter Krishna indicates the goal of human existence. He directs a spiritual practitioner to the ultimate Reality, SAT, using the sacred words OM TAT SAT and says what is contrary to these practices as unreality, ASAT.

I - SATTVIKA, RAJASIKA, TAMASIKA SHRADDHA, FAITH - VERSES 1 – 7

Arjuna asks Krishna to describe the one who worships with Shraddha though acting contrary to scriptures. Would such a person belong to sattvika, rajasika, tamasika category? Krishna explains how shraddha varies according to individual nature. The Sattvika worships gods, rajasika worships demi-gods, and tamasika worships ghosts and spirits. The Lord describes the three types of food they consume, their sacrifice, austerity and charity. The nature of these four factors classifies shraddha as sattvika, rajasika, or tamasika.

II - SATTVIKA, RAJASIKA, TAMASIKA AHARA, FOOD - VERSES 8 – 10

Three types of food are discussed in this section. Food, Ahara, has been classified into three categories viz. sattvika, rajasika, and tamasika. Sattvika food is conducive for spiritual growth, rajasika food suits warrior class and tamasika caters to the lowest class, the idea being that the respective class of people prefer to eat respective type of food.

III - SATTVIKA, RAJASIKA, TAMASIKA YAJNA, SACRIFICE - VERSES 11 – 13

Yajna, sacrifice also falls under three classifications viz. sattvika, rajasika, and tamasika. Sattvika sacrifice is ordained by the scriptures and is undertaken without desire or motive for fruit. Rajasika sacrifice seeks fruit and ostentation. Tamasika sacrifice does not conform to the scriptures and follows no inner faith or external religious tradition.

IV - SATTVIKA, RAJASIKA, TAMASIKA TAPA, AUSTERITY - VERSES 14 – 19

Sattvika Tapa envisages three aspects viz. of body, speech and mind which is to be practised with devoutness and faith, desiring no fruit. The practice of sacrifice with ostentation to gain good name, fame and following is considered rajasika. Such austerity is unstable and transitory. Tamasika austerity is practiced out of foolish notion, torturing oneself and for the purpose of harming others.

V - SATTVIKA, RAJASIKA, TAMASIKA DANA, CHARITY - VERSES 20 – 22

Charity, proceeding from obligatory duty, given to the proper deserving person, place and time is sattvika. That which is given reluctantly, with an idea of earning a return or expecting gain is rajasika. A gift given insultingly, without due respect, to a wrong person, place and time is tamasika.

VI - *OM*-SUPREME, *TAT*-THAT, *SAT*-REALITY, *ASAT*-UNREALITY -VERSES 23 – 28

Brahman has been designated as OM TAT SAT. Out of Brahman arose brahmanas, vedas and sacrifices. Knowledge is the conditioned consciousness which arises from Brahman, the pure consciousness. Action springs from knowledge and from sacrificial action emerge produce, life and people. Hence Knowledge, action and people are said to arise from Brahman. The path to supreme Brahman has been indicated as OM TAT SAT. ASAT refers to the improper practice of dana, tapa and yajna undertaken without shraddha. Such irregular practice leads one to a purposeless life. It doe no good here in this world or hereafter.

<<<000>>>

CHAPTER 18

Moksha Sannyaasa Yogah:

Yoga of Liberation by Renunciation

PREAMBLE

The closing Chapter is a summary of the entire Gita. If the 2nd Chapter were its Profile, the 18th is its Review. This is the longest Chapter in the Gita having 78 Verses.

Moksha consists in securing lasting freedom from the bondage of mundane existence in the form of birth and death and realizing God who is no other than Bliss. Summing up the substance of all the previous Chapters, the present one discusses in detail, under the terms of *'Sannyasa'* and *'Tyaga'* respectively the paths of Knowledge and Action, both of which are the means to the attainment of *Moksha.*

It was explained that there are three types of personalities depending on their temperaments or Gunas. They are Sattwic-good, Rajasic-passionate and Tamasic-dull. This Chapter discusses how these Gunas create differences among individuals in their capacity to sacrifice, in their wisdom, in their actions, fortitude and happiness.

The teaching of the Gita has been wound up in Verse 66 of this Chapter with an exhortation to offer all actions to God who is the same as Moksha. It is for these reasons that this Chapter has been entitled "Moksha Sannyaasa Yoga" or Yoga of Liberation by Renunciation.

THE TEXT

RENUNCIATION: NOT TOWARDS WORK BUT TO THE FRUITS OF WORK

arjuna uvaacha
sannyaasasya mahaabaaho tattwam icchaami veditum
tyaagasya cha hrisheekesha prithak keshinishoodana // 18.1 //

ARJUNA SAID
I DESIRE TO KNOW THE TRUE NATURE OF SANNYAASA AND TYAGA AS DISTINGUISHED FROM EACH OTHER, O MIGHTY HRISHIKESA, O SLAYER OF KESI.

This Chapter begins with Arjuna's question seeking the precise definition of Sannyasa - renunciation and Tyaga - relinquishment. These terms are used in many places in different contexts in the Gita with apparent varying meanings. Sri Krishna replies this question exhaustively.

The central theme of this discourse revolves around the meanings of these two words. It guides us what types of tendencies, urges, impulses and motives are to be relinquished or abandoned so that true renunciation of the non-divinity in oneself can take place.

sri bhagavaan uvaacha
kaamyaanaam karmanaam nyaasam sannyaasam kavayoviduh
sarvakarmaphalatyaagam praahustyaagam vichakshanaah // 18.2 //

SRI BHAGAVAN SAID
THE RENUNCIATION OF WORKS INDUCED BY DESIRE IS UNDERSTOOD BY THE SAGES TO BE SANNYASA WHILE THE SURRENDER OF THE FRUITS OF ALL WORKS IS CALLED TYAGA BY THE WISE.

Total giving up all desire-prompted activities is renunciation while giving up of the fruits of actions is relinquishment. On the face of it these two statements appear to have the same implication because desires are always for the fruits of actions. Although both mean giving up of desire, Sannyasa is giving up of desire motivated action while Tyaga is giving up of desire for the fruits of actions.

Action is the effort put forth at present to attain its fruit in future. The fruit is a culmination in future of the present action. A desire-prompted action relates to the present while anxiety to enjoy its reward which is a mental disturbance relates to the future in the time-frame. A disturbed mind cannot execute any action with efficiency. Thus renunciation is the goal to be reached through abandoning the anxiety for the enjoyment of the fruits of actions.

Both Sannyasa and Tyaga are disciplines in our activities. These terms do not indicate that work should be ignored. On the other hand Gita insists that we must always work. But work can be executed with efficiency if these two factors viz. desire prompted action and desire for its reward are eliminated in which case the work becomes an inspired and noble action.

Inertia or non-action is not the ideal. Action without any selfish desires or expectation of gain, performed in the spirit that 'I am not the doer, I am surrendering myself to the Universal Self' is the ideal set before us. The Gita does not teach the complete renunciation of works but the conversion of all works into *nishkama karma* or desireless action.

tyaajyam doshavadityeke karma praahurmaneeshinah
yajnadaanatapahkarma na tyaajyamiti chaapare // 18.3 //

SOME PHILOSOPHERS DECLARE THAT ALL WORKS SHOULD BE RELINQUISHED AS EVIL; OTHERS DECLARE THAT ACTS OF SACRIFICE, GIFT AND AUSTERITY SHOULD NOT BE GIVEN UP.

As against the principles of work stated in the previous verse, some philosophers (Sankhyas) declare that action itself should be abandoned as an evil because they produce Vasanas obstructing the realization of the Self while some others say that acts of sacrifice (Yajna), charity (Dana) and austerity (Tapas) should never be given up.

However the imports of Sri Krishna's teachings in the Gita is that only evil activities are to be renounced and that all the spiritual activities and one's own duties should be pursued in a spirit of dedicated selfless devotion and thus transform the work itself as a homage to the Supreme.

RELINQUISHMENT

nishchayam shrinu me tatra tyaage bharatasattama
tyaago hi purushavyaaghra trividhah samprakeertitah // 18.4 //

HEAR FROM ME THE CONCLUSION OR THE FINAL TRUTH ABOUT THIS RELINQUISHMENT, O BEST OF THE BHARATAS; RELINQUISHMENT VERILY, O BEST OF MEN, HAS BEEN DECLARED TO BE OF THREE KINDS.

Sri Krishna promises Arjuna that He will explain what constitutes Tyaga or spirit of relinquishment and its various kinds.

yajnadaanataph karma na tyaajyam kaaryameva tat
yajno daanam tapashchaiva paavanaani maneeshinaam // 18.5 //

ACTS OF SACRIFICE, GIFT AND AUSTERITY SHOULD NOT BE GIVEN UP, BUT SHOULD BE PERFORMED; FOR VERILY SACRIFICE, GIFT AND ALSO AUSTERITY ARE THE PURIFIERS OF THE WISE.

The Lord says that practice of worship, charity and austerity should not be given up because these activities bring about a discipline in the mind and its inner peace and equilibrium which are necessary for spiritual unfoldment and final experience of the Infinite.

etaanyapi tu karmaani sangam tyaktwaa phalaani cha
kartavyaaneeti me paartha nischitam matamuttamam // 18.6 //

BUT EVEN THESE ACTIONS SHOULD BE PERFORMED LEAVING ASIDE ATTACHMENT AND THE DESIRE FOR REWARDS, O PARTHA, THIS IS MY CERTAIN AND CONCLUSIVE CONVICTION.

Even these actions viz. sacrifice (Yajna), charity (Dana) and austerity (Tapas) should be performed without any attachment i.e. without any sense of egoism and desire for its rewards. Ego and its desires are the components of attachment. When ego tries to satisfy its desires it develops a relationship with the outside world of things and beings. This relationship is attachment. If any action is performed with attachment, the expectations of its fruits affect the efficiency in the action undertaken.

To be rid of attachment and to be free from anxieties regarding the fruits of actions that will accrue at a future time are the roots of the Krishna doctrine in the Gita. Detachment is not a matter of outward action or inaction; it is the possession of the impersonal outlook and inner renunciation of ego while performing action.

THREE KINDS OF RENUNCIATION

niyatasya tu sannyaasah karmano nopapadyate
mohaattasya parityaagas taamasah parikeertitah // 18.7 //

VERILY THE RENUNCIATION OF OBLIGATORY ACTION IS NOT PROPER; THE RELINQUISHMENT OF THE SAME FROM DELUSION IS DECLARED TO BE TAMASIC.

Relinquishment of obligatory duties is considered as the worst. Obligatory duties mean unavoidable duties such as daily worship and special duties such as certain rituals on special occasions both individually and from the view point of the society in which one lives. As the performance of these duties makes the aspirant's heart pure, giving up of such duties is considered as Tamasic.

duhkhamityeva yat karma kaayakleshabhayaat tyajet
sa kritwaa raajasam tyaagam naiva tyaagaphalam labhet // 18.8 //

HE, WHO ABANDONS ACTION FROM THE FEAR OF BODILY TROUBLE BECAUSE IT IS PAINFUL, DOES NOT OBTAIN THE MERIT OF RENUNCIATION BY DOING SUCH RAJASIC RENUNCIATION.

If anyone gives up his obligatory duties because they are painful or on account of fear of bodily suffering such Tyaga is considered as Rajasic because for a man of action to perform his duties only so long as they are not risky to his person is no heroism at all. Hence The Lord says that such a person shall not attain any fruit of his renunciation.

kaaryamityeva yatkarma niyatam kriyate'rjuna
sangam tyaktwaa phalam chaiva sa tyaagah saatwiko matah // 18.9 //

WHATEVER OBLIGATORY ACTION IS DONE, O ARJUNA, MERELY BECAUSE IT OUGHT TO BE DONE, ABANDONING ATTACHMENT AND ALSO THE FRUIT, THAT RENUNCIATION IS REGARDED AS SATTVIC.

A man of pure nature performs actions that have fallen to his lot in accordance with his capacity and inherent nature. He is not filled with pride in performing action nor does he hope to gain any reward therefrom. When a man performs his obligatory duties without the spirit of doership and selfishness, his mind is purified and becomes fit for Self Realization. This kind of renunciation of attachment in performing action as also the expectation of the rewards of such action is considered Sattvic.

It will be noted from the above three verses that the discussion is not so much about what is to be renounced as to how and where one should act. Thus the concept of Tyaga in the Gita is a subjective renunciation of selfishness and desire in the field of activity and not giving up the world and one's duties and actions in it. Acting in the outside world, renouncing ego and egocentric desires, an individual grows in inward purity.

na dweshtyakushalam karma kushale naanushajjate
tyaagi sattvasamaavishto medhaavee chhinnasamshayah // 18.10 //

THE MAN OF RENUNCIATION, INTELLIGENT AND PERVADED BY PURITY, WITH HIS DOUBTS DISPELLED, HAS NO AVERSION TO DISAGREEABLE WORK AND NO ATTACHMENT TO AGREEABLE ACTION.

The question how does such a person, purified through Sattvic Tyaga, gains the highest spiritual experience is answered here.

A man of Sattvic relinquishment never hates any disagreeable work and environment nor gets attached to any agreeable fields of action and favorable scheme of things. He does his duties under all circumstances, agreeable or disagreeable, without getting elated when successful or dejected when faced with obstacles.

He is not overwhelmed by joy or sorrow; he is always equanimous. He is independent of the happenings around him. Even the low impulses like jealousy, anger, passion, greed etc. do not affect him. He does not become a victim of his own mental impressions, Vasanas.

Such a man is considered to be pervaded by purity. He is said to be educated, cultured and with clear vision of his goal without getting hampered by all sorts of doubts. He is termed a man of understanding, a *Medhavi.*

He knows his field of activity and his own divine nature. He is fully aware of the instruments of action and his relationship with the world outside. But a majority of people identify themselves with doership and live in the world conditioned by the happenings around. Such an average man who works with an ego and attachment must learn to work at least renouncing the fruits of his action which is explained in the next verse.

na hi dehabhritaa shakyam tyaktum karmaanyasheshatah
yastu karmaphalatyaagee sa tyaageetyabhidheeyate // 18.11 //

VERILY IT IS NOT POSSIBLE FOR AN EMBODIED BEING TO RENOUNCE ACTIONS ENTIRELY; BUT HE WHO RELINQUISHES THE REWARDS OF ACTIONS IS VERILY CALLED A MAN OF RENUNCIATION.

Since all of us are embodied and therefore cannot abandon all activities so long as the body is alive, the only course available is to direct all our actions in such a way as to bring harmony in our inner lives.

If Tyaga of Sattva type is not possible due to attachment to the world, relinquishment of attachment or anxiety to the fruits of actions which will materialize at a future time is advised by The Lord. A man who abandons his longing to enjoy the rewards for his action is called a Tyagi.

THREE TYPES OF FRUITS OF TYAGA

anishtamishtam mishram cha trividham karmanah phalam
bhavatyatyaaginaam pretya na tu sannyaasinaam kwachit // 18.12 //

THE THREEFOLD FRUIT OF ACTION - DESIRABLE, UNDESIRABLE AND MIXED - ACCRUES AFTER DEATH TO THOSE WHO HAVE NO SPIRIT OF RENUNCIATION, BUT NEVER TO THE RELINQUISHERS.

Earlier three types of Tyaga were discussed. Now three types of fruits of Tyaga are explained. The fruits of action mean not only the results of actions accruing at a future date but also the changes that take place at the mental plane or in the thought process itself. Such changes or reactions in the mind are of three types viz. the disagreeable - those that are positively bad, the agreeable - those that are positively good and the mixed - those that include both good and bad.

As the present determines the quality of the future, after death, the next embodiment and its environment would depend upon the type of vasanas produced in the present actions. This is called the Theory of Re-incarnation.

The Lord explains that for a man of renunciation (Sannyasa) there cannot be any response to the actions done in the past or in the present; he realizes the Bliss. The pleasant, unpleasant and mixed reactions - Karma Phalam- are applicable only to those who have an ego-centric identification with actions as well as their results. Relinquishment of the sense of ego and the anxiety for the results and serving the world as a service to The Lord is Tyaga.

WORK IS A FUNCTION OF NATURE

panchaitaani mahaabaaho kaaranaani nibodha me
saankhye kritaante proktaani siddhaye sarva karmanaam
// 18.13 //

LEARN FROM ME, O MIGHTY-ARMED ARJUNA, THESE FIVE FACTORS, AS DECLARED IN THE SANKHYA DOCTRINE, FOR THE ACCOMPLISHMENT OF ALL ACTIONS.

adhishthaanam tathaa kartaa karanam cha prithagvidham
vividhaashcha prithakcheshtaa daivam chaivaatra panchamam
/ 18.14 /

(BODY) THE SEAT OF ACTION, (EGO) THE DOER, THE VARIOUS SENSE ORGANS OF PERCEPTION, THE DIFFERENT FUNCTIONS OF ORGANS OF ACTIONS AND THE PRESIDING DEITY ALSO, THE FIFTH

shareeravaangmanobhiryat karma praarabhate narah
nyaayyam vaa vipareetam vaa panchaite tasya hetavah // 18.15 //

WHATEVER ACTION A MAN PERFORMS BY HIS BODY, SPEECH AND MIND, WHETHER RIGHT OR THE REVERSE, THESE FIVE ARE ITS CAUSES.

The concept of work is analyzed in these verses. When it was told that action can be done without egocentric desires and attachments to fruits the consequential question is what constitutes action or work. Sri Krishna says that there are five aspects of action or five-fold division of work which are already laid down in the Sankhyan philosophy.

The five components of action are

1. The body *-Adhishthaanam* -the gateway for the entrance and existence of stimuli
2. The ego *-Karta-* which seeks fulfillment of the action through the body

3. the organs of perception - *Karanam* - through which the inner personality comes into contact with the field of enjoyment and satisfaction
4. The organs of action and
5. the presiding deities of the organs of perception which make them work properly.

The deities represent an unseen power other than the human factors. Each of the sense organs is controlled by a reflection of Consciousness called Presiding deity.

It is this non-human factor that interferes and disposes of human effort. It is the wise, all-seeing will that is at work in the world. In all human actions, there is an unaccountable element which is commonly called luck, destiny, fate or the force accumulated by the acts of one's past lives. It is called here *daiva*.

The task of man is to drop a pebble in the ocean of time and he may not see the ripple reach the other distant shore; he may plant the seed but he may not see the harvest which lies in the hands higher than his own.

As all the items listed above will have to function in a coordinated manner for the accomplishment of any task undertaken, be it by the body, speech or mind or whether they are right or wrong, they are called the causes of all actions.

tatraivam sati kartaaram aatmaanam kevalam tu yah
pashyatyakritabuddhitwaan na sa pashyati durmatih // 18.16 //

SUCH BEING THE CASE, THE MAN OF PERVERSE MIND WHO, OWING TO HIS UNTRAINED UNDERSTANDING,

LOOKS UPON THE PURE SELF AS THE DOER, HE DOES NOT SEE.

The Self is always actionless. It is always the silent witness. But a man of perverted understanding attributes agency to the pure Self as the doer because of misapprehension of the facts. He equates the body with the Self because of his lack of knowledge of the pure, actionless Self. Though he sees with his physical eyes, he does not behold the one eternal essence which is the substratum of everything.

yasya naahankrito bhaavo buddhiryasya na lipyate
hatwaapi sa imaam llokaan na hanti na nibadhyate // 18.17 //

HE WHO IS FREE FROM THE EGOISTIC NOTION, WHOSE UNDERSTANDING IS NOT TAINTED (BY GOOD OR EVIL), THOUGH HE SLAYS THESE PEOPLE, HE SLAYS NOT, NOR IS HE BOUND (BY THE ACTION).

The realm of matter is the field of activity and the life's sorrows and agitations belong to it. Although the Spirit is independent of the field, because of Its identification with the field It feels happy or unhappy according to the condition of the field at any given moment. Similarly ego which is the result of man's self projections and unhealthy contacts with the outside world is the cause of man's sufferings. Therefore Sri Krishna says that those who have no sense of egoism and whose intelligence is not vitiated by false values of possession, acquisition etc. perform no action although they act.

The statement 'performing no action while acting' means that even while a man of above mentioned temperament is acting in the world, such actions leave no mental impressions (Vasanas) in him and he remains detached. An egoless man of wisdom while working in any field is an expression of the Infinite Will and in that attitude of surrender and dedication actions performed by him leave no vasanas in him. Hence The Lord says 'though he kills he does not kill'.

Thus Arjuna is told that if he can act in the world without identifying with things around him and does his duty in the consciousness of the Divine, even if he kills his kith and kin, teachers etc. he would not be committing any crime and the killings would not leave any murderous impressions in him.

In a way we can say that the teachings of the Gita are concluded here. At the beginning Sri Krishna stated the proposition: "The self slays not nor is slain" (2.19) and gave the immutability of the Self as the reason (2.20). He also briefly introduced the idea (2.21) that an enlightened person is not compelled to engage in action and explained it in detail through the treatise. Now He concludes His discourses by saying that "the wise man slays not nor is he bound".

The essence of the teaching is this: A sannyasi is free from ego and identification with the body. He renounces all actions because it is brought about by ignorance of the true nature of the Self. Therefore the threefold fruit of action – desirable, undesirable and mixed – does not affect him. It is only the unenlightened man that is affected by it.

In the following verses Sri Krishna explains why different people act differently under different impulses and keep different basis for their actions. Each one of these factors is divided under three categories of human nature viz. Sattvic, Rajasic and Tamasic.

KNOWLEDGE AND ACTION

jnaanam jneyam parijnaataa trividhaa karmachodanaa
karanam karma karteti trividhah karma sangrahah // 18.18 //

KNOWLEDGE, THE KNOWN (THE OBJECT OF KNOWLEDGE) AND THE KNOWER FORM THE THREEFOLD INCITEMENT TO ACTION; THE INSTRUMENT, THE OBJECT AND THE AGENT FORM THE THREEFOLD BASIS OF ACTION.

The threefold impulse that propels activity *(Karma Chodana)* and also the basis of action *(Karma Sangraha)* are explained here.

The impulse to action is made up of Knowledge *(Jnanam)*, the Known *(Jneyam)* and the Knower *(Parijnata)*. They indicate the experience, the experienced and the experiencer respectively. No action is possible without these three constituents. From the experiencer the impulse for action comes out as a desire, from the experienced as a temptation and from the experience as a memory of enjoyment.

The basis of action comprises of the instruments of action in the form of organs of perception, mind and understanding. The object of action is that which is sought for and reached through action by the doer. The doer is in the form of ego that sets the organs going.

Thus an activity consists of

- an agent having a desire
- who maintains in his mind a clear picture of the end or the goal and

- who possesses all the necessary instruments to act.

The performance of an action, either to obtain or to avoid a thing, is possible only when there is conjunction of these three; if any one of these items is absent no activity can take place. All actions inhere in these three: the instrument, the object and the doer; hence, they form the bases of action.

jnaanam karma cha kartaa cha tridhaiva gunabhedatah
prochyate gunasankhyaane yathaavacchrinu taanyapi // 18.19 //

KNOWLEDGE, ACTION AND THE DOER (AGENT) ARE DECLARED IN THE SCIENCE OF THE GUNAS TO BE OF THREE KINDS, ACCORDING TO THE DISTINCTION OF THE GUNAS; HEAR THEM ALSO DULY.

Knowledge, action and the actor or the doer fall under three categories because of differences in the temperaments or Gunas in an individual at any given time. These classifications are exhaustively discussed in the following verses.

Since knowledge, action and the doer are characterized by the three Gunas, they fall into the nature of Prakriti or Nature or Matter. They have no connection with the Atman or the Self.

THREE KINDS OF KNOWLEDGE

sarvabhooteshu yenaikam bhaavamavyayameekshate
avibhaktam vibhakteshu tajjnaanam viddhi saatwikam // 18.20 //

THE KNOWLEDGE BY WHICH ONE SEES THE ONE INDESTRUCTIBLE REALITY IN ALL BEINGS, UNDIVIDED IN THE DIVIDED - KNOW THAT KNOWLEDGE TO BE SATTVIC.

prithaktwena tu yajjnaanam naanaabhaavaan prithagvidhaan
vetti sarveshu bhooteshu tajjnaanam viddhi raajasam //18.21 //

BUT THAT KNOWLEDGE THROUGH WHICH ONE SEES MULTIPLICITY OF BEINGS IN DIFFERENT CREATURES BY REASON OF THEIR SEPARATENESS - KNOW THAT KNOWLEDGE TO BE RAJASIC.

yattu kritsnavadekasmin kaarye saktamahaitukam
atatwaarthavadalpam cha tattaamasamudaahritam // 18.22 //

BUT THE KNOWLEDGE WHICH IS CONFINED TO ONE SINGLE EFFECT AS IF IT WERE THE WHOLE, WITHOUT CONCERN FOR THE CAUSE, WITHOUT GRASPING THE REAL AND NARROW - THAT IS DECLARED TO BE TAMASIC.

Sattvic:
That knowledge which can recognize the flux of things, which can feel the harmony underlying the unity in the diversity of forms and behaviors, which can live in the awareness of the One Life that pulsates in every living being i.e. Brahman or the Supreme Reality is the genuine achievement of a Sattvic intellect. Through this knowledge one Imperishable Being is seen in all existences. Though the body, mind and intellect equipments take different forms in different living creatures, the Sattvic knowledge recognizes all of them as the expressions of one and the same Non-dual Truth, Atman, which is the Essence in all of them.

Rajasic:
That knowledge which looks upon other living entities as different from one another is passionate or Rajasic. An intellect to which the world is an assortment of various types, behaving

under various moods differently, an intellect that recognizes the world as made up of an endless incomprehensible plurality has Rajasic knowledge. Finding creatures happy or unhappy, wise or ignorant, ugly or beautiful, a man endowed with Rajasic knowledge thinks that different souls dwell in different bodies.

Tamasic:
That knowledge which regards without any reason and understanding a particular path or view as the sole end and sticks to that opinion with arrogance and egoism, that knowledge which considers the entire world of things and beings as meant for its owner and his pleasures alone and which does not recognize anything beyond its ego is Tamasic. This knowledge is of the lowest type of spiritual seekers which ignores totally the Divine Presence.

Thus the knowledge of the Sattvic perceives oneness underlying the universe, that of the Rajasic recognizes the plurality of the world and that of the Tamasic is egoistic with a perverted view of the world.

It has to be noted that this categorization and that which will follow in this Chapter is not for judging others but to evaluate oneself and take corrective steps for self-improvement when wrong tendencies are observed

THREE KINDS OF WORK

niyatam sangarahitam araagadweshatah kritam
aphalaprepsunaa karma yattat saatwikamuchyate // 18.23 //

AN ACTION WHICH IS OBLIGATORY, WHICH IS FREE FROM ATTACHMENT, WHICH IS DONE WITHOUT LOVE

OR HATRED BY ONE WHO IS NOT DESIROUS OF ANY REWARD - THAT ACTION IS DECLARED TO BE SATTVIC.

yattu kaamepsunaa karma saahankaarena vaa punah
kriyate bahulaayaasam tadraajasamudaahritam // 18.24 //

BUT THAT ACTION WHICH IS DONE BY ONE LONGING FOR THE FULFILLMENT OF DESIRES OR GAINS, WITH EGOISM OR WITH MUCH EFFORT - THAT IS DECLARED TO BE RAJASIC.

anubandham kshayam himsaam anavekshya cha paurusham
mohaadaarabhyate karma yattat taamasamuchyate // 18.25 //

THAT ACTION WHICH IS UNDERTAKEN FROM DELUSION, WITHOUT REGARD TO THE CONSEQUENCE, LOSS, INJURY AND ONE'S OWN ABILITY- THAT IS DECLARED TO BE TAMASIC.

The threefold nature of action (Karma) is described.

Sattvic:
Sattvic actions are those that are one's own obligatory duties towards the society, performed without any attachment to the fruits thereof and that are not motivated by likes and dislikes. These duties are just performed spontaneously. Fulfillment and joy are sought in the very work itself. Such Sattvic actions are undertaken only by men who possess Sattvic knowledge. A Sattvic action is the purest producing peace and harmony in the field of activity. It is an obligatory action undertaken for its own sake in an attitude that work itself is worship. Such inspired activities are undertaken without any attachment and

any anxiety for the rewards. They are not guided by likes or dislikes of the performer. Action itself is fulfillment.

Rajasic:

Rajasic activities are those that are propelled by desires waiting for their fulfillment that are performed in a self-centered vainglorious attitude of 'I'-ness and which are undertaken with great strain and labor on the part of the doer. They are undertaken by men of Rajasic knowledge. Rajasic action is undertaken to satisfy one's desire in a spirit of arrogance, egoism and vanity. Such actions involve considerable effort and strain.

The consciousness of suffering, the sense that we are doing something disagreeable, that we are passing through grim agony and toil takes away value from the act. To feel consciously that we are doing something great, that we are sacrificing something vital is a failure of the sacrifice itself.

But when the work is undertaken for the cause, it is a labor of love and sacrifice itself is not felt as a sacrifice. Doing unpleasant things from a sense of duty, feeling the unpleasantness all the time is Rajasic. Doing it gladly in utter unself-consciousness, with a smile on the lips is Sattvic. It is the difference between an act of love and an act of law, an act of grace and an act of obligation.

Tamasic:

Tamasic actions are those that are undertaken without any regard for the consequences thereof and that bring disaster and sorrow to all including the performer. They emanate in an individual out of his misconception about the goal of life. They are undertaken by men of Tamasic knowledge.

THREE KINDS OF DOER

muktasango'nahamvaadi dhrityutsaahasamanvitah
siddhyasiddhyor nirvikaarah kartaa saatwika uchyate // 18.26 //

HE WHO IS FREE FROM ATTACHMENT, NON-EGOISTIC, ENDOWED WITH FORTITUDE AND ENTHUSIASM AND UNAFFECTED BY SUCCESS OR FAILURE IS CALLED SATTVIC.

raagee karmaphalaprepsur lubdho himsaatmako'shuchih
harshashokaanvitah kartaa raajasah parikeertitah // 18.27 //

PASSIONATE, DESIRING TO OBTAIN THE FRUITS OF ACTIONS, CRUEL, GREEDY, IMPURE, EASILY ELATED OR DEJECTED, SUCH AN AGENT IS SAID TO BE RAJASIC.
ayuktah praakritah stabdhah shatho naishkritiko'lasah
vishaadee deerghasootree cha kartaa taamasa uchyate // 18.28 //

UNSTEADY, VULGAR, UNBENDING, CHEATING, MALICIOUS, DEJECTED, LAZY AND PROCRASTINATING - SUCH AN AGENT IS CALLED TAMASIC.

Sattvic:
A doer who has no attachment to the field in which he is acting, who is not egoistic, who is full of persistence and zeal unmindful of obstacles on the path, who is not perturbed by the results of his actions, be they success or failure, is considered a *Sattvic-Karta*. He is ever conscious of the power of the Infinite Light in all his activities at all times.

Rajasic:
A doer who yields to passions, desires and attachments, who eagerly seeks the fruits of his work, who is selfish, greedy and

insatiable, whose acts cause harm to others, who is not pure in his means, who is tossed between joys and sorrows of life is considered *Rajasic Karta.*

Tamasic:
A doer who has no control over his own base mental impulses and instincts, who is arrogant, vulgar and obstinate in his own wrong conclusions, who is unsteady, despondent, deceitful, indolent, procrastinating and malicious is considered *Tamasic Karta.*

THREE KINDS OF UNDERSTANDING

buddherbhedam dhriteshchaiva gunatastrividham shrinu
prochyamaanamasheshena prithaktwena dhananjaya // 18.29 //

HEAR THE THREEFOLD DIVISION OF THE INTELLECT AND FORTITUDE ACCORDING TO THE GUNAS, AS I DECLARE THEM FULLY AND DISTINCTLY, O DHANAJAYA.

pravrittim cha nivrittim cha kaaryaakaarye bhayaabhaye
bandham moksham cha yaa vetti buddhih saa paartha saatwikee // 18.30 //

THAT WHICH KNOWS THE PATH OF WORK AND RENUNCIATION, WHAT OUGHT TO BE DONE AND WHAT OUGHT NOT TO BE DONE, FEAR AND FEARLESSNESS, BONDAGE AND LIBERATION - THAT INTELLECT IS SATTVIC, O PARTHA.

yayaa dharmamadharmam cha kaaryam cha akaaryam eva cha
ayathaavatprajaanaati buddhih saa paartha raajasee // 18.31 //

THAT BY WHICH ONE INCORRECTLY UNDERSTANDS DHARMA AND ADHARMA AND ALSO WHAT OUGHT TO BE DONE AND WHAT OUGHT NOT TO BE DONE - THAT INTELLECT, O PARTHA, IS RAJASIC.

adharmam dharmamiti yaa manyate tamasaavritaa
sarvaarthaan vipareetaamshcha buddhih saa paartha taamasee
// 18.32 //

THAT WHICH, ENVELOPED IN DARKNESS, REGARDS ADHARMA AS DHARMA AND VIEWS ALL THINGS IN A PERVERTED LIGHT - THAT INTELLECT, O PARTHA, IS CALLED TAMASIC.

Three types of understanding (Buddhi) are explained. Understanding or Buddhi means the intellectual capacity in the individual to grasp what is happening around.

Sattvic:
The understanding that can readily judge things that are to be done *(Pravritti)* and things that are to be avoided *(Nivritti)*, that can readily discriminate the beings and situations in its field of activity, that can distinguish between the right field of pursuit and wrong field of false ideas, that understands fear and fearlessness is considered as the *Sattvic Buddhi,* an understanding of purity.

Rajasic:
The understanding that erroneously judges both the right and the wrong that makes faulty conclusions about what should be done and what should not be done due to inaccurate egoistic pre-conceived notions is considered *Rajasic Buddhi.*

Tamasic:
The understanding that deems the wrong as the right, reversing every value due to ignorance, sees all things in a perverted way, always against the truth is considered as the *Tamasic Buddhi.* In fact this is no understanding at all; it can only be a perpetual misunderstanding.

THREE KINDS OF STEADINESS OR FORTITUDE

dhrityaa yayaa dhaarayate manah praanendriyakriyaah
yogenaavyaabhichaarinyaa dhritih saa paartha saatwikee
// 18.33 //

THE UNWAVERING FORTITUDE BY WHICH, THROUGH YOGA, THE FUNCTIONS OF THE MIND, THE LIFE-FORCE AND THE SENSES ARE RESTRAINED - THAT FORTITUDE O PARTHA, IS SATTVIC.

yayaa tu dharmakaamaarthaan dhrityaa dhaarayate'rjuna
prasangena phalaakaangkshee dhritih saa paartha raajasee
// 18.34 //

BUT THE FORTITUDE, O PARTHA, BY WHICH, ONE HOLDS FAST TO DUTY, PLEASURE AND WEALTH, AND CRAVES FOR THE FRUITS OF ACTION FROM ATTACHMENT, THAT FORTITUDE IS RAJASIC.

yayaa swapnam bhayam shokam vishaadam madameva cha
na vimunchati durmedhaa dhritih saa paartha taamasee // 18.35 //

THAT BY WHICH A STUPID MAN DOES NOT GIVE UP SLEEP, FEAR, GRIEF, DESPAIR AND ALSO ARROGANCE - THAT FORTITUDE, O PARTHA, IS TAMASIC.

The three kinds of Fortitude *(Dhriti)* is explained. Fortitude is the consistency of purpose and self-application with which every individual pursues his field of endeavor chosen for him by his Buddhi to achieve a set goal without allowing himself to be distracted by the obstacles on the way. Its power is proportional to the detachment from regrets over the past and anxieties for the future.

Sattvic:
The fortitude by which one controls the activities of the mind, organs of perception and organs of action is the *Sattvic Dhriti.* The stability with which one progressively controls one's mind and sense organs and their activities through single-pointed concentration upon a given goal is of the Sattvic type.

Rajasic:
The consistency with which one firmly holds on to duty, pleasure and wealth, ever desirous of enjoying the fruits of his action is of *Rajasic Dhriti.* He follows Dharma-duty- only to gain the heavens, pursues wealth to gain power in life and works for pleasure to achieve sensual satisfaction.

Tamasic:
The steadiness of purpose with which one does not abandon one's dreams and imaginations, fear and agitation, grief and sorrow, depression and arrogance is of *Tamasic Dhriti* and such a person is called *Durmedha*, a fool.

THREE KINDS OF HAPPINESS

sukham twidaaneem trividham shrinu me bharatarshabha
abhyaasaadramate yatra duhkhaantam cha nigacchati // 18.36 //

AND NOW HEAR FROM ME, O BEST AMONG THE BHARATAS, OF THE THREEFOLD PLEASURE IN WHICH ONE REJOICES BY PRACTICE AND BY WHICH ONE COMES TO THE END OF SORROW.

yattadagre vishamiva parinaame'mritopamam
tatsukham saatwikam proktam aatmabuddhi prasaadajam // 18.37 //

THAT WHICH IS LIKE POISON AT FIRST BUT IN THE END LIKE NECTAR - THAT PLEASURE IS DECLARED TO BE SATTVIC, SPRINGING FROM A CLEAR UNDERSTANDING OF THE SELF.

vishayendriya samyogaad yattadagre'mritopamam
parinaame vishamiva tatsukham raajasam smritam // 18.38 //

THAT PLEASURE WHICH ARISES FROM THE CONTACT OF THE SENSE-ORGANS WITH THE OBJECTS, WHICH IS AT FIRST LIKE NECTAR AND IN THE END LIKE POISON IS DECLARED TO BE RAJASIC.

yadagre chaanubandhe cha sukham mohanamaatmanah
nidraalasyapramaadottham tattaamasamudaahritam // 18.39 //

THAT PLEASURE WHICH AT THE BEGINNING AND AT THE END DELUDES THE SELF, WHICH ARISES FROM SLEEP, INDOLENCE AND HEEDLESSNESS IS DECLARED TO BE TAMASIC.

Happiness is the universal aim of life. Only it is of different kinds according to the Gunas which dominate our nature. If Tamas predominates in us, we are satisfied with violence and inertia, blindness and error. If Rajas prevails, wealth and power, pride and glory give us happiness. True happiness of human beings lies not in the possession of outward things but in the fulfillment of the higher mind and spirit, in the development of what is most inward in us. It may mean pain and restraint but it will lead us to joy and freedom. We can pass from the happiness of knowledge and virtue to the eternal calm and joy, *Ananda* of the Spirit, when we become one with the Highest Self and one with all beings.

Sattvic:
The joy arising out of the inner self-control and consequent self-perfection which looks though painful and arduous in the beginning, is enduring in the long run, in contrast with the fleeting joys of sensual satisfaction. It is the result of inner discipline and contemplation. This brings about tranquility in the intellect and from this tranquility of the intellect emerges Sattvic happiness. This happiness that arises from consistent effort lasts long and yields greater sense of fulfillment which is the result of an individual's balanced and self-disciplined life of high ideals and divine values of life.

Rajasic:
This pleasure arises only when the sense-organs are directly in contact with the sense-objects. In the beginning it is alluring but it creates a sense of exhaustion and dissipation in the enjoyer in the long run. It is also vitiated by the anxiety about its diminution and ultimate loss. Therefore the temporary happiness provided by the sense-objects is termed Rajasic.

Tamasic:
This type of happiness arises from 1. sleep - not the physiological every day sleep but the non-apprehension of Reality and the incapacity to perceive the goal of life - 2.indolence - the

incapacity of the intellect to think correctly about the problems that it faces to arrive at a correct judgment - and 3. Heedlessness - ignoring the values of higher ideals.

Sattva, rajasika and tamasika gunas in different combinations form the basis for the fourfold classification of human beings in a society into Brahmana, Kshatriya, Vaishya and Shudra.

The Lord gives a brief resume of the three spiritual disciplines to reach Brahman - Karma Yoga, path of action for the body, Bhakti Yoga, path of devotion for the mind and Jnana Yoga, Path of knowledge for the intellect.

Pursuing the path of action a seeker drops the bulk of the vasanas, desires. His mind becomes purified. His intellect becomes sharp. He rises to the path of knowledge and acquires spiritual values. He develops commitment to God and thus enters the path of devotion. The three disciplines prepare the seeker for concentration, meditation upon the Supreme through which he realizes Brahman.

Krishna appeals to Arjuna to drop his ego and seek the supreme Self within. Every person functions helplessly according to one's own nature. Krishna assures Arjuna that He has imparted the knowledge necessary to take the plunge, leaving the choice to him to reflect and decide his course of action.

ONE'S NATURE *(SWABHAVA)* AND STATION IN LIFE *(SWADHARMA)*

na tadasti prithivyaam vaa divi deveshu vaa punah
Sattvam prakritijairmuktam yadebhih syaat tribhirgunaih // 18.40 //

THERE IS NO BEING ON EARTH OR AGAIN IN HEAVEN AMONG THE DEVAS, WHO IS FREE FROM THESE THREE GUNAS BORN OF PRAKRITI (NATURE).

This verse concludes the discussion so far made about the three Gunas influencing the personality and the behavioral pattern of the living organisms. Sri Krishna says that there is no creature either on the earth or among the Gods in the heaven who is free from the influences of these three Gunas. The play of these three Gunas is the very expression of Prakriti. Put together they are the manifestations of Maya which make the individuals differ from each other.

With these three measuring rods Sri Krishna classifies the entire humanity under four distinct types. The criterion of this classification of man is the quality of his inner equipments responsible for achievements in the field of his activities.

The fourfold division of society is based on this principle. Certain well defined characteristics determine these four classes in the community. They are never determined by birth. This classification of society is as follows:

- Brahmanas - who have major portion of Sattva and a little Rajas with minimum Tamas.
- Kshatriyas - who have mostly Rajas with some Sattva and very little Tamas.
- Vaishyas - who have more Rajas, very little Sattva and some Tamas.
- Sudras - mostly Tamas, very little Rajas and negligible Sattva.

braahmanaKshatriyavishaam shoodraanaam cha parantapa
karmaani pravibhaktaani swabhaavaprabhavairgunaih // 18.41 //

OF BRAHMANAS, KSHATRIYAS AND VAISHYAS, AS ALSO THE SUDRAS, O ARJUNA, THE ACTIVITIES ARE DISTINGUISHED IN ACCORDANCE WITH THE QUALITIES BORN OF THEIR OWN NATURE.

Sri Krishna applies the characteristics of various Gunas to the social fabric and classifies the entire mankind under four different heads viz. Brahmanas, Kshatriyas, Vaishyas and Sudras.

Different kinds of duties are assigned to each of these categories of individuals depending on their nature *(Swabhava)* which in turn depends on the Gunas predominating in them. This classification is based on the quality of the inner personality of the individuals and not on the accident of their birth.

The fourfold order is not peculiar to Hindu society. It is of universal application. The classification depends on types of human nature. Each of the four classes has certain well defined characteristics though they are not to be regarded as exclusive. They are not always determined by heredity.

The Gita cannot be used to support the existing social order with its rigidity and confusion. The Gita enlarges the scope and meaning of the theory of the fourfold order. Man's outward life must express his inward being; the surface must reflect the depth. Each individual has his inborn nature-Swabhava- and to make it effective in his life is his duty-Swadharma. Each individual is a focus of the Supreme, a fragment of the Divine. His destiny is to bring out in his life this divine possibility. The

Gita lays the utmost emphasis on Swadharma – the dharma or duty of an individual – as determined by his Swabhava, his inner nature formed as a result of his own past actions.

The one Spirit of the universe has produced the multiplicity of souls in the world, but the idea of the Divine is our essential nature, the truth of our being, our Swabhava and not the apparatus of the Gunas, which is only the medium of expression. If each individual does what is appropriate to him, if he follows the law of his being, his Swadharma, then God would express Himself in the free volitions of human beings. All that is essential for the world will be done without a conflict.

But men rarely do what they ought to do. When they undertake to determine events believing that they know the plan of the whole, they work mischief on the earth. So long as our work is done in accordance with our nature, we are righteous and if we dedicate it to God, our work becomes a means of spiritual perfection. When the divine in the individual is completely manifested, he attains the eternal, imperishable status. The problem that human life sets to us is to discover our true self and live according to its truth; otherwise we would sin against our nature.

The emphasis on Swabhava indicates that human beings are to be treated as individuals and not as types. Arjuna is told that he who fights gallantly as a warrior becomes mature for the peace of wisdom. There are four broad types of nature and answering to them are four kinds of social living. The four classes are not determined by birth or colour but by psychological characteristics which enables us for definite functions in society.

shamo damanastapah shaucham kshaantiraarjavameva cha jnaanam vijnaanam aastikyam brahmakarma swabhaavajam // 18.42 //

SERENITY, SELF-RESTRAINT, AUSTERITY, PURITY, FORGIVENESS AND ALSO UPRIGHTNESS, KNOWLEDGE, REALIZATION AND BELIEF IN GOD ARE THE DUTIES OF THE BRAHMANAS, BORN OF THEIR OWN NATURE.

The duties of the *Brahmanas* are enumerated:

- Serenity *(Shama)* - Controlling the mind from running after the world of objects in pursuit of sensual enjoyment.
- Self restraint *(Dama)* - Controlling the sense organs from conveying the external stimuli to the mind.
- Austerity *(Tapas)* - Conscious physical self denial to save human energy from sense indulgence and directing such energy towards spiritual awakening.
- Purity (*Shaucham*)- External cleanliness and internal purity.
- Forgiveness or Forbearance *(Kshanti)*- To be patient and forgiving even against wrongs committed against oneself.
- Uprightness *(Arjavam)*- A quality that makes the individual straightforward in all his dealings and thus becoming fearless.
- Cultivating and practicing these six qualities are the life-long duty of a Brahmana. Three more duties are added by The Lord as a code of conduct or duties in the spiritual side of a Brahmana. They are:
- Knowledge *(Jnanam)* - Knowledge of all that Upanishads deal with.

- Wisdom *(Vijnanam)* - Personal experience of the knowledge so acquired. Knowledge is that which is imparted while wisdom is that which is experienced within oneself. Wisdom is living the knowledge gained by studies.
- Faith *(Astikyam)* - Conviction to live what one has learnt and understood.

shauryam tejo dhritirdaakshyam yuddhe chaapyapalaayanam
daanameeshwarabhaavashcha kshaatram karmaswabhaavajam
// 18.43 //

PROWESS, SPLENDOR, FIRMNESS, DEXTERITY AND ALSO NOT FLEEING EVEN IN A BATTLE, GENEROSITY AND LEADERSHIP ARE THE DUTIES OF KSHATRIYAS, BORN OF THEIR OWN NATURE.

The qualities of a Kshatriya are enumerated:

- Prowess and splendor - Vigor to meet challenges in life.
- Firmness or fortitude - Zeal and consistency of purpose.
- Dexterity - Alertness and foresight.
- Not fleeing even from a battle - Not to accept defeat in any field of activity.
- Generosity - Compassion to those in need of help.
- Lordliness - Self confidence in one's own ability and possessing leadership qualities.

These are the duties of the Kshatriyas, the men of action.

krishigaurakshyavaanijyam vaishyakarma swabhaavajam
paricharyaatmakam karma shoodrasyaapi swabhaavajam
// 18.44 //

AGRICULTURE, CATTLE REARING AND TRADE ARE THE DUTIES OF THE VAISHYA CLASS BORN OF THEIR OWN NATURE; ACTION CONSISTING OF SERVICE IS THE DUTY OF THE SUDRA CLASS BORN OF THEIR OWN NATURE.

The duties of Vaishyas and Sudras are stated in this verse.

Thus the mental temperament of a man determines what class he belongs to and each class has been given a set of duties to perform in the world. If a man does a type of work for which he is not fit temperamentally, chaos follows.

Each class of people mentioned here has to work with a spirit of dedication for their own evolution and sense of fulfillment. When each one works according to Vasanas in him and fully devotes himself to the prescribed duties, he develops within himself and attains gradually the State of Perfection.

It is not a question of identical opportunities but equal opportunities for all men to rise to the highest station in social life, for men differ in their powers. Each one should have the opportunity of achieving his human fullness, the fruits of wisdom and virtue, according to his effort and condition.

The Varna rules recognize that different men contribute to the general good in different ways. Society is a functional organization and all functions which are essential for the health of society are to be regarded as socially equal. Individuals of varying capacities are bound together in a living organic social system; the process is not an attempt to achieve uniformity, which is impossible, but at an integrated variety. All men are not equal in their capacities but all men are equally necessary for society and their contributions from their different stations are of equal value.

swe swe karmanyabhiratah samsiddhim labhate narah
swakarmaniratah siddhim yathaa vindati tacchrinu // 18.45 //

EACH MAN, DEVOTED TO HIS OWN DUTY, ATTAINS PERFECTION. HOW HE ATTAINS PERFECTION WHILE BEING ENGAGED IN HIS OWN DUTY, HEAR NOW.

Within the power of our nature, we must live up fully to our duty. By thus working in the field ordered by one's own vasanas, renouncing ego and its desires and with a spirit of dedication and total surrender to the Infinite, mind's evolution starts. How this is achieved is explained in the following verses.

PERFECTION THROUGH PERFORMANCE OF DUTY

yatah pravrittirbhootaanaam yena sarvamidam tatam
swakarmanaa tamabhyarchya siddhim vindati maanavah // 18.46 //

HE FROM WHOM ALL THE BEINGS HAVE EVOLVED AND BY WHOM ALL THIS IS PERVADED, BY WORSHIPPING HIM THROUGH THE PERFORMANCE OF HIS OWN DUTY, MAN ATTAINS PERFECTION.

When a man acts according to his Swabhava and Swadharma he can attain joy and relief only when he learns to work and achieve in a spirit of total self-surrender.

From whom all beings evolved and by whom all is pervaded: Body, mind and intellect are by themselves inert. They can discharge their functions only if they are prompted by Consciousness. To remember constantly that Consciousness - the Atman - which makes the activities to happen through the body equipments is to become a witness to all the agitations in life without getting agitated.

Work becomes worship, by aligning the mind through the performance of activity, to the consciousness of the Self. This change of attitude towards work removes drudgery in work situations converting dreariness into meditation. Sri Krishna says by so performing one's own duties one can attain the highest Perfection. Apart from yielding the reward work itself becomes a fulfillment and the doer becomes an integrated personality.

shreyaanswadharmo vigunah paradharmaat swanushthitaat
swabhaavaniyatam karma kurvannaapnoti kilbisham // 18.47 //

BETTER IS ONE'S OWN DUTY THOUGH IMPERFECTLY CARRIED OUT THAN THE DUTY OF ANOTHER WELL PERFORMED. HE WHO DOES THE DUTY ORDAINED BY HIS OWN NATURE INCURS NO SIN.

This theme was discussed in Ch.3.35 also. It is no use employing our minds in tasks which are contrary to our nature. Every one has his place and everything has a purpose in the scheme of things for each can do something which the others cannot do so well. In each of us lies a principle of divine expression. It is our real nature, Swabhava, finding partial expression in our various activities. By following its guidance in our thought, aspiration and endeavor, we progressively realize the intention of the Spirit for us.

sahajam karma kaunteya sadoshamapi na tyajet
sarvaarambhaa hi doshena dhoomenaagnirivaavritaah // 18.48 //

ONE SHOULD NOT ABANDON, O KAUNTEYA, THE DUTY SUITED TO ONE'S NATURE, THOUGH IT MAY BE DEFECTIVE, FOR ALL UNDERTAKINGS ARE CLOUDED BY DEFECTS, AS THE FIRE BY SMOKE.

The factors that determine our actions are the temperaments and the environment that bring forth new tendencies in us. Sri Krishna indicates that a spiritual seeker must constantly strive to stand apart from the effects of environments as the man is a master of his circumstances.

The statement that all actions are clouded by defects as fire by the smoke means that actions are always blended with the sense of 'I am the doer' which creates new vasanas and therefore they are full of defects. This defect is as much unavoidable as the smoke in fire. As ventilation reduces the impact of the smoke the more we concentrate on the Consciousness Divine, the less will be the assertion of ego and egocentric desires in us and therefore the work we undertake will be purified to that extent.

KARMA YOGA AND ABSOLUTE PERFECTION

asaktabuddhih sarvatra jitaatmaa vigatasprihah
naishkarmyasiddhim paramaam sannyaasenaadhigacchati // 18.49 //

HE WHOSE INTELLECT IS UNATTACHED EVERYWHERE, WHO HAS SUBDUED HIS SELF, FROM WHOM DESIRE HAS FLED, HE, BY RENUNCIATION, ATTAINS THE SUPREME STATE OF FREEDOM FROM ACTION.

The Gita is not tired of repeating that restraint and freedom from desire are essential to spiritual perfection. Attachments to objects, a sense of ego, are the characteristics of our lower nature. If we are to rise to knowledge of our true Self, we must conquer our lower nature with its ignorance and inertia, its love of worldly possessions, etc.

The state of actionlessness or transcending all work does not mean complete withdrawal from all work. Such a question is not possible so long as we live in the body. The Gita insists on inner renunciation. As the ego and nature are akin, the liberated soul becoming Brahman, the Pure Self, described as silent, calm, and inactive, acts in the world of Prakriti, knowing what the latter is.

The highest state is here described, not positively as entering into The Lord but negatively as freedom from *Kama,* Desire.

PERFECTION AND REALIZING BRAHMAN

siddhim praapto yathaa brahma tathaapnoti nibodha me
samaasenaiva kaunteya nishthaa jnaanasya yaa paraa // 18.50 //

LEARN FROM ME IN BRIEF, O KAUNTEYA, HOW HE WHO HAS ATTAINED PERFECTION REACHES BRAHMAN (THE ETERNAL), THAT SUPREME STATE OF KNOWLEDGE.

When our intellect becomes free from its attachments and thus controls our mind and body, then alone we are fit for renunciation of the lower ego-sense and reach for the Infinite Self which is the process of meditation.

buddhyaa vishuddhayaa yukto dhrityaatmaanam niyamya cha shabdaadeen vishayaamstyaktwaa raagadweshau vyudasya cha // 18.51 //

ENDOWED WITH PURE INTELLECT, FIRMLY RESTRAINING ONESELF, TURNING AWAY FROM SOUND AND OTHER OBJECTS OF SENSE AND ABANDONING BOTH HATRED AND ATTRACTION.

viviktasevee laghwaashee yatvaakkaayamaanasah
dhyaanayogaparo nityam vairaagyam samupaashritah // 18.52 //

DWELLING IN SOLITUDE, EATING BUT LITTLE, WITH SPEECH, BODY AND MIND SUBDUED, ALWAYS ENGAGED IN MEDITATION AND CONCENTRATION TAKING REFUGE IN DISPASSION.

ahamkaaram balam darpam kaamam krodham parigraham
vimuchya nirmamah shaanto brahmabhooyaaya kalpate // 18.53 //

HAVING ABANDONED EGOISM, STRENGTH, ARROGANCE, DESIRE, ANGER AND COVETOUSNESS, FREE FROM THE NOTION OF 'MINE' NESS AND TRANQUIL IN MIND, HE BECOMES WORTHY OF BECOMING ONE WITH BRAHMAN.

The process of meditation and attaining the Supreme - Brahman - is discussed. The prerequisites or the qualities which are necessary for meditation are as follows:

- Pure intellect - An intellect without tendencies to acquire, possess and enjoy sense objects.
- Controlling the mind and senses - By receiving the external stimuli the sense organs distract the mind

from concentrating on the Infinite and hence they have to be controlled.

- Renouncing sense objects - By controlling the sense organs the external stimuli such as sound, form, touch, taste or smell can be prevented from reaching the mind through the respective channels of ears, eyes, skin, tongue and nose. Once this is achieved sense objects automatically lose their value and attraction.
- Abandoning attraction and hatred - When the mind is thus protected it cannot, by itself, get agitated by recapitulating agreeable or disagreeable incidents or things.

Thus a successful meditator is one who has an intellect purified from all extrovert desires, who has brought the mind and sense organs under the control of the intellect, thereby preventing them from running after sense objects and who has given up the ideas of likes and dislikes.

- Dwelling in solitude - seeking a place where there will be least disturbance.
- Eating but little - Temperate eating habits.
- Subduing body, mind and speech - Elimination of egocentric attitude in all our thinking, action and relationship with others.
- Ever engaged in meditation and concentration - After the mind is quietened it has to be kept continuously busy by contemplation on The Lord in an attitude of complete identification with Him.
- Taking refuge in dispassion - It is a state where the mind finds no attraction for the objects of the senses. This attitude of dispassion or *vairagya* is necessary for the spiritual growth.

Thus a true seeker of a higher life must seek solitude, live in temperance, subdue his body, mind and speech and must live in a spirit of dispassion.

The qualities that are to be renounced for meditation are:

Although Sri Krishna lists out these qualities, they are in fact basically only one which is the sense of 'I-ness'. When this sense of doership develops, egocentric vanity takes over the individual claiming a false sense of power, pride and arrogance. For an individual working under the influence of power and arrogance, lust and anger are natural while he tries by any means to acquire more and more wealth and protects what has already been acquired.

The Lord advises to abandon the following six qualities and thus become egoless and tranquil.

- egoism
- strength
- arrogance
- desire,
- anger
- covetousness

This is the peace arising out of wisdom and satisfaction experienced in the Realm of Perfection. When the sense of agency and the endless chase of sense gratifications have been renounced the seeker experiences a relative quietitude within him.

This verse does not say that such an individual has reached Perfection but it only says that he is worthy of becoming one with Brahman. Thus what has so far been discussed is only the preliminary preparation for the final Realization.

THE HIGHEST DEVOTION

brahmabhootah prasannaatmaa na shochati na kaangkshati
samah sarveshu bhooteshu madbhaktim labhate paraam // 18.54 //

HAVING BECOME ONE WITH BRAHMAN, BEING SERENE IN THE SELF, HE NEITHER GRIEVES NOR DESIRES. REGARDING ALL BEINGS AS ALIKE HE ATTAINS SUPREME DEVOTION TO ME.

After eliminating egoism and its manifestations in the form of power, pride, lust, passion and sense of possession the seeker experiences greater peace within as he becomes free from all false evaluations of life.

bhaktyaa maamabhijaanaati yaavaanyashchaasmi tattwatah
tato maam tattwato jnaatwaa vishate tadanantaram // 18.55 //

BY DEVOTION HE KNOWS ME IN ESSENCE, WHAT AND WHO I AM; THEN HAVING KNOWN ME IN MY ESSENCE, HE FORTHWITH ENTERS INTO ME, THE SUPREME.

The knower, the devotee, becomes one with the supreme Lord, the Perfect Person, in Self-knowledge and Self-experience. Jnana, supreme wisdom and bhakti, supreme devotion, have the same goal. To become Brahman is to love God, to know Him fully and to enter His being. Entering Him means that when the ego is replaced by God Consciousness the individuality vanishes. The conception of individuality or 'I-ness' ends and he attains Brahmanhood.

By devotion he knows Me in essence, what and who I am: The devotee knows that the Lord is devoid of all names and forms caused by *maya* and is of the nature of the Absolute. He knows that the Lord alone is the essence of the diverse manifestations caused by His maya.

Then having known Me in My essence, he forthwith enters into Me, the Supreme:
Having known that the Lord is non-dual, unborn, undecaying, unchanging and of the nature of spirit and Consciousness, he attains Brahmanhood. The acts of knowing and entering are not two separate and consecutive actions. To know the Lord truly is to be completely absorbed in Him.

APPLICATION OF THE TEACHING TO ARJUNA'S CASE

sarvakarmaanyapi sadaa kurvaano madvyapaashrayah
matprsaadaadavaapnoti shaashwatam padamavyayam // 18.56 //

DOING ALL ACTIONS, ALWAYS TAKING REFUGE IN ME, BY MY GRACE, HE OBTAINS THE ETERNAL, INDESTRUCTIBLE STATE OR ABODE.

Performing all actions and taking refuge in Him mean rendering selfless service in society which should be without the sense of agency and with a sense of dedication to Him. In an individual to the extent his mind and intellect are available for the spiritual truth, he is under the grace or blessings of The Lord. An individual thus working in the field of activity reaches the Immortal State, the state of Perfection.

The above three verses indicate that the ultimate goal of the paths of knowledge, devotion and action is the realization of the seeker's oneness with the Supreme. This is the Integral *Sadhana* synthesizing the methods of Devotion, Work and Knowledge through disciplining body, mind and intellect.

All disciplines pursued from the body level to control the mind and make it turn towards the Ideal are called KARMA YOGA.

All methods to canalize the emotions for controlling the mind and make it contemplate on the Higher are called BHAKTI YOGA.

All the study and reflection, detachment and meditation practiced at the intellectual level whereby the mind is enabled to experience the Infinitude is called JNANA YOGA.

Practicing all these three Yogas is disciplining the human personality in all its three layers of body, mind and intellect which transforms the perceiver, feeler and thinker in the man. This is the outstanding contribution of Gita to the Hindu culture.

chetasaa sarvakarmaani mayi sannyasya matparah
buddhiyogamupaashritya macchittah satatam bhava // 18.57 //

MENTALLY RENOUNCING ALL ACTIONS IN ME, HAVING ME AS THE HIGHEST GOAL, RESORTING TO THE YOGA OF DISCRIMINATION YOU EVER FIX YOUR MIND ON ME.

macchittah sarvadurgaani matprasaadaat tarishyasi
atha chet twam ahamkaaraan na shroshyasi vinangkshyasi // 18.58 //

FIXING YOUR MIND ON ME, YOU SHALL BY MY GRACE OVERCOME ALL OBSTACLES; BUT IF FROM EGOISM YOU WILL NOT HEAR ME, YOU SHALL PERISH.

Mentally renouncing all actions in Me and having Me as the highest goal: Both the ego and egocentric anxieties for enjoying the rewards are to be renounced and then actions are to be performed keeping The Lord as the goal.

Resorting to the Yoga of discrimination: To discriminate the right from the wrong and pursuing the path of selfless action is the Buddhi Yoga.

Ever fix your mind on Me: One who surrendered himself before The Lord and serves all his creatures can alone fix his attention constantly on Him. A devotee who carries out all his activities in dedication to Him experiences the Immutable State of the Self.

Most of our obstacles in life are imaginary due to false fears and anxieties. By constantly remembering The Lord and through His grace all the obstacles on the path can be overcome. But because of ego and egocentric desires if the path shown by The Lord is not to be followed by the seeker then he will by his own ideas and emotions become incapable of achieving anything worthwhile; he will perish, says Sri Krishna.

In the following verses Sri Krishna tries to go over the philosophical ideas to Arjuna to solve the problem of his despondency and motivate him to accomplish his immediate task ahead.

yadahamkaaram aashritya na yotsya iti manyase
mithyaisha vyavasaayaste prakritistwaam niyokshyati // 18.59 //

IF FILLED WITH EGOISM, YOU THINK 'I WILL NOT FIGHT', VAIN IS YOUR RESOLUTION; FOR YOUR NATURE WILL COMPEL YOU.

swabhaavajena kaunteya nibaddhah swena karmanaa
kartum necchasi yanmohaat karishyasyavasho'pi tat // 18.60 //

O KAUNTEYA, BOUND BY YOUR OWN KARMA (ACTION), BORN OF YOUR OWN NATURE, THAT WHICH FROM DELUSION YOU WISH NOT TO DO, EVEN THAT YOU SHALL DO HELPLESSLY AGAINST YOUR WILL.

Sri Krishna tells Arjuna that if he is under the impression that he would not fight due to self-importance, self-conceit and the temporary illusion of escapism, it would merely be an exercise in futility because being a Kshatriya, his Rajasic temperament will dominate and force him to fight.

The Lord continues that in spite of his determination not to wage war Arjuna will be compelled to fight by the power of his own nature ordered by his Karma or vasanas existing in him at that moment. This is the law of life.

eeshwarah sarvabhootaanaam hriddeshe'rjuna tishthati
bhraamayan sarvabhootaani yantraaroodhaani maayayaa // 18.61 //

THE LORD DWELLS IN THE HEARTS OF ALL BEINGS, O ARJUNA, CAUSING ALL BEINGS, BY HIS ILLUSIVE POWER, TO REVOLVE, AS IF CAUGHT IN A MACHINE.

The relations of our inborn nature and its fateful compulsion are regulated by the Divine who dwells in our hearts and guides our development. The power that determines events is not a blind, unthinking will which we call fate or destiny. The Spirit that rules the cosmos, The Lord who presides over the evolution of the cosmic plan, is seated in the heart of every being and will not let him rest.

The Supreme is the inmost self of our existence. All life is a movement of the rhythm of His life and our powers and acts are all derived from Him. If, in our ignorance, we forget this deepest truth, the truth will not alter. If we live consciously in His truth, we will resign all actions to God and escape from our ego. If we do not, even then the truth will prevail. Sooner or later we will yield to the purpose of The Lord. The Supreme desires our free co-operation. When we become the media for the light of God, He uses us for His work.

As puppets are moved by a string-puller seated behind the scene, so also the created beings move and act on the stage of the world under the control of the Lord seated in the hearts of all. Compare this with 9.10.

tameva sharanam gaccha sarvabhaavena bhaarata
tatprsaadaatparaam shaantim sthaanam praapsyasi shaashwatam // 18.62

TAKE REFUGE IN HIM ALONE WITH ALL YOUR SOUL, O BHARATA. BY HIS GRACE YOU WILL GAIN SUPREME PEACE AND THE EVERLASTING ABODE.

We must be conscious of the Divine on all the planes of our existence. Arjuna is called upon to understand the will of

God and do his duty. He must change the whole orientation of his being; give up self-conceit, for all creatures are under the control of the Supreme Lord. He must put himself at the service of the Supreme. His illusion will then be dispelled; the bond of cause and consequence will be broken. He will attain shadowless light, perfect harmony and Supreme Blessedness.

iti te jnaanamaakhyaatam guhyaad guhyataram mayaa
vimrishyaitadasheshena yathecchasi tathaa kuru // 18.63 //

THUS HAS THE WISDOM MORE PROFOUND THAN ALL PROFUNDITIES BEEN DECLARED TO YOU BY ME. REFLECT ON IT FULLY, AND THEN DO AS YOU CHOOSE.

This verse can be considered as the conclusion of The Lord's discourses to Arjuna in the battlefield of Kurukshetra. Sri Krishna says that he has declared to Arjuna (through him to the entire humanity) all the essential features of the right way of living and its noble endeavors for which there is nothing more to add.

This knowledge is more secret than all the secrets because it is not easy for one to understand the Gita way of life and its vision of the goal in all their implications unless one is initiated into them. Even the very sharp intellect will fail to feel the presence of the subtle, eternal and infinite Self. Sri Krishna advises Arjuna to think and reflect over what all He had declared and thereafter take such decision as he thinks proper without blindly accepting what has been told to him. Teaching is not indoctrination. Thus The Lord leaves the decision to act and lead a higher life to Arjuna's own free and sweet choice after considering all the points brought to his notice.

There is no compulsion involved and free choice is the characteristic of Hinduism as the human personality cannot grow morally and ethically through coercion. The Supreme does not impose His command; we are free at any moment to reject or accept the Divine call. The integral surrender should be made with the fullest consent of the seeker. God does not do the climbing for us but supports us whenever we stumble, comfort us when we fall. He is prepared to wait till we turn to Him. Thus The Lord's approach is counseling but not commanding. The scriptures serve the purpose of telling man what he should do and what he should not. It is up to man himself to choose the right and to reject the wrong

Thus Sri Krishna helps out Arjuna, indicating what is good for him i.e., to rise above this world of perception, emotion and thought and reach the Supreme Being. The lord assures his teaching will liberate his devotees. The Lord emphasizes the importance of communicating His message to mankind thereby both the teacher and the taught will evolve spiritually. Free from delusion, with faith and dedicated effort they would reach the ultimate state of Enlightenment.

Arjuna understands Sri Krishna's message and decides to pursue the higher objectives enunciated by the Lord. Sanjaya glorifies Sri Krishna and His wonderful dialogue. Sanjaya is in ecstasy having heard the wonderful dialogue between Lord Krishna and Arjuna.

He bows in gratitude to Vyasa whose grace enabled him to hear the holy dialogue. He pronounces to King Dhritarashtra his immense joy beholding the divine form of Krishna and remembering His great message over and over again. Finally, he declares that the Lord's firm principles will bless this world with success, prosperity and peace.

FINAL APPEAL

sarva guhyatamam bhooyah shrinu me paramam vachah
ishto'si me dhridhamiti tato vakshyaami te hitam // 18.64 //

LISTEN AGAIN MY SUPREME WORD, MOST SECRET OF ALL; BECAUSE YOU ARE DEARLY BELOVED OF ME, I WILL TELL YOU WHAT IS GOOD FOR YOU.

Although Arjuna was given a free choice to make his independent decision he gave an impression that still some doubts and misgivings were lurking in his mind. Therefore Sri Krishna tells Arjuna that He will again confide in him the profoundest wisdom, the supreme secret because he is His dearest friend. This secret is revealed in the following two verses.

manmanaa bhava madbhakto madyaajee maam namaskuru
maamevai'shyasi satyam te pratijaane priyo'si me // 18.65 //

FIX YOUR MIND ON ME, BE DEVOTED TO ME, WORSHIP TO ME, BOW DOWN TO ME, YOU SHALL EVEN COME TO ME; TRULY THIS IS MY PLEDGE TO YOU, FOR YOU ARE DEAR TO ME.

Sri Krishna repeats the salient features of the philosophy of the Gita for the benefit of Arjuna and through him for all of us.

The Lord lays down four conditions for the success of a seeker. To the one in whom these are present an assurance of reaching Him is given. In order to avoid anybody taking His words lightly He adds that this is His true promise and specifically conveys this secret to Arjuna because he is dear to Him and The Lord loves him.

These conditions are:

- *Fix the mind on The Lord, ever remembering Him.*
- *Regard Him as the sole refuge.*
- *Ever devotedly identify with Him through the process of performing selfless activities and*
- *Dedicate them to Him in an attitude of reverence and sacrifice.*

The ultimate mystery, the supreme teaching with which The Lord wound up Chapter 9.34 is repeated here. Thought, worship, sacrifice and reverence, all must be directed to The Lord. We must surrender ourselves to God. Our spiritual life depends as much on our going to Him, as on His coming to us. It is not only our ascent to God but His descent to man. He is waiting only for our trustful appeal to Him.

sarva dharmaan parityajya maamekam sharanam vraja
aham twaa sarvapaapebhyo mokshayishyaami maa shuchah // 18.66 //

ABANDONING ALL DHARMAS (OF THE BODY, MIND AND INTELLECT), TAKE REFUGE IN ME ALONE; I WILL LIBERATE YOU FROM ALL SINS, DO NOT GRIEVE.

This is the noblest of all the verses in the Gita having brilliant import and yet this is the most controversial. Philosophers, translators, reviewers, critics and commentators have put forward several interpretations of this verse each maintaining his own point of view.

To Sri Ramanuja, this is the final verse (*Charama-Shloka*) of the whole Gita.

It is the answer given by The Lord to the question put by Arjuna in Chapter 2.7 – 'My heart is overpowered by the taint of pity, my mind is confused as to duty. I ask you. Tell me decisively what is good for me, I am your disciple. Instruct me who has taken refuge in You'.

Leaving aside all these divergent opinions we can understand this verse as follows.

The essential property of a substance is called its *Dharma*. Therefore, the "essential *Dharma*" of man is the Divine Spark of Existence, the Infinite Lord, and the Atman. With this understanding of the term *Dharma*, we can appreciate that it differs from mere ethical and moral rules of conduct, all duties in life, all duties towards relations, friends, community, nation and the world, all our obligations to our environment, all our affections, reverence, charity, and sense of goodwill etc. Thus to live truly as the *Atman*, and to express Its Infinite Perfection through all our actions and in all our contacts with the outer world is to rediscover our *Dharma*.

In this Verse, the Lord wants us to accomplish three distinct adjustments in our inner personality. They are: (1) Renounce all Dharmas through meditation; (2) surrender to My refuge alone; and while in the state of meditation, (3) stop all worries. And as a reward He promises: "I shall release you from all sins". This is a promise given to all mankind.

Abandoning all *dharma* (*Sarva-Dharman Parityajya*) - As a mortal, finite ego, the seeker is living with the *Dharmas* of his body, mind and intellect, and exists in life as a mere perceiver, feeler, and thinker. The perceiver-feeler-thinker personality in us is the "individuality" which expresses itself as the "ego."

These are not our 'essential' *Dharmas*. And since these are the 'non-essentials,' "renouncing all *dharmas*" means "ending the ego." "To renounce" therefore means "not to allow ourselves to fall again and again into this state of identification with the outer envelopments of matter around us". Extrovert tendencies of the mind are to be renounced. "Develop introspection diligently" is the deep suggestion in the phrase "renouncing all *dharmas*."

Come to me alone for shelter (*Mam-ekam Sharanam Vraja*) - Self-withdrawal from our extrovert nature will be impossible unless the mind is given a positive method of developing its introvert attention. By single-pointed, steady contemplation upon Me, the Self, which is the One-without-a-second, we can successfully accomplish our total withdrawal from the misinterpreting equipments of the body, mind and intellect. Lord Krishna commands His devotees to come to His shelter whereby they can accomplish the renunciation of all their false identifications.

I shall release you from all sins *(aham twaa sarvapaapebhyo mokshayishyaami)* - That which brings about agitations and causes dissipation of the energies is called "sin". The actions themselves can leave their "foot prints" upon the mental stuff, and these marks are called *vasanas*. To erase all *vasanas* completely is to stop all thoughts - the total cessation of thought-flow viz. "mind". Transcending the mind-intellect-equipment is to reach the plane of Pure Consciousness, the Krishna-Reality.

Be not grieved (*Maa shuchah*) - When both the above conditions are accomplished, the seeker reaches a state of tranquility in meditation. Lord Krishna wants the seeker to renounce all his "anxieties to realize." Even a desire to realize is a disturbing thought that can obstruct the final achievement. Arjuna was perturbed by the various duties, ritualistic and ethical, that the war will result in the confusion of castes and indifference to the ancestors as well as in the violation of sacred duties of reverence for the teachers etc. Sri Krishna tells him not to worry about these laws and usages, but to trust Him and bow down to His will. If he consecrates his life, actions, feelings and thoughts, and surrenders himself to God, He will guide him through the battle of life and he need have no tears or fears. Surrender is the only way to self-transcendence. This is the Lord's assurance to all humanity.

The stanza is important inasmuch as it is one of the most powerfully worded verses in the Gita wherein the Lord undertakes to do something helpful for the seeker in case he is ready to obliterate his ego and put forth his best efforts.

"We should willingly yield to His pressure, completely surrender to His will and take shelter in His love. If we destroy confidence in our ego and replace it by perfect confidence in God, He will save us. He asks us of total self-giving and gives in return the power of the Spirit which changes every situation.

When we turn to Him and let Him fill our whole being, our responsibility ceases. He deals with us and leads us beyond all sorrow. It is an unreserved surrender to the Supreme who takes us up and raises to our utmost possible perfection. Though the Lord conducts the world according to the fixed laws and expects us to conform to the law of right action based on our nature and station in life, if we take shelter in Him, we transcend all these. A seemingly outer help must come to man, for his soul cannot deliver itself from the trap in which it is caught by his own effort". Dr.S.Radhakrishnan.

The teachings of the Gita are concluded here.

HOW TO FOLLOW THE DOCTRINE?

idam te naatapaskaaya naabhaktaaya kadaachana
na chaashushrooshave vaachyam na cha maam yo'bhyasooyati // 18.67 //

THIS IS NEVER TO BE SPOKEN BY YOU TO ONE WHO IS DEVOID OF AUSTERITIES OR DEVOTION, NOR TO ONE WHO DOES NOT RENDER SERVICE, OR WHO DOES NOT DESIRE TO LISTEN, NOR TO ONE WHO TALKS ILL OF ME.

Having elaborated the entire doctrine of Gita and re-stated its philosophy, Sri Krishna prescribes the rule that should be followed for imparting this knowledge to others. The Lord enumerates the necessary qualifications which are in the nature of adjustments in the inner personality that are necessary for a sincere student of the Gita.

In other words the following types of people cannot be benefited by the study of Gita.

- Those who do not live an austere life i.e. those who do not have control over their body and mind.
- Those who do not have any devotion i.e. those who do not have any capacity to identify themselves with the ideal that they want to reach.
- Those who do not render service, i.e. those who are not able to serve others and who are selfish having no sympathy for others and
- Those who criticize The Lord i.e. those who do not have any respect or desire even to listen the philosophy of Gita.

Only those who are disciplined, loving and have a desire to serve are capable of understanding the message; others may listen to it and abuse it.

ya imam paramam guhyam madbhakteshwabhidhaasyati
bhaktim mayi paraam kritwaa maamevaishyatyasamshayah
// 18.68 //

HE WHO WITH THE HIGHEST DEVOTION TO ME WILL TEACH THIS SUPREME SECRET TO MY DEVOTEES, SHALL DOUBTLESS COME TO ME.

na cha tasmaanmanushyeshu kashchinme priyakrittamah
bhavitaa na cha me tasmaadanyah priyataro bhuvi // 18.69 //

THERE IS NONE AMONG MEN WHO DOES DEARER SERVICE TO ME THAN HE; NOR SHALL THERE BE ANOTHER ON EARTH DEARER TO ME.

It is an Upanishadic commandment that not only one should study the scripture himself but must pass on the benefit of such knowledge to others in the society according to the best of his ability. If the knowledge is not so conveyed to others there cannot be any mobility of intelligence or fluidity of inspiration in him.

Sri Krishna promises the highest reward of reaching Him to the one who is capable of conveying the truths of Gita to others. The Lord also suggests that such a teacher who spreads the knowledge of Gita is dearest to His heart as there is none equal to him in the world either at present or in times to come. Sri Krishna says that there can be none else more dear to Him than such a preacher for he is doing the greatest service to

Him by earnestly and devotedly trying to spread the immortal principles expounded in the Gita.

It is not necessary that one should become first a master of the entire Gita. Whatever one has understood one must immediately learn to give it out to those ignorant of even that much.

The great ones who have crossed the ocean of Samsara and help others to cross are the dearest to The Lord. More important than this is that one must honestly try to live the eternal principles of the Gita in one's own life so that he becomes eligible to be the dearest to The Lord.

adhyeshyate cha ya imam dharmyam samvaadamaavayoh
jnaanayajnena tenaaham ishtah syaamiti me matih // 18.70 //

AND HE WHO STUDIES THIS SACRED DIALOGUE OF OURS, BY HIM I WOULD BE WORSHIPPED THROUGH THE YAJNA OF KNOWLEDGE; SUCH IS MY CONVICTION.

After glorifying the teachers who spread the wisdom of Gita, even those who study this sacred text are applauded. The philosophy of life as given out in Gita in the form of a dialogue between Sri Krishna, the Infinite and Arjuna, the Finite Man, will attract a student to its profundity and transform him to the highest through what The Lord calls as Gyan Yagna.

Just like the Fire God is invoked in a sacrifice and then oblations are offered into it, the study of Gita and regular contemplation on its significance ignites the Fire of knowledge in the student into which he offers his own false values and negative tendencies as oblations. This is what is implied in the phrase Gyan Yagna. Sri Krishna says that such students are the greatest devotees of the Infinite.

shraddhaavaan anasooyashcha shrinuyaadapi yo narah
so'pi muktah shubhaamllokaan praapnuyaat punyakarmanaam
// 18.71 //

EVEN THE MAN WHO LISTENS TO IT WITH FAITH AND WITHOUT MALICE, HE TOO, BEING LIBERATED, SHALL ATTAIN TO THE HAPPY WORLDS OF THE RIGHTEOUS.

The Lord suggests that even listening to the Gita discourses is immensely useful. Sri Krishna indicates two conditions by fulfilling which alone one can gain the maximum joy and perfection out of the discourses on Gita viz.

- Full Faith: One should have the capacity to discover, understand and live upto the ideals contained in the subtle meanings of the spiritual declarations and
- Free from Malice: One should not have any prejudice against the very philosophy of Gita; otherwise its teachings will never appeal to the listener.

To the extent we learn and live the principles of right living as propounded in the Gita, to that extent we can live a life of achievement.

kacchidetacchrutam paartha twayaikaagrena chetasaa
kacchid ajnaanasammohah pranashtaste dhananjaya // 18.72 //

HAS THIS BEEN HEARD BY YOU, O PARTHA, WITH AN ATTENTIVE MIND? HAS THE DELUSION CAUSED BY YOUR IGNORANCE BEEN DISPELLED, O DHANANJAYA?

Sri Krishna enquires Arjuna whether he has understood what has been expounded by Him all along and whether his distraction of thought, caused by false values and judgment of affairs, has been dispelled. The implication is to hear from Arjuna to what extent these discourses benefited him.

CONCLUSION

arjuna uvaacha
nashto mohah smritirlabdhaa twatprasaadaanmayaachyuta
sthito'smi gata sandehah karishye vachanam tava // 18.73 //

ARJUNA SAID
DESTROYED IS MY DELUSION, AS I HAVE GAINED MY MEMORY (KNOWLEDGE) THROUGH YOUR GRACE, O ACHYUTA. I STAND FIRM WITH MY DOUBTS DISPELLED. I SHALL ACT ACCORDING TO YOUR WORD.

Arjuna confesses that his confusions have ended as if he were woken up from a state of unconsciousness. This statement of Arjuna is not a mere meek acceptance of the arguments of Sri Krishna.

It is an affirmation of re-gaining and re-cognizing his own real nature on account of the awakening of the hero in him as well as his confirmation that the neurosis which conquered his mental make up temporarily has vanished. The awakening of wisdom is the end of ignorance. In this state all vacillations of the mind, doubts and despairs, dejections and hesitations, fears and weaknesses disappear.

With such a rejuvenated mind Arjuna declares that he will do according to the word of The Lord who is nothing but Pure

Existence. This is the surrendering of oneself to one's own inner personality. To surrender oneself and declare that he would do The Lord's bidding is the beginning and the end of all spiritual life. There is no more sense of separate existence for the declarer apart from the Godhead. This evolution means shedding of all pretences and evasions.

"Arjuna turns to his appointed action, not with an egoistic mind but with Self-Knowledge. His illusions are destroyed, his doubts are dispelled. The chosen instrument of God takes up the duty set before it by The Lord of the world. He will now do God's bidding. He realizes that He made us for His ends, not our own. Arjuna had the onset of temptation and won his way to a liberating victory. He now feels that he will fulfill the command of The Lord. It is our duty to live in the spirit of this verse and remember that we seek not our own will but the will of Him who sent us. To will what God wills is the secret of Divine Life". Dr.S.Radhakrishnan.

When Arjuna uttered the words *"karishye vachanam tava"* ("thy will be done" as a Westerner would say) he gave up his separate existence and identified himself with the work of the Lord. This evolution means a great shedding of all pretences, assumptions and evasions. It is a kind of *vastrapaharana*, a stripping-off of the mind and intellect.

sanjaya uvaacha
ityaham vaasudevasya paarthasya cha mahaatmanah
samvaadam imam ashrausham adbhutam romaharshanam
// 18.74 //

SANJAYA SAID
THUS HAVE I HEARD THIS WONDERFUL DIALOGUE BETWEEN VAASUDEVA AND THE HIGH-SOULED PARTHA CAUSING MY HAIR TO STAND ON END.

Earlier, Arjuna proclaimed that he will not fight and became despondent. It is the same Arjuna now entirely revived who declared that all his doubts were cleared and he shall abide by 'His Will'. Thus the Arjuna disease has been cured by the Krishna Therapy.

Sanjaya concludes his running commentary in the last five verses of the Gita. They contain his expressions of the glory of the Gita, the revival of Arjuna, his own reaction as he listened to the dialogue between The Lord and Arjuna and the affirmation of his faith in the true culture of the Hindus.

The conversation between Vaasudeva and Arjuna is a dialogue between the 'Higher' and the 'Lower' in man. It is between the Spirit and the Matter.

Vaasudeva is a symbolism that stands for the Consciousness that illumines the concept of time projected by the intellect of man. Vaasudeva is the Atma, the Self. Partha represents the matter. The act of understanding oneself as the matter vesture is the art of unveiling the Infinite through the finite, the technique of which is the theme of the Gita.

Sanjaya describes the philosophy of the Gita so far heard by him as marvelous and wonderful because it revealed the real personality of Arjuna. Arjuna is referred as high souled because of his great achievement in understanding the philosophy of the Gita and shedding all his confusions which is something worthy of admiration. This is also a warning to Dhritarashtra about the consequences of war with the rejuvenated Arjuna.

vyaasaprasaadaacchhrutavaan etad guhyamaham param
yogam yogeshwaraat krishnaat saakshaat kathayatah swayam
// 18.75 //

THROUGH THE GRACE OF VYASA, I HEARD THIS SUPREME AND MOST SECRET YOGA TAUGHT BY KRISHNA HIMSELF, THE LORD OF YOGA, IN PERSON.

In this verse Sanjaya expresses his gratitude to Sage Veda Vyasa who had given him the special faculty to see and hear from a distance all that transpired in the battlefield of Kurukshetra so that he might report the events to the blind king, Dhritarashtra.

He terms what had been heard by him from Sri Krishna as the supreme and the most profound Yoga. His joy is more due to his hearing the philosophy of Gita directly from the Lord than listening to the discourse itself and hence Sri Krishna is referred to as the Lord of all Yogas. This is also an indirect reminder to the blind king about the futility of war with Pandavas.

raajan samsmritya samsmritya samvaadamimam adbhutam
keshavaarjunayoh punyam hrishyaami cha muhurmuhuh
// 18.76 //

O KING, AS I RECALL AGAIN AND AGAIN THIS WONDERFUL AND HOLY DIALOGUE BETWEEN KESAVA AND ARJUNA, I AM THRILLED WITH JOY AGAIN AND AGAIN!

Sanjaya describes the deep impression created in his mind by listening to the Gita Philosophy. He says the discourse between Sri Krishna and Arjuna - between God and Man, between the Perfect and the Imperfect, between the Higher and the Lower - is at once wonderful and holy. The response in Sanjaya is so powerful that he says it had given him the utmost thrill of joy again and again.

The implication is that the Gita should be studied and reflected upon continuously until we are re-educated in the way of life as expounded in It. The reward for such a study is to know the very purpose of our existence and to activate the power in us to tackle intelligently the chaotic happenings around us.

taccha samsmritya samsmritya roopamatyadbhutam hareh
vismayo me mahaan raajan hrishyaami cha punah punah // 18.77 //

AND AS OFTEN AS I RECALL THAT MOST WONDERFUL FORM OF HARI, GREAT IS MY ASTONISHMENT, O KING! AND I THRILL WITH JOY AGAIN AND AGAIN!

Sanjaya confesses that he had been enchanted not only by the philosophy of the Gita but also even by the memory of The Lord's magnificent form as the total manifested Universe.

The dialogue of Sri Krishna and Arjuna and the fact of God are not philosophical propositions but are spiritual facts. We do not learn their meaning by simply recounting them but by dwelling upon them in a spirit of prayer and meditation.

yatra yogeswarah krishno yatra paartho dhanurdharah
tatra shreervijayo bhootirdhruvaa neetirmatirmama // 18.78 //

WHEREVER THERE IS KRISHNA, THE LORD OF YOGA AND WHEREVER THERE IS PARTHA, THE ARCHER, I THINK, THERE WILL SURELY BE PROSPERITY, VICTORY, WELFARE AND MORALITY.

In this concluding verse of the Song Divine Sanjaya summarizes the assessment of his total experience of hearing the conversation between Sri Krishna and Arjuna.

Sri Krishna, The Lord of Yoga - All through the Gita Sri Krishna represented the Self, the Atman, and the substratum upon which everything happens. He can be invoked within us by means of any one of the techniques of Yoga taught in the Gita.

Arjuna, ready with the bow - Partha represents in the Gita a confused, limited, ordinary mortal with all his weaknesses, agitations, fears and pairs of opposites. When he has thrown out his instruments of action i.e. bow and arrows, there can be no hope of success or prosperity for him. But when he is ready with his bow he is prepared and willing to use his faculties to face the challenges of life.

Taken these two together - Sri Krishna, the Yogeswara and Arjuna, the Dhanurdhara - they symbolize a way of life wherein man, with the spiritual understanding, gets ready to face the battle of life. For him success is assured.

The teaching of the Gita is Yoga and the teacher is Yogeswara. When the human soul becomes enlightened and united with the divine, fortune and victory, welfare and morality are assured.

Today's confusions and conflicts in society and man's helplessness against the flood of events, in spite of his achievements in science and mastery over matter, is due to his failure to invoke the Yogeswara in him. A happy blending of the sacred and the secular is what is advised in the Gita as a policy for right living.

Sage Veda Vyasa visualizes a world order in which man pursues a way of life in which the spiritual and material values are well balanced. Material prosperity without inner peace is savagery while spirituality without material well being is madness. Spiritual vision and social service should go together.

The double purpose of human life, personal perfection and social efficiency is indicated here. Human perfection is a kind of marriage between high thought and just action where the priesthood and the kingship move together. This, according to the Gita, must be, for ever, the aim of man.

This last Chapter of the Gita is called 'The Yoga of Liberation by Renunciation' because to renounce false values in us is at once to rediscover the Divine nature in each one of us which is the essential heritage of man. To discard the animal in us (Sannyasa) is the discovery of the Divine in us which is Liberation (Moksha).

om tat sat iti srimadbhagavadgeetaasu upanishatsu brahma vidyaayaam yogashaastre sri krishnaarjuna samvaade moksha sannyaasa yogo naama ashtaadasho'dhyaayah ||

THUS IN THE UPANISHADS OF THE GLORIOUS BHAGAVAD GITA, THE SCIENCE OF THE ETERNAL, THE SCRIPTURE OF YOGA, THE DIALOGUE BETWEEN SRI KRISHNA AND

ARJUNA, ENDS THE EIGHTEENTH DISCOURSE ENTITLED THE YOGA OF LIBERATION BY RENUNCIATION.

AN OUTLINE VIEW OF THIS CHAPTER

This chapter begins with the definitions of sanyasa, renunciation and tyaga, relinquishment. Since these terms are related to action a dissertation of action, an examination of its anatomy and a study of its causes, incentives and constituents follow.

Thereafter definitions of the sattvika, rajasika and tamasika qualities of jnana-knowledge, karma-action, karta-actor, buddhi–intellect, dhriti–steadfastness, and sukha–happiness are given. This analysis helps in the evaluation of human personality.

The three qualities orr gunas also define the four castes known as brahmana, kshatriya, vaishya and shudra which are presented along with their respective duties.

After defining the structure of a human being a seeker is directed to the main spiritual paths of kama-action, bhakti-devotion, and jnana-knowledge. Krishna appeals to Arjuna to follow these paths and reach the eternal abode of Brahman. The Lord assures the seekers that His teaching will help them attain spiritual liberation.

The chapter ends with Sanjaya's ecstatic glorification of Lord Krishna and His wonderful dialogue with Arjuna.

I - SANYASA AND TYAGA - VERSES 1 – 6

Arjuna asks Krishna to explain the distinction between sanyas and tyaga. Krishna quotes the ancient declarations in

His answer. Some declare Sanyas as renunciation of desire-ridden action and tyaga as relinquishment of fruit of action. Some others declare all action has to be relinquished as evil. Some more declare that acts of sacrifice, charity and austerity should not be relinquished. Krishna endorses the last view that these three acts ought not to be relinquished but performed relinquishing attachment and fruit.

II - TAMASIKA, RAJASIKA AND SATTVIKA TYAGA - VERSES 7 – 12

This topic defines the three distinct types of tyaga relinquishment. Tamasika tyaga is relinquishing obligatory action out of one's ignorance, confusion, delusion. Rajasika tyaga is relinquishing action from fear of bodily pain or sorrow. Sattvika tyaga is performance of action relinquishing attachment and fruit thereof. One who practises sattvika tyaga is a true relinquisher. He does not act on impulse or emotion, likes or dislikes of the mind. He operates from his intellect. He neither courts pleasant action nor avoids unpleasant. He merely performs obligatory action without concern for fruit. Consequently, he acquires no further vasanas, desires, be they good, bad or indifferent.

III - CAUSES, INCENTIVES AND CONSTITUENTS OF ACTION - VERSES 13 – 18

The Lord enumerates the five causes for accomplishing any acion in the world. Viz., 1-the body, 2-actor, 3-instrument of action, 4-its function and 5-conscious-principle. The knower, knowledge and known are the threefold cause of action. The constituents of action comprise the actor, instrument of action and actual acting.

IV - SATTVIKA, RAJASIKA AND TAMASIKA JNANA, KARMA AND KARTA (ACTOR) - VERSES 19 – 28

The nature of an individual comprises three basic qualities known as sattvaguna, rajoguna and tamoguna. Sattvaguna is the highest quality reflecting purity and serenity, poise and maturity. Rajoguna is of the middle order manifesting as passion packed with action and agitation. Tamoguna, the lowest, is the quality of inertia and lethargy, heedlessness and indifference. Action consists of actor, knowledge and execution. An action requires an actor to execute it. The actor must possess the knoledge of action to be executed. And he must actullay execute the action. The topic defines sattvika, rajasika and tamasika qualities of knowledge, action and actor.

V - SATTVIKA, RAJASIKA AND TAMASIKA BUDDHI (INTELLECT), DHRITI (STEADFASTNESS) AND SUKHA (HAPPINESS) - VERSES 29 – 39

The topic continues further defining the gunas of intellect, steadfastness and happiness. These three are appendages to action. Besides the ingredients of action covered in the previous topic, a doer needs to use his intellect to direct the course of his action. He must continue to perform steadfastly until the action undertaken is accomplished. As every action is undertaken to gain happiness, the quality of happiness obtained reflects the quality of action.

VI - FOUR CASTESAND THEIR DUTIES - VERSES 40 – 44

Sattva, rajasika and tamasika gunas in different combinations form the basis for the fourfold classification of human beings in a society into Brahmana, Kshatriya, Vaishya and Shudra castes. This classification demonstrates the distinct types of character, behaviour and conduct of people and their traits.

VII - THROUGH ACTION, DEVOTION, KNOWLDEGE AND MEDITATION ONE REACHES BRAHMAN - VERSES 45 – 58

The Lord gives a brief resume of the three spiritual disciplines to reach Brahman - Karma Yoga, path of action for the body, Bhakti Yoga, path of devotion for the mind and Jnana Yoga, Path of knowledge for the intellect. Pursuing the path of action a seeker drops the bulk of the vasanas, desires. His mind becomes purified. His intellect becomes sharp. He rises to the path of knowledge and acquires the twelve spiritual values. He develops commitment to God and thus enters the path of devotion. The three disciplines prepare the seeker for concentration, meditation upon the Supreme through which he realises Brahman.

VIII - KRISHNA APPEALS TO ARJUNA TO REACH THE ETERNAL ABODE - VERSES 59 – 66

Krishna appeals to Arjuna to drop his ego and seek the supreme Self within. Every person functions helplessly according to one's own nature.. Krishna assures Arjuna that He has imparted the knowledge necessary to take the plunge, leaving the choice to him to reflect and decide his course of action. Thus the Lord helps out Arjuna, indicating what is good for him i.e., to rise above this world of perception, emotion and thought and reach the Supreme Being.

IX - THE LORD ASSURES HIS TEACHING WILL LIBERATE HIS DEVOTEES - VERSES 67 – 73

The Lord emphasizes the importance of communicating His message to mankind. Both teacher and the taught will evolve spiritually. Free from delusion and with faith and dedicated effort they would reach the ultimate state of Enlightenment. Arjuna receives the Lord's message and decides to pursue the higher.

X - SANJAYA GLORIFIES KRISHNA AND HIS WONDERFUL DIALOGUE - VERSES 74 – 78

Sanjaya is in ecstacy having heard the wonderful dialogue between Lord Krishna and Arjuna. He bows in gratitude to Vyasa whose grace enabled him to hear the holy dialogue. He pronounces to king Dhritarashtra his immense joy beholding the divine form of Krishna and remembering His great message over and over again. Finally, he declares that the Lord's firm principles will bless this world with success, prosperity and peace.

<<<000>>>

Gita Mahatmyam: Greatness of the Bhagavad Gita

(It is customary to read this at the end of the day's Gita study)

The greatness of Gita is described in the Varaha Purana. Bhagavan Vishnu Himself says therein that if one is devoted to the constant practice of the Gita he would be happy in this very world in spite of his Prarabdha Karma. No evil, however great, can affect him who meditates on Gita; he will be like the lotus leaf untouched by the water. Where there is a book of Gita, where it is studied, they are all holy places - in fact they are Prayaga and similar other places where Devas, Rishis, Yogis, etc. reside. Where Gita is read, help comes forthwith. Where Gita is discussed, recited, taught or heard, there Sri Bhagavan Vishnu Himself invariably resides without any doubt. Gita is The Lord's abode standing on whose wisdom He maintains the three worlds.

The Gita is His Supreme Knowledge. It is inseparable from Brahman - this Knowledge is Absolute, Imperishable, Eternal, and the Essence of His Inexpressible State. It is the Knowledge encompassing the whole of the three Vedas, supremely blissful and consisting of the realization of the true nature of the Self.

The one who recites Gita daily either wholly or partly acquires merit or attains the highest plane of human evolution. By practicing the Gita, he attains the supreme *Mukti.* Even a dying man uttering the word "Gita" attains the life's goal. Even the one who hears the meaning of the Gita is freed from sin. He who meditates on the meaning of Gita is regarded as *Jivanmukta* and after the destruction of his body he attains the highest plane of knowledge.

Finishing the reading of Gita without reading its Mahatmya as declared in the Varaha Purana is an exercise in futility and a wasted labor. On the other hand he who studies Gita followed by the reading of its Mahatmya obtains the fruit stated herein and reaches that goal which is difficult to attain.

Sage Suta confirms that he who after having finished the reading of Gita studies this eternal greatness of Gita will obtain the fruit described therein.

Thus ends in the Varaha Purana the discourse entitled The Greatness of the Gita

Note: Leaving aside the poetic liberty, it may be construed from the above that the one who assimilates the teachings of the Gita as "A User's Manual for Every Day Living" in his practical life is an embodiment of the Gita itself. He would be a true Jnani, a *Jivanmukta.*

<<<000>>>

Finale with a Prayer to The Lord

If the Bhagvad Gita can be called *Madhura Gitam* (Sweet Song), then its singer is *Madhura Murthy* (Sweetness Personified). Hence let us pray to that Lord of Sweetness through the popular poem *Madhurashtakam* by Shri Vallabhacharya and draw the curtains down.

Madhurashtakam, written in melodious lyrical Sanskrit, is easy to understand and rhythmic to recite. A*shtakam* means a poem with eight stanzas. Madhurashtakam uses just one adjective, *"madhuram",* meaning sweet or beautiful etc., to describe the lovely attributes of Bhagavan Sri Krishna who is depicted as the master of Sweetness and Sweetness personified as also the Lord of Mathura (meaning both as a city and sweetness).

THE POEM MADHURASTHAKAM

adharam madhuram vadanam madhuram
nayanam madhuram hasitam madhuram
hrdayam madhuram gamanam madhuram
madhuradi-pater akhilam madhuram

"His lips are sweet, His face is sweet. His eyes are sweet, His smile is sweet. His heart is sweet, His walk is sweet. Everything is sweet about the Lord of sweetness." (1)

vacanam madhuram caritam madhuram
vasanam madhuram valitam madhuram
calitam madhuram bhramitam madhuram
madhuradi-pater akhilam madhuram

"His words are sweet, His character is sweet. His garments are sweet, His navel is sweet. His movement is sweet, His wanderings are sweet. Everything is sweet about the Lord of sweetness." (2)

venur madhuro renur madhurah
panir-madhurah padau madhurau
nrtyam madhuram sakhyam madhuram
madhuradi-pater akhilam madhuram

"His flute is sweet, His dust is sweet. His hands are sweet, His feet are sweet. His dancing is sweet, His friendship is sweet. Everything is sweet about the Lord of sweetness." (3)

gitam madhuram pitam madhuram
bhuktam madhuram suptam madhuram
rupam madhuram tilakam madhuram
madhuradi-pater akhilam madhuram

"His singing is sweet, His yellow dress is sweet. His eating is sweet, His sleeping is sweet. His form is sweet, His tilaka is sweet. Everything is sweet about the Lord of sweetness." (4)

karanam madhuram taranam madhuram
haranam madhuram ramanam madhuram
vamitam madhuram samitam madhuram
madhuradi-pater akhilam madhuram

"His activities are sweet, His liberation is sweet. His thieving is sweet, His loving sports are sweet. His offerings are sweet, His peacefulness is sweet. Everything is sweet about the Lord of sweetness." (5)

gunja madhura mala madhura
yamuna madhura vici madhura
salilam madhuram kamalam madhuram
madhuradi-pater akhilam madhuram

"His gunja-mala is sweet; His flower-garland is sweet. Is Yamuna is sweet, His ripples are sweet. His water is sweet, His lotuses are sweet. Everything is sweet about the Lord of sweetness." (6)

gopi madhura lila madhura
yuktam madhuram bhuktam madhuram
hrstam madhuram sistam madhuram
madhuradi-pater akhilam madhuram

"His Gopis are sweet, His pastimes are sweet. His meeting is sweet, His food is sweet. His happiness is sweet, His etiquette is sweet. Everything is sweet about the Lord of sweetness." (7)

gopa madhura gavo madhura
sastir madhura srstir madhura
dalitam madhuram phalitam madhuram
madhuradi-pater akhilam madhuram

"His cowherd boys are sweet, His cows are sweet. His herding-stick is sweet, His creation is sweet. His trampling is sweet; His fruitfulness is sweet. Everything is sweet about the Lord of sweetness." (8)

KRISHNAM VANDE JAGADGURUM

I submit before that Lord of Sweetness.

"ekam jyoti bahudha vibhati'
-The one light manifests itself in various forms-
The Atharva Veda (XIII.3.17)

om poornamadah poonamidam poornaat poornamudachyate
poornasya poornamaadaaya poornamevaa vasishyate
Om Shantih Shantih Shantih ||

THAT IS INFINITE; THIS IS INFINITE
FROM THAT INFINITE THIS INFINITE COMES
FROM THAT INFINITE THIS INFINITE REMOVED OR
ADDED INFINITE REMAINS
INFINITE [BRAHMAN] IS LIMITLESS
INFINITE NUMBER OF UNIVERSES COME OUT FROM
AND GO INTO THE INFINITE BRAHMAN
YET BRAHMAN REMAINS UNCHANGED.

About the Author

Sri T.N.Sethumadhavan is a Retired Bank Executive, devoted to the study of Hindu Scriptures and Philosophy. He is a Vedantic seeker by choice enjoying co-relating ancient Hindu thoughts to modern behavioral sciences and management studies. He is engaged in actively promoting this goal through lectures, writings etc. His extensive writings on the Sanatana Dharma are easy to read and understand, thus being instrumental in enlivening the zeal to learn more about Hinduism. He can be contacted at tnsethumadhavan@gmail.com.

Human Society

"There can be no complete peace anywhere. Human society is a conflict-prone society; it is not conflict-free. This sort of conflict will happen so long as there is society, you cannot totally stop it but you can minimize it.

There can be no ideal situation. Within the minimum conflict situation, we should try to progress. You cannot have complete peace of the graveyard.

Someone gave that example -- that Switzerland had 500 years of peace and democracy and what did they produce? The Cuckoo Clock. Italy had always been in turmoil and they produced Michelangelo, Leonardo da Vinci and the Renaissance.

So don't be frustrated by this conflict, it will be there, we have to be able to minimize it."

Meghalaya Governor Ranjit Shekhar Mooshahary, a former head of the Border Security Force and the National Security Guard, in a rare and candid interview with Rediff.com*'s Archana Masih.*

Rediff.Com dt 28/02/2013